HANDBOOK *of*
AUTOETHNOGRAPHY

*This Handbook is dedicated to the work and lives of
H. L. (Bud) Goodall, Jr. (1952–2012),
Nicholas L. (Nick) Trujillo (1956–2012),
and John T. Warren (1974–2011),
three of our most extraordinary writers and scholars.*

You left us too soon.

HANDBOOK *of* AUTOETHNOGRAPHY

Stacy Holman Jones, Tony E. Adams, and Carolyn Ellis

Left Coast Press Inc.

Walnut Creek, California

LEFT COAST PRESS, INC.
1630 North Main Street, #400
Walnut Creek, CA 94596
www.LCoastPress.com

Copyright © 2013 by Left Coast Press, Inc.
First paperback edition 2015.

All rights reserved. No part of this publication may be reproduced, stored in a retrieval system, or transmitted in any form or by any means, electronic, mechanical, photocopying, recording, or otherwise, without the prior permission of the publisher.

ISBN 978-1-59874-600-6 hardback
ISBN 978-1-61132-712-0 consumer eBook
ISBN 978-1-59874-601-3 paperback

Library of Congress Cataloging-in-Publication Data:
Holman Jones, Stacy Linn, 1966-
  Handbook of autoethnography / Stacy Holman Jones, Tony E. Adams, and Carolyn Ellis.
    pages cm
  Includes bibliographical references.
  ISBN 978-1-59874-600-6 (hardback : alk. paper)—ISBN 978-1-59874-601-3 (paperback)—ISBN 978-1-61132-712-0 (consumer eBook)
  1. Ethnology—Authorship. 2. Ethnology—Research. 3. Ethnology--Methodology. I. Title.
  GN307.7.H65 2013
  305.8—dc23
                              2012048860

Printed in the United States of America

♾™ The paper used in this publication meets the minimum requirements of American National Standard for Information Sciences—Permanence of Paper for Printed Library Materials, ANSI/NISO Z39.48–1992.

Contents

Exemplars

Preface

Carrying the Torch
for Autoethnography

Carolyn Ellis

"Time to write the preface," I say, pretending to speak to my dogs to mask that I am talking out loud to myself again. *You didn't really think I'd write an autoethnography without the dogs in it, did you?* Since what I say does not contain the words "treat," "cookie," "outside," "ball," "toy," or "hello" (as to a visitor), the dogs ignore me. Zen is busy herding her five stuffed animals into the small doggy bed in the corner of my study, while Buddha is stretched out and sleeping under my chair. Art has left for school to teach his narrative class, and I'm "finished" for the day with all the administrative tasks I've taken on as Chair-Elect of my department. *What was I thinking?* Finally, time to write and no time to waste. I tackle the blank page, hoping that I can say something meaningful that is up to the quality of this Handbook. *The feeling of nervousness upon starting a new piece never goes away.*

I recall the first time I typed the word "autoethnography." It was 1995. I spelled it first with a hyphen, and then without. "Without," I said to myself, "because autoethnography is a thing all its own, not just 'auto' linked to 'ethnography'." At that point, of course, it was a fantasy to think that autoethnography was anything more than a word that had been used by a few folks interested in reflexivity, or to think the term would ever be more than something I had fabricated to make sense of *Final Negotiations*, the ethnographic novel I had been writing for the last decade about love and loss in a nine-year romantic relationship.

Handbook of Autoethnography, edited by Stacy Holman Jones, Tony E. Adams, and Carolyn Ellis, 9–12. © 2013 Left Coast Press, Inc. All rights reserved.

Then, after attending my workshop on autoethnography in 1999, Karen Scott-Hoy painted "Autoethnography" to depict visually the methods in her dissertation about being a health worker with the Vanuatu. Affecting me viscerally, this painting solidified for me that autoethnography was real and not just something imagined. I saw and felt the power of autoethnography as an opening to honest and deep reflection about ourselves, our relationships with others, and how we want to live. I saw and felt the reciprocal relationships between knowing and feeling, self and other, author and respondents. The power of Karen's art reinforced what my partner Art Bochner and I had sought to do in our work together, especially in our edited collection, *Composing Ethnography*, and then later in *Ethnographically Speaking*: to add to our canonical qualitative texts an evocative and vulnerable heart, our intimate autobiographical experiences, and other artful and evocative forms of expression—short stories, poetry, performance, music, and art.

From then until now has been a fabulous journey, one I could not have predicted when a handful of us began writing and teaching about autoethnography in the 1990s. We have moved from defending autoethnography as research to witnessing its explosion in many disciplines and applied research fields all over the world. Signs of autoethnography's influence abound: the large number of e-mails many of us receive in response to our autoethnographic stories; the increasing number of published articles, chapters, books, book series, edited volumes, conferences—even critiques—that showcase or discuss autoethnography. At the International Congress of Qualitative Inquiry (ICQI), for example, presentations on and about autoethnography take center stage. This is why some of us think of ICQI as "our" annual meeting place. And now—this Handbook. *For those who predicted autoethnography would be a fad—if you're reading this, "You were wrong!" And if you aren't reading this Handbook, you're missing out.*

For most of us, autoethnography is not simply a way of knowing about the world; it has become a way of being in the world, one that requires living consciously, emotionally, and reflexively. It asks that we not only examine our lives but also consider how and why we think, act, and feel as we do. Autoethnography requires that we observe ourselves observing, that we interrogate what we think and believe, and that we challenge our own assumptions, asking over and over if we have penetrated as many layers of our own defenses, fears, and insecurities as our project requires. It asks that we rethink and revise our lives, making conscious decisions about who and how we want to be. And in the process, it seeks a story that is hopeful, where authors ultimately write themselves as survivors of the story they are living. For many of us in this volume, autoethnography has enhanced, even saved, our academic careers. It might not be hyperbole to say that sometimes it has saved our lives.

I have thrived as a result of living the autoethnographic life. In addition to examining my life, this approach has motivated me to love and care for others and equipped me to bear witness to their pain and struggles; as well, it has increased

"Autoethnography." *Painting by Karen Scott-Hoy.*

my desire to contribute to the betterment of life and act on behalf of the good. My life has been enriched by the folks autoethnography has brought into my life—from my partner to colleagues and friends of my generation; from enthusiastic next-generation professors and students at my university to the passionate new professors and students who make the pilgrimage from many parts of the world to bask each year in Norman Denzin's ICQI.

Now the myriad and diverse topics, authors, and approaches to autoethnography in the pages of this Handbook further break open the world of autoethnography, expanding and extending what it can be and do. It is with great honor and humility that I applaud the authors here and pay tribute to my co-editors, Stacy Holman Jones and Tony Adams. Two of the most creative and committed autoethnographers I know, they have worked tirelessly and lovingly on this Handbook and have invited me along for the ride, an e-ticket adventure if ever there was one. Thank you both.

Finally, autoethnography depends on response. You, the readers, have always made it worth the effort. Join us now in carrying the torch of and for autoethnography into the future. Enjoy.

Acknowledgments

Editing a handbook is a joint venture. Not only did we solicit and work with the authors of individual chapters, we also solicited reviewers for these chapters; nearly every chapter was reviewed by at least four, most often five, people. We also requested feedback from numerous scholars on the topics and organization of the Handbook.

We celebrate our authors, who approached their work, the reviewer's feedback, and the timeline of the Handbook project with enthusiasm, rigor, and grace. This collection is a reflection and demonstration of their insights, dedication, and talents.

We would like to thank our editorial board for their suggestions about chapter authors and Handbook themes as well as their commitment to reviewing the chapters. They are (listed alphabetically): Bryant Alexander, Leon Anderson, Brydie-Leigh Bartleet, Heewon Chang, Norman Denzin, Kim Etherington, Bud Goodall (who passed away on August 24, 2012), Valerie Janesick, Pranee Liamputtong, Ron Pelias, Chris Poulos, Deborah Reed-Danahey, Laurel Richardson, Andrew Sparkes, Tami Spry, Lisa Tillmann, Nick Trujillo (who passed away on October 29, 2012), and Philip Vannini.

We would also like to thank the ad-hoc reviewers of the chapters (listed alphabetically): Jacquelyn Allen-Collinson, Wilfredo Alvarez, Ahmet Atay, Ambar Basu, Keith Berry, Derek Bolen, Robin Boylorn, Jay Brower, Devika Chawla, Courtney Cole, Christopher Collins, Joshua Collins, Julia Colyar, Julie Cosenza, Christine Crouse-Dick, Summer Cunningham, Marissa Doshi, Kitrina Douglas, Shirley Drew, Jenn Freitag, Susanne Gannon, Grace Giorgio, Joseph Hassert, Andrew Herrmann, Richard G. Jones, Jr., Kurt Lindemann, Lesa Lockford, Rebecca Mahfouz, Jimmie Manning, Amir Marvasti, Janet McKeown, Chris McRae, Marilyn Metta, Michaela D. E. Meyer, Michelle Millard, Melanie Mills, Rahul Mitra, Shane Moreman, Cheryl Nicholas, Blake Paxton, Sandy Pensoneau-Conway, Steve Phalen, marcela polanco, Joshua Potter, David Purnell, Leslie Rossman, Christina Saindon, Patrick Santoro, Dana Schowalter, Lara Stache, Danielle Stern, David Ta, Sherri Ter Molen, Keyan Tomaselli, Satoshi Toyosaki, Eve Tuck, Jillian Tullis, Adam Tyma, David Van Bebber, Sarah Wall, Julie Wight, Jonathan Wyatt, Stephanie Young, and Amber Zimmerman.

Tony

My life is a story made possible by the stories and lives of many others. I first want to thank the people who have built, and continue to build, my confidence about living and about writing: Brett Aldridge, Nilanjana Bardhan, Christopher Birdsong, Derek Bolen, Robin Boylorn, Jay Brower, Marcy Chvasta, Ken Cissna, Norm Denzin, Rachel Dubrofsky, Brian Flowers, Brad Gangnon, Craig Gingrich-Philbrook, Jonny Gray, Andrew Herrmann, Kim Kline, Lenore Langsdorf, Patricia Leavy, Michael LeVan, Nicole Neuman, Mark Neumann, Ron Pelias, Jillian Tullis, John Warren, and Jonathan Wyatt. I also want to thank my students and my colleagues at Northeastern Illinois University, especially Wilfredo Alvarez, Anna Antaramian, Katrina Bell-Jordan, Bernard Brommel, Rodney Higginbotham, Nancy McVittie, Cyndi Moran, Seung-Hwan Mun, Shayne Pepper, Nanette Potee, Edie Rubinowitz, and Angie Sweigart-Gallagher.

I thank Mitch Allen for his continued faith in my work and for granting me the privilege of publishing with Left Coast Press, Inc. I also thank the Left Coast team, especially Ryan Harris, for their enthusiastic support of my/our work.

I thank my co-editors, Stacy Holman Jones and Carolyn Ellis, for making this Handbook a possibility and for always infusing the writing and editing process with care and love. Stacy, I especially thank you for giving me the honor and privilege of working with you on a queer, autoethnographic project—to see how and if we were, in your words, "good for each other." Your faith in me continues to make the faith in myself possible, and I look forward to venturing into new personal and professional territory with you. Carolyn, I especially thank you for teaching me about the importance of the mundane, of being attentive to others who may make us uncomfortable, and of turning off my intellect and worry and over-theorizing when it just becomes too much. I also appreciate the unwavering support you have had in me and in our collaborations, and I look forward to living together on/through future projects.

I am thankful for the mentorship of Art Bochner. You have taught me about the importance of forgiveness, strategies for healing troubled relationships, and ways of making my life better. Your feedback and laughter, patience and constructive criticism, tough questions and warm hugs continue to inspire; I am forever grateful for your love and friendship.

I conclude by thanking my best friend, Keith Berry, my stepfather, Michael Rome, and my parents, Phil Adams and Sheri Rome, for providing me with unconditional love. And I thank Gerardo (Jerry) Moreno for supporting me throughout the long days and nights of writing and editing. I hope I continue to make you happy for a very long time.

Stacy

A project like this one is a lifetime in the making with so many to thank along the way. I'll begin by thanking Tony Adams and Carolyn Ellis for making this work so rewarding and enjoyable. You are both wonderful co-authors, editors, friends, and mentors. I can't imagine working so hard or so well with anyone else. Carolyn, I am so very grateful that you gave me and my writing a chance all those years ago and for being my unwavering champion and cheerleader ever since. I hope I have rewarded your faith in me. Tony, I thank you for always being willing to take on projects, to talk and write, and to laugh and kvetch with me. I always wondered how people managed to create and sustain lifetime writing and research collaborations, and now I know.

I am deeply grateful to Nick Trujillo, my mentor, writing guru, and friend. Nick taught me the joys of living the ethnographic life, and I aspire to work, write, and live with his fearlessness, joy, and appreciation. Nick, you are deeply loved and missed.

I'd like to also thank Mitch Allen at Left Coast for his enthusiasm and encouragement and for being an honest and willing guide for those of us writing autoethnography. I also thank the Left Coast editorial team, including Ryan Harris, for their support and expertise. And, of course, I thank all of the authors who contributed to making this Handbook possible. Working with each of you was an honor and a pleasure.

I also thank all of my wonderful colleagues and students at California State University Northridge and at the University of South Florida, especially Ben Attias, Ashley Beard, Aimee Carillo Rowe, Ken Cissna, Eric Eisenberg, Sara Dykins Callahan, Elizabeth Edgecomb, Michael LeVan, Kathryn Sorrells, Jillian Tullis, Lori Roscoe, and Rachel Silverman. I am grateful to the people who've taught me all I know about writing and performance: Art Bochner, Tessa Carr, Norm Denzin, Craig Gingrich-Philbrook, Bud Goodall, Paul Gray, Chris McRae, Lynn Miller, Jeanine Mingé, Omi Osun, Ron Pelias, Deanna Shoemaker, and Kathleen Stewart. And I thank my longtime reading and writing friends Brenna Curtis, Georgine Hodgkinson, and Linda Yakle for being just that.

Doing the editorial work on the Handbook wouldn't have been possible without the love and support of my family. I thank my grandparents, William Blackburn and Bernice Holman, for encouraging the writer in me. I thank my parents, Dean and Mary Holman, for their love and support. I thank my extended California family, including Jeanine Mingé and Johnny Sterner, for making Los Angeles feel like home. And I thank my partner, Keely Masino, and my beautiful child for, well, everything.

Carolyn

I write this acknowledgment after reading Tony's and Stacy's words of appreciation. My heart fills full. I know we autoethnographers have a reputation for being mushy, but to me that's part of what makes this approach and this community so special. Thus, I hereby reclaim the terms "mushy" and "sentimental" without fear of retribution or critique. Tony and Stacy are just the best; I love them as co-authors and colleagues, and for the kind, responsible, and loving friends and family they are.

I'd like to thank Mitch Allen for always being there—as a publisher, intellectual, supportive critic, and, most of all, dear friend. Thanks to Norman Denzin for all he has done and continues to do to support and help our community grow and thrive; to Laurel Richardson for her inspiring creativity and friendship; to Ron Pelias and Buddy Goodall for leading the way from the beginning; to Chris Poulos for his dedication to continuing the autoethnographic story. Thanks to all the wonderful students who have challenged, stimulated, encouraged, and supported me through the years. Thanks for your continuing commitment to and passion for autoethnography and your willingness to put your vulnerable selves out there. I feel appreciative for all I have learned from each of you. You are the future.

I appreciate the University of South Florida Department of Communication, the Ethnography Division of the National Communication Association, and the International Congress of Qualitative Inquiry (ICQI)—and how welcomed and at home I feel among the folks in these venues. As well, I feel appreciative for the past—the continuous bonds I share with those who influenced me earlier in life and continue to do so in their deaths, especially my parents, Arthur and Katherine Ellis, who gave me opportunities to be who I wanted to be when what I wanted seemed so foreign to them.

And, finally, I want to say thanks to the family that surrounds me now—especially Art, Buddha, and Zen. All that I write has the imprint of conversations with Art. Together he and I have created a haven of love and safety and a remarkably adventurous, intellectual and romantic partnership. I still pinch myself to make sure our life together is real; if it turns out to be socially constructed, well… that is good enough for me.

Introduction

Coming to Know Autoethnography as More than a Method

Stacy Holman Jones, Tony Adams, and Carolyn Ellis

Coming to Autoethnography

Carolyn

I have been an ethnographer all my life. I also have been interested in peoples' emotions and intentions and how they create meaningful lives and cope with the problems of living. During the 1970s, I had the good fortune of being at Stony Brook University, majoring in sociology. Thankfully, I was able to pursue my interests and immerse myself in the ethnographic study of community. Positivism ruled in those days, particularly in sociology departments—it still does—and thus I also was encouraged to emphasize systematic data collection and traditional analysis over imagination and storytelling. In 1982, while an assistant professor at the University of South Florida, I lost my brother in a plane crash. That and having a partner in the last stages of emphysema led me to begin keeping notes on my relational and personal experiences of grief and loss, which eventually resulted in some of my first autoethnographic writing (Ellis, 1993, 1995). In 1996 I moved to the Communication Department, and there I was able to continue the work that would connect my sociological eye with a communicative heart. Autoethnography felt perfect to me because it combined my interests in ethnography, social psychology of the self and role-taking, subjectivity and emotionality, face-to-face communication and interaction, writing as inquiry and for evocation, storytelling, and my social work orientation toward social justice and giving back to the community.

Handbook of Autoethnography, edited by Stacy Holman Jones, Tony E. Adams, and Carolyn Ellis, 17–48. © 2013 Left Coast Press, Inc. All rights reserved.

Unlike the stories that Stacy Holman Jones and Tony Adams will tell later in this introduction, I did not have "mentors" in autoethnography, and initially it was challenging to get this work accepted and published. What I did have though were like-minded colleagues and friends—Arthur Bochner, Norman Denzin, Laurel Richardson, Buddy Goodall, Mitch Allen, Ron Pelias, and many, many more—who encouraged and supported this work within an intellectual environment where postmodern, poststructuralist, and feminist writers were contesting issues of authority, representation, voice, and method. Once Art and I joined work and lives, the synergy propelled our autoethnographic and narrative project forward (Ellis & Bochner, 1996; 2000; Bochner & Ellis, 2002). We turned our energy to joining social science and humanities to make scholarship more human, useful, emotional, and evocative; to developing a research program in which we could mentor students in interpretive social science with a focus on narrative and autoethnography; and to contributing to the world in which we live.

Again, I was fortunate to have supportive colleagues in the discipline of communication and in my department, especially Stacy who early on embraced autoethnography and continues to carry the torch in so many wonderful ways. Together, she and I were privileged to have so many superb students, such as Tony, who came to us already versed in autoethnography and eager to get on with telling their stories. We continue to learn much from this younger generation of autoethnographers, and I am confident in their ability and desire to carry on the autoethnographic movement in academia.

I continue to write stories that start from and explore my relational and emotional life, though now I concentrate on the lives of Holocaust survivors. My focus has turned to collaborative witnessing, a form of relational autoethnography that works to evocatively tell the experiences of others in shared storytelling and conversation (Ellis & Rawicki, in press a, b; Rawicki & Ellis, 2011). I continue to feel I am doing work that is a "calling," and the cornerstone of that work is autoethnography.

Stacy

I grew up in a research tradition that included personal experience, valued story, and sought the literary. In a collaborative graduate seminar on ethnographic methods, Nick Trujillo taught Rona Halualani, Donna Knifong and me to consider every moment of our work—conducting fieldwork (and hanging out), creating field notes, reading the literature, discussing our research in the classroom, all of it—as experiences worth writing about deeply, analytically, and creatively. He also insisted that what we were doing constituted a worthwhile turn in the larger conversation about ethnography and autoethnography happening in and around qualitative research (see Communication Studies 298, 1997). Later, as I worked on my MA thesis, Nick encouraged, cajoled, and demanded—again and again—that I write the story, that I keep writing the story, that I just write the story. And so I wrote stories, lots of them.

When I left California State University, Sacramento in 1996 for the University of Texas (UT), I carried my love of story into the performance studies classrooms of Paul Gray, Lynn Miller, and Omi Osun. Omi taught me that working at the intersections of performance and ethnography meant understanding fieldwork as personal and knowledge as an embodied, critical, and ethical exploration of culture (see Jones, 2002). Performance was a stage and means for writing, telling, and living the story of my research, and I did this alongside wonderful colleagues including Tessa Carr, Heather Carver, Deanna Shoemaker, Elizabeth Lee-Brown, Clarie Van Ens, and Lisa Weckerle. While I was at UT, I took a course titled "Fictocriticsm and Cultural Critique" with anthropologist Kathleen Stewart, who taught me that writing stories offers us a powerful form for theorizing the daily workings of culture. During this time, Nick introduced me to Carolyn Ellis and Art Bochner, who understood and encouraged my commitments to autoethnography, performance, and critical scholarship as complementary and of equal importance. And so I performed and wrote critical stories and merged the two in/as performative personal writing, work I have been doing ever since.

Much of that work focuses on telling stories that clearly locate the personal in the field, in the writing, and in the political contexts of the research. In my essay on autoethnography for the *Handbook of Qualitative Methods* (2005a), I told some of my story of coming to autoethnography as an effort to create work that changes the world (p. 765). Tony and I have continued to tell these stories, particularly in our efforts to write autoethnography as a queer method (see Adams & Holman Jones, 2008, 2011; Holman Jones & Adams 2010a, 2010b).

Today, my writing focuses less on the personal experience of doing research and more on storytelling as a relational accomplishment. I do autoethnography less as a way to live and relate the story of research and more as a way *into* researching and storying living. My most recent work (2011) considers the power of texts to write us into and out of being, as well as how identities and lives are performed in relation to others (p. 322).

What autoethnography is teaching me today is this: telling our stories is a way for us to be present to each other, provides a space for us to create a relationship embodied in the performance of writing and reading that is reflective, critical, loving, and chosen in solidarity (2011, p. 333). I grew up and was nurtured in a research tradition that embraced autoethnography as a legitimate, important, and *telling* methodology. While choosing autoethnography wasn't a professional risk during my graduate education or early in my publishing career, telling personal stories in/as research always carries personal, relational, and ethical risks. More and more, I view these risks as necessary not only for our research but also for living full lives and changing our world in important and essential ways. This is so because, as Butler (2005) writes, our willingness to risk ourselves—our stories, our identities, our commitments—"in relation to others constitutes our very chance of becoming human" (p. 136).

Tony

I first encountered autoethnography when I entered the MA program in Speech Communication at Southern Illinois University Carbondale (SIUC) in 2001. Lenore Langsdorf, my thesis advisor, advocated for the use of narrative and personal experience in research, and I took courses on performance theory and autoethnography with Ron Pelias. Craig Gingrich-Philbrook and Elyse Pineau were doing innovative work on auto-performance and embodiment, and I took classes alongside many contemporary autoethnographers, including Keith Berry, Nicole Defenbaugh, Ben Myers, Sandy Pensoneau-Conway, Satoshi Toyosaki, and Amber Zimmerman.

I continued my graduate work by entering the doctoral program at the University of South Florida (USF) in 2004. In my first semester, I took a course on narrative inquiry with Art Bochner, and my final paper evolved into my first autoethnographic publication about the strained relationship I had with my father (Adams, 2006). I took another course with Art on the social construction of reality and completed an independent study with him the following semester on narrative ethics (Adams, 2008). Art soon agreed to direct my dissertation on narratives of coming out and continued working with me to publish my dissertation as a book (Adams, 2011).

At USF I also took a course on autoethnography and a course on qualitative research with Carolyn, and Stacy and I began to investigate the fertile relationship between autoethnography and queer theory. Many of my peers were working in/with autoethnography, including Robin Boylorn, Jeanine Mingé, Andrew Herrmann, and Jillian Tullis, and I continued to find myself supported by the legacy of prior USF-autoethnographers, including Jay Baglia, Laura Ellingson, Elissa Foster, Christine Kiesinger, and Lisa Tillmann.

Even though I attended graduate programs that cultivated and embraced the use of personal narrative and lived experience, I initially steered clear of autoethnography as the primary research method for my dissertation; stubbornly, and ignorantly, I thought that the method would thwart the possibility of having an academic career. I worried about pleasing (imagined) traditional scholars at other schools instead of pleasing the professors with whom I worked and instead of doing the work that I felt mattered. And so, for the first two years of my doctoral program, I formulated a more traditional ethnographic study to investigate mediated representations of the environment found at The Florida Aquarium. Though this research was intriguing, it did not satisfy me in the way that autoethnographic research on relationships would once I allowed myself to embrace this research.

On February 28, 2006, near the end of my second year in the doctoral program, my life changed abruptly: Brett Aldridge, an ex-boyfriend and close friend from my time at SIUC, passed away. His sister told me that he died of diabetes-related causes, but two of his friends told me that Brett might have committed suicide after coming out to his father—that is, after telling his father that he was gay (see Adams, 2011).

While I recognized that I could not find out for sure how Brett died—and his embodied presence was gone regardless of how he passed—I did find myself reflecting on the onslaught of negative commentary tied to coming out and sexual orientation that I had been experiencing. I found myself reflecting on various homophobic experiences in the classroom and with students who tried to save me from my homosexuality, discriminatory practices that others relayed to me that happened to them because of their sexual orientation, and the criticism from family members to my coming out, as well as their attempts to silence any discussion of same-sex attraction.

This barrage of reflection forced me to contend with some of the ways people were ostracized because of their sexuality and how they, as could have been the case with Brett, might turn to suicide after experiencing such pain. I also realized that while my work on the environment and at the aquarium may have been important, the intimate, personal, and relational work of same-sex attraction mattered much more; lesbian, gay, bisexual, and queer persons were being harmed by ignorance and hate, and I could not let such ignorance and hate proceed unchallenged. Thus, I turned to doing the kind of work that mattered more to me and to bringing my emotions and experiences into the research process. I turned to writing stories that others could use in times of relational distress, and I re-turned to the original principles of my graduate education, especially by doing and living autoethnography.

○

As our stories illustrate, autoethnography creates a space for a turn, a change, a reconsideration of how we think, how we do research and relationships, and how we live. These stories constitute a narrative of coming to an experience and a moment in time when excluding or obscuring the personal in research felt uncomfortable, even untenable. These stories are not unique to us—many of the essays in this volume include stories of coming to autoethnography.

Numerous researchers also have turned to autoethnography, forever changing the landscape of qualitative and interpretive methods. The method flourishes in professional journals and at academic conferences, and numerous books (e.g., Bochner & Ellis, 2002; Chang, 2008; Chang & Boyd, 2011; Ellis, 2004, 2009a; Hayler, 2011; Muncey, 2010; Poulos, 2009; Spry, 2011; Tamas, 2011) and special issues of journals (e.g., Berry & Clair, 2011; Boyle & Parry, 2007; Ellis & Bochner, 1996; Gingrich-Philbrook, 2000; Hunt & Junco, 2006; Myers, 2012; Ngunjiri, Hernandez, & Chang, 2010; Poulos, 2008) are devoted to autoethnographic inquiry. Disciplines such as nursing (e.g., Wright, 2008; Foster, McAllister, & O'Brien, 2006) and music (e.g., Bartlett & Ellis, 2009), criminology (e.g., Jewkes, 2011), education (e.g., Duncan, 2004), sociology (e.g., Wall, 2006, 2008), anthropology (e.g., Behar, 1996, 1998; Reed-Danahay, 1997), psychology (e.g., Philaretou & Allen, 2006), political science (e.g., Burnier, 2006), social work (e.g., Averett & Soper, 2011), communication (e.g., Holman Jones, 2007), and business (e.g., Doloriert & Sambrook, 2011; Vickers, 2007) have embraced the method. Courses solely devoted to autoethnography are taught at many colleges and universities, and many texts on qualitative research methods now include chapters about the method (e.g., Denzin & Lincoln, 2000b, 2005, 2011; Ellis & Adams, forthcoming; Lapan, Quartaroli, & Riemer, 2012). Further, in 2005, Norman Denzin began the International Center for Qualitative Inquiry and the International Congress of Qualitative Inquiry, an organization and a conference that recognize the importance of reflexivity and personal experience in research, and, in 2011, Derek Bolen created the first-ever "Doing Autoethnography" conference, at Wayne State University. While we do not envision this Handbook as the definitive book about autoethnography, we do see it as a text that will further develop and refine autoethnographic inquiry and serve as a resource to seasoned and new autoethnographers alike.

Next, we briefly define what autoethnography is and identify key characteristics of autoethnographic practices. We then provide a brief history of the method as well as describe purposes of autoethnographic projects. We conclude by discussing the ways in which we assembled the Handbook and point out the important features of this collection.

Conceptualizing Autoethnography

One characteristic that binds all autoethnographies is the use of personal experience to examine and/or critique cultural experience. Autoethnographers do this in work that ranges from including personal experience within an otherwise traditional social scientific analysis (Anderson, 2006; Chang, 2008) to the presentation of aesthetic projects—poetry, prose, films, dance, photographic essays, and performances—as autoethnographic research (Bartleet & Ellis, 2009; Cancienne, & Bagley, 2008; Harrison, 2002; Pelias, 2011; Saldaña, 2008; Spry, 2011; Williams, 2011). While all personal writing could be considered examinations of culture, not all personal writing is autoethnographic; there are additional characteristics that distinguish autoethnography from other kinds of personal work. These include (1) *purposefully commenting on/critiquing of culture and cultural practices*, (2) making *contributions to existing research*, (3) *embracing vulnerability with purpose*, and (4) *creating a reciprocal relationship with audiences in order to compel a response.*

Autoethnographies Comment on/Critique Culture and Cultural Practices

First, autoethnographers intentionally *highlight* the relationship of their experiences and stories to culture and cultural practices, with many authors choosing to launch a critique of this relationship in their work. If an author experiences an epiphany, reflects on the nuances of that experience, writes to show how the aspects of experience illuminate more general cultural phenomena and/or to show how the experience works to diminish, silence, or deny certain people and stories, then the author writes autoethnographically. If an author writes to tell a story to illustrate a sad, joyful, or problematic experience but does not interrogate the nuances of this experience in light of general cultural phenomena and cultural practices, then the author writes autobiographically. Some autoethnographers further distinguish autoethnography from autobiography and personal narrative by making the distinction between autoethnographic writing that includes the perspectives of multiple subjects (through interviews and/or fieldwork) and autobiographic or personal narrative work that presents the perspective of a single subject. As our discussion indicates, determining an author's purpose and approach and assigning a label—autoethnography or autobiography—is a complex and uncertain activity. However, autoethnographic texts typically feel more self and socially conscious than autobiographic works; the intent to describe cultural experience marks this difference.

Autoethnographies Make Contributions to Existing Research

Second, autoethnographic texts demonstrate knowledge of past research on a topic and seek to contribute to this research. This characteristic is often noted as the difference that marks autoethnography as *scholarship* in contrast with writing that does not work to contribute to a scholarly conversation. Autoethnographers strive to write accessible prose that is read by a general audience, but they also try to construct the work so that it steps into the flow of discussion around a topic of interest to researchers. For example, when Tony (2011) writes about coming out in everyday interactions, he does so acknowledging what other people have said about coming out, situating his work within these discussions. He also extends this existing work by critiquing current conceptualizations of coming out, by making new claims about the coming out process, and by asking questions that can be explored in future projects. When Stacy writes about her experience with international adoption (2005b, 2011), she references existing ideas on the experience and the possible impacts of adoption for adopted children and adoptive and birth parents. She also asks questions about what these ideas obscure or leave out, and she makes claims based on her interpretation of adoption stories as performative and relational accomplishments. The work of both Tony and Stacy makes explicit references to existing research and marks their work in conventions recognizable to scholars through the use of in-text or endnote citations and scholarly commentary.

But this does not mean that all autoethnographies use these conventions to demonstrate knowledge of and contribute to past research. Consider Carolyn's "Maternal Connections" (1996). While she does not formally cite or situate her account among existing daughter-mother stories, her text offers a description of and a counter story to dominant stories about beauty, aging, and parental care. Or consider Ron Pelias's "The Critical Life" (2000). Though he does not cite any sources, the craft of the text and the specificity of detail demonstrate that Pelias intimately knows about the nuances, complications, and possible distress that can stem from having to perpetually evaluate others.

Autoethnographies Embrace Vulnerability with Purpose

Third, autoethnographic works present an intentionally vulnerable subject. Unlike more traditional research methods, secrets are disclosed and histories are made known. Given that we ground our stories in personal experience, we write, dance, paint, and perform the ways we have lived. As such, authoethnographic texts open the door to criticisms that other ways of knowing do not; as Carolyn (2004) notes, "We open ourselves up for criticism about how we've lived" (p. 34). These criticisms sometimes are couched in charges of self-indulgence and narcissism (Anderson, 2006; Buzard, 2003; Delamont, 2009), though such critiques often ignore the dialogic relationship of self and culture—the "I" and "we"—that autoethnographers emphasize when making themselves vulnerable by making personal experiences available for consideration.

Autoethnographers also make choices about which selves and experiences to share as a way of mitigating vulnerability and potential exposure to criticism. Some authors choose to explore a particular aspect of themselves or their experiences. For example, Allen-Collinson and Hockey (2001) write about their experiences as long-distance runners, and Ngunjiri (2011) writes about the intersections of her spiritual and academic selves. Some authors intertwine their stories with interviews in order to indicate the sharing of experience among multiple subjects (Marvasti, 2006), and other authors situate their experiences within the flow of their entire lives. For example, Boylorn (2013) describes how being raised by a collective of strong black women in a small town in the South has shaped her writings and ways of being in the world. Metta (2010) writes through the memory of her experience of spousal and family abuse to consider how those experiences shaped her way of viewing and coming-to-know the world, her relationship with her children, and her work as a psychotherapist. Other authors make themselves vulnerable by exploring aspects of their experiences that may be particularly stigmatizing—for example, Tamas's (2011) explorations of spousal and family abuse, Rambo's (2007) consideration of the ethics and politics around an article she wrote about incest and sexual harassment, and Jago's (2002, 2011) chronicles of depression. All of these authors purposefully open themselves up to "the possibility of being wounded or attacked" (Behar, 1998) in order to call attention to the vulnerabilities that other human beings may endure in silence and in shame.

Autoethnographies Create Reciprocity in order to Compel a Response

Fourth, autoethnography actively seeks a reciprocal relationship with audiences—one marked by mutual responsibility and participation—in order to compel a response (Holman Jones, 2005a). This is not to say that other forms of scholarship do not seek a response from readers, but rather that autoethnography explicitly acknowledges, calls to and seeks contributions from audiences as part of the ongoing conversation of the work. Indeed, the choice to make a self vulnerable to the kinds of critiques we noted earlier is often made with the hope that audiences will engage with and respond to our work in constructive, meaningful—even vulnerable—ways.

The idea of reciprocity also suggests that audiences approach and act on the work they read with a sense of responsibility—they are not passive receivers of a text or performance but are, instead, positioned as active participants expected to act in and on the unfolding story (Elam, 1997). The oft-cited standard that autoethnographies seek to show—rather than only tell about—experience, along with the use of literary, poetic and aesthetic conventions for creating engaging texts and performances, marks an autoethnographer's efforts to connect with readers. Some autoethnographers address this reciprocal relationship by explicitly evoking the audience in their stories, using the second person to call participants to simultaneously witness and act with the text as it unfolds (e.g., Adams, 2011; Glave, 2003/04; McCauley, 1996; Pelias, 2000). As an example of this call to witness and act, Stacy (2011) writes:

> [I]f writing beyond recognition is the price we must pay for working at the limits of self-knowledge and mastery, of piecing together radically incomplete accounts as they are performed in the "crucible of social relations" (Butler, 2005, p. 132), let it be *you* who reads with feeling and solidarity. Let it be you who takes what
>
> > experience tells
> > and makes it into something
> > you can use, something
> > yours. (p. 333)

Cultivating reciprocity with and expecting a response from audiences thus becomes the means by which our autoethnographies embrace *vulnerability with purpose*, make *contributions to existing scholarship*, and *comment on/critique culture and cultural practices*. These four characteristics respond to several perceived needs in research: to create particular and contingent knowledges and ways of being in the world that honor story, artfulness, emotions, and the body; to treat experience and individuals with responsibility and care; and to compel all who do, see, and listen to this work to make room for difference, complexity, and change. These characteristics also hint at the history of how and why autoethnography developed as a qualitative, interpretive, and critical research method.

Autoethnography: A Brief History

Four interrelated historical trends contributed to the formation of autoethnography: (1) *a recognition of the limits of scientific knowledge and a growing appreciation for qualitative research*; (2) a *heightened concern about the ethics and politics of research*;

(3) *a greater recognition of and appreciation for narrative, the literary and aesthetic, emotions and the body*; and (4) the *increased importance of social identities and identity politics*.

Qualitative Research and the Limits of Scientific Knowledge

Quantitative research offers an understanding of the overarching facets of social life. It is good at providing a snapshot of widely held beliefs, commonly practiced behaviors, and underlying cultural values. Quantitative research also is helpful in illustrating social trends, such as what populations of people tend to vote for which political candidates or what social issues might be important to these populations. In sum, quantitative research is useful to us because it focuses on generalized knowledge based on data gathered from large numbers of people. What quantitative research is less adept at is accounting for or describing the particular, the micro, and the situated elements of our lives. Further, the goals of predictability and controlling for error in quantitative analysis also can mean that research may lack nuance or even generate erroneous assumptions about social life (e.g., Fischer, 1998; Herrnstein & Murray, 1994; Zuckerman, 1990). Regardless of methodology, all researchers of humans should understand that we are not (static) rocks or telephones; rather, we are dynamic, unpredictable, and ever-changing beings. Given that society is made of humans, society is necessarily a dynamic and unpredictable concept, too. We might be able to make informed, educated guesses about human behavior, and there might be significant, knowable social constraints (e.g., geography, economy), but to know, with full certainty, what others will do, say, or think is impossible.

A greater appreciation for qualitative research and a growing acceptance of qualitative methods thus provided a way for scholars to answer questions about the nature of reality, knowledge, action, and values that were generated in response to developments and events in human history. In the wake of war, colonial domination, and the genocide of slavery and the Holocaust (and the war, colonial rule, and genocide of our current times), people began to question the ability of Enlightenment thinking and objectivist methods to articulate covering laws (akin to the laws of physics, for example) in order to understand society. The ensuing "crises" of legitimation, representation, and praxis questioned the notion of a world "out there" to be discovered in the articulation of ultimate truths and certain knowledges—truths and knowledges that helped create predictable and stable standards for human behavior (Denzin & Lincoln, 2000a). Questions about what we can know, who can know it, and what actions we can and should take prompted scholars to embrace a view of knowledge as context-bound, partial, contingent, and constituted in and mediated by discourse (Bochner, 2001). These questions also prompted qualitative researchers to examine the mundane, particular, and personal details of experience as a means for understanding the reciprocal relationships of self and culture, communities, and social worlds.

As a result, qualitative research tends to focus on the happenings and politics of a particular culture, a single organization, or one kind of text in order to offer insight about the workings of this particular phenomenon. Qualitative researchers also tailor their methods to delve deeply into the experiences and actions of a particular person, community, or context, heralding the value of interviewing a small number of people, investigating a unique context (Droogsma, 2007; Waskul, Vannini, & Wiesen, 2007), or analyzing a handful of texts (Tourigny, 1998; Carlin & Winfrey, 2009). Qualitative research treats humans as patterned but not fully predictable beings whose thought practices are internally closed off from others (Peters, 1999) and embraces the idea that we are creatures who are never fully and completely knowable, even to ourselves (Mead, 1962). Qualitative researchers, therefore, embrace the contingencies of knowledge and the unique experiences of individuals—contingencies and experiences often disregarded in large-scale social scientific research projects.

The Ethics and Politics of Research

Another trend in research that helped cultivate the creation of autoethnography was a heightened concern about the welfare of research participants and "relational ethics" (Ellis, 2007). Concern about how cultural members will be studied—how they will be probed and prodded, what questions they will be asked, who will be interviewed, how the data will be used—were also generated in the wake of research abuses and manipulations—most famously documented in responses to and critiques of Stanley Milgram's obedience studies and the Tuskegee Syphilis experiments.

Stanley Milgram conducted a series of experiments in order to investigate "destructive obedience" (1964, p. 848)—the obedience that occurred when, from 1933 to 1945,

> millions of innocent persons were systematically slaughtered on command. Gas chambers were built, death camps were guarded, daily quotas of corpses were produced with the same efficiency as the manufacture of appliances. These inhumane policies may have originated in the mind of a single person, but they could only be carried about on a massive scale if a very large number of persons obeyed orders. (1963, p. 371)

Milgram designed a study to test obedience and to illustrate how everyday people would succumb to the perceived authority of a researcher by administering shocks to others upon the researcher's command. While Milgram's (1963, 1964) intentions were commendable, there were concerns about his research design and implementation. In particular, others (e.g., Baumrind, 1964) questioned whether a researcher has the right and responsibility to make people "sweat, tremble, stutter, bite their lips, groan, and dig their fingernails into their flesh" for the purposes of knowledge (Milgram, 1963, p. 375). Should researchers be concerned if they cultivate "serious embarrassment" among research participants (Milgram, 1963, p. 375)? Do the benefits of social scientific inquiry, of achieving understanding by examining "situations in which the end is unknown," justify the use of risk among participants (1964, pp. 848–849)?

The Tuskegee Syphilis Study also introduced numerous ethical issues into research. The study, which began in 1932 and continued until 1972, investigated the long-term effects of untreated syphilis. The researchers—all of whom where white—solicited poor, rural black men with the promise of free medical care; though the investigators monitored the participants and offered largely ineffective (and in many cases harmful) treatments to participants, they did not tell the men they were suffering with syphilis. Even after effective treatments (in the form of penicillin) were identified beginning in the 1940s, investigators refused to offer treatment to some of the infected men out of a "scientific" need to study these men until death (see Thomas & Quinn, 1991).

In response to the exposure of these manipulative and abusive research practices, Congress passed the National Research Act in 1974. This act called for the creation of the National Commission for the Protection of Human Subjects of Research. The commission soon authored the Belmont Report, which summarizes the basic ethical principles and guidelines for conducting research with human subjects, including a *respect for persons* (treating participants as autonomous persons and providing protections for those who have diminished autonomy), *beneficence* (ensuring a subject's well-being by doing no harm and maximizing possible benefits of the research for participants), and *justice* (ensuring a fair distribution of the research benefits and burdens). The practices of seeking informed consent from participants, engaging in an assessment of the risks and benefits of the research that is evaluated by an independent review board, and using guidelines for the fair selection of subjects were devised to carry out these ethical principles in research (United States Department of Health and Human Services, 1979; see Tullis's essay in this Handbook).

If the concerns about ethically and responsibly doing research with human participants began with quantitative researchers engaging in biomedical and behavioral research, these concerns certainly extend to qualitative researchers who work with others. Concurrent with the questioning of objectivist science (raised by war, colonialism and genocide), concerns were raised about anthropologists and ethnographers who entered the field, conducted fieldwork and observations, and then (often) left to write and publish about the studied others (see Conquergood, 1991; Pathak, 2010). As Geertz (1973) notes, "The decline in faith in brute fact, set procedures, and unsituated knowledge in the human sciences, and indeed in scholarship generally, altered no less radically the askers' and lookers' conception of what it was they were trying to do" (pp. 131–132). This rethinking of what qualitative researchers—the askers and lookers—were trying to do also led ethnographers to consider how their research findings functioned as rhetorical and poetic representations and ushered in the "crisis of representation" (Clifford & Marcus, 1986; Van Maanen, 1988).

The Call for Narrative, the Literary and Aesthetic, Emotions and the Body

The crisis of representation drew attention to the absence of human stories, aesthetic considerations, emotions, and embodied experiences in research projects. Storytelling, locating the researcher's point of view within a text, and scholarly writing as a literary and aesthetic event were devalued and even quashed by researchers (see Bochner, forthcoming). This is perhaps no better illustrated than in the oft-cited contrast between the writing in anthropologists' research publications and in their field diaries (Heath, 2012), though a commitment to telling personal and reflexive stories using the conventions of literature has been a long-standing (but often discounted or ignored) practice of women anthropologists (Holman Jones, 2005b; see Abu-Lughod, 1990; Gordon, 1988; Tedlock, 2000; Visweswaran, 1997). Scholars began to speak out about these absences and silences, emphasizing that the form and medium in which we present our work are impacted by race, class, sexuality and gender identities (Lorde, 1984).

Similarly, emotions and lived experience of phenomena were noticeably lacking, relegated to the realm of the "feminine" and thus considered inferior to and a barrier against objectivity, rationality, and masculinity (Keller, 1995). Likewise, researchers' and participants' bodies were abstracted, disregarded or relegated to the periphery of social scientific inquiry, despite the privileged positioning of the (researcher's) body in the ethnographic field (Conquergood, 1991; Leder, 1990). The fallible, messy, and uncontrollable body was just too uncertain—too leaky (Lindemann, 2010)—to include in published research texts.

However, qualitative researchers became increasingly aware of the impossibilities and violence of bodily erasure wrought in our research (Conquergood, 1991; Stoller, 1997). For example, how could a study of death and dying dismiss or disguise the physical experience and embodiment of experience of a dying person and that person's close others and still offer insight to these processes (Ellis, 1995; Trujillo & Vande Berg, 2008)? How could a person study speech anxiety without ever having embodied such anxiety (Pelias, 1997)? In his account of disruptive moments in relational interactions, Pelias (2011) describes the tense body, the body in conflict, the "physically and psychologically *heightened*" body, the "momentarily *speechless*" body, the body that feels "*inadequate,*" "*torn,*" "*doubled,*" and "*wondering*" (p. 39, emphasis in original). As these examples and others show, objective, sterile, and impersonal prose was simply inadequate to articulating the stories, the creative use of language, and image, emotion and human feeling and bodily experience (Ellis, 1995; Frank, 1995). This seemingly objective prose also disregarded the experiences, challenges and concerns of the disenfranchised, though this, too, would be challenged with the rise of identity politics.

The Importance of Social Identities and Identity Politics

In the United States, the 1960s and 1970s often are characterized as a time of social and political questioning and unrest. It was the era of Black Power, disability rights, and second-wave feminism, *Loving vs. Virginia*, the Stonewall Riots, and the Vietnam War. One facet of this questioning and unrest was the battle over social identities and the emergence of identity politics: People were fighting to illustrate that who you are, how you are classified, and what you believe and desire impacts how you perceive society, how society perceives you, and, as a result, how you can move in and act on the world. For example, these identities determined who you could love and marry, if and where you could work or eat or go to school, as well as what you could study in school. People were speaking out, publically, about how some people were treated in humane and privileged ways while others were silenced, disregarded or abused. One academic response to this questioning and unrest was the emergence of new areas of study: African American studies, women's and gender studies, Latin studies, Asian studies, labor and class studies, religious and spirituality studies, and, later, LGBTQ studies, which focused specifically on the identities as well as the personal, social, and political experiences of those who suffered from social injustice.

Not enough has changed in the United States during the last four decades. There might be more structures in place to discourage prejudice and mistreatment, but years, decades, and centuries of prejudice and mistreatment—and their byproduct, distrust—cannot be changed definitively or quickly. As well, the academic safe spaces in which scholars and students can explore identity politics are rapidly disappearing from university campuses (Brown, 2007; Warren, 2011). One thing that has changed, however, is the emphasis on reflexivity in qualitative research (Alvesson & Sköldberg, 2009; Berry & Clair, 2011; Ellis & Bochner, 2000) and a recognition of the ways in which social identities—such as race, class, age, gender, sexuality, religion, and health, among others—impact what and how we study as well as what we see and how we interpret what we study. For instance, Boylorn (2006) and Brown and William-White (2010) describe what it means to be black in predominantly white academic settings. Pelias (2011) describes enactments of gender—of being a "girly man" and of (not) doing gender "right." Defenbaugh (2011) describes what it means to be an ill body in everyday contexts. Chang and Boyd's (2011) edited collection of essays explores how scholars understand, express, and integrate their spiritual lives into their work as academics. Numerous authors (Bornstein, 2012; Newton, 2000; White & Pugh, 1998) have explored how being gay, lesbian, bisexual, queer, and transgender have impacted their research and their lives.

An emphasis on identity politics and reflexivity brings the questioning of the knowledge of scientism, the ethical considerations of research, and the shift in representational practices in qualitative research full circle. While we have treated them separately in the preceding discussion, (1) *the particular, partial, contingent, and shifting nature of knowledge,* (2) *the importance of treating research participants with ethics and care,* (3) *the value of stories, literary and aesthetic modes of communication, emotions, and embodiment in our work,* and (4) the *significance of social identities and identity politics for understanding and honoring positionality and difference* are interrelated and mutually influencing concerns. Concerns about the colonialism of research are directly tied up with the ethics of researching and representing others. The use of qualitative research methods, particularly narrative and storytelling, are crucial ways of knowing for some populations. Similarly, performance studies scholars—scholars who have long valued storytelling, narrative, and the body—have emphasized the ways in which identity is manifest in bodies in motion (Conquergood, 1991; Pineau, 1995; Spry, 2011). And in addition to tearing down the unquestioned legitimacy of scientific design, the ethics violations of the Tuskegee Syphilis Study also highlighted the dilemmas of identity politics, particularly when black populations became (more) fearful of researchers, especially white researchers (Thomas & Quinn, 1991). Yet, stunningly, most all of these dilemmas did not receive much academic attention until the 1960s and 1970s, a moment in United States history where identities began to matter, when positivism was questioned, when research participants began to be appreciated, and when other ways of knowing became valued.

These interrelated and mutually influencing concerns contributed to the emergence of autoethnography as a methodological practice that takes seriously the admonitions about what we no longer can do, be, or tolerate as researchers. No longer can we exude "arrogance" through our "judgmental interpretations of Others" (Clair, 2003, p. 4). No longer can we set out to conquer "strange" and "exotic" cultures. No longer can a researcher *not* identify possible formative characteristics of himself or herself or engage in rigorous self-reflexivity; as Pathak (2010) observes, autoethnographers must work to identify the "systems that shape, constrict, disrupt, inform both the story and the storyteller in autoethnography" (p. 8). No longer can we hide behind positivist ideologies or the power we, as researchers, might have over Others. No longer can we uncritically question or take the beliefs and practices of Others as our own, nor can we represent Others without their input. No longer can we think that we are the ones who should give the Others a voice or to articulate for them the knowledges of their lives and cultures.

These concerns and caveats are demonstrated throughout the essays in this Handbook, with all of the authors touching on several of the concerns raised in this introduction. For example, many of the essays show how autoethnography constitutes a rigorous, nuanced, and legitimate research practice (e.g., Anderson & Glass-Coffin, Chang, Denzin) and critique extant and ethically questionable ways of doing research (e.g., Douglas & Carless; Dutta & Basu; Tomaselli, Dyll-Myklebust, & van Grootheest). Several essays dwell in and conjure up emotions (e.g., Allen-Collinson, Metta; Giorgio, Richardson), demonstrate the importance of literary and aesthetic approaches to scholarship (e.g., Bartleet, Colyar, Mingé,

Pelias), illustrate the use and importance of reflexivity (e.g., Berry, Chawla, Tamas) and the complexities of story (e.g., Gannon, Shoemaker, Stewart, Wyatt & Gale), and take seriously the necessity and challenges of embodiment (e.g., Alexander, Boylorn, Rambo). Other essays explore the creation and negotiation of identities and identity politics (e.g., Crawley & Husakouskaya, Poulos, Tillmann, Weems), consider the role autoethnography might play in critiques of culture and the practice of critique (e.g., Gingrich-Philbrook, Pathak, Toyosaki & Pensoneau-Conway, Tuck & Ree), and address the ethical demands involved in doing autoethnography (e.g., Hernandez & Ngunjiri, Tullis).

Purposes of Autoethnography

Given the concerns and caveats we have enumerated, why would a person use or do autoethnography? What are the benefits of the method as well as the ethical, emotional, professional, and literary and creative risks of doing autoethnographic work? The following purposes are what make autoethnography, as a method, unique and compelling. They include (1) *disrupting norms of research practice and representation*; (2) *working from insider knowledge*; (3) *maneuvering through pain, confusion, anger, and uncertainty and making life better*; (4) *breaking silence/(re) claiming voice* and *"writing to right"* (Bolen, 2012); and (5) *making work accessible*.

Disrupting Norms of Research Practice and Representation

In "A Feminist Critique of Family Studies" (2009), a chapter in the *Handbook of Feminist Family Studies*, Alexis Walker reflects upon her six-year term as editor of the *Journal of Marriage and Family*. Throughout the essay, Walker describes feeling conflicted between publishing traditional research essays—impersonal essays that often perpetuated hegemonic ideals (e.g., the inappropriateness of women working, the dangers of cohabitation)—and publishing much more feminist essays, ones that used lived experience and ones that addressed social inequalities, the workings of power and privilege, and the ways in which hegemonic ideals of families were perpetuated.

At the end of the chapter, Walker included some of her behind-the-scenes experiences while editing the journal. She wrote about her brother being shot on a hunting trip and her sister committing suicide after having suffered for years with mental illness. She mentioned her father being diagnosed with cancer and how her partner had to give up parts of her career and take a significant pay cut. And she mentioned how she herself was diagnosed with non-Hodgkin's lymphoma.

"As a sister, daughter, partner, and individual, I was negotiating the daily family life experience of adult sibling relationships, life threatening health crises, aging parents, mental illness, income loss, and chronic illness" (p. 26), she wrote.

Was I reading about these things in manuscripts submitted to [the *Journal of Marriage and Family*]? No. Instead, I was reading about the effects of cohabitation on children's math scores, the ways in which number and type of marital status transitions affect adolescent externalizing behavior, and how fathers would be more involved with their children if mothers worked hard to foster their involvement. (2009, p. 26)

Walker concluded by calling for research that "makes life experience come alive," research that uses subjectivity and reflexivity, and research that commits to social change (p. 26).

Such life experiences would have no place in traditional social scientific research. If a person had breast cancer and was doing research on that topic, nowhere could the personal ties to the experience be disclosed, or else the research would be biased (Kleinman, 2003). However, the assumption of objectivity is one of the most problematic notions in traditional social scientific work. In addition, objectivity obscures the twists and turns research projects often take. As Ronai (1995) notes, traditional social scientific research is impersonal; it fails to account for the "intuitive leaps, false starts, mistakes, loose ends, and happy accidents that comprise the investigative experience" (p. 421). Autoethnography emerged to account for the role of personal experience in research, to illustrate why the personal is important in our understanding of cultural life, and to more fully articulate the complex research and decision-making processes researchers engage in in the conduct of their work. Again, autoethnography does not claim to produce better or more reliable, generalizable and/or valid research than other methods, but instead provides another approach for studying cultural experience.

Working from Insider Knowledge

Working from insider knowledge, autoethnographers use *personal* experience to create nuanced and detailed "thick descriptions" of *cultural* experience in order to facilitate understanding of those experiences (Geertz, 1973). For instance, Carolyn (1996, 2001, 2003) describes taking care of her aging mother, including the loving work of giving her baths, reminiscing about the past, and talking about death and dying. Jonathan Wyatt (2005, 2008, 2012) describes his relationship with his deceased father, discerns what it may mean to be fathers and sons, and, in writing, explores his efforts to keep his father's spirit alive. Laurel Richardson (2007) provides insight into friendship, companionship, and grief.

Other autoethnographers offer vivid descriptions of and insights into taboo and terrifying experiences. For instance, Lisa Tillmann has published several essays describing the day-to-day feelings associated with eating disorders—essays that provide insights that a detached observer could not offer (see Ellis, Kiesinger, & Tillmann-Healy, 1997; Tillmann-Healy, 1996; Tillmann, 2009b). Or consider Carol Rambo's writings about her experiences of childhood sexual abuse (Ronai, 1995, 1996; Rambo, 2005). She describes being tied up and strapped down, her father performing oral sex on her, faking orgasms, being ridiculed and neglected by her grandmother, and fluctuating in and out of love with her mother. Ronai does not write about these experiences just to tell them "as a survivor of child sex abuse," she writes to illustrate the personal, often hidden nuances of such traumatic experiences—nuances difficult to discern via surveys or interviews with others, or by someone who has never personally experienced this kind of abuse.

Carolyn, Wyatt, Tillmann, Rambo, and numerous other autoethnographers offer intimate and explicit insight into important cultural experiences through relating the lived, day-to-day moments of personal experience and insight that other research methods (e.g., surveys, content analysis, traditional forms of ethnography) could not solicit; as Philaretou and Allen (2006) contend, autoethnography can help address "questions that would be hard to obtain through conventional research methods" (p. 67). Because autoethnography presents a person's experience in the context of relationships, social categories, and cultural practices (or the violation of these relationships, categories and practices), the method revels in sharing insider knowledge about a phenomenon. Further, the autoethnographer is not a traditional participant-observer, someone who infiltrates a cultural group and tries to become part of the group (without going "native") while simultaneously trying to write about the group, and then leaves to write, sometimes never again making contact with cultural group members. Centering the work inside personal experience, autoethnographers not only have an investment in the experience they study but can also articulate aspects of cultural life traditional research methods leave out or could not access.

Maneuvering through Pain, Confusion, Anger and Uncertainty and Making Life Better

Andrew Herrmann (2012a) describes his turbulent experience of the academic job market. He offers readers insight into how the search for an academic job might feel along with the sense that his writing has been a cathartic process, a way to purge or curb negative feelings and channel them into something that feels better (even though material circumstances might suggest otherwise). Throughout the essay, he wrestles with a mess of feelings: the pain of becoming/being unemployed and feeling as though he is a failure; confusion in not knowing what he did wrong or what he could have done differently; anger at those who tell him that he made the wrong choice to pursue a PhD and toward others who have acquired tenure-track jobs; and uncertainty about how, during his job search, he never knew exactly what to do or say, how to juggle a variety of professional interests, and how to behave in tempered but appealing, direct but non-aggressive ways.

Herrmann's (2012a) essay illustrates another purpose of autoethnography: The method allows researchers to write through painful, confusing, angering, and uncertain experiences. As Carolyn (2004) notes, "I tend to write about experiences that knock me for a loop and challenge the construction of meaning I have put together for myself. I write when my world falls apart or the meaning I have constructed for myself is in danger of doing so" (p. 33). Tami

Spry (2011) makes a similar observation: "After years of moving through pain with pen and paper," she says, "asking the nurse for these tools in the morning after losing our son in childbirth was the only thing I could make my body do" (p. 36). This characteristic of autoethnography—as a method for figuring out life and writing through difficult experiences—is beneficial for the author, who can use writing as inquiry (Richardson, 2000) in order to figure out how to live better (see Adams, 2012).

Further, while writing and performing can be cathartic processes, Herrmann (2012a), Carolyn (2004), and Spry (2011) do not write or perform only for themselves; they also write and act for others, offering reflection, insight and hope to readers and audiences who might have had, as well as to readers interested in, the experiences chronicled. If a person only wanted to write or act for herself or himself, then there would be little need to publish or perform. But in autoethnography we see an explicit and intentional directedness toward others, either through the offering of insight that might help those who relate to a person's experience or in a desire for others to bear witness to particular struggles. By processing painful, confusing, angering, and uncertain cultural experiences, the autoethnographer can make life better by giving others "equipment for living" (Burke, 1974), a story and an account to live *with* rather than only think about (Coles, 1989; Bochner, 2002).

Breaking Silence, (Re)Claiming Voice, and Writing to Right

Another purpose of autoethnography is to break silences surrounding experiences as they unfold within cultures and cultural practices. In privileging subjectivity, personal voice, and emotional experience, autoethnographies subvert traditional norms of scholarship that silence the "complexity and fragility" of life (Tillmann, 2009a, p. 95; see DeLeon, 2010). As we noted in the previous section, traditional research often adheres to hegemonically masculine traits, particularly objectivity, control, and predictability. Other traits, such as subjectivity, uncertainty, and emotions, are often gendered as feminine and, consequently, considered inadequate, insufficient, and irrational (Keller, 1995; Pelias, 2011; Walker, 2009). However, by valuing personal experience, autoethnography calls into question such supposedly superior masculine traits. The method embraces uncertainty and emotionality, and it attempts to make sense of the ways in which our identities as raced, gendered, aged, sexualized, and classed researchers impact what we see, do, and say. Autoethnography thus breaks the silences embedded in traditional research; the method conceives of humans as possibly-patterned-but-unpredictable beings and not static and stoic machines (Soukup, 1992; Ellis, 1991).

Autoethnographies can also break silence by addressing understudied, hidden, and/or sensitive topics (Philaretou & Allen, 2006)—topics such as race and racism in educational settings (Boylorn, 2006, 2011; Pennington, 2007), depression (Jago, 2002, 2011), abuse (Ronai, 1996; Tamas, 2011), disorders and illnesses (Brooks, 2011; Defenbaugh, 2011; Fox, 2010b), and sexual violence, heteronormativity, and refiguring women's desires (Mingé & Zimmerman, 2008). In these and many other autoethnographic works, authors write through silence and (re)claim the voices of subverted and subjugated experience. These autoethnographers write toward a cautious and contingent liberation; they illustrate the value of personal experience, the importance of self-reflexivity, and the desire for change around identity politics and disenfranchisement while simultaneously recognizing that breaking silence and reclaiming voice need not—and might never—be ordered, possible, or desirable (Tamas, 2008, 2012).

Despite the contingencies and difficulties of writing toward and for liberation, some autoethnographers use personal experiences to describe cultural experiences with the explicit goal of *changing* experience; they "write to right" (Bolen, 2012) and to go "against the current social order" (DeLeon, 2010, p. 409). These autoethnographers openly challenge Hammersley's (2011) suggestion that social research cannot, and should not, advocate on behalf of social change. For some autoethnographers, this is the most important purpose of/reason for using the method.

For instance, Carolyn (2009b) calls out the racist and classist aspects of rural life, from dating someone of a different race to discussions about race with her neighbors. Ragan Fox (2010a) uses what he terms "auto-archaeology" in an analysis of his high school artifacts as a means of examining how institutional structures and discourses "constrain and enable LGBTQ identities and [challenge] educators to improve their efforts to fight institutionalized homophobia" (p. 122). Rachel Simon's (2003) book about riding the bus with her mildly retarded sister shows how laws, economics, institutions, racism and ableism constrain the life of an otherwise independent and content woman (see Couser [2005] for an analysis of this text). In all of these works, the authors do not use personal experiences solely to describe or to facilitate understanding about cultural experiences or to do the important work of moving through pain, confusion and anger, or to break silences and reclaim voices and identities. Instead, they use personal experiences to promote social change by compelling readers to think about taken-for-granted cultural experiences in astonishing, unique, and often problematic ways and, further, to take new and different action in the world based on the insights generated by the research.

Making Work Accessible

Traditional academic writing is often characterized by, and sometimes criticized for, being inaccessible and jargon-laden. Fledderus (2003) calls such writing "esoteric," "impenetrable," and "elite"; Mykhalovskiy (1996) characterizes "the university" as an "insular" and "isolated" institution of intellectuals who produce books and articles that are only read "by a handful of other academics" (p. 137; see Herrmann, 2012b); and Pelias (2000) notes that much of the work published using the "paradigmatic logic" of sciences continues to ignore the prevalent and persuasive arguments for "why the heart needs to accompany the head" (p. 223; see Tillmann, 2009a).

Another purpose of autoethnography is, therefore, to create work that appeals to a variety of audiences, not just academics. As Carolyn (2004) has said, one of the "great rewards" of autoethnographic work is readers' responses to it: "I can count on one hand how many people ever wrote to me about my more orthodox social science work, but I have gotten hundreds of responses to my autoethnographic stories" (p. 35). Rather than produce inaccessible, esoteric, and jargon-laden texts, autoethnographers work to connect with multiple and diffuse audiences by writing and performing in clear, concise and engaging ways. They strive for an expanded audience by using the tools of literary and aesthetic (visual art, dance, film, performance and multimedia projects) practitioners. They appreciate storytelling as a way of knowing, sharing, and relating, and value a variety of representational mediums (e.g., performance, writing, film) and genres (e.g., poetry, prose, moving images). Not only do these practices make research more accessible—and, we believe, more valuable in that more than just a select few can engage particular works—but they also help satisfy some autoethnographers' commitment to cultural critique and social justice.

○

Similar to the ways autoethnography emerged in research, the purposes of autoethnography we've enumerated above are intertwined and mutually implicating. For instance, an autoethnography that describes and critiques cultural beliefs and practices often also works to break silences and reclaim lost voices (Boylorn, 2006; Granger, 2012; Holman Jones, 2011; Metta, 2010; Tamas, 2011). Many autoethnographies are designed to help others and to make life better, and, given the use of personal experience, offer insider knowledge into the workings of cultural beliefs and practices (Adams, 2011; Tillmann-Healy, 1996). Many autoethnographies are written with the dual goals of breaking research norms and practices of representation and creating accessible texts for a range of audiences (Ellis, 1995; Goodall, 2006; Mingé & Zimmerman, 2012). These intertwined and mutually implicating purposes of autoethnography also reflect the organization of this Handbook, which is designed to consider contemporary issues surrounding the method and to look to the future of autoethnographic inquiry.

More than Method: Contemporary Issues in Autoethnography

We've envisioned this Handbook as a resource for researchers and graduate students across the humanities, social sciences, communication, education, social work, and health. We wanted to create a volume that contextualizes the development and practices of autoethnography; points to future practices, themes, and commitments; and provides examples of thoughtful, effective, and innovative autoethnography. This Handbook is organized into four sections: (1) *reflecting and engaging*; (2) *making and relating*; (3) *representing, breaking and remaking*;

and (4) *moving and changing*. The titles and focuses of these four sections reflect our adaptation of Conquergood's (1992) tripartite scheme of *mimesis, poiesis,* and *kinesis* in the evolution of performance and performance ethnography.

Reflecting and Engaging

Mimesis is the idea that autoethnography acts as a mirror or reflection of life and living in ways that are useful for contemplation as well as a mode of engagement with understanding. Or, as Art Bochner's introduction to the first section puts it, autoethnography is a "form of inquiry, writing, and/or performance that puts questions and 'issues of being' into circulation and dialogue." Our first section reflects on the state of the art of autoethnography as a research practice, mode of inquiry, and mode of engagement. The chapters in this section also look forward to the future of autoethnography through the lenses of reflection and engagement—as a means of answering what Bochner describes as autoethnography's call to "do meaningful work and lead a meaningful life."

The first five chapters in this section *tell about* their topics. In particular, they chart the development of autoethnographic practices and commitments as they relate to the chapter topics and themes, providing readers with a map of current concerns/questions/issues and suggesting future directions/challenges/concerns for exploration. These chapters include Leon Anderson and Bonnie Glass-Coffin's tales of coming to autoethnography; Kitrina Douglas's and David Carless's personal histories of autoethnographic inquiry; Heewon Chang's explication of the workings of autoethnography as a method for connecting self to society; Norman Denzin's charting of the development of interpretive autoethnography through his and others' writing practices; and Mohan Dutta and Ambar Basu's telling stories of negotiating postcolonial selves and politics in the academy and in research practice.

The remaining three chapters—exemplars—in the section *show* the ways in which autoethnography can be a practice of reflection and engagement. These original contributions demonstrate the practices, commitments, possibilities, and critical questions around autoethnographic inquiry. They also provide examples of the authors' unique approaches to autoethnographic writing in both form and voice. The exemplars in this section include Devika Chawla's stories of walking with her grandmother, Indian women, and home; the "sayin's" Robin Boylorn was taught by her mother and the women in her family in her rural south childhood; and Sophie Tamas's exploration of a (academic) subject in writing, body, time and space.

Making and Relating

The next section of the Handbook illustrates the idea of *poiesis* in autoethnography. If *mimesis* focuses our attention on reflection and engagement, *poiesis* asks us to consider autoethnography as a creation that makes something happen—a poetics and way of relating to self and culture that shows how we make meaning and construct relationships on the page and in the world. The chapters in this section consider the specifics of autoethnography as it is currently practiced, the creation and shifting of various autoethnographic subjectivities (selves, collaborators, audiences, and communities), the practice of autoethnography as a relational and collaborative endeavor, and autoethnography as a doing that creates, marks, and makes visible various voices and ways of knowing. As Bud Goodall's section introduction points out, the autoethnographer's awareness of the interplay of meaning, selves, and culture and the recognition of ourselves as makers of meaning—as storytellers—creates a sensitivity and commitment to the power and responsibility of world-making and representation.

The first five chapters in this section include the tales Keith Berry spins on and around autoethnographic reflexivity and cultural critique; Susanne Gannon's letters on and to subjectivities in autoethnography; Jillian Tullis's consideration of the ethical considerations and obligations of autoethnographic work; Kathy-Ann Hernandez and Faith Ngunjiri's reflection on collaborative autoethnography; and Jacquelyn Allen-Collinson's consideration of autoethnography as a relational research practice centered in lived and embodied experience. The four exemplars in this section include Jonathan Wyatt's and Ken Gale's assembled letters to (them)selves; Mary Weems's charting of a year and life in poems; Sara Crawley and Nadzeya Husakouskaya's globally queer drag performances of academic selves; and Laurel Richardson's tale of a fiftieth high school reunion as a journey of discovery through the lens of her childhood experience, particularly of straddling a Jewish/Gentile split within the entanglements of family, culture, and class.

Representing, Breaking and Remaking; Moving and Changing

The next two sections of the Handbook focus on autoethnography as *kinesis*, a dynamic practice that creates movement and change. As Soyini Madison (2012) notes, "Kinesis is the point at which reflection and meaning now evoke intervention and change" (pp. 188–189).

The chapters in *Representing, Breaking, and Remaking* cover the movement of autoethnographic methods, modes of inquiry and representational practices that range from language- and text-based to geographic, symbolic, and embodied. The chapters in this section also consider how autoethnographic approaches can be used to intervene in systems and practices of bearing witness to and creating change within selves, communities, and cultures. As Barbara Tedlock observes in her section introduction, "writing and performing vulnerably from the heart with analytic accuracy" allows autoethnographers to "emerge from a flat soulless description of social worlds" into "sensuous, evocative research that encourages and supports both personal development and social justice."

The first five chapters in this section include essays by Julia Colyar on the writing process and Ron Pelias on compositional strategies in autoethnography; Grace

Giorgio's writing on and as memory, memorial and bearing witness; Jeanine Mingé's lessons on creating mindful autoethnographic knowledges within stories of biological, academic and chosen families; and Brydie-Leigh Bartleet's charting of artful and embodied modes of autoethnographic inquiry from the visual and poetic to the musical and performative. The three exemplars in the section include Chris Poulos's stories of writing as a way through and to voice, identity and hope; Lisa Tillmann's poetic call for the equality of all in marriage, health and safety, and human rights; and Marilyn Metta's poetic and painterly journey through embodied writing and recovery from abuse.

Andrew Sparkes, in his introduction to the chapters in the *Moving and Changing* section, sees autoethnography as both a mode of knowing and a way of being. He points out how the essays in this section privilege autoethnography "not only as a way to know, but also as a way to critically act in the world and a way to understand the construction of the self." As such, the essays in this section explore how autoethnography can be used to move and change selves, communities, and worlds, particularly through the practices of autoethnographic approaches to teaching autoethnographic methods/modes of inquiry/means of representation; through exploring autoethnographic performances of possibilities, utopias, and futures; and through concrete efforts to make the world a more hospitable and just place to live. The final chapters in this section consider how autoethnographic approaches can work as an imaginative criticism and be critiques based on the context, point of view, and aims of the work.

The first six chapters in this section include Deanna Shoemaker's journey through autoethnography as a performance of possibilities, utopias and futures; Bryant Alexander's pedagogy for teaching autoethnography and approach to teaching autoethnographically; Satoshi Toyosaki and Sandy Pensoneau-Conway's consideration of autoethnography as an ontology and praxeology of social justice; Keyan Tomasellli, Lauren Dyll-Myklebust and Sjoerd van Grootheest's exploration of autoethnography as a personal, political and egalitarian intervention in research with Africans in Africa; Archana Pathak's consideration of the intersections of post-colonial theory and autoethnography; and Craig Gingrich-Philbrook's evaluation of the power, politics, and unequal distribution of entitlements in the telling of stories and in evaluations of autoethnography. The three exemplars in the section include Carol Rambo's story of an embodied, chronic, personal, psychological, and relational liminality; Eve Tuck and C. Ree's exploration of haunting as a form of social justice; and Kathleen Stewart's autoethnography of what happens at the inter-section of theory and experience.

○

We see the trajectory of autoethnography, "from the mirroring of *mimesis* to the enlightenment of *poiesis*, and finally to the intervention of *kinesis* [as] a testament" to the understanding of autoethnography as a practice that "does not simply describe the world, but offers great possibility for changing it" (Madison, 2012, p. 189). The concluding chapter in the Handbook points to these possibilities for change and points toward the future of autoethnography as a "what if" practice.

Beyond the intellectual and emotional, instrumental and evocative, and poetic and political contributions that each chapter makes to enhancing our understandings of the reasons for and purposes and practices of autoethnography, the authors included in this Handbook tell stories of coming to autoethnography that feature how the method and practice has added something new, exciting, and important to their (writing) lives. Reflective and engaging, focused on creation and making something happen, and providing means for movement and change, autoethnography is more than a method. As you will see, it is a way of living and of writing life honestly, complexly, and passionately.

References

Abu-Lughod, L. (1990). Can there be a feminist ethnography? *Woman and Performance: A Journal of Feminist Theory, 5*, 7–27.

Adams, T. E. (2005). Phenomenologically investigating mediated "nature." *The Qualitative Report, 10*(3), 512–532. Retrieved August 10, 2012, from /www.nova.edu/ssss/QR/QR1-3/adams.pdf.

Adams, T. E. (2008). A review of narrative ethics. *Qualitative Inquiry, 14*(2), 175–194.

Adams, T. E. (2011). *Narrating the closet: An autoethnography of same-sex attraction*. Walnut Creek, CA: Left Coast Press, Inc.

Adams, T. E. (2012). The joys of autoethnography: Possibilities for communication research. *Qualitative Communication Research, 1*, 181–194.

Adams, T. E., & Holman Jones, S. (2008). Autoethnography is queer. In N. K. Denzin, Y. S. Lincoln, & L. T. Smith (Eds.), *Handbook of critical and indigenous methodologies* (pp. 373–390). Thousand Oaks, CA: Sage.

Adams, T. E., & Holman Jones, S. (2011). Telling stories: Reflexivity, queer theory, and autoethnography. *Cultural Studies ↔ Critical Methodologies, 11*, 108–116.

Allen-Collinson, J., & Hockey, J. (2001). Runners' tales: Autoethnography, injury and narrative. *Auto/Biography, 9*, 95–106.

Alvesson, M., & Sköldberg, K. (2009). *Reflexive methodology*. London: Sage.

Anderson, L. (2006). Analytic autoethnography. *Journal of Contemporary Ethnography, 35*, 373–395.

Averett, P., & Soper, D. (2011). Sometimes I am afraid: An autoethnography of resistance and compliance. *The Qualitative Report, 16*, 358–376.

Bartleet, B.-L., & Ellis, C. (Eds.). (2009). *Music autoethnographies: Making autoethnography sing/making music personal*. Bowen Hills, Australia: QLD Australian Academic Press.

Baumrind, D. (1964). Some thoughts on ethics of research: After reading Milgram's "Behavioral Study of Obedience." *American Psychologist, 19*, 421–423.

Behar, R. (1996). *The vulnerable observer*. Boston: Beacon Press.

Behar, R. (1998). A sixth memo for the millennium: Vulnerability. Retrieved August 10, 2012, from www.mit.edu/~bhdavis/BeharLec.html

Berry, K., & Clair, R. P. (2011). Special issue: The call of ethnographic reflexivity: Narrating the self's presence in ethnography. *Cultural Studies ↔ Critical Methodologies, 11*(2).

Bochner, A. P. (2001). Narrative's virtues. *Qualitative Inquiry 7*(2), 131–157.

Bochner, A. P. (2002). Perspectives on inquiry III: The moral of stories. In M. L. Knapp & J. A. Daly (Eds.), *Handbook of interpersonal communication* (3rd ed., pp. 73–101). Thousand Oaks, CA: Sage.

Bochner, A. P. (forthcoming). *Coming to narrative: Method and meaning in a university life*. Walnut Creek, CA: Left Coast Press, Inc.

Bochner, A. P., & Ellis, C. (2002). *Ethnographically speaking: Autoethnography, literature, and aesthetics*. Walnut Creek, CA: AltaMira Press.

Bolen, D. M. (2012). *Toward an applied communication relational inqueery: Autoethnography, co-constructed narrative, and relational futures*. Unpublished doctoral dissertation, Wayne State University.

Bornstein, K. (2012). *A queer and pleasant danger*. Boston: Beacon Press.

Boyle, M., & Parry, K. (2007). Special issue on organizational autoethnography. *Culture and Organization 3*(3).

Boylorn, R. M. (2006). E pluribus unum (out of many, one). *Qualitative Inquiry, 12*, 651–680.

Boylorn, R. M. (2011). Gray or for colored girls who are tired of chasing rainbows: Race and reflexivity. *Cultural Studies ↔ Critical Methodologies, 11*, 178–186.

Boylorn, R. (2013). *Sweetwater: Black women and narratives of resilience*. New York: Peter Lang.

Brooks, C. F. (2011). Social performance and secret ritual: Battling against obsessive-compulsive disorder. *Qualitative Heath Research, 20*, 249–261.

Brown, C. (2007). *Dude, where's my Black studies department?: The disappearance of Black Americans from our universities*. Berkeley: North Atlantic Press.

Brown, A. F., & William-White, L. (2010). "We are not the same minority": The narratives of two sisters navigating identity and discourse at public and private White institutions. In C. C. Robinson & P. Clandy (Eds.), *Tedious journeys: Autoethnography by women of color in academe* (pp. 149–175). New York: Peter Lang.

Burke, K. (1974). *The philosophy of literary form: Studies in symbolic action* (3rd ed.). Berkeley: University of California Press.

Burnier, D. (2006). Encounters with the self in social science research: A political scientist looks at autoethnography. *Journal of Contemporary Ethnography, 35*, 410–418.

Butler, J. (2005). *Giving an account of oneself*. New York: Fordham Press.

Buzard, J. (2003). On auto-ethnographic authority. *The Yale Journal of Criticism, 16*, 61–91.

Cancienne, M. B., & Bagley, C. (2008). Dance as method: The process and product of movement in educational research. In P. Liamputtong & J. Rumbold (Eds.), *Knowing differently: Arts-based and collaborative research methods* (pp. 169–187). New York: Nova Science.

Carlin, D. B., & Winfrey, K. L. (2009). Have you come a long way, baby? Hillary Clinton, Sarah Palin, and sexism in 2008 campaign coverage. *Communication Studies, 60*, 326–343.

Chang, H. (2008). *Autoethnography as method*. Walnut Creek, CA: Left Coast Press, Inc.

Chang, H., & Boyd, D. (2011). *Spirituality in higher education: Autoethnographies*. Walnut Creek, CA: Left Coast Press, Inc.

Clair, R. P. (2003). The changing story of ethnography. In R. P. Clair (Ed.), *Expressions of Ethnography* (pp. 3–26). Albany: State University of New York Press.

Clifford, J., & Marcus, G. E. (Eds.). (1986). *Writing culture: The poetics and politics of ethnography*. Berkeley: University of California Press.

Coles, R. (1989). *The call of stories*. Boston: Houghton Mifflin.

Communication Studies 298. (1997). Fragments of self at the postmodern bar. *Journal of Contemporary Ethnography, 26*, 251–292.

Conquergood, D. (1991). Rethinking ethnography: Towards a critical cultural politics. *Communication Monographs, 58*, 179–194.

Conquergood, D. (1992). Ethnography, rhetoric, and performance. *Quarterly Journal of Speech, 78*, 80–97.

Couser, G. T. (2005). Disability and (auto)ethnography: Riding (and writing) the bus with my sister. *Journal of Contemporary Ethnography, 34*, 121–142.

Defenbaugh, N. L. (2011). *Dirty tale: A narrative journey of the IBD body*. Cresskill, NJ: Hampton Press.

Delamont, S. (2009). The only honest thing: Autoethnography, reflexivity and small crises in fieldwork. *Ethnography and Education, 4*, 51–63.

DeLeon, A. P. (2010). How do I begin to tell a story that has not been told? Anarchism, autoethnography, and the middle ground. *Equity & Excellence in Education, 43*, 398–413.

Denzin, N. K., & Lincoln, Y. S. (2000a). Introduction: The discipline and practice of qualitative research. In N. K. Denzin & Y. S. Lincoln (Eds.), *The SAGE handbook of qualitative research* (2nd ed., pp. 1–28). Thousand Oaks, CA: Sage.

Denzin, N. K., & Lincoln, Y. S. (Eds.). (2000b). *Handbook of qualitative research* (2nd ed.). Thousand Oaks, CA: Sage.

Denzin, N. K., & Lincoln, Y. S. (Eds.). (2005). *The SAGE handbook of qualitative research* (3rd ed.). Thousand Oaks, CA: Sage.

Denzin, N. K., & Lincoln, Y. S. (Eds.). (2011). *The SAGE handbook of qualitative research* (4th ed.). Thousand Oaks, CA: Sage.

Doloriert, C., & Sambrook, S. (2011). Accommodating an autoethnographic PhD: The tale of the thesis, the viva voce, and the traditional business school. *Journal of Contemporary Ethnography, 40*, 582–615.

Droogsma, R. A. (2007). Redefining Hijab: American Muslim women's standpoints on veiling. *Journal of Applied Communication Research, 35*, 294–319.

Duncan, M. (2004). Autoethnography: Critical appreciation of an emerging art. *International Journal of Qualitative Methods, 3*(4).

Elam, H. J., Jr. (1997). *Taking it to the streets: The social protest theater of Luis Valdez and Amiri Baraka*. Ann Arbor: University of Michigan Press.

Ellis, C. (1991). Sociological introspection and emotional experience. *Symbolic Interaction, 14*, 23–50.

Ellis, C. (1993). "There are survivors": Telling a story of sudden death. *The Sociological Quarterly 34*, 711–730.

Ellis, C. (1995). *Final negotiations: A story of love, loss, and chronic illness*. Philadelphia: Temple University Press.

Ellis, C. (1996). Maternal connections. In C. Ellis & A. P. Bochner (Eds.), *Composing ethnography: Alternative forms of qualitative writing* (pp. 240–243). Walnut Creek, CA: AltaMira Press.

Ellis, C. (2001). With mother/with child: A true story. *Qualitative Inquiry, 7*, 598–616.

Ellis, C. (2003). Grave tending: With mother at the cemetery. *Forum: Qualitative Social Research, 4*(2). Retrieved August 10, 2012, from www.qualitative-research.net/fqs- texte/2-03/2-03ellis-e.html

Ellis, C. (2004). *The ethnographic I: A methodological novel about autoethnography*. Walnut Creek, CA: AltaMira Press.

Ellis, C. (2007). Telling secrets, revealing lives: Relational ethics in research with intimate others. *Qualitative Inquiry, 13*, 3–29.

Ellis, C. (2009a). *Revision: Autoethnographic reflections on life and work*. Walnut Creek, CA: Left Coast Press, Inc.

Ellis, C. (2009b). Telling tales on neighbors: Ethics in two voices. *International Review of Qualitative Research, 2*, 3–28.

Ellis, C., & Adams, T. E. (forthcoming). The purposes, practices, and principles of autoethnographic research. In P. Leavy (Ed.), *The Oxford handbook of qualitative research methods*. New York: Oxford University Press.

Ellis, C., & Bochner, A. P. (Eds.). (1996). Special issue: Taking ethnography into the twenty-first century. *Journal of Contemporary Ethnography, 25*(1).

Ellis, C., & Bochner, A. P. (2000). Autoethnography, personal narrative, reflexivity. In N. K. Denzin & Y. S. Lincoln (Eds.), *Handbook of qualitative research* (2nd ed., pp. 733–768). Thousand Oaks, CA: Sage.

Ellis, C., Kiesinger, C. E., & Tillmann-Healy, L. M. (1997). Interactive interviewing: Talking about emotional experience. In R. Hertz (Ed.), *Reflexivity and voice* (pp. 119–149). Thousand Oaks, CA: Sage.

Ellis, C., & Rawicki, J. (in press a). Collaborative witnessing of survival during the Holocaust: An exemplar of relational autoethnography. *Qualitative Inquiry*.

Ellis, C., & Rawicki, J. (in press b). Collaborative witnessing in conversations with Holocaust survivors. In S. High (Ed.), *Beyond trauma and testimony*. Vancouver: University of British Columbia Press.

Fischer, F. (1998). Beyond empiricism: Policy inquiry in post positivist perspective. *Policy Studies Journal, 26,* 129–146.

Fledderus, F. (2003). Insights and outlooks: Why highfalutin language has to go. *Discourses in Music, 4*(2). Retrieved August 10, 2012, from www.discourses.ca/v4n2io.html

Foster, K., McAllister, M., & O'Brien, L. (2006). Extending the boundaries: Autoethnography as an emergent method in mental health nursing research. *International Journal of Mental Health Nursing, 15*(1), 44–53.

Fox, R. (2010a). Tales of a fighting bobcat: An 'auto-archaeology' of gay identify formation and maintenance. *Text and Performance Quarterly, 30,* 122–142.

Fox, R. (2010b). Re-membering Daddy: Autoethnographic reflections of my father and Alzheimer's disease. *Text and Performance Quarterly, 30,* 3–20.

Frank, A. W. (1995). *The wounded storyteller.* Chicago: University of Chicago Press.

Geertz, C. (1973). *The interpretation of cultures.* New York: Basic Books.

Gingrich-Philbrook, C. (2000). Special issue: The personal and political in solo performance. *Text and Performance Quarterly, 20*(1).

Glave, T. (2003/04). On the difficulty of confiding with complete love and trust, in some heterosexual 'friends.' *Massachusetts Review, 44,* 583–595.

Goodall, H. L. (2006). *A need to know: The clandestine history of a CIA family.* Walnut Creek, CA: Left Coast Press, Inc.

Gordon, A. (1988). *Ghostly matters: Haunting and the sociological imagination.* Minneapolis: University of Minnesota Press.

Granger, C. (2012). *Silent moments in education: An autoethnography of learning, teaching, and learning to teach.* Toronto: University of Toronto Press.

Hammersley, M. (2011). *Methodology: Who needs it?* Los Angeles: Sage.

Harrison, B. (2002). Photographic visions and narrative inquiry. *Narrative Inquiry, 12,* 87–111

Hayler, M. (2011). *Autoethnography, self-narrative and teacher education.* Rotterdam, Netherlands: Sense.

Heath, S. B. (2012). *Words at work and play: Three decades in family and community life.* Cambridge, UK: Cambridge University Press.

Herrmann, A. F. (2012a). "I know I'm unlovable": Desperation, dislocation, despair, and discourse on the academic job hunt. *Qualitative Inquiry, 18,* 247–255.

Herrmann, A. F. (2012b). "Criteria against ourselves?" Embracing the opportunities of qualitative inquiry. *International Review of Qualitative Research, 5,* 135–152.

Herrnstein, R. J., & Murray, C. (1994). *The bell curve: Intelligence and class structure in American life.* New York: Free Press.

Holman Jones, S. (2005a). Autoethnography: Making the personal political. In N. K. Denzin & Y. S. Lincoln (Eds.), *Handbook of qualitative research* (pp. 763–791). Thousand Oaks, CA: Sage.

Holman Jones, S. (2005b). (M)othering loss: Telling adoption stories, telling performativity. *Text and Performance Quarterly, 25,* 113–135.

Holman Jones, S. (2007). *Torch singing: Performing resistance and desire from Billie Holiday to Edith Piaf.* Lanham, MD; AltaMira Press.

Holman Jones, S. (2011). Lost and found. *Text and Performance Quarterly, 31,* 322–341.

Holman Jones, S., & Adams, T. E. (2010a). Autoethnography and queer theory: Making possibilities. In N. K. Denzin & M. D. Giardina (Eds.), *Qualitative inquiry and human rights* (pp. 136–157). Walnut Creek, CA: Left Coast Press, Inc.

Holman Jones, S., & Adams, T. E. (2010b). Autoethnography is a queer method. In K. Browne & C. J. Nash (Eds.), *Queer methods and methodologies* (pp. 195–214). Burlington, VT: Ashgate.

Hunt, S. A., & Junco, N. R. (2006). Two thematic issues: Defective memory and analytical autoethnography. *Journal of Contemporary Ethnography, 35*(4).

Jago, B. J. (2002). Chronicling an academic depression. *Journal of Contemporary Ethnography, 31,* 729—757.

Jago, B. J. (2011). Shacking up: An autoethnographic tale of cohabitation. *Qualitative Inquiry, 17,* 204–219.

Jewkes, Y. (2011). Autoethnography and emotion as intellectual resources: Doing prison research differently. *Qualitative Inquiry, 18,* 63–75.

Jones, J. L. (2002). Performance ethnography: The role of embodiment in cultural authenticity. *Theatre Topics, 21,* 1–15.

Keller, E. F. (1995). *Reflections on gender and science.* New Haven, NJ: Yale University Press.

Kleinman, S. (2003). Feminist fieldworker: Connecting research, teaching, and memoir. In B. Glassner & R. Hertz (Eds.), *Our studies, ourselves: Sociologists' lives and work* (pp. 215–232). New York: Oxford University Press.

Lapan, S. D., Quartaroli, M. T., & Riemer, F. J. (2012). *Qualitative research: An introduction to methods and designs.* San Francisco: Jossey-Bass.

Leder, D. (1990). *The absent body.* Chicago: University of Chicago Press.

Lindemann, K. (2010). Cleaning up my (father's) mess: Narrative containments of 'leaky' masculinities. *Qualitative Inquiry, 16*(1), 29–38.

Lorde, A. (1984). *Sister outsider.* Berkeley, CA: The Crossing Press.

Madison, D. S. (2012). *Critical ethnography: Method, ethics, and performance* (2nd ed.). Los Angeles: Sage.

Marvasti, A. (2006). Being Middle Eastern American: Identity negotiation in the context of the war on terror. *Symbolic Interaction, 28,* 525–547.

McCauley, S. (1996). Let's say. In P. Merla (Ed.), *Boys like us: Gay writers tell their coming out stories* (pp. 186–192). New York: Avon.

Mead, G. H. (1962). *Mind, self, and society from the standpoint of a social behaviorist.* Chicago: University of Chicago Press.

Metta, M. (2010). *Writing against, alongside, and beyond memory.* New York: Peter Lang.

Milgram, S. (1963). Behavioral study of obedience. *Journal of Abnormal and Social Psychology, 67,* 371–378.

Milgram, S. (1964). Issues in the study of obedience: A reply to Baumrind. *American Psychologist, 19,* 848–852.

Mingé, J., & Zimmerman, A. L. (2008). Power, pleasure, and play: Screwing the dildo and rescripting sexual violence. *Qualitative Inquiry, 15,* 329–349.

Mingé, J., & Zimmerman, A. L. (2012). *Concrete and dust: Mapping the sexual terrain of Los Angeles.* New York: Routledge.

Muncey, T. (2010). *Creating autoethnographies.* Thousand Oaks, CA: Sage.

Myers, W. B. (2012). Special issue: Writing autoethnographic joy. *Qualitative Communication Research, 1*(2).

Mykhalovskiy, E. (1996). Reconsidering table talk: Critical thoughts on the relationship between sociology, autobiography and self-indulgence. *Qualitative Sociology, 19,* 131–151.

Newton, E. (2000). *Margaret Mead made me gay: Personal essays, public ideas.* Durham, NC: Duke University Press.

Ngunjiri, F. W. (2011). Studying spirituality and leadership: A personal journey. In H. Chang & D. Boyd (Eds.), *Spirituality in higher education: Autoethnographies* (pp. 183–198). Walnut Creek, CA: Left Coast Press, Inc.

Ngunjiri, F. W., Hernandez, K-A. C., & Chang, H. (2010). Special issue: Autoethnography as research practice. *Journal of Research Practice, 6*(1).

Pathak, A. A. (2010). Opening my voice, claiming my space: Theorizing the possibilities of postcolonial approaches to autoethnography. *Journal of Research Practice, 6*(1). Retrieved March 15, 2011, from jrp.icaap.org/index.php/jrp/article/view/231/191

Pelias, R. J. (1997). Confessions of apprehensive performer. *Text and Performance Quarterly, 17,* 25–32.

Pelias, R. J. (2000). The critical life. *Communication Education, 49,* 220–228.

Pelias, R. J. (2011). *Leaning: A poetics of personal relations.* Walnut Creek, CA: Left Coast Press, Inc.

Pennington, J. L. (2007). Silence in the classroom/whispers in the halls: Autoethnography as pedagogy in White pre-service teacher education. *Race, Ethnicity, and Education, 10*(1), 93–113.

Peters, J. D. (1999). *Speaking into the air: A history of the idea of communication.* Chicago: University of Chicago Press.

Philaretou, A. G., & Allen, K. R. (2006). Researching sensitive topics through autoethnographic means. *The Journal of Men's Studies, 14*(1), 65–78.

Pineau, E. L. (1995). Re-casting rehearsal: Making a case for production as research. *Journal of the Illinois Speech and Theatre Association, 46,* 43–52.

Poulos, C. N. (2008). Autoethnography special issue. *Iowa Journal of Communication, 40*(1).

Poulos, C. N. (2009). *Accidental ethnography: An inquiry into family secrecy.* Walnut Creek, CA: Left Coast Press, Inc.

Rambo, C. (2005). Impressions of Grandmother: An autoethnographic portrait. *Journal of Contemporary Ethnography, 34,* 560–585.

Rambo, C. (2007). Handing IRB an unloaded gun. *Qualitative Inquiry, 13,* 353–367.

Rawicki, J., & Ellis, C. (2011). Lechem hara (bad bread) lechem tov (good bread): Survival and sacrifice during the Holocaust. *Qualitative Inquiry, 17,* 155–157

Reed-Danahay, D. E. (Ed.). (1997). *Auto/ethnography.* New York: Berg.

Richardson, L. (2000). Writing: A method of inquiry. In N. K. Denzin & Y. S. Lincoln (Eds.), *Handbook of qualitative research* (pp. 923–948). Thousand Oaks, CA: Sage.

Richardson, L. (2007). *Last writes: A daybook for a dying friend.* Walnut Creek, CA: Left Coast Press, Inc.

Ronai, C. R. (1995). Multiple reflections of child sex abuse. *Journal of Contemporary Ethnography, 23,* 395–426.

Ronai, C. R. (1996). My mother is mentally retarded. In C. Ellis & A. P. Bochner (Eds.), *Composing ethnography: Alternative forms of qualitative writing* (pp. 109–131). Walnut Creek, CA: AltaMira Press.

Saldaña, J. (2008). Second chair: An autoethnodrama. *Research Studies in Music Education 30,* 177–191.

Simon, R. (2003). *Riding the bus with my sister: A true life journey.* New York: Penguin.

Soukup, P. (1992). Interpersonal communication. *Communication Research Trends, 12*(3).

Spry, T. (2011). *Body, paper, stage: Writing and performing autoethnography.* Walnut Creek: Left Coast Press, Inc.

Stoller, P. (1997). *Sensuous scholarship.* Philadelphia: University of Pennsylvania Press.

Tamas, S. (2008). Writing and righting trauma: Troubling the autoethnographic voice. *Forum: Qualitative Social Research, 10*(1). Accessed August 10, 2012, from nbn-resolving.de/urn:nbn:de:0114-fqs0901220

Tamas, S. (2011). *Life after leaving: The remains of spousal abuse.* Walnut Creek, CA: Left Coast Press, Inc.

Tamas, S. (2012). Love and happiness? *Qualitative Communication Research, 1*(2), 231–251.

Tedlock, B. (2000). Ethnography and ethnographic representation. In N. K. Denzin & Y. S. Lincoln (Eds.), *Handbook of qualitative research* (2nd ed., pp. 455–486). Thousand Oaks, CA: Sage.

Thomas, S. B., & Quinn, S. C. (1991). The Tuskegee Syphilis Study, 1932 to 1972: Implications for HIV education and AIDS risk education programs in the Black community. *American Journal of Public Health, 81,* 1498–1505.

Tillmann-Healy, L. M. (1996). A secret life in a culture of thinness: Reflections on body, food, and bulimia. In C. Ellis & A. P. Bochner (Eds.), *Composing ethnography: Alternative forms of qualitative writing* (pp. 76–108). Walnut Creek, CA: AltaMira Press.

Tillmann, L. M. (2009a). Speaking into silences: Autoethnography, communication, and applied research. *Journal of Applied Communication Research, 37,* 94–97.

Tillmann, L. M. (2009b). Body and bulimia revisited: Reflections on "A secret life." *Journal of Applied Communication Research, 37,* 98–112.

Tourigny, S. C. (1998). Some new dying trick: African American youths "choosing" HIV/AIDS. *Qualitative Health Research, 8*(2), 149–167.

Trujillo, N., & Vande Berg, L. (2008). *Cancer and death: A love story in two voices.* New York: Hampton Press.

United States Department of Health and Human Services. (1979). *The Belmont report: Ethical principles and guidelines for the protection of human subjects of research.* Retrieved August 30, 2012, from www.hhs.gov/ohrp/humansubjects/guidance/belmont.html

Van Maanen, J. (1988). *Tales of the field: On writing ethnography.* Chicago: University of Chicago Press.

Vickers, M. H. (2007). Autoethnography as sensemaking: A story of bullying. *Culture and Organization, 13,* 223–237.

Visweswaran, K. (1997). *Fictions of feminist ethnography.* Minneapolis: University of Minnesota Press.

Walker, A. (2009). A feminist critique of family studies. In S. A. Lloyd, A. L. Few, & K. R. Allen (Eds.), *Handbook of feminist family studies* (pp. 18–27). Thousand Oaks, CA: Sage.

Wall, S. (2006). An autoethnography on learning about autoethnography. *International Journal of Qualitative Methods, 5*(2). Retrieved from ejournals.library.ualberta.ca/index.php/IJQM/article/viewFile/4396/3522

Wall, S. (2008). Easier said than done: Writing an autoethnography. *International Journal of Qualitative Methods, 7*(1). Retrieved from ejournals.library.ualberta.ca/index.php/IJQM/article/view/1621

Warren, C. (2011). From the editor: Belts and corsets. *Academe Online.* Retrieved August 10, 2012, from www.aaup.org/AAUP/pubsres/academe/2011/SO/col/fte.htm

Waskul, D. D., Vannini, P., & Wiesen, D. (2007). Women and their clitoris: Personal discovery, signification, and use. *Symbolic Interaction, 30,* 151–174.

White, W., & Pugh, T. (1998). "It's just my job to be out": Tenure stories of lesbian, gay, and bisexual academics. *International Journal of Sexuality and Gender Studies, 3,* 93–112.

Williams, C. (2011). *Capturing Southern identities: Auto-ethnographic documentaries of the Southern United States.* Unpublished M.A. Thesis. Georgetown University.

Wright, J. (2008). Searching one's self: The autoethnography of a nurse teacher. *Journal of Research in Nursing 13*(4), 338–347.

Wyatt, J. (2005). A gentle going? An autoethnographic short story. *Qualitative Inquiry, 11,* 724–732.

Wyatt, J. (2008). No longer loss: Autoethnographic stammering. *Qualitative Inquiry, 14,* 955–967.

Wyatt, J. (2012). Fathers, sons, loss, and the search for the question. *Qualitative Inquiry, 18,* 162–167.

Zuckerman, M. (1990). Some dubious premises in research and theory on racial differences: Scientific, social, and ethical issues. *American Psychologist, 45,* 1297–1303.

Section One

Reflecting and Engaging

Section One Introduction

Putting Meanings into Motion

Autoethnography's Existential Calling

Arthur P. Bochner

But this too is true: stories can save us.

Tim O'Brien (1990)

In high school, I wrote my senior thesis on Albert Camus, an audacious choice for a seventeen-year-old, but one I eagerly embraced. "One must imagine Sisyphus happy," wrote Camus, because he continues to struggle to achieve new heights (1955, p. 123). This is what "fills one's heart," a human being deciding to rise above the absurd struggles of life by accepting rather than denying his plight (p. 123). Sisyphus understands the absurdity of his situation, yet still expresses an intense passion for life, which makes it possible to imagine him happy. He recognizes that the only real thing is human experience. For Camus (1955), the real is what one can feel in his heart or touch in the world and, thus, there is no truth beyond experience. It is what we create ourselves, what we experience and do, that gives meaning to our lives.

As a graduate student in the School of Speech at Syracuse University, I was introduced to the humanistic psychologists—Frankl (1959), Rogers (1961), Maslow (1968), and May (1953, 1967). Their books spoke to me in a deeper and more personal way than anything I had studied in rhetoric and public address. These psychologists concentrated on subjective experience—inner lives, feelings and thoughts—but they also brought to light the importance of how humans

Handbook of Autoethnography, edited by Stacy Holman Jones, Tony E. Adams, and Carolyn Ellis, 50–56. © 2013 Left Coast Press, Inc. All rights reserved.

interact with others and deal with social relationships. They introduced me to terms and ideals that had obvious relevance to human communication but had rarely come up in my graduate studies—concepts such as compassion, empathy, spontaneity, identity, and relatedness. I felt inspired by their concern for human suffering and healing, spiritual experience, and the "will to meaning" (Frankl, 1959, p. 121). The humanistic psychologists wanted a human science that addressed the full range of human experience—much of which had been removed from psychology by its obsession with scientific stature, focus on method, aversion to value-centered inquiry, and uncritical commitment to the mechanism and reductionism of the positivists' spectator theory of knowledge with its emphasis on objectivity, detachment, and neutrality. Attempting to insert what was unique about a person back into the human sciences, humanistic psychologists highlighted subjectivity, feeling, empathy, authenticity, intimacy, death and dying, and everything involved with finding meaning in life.

As a doctoral student at Bowling Green State University, however, I was taught that the sorts of human experiences embraced by humanistic psychologists were too elusive, crude, and uncontrollable to be subjected to scientific inquiry. My mentor was a tenacious and intractable empiricist. "In the name of science," he told me, "we have to bracket experiences that can't be organized into coherent systems, explained by theories, predicted and/or controlled. If you can't measure it, then, as far as science is concerned, it doesn't exist." Gradually, I was indoctrinated into the belief system of empiricism in which it was taken for granted that the object of knowledge can be entirely separated from the knowing subject—the researcher.

By the time I graduated with a PhD in 1971, I had a thorough understanding of scientific method—reliability, validity, research design, and statistical inference. I was a competent technician, yet uncertain about how these skills could be applied in the real world of human communication, where so much was riding on the creation and performance of meaning.

In the social sciences of the 1970s, we were teaching how to know, not inquiring into how to live. Method trumped meaning. One's technical skills—methodological competencies—were crucial to academic success. Bemoaning the ways in which social science had divorced itself from the moral problems of life and living, which was its original calling in the seventeenth century (Smith, 1997), Ernest Becker (1968, p. xiii) lamented how "we are becoming mired in data and devoted to triviality," which is bound to happen when the shape of a scientific field follows from rather than precedes its method.

Devotion to triviality can lead to alienation, and by the late 1970s I had become one of those alienated academics. Applying my well-honed technical skills as a traditional, quantitative empiricist, I had accumulated numerous publications. I was one of the worker bees who Thomas Kuhn (1962) characterized as endemic to normal science because they nourish the paradigm, stabilizing the disciplinary matrix. But something was missing from my academic life. I believed research was a moral obligation, that you couldn't be a good professor if you didn't conduct and publish research. But I had my doubts about the importance and value of the research I was publishing. Moreover, I couldn't ignore the crisis of confidence that was cascading through social science, raising doubts about the political, philosophical, ethical, and ideological foundations of mainstream social science (Coser, 1975; Elms, 1975; Gergen, 1973; Koch, 1976; Rorty, 1979; Sampson, 1978; Taylor, 1977).

The disciplinary matrix in my own field, communication, was particularly troubling. Empiricism in communication studies rested largely on the premise that communication between humans could be described as an object. But human communication is not an object, and thus the field of communication had no genuine calling to study objects. Communication is a process consisting of sequences of interactions, and studying these sequences and performances is itself a dynamic, communicative activity. Moreover, as communicating humans studying humans communicating, we are inside what we are studying. This reflexive quality of human communication cannot be meaningfully bracketed in the name of science. It must be accommodated and integrated into research and its products.

Enter the *narrative turn* provoked by poststructuralist, postmodernist, and feminist critics who had waged an unrelenting attack on the postpositivist's presumptions about the authority of a humanly constructed text, casting serious doubt on the sanctified scientific doctrine of truth through method (Bakhtin, 1981; Barthes, 1977; Derrida, 1978, 1981; Foucault, 1970; Haraway, 1988; Harding, 1991; Hartsock, 1983; Lyotard, 1984; Rorty, 1979, 1982; Toulmin, 1969). I turned toward narrative as a mode of inquiry because stories seemed to offer the best possibility for constructing and embodying a different relationship between researchers and research participants, and between writers and readers of social science inquiry. Returning to where I had started with my high school thesis on Camus and the allure of the existential/humanistic psychologists, I anticipated that narrative inquiry could be used to create a more personal, collaborative, performative, and interactive mode of research, one centered on the question of how human experience is endowed with meaning and on the moral and ethical choices we face as human beings who live in an uncertain and changing world (Bochner, 1994, 2002, 2012a). The texts produced within the paradigm of personal narrative inquiry would take the form of stories intended to create the effect of reality. The stories would show characters embedded in the complexities of lived moments of struggle, resisting the intrusions of chaos, disconnection, fragmentation, marginalization, and incoherence; and trying to preserve or restore continuity and coherence to their lives in the face of unexpected blows of fate that call meanings and values into question. These stories would be a "narrative quest...for the good life" (MacIntyre, 1984, p. 219; see also Freeman, 2010), a concern for the question, "What kind of life is worth living?" communicated in the form of personal stories that put meanings into motion (Bochner, 2012b).

Enter autoethnography, "an autobiographical genre of writing and research that displays multiple layers of consciousness, connecting the personal to the cultural" (Ellis & Bochner, 2000, p. 739). Though the term *autoethnography* had been introduced into the vocabulary of the social sciences in the 1970s (Hayano, 1979), its formidable potential as a mode of inquiry, writing, performing and living had not been exploited prior to the publication of several edited collections (Banks & Banks, 1998; Bochner & Ellis, 2002; Ellis & Bochner, 1996), handbook essays (Ellis & Bochner, 2000; Holman Jones, 2005), and research texts (Ellis, 2004, 2009). During this period, autoethnography blossomed as an alternative to the excesses and limitations of theory-driven, empiricist social science. Whereas empiricist social science fuels an appetite for abstraction, facts, and control, autoethnography feeds a hunger for details, meanings, and peace of mind.

As a form of writing and communicating, autoethnography has become a rallying point for those who believe that the human sciences need to become more human. As the philosopher Charles Taylor (1985) argues, we human beings are selves only insofar as certain issues matter to us. We attribute significance and meaning to our actions and experiences. Indeed, a person's identity is contingent on the significance these things have for him or her. If we grant Heidegger's (1927/1962) point that humans are beings whose lives are "at issue" or "in question," (Richardson, Fowers, & Guignon, 1999, p. 220), then we can understand autoethnography as a form of inquiry, writing, and/or performance that puts questions and "issues of being" into circulation and dialogue.

Autoethnography is an expression of the desire to turn social science inquiry into a non-alienating practice, one in which I (as a researcher) do not need to suppress my own subjectivity, where I can become more attuned to the subjectively felt experiences of others, where I am free to reflect on the consequences of my work, not only for others but also for myself, and where all parts of myself—emotional, spiritual, intellectual, embodied, and moral—can be voiced and integrated in my work (Bochner, 2005; Richardson, 1992). It's a response to an existential crisis—a desire to do meaningful work and lead a meaningful life.

In practice, autoethnography is not so much a methodology as a way of life. It is a way of life that acknowledges contingency, finitude, embeddedness in storied being, encounters with Otherness, an appraisal of ethical and moral commitments, and a desire to keep conversation going. Autoethnography focuses on the fullness of living and, accordingly, autoethnographers want to ask, how can we make life better? We autoethnographers are reluctant to commit to removing pain from our work because, as Soni (2010) observes, "the idea of happiness is a tragic one, inseparable from the experience of mourning" (p. 15). We believe that this does not make us heavy, depressing, or pain-obsessed individuals. On the contrary, the question of happiness is the most urgent calling of autoethnography (Bochner,

2012a). Our work as autoethnographers invites others to become involved with a life, engaged with it, and responsible for doing something about what its tragic qualities may signal or foreshadow; to commit to alleviate the narrative situation; in short, to make happiness more probable. Readers or listeners who take up this calling, accepting the responsibility, can show concern for the other's life, what Frankfurt (2004, p. 11) calls "caring" and Hyde (2006, p. ix) calls "the life-giving gift of acknowledgement," even when they share little or nothing with the other.

Autoethnographers need not treat those committed to other "ways of knowing" as enemies. It is what we are for, not what we are against, that should form the basis of how our work is judged. The human sciences ought to be wide enough to accommodate the diverse goals of prediction and control, understanding and interpretation, and social change and transformation (Bochner, 1985). As Richard Rorty (1982) said, "these [different research purposes] aren't issues to be resolved, but differences to be lived with" (p. 197).

Autoethnography is inquiry; something we call experience is being inquired into, interpreted, made sense of, and judged. Facts are important to an autoethnographic storyteller; they can and should be verified. But facts don't tell you what they mean or how they may make you feel. The burden of the autoethnographer is to make meaning of all the stuff of memory and experience—how it felt then and how it feels now. The truth of autoethnographies can never be a stable truth because memory is active, dynamic, and ever changing. As we grow older and/or change our perspective, our relationship to the events and people of the past changes, too. The past is always open to revision and so, too, are our stories of the past and what they mean now (Ellis, 2009).

There may be no better way to come to terms with how we want to live and what we can say about how others live than to listen to their stories. The problem, as Henry Greenspan (1998) observed, is not what we can get out of stories but how we can get into them.

The writers in this section of the Handbook show a strong commitment to the development of a more human and humanizing social science, one that seeks greater understanding and a more just and caring world. Their work is a powerful exemplar of what it means to put meanings into motion, inviting us to take notice of what attracts us to autoethnographies and what makes some people resist them. Now I must step aside and allow you, our readers, to reflect and engage with the stories that the writers in this section tell, their personal and academic histories, as well as the tales that bear the mark of their imagination, memory, and capacity to care, to love, and to make their lives an issue for themselves as well as for us.

References

Bakhtin, M. M. (1981). *The dialogical imagination*. Austin: The University of Texas Press.

Banks, A., & Banks, S. (Eds.) (1998). *Fiction & social research: By ice or fire*. Walnut Creek, CA: AltaMira Press.

Barthes, R. (Ed.). (1977). *Image, music, text*. New York: Hill and Wang.

Becker, E. (1968). *The structure of evil: An essay on the unification of the science of man*. New York: The Free Press.

Bochner, A. P. (1985). Perspectives on inquiry: Representation, conversation, and reflection. In M. Knapp & G. R. Miller (Eds.), *Handbook of interpersonal communication* (pp. 27–58). Thousand Oaks, CA: Sage.

Bochner, A. P. (1994). Perspectives on inquiry II: Theories and stories. In M. Knapp & G. R. Miller (Eds.), *Handbook of interpersonal communication* (2nd ed., pp. 21–41). Thousand Oaks, CA: Sage.

Bochner, A. P. (2002). Perspectives on inquiry III: The moral of stories. In M. Knapp & J. A. Daly (Eds.), *Handbook of interpersonal communication* (3rd ed., pp. 73–101). Thousand Oaks, CA: Sage.

Bochner, A. (2005). Surviving autoethnography. In N. Denzin (Ed.), *Studies in symbolic interaction*, (Vol. 28, pp. 51-58). Amsterdam: Elsevier Science Ltd.

Bochner, A. P. (2012a). Suffering happiness: On autoethnography's ethical calling. *Qualitative Communication Research, 1*, 209–229.

Bochner, A. P. (2012b). On first-person narrative scholarship: Autoethnography as acts of meaning. *Narrative Inquiry* (in press).

Bochner, A. P. (2013). *Coming to narrative: Method and meaning in a university life*. Walnut Creek, CA: Left Coast Press, Inc.

Bochner, A. P., & Ellis, C. (2002). *Ethnographically speaking: Autoethnography, literature, aesthetics*. Walnut Creek, CA: AltaMira Press.

Camus, A. (1955). *The myth of Sisyphus and other essays*. New York: Vintage Books.

Coser, L. A. (1975). Presidential address: Two methods in search of some substance. *American Sociological Review, 40*, 691–699.

Derrida, J. (1978). *Writing and difference*. London: Routledge & Kegan.

Derrida, J. (1981). *Positions*. Chicago: University of Chicago Press.

Ellis, C. (2004). *The ethnographic I: A methodological novel about autoethnography*. Walnut Creek, CA: AltaMira Press.

Ellis, C. (2009). *Revision: Autoethnographic reflections on life and work*. Walnut Creek, CA: Left Coast Press, Inc.

Ellis, C., & Bochner, A. P. (Eds.). (1996). *Composing ethnography: Alternative forms of qualitative writing*. Walnut Creek, CA.: AltaMira Press.

Ellis, C., & Bochner, A. P. (2000). Autoethnography, personal narrative, reflexivity: Researcher as subject. In N. K. Denzin & Y. S. Lincoln (Eds.), *The handbook of qualitative research* (2nd ed., pp. 733–768). Thousand Oaks, CA: Sage.

Elms, A. (1975). The crisis of confidence in social psychology. *American Psychologist, 30*, 967–976.

Foucault, M. (1970). *The order of things: An archaeology of the human sciences*. New York: Random House.

Frankfurt, H. G. (2004). *The reasons of love*. Princeton, NJ: Princeton University Press.

Frankl, V. (1959). *Man's search for meaning*. Boston: Beacon Press.

Freeman, M. (2010). *Hindsight: The promise and peril of looking backward*. New York: Oxford.

Gergen, K. (1973). Social psychology as history. *Journal of Personality and Social Psychology, 26*, 309–320.

Greenspan, H. (1998). *On listening to Holocaust stories: Recounting and life history*. New York: Prager.

Haraway, D. (1988). Situated knowledges: The science question in feminism and the privilege of partial perspective. *Feminist Studies, 14*, 575–599.

Harding, S. (1991). *Whose science? Whose knowledge? Thinking from women*. Ithaca, NY: Cornell University Press.

Hartsock, N. (1983). *The feminist standpoint: Developing the ground for a specifically feminist historical materialism*. In S. Harding & M. Hintikka (Eds.), *Discovering reality* (pp. 283–310). Boston: Reidel.

Hayano, D. M. (1979). Auto-Ethnography: Paradigms, problems, and prospects. *Human Organization, 38*, 113–120.

Heidegger, M. (1962). *Being and time* (J. Macquarrie & E. Robinson, Trans.). New York: HarperCollins. (Original work published in 1927.)

Holman Jones, S. (2005). Autoethnography: Making the personal political. In N. K. Denzin & Y. A. Lincoln (Eds.), *The SAGE handbook of qualitative research* (3rd ed., pp. 763–791). Thousand Oaks, CA: Sage.

Hyde, M. (2006). *The life giving gift of acknowledgement.* West Lafayette, IN: Purdue University Press.

Koch, S. (1976). Language communities, search cells, and the psychological studies. In W. J. Arnold (Ed.), *Nebraska symposium on motivation 1975* (pp. 477–559). Lincoln: University of Nebraska Press.

Kuhn, T. (1962). *The structure of scientific revolutions.* Chicago: University of Chicago Press.

Lyotard, J-F. (1984). *The postmodern condition: A report on knowledge.* Minneapolis: University of Minnesota Press.

MacIntyre, A. (1984). *After virtue: A study in moral theory.* Notre Dame, IN: University of Notre Dame Press.

Maslow, A. (1968). *Toward a psychology of being.* New York: Von Nostrand.

May, R. (1953). *Man's search for himself.* New York: W. W. Norton.

May, R. (1967). *Existential psychology.* New York: Random House.

O'Brien, T. (1990). *The things they carried.* New York: Houghton Mifflin Harcourt.

Richardson, L. (1992). The consequences of poetic representation: Writing the other, rewriting the self. In C. Ellis & M. Flaherty (Eds.), *Investigating subjectivity: Research on lived experience* (pp. 125–137). Newbury Park, CA: Sage.

Richardson, F. C., Fowers, B.J., & Guignon, C. B. (1999). *Re-envisioning psychology: Moral dimensions of theory and practice.* San Francisco: Jossey-Bass.

Rogers, C. (1961). *On becoming a person.* Boston: Houghton Mifflin.

Rorty, R. (1979). *Philosophy and the mirror of nature.* Princeton, NJ: Princeton University Press.

Rorty, R. (1982). *Consequences of pragmatism (essays 1972–1980).* Minneapolis: University of Minnesota Press.

Sampson, E. E. (1978). Scientific paradigms and social values. Wanted—a scientific revolution. *Journal of Personality and Social Psychology, 36*, 1332–1343.

Smith, R. (1997). *The Norton history of the human sciences.* New York: W. W. Norton.

Soni, V. (2010). *Mourning happiness: Narrative and the politics of modernity.* Ithaca, NY: Cornell University Press.

Taylor, C. (1977). Interpretation and the sciences of man. In F. R. Dallmayr & T. A. McCarthy (Eds.), *Understanding social inquiry* (pp. 101–131). Notre Dame, IN: University of Notre Dame Press.

Taylor, C. (1985). Self-interpreting animals. In C. Taylor (Ed.), *Philosophical papers: Vol. 1 Human agency and language* (pp. 45–76). Cambridge, UK: Cambridge University Press.

Toulmin, S. (1969). Concepts and the explanation of human behavior. In T. Mischel (Ed.), *Human action* (pp. 71–104). New York: Academic Press.

Chapter 1

I Learn by Going
Autoethnographic Modes of Inquiry

Leon Anderson and Bonnie Glass-Coffin

> I wake from sleep to take my waking slow,
> I learn from going, where I have to go.
>
> Theodore Roethke, "The Waking"

Introduction

"I learn from going," the poet Theodore Roethke writes in the epigraph to this chapter. This emergent quality of autoethnographic writing is one of autoethnography's key features. In contrast to more traditional ethnographic forms, autoethnographic writing is based upon and emerges from relationship and context. It is open to experimentation in ways that set it apart from more "scientific" approaches to inquiry, both in theory and in method. But, although it is generally accepted that autoethnographers "learn by going," little attention has been paid to the question of "how" one learns and how one "does" autoethnography as a stance, as a position, as a contribution to emerging scholarship. What are the modes of inquiry associated with autoethnographies and how can these be best presented to provide some guidance for scholars who are drawn to this genre where Self and Other(s) interact, relate and dance together in ways that challenge the received wisdom of more traditional social science?

These methodological issues, and how such issues contribute to the scholarship on autoethnographic inquiry, are the focus of this chapter, and how a

Handbook of Autoethnography, edited by Stacy Holman Jones, Tony E. Adams, and Carolyn Ellis, 57–83. © 2013 Left Coast Press, Inc. All rights reserved.

consideration of such issues contributes to the scholarship on autoethnographic inquiry. It would be easy for us to fall into presenting an overly intellectualized and reified map of different social science traditions and their prescriptive assumptions for how to conduct "autoethnography" within different disciplinary paradigms. Indeed, the first author now looks at his efforts to carve out a space for "analytic autoethnography" (Anderson, 2006) as, in part, falling prey to just such a misstep. Our goal in this chapter is panoramic rather than partisan. We examine a wide range of autoethnographic scholarship to identify a set of features that such inquiry holds in common.

We start by reflecting on our personal experiences with autoethnography; we have come to see that autoethnographic inquiry is shaped not just by scholarly traditions, but also by life and career trajectories of individual scholars. A key feature, in fact, is that autoethnographic inquiry takes shape in the lives of scholars who have been trained in specific forms of inquiry within and because of the context of our own life experiences. In this chapter, we present these stories first, as a way of orienting the reader towards the assertion that, by connecting scholarship to lived experience, autoethnography *expands* the paradigm of what ethnography is. As our stories show, ethnography can be personal *and* academic. It can be scientific *and* spiritual. When ethnography is located in the particularities of emergence and the bricolage of personal encounter rather than in generalizations, reifications, or objectifications, it is often defined as being "autoethnographic." But, do ethnography and autoethnography differ in other fundamental ways? We ponder this question throughout this chapter.

After presenting our own trajectories as social science researchers who have come to view autoethnographic modes of inquiry as critical to our scholarship—and our lives—we present a broad overview of the varieties of inquiry and the key features and commitments that characterize them. We look first at the key methods used in collecting the "stuff" of autoethnographic research. Autoethnographic inquiry incorporates many of the standard forms of traditional qualitative data collection—such as fieldnotes, interviews, and personal documents. But, as we will show, such data are often "collected" and incorporated into analysis in autoethnographic projects differently than from traditional ethnographic work. Autoethnographic inquiry, we argue, integrates distinctive features of the "new language of qualitative methods" (Gubrium & Holstein, 1997), including the visibility of researcher's self, strong reflexivity, relational engagement, personal vulnerability, and open-ended rejection of finality and closure. In the latter part of this chapter, we talk about each of these key features of autoethnographic research and writing in some depth, concluding with the optimistic prediction that autoethnography will continue to push the boundaries of "acceptable" or "respectable" social science in ways that enrich and empower both the work that we do as social scientists and the expressions of humanity and connection that we are.

Our work as autoethnographers challenges scientific approaches to inquiry that intentionally separate the Observer and the Observed. In challenging this received wisdom that "science" has to equal "separate," we have re-framed the boundaries and relations between Self and Other(s), Actor and Acted-Upon, Author and Story, presenting instead a genre of writing that, "at minimum, places the author's lived experience within a social and cultural context" (Reed-Danahay, 2009, p. 30). It is our hope that this introduction into autoethnographic modes of inquiry will reflect favorably on both our legacy as ethnographers and our futures. For as autoethnographers, we are, first and foremost, ethnographers who recognize and honor our deep connections with, rather than separation from, the communities of which we are a part.

Autoethnographic Trajectories

So, how did we, the authors of this chapter, come to embrace autoethnography? We asked ourselves this question and found, in the narratives that emerged, some significant moments in our own lives that influenced our respective commitments to this approach.

Bonnie

I came to the study of anthropology as a spiritual-seeker and an aspiring writer—a bridge builder and cultural translator. In high school, I was a devoted Christian, a journalist, and an avid reader. I saw myself as an English major and investigative reporter when I envisioned college. But, these plans took a hard right turn when I was selected as a foreign exchange student for a year-length trip to Peru during my last year of high school. For most of 1975, I found myself in a completely foreign culture, with very little ability to speak Spanish, and struggling with daily studies in a Spanish speaking high school of 4,000 girls where only the English teacher and I spoke a common language. Over the months, we became fast friends and, like friends back home, I presumed we were alike in most every way. Then, one day, she told me very simply that her grandmother had been killed by a witch, and that the local shaman had been unable to save her because the family had not believed strongly enough in his powers, nor acted soon enough on his diagnosis. "How could that be?" I wondered in disbelief. "How could someone whom I thought I knew so well be so fundamentally different than me?" In that moment, my passions for investigating both anthropology and shamanism studies were ignited, and I vowed to study anthropology in college to better understand.

At the beginning of my undergraduate studies in anthropology, though, I felt my identity as a spiritual being to be at odds with my immersion in the social sciences. In my undergraduate years, I found it difficult to reconcile the assumption that world-view, ethos, and spirituality were epiphenomenal reflections of material constraints. I chafed at the functionalist understanding of religion as little more than an expression of society's need to control the hearts and minds of its people. As a humanist, a musician, a romantic, a poet, and one deeply inspired by all-things-spiritual, I had been drawn to anthropology because of that cultural immersion experience during my senior year of high school. After a year living and studying in northern Peru, I returned to the United States a marginalized being. Unlike those I had left behind on my travels and now returned to, I saw the power of Culture as both generator and constraint of all my beliefs and behaviors. I felt marginalized when interacting with those who had never left their home-lands because they couldn't see this simple fact. In anthropology, where culture is recognized as the lens which colors worlds, I found both a language to express the intense longing I felt to "return home" to the person that I had been before this awakening as well as a community of peers who understood the impossibilities of putting this particular Pandora back in the box. Yet, after being thoroughly socialized into the objectivist and comparative frame of "cultural materialism" (an anthropological theory that posits world view and beliefs as epiphenomenal to economic organization and technology that was much in vogue during the mid-1970s), I felt more than a little empty when I graduated from Whitman College in 1980. I felt, in some way I could not articulate, that I had sold-out to science, even as I gratefully acknowledged my membership in the world of anthropological inquiry. Still, I felt somehow that the only legitimate path to social science required me to abandon the worlds of inspiration, of emotion, of poetry and humanism that had sustained me during my formative years.

In the time between my undergraduate degree and my graduate studies, that emptiness deepened. I knew something of Peruvian shamanism because of the friendships I had made while in Peru, so I was especially intrigued when I found the works of Carlos Castaneda (1968, 1971, 1972, 1974) and Michael Harner (1980) who reported on the transformative impact of their own field experiences with shamanic healers. To say that I devoured these books is an understatement. More accurately, these books became touchstones as they showed me a way to rekindle my own interests in all things spiritual, even in the context of anthropological fieldwork.

When I began thinking about applying to graduate school, I knew only two things: I wanted to study shamanism as a possible way back to the spiritual that had been such an important part of my youth, and I wanted to go back to the north coast of Peru, because of the deeply transformative experiences I had felt in high school. As fate would have it, I found an ideal fit for myself at UCLA, in the same program where three recent student projects had focused on shamanism on the north coast of Peru (Joralemon, 1983; Sharon, 1978; Skillman, 1990). When the time came, my own dissertation research focused on the lives of female Peruvian shamanic healers (called *curanderas*) to add the voice of female healers to the record. As I immersed myself in my project, I found that a significant difference between male healers my UCLA colleagues had investigated and the women who became the focus of my research was in the way they framed how healing occurs.

The male healers whom my colleagues at UCLA had studied all took an active role in moving their patients from affliction to relief. On the other hand, the female

healers with whom I worked felt their main role as healers was to "awaken" sufferers to their own agency and power-over-themselves. In essence, these *curanderas*
emphasized that sufferers needed to "come into relationship with themselves," and
accept/embody/celebrate all parts of their own lives as valid in order to become
healed. Lived experience became the lens through which my understanding of
female healing in Peru was organized. And, this emphasis on experience became
my touchstone for writing about my relationship to the process of fieldwork itself.
As one of the healers told me during our very first ceremony together,

> To live is to experience....You should save your tapes. They are expensive and
> you will learn very little from them. What you write won't come from what
> you record but from what you live—from what you experience. Reality isn't
> observed or recorded, it is lived! (Glass-Coffin, 1998, p. xi)

I began writing autoethnographically very early in my career as a way of honoring the lessons I had learned from the women who had been the focus of my
research.

Much later on, I had a kind of spiritual awakening with another shamanic
healer by the name of Oscar Miro-Quesada that further impacted how I write
myself into my published work. As I have reported elsewhere,

> On the day of my awakening I had trekked to his home in Florida to interview
> him for a book project. When we met the previous September, I expressed inter-
> est in documenting how his adaptations of Peruvian traditions meet the needs
> of U.S. seekers. His response to my request was bracketed by a question: "Sure,
> I'm happy to have these transformations be the subject of your ethnography, but
> before I do, are you also willing to be transformed?" (Glass-Coffin, 2009, p. 64)

What followed was a profoundly transformative experience that turned my
way of thinking and being in the world, quite literally, upside-down. Until that
time, I had simply assumed, as an anthropologist trained in cultural materialism,
that my way of thinking about the world as well as consciousness itself was a *product* of material constraints. But, during that visit with don Oscar, I had an experience where I "saw" plants interact with me as sentient beings who responded to
my every action and intention. I realized that "consciousness structures matter"
rather than the other way around. As I started writing even more explicitly about
how my research into shamanism created a vehicle for my *own* growth and transformation, I more formally discovered autoethnography as a legitimate tool for
the expression of my own personal transformation (Glass-Coffin, 2009, 2010). In
researching how to best locate myself in these new texts, I found great models in
the work of "experiential" anthropology and "ecstatic" anthropology, especially
in the works of Behar (1997), Fabian (2000), Jackson (1989), Young and Goulet
(1994), Goulet and Miller (2007), and Turner (1994). In the work I've published
in recent years, I've insisted on treating "unseen worlds" as ontologically real

rather than treating discussions of non-human sentience as a culturally relative belief (Glass-Coffin, 2009, 2010). Most recently, I have discussed at length how honoring the sentient beings who inhabit these planes is not only relevant but urgently needed if we are to live in a truly sustainable way with our planet (Glass-Coffin & Kiiskeentum, in press).

Leon

How did I come to autoethnography? Where did I come from and what drew me to this genre of research and writing? And how has my trajectory as a writer and a sociologist influenced my views of autoethnographic inquiry? Looking back, I think it boils down to a few simple biographical experiences, influences, and choices. I was a writer well before I became a sociologist. I've long enjoyed playing with different genres of writing, but I have found my voice most strongly in the tradition of second Chicago School ethnography. As a result, I find my perspective on and practice of autoethnography grounded in traditional symbolic interactionist theory and methods. Yet unlike some of my interactionist colleagues, I see no reason for minimizing or rejecting the presence of the researcher in ethnographic research or in published work. Indeed, I believe there is much to recommend it.

From my earliest childhood, I have seen myself as a writer and storyteller. The first story I remember writing was a six-year-old's fiery account of the end of the world, written on a Sunday afternoon after I had heard a sermon on the Book of Revelation. Following the lead of the pastor who had so impressed me by that sermon, and the many other Free Methodist, Baptist, and Assembly of God pastors whose sermons I devoured in my youth, I spent the next decade writing sermonettes and dramatic morality tales that my mother today occasionally uncovers in her cedar chest and sends to me with pride, not knowing I find them so painfully moralistic that it hurts me to imagine that young writer was me.

But by the late 1960s I had found another voice and model for writing in the Beat poetry and folksong writers of the era. With my brother Gene, I wrote song lyrics that he put to music and played in coffee shops and student unions around the Northwest, and in the mid-70s I had the glorious opportunity to spend time reading and writing poetry with a passionate group of west coast poets in Portland and Missoula. With visions of Jack Kerouac and Gary Snyder at my side, I rode freight trains across the country and chased mountain goats in the Bitter Root Mountains. In search of my muse, I read and re-read Robert Graves's *The White Goddess*, seeking to tap some mythopoetic well-spring of creativity.

Then in 1973, I read two of the most powerful books I had ever found, C. Wright Mills's *White Collar* and John Dos Passos's *USA* trilogy. It was a turning point in my perspective. Powerful, critical, and playful writing, but not just all coming out of the author's inspiration and experience. You needed to know a lot to write like these guys. One hell of a lot. It wasn't all about me. I got serious about school and understanding the world I lived in. And inquiry became different for me: not just a quest for muse-inspired understanding, but an interest in the expe-riences of those around me. I moved away from poetry and English departments and toward history, sociology, and journalism.

But not completely away. The "new journalism" of the 1970s blurred the boundaries between reporting and fiction—already provocatively challenged for me in Dos Passos's *USA* and Mills's *White Collar*. In my peregrinations in search of work, I carried Dos Passos with me to Alaska, where I worked with "emotion-ally disturbed" kids who seemed a lot like the boy I had so recently been. And when, by a chance of luck in the late 1970s, the city desk editor of the *Anchorage Daily News* asked me to start writing feature stories for *We Alaskans*, the newspa-per's Sunday magazine, I felt free to fictionalize my stories of crab fisheries in the Aleutians, tundra firefighting north of the Arctic Circle, and teen romance at the Anchorage roller rink. As William Faulkner's Rosa in *Absalom! Absalom!* had put it so well, "there's a might-have-been that is truer than truth."

But my penchant for often reporting the seedy side of social life didn't fit well with the editor's vision for stories in the soon-to-be premiere newspaper of the Last Frontier, and when a promotion to associate editor for the magazine didn't come through, I looked to other opportunities, finally moving to Texas to get a PhD in sociology. In Alaska I'd felt privileged to have a week or two to investigate a story: get to the people, talk and see what they were up to, and get the story written. And fictionalizing offered a way to flesh out details that I didn't have time to get in the field. When I got to Texas, I was primed to do the same thing, but my new mentor, David Snow, slowed me down and introduced me to rigorous research. From Dave I learned not to hurry and to listen more deeply than I ever had taken time to listen before. I learned the history and methods of Chicago School ethnography from the early empirical classics of Robert Park's students, like Nels Anderson's *The Hobo* (1932) and Paul Cressey's *The Taxi Dance Hall* (1932), to the more theoretically-focused "second Chicago School" ethnographies in the 1950s and 1960s of Everett Hughes's masterful students Howard Becker and Erving Goffman. I was deeply moved by what has come to be termed "realist ethnography," participant observation research like Elliot Liebow's *Tally's Corner* (1967) and Carol Stack's *All Our Kin* (1974), with its commitment to sustained immersion in the social world being studied and a willingness to be guided by the voices of those who live there. With Dave I embarked on a decade-long path of studying homelessness in America through which I developed an enduring com-mitment to studying social life *in situ* and to striving to understand the meanings and experiences of those beyond myself.

As a disciple of Chicago School ethnography, I have felt a responsibility to con-tribute to improving—not just replicating—our craft. And in the 1990s and early 2000s as I witnessed the emergence of the rich new genre of autoethnographic writing, I saw opportunities to bring myself, as a Chicago School ethnographer, into a more visible and reflexive position in my research and writing. In March

2001, I quite literally dove into autoethnography, as I found myself drawn to study my new hobby of skydiving. But just how to do autoethnographic research consistent with "realist" and "analytic" ethnography vexed me. In 2006 I published an article outlining my thinking on the subject. Upsetting some Chicago School and traditional anthropological ethnographers, I argued (and continue to argue) that acknowledging—and embracing—the researcher as part of our research improves our craft in general—particularly when researchers are "members" of the social world they are studying. Frustrating some alternative qualitative methodologists, I made (and continue to make) the case that many autoethnographic sensitivities, such as heightened reflexivity, engagement, and vulnerability, are not so much a rupture from what many of us have been doing all along as they are a refinement of long-standing ethnographic impulses. Finally, in 2011, after a decade of autoethnographic research, I began to publish research that modeled the analytic autoethnography I espoused (Anderson, 2011). In the meantime, as I explored autoethnographic writings, I developed a more nuanced and appreciative understanding of autoethnography in general, and especially of the range of potential analytic autoethnographic styles. If in the end I remain committed to an analytic model of autoethnographic writing, I do so today with a greater sense of blurred boundaries as opposed to clear distinctions. And in writing this chapter with Bonnie I've become convinced that the modes and key features of autoethnographic inquiry are similar no matter where along the spectrum from "evocative" (e.g., Ellis, 1997) to "analytic" (e.g., Anderson, 2006) one stands.

Autoethnographic Inquiry

Autoethnography, as Allen-Collinson notes in Chapter 13 in this volume, "offers a variety of modes of engaging with self, or perhaps more accurately with selves, in relation to others, to culture." Yet scholars new to the field may find it difficult to gain a grasp of the varieties of engagement or inquiry used by autoethnographers. There are two reasons for this lack of methodological clarity that we want to briefly acknowledge.

The first is that autoethnographers are often eclectic bricoleurs in their methods, drawing upon a range of materials, from "impressionistic" personal memories and musings to more traditionally "objective" data like fieldnotes and informant interviews. Not only do various autoethnographic scholars collect and interpret their "data" in different ways, but even individually they often improvise and experiment, changing their methods and ways of interpreting their data as they go. Indeed, for many, a key virtue of autoethnography is its methodological openness. But that virtue can be a challenge as well, for an aspiring new autoethnographic scholar can miss the trees for the forest, failing to get a grasp of how to collect the basic data that create the bigger autoethnographic story or mosaic.

A second reason for a lack of methodological clarity in autoethnographic scholarship is that autoethnographic texts often do not conform to traditional social science journal article structure, characterized by an extended "methods" section. While many traditional social science scholars (and journal editors) may view this as indicating a lack of discipline and rigor in research, for many autoethnographers, there is a sense of principle involved. Their goal is not to highlight methodological criteria, but rather to tell a story in a way that reveals the self as a central character with rich emotional evocation that serves to ground the story being told. But again, the lack of explicit methodological discussion can create a problem for would-be autoethnographers, particularly for graduate students seeking to pursue autoethnographic research for theses and dissertations. Lacking explicit and accepted guidelines to structure their research, they may find their academic mentors and advisors resistant to seeing their proposed research as rigorous and worthwhile social science. Published articles that tend more toward "analytic autoethnography" are more likely to articulate an explicit methodology than do more evocative autoethnographic texts. But even there, the methodological discussions in the more analytic autoethnographic texts tend to focus much more on issues of researching others than on self-focused inquiry. In short, autoethnography often (although by no means always) blends methodological description into the narrative of the text, if in fact it addresses methodological issues explicitly at all.

Still, it is possible to pull together descriptions of some autoethnographic modes of inquiry by combining the relatively limited literature on autoethnographic methods per se with the rich autoethnographic literature itself—a considerable amount of which is referenced and described below. We pursue this goal first by describing the most common methods or techniques of data collection in autoethnographic inquiry and, second, by exploring a set of integral features or characteristics shared by each of these modes of inquiry. We conclude with the argument that autoethnographic inquiry is guided less by specific techniques of data collection than it is by a set of ethical, aesthetic, and relational sensitivities that can be—and are being—incorporated into a wide variety of autoethnographic modes of inquiry.

Types of Inquiry

Our examination of published autoethnographic scholarship clearly suggests that the kinds of "data" collected by autoethnographers is broadly similar to the kinds of data collected in ethnographic research more generally. Three types of "data" stand front-and-center as the most common in the autoethnographic writings we have read: fieldnotes, personal documents, and interviews. But in each case, the autoethnographic focus of research influences just how these data are conceptualized and collected.

Fieldnotes

As the signature form of data collection in ethnography, fieldnote writing not surprisingly represents a core method of inquiry in autoethnographic research. Van Maanen (1988) speaks of ethnography as "the peculiar practice of representing the social reality of others through the analysis of one's own experience in the world of these others" (p. ix). The writing of autoethnographic fieldnotes, on the other hand, involves not only the "representation of the social reality of others," but of oneself as well. As Emerson, Fretz, and Shaw (2011) observe, ethnographers vary in their fieldnote writing practices from writing fieldnotes in and immediately following participant observation to going for long stretches focused on immersion in the lived experience of the social world they are studying, followed by focused recollection. Autoethnographic inquiry can involve both of these kinds of fieldnote writing. In the first case, researchers use contemporaneously written fieldnotes to document an experience or slice of experience. In his autoethnographic exploration of base-jumping, for instance, Jason Laurendeau (2011) draws upon fieldnotes written up following specific base-jumping activities and events. Similarly, Elaine Bass Jenks (2002) created a set of "notepad" fieldnotes while spending six weeks with her son at a summer camp for visually impaired children. In both cases, the researchers recorded their observations close in time to specific activities and events.

In contrast to Laurendeau and Jenks, many (perhaps most) autoethnographers create fieldnotes from more distant memories. As an autoethnographer identified as "Valerie" explains in a discussion of writing ethnographic fieldnotes about her experience with breast cancer in Ellis's *Ethnographic I* (2004), "Carolyn told me to start by writing my story as fieldnotes organized chronologically" (p. 113). While many autoethnographers build such fieldnote chronicles, others focus on writing more fragmented "autoethnographic vignettes," revisiting and retelling specific emotionally memorable events in their lives. While the self-focus of fieldnote chronicles and vignettes may distinguish autoethnography from traditional ethnography, traditional ethnographers often do life history interviews as well—albeit of others, not themselves.

The issue of self-description and introspection in general is central to autoethnographic fieldnote writing. While virtually all ethnographers recognize the importance of the researcher's self in research, the degree of self-presence and the point in time and in analysis at which the self is engaged can differ. Even in autoethnographic inquiry, where self-presence tends to be maximized, there seems to be considerable variability in just where and how the self is inserted into fieldnotes and analysis. On the one hand, fieldnotes may be heavily laden with self-reference and introspection—as much personal diary as "fieldnotes" per se (see next section on personal documents). Autoethnography that builds primarily on self-recollections from sometimes distant events (as in Valerie's story just referenced) would seem to be particularly open to interrogation by the researcher's self at a new point in time, thus opening opportunities for reflexive engagement in the fieldnotes themselves. On the other hand, contemporaneously written fieldnotes may at times involve less detailed reflexivity in the moment, followed by more reflexive engagement at a later point in time—as in the case of Jenks's previously referenced fieldnote writing at a summer camp for visually impaired children.

Autoethnographic fieldworkers are encouraged to reflect upon the ways in which their engagement with the "field" has contributed to their understanding of themselves as contingent upon and emerging from the experiences of their lives. The "field" in this case may involve experiences with other people or it may not; instead, the field may be the "state of mind" that one assumes when recording one's own experiences and how one is changed by these. In this sense, fieldnote writing can become a kind of (at least for the moment) self-defining "mystory" because, as Laurel Richardson (1994) reminds us, "Writing is also a way of 'knowing'—a method of discovery and analysis. By writing in different ways, we discover new aspects of our topic and our relationship to it" (p. 516).

The following excerpt from Bonnie's fieldnotes illustrates this point. In this case, the boundary between fieldnotes and personal documents is especially blurred as the text that she recorded in her notes while working on a project in Trujillo, Peru, was later used to craft a letter that she then sent to a fellow anthropology student in California. In the letter/fieldnotes, Bonnie describes the experiences surrounding a miscarriage and an ensuing infection that forced her into bed (and that eventually forced her to return home) during October of 1987:

> Dear B: I'm writing you from that reverie that comes with forced recuperation…from that forced reflection that washes over mind and body when the outer static of daily living quiets; when inner conversations fill the gaps left by absent visitors.…The miscarriage itself occurred while I was on a four-day jaunt to a nearby mountain town, a holiday of sorts away from the interview anthropology that was literally my bread and butter. Yet I learned more about anthropology in those four days than perhaps in all the time I have spent in the field to date.…I learned about stepping into the picture and becoming part of the ongoing movie instead of trying just to describe it.…[Yet] even as I write, I know that the written word hardens and sets the essence into the shell of experiences lived. Still, perhaps this shell can serve as a valuable reminder and a sign-post along the continuing path…as one expression of the interplay between chaotic, unorganized, unsynthesized experience and the retelling of it in stories which are such an important part of daily living here. (Glass-Coffin, fieldnotes, October 27, 1987)

In writing this letter, Bonnie found herself reflecting more deeply on her relationship to fieldwork in anthropology than had been the case before writing these words. It was an aha! moment that she wanted to remember. "The 'field' is a state of mind," she commented in her field journal as she copied the text of this letter there so that she might later remember the exact moment when she had gained this new perspective. And, of course, it is the copy of the letter, still recorded in that field journal that she drew from here, as the original was mailed long ago to her friend back home.

Personal Documents and Artifacts

In addition to fieldnotes (whether explicitly reflexive or not), autoethnographers can tap a wide range of personal documents to chronicle and examine their lives. We live in a world rich with personal documents, from college transcripts to medical reports to Facebook "likes." Further, our lives are embodied and reflected through many artifacts and personal belongings. The range of such materials that may be incorporated into autoethnographic inquiry seems limited only by researchers' interests and imaginations.

Personal documents, such as letters and diaries, have long been used in humanistic sociological research, from the early classic *The Polish Peasant* (Thomas & Znaniecki, 1927) to contemporary life-story narratives (e.g., Plummer, 2001). Many autoethnographic scholars draw upon diaries and journals that overlap with, or take the place of, more traditional fieldnotes. Simone Fullagar (2002), for instance, uses her extensive travel diaries in her autoethnographic study of "feminine desire" in leisure. Her richly descriptive diary entries capture a range of experiences, from exhaustion in the mountains of Nepal to deeply sensual pleasure riding camels in an Indian desert, that she draws upon to "write the embodied feminine self into knowledge as a strategy of disrupting the binary oppositions that are so central to phallocentrism" (p. 72). In his autoethnographic exploration of the challenges he has faced in balancing work, family, and leisure activities, Leon (2011) has similarly drawn upon personal diary entries that he has written over the past decade, chronicling conversations, dreams, and personal reflections that supplement his separate fieldnote files, which are directed more toward specifically describing skydiving activities and relationships. Most autoethnographers would make little distinction between fieldnotes and diaries; all such materials provide valuable data for autoethnographic inquiry.

The range of personal documents and artifacts that can be brought to bear on autoethnographic inquiry extends far beyond diaries and letters. The value of any document or artifact for such research depends on its evocative potential—its ability to either open the researcher to deeper reflection on relevant experiences and relationships or to evoke compelling images, emotions, or understandings in other readers. Andrew Sparkes (1996) utilizes medical reports describing the analysis of MRIs of his back as an avenue into reflecting on the relationship between his experience of his "flawed" embodied self and more distanced, "factual" medical discourse. Other scholars turn to familial and personal documents, especially photographs, as vehicles or media for autoethnographic inquiry. Indeed, the use of photographs is so common that it has led some to refer to "visual autoethnography" as a special genre in the field (Smith-Shank & Keifer-Boyd, 2007).

Questions of categorization aside, photographs provide rich media for both autoethnographic introspection and evocative presentation. Often photographic images are presented in autoethnographic texts in tandem with the researchers' narratives of their interpretations and contextual understandings of the photos. In her self-proclaimed "autoethnographic rant" on hating dresses, Sara Crawley (2002) juxtaposes photographs taken of her in a bridesmaid dress and in a tuxedo to capture the social challenges of living as a butch lesbian in a heteronormative culture. Similarly, Anniina Guyas (2007) uses a photograph of her grandmother as a base for reflective inquiry on her changing perceptions of her grandmother, her family, and herself at different stages of her life.

The massive proliferation of media in the internet age has dramatically expanded the range of personal documents upon which autoethnographers and other social scientists may draw, including textual documents like email and text messaging, digital videos, and even documents chronicling virtual world experiences such as self-creation and presentation in Second Life (e.g., Dumitrica & Gaden 2009). The range of such potential materials for autoethnographic data and inquiry—as well as for autoethnographic texts and performances—is extensive and can be expected to expand even more dramatically in the coming decade. The kinds of products that will emerge as a result of these new technologies are likely to take forms that we cannot yet even imagine.

Interviews

At first glance, the term "autoethnographic interview" may seem an oxymoron. If the purpose of an interview is to obtain new information or "data," what possibly can I tell myself that I do not already know? The answer, autoethnographers would reply, is, "A lot." As life-story scholars have long recognized, our memories of the past are filtered through the interpretive lenses we bring to our self-reflections. Indeed, insofar as the self is a multifaceted and fragmented social construct, our memories and understandings of events may shift significantly over time and context. In keeping with Holstein and Gubrium's (1995) conception of an interview as "an occasion for purposefully animated participants to *construct* versions of reality interactionally rather than merely purvey data" (p. 79), an autoethnographic self-interview involves dialogue between one's past and present selves, at times actively with others as well, in which memories and understandings about the past are constructed anew.

But just what does an autoethnographic interview look like? Seldom, if ever, have we read about autoethnographers approaching themselves orally with interview guides and probes. The process seems much more episodic and textual. Sara Crawley (this volume) refers to self-interviewing as reconstructing "scenes from one's reflected life experiences." In a workplace autoethnography of a youth employment agency, where he worked over a four-year span (but only turned into a research study in the final year), Leon (1999) continually "interviewed" himself as he wrote fieldnotes, to recall past experiences that came to memory in light of on-going fieldwork experiences and issues.

Further, autoethnographic researchers interview others as well as themselves, and in conjunction with themselves, to gain deeper understandings of topics and events. A variety of types of interviews are valuable instruments in the autoethnographic toolkit, as illustrated by three types of interviews described by Ellis and Berger (2002): reflexive dyadic interviews, interactive interviews, and co-constructed narratives.

Reflexive dyadic interviews resemble a traditional interview protocol, with the interviewer asking questions and the interviewee answering them, but with the added dimension of the interviewer sharing personal experience with the topic:

> The researcher's disclosures are more than tactics to encourage the respondents to open up; rather the researcher often feels a reciprocal desire to disclose, given the intimacy of the details being shared....The interview is conducted more as a conversation between two equals than as a distinctly hierarchical, question-and-answer exchange. (Ellis & Berger, 2002, p. 845)

And when telling the story (in publication) later, the interviewer/author reflects on the personal biographical experiences that brought them to the topic and what they learned, both cognitively and emotionally, from their sharing.

Interactive interviews involve collaborative interviewing among a small group of individuals where "each is given the space to share his or her story in the context of the developing relationships among all participants" (Ellis & Berger, 2002, p. 847). The focus is on the understandings that emerge among the participants during interaction—what they learn together. It is helpful for the researcher to have personal experience with the topic being discussed. So, for instance, as a married male skydiver, Leon spent an evening at a skydiving airport pub with three other married male skydivers, drinking beer and sharing stories about the challenges of fitting their hobby into family and work life. Through the interactive interview, each of the skydivers left the conversation with a greater awareness that he was not alone in facing such challenges.

In *co-constructed narratives* the focus turns directly to the self or selves, as researchers examine their own relationships rather than the relationships of others. A compelling example of just such an interview is provided by Ellis and Bochner's (1992) "self-consciously therapeutic" venture into exploring a deeply emotional decision for Carolyn to have an abortion early in their relationship. Ellis and Bochner individually wrote narratives of the events, decisions, and their coping strategies, followed by sharing their narratives and discussing their experiences surrounding the abortion. They also sought out contributions from others who had played roles in the unfolding of the events and decisions.

As the foregoing examples illustrate, across the range of interview styles used by autoethnographic researchers we see movement beyond the outdated conception of interviews as one-way communication. For autoethnographic scholars, interviews—of both self and others—are an active co-construction of "reality," feelings, and understanding as well as a means for recreating scenes from past and present life experiences.

Key Features

In the foregoing section we described a variety of methods of inquiry used in autoethnographic research. Several of the methods we described, such as field-notes and interviews, are standard tools in ethnographic research in general, albeit adapted to an autoethnographic focus. But in the process of adapting these methods to autoethnography, researchers have significantly modified them to incorporate or emphasize aesthetic, cognitive, emotional, and relational values that have received less attention in traditional ethnographic research. Whether these changes are viewed as a rupture with previous ethnographic research (e.g., Denzin, 2006; Ellis & Bochner, 2000) or as new developments consistent with longstanding (if often submerged) sensitivities within Chicago School ethnography (e.g., Anderson, 2006), the bottom line is that autoethnographic inquiry can be distinguished from traditional ethnography most in terms of these distinguishing features. In particular, we point to five key distinctive characteristics. Taken together, we believe, these features capture the ethos and spirit of autoethnographic inquiry.

Visibility of Self

Key to autoethnographic inquiry today is the visibility of the self in research and in writing. As critical as it is now, however, this emphasis on the visibility of self hasn't always been key to autoethnographic inquiry. In anthropology, autoethnography was first used as a gloss for describing an ethnography of one's own people (Hayano, 1979, p. 99), and the only criteria for autoethnographic writing was the researcher's membership as an "insider" to the culture that was the subject of investigation. Thus, early autoethnography in anthropology was a kind of "insider anthropology" regardless of whether the self was made visible in the writing. Yet, with the turn towards reflexivity of the 1980s and the 1990s and its related critiques of objectivity, this visibility of self became a hallmark of autoethnographic research and writing (Meneley & Young, 2005).

This very visible "Ethnographic I" (Ellis, 2004) is not just present, but is multi-vocal in its meaning. It is the "I" of the researcher made visible in the research process. It is the "I" that "not only looks but is looked back at, that not only acts but is acted back upon by those in her focus" (p. xix). It is the "I" of emergence, the "I" of dialogue, the "I" of being-changed-by inquiry. The ethnographic "I" is visible as an actor and an agent, acting and reacting visibly to the implications and the consequences of inquiry. Yet, ironically perhaps, the "I" that may seem deliciously in control by virtue of its visibility is not autonomous at all. Instead, the ethnographic "I" exists *only* as it is both framed and opened by the

Other. In autoethnographic inquiry, the "I" that is emphasized and celebrated is, therefore, the "I" of connection and position and unfolding.

Thus, as mentioned in the introduction to this chapter, a cornerstone to autoethnographic inquiry as it is understood today is "self-narrative that places the self within a social context. It is both a method and a text" (Reed-Danahay, 1997, p. 9). Because autoethnographic inquiry takes as a given the connections between rather than the separation of self and context, autoethnographic writing is theoretically more congruent with postmodern, feminist, queer, post-Colonial, and poststructural approaches to social science inquiry than with modernist orientations and sensibilities. It is "active, reflexive, and reflective...decentered, deconstructed and self aware" (Kong, Mahoney, & Plummer, 2002, p. 241). Its focus is on issues of identity and selfhood, voice and authenticity, cultural displacement and exile, boundary-crossing and a double-consciousness that foreground the multiple nature of selfhood while opening up new ways of writing about social life (Reed-Danahay, 1997, pp. 2–4).

Obviously, if the researcher is to be visible in published texts, it is critical for her or him to be visible in the data. Autoethnographers are self-consciously involved in the construction of meaning and values in the social worlds they investigate, and the data they collect or create in the course of inquiry should reflect this personal connection. Interestingly, as Atkinson, Coffey, and Delamont (2003) have observed, "the personal has never been subordinate in the private world of fieldnotes" (p. 60). However, even though the presence of an active researcher has often been acknowledged as appropriate in fieldnotes, many qualitative textbooks have suggested that personal reflections be clearly separated from more "objective" fieldnote descriptions, whether in sidebar "memos to self" within the fieldnotes or in separate personal journals. In contrast, autoethnographic inquiry rejects the distinction between the subjective and the objective, seeking, as Davies (1999) puts it, "to develop forms of research that fully acknowledge and utilize subjective experience as an intrinsic part of research" (p. 5). So, for instance, while Leon has in a sense kept "double books" by writing both fieldnotes on his skydiving forays and a diary reflecting on more personal day-to-day life, he has merged both sets of writings into one corpus of autoethnographic data, thus building a richer and more expansive autoethnographic record.

Strong Reflexivity

A second fundamental characteristic of autoethnographic inquiry, incorporated across the range of research "methods" discussed previously, is what McCorkel and Myers (2003) have termed "strong reflexivity." Over the past fifteen years reflexivity has become a buzzword in the social sciences, with a multiplicity of often ambiguous meanings. "In its most transparent guise," Charlotte Davies (1999) has written in her review of the concept, "reflexivity expresses researchers' awareness of their necessary connection to the research situation and hence their effects upon it" (p. 7). At a deeper level, "strong reflexivity" involves an aware-ness of reciprocal influence between autoethnographers and their settings and co-participants. It entails self-conscious introspection guided by a desire to better understand both self and others through examining one's actions and perceptions in reference to and dialogue with those of others. For autoethnographers this is part of a holistic process of inquiry. As Atkinson, Coffey, and Delamont (2003) observe:

> [Auto]ethnographers-as-authors frame their accounts with personal reflexive views of the self. Their ethnographic data are situated within their personal experience and sense making. They themselves form part of the representa-tional processes in which they are engaging and are part of the story they are telling. (p. 62)

Not only do autoethnographers "form part of the representational processes," they are also informed by those processes as the cultural meanings they co-create are constituted in conversation, action, and texts. While it can be argued that all "ethnographers use their experience among and knowledge of others to expand their knowledge of self" (Davies, 1999, p. 180), strong reflexivity represents a deeper and more self-conscious informative reciprocity between the researcher and other group members.

Strong reflexivity can be written in many ways. One common strategy of reflexive inquiry involves describing and reflecting on one's self and experience at different points in time. Michael Humphreys (2005), for instance, draws upon three vignettes from his diary entries over the years to pursue a reflexive under-standing of the challenges, successes, and failures of an academic life. Anniina Guyas (2007), as previously noted, similarly uses self-experience at different points in her life to gain deeper insight into her relationship with her grandmother in a broader personal, familial, and cultural context. Amy Pinney (2005) takes a different tack for pursuing reflexive perspective in her autoethnographic study of personal agency and desire by juxtapositioning herself in two roles, first as a strip club dancer and then as a strip club patron. In each case, the researcher seeks to self-consciously problematize a definitive sense of self and others, pursuing instead a richer understanding of the fragmented, temporally and contextually shifting nature of selves and relationships.

Engagement

Autoethnography lies at the intersection of discourses and experiences of Self and Other, Insider and Outsider, Native and Colonialist. Because of this, engage-ment, negotiation, and hybridity emerge as common themes of all the varieties of autoethnographic texts described by Reed-Danahay (1997). Feminist method-ologists like Fonow and Cook (1991), Naples (2003), and DeVault and McCoy (2006) argue that researchers should subject themselves to the same level of scru-tiny they direct toward the subjects of their inquiry. Doing so requires not only that researchers present the results of their research to the affected communities, but also that the agent of knowledge be placed along the same critical plane as the object of inquiry. In this way, the researcher gazes back at her or his socially situated research project and examines the cultural assumptions that undergird and historically situate it (see Harding, 1991). While traditional positivism assumes the necessity of detachment and objectivity, autoethnographic inquiry calls for personal engagement as a medium through which deeper understanding is achieved and communicated.

So, for instance, when Leon was studying the homeless with David Snow (Snow & Anderson, 1993), he did not feel it was appropriate for him to argue with a homeless person on the streets about the best way to panhandle. But since he has been pursuing research with fellow skydivers, he feels a need and responsibility to share his views—and even to argue—with his skydiving companions over a wide variety of topics, from the pros and cons of training procedures and equipment to handling conflictual airport politics. Through such reflexive discourse with other members of the group, setting, or subculture one is studying, the "complete member researcher" (P. A. Adler & P. Adler, 1987, pp. 67–84) as autoethnographer uses collective experiences and interactions to more richly understand and define both self and others in our communities and in the broader social world.

But while engaged research carries great rewards, it also carries risks for the social scientist whose livelihood depends upon continued publication. This lesson hit close to home when Bonnie's book about her work with female *curanderas* was released (Glass-Coffin, 1998). A Peruvian colleague suggested that the book would be of great interest to Peruvian audiences, and he offered to translate the text into Spanish and look for a publisher in Peru. She asked the primary informants with whom she had the most affinity and access (since, unlike some of the other healers in Bonnie's book, they had telephones) their opinion, and they admonished her not to proceed with the idea because "there are pieces of our life story in your book that we don't want our neighbors to see." Bonnie decided to honor this commitment and did not pursue the translation. The consequences of this single decision are multiple and continue to ripple outward. Publication opportunities were lost on the way to Bonnie's tenure and promotion. Peruvian audiences were denied the opportunity to know the work of women *curanderas* in their country, and the other four healers documented in Bonnie's book lost an audience for their voices without being asked their thoughts on the subject.

Now, more than ten years later, the same informants who admonished Bonnie not to publish are writing their own Spanish-language book about their healing arts. Their son recently asked Bonnie if she would be interviewed for the book project as "someone who was greatly influenced by my mothers' work." When this book is released, the fame of these two women will continue to spread, and all the other voices who were part of the original research will further fade into the background. The call for engagement in autoethnographic inquiry is consistent with a wide range of critical ethnography (Madison, 2005), including feminist scholarship, participatory action research, and post-Colonial ethnography, each of which emphasizes the ethical and relational dimensions, as well as the analytic aspects, of ethnographic practice. Yet, even as research is decolonized, the particularities of personal affinity between researcher and subject, as well as simple logistics of who lives on- and off-the-grid challenge on-going quests toward democratization of knowledge and power.

Vulnerability

Autoethnographic writing is most successful when it is evocative, emotionally compelling, and when readers can feel their lives deeply touched by the stories that they read: As Ruth Behar (1997) has told it, there's little point to anthropology that doesn't "break your heart" (p. 1). Certainly, inquiry that is vulnerable, forthright in exploring the character weaknesses, struggles, and ambiguities of the researcher, can touch readers deeply and evoke an open heart and mind to self-scrutiny as well. Vulnerability, defined by *Webster's Dictionary* as "being exposed to the possibility of harm," creates a strong ethos and compelling rhetoric for autoethnographic writing—presenting the author as willing to embrace self-exposure in a public domain. But the call to vulnerability also presents several challenges for autoethnographic inquiry. Indeed, as Allen-Collinson (Chapter 13) notes, we have only recently come to grapple with the issue of self-protections in autoethnographic research that we address routinely in research with other human subjects.

Autoethnographic research presents the ethnographer with vulnerability on many fronts. In the early stages of inquiry, many autoethnographers have found themselves facing the challenge of reliving or reinterpreting past experiences in painful ways. As Brett Smith (1999) reports in his autoethnographic chronicle of his battle with serious depression, "the telling, reading, enacting, and listening [of autoethnographic inquiry] for some, does not come easy" (p. 277). April Chatham-Carpenter (2011) recalls the struggle she faced in confronting the disturbing urge to return to past bulimic behaviors and self-perceptions as she wrote about those experiences. "Valerie" in Ellis's *The Ethnographic I* (2004) discovers in the self-analysis of autoethnography that "what I had to face as I wrote my story is that I am scared all the time that the cancer will come back" (p. 114). These stories serve as cautionary tales that autoethnography often requires a courageous persistence in confronting painful memories and insights. Yet for many who explore "traumatic truths" in autoethnographic work, there seems to be a powerful urge for self-revelation and, hopefully, therapeutic disclosure. Recognizing the possibility of emotional challenges, it is important for those travelling into painful personal terrain to follow Chatham-Carpenter's (2011) strategies for self-protection: I "surrounded myself with supportive individuals who knew my background and pain, to whom I could confide the twin compulsions of anorexia and needing to be published on this topic."

In a related vein, several scholars have observed that one of the difficulties of pursuing vulnerability in autoethnography is that one's life is intertwined with others. As Ellis (2009) observes, "When we write autoethnographically about our lives, by definition we also write about intimate others with whom we are in relationships" (p. 307). Writing revealingly and vulnerably about oneself is one thing, but writing revealingly about other family members or intimates can be felt as quite another. And while many autoethnographers have written deeply revelatory and uncomfortable stories of family members, yet others—how many is impossible to know—have written in ways that protected at least some of their intimates from such scrutiny. The problem in pursuing autoethnography in such a guarded manner is as obvious as the urge to do so. But if it is important to be vulnerable in your fieldnotes and recollections, it may nonetheless be wise to be judicious and self-protective to some degree in published work. Laurel Richardson (2001) has provided sound guidance on this issue. In writing as data and inquiry, she argues it is valuable to include "everything and everyone" (p. 36). The advantage of this is to build the richest set of data possible. But when it comes to publishing from autoethnographic work, one can use more personal discretion and professional judgment. Indeed, while vulnerability has compelling dramatic and evocative virtues, most of us have parts of our lives that we consider too sensitive to reveal to scholarly or other audiences.

An additional concern about self-revealing portrayals raised by Ellis (2009) is that the choice to be vulnerable in a publication may reify that choice in ways that the author never intended. In discussing her choice to write about a minor speech impediment Ellis notes,

> There will be times when [the speech impediment] bothers me…[and now that I've written about it] it also may bother me because I made such a big deal about it. What if people now don't think I have a speech problem? Then that will bother me *too*—here I've made this big deal out of something that shouldn't have been a big deal. (Flemons & Green, 2002, pp. 92–93)

Finally, there is a concern that to "open up the realm of the interior and the personal" (Fiske, 1990, p. 90) can also open the autoethnographer to charges of narcissistic self-indulgence, as well as setting her or him on a challenging, potentially emotionally painful, voyage of self-investigation. Sometimes, as Chatham-Carpenter (2011) notes, autoethnographers choose to be self-protective when going public and when dealing with their careers:

> In the process of trying to keep anorexia at bay, I kept coming face to face with the ultimate ethical question about this type of research—at what cost am I willing to be published about such a personal topic? Is the pain involved for me as the storyteller too much to make the storytelling worthwhile? I had to experiment with how much I was willing to tell, and risk not telling all, being

"rejected" from certain publication outlets as a result, and then decide whether to ultimately pursue the advice the reviewers gave me. Their advice ended up being useful, in helping me understand the voices behind my pain, and in separating those voices from myself. But it took several years before I was healthy enough to follow through with this. By that time, I had surrounded myself with supportive individuals who knew my background and pain, to whom I could confide the twin compulsions of anorexia and needing to be published on this topic.

As a "spiritual seeker," in a public university for instance, Bonnie has also wondered about how much she should admit to that in her publications. She has always felt somewhat at odds with her social-scientist peers. Like Cozart (2010) and Chang (2011), she has often sensed resistance to, and even feared that discussions of, personal spirituality have no place in the academy. Indeed, she began her employment at Utah State University not long after a number of Brigham Young University faculty members were both fired from the university and excommunicated from the Church of Jesus Christ of Latter Day Saints as a result of publishing activities. In those cases, it was the lack of spiritual commitment to Church-defined doctrinal truths that caused such heartache for these colleagues. But, for an untenured faculty member at a public university just up the road, the back-lash from that incident was something frequently heard in the hallways and just as quickly internalized. For an untenured scholar, allegiance to an openly engaged spirituality is definitely a kind of vulnerability that gives one pause when considering just how "out" to be with this positioning in scholarly publications.

Yet—after tenure—Bonnie has chosen to write about her spiritual experiences without contextualizing these as culturally relevant beliefs without ontological significance. She has done so as a way of challenging the boundaries that she feels need to be expanded in order to make social science inquiry more relevant to the more than 70 percent of students *and* faculty at more than 200 universities around the country who *do* define themselves as religious or spiritual (Chang, 2011). Now, instead of alluding to the consciousness of non-human entities "as if" this was something real and to be reckoned with, she presents the results of her "peek behind the veil" where plants bowed to her and responded to her attentions just as she saw it rather than as the result of some epiphenomenal deception that needs to be framed in terms of received "scientific" wisdom. As she has recently reflected,

> Some changes to my scholarship I make willingly, including my own experiences as I now move from the role of anthropological observer to shamanic initiate, and as I accept my birthright as a full-member of an earth-honoring spiritual community. Others, I fear, but cannot reject, wondering only whether the record of my adventures with a family that includes plants and animals, rocks and trees, can ever be made palatable to my academic peers.…[But] I believe that in our discipline…the time has come for new beginnings and a new acknowledgment of belonging. I believe that it is time to proudly verbalize the perspectives of engagement, transformation, connection, and consequence that

some of us have experienced....Whether or not my peers choose to accept these narratives, however, they continue to serve as bridges between consciousness and matter, between Self and Other, and between participant and observer, in ways that I am confident reflect the resilient legacy of our discipline. (Glass-Coffin, 2010, pp. 214–215)

While the verdict is still out as to whether Bonnie's decisions will be admired or ridiculed by her colleagues in anthropology, she has found the rewards of this vulnerability to be worth whatever risks it means to her professional standing or her career. Although the outcomes might have been different if she were not yet tenured, she has not felt any negative impacts as a result of her spiritual "coming-out." Instead, she has found herself re-energized as a scholar because of the honesty of self-disclosure. By pushing the paradigms of her discipline, she has also found new venues opening to her for publication, discussion and debate.

Open-endedness/Rejection of Finality and Closure

The final feature of autoethnographic research that we wish to highlight is the open-endedness of this form of inquiry. Autoethnography is characterized by a principled resistance to what Ellis and Bochner (2000) have referred to as "undebatable conclusions" (p. 744). Autoethnographic inquiry itself, as well as autoethnographic publications, represents understandings and insights captured at one point (or more) in temporal and sociocultural contexts. Often published autoethnographic stories seek to explicitly portray this processual nature of social life, as in Anniina Guyas's (2007) rendering of her changing perceptions of a photograph of her grandmother over time. Social life, identities, and relationships are fluid, not static, and autoethnographic inquiry is self-consciously situated ethnography. Jason Laurendeau (2011) concludes his account of his base-jumping pursuits with the observation, "That was part of how I was growing at that time" (p. 417). And if inquiry captures a point in time, it is with the awareness of a broad horizon stretching into the future. As Andrew Sparkes (1996) writes in his autoethnography of struggling with spinal degeneration, "In seeking, I find that new narratives of the body are in the making, and that with the end of one kind of body comes the beginning of other kinds. I remain unsure as to where that leaves me" (p. 490). Similarly, Brett Smith (1999) concludes, "This story has no final 'transcendent epiphany.'...I am no Phoenix who heroically and cleanly rises out of its own ashes. My life, like stories, has no neat and tidy ending" (p. 274).

The open-endedness of autoethnographic inquiry is grounded in the "obdurate reality" (Blumer, 1969, pp. 23–24) of change, but also often, if not always, in the belief in agency and the hope of healing. As Valerie writes of her autoethnographic research on her cancer experience, "Maybe through talking and writing with other women about their experiences, I can figure out another story to live....I hope to write myself as a survivor in a deeper and more meaningful way" (cited in Ellis, 2004, p. 114). The autoethnographic resistance to finality and closure reflects a conception of the self (and society) as relational and processual, mutably written in a moment that opens onto a panoramic, albeit not unlimited, future of possibilities.

Conclusion

While there has been considerable scholarly dialogue about proposed criteria for judging the quality autoethnographic writing (e.g., Bochner, 2000; Schwandt, 1996; Smith & Hodgkinson, 2005), there has been far less extensive discussion of the practical work of conducting autoethnographic research itself. In this chapter we have tried to fill this gap by examining various modes of inquiry that autoethnographic scholars, including ourselves, draw upon in the course of their research. Not surprisingly, we find that autoethnographic inquiry involves many of the same kinds of data collection that typify ethnography more generally. Fieldnotes, qualitative interviews, and analysis of personal documents are among the most common types of data discussed in autoethnographic research. But in the process of adapting these data collection tools to autoethnography, researchers have emphasized aesthetic, cognitive, emotional, and relational values that have received less attention in traditional ethnographic research. These values frame several key features of autoethnographic inquiry, including the visibility of the researcher's self in the inquiry process, a push toward strong reflexivity, and deeply personal engagement with the social group or setting being studied. Additionally, autoethnography places demands and challenges of vulnerable inquiry upon the researcher, challenging us to risk facing our own personal weaknesses as we pursue deeper social understanding through examining our own lives. Finally, autoethnography is characterized by an open-ended rejection of finality and closure—in inquiry during the research process as well as in published scholarship.

Taken together, we believe, the features we have described in this chapter reveal the ethos and spirit of autoethnographic inquiry. It is instructive to note that the sensitivities and values captured in the key features of autoethnographic inquiry have been part of the broader discourse and practice of progressive qualitative research for decades now, elaborated in various ways in feminism, postmodernism, cultural studies, post-Colonial ethnography, and queer theory—among other academic perspectives. Indeed, in our own career trajectories we were first introduced to many features of autoethnography in these earlier cultural and academic movements. We were initially trained in more positivistically oriented research methods, but we resonated with the insights and commitments advanced by critical and poststructural scholars. The intellectual movements of feminism and post-Colonial theory have played major roles in Bonnie's affinity for autoethnography. Similarly, Leon's interests in autoethnography emerged in large part through his engagement with cultural studies and social constructionism. In both of our cases, our personal biographies, intellectual inclinations, and career trajectories have led us to craft our scholarly inquiry in ways that have to some degree transformed that inquiry. While autoethnographic scholarship will continue to depend on many of the same methods as other ethnography, we believe that, like us, other scholars engaged in autoethnography will continue to distinguish themselves by greater allegiance to progressive sensitivities in the social sciences and humanities. Indeed, autoethnographic inquiry is in many ways epitomized in Kong, Mahoney, and Plummer's (2002) description of "the queered interview" as "much more active, reflexive, and reflective; decentered, deconstructed, and self-aware...embracing the mutuality of interviewer and subject" (p. 241).

In embracing the challenge of such inquiry, autoethnography will continue to push the boundaries of "acceptable" or "respectable" social science. As the digital age and global interconnection expand social life and opportunities for self-creation, autoethnographic inquiry will undoubtedly unfold in new directions—incorporating both new technologies and new forms of social engagement. We cannot say what specific methods of inquiry will guide future autoethnographic work. We can, however, with confidence suggest that the key features and values—of authorial visibility, reflexivity, evocative writing, relational engagement, vulnerability, and openness to new directions—will be incorporated into autoethnographic inquiry wherever it goes. Indeed, insofar as these features are key to the "new language of qualitative research" (Gubrium & Holstein, 1997), autoethnography is currently leading the way.

References

Adler, P. A., & Adler, P. (1987). *Membership roles in field research*. Newbury Park, CA: Sage.

Anderson, L. (1999). Witcraft in a state employment agency: Rhetorical strategies for controlling clients. *Perspectives on Social Problems, 11*, 219–238.

Anderson, L. (2006). Analytic autoethnography. *Journal of Contemporary Ethnography, 35*, 373–395.

Anderson, L. (2011). Time is of the essence: An analytic autoethnography of family, work, and serious leisure. *Symbolic Interaction 34*, 133–157.

Atkinson, P., Coffey, A., and Delamont, S. (2003). Key themes in qualitative research: Continuities and changes. Walnut Creek, CA: AltaMira Press.

Behar, R. (1997). *The vulnerable observer: Anthropology that breaks your heart*. Boston: Beacon Press.

Blumer, H. (1969). *Symbolic interactionism: Perspective and method*. Englewood Cliffs, NJ: Prentice-Hall.

Bochner, A. P. (2000). Criteria against ourselves. *Qualitative Inquiry, 6*, 266–272.

Castaneda, C. (1968). *The teachings of Don Juan: A Yaqui way of knowledge*. Berkeley: University of California Press.

Castaneda, C. (1971). *A separate reality: Further conversations with Don Juan*. New York: Simon and Schuster.

Castaneda, C. (1972). *Journey to Ixtlan: The teachings of Don Juan*. New York: Simon and Schuster.

Castaneda, C. (1974). *Tales of power*. New York: Simon and Schuster.

Chang, H. (2011). Autoethnography as method for spirituality research in the academy. In H. Chang & D. Boyd (Eds.), *Spirituality in higher education* (pp. 11–29). Walnut Creek, CA: Left Coast Press, Inc.

Chatham-Carpenter, A. (2011). Do thyself no harm: Protecting ourselves as autoethnographers. *Journal of Research Practice 6*. Accessed December 30, 2011, at jrp.icaap.org/index.php/jrp/article/view/213/183

Cozart, S. C. (2010). When spirit shows up: An autoethnography of spiritual reconciliation with the academy. *Educational Studies, 46,* 250–269.

Crawley, S. (2002). "They *still* don't understand why I hate wearing dresses": An autoethnographic rant on dresses, boats and butchness. *Cultural Studies ↔ Critical Methodologies, 2,* 69–92.

Davies, C. A. (1999). *Reflexive ethnography: A guide to researching selves and others.* London: Routledge.

Denzin, N. K. (2006). Analytic autoethnography or déjà vu all over again. *Journal of Contemporary Ethnography, 35,* 419–428.

DeVault, M., & McCoy, L. (2006). Feminist interviewing: Experience, talk, and knowledge. In S. N. Hesse-Biber (Ed.), *Handbook of feminist research: Theory and praxis* (pp. 173–197). Walnut Creek, CA: Sage.

Dumitrica, D., & Gaden, G. (2009). Knee-high boots and six-pack abs: Autoethnographic reflections on gender and technology in *Second Life. Journal of Virtual Worlds Research 1.* Accessed December 30, 2011, at journals.tdl.org/jvwr/article/view/323/422

Ellis, C. (1997). Evocative autoethnography: Writing emotionally about our lives. In W. G. Tierney & Y. S. Lincoln (Eds.), *Representation and the text: Re-framing the narrative voice* (pp. 115–142). Albany, NY: State University of New York Press.

Ellis, C. (2004). *The ethnographic I: A methodological novel about autoethnography.* Walnut Creek, CA: AltaMira Press.

Ellis, C. (2009). *Revision: Autoethnographic reflections on life and work.* Walnut Creek, CA: Left Coast Press, Inc..

Ellis, C., & Berger, L. (2002). Their story/my story/our story. In J. F. Gubrium & J. A. Holstein (Eds.), *Handbook of interview research* (pp. 849–875). Thousand Oaks, CA: Sage.

Ellis, C., & Bochner, A. P. (1992). Telling and performing personal stories: The constraints of choice in abortion. In C. Ellis & M. Flaherty (Eds.), *Investigating subjectivity: Research on lived experience* (pp. 79–101). Newbury Park, CA: Sage.

Ellis, C., & Bochner, A. P. (2000). Autoethnography, personal narrative, reflexivity. In N. K. Denzin & Y. S. Lincoln (Eds.), *Handbook of qualitative research* (2nd ed., pp. 733–768). Thousand Oaks, CA: Sage.

Ellis, C. S., & Bochner, A. P. (2006). Analyzing analytic autoethnography: An autopsy. *Journal of Contemporary Ethnography, 35,* 429–449.

Emerson, R. M., Fretz, R. I., & Shaw, L. L. (2011). *Writing ethnographic fieldnotes* (2nd ed.). Chicago: University of Chicago Press.

Fabian, J. (2000). *Out of our minds: Reason and madness in the exploration of Central Africa.* Berkeley: University of California Press.

Fiske, J. (1990). Ethnosemiotics: some personal and theoretical reflections. *Cultural Studies, 4,* 85–99,

Flemons, D., & Green, S. (2002). Stories that conform/stories that transform: A conversation in four parts. In A. P. Bochner & C. Ellis (Eds.), *Ethnographically speaking: Autoethnography, literature, and aesthetic* (pp. 115–121). Walnut Creek, CA: AltaMira Press.

Fonow, M. M., & Cook, J. A. (1991). *Beyond methodology: Feminist scholarship as lived experience.* Bloomington: Indiana University Press.

Fullagar, S. (2002). Narratives of travel: Desire and the movement of feminine subjectivity. *Leisure Studies, 21,* 57–74.

Glass-Coffin, B. (1998). *The gift of life: Female spirituality and healing in Northern Peru.* Albuquerque: University of New Mexico Press.

Glass-Coffin, B. (2009). Balancing on interpretive fences or leaping into the void: Reconciling myself with Castaneda and the teachings of Don Juan. In B. Hearne & R. Trite (Eds.), *A narrative compass: Women's scholarly journeys* (pp. 57–67). Urbana: University of Illinois Press.

Glass-Coffin, B. (2010). Anthropology, Shamanism and alternate ways of knowing/being in the world: One anthropologist's journey of discovery and transformation. *Anthropology and Humanism 35,* 204–217.

Glass-Coffin, B., & Kiiskeentum (in press). Ontological relativism or ontological relevance: An essay in honor of Michael Harner. *Anthropology of Consciousness.*

Goulet, J-G., & Miller, B. G. (2007). *Extraordinary anthropology: Transformations in the field.* Lincoln: University of Nebraska Press.

Gubrium, J. F., & Holstein, J. A. (1997). *The new language of qualitative method.* New York: Oxford University Press.

Guyas, A. S. (2007). Reconstructing self within the family: Rebuilding the family album. *Visual Culture & Gender, 2,* 16–23.

Harding, S. (1991). *Whose science? Whose knowledge? Thinking from women's lives.* Ithaca, NY: Cornell University Press.

Harner, M. (1980). *The way of the Shaman.* Toronto: Bantam Press.

Hayano, D. M. (1979). Autoethnography: Paradigms, problems and prospects. *Human Organization, 38,* 99–104.

Holstein, J. A., & Gubrium, J. F. (1995). *The active interview.* Thousand Oaks, CA: Sage.

Humphreys, M. (2005). Getting personal: Reflexivity and autoethnographic vignettes. *Qualitative Inquiry, 11,* 840–860.

Jackson, M. (1989). *Paths towards a clearing: Radical empiricism and ethnographic inquiry.* Urbana: University of Illinois Press.

Jenks, E. B. (2002). Searching for autoethnographic credibility: Reflections from a mom with a notepad. In A. P. Bochner & C. Ellis (Eds.), *Ethnographically speaking: autoethnography, literature, and aesthetic* (pp. 170–187). Walnut Creek: AltaMira Press.

Joralemon, D. (1983). *The symbolism and physiology of ritual healing in a Peruvian coastal community.* Unpublished doctoral dissertation. University of California, Los Angeles.

Kong, T. S. K., Mahoney, D., & Plummer, K. (2002). Queering the interview. In J. F. Gubrium & J. A. Holstein (Eds.), *Handbook of interview research* (pp. 239–258). Thousand Oaks, CA: Sage.

Laurendeau, J. (2011). "If you're reading this, it's because I've died": Masculinity and relational risk in BASE jumping. *Sociology of Sport Journal, 28,* 404–420.

Madison, D. S. (2005). *Critical ethnography: Methods, ethics, and performance.* Thousand Oaks, CA: Sage.

McCorkel, J., & Myers, K. (2003). What difference does difference make? Position and privilege in the field. *Qualitative Sociology, 26,* 199–231.

Meneley, A., & Young, D. (2005). *Auto-ethnographies: The anthropology of academic practices.* Toronto: University of Toronto Press.

Mills, C. W. (1959). *The sociological imagination.* New York: Oxford University Press.

Naples, N. A. (2003). *Feminism and method: Ethnography, discourse analysis, and activist research.* London: Routledge.

Pinney, A. (2005). Ethics, agency, and desire in two strip clubs: A view from both sides of the gaze. *Qualitative Inquiry, 11,* 716–723.

Plummer, K. (2001). *Documents of life 2.* London: Sage.

Reed-Danahay, D. (Ed.). (1997). *Auto/ethnography: Rewriting the self and the social.* Oxford: Berg.

Reed-Danahay, D. (2009). Anthropologists, education, and autoethnography. *Reviews in Anthropology, 38,* 28–47.

Richardson, L. (1994). Writing: A method of inquiry. In N. K. Denzin & Y. S. Lincoln (Eds.), *Handbook of qualitative research* (pp. 516–529). Thousand Oaks, CA: Sage.

Richardson, L. (2001). Getting personal: Writing-stories. *Qualitative Studies in Education, 14,* 33–38.

Schwandt, T. (1996). Farewell to criteriology. *Qualitative Inquiry, 2,* 58–72.

Sharon, D. (1978). *The wizard of the four winds.* New York: The Free Press.

Skillman, R. D. (1990). Huachumero. *San Diego Museum of Man Ethnic Technology Notes, 22,* 1–31.

Smith, B. (1999). The abyss: Exploring depression through a narrative of the self. *Qualitative Inquiry, 5,* 264–279.

Smith, J., & Hodkinson, P. (2005). Relativism, criteria and politics. In N. K. Denzin & Y. S. Lincoln (Eds.), *Handbook of qualitative research* (3rd ed., pp. 915–932). London: Sage.

Smith-Shank, D., & Keifer-Boyd, K. (2007). Editorial: Autoethnography and arts-based research. *Visual Culture and Gender 2.* Accessed December 30, 2011, at explorations.sva.psu.edu/vcg/2vol/vcg_v2_editorial.pdf

Snow, D., & Anderson, L. (1993). *Down on their luck: A study of homeless street people.* Berkeley: University of California Press.

Sparkes, A. C. (1996). The fatal flaw: A narrative of the fragile body-self. *Qualitative Inquiry, 2,* 463–494.

Thomas, W. I., & Znaniecki, F. (1927). *The Polish peasant in Europe and America.* New York: Knopf.

Turner, E. (1994). A visible spirit in Zambia. In D. Young & J-G. Goulet (Eds.), *Being changed by cross cultural encounters: The anthropology of extraordinary experiences* (pp. 71–95). Peterborough, ON: Broadview Press.

Van Maanen, J. (1988). *Tales of the field: On writing ethnography.* Chicago: University of Chicago Press.

Young, D., & Goulet, J-G. (Eds.). (1994). *Being changed by cross cultural encounters: The anthropology of extraordinary experiences.* Peterborough, ON: Broadview Press.

Chapter 2

A History of Autoethnographic Inquiry

Kitrina Douglas and David Carless

How to tell a history? How might we[1] write a story of what has gone before—concerning the origins and development of a research methodology we now know as autoethnography? How should we recount a history of something that, although it includes us, stretches far beyond us in terms of people, practices, places and times?

When we received an invitation to contribute to this Handbook, we were asked to write a chapter on the history of autoethnography. Of course, as the editors and other contributors would probably attest, *the* history of anything does not exist—it is instead an illusion, a fiction, or a fallacy because there can be no one definitive telling of any story, history or otherwise. History, like any other story, is subject to amendment, development, alteration, expansion and change—forever re-written as new insights, stories, perspectives, contexts or understandings are uncovered. *And history, like any other story, depends on who is doing the telling.*

So what we have here is *a* history of autoethnography. In fact—and we may as well be clear about it from the outset—it is *our* history of autoethnography. To do otherwise would be to write against some of the core premises that autoethnography is built upon. In particular, it would risk working against the realization that knowledge about the social and human world cannot exist independent of the knower; that we cannot know or tell anything without (in some way) being involved and implicated in the knowing and the telling. In addition, it would fail to capitalize on one of the unique opportunities that autoethnography provides: to learn about the

Handbook of Autoethnography, edited by Stacy Holman Jones, Tony E. Adams, and Carolyn Ellis, 84–106. © 2013 Left Coast Press, Inc. All rights reserved.

general—the social, cultural and political—through an exploration of the personal. Carolyn Ellis (2004) writes that autoethnographic researchers work to "connect the autobiographical and personal to the cultural and social" by privileging "concrete action, emotion, embodiment, self-consciousness, and introspection" (p. xix). How might we draw upon this approach in writing this chapter? How might *our* (personal) experiences and stories regarding autoethnography contribute to a (general) history of the methodology? Stacy Holman Jones (2005) suggests that

> autoethnography is setting a scene, telling a story, weaving intricate connections among life and art, experience and theory, evocation and explanation... and then letting go, hoping for readers who will bring the same careful attention to your words in the context of their own lives. (p. 765)

We follow this counsel in our approach to this chapter by sharing stories from four key phases in our own histories of autoethnography. These moments—epiphanies if you prefer—relate to: (1) an initially ill-defined sense or awareness that *something was missing* from the academic writings and communications we were studying and accessing; (2) a significant exposure or *encounter* with autoethnography which signaled the possibility of a different way of working; (3) the *doing* of autoethnography, with reference to some of the practical and ethical challenges that can arise; and (4) navigating others' *responses* to autoethnographic scholarship.

Our re-telling of these moments is like all the stories we tell of our lives and experiences: partial, situated, and incomplete. Nonetheless, it provides a starting place to consider why and how autoethnography has developed, while recognizing the kinds of challenges and rewards autoethnographers have and are likely to experience. This chapter also provides a kind of journey through autoethnography's history as experienced by two particular researchers. In telling our story, we hold fast to the conviction that evoking the personal can illuminate the general,[2] and we hope that *our* history of autoethnography will resonate in some way for you, and perhaps chime with your own experience. We begin where it began for us, at a place that at once provides a stimulus and rationale for autoethnography.

Something Is Missing

Where and why?

What is the problem?

I feel a need—that is not being met

Now, you might not be wrong

I hear the tale you are telling

But it's partial, incomplete

...something is missing

○

"Before I begin, could we have a show of hands of who here has medical training?" The first speaker of the day, a slightly balding, slightly overweight professor of psychiatry, wears an immaculate gray suit topped off with a crimson tie. He steps out from behind the podium towards the front of the stage as he asks the question.

Should I raise my hand? Does a Bachelor's degree in physical education, a Master's in kinesiology, and a PhD in exercise and health science count as "medical training"? If I do raise my hand, does that separate me in some way from those in the audience who don't? I look around the room, at the backs of the heads in front of me, the faces behind me and to the side, at the hands in the laps. Two hundred delegates—here to attend a conference advertised for users of mental health services, carers, family members, and health professionals—and see only a scattering of raised hands. "Ah, OK," he says with a smile, "then I better mind my P's and Q's."[3] He steps back behind the podium and clicks onto his first slide. "Let me start by looking at the symptomatology of mental illness…"

o

Some symptoms of schizophrenia, from the surgeon general's report on mental health (United States Department of Health and Human Services, 1999):

> *Disorganized speech/thinking,* also described as "thought disorder" or "loosening of associations," is a key aspect of schizophrenia….Tangential, loosely associated, or incoherent speech severe enough to substantially impair effective communication is used as an indicator of thought disorder….*Alogia*, or poverty of speech, is the lessening of speech fluency and productivity, thought to reflect slowing or blocked thoughts, and often manifested as laconic, empty replies to questions. (p. 271)

o

Some moments documented in Stuart's—a person diagnosed with schizophrenia and one of the participants in my PhD dissertation—medical records:

- Left school with no qualifications, government training schemes since leaving school, range of short-term jobs since

- Several relationships with women, one had bipolar disorder and committed suicide

- Six-month period suffering from loss of identity—prescribed Trifluoperazine

- Admitted to hospital—diagnosed with emerging psychosis with overlays of obsessional thoughts

And it is said (by some) that schizophrenia is genetically determined. But if this catalog of events—and more besides, in many cases—had happened to *me*, I remember thinking, I reckon I'd become psychotic, too. Reading the participants' lengthy medical records, it sounded like everyone—genetic predisposition aside—had experienced a tough and challenging set of life events, enough to knock any of us off our stride.

○

Stuart carried the extra weight well. He didn't let the sixty pounds he'd put on—one of the more visible side effects of antipsychotic medication—intrude on his game. Of course it slowed him down. But he adjusted his tactics accordingly, taking the role of vocal playmaker, occupying the midfield, calling the moves and making telling passes to other players.

"Andy, man on! You're alright, I'm with you," he called, drifting infield, eyes flitting between the ball Andy danced around and Len, who was trying to lose his marker with a break down the wing. The whistle finally went after Andy succumbed to an enthusiastic challenge, losing the ball and protesting, with mock-horror on his face, "*Referee!*"

Stuart turned towards me, clapping his hands in my direction. "Alright, Dave?" he shouted, a huge grin on his face, jogging towards the goal mouth. "I know you're new to the team, but come on, don't be shy," he said, with a hearty pat on my back. "We let our goalies in on the up-front action too! There ain't nothing wrong with breaks *right* from the back in this game, mate!"

"Alright, Stuart, thanks," I replied, laughing. "I'm waiting for just the right moment before I step into the spotlight!"

Stuart laughed and jogged back to take the free kick. Spinning the ball in his fingertips before placing it with precision on the ground, he turned towards me again. "We'll switch positions at half time, unless you want me to swap with you now?" he half-shouted, before chipping the ball into the air, towards the edge of the penalty box.

○

Stuart talked to me for two hours that day about his life. He'd showed me photographs of moments, people, places, trophies. He told me about when he'd first become "unwell," about the psychiatrist, about his father's funeral, how he'd become unwell again. He talked about being in the hospital, about the swimming teacher who'd helped him overcome his fear of the water, how he'd been unwell some more, about the football teams he'd played for over the years, and about his current team which he'd helped set up. He told about the flat he shared, his trip to America, how he'd been unwell again, about the people—"like family really"—who'd helped him out, about the sausages he liked to eat, the phone calls with his mother, and about how he was "nearly 100 percent now."

What did I *now* know about mental illness? How much did I understand of Stuart and his experiences? Not much perhaps? But then again, a lot more beyond the symptoms, deficits, and dysfunctions catalogued in the scientific literature on mental health. In fact, I wouldn't mind betting that I'd learned some things that the slightly balding, slightly overweight professor of psychiatry would do well to understand.

There was something missing from the story the professor had told. And there was something missing from the journal articles and books I was reading. *Something didn't fit.* And it wasn't only when I compared those stories to Stuart's stories. The academic literature on mental illness didn't tally with what I was learning through being with, talking to, getting to know a group of men diagnosed with severe mental illness. It didn't fit with my own experience of the ups and downs of life, either. And I couldn't *make* it fit: no matter how many journal articles and books I read, something wasn't quite right. Until, that is, I stumbled upon the work of Peter Chadwick (e.g., 2001a)—a psychologist who wrote about his own experience of psychosis, as he put it, "from the inside."

○

But what is *the something* that is missing, that causes this lack of "fit"? We are not alone in coming to the view that it is understandings about the subjective dimensions of personal experience that are missing from many existing academic texts—subjective dimensions that are best expressed through the personal voice. A sense (expressed above) that people are *not like that* emerges as our personal knowledge of others collides with the more distant representations produced through traditional scientific methods. Arthur Bochner (1997) has reflected on how although he "had studied, theorized, and taught about loss and attachment for more than two decades," he "didn't really begin to *know* loss until [he] experienced [his] father's death" (p. 424). Here, *personal experience* challenges theories, categories, and interpretations.

Related to this is a potential "reality clash" when individuals who come into contact with academic texts come away with the feeling "*I* am not like that!" Here, then, a dominant representation fails to fit the experiences of those it purports to represent. This kind of collision is not unusual, and numerous autoethnographic texts present a self who contravenes (in some important way) dominant representations of a particular experience or identity. Mental health is one field in which such issues have particular potency. Patricia Deegan (1996), Peter Chadwick (2001a), Brett Smith (1999), and Stuart Baker-Brown (2006) are among those who have published personal accounts of their experience of mental health problems that contravene or challenge medical portrayals of mental illness. While not always specifically presented as autoethnography, these accounts share some common ground in that they both *include* and *focus on* personal experience as part of the analysis/representation of phenomena. More recently, others have moved explicitly in an autoethnographic direction to provide insights into mental health problems on the basis of personal experience (e.g., Burnard, 2007; Grant, 2010; Grant, Biley, & Walker, 2011; Muncey & Robinson, 2007; Short, Grant, & Clarke, 2007).

Similar developments can be observed in other fields including health and illness (e.g., Martin, 1997; Sparkes, 1996; Spry, 1997; Tillmann-Healy, 1996; Vickers, 2002), gender and sexuality (e.g., Adams, 2006, 2011; Carless, 2010a,

2012a; Gust & Warren, 2008; Holman Jones & Adams, 2010; Pinney, 2005), sports and physical education (e.g., Douglas, 2009; Duncan, 2000; Gilbourne, 2010; Kosonen, 1993; Purdy, Potrac, & Jones, 2008; Tiihonen, 1994; Tsang, 2000;), and race and ethnicity (e.g., Gatson, 2003; McLaurin, 2003; Moreira, 2008a, 2008b). Scanning across these and other fields, it seems that the development and progress of autoethnography has, to some extent, been independent across disciplines, with some starting earlier, or progressing faster, than others. Across fields, however, is recognition of a growing need for a way to address, consider, and include what is found to be missing from writings based solely on scientific research methods: the voice of personal experience.

If it is indeed the personal voice of experience that is an "antidote" to balance or reposition existing research texts, what led to this imbalance in the first place? William James was drawing on his own experience as a way to illuminate psychological phenomena in the 1890s (James, 1892), while Michel de Montaigne was offering meditations based on personal reflection as long ago as 1500 (see de Montaigne, 1991). These examples suggest there is little that is new in drawing on the personal to illuminate the general. Rather than appearing now for the first time, personal and subjective experience has instead *been systematically removed* from human and social science research over the course of the past century in response to calls for methods that more closely parallel research in the natural sciences. Thus, it is not by chance that "something is missing" from human and social science research texts of our times—this omission can be understood as a result of the dominant cultural (e.g., scientism, positivism) and political (e.g., neo-liberal) conditions of our times. This absence or gap can usefully be construed as a "problem" for which autoethnography offers a solution.

Encountering Autoethnography

The self appears,

The textual self appears,

We, writing the self

And then

The body appears

o

Instant porridge? I never knew there was such a thing. "Just add milk and microwave for 60 seconds" it says. *Hmm.* I'm suspicious of "instant" anything, but I'm willing to give it a go. I pour the oat mix into the flimsy plastic bowl and put the bowl into the motel's microwave, wondering why no other guests are taking breakfast this morning. I open the book of abstracts for today's schedule and scan the text as the microwave whirs. "Panel P040, Autoethnography as Relational Practice" catches my eye, perhaps because I recognize the name of the panel's chair. I've heard about this guy—I've even read some of his work. What time does it start? 9:45, I can make that… I get up and look for a cup and saucer, or a mug, for coffee. I can't find one. Perhaps we're supposed to use these paper cups? Seems strange—it can't be that a paper cup is thrown away every time every person in this massive country finishes a drink. Can it? Surely it'd be better if the motel just washed… *Beep, beep, beep, beep!* I cross to the microwave, open the door, *Aaagh!* The porridge mix has bubbled over… *Ouch!* That plastic bowl is so hot! I half drop it, blow on my fingers, pick up the mess with a paper napkin, and quickly plonk it down in front of my seat. Should I clean the microwave? Probably. But after I've finished… "Tension plagues the relationship between me and my father especially when it comes to golf- and gay-related issues" (Adams, 2005). *Golf and gay?* Did I just read what I thought I read? Golf and gay in the same sentence? In a book of abstracts? At an academic conference? But there are no gay men in sports! Well, hardly any, it seems. Except me of course… and I'm not sure I want to label myself anyway. "My story interrogates the troubled relationship that separates us. It's a story of sexuality and sports, of gayness and hegemonic masculinity, of a fag and his golf clubs." *My* story? *Me* and *my* father? Not *them* and *their?* Not *those homosexuals?* This sounds different. OK, it doesn't relate to my PhD and it probably won't help us win an evaluation or research contract, but maybe I should give this a chance…

(Later that morning) I sidle in with four or five others, through the door at the back. It's quite an elegant room. *Huh,* it's quite a large room. *Ooh,* there's quite a sizeable audience, more than came to my session. *Hmm,* all the seats are taken. Well, apart from a few in the front row.

"Come on in!" a tanned, bearded, healthier-than-usual-for-an-academic-looking man in a colorful shirt says with a welcoming wave, "there are empty seats down the front here." *Err,* not sure I want to be *right* at the front, so I shuffle along the back wall and stand, leaning against it, in the far corner. The man with the tan introduces the next speaker, at the same time a young man stands up at the front and smiles, a little nervously I think. Why is *he* standing up? He's obviously not the… "My mom always told me that I'd either be gay *or* that I'd marry a black woman," he says. *He is! And he's telling a story.* More: he's *starting* with a story! What about the pre-amble? What about the stats on prevalence? What about the methods section? And the bit about the participants? I thought I was being bold using a story *in the middle* of a presentation about my *participants.* That caused enough reaction when I spoke at the department student conference. And he is *starting* with a story… and not just *a* story, but *his* story!

"I'm often asked how long I've *known* that I've been gay. Well, that depends. I've known that I've been attracted to men since an early age, but I didn't know that I fit into the category of 'gay' until…" *But this is my story!* Well, it can't be, can it, because I haven't *told* my story… but, but… yes… yes… and he's not an old guy looking back on harassment and homophobia and secrets and lies… he isn't reminiscing about "the bad old days"… and he's not camp or effeminate either, like the gay men on TV. Instead he's standing up and telling stories, from the inside, about a life that is being lived now—a life that includes sports, being a student, being a son, and being sexually attracted and involved with another man. And the most useful paper (Sparkes, 1997) I've read to date on gayness in sports is *a fiction*—because the researcher *couldn't find any gay physical education teachers or students to interview!*

At the end, I wanted to speak with the presenter—to thank him for this honest, open, trusting, brave work. For those twenty minutes in which by speaking of *his* life, he had somehow spoken of mine: of experiences, doubts, separations, distance, desires, hopelessness, dreams, silences that I had never shared and that I had never heard anyone else speak of—in academia or beyond. I wanted to speak with him about the excitement and fear I felt experiencing and contemplating the methodology he had demonstrated: an approach that I had found so powerful, so affecting, so revealing; that had lifted a lid—for me—on what research could be and what it might achieve. But there was a crowd gathered now at the front, around him, around the other presenters, smiling, hugging, talking—ah, they seem to know each other. *Hmm*, I don't know any of them… perhaps I'll get in touch via email…

○

Despite a sense that "something is missing," and even a seeking of an alternative way of working, it is hard to see how the step to actually working in other ways can happen without the spark and direction created by encountering a concrete example of autoethnography. We need, in Gubrium and Holstein's (1997) terms, a *language* that authorizes self-exploration. We have both—at different times and in different ways—been fortunate enough to be exposed to excellent examples of autoethnography, which crystallized and embodied a solution to the "problems" we were experiencing with traditional methodologies. This encounter might take the form of, for example, sharing a published autoethnography with a colleague or an academic witnessing autoethnography as a conference presentation (as in the preceding story). It might also come from an encounter with a work in the arts or performance studies (e.g., Pelias, 2004; Spry, 2011). Arguably, it is less likely to come through being taught autoethnography as part of a research methods course as many still privilege traditional approaches. Thus, each person's initial *encounter* with autoethnography—which might be through a range of different channels— is especially significant in terms of the uptake, development, and influence of autoethnography within the academy.

The uptake and development of *autoethnography* as an explicitly defined method can be traced back to the late 1970s where a more sophisticated and complex understanding of the field researcher and his or her connection to a particular phenomenon stemmed from post-Chicago School developments in phenomenology, ethnomethodology and existential sociology (P. A. Adler & P. Adler, 1987). Patricia and Peter Adler (1987) mandate for an epistemology of membership roles whereby a researcher would value and document his or her own experiences and emotions alongside participants', using these insights to benefit members of a community to which the research relates. Of the types of membership roles described by Adler and Adler the *opportunistic* and *convert* complete member researcher seems most akin to a current understanding of what autoethnographers do, and perhaps provides some background for how field researchers began to embrace the importance of documenting their own subjective experience of a phenomenon prior to their being "concrete examples" to follow. Early examples of opportunistic approaches—where a connection to the subject or phenomena pre-exists a research interest—can be seen in David Sudnow's *Ways of the Hand* (1978) in which the author explored his experiences of becoming a jazz pianist. Another early example is the work of David Hayano (1979) who used the term *auto-ethnography* in making the case for self-observation in cultural anthropology and then later demonstrated this approach in *Poker Faces* (1982).

A decade after Adler and Adler (1987) set out their vision for field researcher roles, Ellis and Bochner (2000) documented how feminist (e.g., Behar, 1996; Kreiger, 1991; D. Smith, 1992) and indigenous or native (e.g., L. Smith, 1999) epistemologies have contributed to an explosion of personal narratives. They note how a continued and sustained interest with concerns over power and praxis has generated more reflexive, emotional accounts that challenge taken for granted assumptions as to what counts as knowledge and how this is presented. It is perhaps unsurprising, therefore, that Ellis and Bochner identify over forty different terms that have been used to describe autoethnographic approach-es between the late 1970s and 2000, which include, for example, *narratives of the self* (Richardson, 1994), *self-stories* (Denzin, 1989), *critical autobiography* (Church, 1995), *confessional tales* (Van Maanen, 1988), and *autobiographical ethnography* (Reed-Danahay, 1997).

As we now survey the scene it appears that the researchers who have included personal accounts, who have become visible in their work and who have begun to embrace reflexivity, have served—among other things perhaps—as trailblaz-ers whose work has shown that there is another way of *doing* social and human science research. Encountering an excellent example of autoethnographic inqui-ry—as the preceding story portrays—can serve as a beacon which illuminates anew, not so much by adding to or building onto an existing picture, bit by bit or piecemeal, but instead by turning on a new light in a new room. This kind of striking experience or epiphany can, in our experience, cut through the clutter of day-to-day life as a researcher, academic, or student. In so doing it has the poten-tial not only to inspire others but also to help legitimize autoethnography as a valid, useful, and important way of *doing* social research.

Doing Autoethnography

So you read my words
Sketched on the page
And learned of entanglement
Well, here now is my flesh
What say you, as I sing my song?
Where do you belong?

○

It niggled,[4] it gnawed, it tugged, there was something in it. It unsettled me, it wouldn't let go, it wouldn't go away, it had me in its grip.

"You should include your autoethnography," was all Professor Andrew Sparkes had said before taking a sip of his beer and placing it gently on the table. Of course, his *Fatal Flaw* (1996) and *Telling Tales in Sport and Physical Activity* (2002) were ground breaking in our field, so he wasn't asking me to attempt something he hadn't already done. His huge hands made the pint glass seem small, and those five words, *You-should-include-your-autoethnography,* made the problem seem small—at least in the Highbury Vaults pub, one of six havens where scholars from our department regained their sanity *post-lecture*. So here we all sat, Andrew, our invited guest speaker at the student conference, David, Ken, Lucy, Mark, and Jim, with me staring at my orange juice contemplating what he'd just said as the conversation moved on around me. All I needed to do was to include my story alongside all the other stories being deposited in my vault. You would never have guessed his little provocation could start an avalanche. It was just a little whisper, a call, a crack. But…

○

A wry smile came over my face as I read, "Nothing like these forays out into the other world to make you realize how fortunate we are to have created what we have in the Communication Department" (Ellis & Bochner, 2000, p. 760). "Yes," I talked back to the text, "well I'm not in a Communication Department. I'm in the Exercise, Nutrition and Health SCIENCES department. We take blood samples, fit calorimeters, take anthropometric measurements, and estimate energy expenditure." I allowed the heavy tome to fall onto my lap and revisited the niggle as I lay awake in bed. Though late at night, I couldn't help line up Andrew Sparkes, Laurel Richardson and Harry Wolcott, as usual, at the end of my bed where I posed questions for them, and then listened to them debate with each other. "I'll tell you what I'm struggling with," I said. Andrew always answers first, perhaps because I know him more than the others. He taught me as an undergraduate, and he's a "piss or get off the pot" person. The other two are bodyless texts as I know them only through their written words, and it is these words I bring to mind as I ask them questions. Although I don't know these people phys- ically, they guide me, and even though I've never heard them speak, I hear their words in my head. I also give them bodies as I look toward the foot of my bed; Harry, sitting in the middle is wiry; Laurel Richardson is tall and skinny. All three are wise.

"How can I include myself?" I ask with a shrug. "Which stories? How can I engage with autoethnography when I'm barely permitted a poetic chapter in my PhD?"

"Well, yes, the department you are in can cause problems, try not to worry about that just now," Laurel Richardson says. "You have to start writing!" Harry interrupts. "Get something down, and don't start judging it or editing it before you finish it."

o

Two bare pectoral muscles, beautifully shaped, came into view. Lucy's eyes enlarged and her mouth opened as she turned towards me at the moment a pink sheen began to spread across her face—her blushing made me smile even more as I watch her notice David stripping off his shirt in the August sun. We held our "research team" meetings on the lawn outside our department. Lucy and David agreed to be my "research team" after the ethics committee had refused me eth- ical approval.

Study E4972: *Motivation, High Achievement and Persistence in Women Professional Golfers* was deferred, on the grounds that:

> The committee have serious misgivings about the scientific validity, methodol- ogy, and approach to subjects...please allude in the protocol [to] how reliable this data will be, and steps that will be taken to ensure that the data is [*sic*] not biased given that the researcher knows the subjects. (Chairman, UBHT Ethics Committee, 2001)

The study was resubmitted including a new protocol.

> The committee now understands the reasons behind this research project, but still has concerns related to the validity of any findings in the sense that the researcher "knows" all of the subjects and therefore there is potential for a sig- nificant element of bias with qualitative interviews. (Chairman, UBHT Ethics Committee, 2001)

When you play sports people think: "Thick jock!" They make jokes about us. Even friends in the department made jokes about my participants not having "an intelligent thought between them." And here I was, the only person in the depart- ment refused ethical approval—kind of proving that *I* shouldn't be *there*. *Who I am* was the problem. So as well as allegedly being stupid, I was learning that I'm not reliable and that I'm biased. But there it was again: the niggle. I felt I knew something that they were missing, and it was hidden in my body.

Lucy turned to her notes—she'd been reading my interview with Kandy. "I was shocked that Kandy doesn't enjoy playing golf," Lucy said. "Comparing golf with a butcher who cuts meat isn't how I think of a professional athlete." Rather ironic, I thought to myself, that she and David were supposed to bring objectivity, and here she was full of assumptions. "What makes you think professional athletes would enjoy their work?" I asked.

Later that night I was drawn to revisit that moment. I wondered what I was doing while we talked. As I thought more about that moment in the sun with David and Lucy, I became more aware of how extracts from *my stories* had shown life "as a pro" differently; they began to open up political edges, and they persuaded Lucy. So, I began writing them down: little scenes, snippets and conversations, the things that niggled me, and then I began trying to understand why they niggled me.

○

I always run in the morning. There is something about the movement of my body, the rhythm of my stride, energy being channeled through my muscles, deep breathing, the slight breeze against my face. Sooner or later, as I run, words fill my head, pictures arrive, I see scenes, remember conversations, talk back, argue, cry, become upset, become lost in one story, laugh at another. Five miles pass, I begin to see, I see myself, a scene unfolds, a topic comes into vision, sometimes ten miles pass, sometimes I lose sight, become worried I'll lose the plot before I get back, and then I'm home. At that moment I want to unleash my thoughts on a page, something has been brewing, I must get it down.

○

"About bloody time, too!" was all my sister said. Well, that and: "You're so closed off." No wonder I am, I thought, retrieving the three short vignettes from her hand and retreating rapidly. As I waited, two years later, for her to call, I wondered what her response would be this time, because this time the stories included *her.* My story *Winning and Losing* (Douglas, 2009) described different aspects of our relationship—on and off the golf course—about her bullying and protecting me, trying to influence the presentation of my body, and included her miscarriage while she was caddying for me. While I ran, I practiced responses to what I imagined she would say. I hated feeling vulnerable as I opened my world to her. I hated feeling disempowered having to ask for her approval. I called her up.

"So, have you had time to read it?" I ventured. "I need to know. It's important to me to get your okay before I submit it." "Oh yeah, it's fine," she said, sounding like she was painting her nails or plucking her eyebrows while on the phone. "Carry on. I don't remember any of it actually. I'm not bothered." Yeah right, I thought. I think *I ticked the box...* but a tick was all.

○

I'd been around David for over a decade, watching him write papers, observing him hone and chisel evaluations, and I'd been there, in the background, while he wrote songs that embodied his life experiences, and those of others, playing music and singing songs. I also listened to him talk about song writing: "You've got to let a song breathe," he'd say, "give it a chance." "You want the melody and guitar to hold back during some parts of the song to let the words take center stage." My body absorbed his teaching; he was planting seeds he didn't even realize he was planting, scattering them on fertile ground. I began to thirst after working that way without even thinking. I knew our data was more than a list of logical categories, but I hadn't considered that writing a song could also be an embodied autoethnographic act, that when I wrote a song, my story, and the stories of others, may be there, too. So when it happened I didn't even notice it.

I was alone in Cornwall, and in a similar way to how David worked, I was simply playing songs. Then, after a while, I began experimenting and tuned one string differently, dropping the "E" string to a "D." That little change set the stage. I fiddled with a different strumming pattern. I liked how it felt, how it sounded. In my spirit, and in the work I'd been doing earlier in the evening, I was still searching for BIG answers, but a few words turned up and sat down next to the melody: "Light the candle, strike the match, open up that battened hatch, I want to see," seemed to fit my mood. I immediately stopped and wrote them down in case I forgot them. Then, I sang them again and again and carried on plucking the top string followed by the other strings when I got to the end of the line. In the space created by the resonating guitar my eyes gazed randomly round the room and, the next thing, I'm looking into the mirror: "In the mirror is this me, am I all you want me to be?" I wasn't thinking about my sports career, but it was present, in my body, and I knew where it had taken me, all those trophies and the costs, and carried on writing:

> *Climb upon the mountain, too, but it's in the valley that I find you,*
> *and I see what is true*
> *In the mirror is this me? Am I all that I could be?*
> *They tell you follow a distant star, a journey that will take you far*
> *from all, that you might be*
> *In the mirror is this me? Am I all that I might be?*
> *Just imagine how it might be, if only we could see*

o

I lay back and looked out of my bedroom window; in the darkness the constellation came into view. My friends Andrew, Harry, and Laurel had disappeared, they seldom sit at the foot of my bed now. So many stars in the cosmos I thought, and like us, they appear at different times, arc different trajectories, share a similar journey. We share pain, creative moments; we are searching spirits; we worry, become outsiders in our own solar systems, and attempt to remain true to some force that drives us on.

○

As we revisit the tales of those who have engaged with autoethnography and as we listen to other tales of doing autoethnography (e.g., Adams, 2011; Ellis, 1997, 2001, 2004; Ellis & Berger, 2003; Etherington, 2003, 2004; Martin, 1997; Muncey, 2010; Pelias, 1999, 2004; Richardson, 1997, 2000; Sparkes, 1996, 2000; Spry, 2001, 2011) it seems vulnerabilities and insecurities lurk at the door of each individual's journey. Even when our work is valued by others, most autoethnographers still appear to have questions, doubts, and ethical concerns. It seems this is our mantle. Autoethnographers claim no right to have "got it right" simply on the bases of linking the personal to the political and cultural or through attempting to use personally evocative texts, by employing artistic and creative methods, or because we can sing or dance our bodies. We live with tensions, and because our lives, bodies and stories are neither fixed nor finished, we are never certain of where our work will take us.

For those who come to autoethnography from an artistic or creative background, or from performance or communication studies (e.g., Law, 2002; Pelias, 1999), it seems that there is greater opportunity and possibility to be mentored, educated, and supported at an early stage. However, for individuals who perform autoethnography, sing songs or dance, there is the challenge of taking an embodied act of singing/dancing/performing and transforming it to a textual presentation if we are to resist silence (Pelias, 1999, p. ix). As Etherington (2004) points out, failure to publish for some academics will result in career stagnation, employment difficulties, and lack of tenure. In contrast, others come to autoethnography after being systematically trained to value neutrality and to distance the self from their subjects and selves (see Bochner, 1997; Brackenridge, 1991). Like many others before us and since, we were (academically speaking) birthed into a tradition and a history that seeks objectivity and to remove all aspects of self, including the body, from the research process in order to diligently focus on (different) others. It would be naive to think that these academic traditions leave no scars. As Alasdair MacIntyre (1984) reminds us:

> What I am, therefore, is in key part what I inherit, a specific past that is present, to some degree in my present. I find myself part of history and that is generally to say, whether I like it or not, whether I recognise it or not, one of the bearers of a tradition. (pp. 205–206; see also Freeman, 2010, p. 123)

Whether we like it or not, and whether we recognize it, not only are we part of a cultural tradition in terms of ethnicity, gender, and sexuality, but the type of department we are affiliated with, our subject areas, and our choice of scientific ways of valuing and "doing" research.

Given the profusion of experiences, backgrounds, and disciplines represented by those who engage with autoethnography, it is not surprising that practical approaches, the how we "do autoethnography," differ. As we gaze across histories it seems many of us begin by using what we know best, or what is at our fingertips, and then blend, borrow, add to, adapt, and transform our approach as we gain understanding, experience and insight. In order to mine for personal experiences some autoethnographers have drawn on systematic sociological introspection and emotional recall, "memory work," introspection, self-introspection, and interactive introspection, self ethnography, diaries, free writing, and song writing (for examples, see Bochner & Ellis, 2002; Carless & Douglas, 2009; Douglas, 2012; Laine, 1993; Reed-Danahay, 1997; Sironen, 1994). Autoethnographers have then used a variety of genres to share their experiences, including short stories, fiction, novels, layered accounts, poetry, memoirs, diaries, songs, dance, photos, and performances. Additionally, as mentioned earlier, it seems that as autoethnographers have become exposed to the work of others many have been inspired to experiment and take chances. This seems to have shaped how the field is maturing and developing, and it seems as though the process we each transverse feels to be simultaneously a refining in the fire and stumbling in the dark.

As a great deal of autoethnographic work centers on sensitive issues, taboo subjects, the sacred or hidden aspects of our lives, and on stories and bodies that have been silenced, marked, stigmatized, and forgotten, it shouldn't be surprising that autoethnographers are aware, or have become aware, of many ethical and moral dilemmas and challenges. The types of ethical consideration, however, may not be addressed or understood by traditional ethical approval forms or committees where beliefs and views are often polarized. Given that autoethnographies have been an act of witnessing (Ropers-Huilman, 1999; B. Smith, 2002), a testimony (Frank, 1991), a sacrament (Richardson, 2000), and an aid to healing and strength (Etherington, 2004), one thorny ethical issue to continually question is how it is possible not to implicate or include others, unwittingly or otherwise, in the weft and weave of *our story plot* (Adams, 2006; Ellis, 2001; Kiesinger, 2002).

In considering this ethical dilemma, Ellis (2001) suggests, "You have to live the experience of doing research on the other, think it through, improvise, write and re-write, anticipate and feel its consequences" (p. 615). For some, the fragile nature of a relationship means relationships could be irrevocably damaged by sharing (e.g., Kiesinger, 2002), while at other times relationships may be cemented and we feel greater communion and comradeship. Ultimately, Ellis (2007) acknowledges that writing about others in our stories can be a "muddle" that we must attempt to work through. On this point, Kim Etherington (2004) urges autoethnographers, at the very least, to be transparent about how we come to make our decisions and to document the factors that led to our choices (see also Tullis, this volume).

But the ethical dimension of autoethnography is not static and continues to expand to include not only relational ethics, but moral ethics, ethical mindfulness, an ethic of trust, an ethic of care, and an ethic to look out for the well-being of ourselves as well as the other as we engage in emotionally laden journeys (Adams, 2008; Guillemin & Gillam, 2004; Ellis, 2007; Etherington, 2007). For Alec Grant (2010), the ethical journeys autoethnographers are now encouraged to chart are ones where we not only tell our stories, but take lessons from our stories in order to "live the person that is storied" (p. 115), all the while working towards a better world.

Responding to Autoethnography

I remember: I had been invited to lead a one-off creative methods workshop for a small group of academics who were interested in arts-based research and—perhaps—the possibility of using such approaches in their own work. The organizer suggested I share an example of arts-based research to give those who may not have experienced it an idea about the form that it might take. Following an introduction in which I described some of my own reasons for turning to arts-based methods, I planned to share a short performance autoethnography I had been working on (Carless, 2012b). In the performance, I draw on my own biography to voice and explore experiences of same-sex attraction and desire which often remain "taboo" and unspoken within sports culture.

Because I have generally received supportive responses to my autoethnographic and arts-based work, I felt fairly positive towards the task. However, I harbored some doubts and concerns about possible responses related to sharing aspects of my own experience of same-sex attraction to an audience of sports scholars *and* my use of an arts-based/poetic/performative methodology before an audience more used to traditional scientific methods.

Eight academics attended the workshop—five female and three male—some of whom I knew and some I didn't. I performed the piece and invited responses, comments or questions. A (male) professor in the audience was the first to respond:

> *Professor A:* "I didn't learn anything from this. It didn't tell me anything about homophobia…"

Next, a (male) senior lecturer:

> *Dr. B:* "I couldn't see me ever using this with students…"

Third, the response of another (male) lecturer:

> *Mr. C:* "You said you weren't sure if they were poems. I can tell you they definitely are. But I can also tell you that they are not research…"

Bang. Bang. Bang. The most senior professor immediately dismissed my work. No questions, no doubts. Certainty. Would he be that dogmatic about a quantitative study? Or a grounded theory study? Or a phenomenological study?

Perhaps he set the tone for the next person, the less-senior Dr. B, to dismiss me. Did the pair of them authorize Mr. C to step in and follow-up with his finalized perspective on reality, art, and research? The three of them had got their bit in before any of the women spoke. How can I defend myself/my work in this context? Should I "do a Germaine Greer" and say: "My only stipulation is that the first question must come from a woman"? But then, some women might be similarly aggressive. How can I—after that—go on to share my experiences of *creating* this kind of work? I left the campus that day feeling I should perhaps keep my "taboo stories" to myself.

○

Some weeks later, an email conversation ensued after sharing a written version of the same piece with a colleague:

> **From:** Grant, Alec, **Sent:** 13 April, **To:** Carless, David
>
> Dear David,
>
> I love your attachment. I felt a whole range of emotions, including sadness while reading it. Thinking and feeling with it, it took me back to my days as an adolescent/young man in the RAF [Royal Air Force] in the late 1960s. The tension between living and working in a forbidding oppressive normative sexual discourse for many people was absolutely cruel. Not much has changed, even arguably in competitive sports. More power to your ethical and representational elbow David. Speak soon.

> **From:** Carless, David, **Sent:** 14 April, **To:** Grant, Alec
>
> Dear Alec,
>
> Thank you for your response on my "autoethnographette" (I'm citing your term now!) That is valuable feedback, particularly after a creative methods workshop I ran a couple of weeks ago in which this piece was rather slated by (interestingly) the 3 male (straight identifying, white) academics in the room (the 5 female academics were much more positive). One said he learnt nothing from the piece, which was disappointing to hear... So, I'm glad it reached you in some fashion—and I appreciate you articulating that for me. Keep well Alec—and keep writing!

> **From:** Grant, Alec, **Sent:** 15 April, **To:** Carless, David
>
> I'm saddened to hear about the reaction to your piece. I've been thinking and feeling a lot with it over the last few days. There's loads in it, and load of obvious theory in it (corporeality, Bourdieu, Foucault and on). And it's great, and moving, performance ethnography. I'm tempted to speculate that it may have triggered defensiveness (institutional Homophobia?) among the white straighties, but perhaps that's too much of a gloss. Anyway, don't let them get to you... Very best for now.

○

Over the past few years, we have both created a number of autoethnographies (e.g., Carless, 2010a, 2010b, 2012a; Carless & Douglas, 2009; Douglas, 2009, 2012; Douglas & Carless, 2008) that we present at conferences and through seminars and lectures. The story above portrays just an example of the strong responses this work can at times evoke from academics, students, practitioners, or friends. These responses range from "inspiring" right through to "useless." And we are not alone in this. Other proponents of autoethnography have documented comparable responses—both favorable and critical—to their autoethnographic work and/or the creative or artistic approaches that this work often relies upon (e.g., Adams, 2011; Ellis & Bochner, 2000; Richardson, 2000; Sparkes, 1996). It seems to us that often the same work has the potential to lead to extremely positive responses *and* extremely negative or hostile responses—sometimes simultaneously. In a sense, an individual's response perhaps tells us more about that individual—about his or her assumptions, beliefs, orientation—than it does about the quality, contribution, or value of the research itself.

At the same time, however, the responses of others clearly *do matter* both in terms of the well-being and professional prospects of the individual and of the development and prospects of the methodology. Besides personal and/or public snubs (see, e.g., Richardson, 1997; Sparkes, 2007), some academics have sought, on various grounds, to exclude autoethnographic methods from social research on the basis, for example, that there are more relevant and pressing issues to research (e.g., Walford, 2004). Other scholars, while acknowledging that authoethnography has a place, criticize moves towards evocative and emotional autoethnographies (e.g., Ellis, 2004), which, to them, neither challenge/transform public life nor offer theoretical "development, refinement and extension" (Anderson, 2006, p. 387).

A number of scholars have reflexively documented and explored the costs—both personal and professional—of these kinds of attacks on their (autoethnographic) work (e.g., Bond, 2002; Flemons & Green, 2002), which has been criticized as being—among other things—self-indulgent and narcissistic (see Coffey, 1999; Sparkes, 2000). In response, a number of authors (e.g., Church, 1995; Eakin, 1999; Freeman, 1993; Gergen, 1999; Mykhalovskiy, 1996; Sparkes, 2000; Stanley, 1993) have critically and comprehensively addressed the charges and, in the process, reminded us of the important contribution that autoethnography makes. Others have reflected on the potential consequences of eliminating autoethnographic methods (particularly their focus on the personal and their utilization of alternative forms of representation) might have on the development of particular topics or fields (e.g., Bochner, 1997; Chadwick, 2001b; Pelias, 2004).

In light of both these arguments—that excluding autoethnography harms research *and* researchers—the existence of journals (such as *Qualitative Inquiry*) and international conferences (such as the *International Congress of Qualitative Inquiry* in the United States, *Contemporary Ethnography Across The Disciplines [CEAD] Hui* in New Zealand, and the *Arts Based Educational Research* conferences in Europe) are critically important. These venues have, for a number of years now, provided a fertile seeding ground where non-mainstream methods such as autoethnography can be shared, explored, developed, and nurtured. Like many others, we have found these venues to be essential to the development of our autoethnographic work.

At the same time, for autoethnography to grow and develop—and for the insights this approach can bring to be more widely appreciated—it is essential that we present and publish our work in other, more diverse venues, too. In our fields, journals such as *Qualitative Research in Psychology, Sport Education and Society, Qualitative Research in Sport, Exercise and Health, Sociology of Sport,* and *Journal of Psychiatric and Mental Health Nursing* have proved receptive to autoethnographic work, while conferences such as the *International Human Sciences Research Conference,* the *International Qualitative Conference in Sport and Exercise,* and *The British Sociological Association Auto/Biography Conference* have offered us a warm welcome. In these venues, readers/audiences are not necessarily familiar with autoethnographic inquiry, so a more extensive review and/or rationale for the approach may be requested by editors or reviewers. Given the importance of continuing to widen acceptance of autoethnography beyond the current "strongholds" into "fledgling" venues, we take the view that this work is well worth the effort.

In this sense, the history of autoethnography as we have outlined it here is not so much a fixed thing of the past, but instead something that is continually relived, revisited, and revised. As we write, some are as unaware of—and uninformed about—autoethnography as we ourselves were as students in the 1990s. There are others who are experiencing the kind of awakenings—now through, perhaps, encounters with our own work—that we experienced ourselves in the 2000s. And there are others still who have now been practicing the art for two decades. As we write, there are students fortunate enough to be taught the skills and philosophy of the approach by experienced proponents. There are other students—experiencing frustrations with the distanced, "neutral," and "objective" methods they are being taught—desperately searching for an alternative. And there are others still who will tomorrow submit their autoethnographic doctoral dissertations. All of these scholars and students—positioned at different places along our articulation of a history of autoethnography—exist, relate, and interact in the present chronological moment.

In this light, all of the "past" contested and marginal moments in autoethnography's history are happening now—again and again, over and over. Given the current political and cultural context that underlies academic research, we would suggest they are likely to do so for the foreseeable future. The kinds of trailblazers who populate autoethnography's history are still needed now—and will be tomorrow. New scholars will be asked to step forward and take their place—and they must do so if the autoethnographic tradition is to continue. At the same time, methodological innovation will be required if autoethnography is to remain fresh and relevant. Indeed, perhaps methodological innovation is a hallmark of the approach and a requirement in *every* autoethnographic study. From this perspective, we might see the past, present, and future history of autoethnography as a continual "coming out"—over and again—for each new student, colleague, editor, and conference delegate we encounter. Moments of autoethnography's history are thus happening simultaneously and repeatedly (in different contexts, for different people). And so the future of this always contested, often marginal methodology hangs in the balance, as autoethnography itself seems to be always and at once a threat and a promise.

Notes

1. During discussion sections of the text, we use the first person voice ("we") to communicate our shared perspective. During autoethnographic sections, we use first person singular voice ("I") to designate either Kitrina's or David's personal experience.
2. We hold the view that autoethnography should reach beyond the author's experience to, in some way, speak to the experiences of others.
3. In post-Victorian Britain this axiom is used as an abbreviation of "mind your manners" or, more specifically, to say both please (p's) and thank you (thank-q). The phrase "mind your p's and q's" is used to remind people, especially children, to speak politely.
4. *Niggle,* or niggled (past tense), means to cause, or have caused, a slight but persistent annoyance, discomfort, or anxiety.

References

Adams, T. E. (2005). *Seeking father: Relationally reframing a troubled love story.* Paper presented at the First Congress of Qualitative Inquiry, University of Illinois, May 2005.

Adams, T. E. (2006). Seeking father: relationally reframing a troubled love story. *Qualitative Inquiry, 12,* 704–723.

Adams, T. E. (2008). A review of narrative ethics. *Qualitative Inquiry, 14,* 175–194.

Adams, T. E. (2011). *Narrating the closet: An autoethnography of same-sex attraction.* Walnut Creek, CA: Left Coast Press, Inc..

Adler, P. A., & Adler, P. (1987). *Membership roles in field research.* Newbury Park, CA: Sage.

Anderson, L. (2006). Analytic autoethnography. *Journal of Contemporary Ethnography, 35,* 373–395.

Baker-Brown, S. (2006). A patient's journey: Living with paranoid schizophrenia. *British Medical Journal, 333,* 636–638.

Behar, R. (1996). *The vulnerable observer: Anthropology that breaks your heart.* Boston: Beacon.

Bochner, A. (1997). It's about time: Narrative and the divided self. *Qualitative Inquiry, 3,* 418–438.

Bochner, A. & Ellis, C. (2002). *Ethnographically speaking: Autoethnography, literature, and aesthetics.* Walnut Creek, CA: AltaMira.

Bond, T. (2002). Naked narrative: Real research? *Counselling and Psychotherapy Research, 2,* 133–138.

Brackenridge, C. (1991). Managing myself. *International Review for the Sociology of Sport, 34*(4), 399–410.

Burnard, P. (2007). Seeing the psychiatrist: An autoethnographic account. *Journal of Psychiatric and Mental Health Nursing, 14,* 808–813.

Carless, D. (2010a). Who the hell was *that*? Stories, bodies and actions in the world. *Qualitative Research in Psychology, 7,* 332–344.

Carless, D. (2010b). The autoethnographic process: Starting a new story. In T. Muncey (Ed.), *Creating autoethnographies* (pp. 132–146). London: Sage.

Carless, D. (2012a). Negotiating sexuality and masculinity in school sport: An autoethnography. *Sport, Education and Society, 17*(5), 607–625.

Carless, D. (2012b). Young men, sport and sexuality: A poetic exploration. In F. Dowling, H. Fitzgerald, & A. Flintoff (Eds.), *Equity and difference in physical education, youth sport and health: A narrative approach* (pp. 67–71). London: Routledge.

Carless, D., & Douglas, K. (2009). Songwriting and the creation of knowledge. In B. Bartleet, & C. Ellis (Eds.), *Musical autoethnography: Creative explorations of the self through music* (pp. 23–38). Queensland: Australian Academic Press.

Chadwick, P. K. (2001a). Psychotic consciousness. *International Journal of Social Psychiatry, 47,* 52–62.

Chadwick, P. K. (2001b). *Personality as art: Artistic approaches in psychology.* Ross-on-Wye, UK: PCCS Books.

Church, K. (1995). *Forbidden narratives: Critical autobiography as social science.* Newark, NJ: Gordon and Breach.

Coffey, A. (1999). *The ethnographic self: Fieldwork and the representation of identity.* London: Sage.

Deegan, P. (1996). Recovery as a journey of the heart. *Psychiatric Rehabilitation Journal, 19,* 91–97.

Denzin, N.K. (1989). *Interpretive biography.* Newbury Park, CA: Sage.

Douglas, K. (2009). Storying my self: Negotiating a relational identity in professional sport. *Qualitative Research in Sport and Exercise, 1,* 176–190.

Douglas, K. (2012). Signals and signs. *Qualitative Inquiry, 18,* 525–532.

Douglas, K., & Carless, D. (2008). The team are off: Getting inside women's experiences in professional sport. *Aethlon: The Journal of Sport Literature, 25,* 241–251.

Duncan, M. C. (2000). Reflex. *Sociology of Sport Journal, 17,* 60–68.

Eakin, P. (1999). *How our lives become stories.* Ithaca, NY: Cornell University Press.

Ellis, C. (1997). Evocative autoethnography: Writing emotionally about our lives. In W. G. Tierney & Y. S. Lincoln (Eds.), *Representation and the text: Re-framing the narrative voice* (pp. 115–142). Albany: State University of New York Press.

Ellis, C. (2001). With mother/with child: A true story. *Qualitative Inquiry, 7,* 598–616.

Ellis, C. (2004). *The ethnographic I: A methodological novel about autoethnography.* Walnut Creek, CA: AltaMira Press.

Ellis, C. (2007). Telling secrets, revealing lives: Relational ethics in research with intimate others. *Qualitative Inquiry, 13,* 3–29.

Ellis, C., & Berger, L. (2003). Their story/my story/our story: Including the researcher's experience in interview research. In J. Gubrium & J. Holstein (Eds.), *Postmodern interviewing* (pp. 157–186). Thousand Oaks, CA: Sage.

Ellis, C., & Bochner, A. (2000). Autoethnography, personal narrative and reflexivity. In N. Denzin & Y. Lincoln (Eds.), *The handbook of qualitative research* (2nd ed., pp. 733–768). Thousand Oaks, CA: Sage.

Etherington, K. (2003). *Trauma, the body and transformation: A narrative inquiry.* London: Jessica Kingsley.

Etherington, K. (2004). *Becoming a reflexive researcher.* London: Jessica Kingsley.

Etherington, K. (2007). Ethical research in reflexive relationships. *Qualitative Inquiry, 13,* 599–616.

Flemons, D., & Green, S. (2002). Stories than conform/stories that transform: A conversation in four parts. In A. P. Bochner & C. Ellis (Eds.), *Ethnographically speaking: Autoethnography, literature, and aesthetics* (pp. 87–94) Walnut Creek, CA: AltaMira Press.

Frank, A. (1991). *At the will of the body: Reflections on illness.* Boston: Houghton Mifflin.

Freeman, M. (1993). *Rewriting the self.* London: Routledge.

Freeman, M. (2010). *Hindsight.* New York: Oxford University Press.

Gatson, S. (2003). On being amorphous: Autoethnography, genealogy and a multiracial identity. *Qualitative Inquiry, 9,* 20–48.

Gergen, K. (1999). *An invitation to social construction.* London, Sage.

Gilbourne, D. (2010). Edge of darkness and just in time: Two cautionary tales, two styles, one story. *Qualitative Inquiry, 16*, 325–331.

Grant, A. (2010). Writing the reflexive self. *Journal of Psychiatric and Mental Health Nursing, 17*, 577–582.

Grant, A., Biley, F., & Walker, H. (2011). *Our encounters with madness*. Ross-on-Wye, UK: PCCS Books.

Gubrium, J. F., & Holstein, J. A. (1997). *The new language of qualitative method*. New York: Oxford University Press.

Guillemin, M., & Gillam, L. (2004). Ethics, reflexivity, and 'ethically important moments' in research. *Qualitiatve Inquiry, 10,* 261–280.

Gust, S., & Warren, J. (2008). Naming our sexual and sexualized bodies in the classroom—and the important stuff that comes after the colon. *Qualitative Inquiry, 14,* 114–134.

Hayano, D. (1979). Auto-ethnography: Paradigms, problems, and prospects. *Human Organization, 38*, 113–120.

Hayano, D. (1982) *Poker faces: The life and work of professional card players*. Berkeley: University of California Press.

Holman Jones, S. (2005). Autoethnography: Making the personal political. In N. K. Denzin & Y. S. Lincoln (Eds.), *Handbook of qualitative research* (3rd ed., pp. 763–791). Thousand Oaks: Sage.

Holman Jones, S., & Adams, T. E. (2010). Autoethnography and queer theory: Making possibilities. In N. Denzin & M. D. Giardina (Eds.), *Qualitative inquiry and human rights* (pp. 136–157). Walnut Creek, CA: Left Coast Press, Inc.

James, W. (1892). *Psychology: The briefer course*. New York: Henry Holt.

Kiesinger, C. E. (2002). My father's shoes: The therapeutic value of narrative reframing. In A. P. Bochner & C. Ellis (Eds.), *Ethnographically speaking: Autoethnography, literature, and aesthetics* (pp. 95–114). Walnut Creek, CA: AltaMira Press.

Kosonen, U. (1993). A running girl. Fragments of my body history. In L. Laine (Ed.), *On the fringes of sport* (pp. 16–25). Sankt Augustin, Germany: Akademie Verlag.

Kreiger, S. (1991). *Social science and the self: Personal essays on an art form*. New Brunswick, NJ: Rutgers University Press.

Laine, L. (1993). *On the fringes of sport*. Sankt Augustin, Germany:Akademie Verlag.

Law, S. (2002). *Hope, hell and highwater: An autoethnographical journey from addiction to recovery*. Unpublished MSc. Dissertation. University of Bristol, UK.

MacIntyre, A. (1984). *After virtue: A study in moral theory (2nd ed.)*. Notre Dame, IN: University of Notre Dame Press.

Martin, V. (1997). *Out of my head: An experience of neurosurgery*. Lewes, UK: Book Guild.

McLaurin, S. (2003). Homophobia: An autoethnographic story. *Qualitative Report, 8*, 481–486.

de Montaigne, M. (1991). *The complete essays of Michel de Montaigne, Book 1* (Trans. M. Screech). London: Penguin.

Moreira, C. (2008a). Life in so many acts. *Qualitative Inquiry, 14*, 590–612.

Moreira, C. (2008b). Fragments. *Qualitative Inquiry, 14*, 663–683.

Muncey, T. (2010). *Creating autoethnographies*. London: Sage.

Muncey, T., & Robinson, R. (2007). Extinguishing the voices: Living with the ghost of the disenfranchised. *Journal of Psychiatric and Mental Health Nursing, 14*, 79–84.

Mykhalovskiy, E. (1996). Reconsidering table talk. *Qualitative Sociology, 19*, 131–151.

Pelias, R. J. (1999). *Writing performance: Poeticizing the researcher's body* . Carbondale: Southern Illinois University Press.

Pelias, R. J. (2004). *A methodology of the heart*. Walnut Creek, CA: AltaMira Press.

Pinney, A. (2005). Ethics, agency, and desire in two strip clubs: A view from both sides of the gaze. *Qualitative Inquiry, 11,* 716–723.

Purdy, L., Potrac, P., & Jones, R. (2008). Power, consent and resistance: An autoethnography of competitive rowing. *Sport, Education and Society, 13*, 319–336.

Reed-Danahay, D. (1997). *Auto/ethnography: Rewriting the self and the social*. Oxford: Berg.

Richardson, L. (1994). Writing: A method of inquiry. In N. K. Denzin & Y. S. Lincoln (Eds.), *Handbook of qualitative research* (pp. 516–529). Thousand Oaks, CA: Sage.

Richardson, L. (1997). *Fields of play: Constructing an academic life*. New Brunswick, NJ: Rutgers University Press.

Richardson, L. (2000). Writing as a method of inquiry. In N. K. Denzin & Y. S. Lincoln (Eds.), *Handbook of qualitative research* (2nd ed., pp. 923–948). Thousand Oaks: Sage.

Ropers-Huilman, B. (1999). Witnessing. *Qualitative Studies in Education, 12,* 21–35.

Short, N., Grant, A., & Clarke, L. (2007). Living in the borderlands; writing in the margins: An autoethnographic tale. *Journal of Psychiatric and Mental Health Nursing, 14,* 771–782.

Sironen, E. (1994). On memory-work in the theory of body culture. *International Review of the Sociology of Sport, 29,* 5–13.

Smith, B. (1999). The Abyss: Exploring depression through a narrative of the self. *Qualitative Inquiry, 5,* 264–279.

Smith, B. (2002). The invisible wound: Body stories and concentric circles of witness. *Auto/Biography, 10,* 113–121.

Smith, D. (1992). Sociology from women's perspective: A reaffirmation. *Sociological Theory, 10,* 88–97.

Smith, L. T. (1999). *Decolonizing methodologies: Research and indigenous peoples*. New York: St. Martin's Press.

Sparkes, A. C. (1996). The fatal flaw. *Qualitative Inquiry, 2*(4), 463–494.

Sparkes, A. C. (1997). Ethnographic fiction and representing the absent Other. *Sport, Education and Society, 2,* 25–40.

Sparkes, A. C. (2000). Autoethnography and narratives of self: Reflections on criteria in action. *Sociology of Sport Journal, 17,* 21–43.

Sparkes, A. C. (2002). *Telling tales in sport and physical activity*. Champaign, IL: Human Kinetics.

Sparkes, A. C. (2007). Embodiment, academics, and the audit culture: A story seeking consideration. *Qualitative Research, 7,* 521–550.

Spry, T. (1997). Skins: A daughter's (re)construction of cancer. *Text and Performance Quarterly, 17,* 361–365.

Spry, T. (2001). Performing autoethnography: An embodied methodological praxis. *Qualitative Inquiry, 7,* 706–732.

Spry, T. (2011). *Body, paper, stage: Writing and performing autoethnography*. Walnut Creek, CA: Left Coast Press, Inc.

Stanley, L. (1993). On auto/biography in society. *Sociology, 27,* 41–52.

Sudnow, D. (1978). *Ways of the hand*. Cambridge, MA: Harvard University Press.

Tiihonen, A. (1994). Asthma. *International Review for the Sociology of Sport, 29*(1), 51–62.

Tillmann-Healy, L. (1996). A secret life in a culture of thinness. In C. Ellis & A. Bochner (Eds.), *Composing ethnography* (pp. 76–108). Walnut Creek, CA: AltaMira Press.

Tsang, T. (2000). Let me tell you a story. *Sociology of Sport Journal, 17,* 44–59.

United States Department of Health and Human Services. (1999). *Mental Health: A Report of the Surgeon General*. Rockville, MD: U.S. DHHS.

Van Maanen, J. (1988). *Tales of the field: On writing ethnography*. Chicago: University of Chicago Press.

Vickers, M. (2002). Researchers as storytellers: Writing on the edge—and without a safety net. *Qualitative Inquiry, 8,* 608–621.

Walford, G. (2004). Finding the limits: Autoethnography and being an Oxford University proctor. *Qualitative Research, 4,* 403–414.

Chapter 3

Individual and Collaborative Autoethnography as Method

A Social Scientist's Perspective

Heewon Chang

Autoethnography is a highly personal process. It is personal because the personal experiences of researchers themselves are the foundation of autoethnography. It is also a highly social process. Autoethnographers carefully examine how they have interacted with other people within their socio-cultural contexts and how social forces have influenced their lived experiences. Therefore, in a public light, autoethnographies reveal their author's personal, professional, relational, and socio-cultural identities. Authors' scholarly orientations and the writing preferences cradling their stories also show. This chapter will reflect my social scientist's training and offer the perspective of an anthropological ethnographer. Acknowledging that many others do autoethnography differently, I hope to add my perspective on what autoethnography is and how it can be done. After defining autoethnography, I share the iterative process of autoethnography from deciding on a topic and research method, to collecting and analyzing material, and finally to writing. I also share my on-going study of mentoring and leadership as an illustration of my own autoethnographic practices. In addition, understanding the inherently experimental spirit of autoethnography, I offer yet another ethnography experiment—mixing individual and collaborative autoethnography.

Handbook of Autoethnography, edited by Stacy Holman Jones, Tony E. Adams, and Carolyn Ellis, 107–122. © 2013 Left Coast Press, Inc. All rights reserved.

Autoethnography: What and Why

The use of autoethnography as a research method has been expanding in a multitude of academic disciplines (e.g., anthropology, communication, education, humanities, leadership, management, nursing, religious studies, social work, sociology, performing arts, and many other disciplines). With the growing popularity of the method, autoethnography has evolved in different directions since the term "auto-ethnography" was first used by anthropologist Hayano in 1979. The growing diversity of autoethnographic approaches makes it risky to distill the method down to a set of simple characteristics. However, for the novice autoethnographers, I make such a risky attempt, noting the following characteristics of autoethnography:

- Autoethnography uses the researcher's personal experiences as primary data.

- Autoethnography intends to expand the understanding of social phenomena.

- Autoethnographic processes can vary and result in different writing products.

Autoethnographers use their personal experiences as primary material (data) for social investigation. They draw from autobiographic data such as memories, memorabilia, documents about themselves, official records, photos, interviews with others, and on-going self-reflective and self-observational memos. Autoethnographers are uniquely qualified to access personal data that may be off limit to other researchers. De Vries (2012) expressed autoethnographers' "easy" access to their personal data: "You are the central character in the research so access is not problematic. You can revisit and rethink the data you collect about yourself in an ongoing way" (p. 362). Accessing and utilizing personal data enables autoethnography to make distinctive contributions to the understanding of human experiences within socio-cultural contexts. In his review of my autoethnography method book (Chang, 2008), Anderson (2010) questioned where autoethnographers do ethnographic "fieldwork" if autoethnography is claimed to stem from the tradition of ethnography. I would respond that autoethnographic fieldwork takes place in the autoethnographers' offices or homes, archival libraries, their significant others' places, interviewees' locations, and other locations pertaining to studies: anywhere where they can create encounters and re-encounters with their memories, with objects, and with people. Anywhere they can find their autoethnographic material is where their ethnographic fieldwork happens. Autoethnographers enter their field with a unique familiarity with how and where they may locate relevant data.

The purpose of autoethnography, at least from the social science perspective, is not only to tell personal stories. It intends to expand the understanding of social realities through the lens of the researcher's personal experiences. For example, when Poplin (2011) shared her spiritual transformation experience after meeting Mother Teresa and its impact on her professional life in higher education, she connected it with her critique of cultural resistance to the spiritual discourse in

US higher education. When Muncey (2010) wrote about her personal experience with teen pregnancy as a result of "repeated incestuous sexual abuse" (p. 7), she offered a social critique of the dominant discourse equating teen pregnancy with teen promiscuity and ignorance, which in turn protected the perpetrators of violence and blamed the victims. Personal stories become vehicles for social critiques through which readers gain understandings of autoethnographers' social realities and of the social forces contextualizing their experiences.

Autoethnography uses different processes and is produced in various formats and writing styles. As a teacher and producer of qualitative research, I pay attention to the analytical-interpretive process of research (Chang, 2008; Charmaz, 2006; Creswell, 2012; Maxwell, 2004; Patton, 2001; Reed-Danahay, 1997; Saldaña, 2009; Wolcott, 1992). I encourage autoethnographic researchers to think carefully and analytically about their research process and to report on their methods within their autoethnographies when possible. Other autoethnographers emphasize the importance of writing as a holistic way of thinking, processing, and producing autoethnography without delineating data collection, analysis, and interpretation as distinctive stages of the autoethnographic process (Ellis, 2004; Goodall, 2000, 2008; Muncey, 2010). Given my social scientist's bent, I begin with the first step of research—identifying a research topic and method.

Making Decisions on Topic and Method

I have been pressuring myself to do more research on leadership issues since my education-leadership joint faculty appointment began four years ago. What should my research niche be in the leadership department? Until the appointment I had been building my scholarly agenda primarily around multicultural education. How can I now expand my research agenda to embrace leadership topics without discarding what I had been building for almost fifteen years? How can the issues of culture, enculturation/education, diversity, and justice converge with my new interest in leadership? I want to know how individuals are groomed and mentored to become effective and justice-oriented organizational leaders. With my long-term interest in autoethnography, I decided to turn the focus of the investigation on myself. I have wondered how my mentors have contributed to my development as a faculty member who aspires to be an effective and fair leader in higher education.

Now that I have a topic to pursue for my autoethnography, I need to make methodological decisions. Should I do the study by myself or invite others to join me? The research opportunity of working with leaders of color from multiple universities feels more promising than ever. I want to study "with" them, not "on" them. I am painfully aware of many research efforts in my field that ended up "exploiting," albeit unintentionally, vulnerable participants—the voiceless, the marginalized, and often people of color. I want a participatory study in which the leaders and I can create reciprocal relationships as equals and gain something meaningful from each other in the process. Collaborative autoethnography will allow me to make myself as vulnerable to others as others to me. Later, I discover that none of the leaders knows about autoethnography, but all are eager to learn about this new method and write about themselves. I invite them to experiment with me on the research design of embedding individual autoethnography within collaborative autoethnography. This means that we "collect" our individual mentoring-related data to construct our own autoethnography and simultaneously contribute our individual data to the community data for collective analysis. A few seasoned qualitative researchers from the group will do the group analysis. I'm one of the "seasoned researchers." So I am doing my individual autoethnography as well as our group's collaborative autoethnography.

○

I located my topic by looking first at my professional interest. Although my topic was initially drawn out of my professional interest, my personal interest in mentoring and personal stories is wrapped up with my personal interests. I see a similar convergence in Romo's (2004) autoethnography of his educational journey from a student to a classroom teacher to a principal, then finally to a teacher educator. This professional topic is closely intertwined with his personal identity as a Chicano activist. His personal experience with ethnic discrimination brings his professional focus on educational leadership and social critique of racism together.

Others may start their autoethnographies with personal experience. Ellis and Bochner (2006) describe their approach as follows: "I start with my personal life. I pay attention to my physical feelings, thoughts, and emotions. I use what I call systematic sociological introspection and emotional recall to try to understand an experience I've lived through" (p. 737). Close attention to personal feelings, thoughts, and emotions opens up autoethnography to a deep well of self-reflexivity. For example, Poulos's (2008) autoethnography of family secrets illustrates how he found his autoethnographic material from his dreams and nightmares, reflections on family secrets, and introspection about his struggles with family relationships.

Whether autoethnography starts from the researchers' professional interests or from personal experience, it is helpful to keep a running list of compelling experiences, professional curiosities, nagging issues, and intense emotions. Thoughts and emotions returning to the researchers' consciousness may be worthy to be noted. Several autoethnographers have discussed how they engaged other researchers in conversations to identify their research topics (Cann & DeMeulenaere, 2010; Ngunjiri, Hernandez, & Chang, 2010; Phillips, Harris, Larson, & Higgins, 2009). Many different personal, relational, professional, and social topics covered by published autoethnographies are likely to stimulate researchers' further thinking on possible topics.

Once a research topic is nailed down, a methodological decision needs to be made about whether to do autoethnography alone or in a group. For an individual autoethnography, researchers focus on their personal experiences and work primarily alone to complete the research process, including writing. In a collaborative autoethnography, researchers must decide how many collaborators they will invite to participate before beginning the study. Collaborative autoethnography can be done with "full" collaboration, in which researchers work together from the beginning (data collection) to the end (writing), or with "partial" collaboration in which researchers work together at selected stages of their process (Chang, Ngunjiri, & Hernandez, 2012). My mentoring and leadership study involved partial collaboration, in that all autoethnographers worked together in pooling autobiographic data, but only a few researchers analyzed community data used in writing a group autoethnography.

Individual and collaborative approaches to autoethnography have both benefits and limitations. In individual autoethnographies, autoethnographers negotiate with themselves and consider "relational ethics" involving others when selecting material for writing. Relational ethics refers to recognizing and valuing "mutual respect, dignity, and connectedness between researcher and researched, and between researchers and the communities in which they live and work," ethical standards that researchers follow when acting and taking "ethical responsibilities toward intimate others who are implicated in the stories we write about ourselves" (Ellis, 2007, pp. 4–5). Despite careful consideration of relational ethics, ultimate decisions about their research topics and methods lie with the individual autoethnographers. The autonomy of individual autoethnographers enables them to delve into their personal experiences as deeply and widely as they desire. In individual autoethnographies, the unique gifts of authors as researchers and writers shine. However, individual autoethnography is at risk of privileging one perspective. Researcher subjectivity in qualitative research is a long standing topic of debate; to this debate autoethnography adds one more dimension—mixing the researcher role with the participant role. The concern with the privileged perspective of the author-researcher-participant, raised by Anderson (2006) and defended by other autoethnographers (Denzin, 2006; Ellis & Bochner, 2006), should be carefully considered as researchers undertake individual autoethnography. The researchers may either maximize the full benefit of individual autoethnography—delving deeply into the researcher's experiences with the recognition of their limited perspectives—or incorporate perspectives of others in their individual autoethnographies.

Collaborative autoethnography, on the other hand, engages multiple authors and multiple, although not always diverse, perspectives. This means that collaborative autoethnographers need to consider one more layer of intersubjectivity, namely among researchers. In the struggle of balancing diverse perspectives, author-researcher-participants are encouraged to listen to each other's voices, examine their own assumptions, and challenge other perspectives. This process sharpens their collective interpretation of multiple perspectives and keeps everyone accountable for the process and product. However, the benefit of including multiple voices is also accompanied by the limitation of added complexity. Because collaborative autoethnography involves more than one researcher, the research team may end up spending significant time coming to consensus about the process, negotiating conflicting perspectives, and addressing miscommunication within the team. In the negotiating process, the brilliance of individual stories may be dulled by the need to reach a consensus or be marginalized by a dominant voice.

After decisions about topic and method are made, autoethnographers are ready to take the next step of collecting autobiographic data for their studies.

Collecting Autobiographical Material

I have been sitting in front of my laptop for five hours. My fingers are moving steadily on the keyboard today like yesterday and the day before yesterday. I'm in a "wet" season of writing. I'm in heaven. Stories are pouring out about my dad and mom, graduate school advisor, pastor of college days, work colleague, and husband. These are people who have shaped and developed me in my personal and professional journey—from growing up in multi-religious Korea in a modest household as a daughter of two academics from Christian backgrounds, to moving to the University of Oregon for graduate studies in anthropology and education, to getting married to a German mathematician, to raising two Eurasian American children, and to settling in a faith-based academic institution in the United States as a scholar of multicultural education and leadership studies. I am writing about how these individuals have mentored me in life. Occasionally my fingers pause. I savor fond memories. Disturbing memories also halt the seemingly automatic move of my fingers. This time my brain is censoring; I hesitate for a moment, deciding if I should write secrets that may reflect badly on some of my mentors. I suppress my self-censoring urge and keep writing. "I will decide later," I say to myself. I don't know if any of the secrets will make it to my final autoethnography, but it feels good to record them because I know they are part of my history. I am doing the writing for me, for my autoethnography.

o

As one of the lead researchers, I am making decisions about what kinds of data we could collect as a group: mentors in life, critical mentoring experiences with leadership development, current leadership roles, current work environments… Like my fellow autoethnographers who are exploring their mentoring experiences as leaders of color in higher education, I am writing my stories on these topics and sharing my writings with others through an online learning platform. We also meet once or twice virtually to discuss what we have written. Some new topics of discussion come up during our conversation. If I do autoethnography by myself, I will not need to follow the group writing prompts or share my snapshot stories with others until my autoethnography is finished. I feel vulnerable with my unedited writing riddled with errors and raw emotions. But I must expose my imperfections to my teammates as they do with me. I'm doing individual autoethnography and also collaborative autoethnography.

o

My fingers are not moving as fast as before. They have stopped to give me time to look elsewhere for missing information. My memories have faded on many accounts. I'm thinking about asking my sisters to confirm my memory of the "honesty" lesson we got from our parents. I wonder if they remember the spanking we got together for stealing coins for candies from our parents' piggy bank. Was I in first grade or second grade? Perhaps I will also ask them about their perspectives about Mom and Dad. Do they think of them as "mentors in life"? While thinking about others to call, I pick up the phone to talk to my old professor about how he remembered me as a first-year graduate student freshly arrived from Korea a few decades ago. Would he remember my broken English? I also shoot an email to my work colleague to request a chat about our mutually developmental relationship. I am making a list of people I want to talk to. They may have different perspectives about me and our relationships than I do, but I want to know what they think about our relationships.

I am also making a list of records I need to get from my parents' house and my basement: the many letters I had written to my parents in Korea during my graduate school days in Oregon, letters from my parents, graduate school records for me that my advisor had kept until he retired, my old photos, my journals from different stages of life, sermons my pastors published. I am also developing a map of my constellation of developmental relationships. With me at the center, I note on this map various individuals who have contributed to my development as an academic and leader in my work place. I put those who are still in close relationship with me in a closer orbit and mentors from the past in a distanced orbit around me. My box of "artifacts" is being filled, and my piles of books and files of articles are growing. But I am worried! I have not been sitting in front of my laptop for several days. No stories are gushing out like last week or last month. Am I still doing autoethnography?

o

Autoethnographic data can be gathered in a variety of ways: recalling, collecting artifacts and documents, interviewing others, analyzing self, observing self, and reflecting on issues pertaining to the research topic. Recalling is a free-spirited way of bringing out memories about critical events, people, place, behaviors, talks, thoughts, perspectives, opinions, and emotions pertaining to the research topic.

Physical evidence of the past, such as memorabilia, photos, multimedia materials, official records, and texts including blogs, personal journals and newspaper articles, can stimulate the researchers' multiple senses to connect the present to the past. They can help researchers capture "snapshots" of memories (Muncey, 2010, p. 55).

While recalling captures autobiographic data from the past, self-analysis, self-observation, and reflection bring out present thinking, attitudes, perceptions, habits, and emotions of autoethnographers. One example of self-analysis is constructing a "culturegram" (Chang, 2008, pp. 97–100), a chart in which autoethnographers display their multiple cultural identities in self-selected categories (e.g., race, ethnicity, nationality, language, religion, gender, sexuality, education, socio-economic status, political orientation, interest groups, and geographic affiliation). This exercise also urges autoethnographers to evaluate their primary identities—what they consider more important—based on their *present* analysis of self. Self-observation is another technique for capturing "taken-for-granted, habituated, and/or unconscious matter that…[is] unavailable for recall" (Rodriguez & Ryave, 2002, p. 4). Autoethnographers may take a narrative approach by recording their present actions or describing their present environments in free writing or experimenting with a systematic approach by using a pre-constructed self-observation log. For example, I observed how I spent my waking hours for a week to see patterns in my relationships, activities, and use of time. Galman (2011) used a daybook as a device for self-observation by recording her daily activities. Self-reflection is yet another way of capturing the present. Whereas self-observation focuses on taken-for-granted yet observable matters, self-reflection allows autoethnographers to focus on their present perspectives on issues related to the research topic. In my autoethnography of mentoring and leadership, for instance, I kept memos about my positionality regarding mentoring, minority leaders in higher education, and women in leadership.

Autoethnographic data collection does not have to be a solitary activity. Autoethnographers can interview others implicated or participating in their studies as well as others related to their research topic. In collaborative autoethnography, interaction among researchers also occurs. In my study of mentoring and leadership, my fellow collaborative autoethnographers, scattered around the country, met virtually one or two times each month to engage each other in conversations about our writings pertaining to the study. Ngunjiri, Hernandez, and Chang (2010) call such meetings "probing sessions," during which participants interview each other to draw out more details about data they collected and shared prior to such sessions. Ellis, Kiesinger, and Tillmann-Healy (1997) utilized "interactive interviews" in their collaborative autoethnography of body image and eating disorders. In their case, they gathered for open conversations on their personal experiences with and the personal and social implications of eating disorders. Their open conversations became the foundation of their collaborative write-up. In his individual autoethnography, Adams (2011) skillfully integrated interviews into his autoethnography process. By interviewing self-identified LGBQ persons and having conversations with others about same-sex attraction, he was able to enrich his autoethnography of "same-sex attraction" with such interactive material.

As autobiographic data grow in the form of texts, artifacts, media material, researchers organize and work with them to make sense of what all these "snapshots" are about.

Meaning-Making

I remind myself that doing autoethnography is more than recalling stories, interviewing others, collecting artifacts, and digging into my past. It is about holding collected (or written) fragments of life against the present light and making sense of their significance within the bigger context of my life. I am sure that my intellectual orientation as an educational anthropologist and leadership scholar will color my interpretation. The multicultural prism of Korea, Germany, and the United States will refract the interpretation of my racial, ethnic, gender, religious, linguistic, and socio-economic experiences. I find it hard to piece fragments into a cohesive story, connecting me with others and to our socio-cultural contexts. To help myself organize the vast amount of data fragments, I look for recurring themes among my stories, others' perspectives on our relationships, and artifacts. I also take note of outlying stories, critical moments, and quotable statements. I pay particular attention to how multicultural contexts have influenced my relationships with mentors and my perspective on leadership as a woman, now redefined as a woman of color, within the US context. I realize that who I am is not a simple reflection of my family, institution, and nation. I am finding out that who I am (self) sometimes contradicts where I come from (society). My lived experience as a woman offers a critique to male privileges in Confucian Korea; my cross-cultural marriage contradicts the normalcy of within-group marriages in Korea and Germany; my assertiveness as an Asian female academic leader defies the stereotype of subordinate Asian women. How have my mentors in life helped me navigate in my socio-cultural contexts riddled with contradictions, uncertainties, and confusions? I am trying to understand the intersubjectivity between myself and my mentors in my complex world.

○

The progress with my autoethnography has now slowed considerably I get frustrated about long pauses of my fingers on the keyboard. I am disappointed by the ever more slowly growing lines on my computer screen. I strike out what I have labored over for the last hour and start my paragraph over. How many times have I done this today? I wish I were a gifted writer like some towering autoethnographers. Sometimes I wonder if I would have been a better (effective) or a faster (efficient) writer if English were my first language or if I wrote my autoethnography in Korean. Then I remind myself that it is not the writing of stories that grounds me now, but the analysis of my stories and their connectivity to socio-cultural contexts. Although I seem to have entered a dry season of writing, I know this seemingly "dormant" period is necessary for my autoethnography to bloom. My fingers might have stopped moving for a while but my mind is going steadily to search for meanings and make connections between my stories and a bigger world.

○

How can a big pile of "data" be eventually transformed into a beautifully constructed, compelling autoethnographic text? The transforming process is difficult to delineate because there is no one-size-fits-all approach. Some autoethnographers may elect an organic, intuitive approach to meaning-making (Ellis, 2004; Goodall, 2008; Muncey, 2010); others take an analytical approach to arriving at cohesive meanings out of fragments of life (Anderson, 2006; Lietz, Langer, & Furman, 2006).

For meaning-making, an important preparatory activity begins with reviewing data holistically. Reviewing may mean reading textual data, examining artifacts, and listening to and watching recordings and transcribing them if necessary. This holistic examination will help researchers become acquainted and re-acquainted with the body of data. During this time, researchers are advised to take notes on (or "memo") recurring topics, dominant themes, unusual cases, and notable statements. They also section/fragment data based on dominant topics. This activity is called "coding," "segmenting," or "fragmenting" data (Maxwell, 2004; Saldaña, 2009). At earlier stages of coding, researchers are advised not to impose external categories too soon so as to avoid losing sight of meanings emerging from raw data. Codes (and attached fragmented data) can be combined later to form larger categories. Through the process of moving in and out of small and large categories and of fragmenting, grouping, and resorting activities, researchers will discover bigger themes that hold the fragmented/coded data together.

This analytical process of dissecting and grouping is a way to make meaning but is not meaning-making per se. Meaning-making is like holding chunks of data against a backdrop and understanding what the data mean in relation to other segmented data and within the broader context. Meaning-making also requires determining how the data are connected to the realities of other people with similar experiences and to existing research. To make meaning of seemingly unconnected data, researchers need to transcend minute details and see a big picture, hear an overtone, or imagine a smell that is not buried in data. By reading others' work, reviewing data over and over, using intuition to grab something out of thin air, and imagining what they hope for researchers will reach "aha" moments—moments when they begin to see contours of data that were not there previously and connections among fragments that they had not noticed before.

One aha moment is unlikely to illuminate the whole understanding of data or lead to a neat interpretation of the entire range of phenomena researchers have been working on for a while. With patience, steady application of data analysis techniques, and thoughtful pauses, however, autoethnographers can hope that the meanings they find in the data are worthy of being captured in text or other forms of representation.

Writing Autoethnography

I have been writing much for this research project. I have been writing about my mentors and my mentoring experiences. I have been responding to writing prompts I constructed for my collaborative autoethnographers to ponder together. My writing has produced many snapshots and fragmented stories. Yet, I know that the final autoethnography has to pull these fragments together and simultaneously transcend them to reach to the world. It does not take too long to glance at what I have written and conclude that not all material I have been collecting will make it into my final writing. Way too much material and way too little room in my paper! I am confronted with the challenge of reducing voluminous data into a cohesive story of the role of mentoring in leadership development through my personal experiences.

❂

I am mindful of my audience—anthropologists, educators, leadership scholars, qualitative researchers, and, of course, autoethnographers. I search for possible journals to which I may submit this writing. I am reading a variety of autoethnographies. I'm assessing my comfort level for different types of writing. I am not much of a poet, so I decide not to experiment with autoethnographic poetry, at least for now. Evocative autoethnography? I do not think so—I am not gifted with engaging emotion in my writing or drawing emotion out of my readers. Critical autoethnography? My analysis of the collective data reveals that leaders of color feel isolated as token minorities in their higher educational institutions without mentors from their own ethnic and racial groups. My interpretation is pointing to cultural and institutional racism. Am I shaping my autoethnography as a critical analysis? I have many compelling stories to tell; should I consider narrative autoethnography? I am again visiting my graduate school mentor's work on description, analysis, and interpretation. I wonder how I may balance them in my own writing and how I may make my interpretation cultural and ethnographic. For my individual autoethnography, I'm pulling out my mentor stories. I am thinking about couching the stories within the themes of mentoring relationships I have identified during data analysis—providing, encouraging, developing new skills, stretching, and modeling leadership. For my collaborative autoethnography, what are common themes connecting the diverse lived experiences of ten autoethnographers? I know that the editors, reviewers, and readers of the journals I'm interested in publishing in want a submission prepared in a more traditional research report format. "I can do it. This is what I am most familiar with." With a big sigh of relief, I begin to write my journal article. So an analytical autoethnography with a critical bent becomes my choice of writing style this time. Still, I feel a pang of regret about not taking a risk to try something different, something bold, and something that would make me uncomfortable. Maybe next time!

○

The end product of autoethnography takes different forms: research reports, poetry, performative scripts, songs, films, performing arts. More artistic endeavors have taken autoethnographies in the direction of evocative autoethnography. In all honesty, it is beyond my reach to introduce and discuss evocative autoethnography intelligently because I have never written one. I will stick to what I started this chapter with—writing about doing autoethnography with a social scientific bent. Here I focus on presentations of autoethnographic research in the form of social science research reports. Such reports usually contain narratives (description) with vivid details, the analysis of the experiences, and the interpretation of the meaning of these experiences framed within sociocultural explanations.

Wolcott (1992) differentiates description, analysis, and interpretation to explicate the purpose of each activity for qualitative research, although he did not believe that ethnographic texts had to separate these activities in their final outcomes. According to Wolcott, the "description" of data refers to presenting details of the past and present reality. It addresses the question of "what is?" The "analysis" of data shows the researcher's work in "the identification of essential features and the systematic description of interrelationships among them—in short, how things work" (p. 12). In the "interpretation" of data, the researcher goes beyond explaining how data fragments are interconnected and "addresses processual questions of meanings and context. 'How does it all mean?' 'What is to be made of it all?'" (p. 12). There is no need to separate three elements artificially in autoethnographic reports. How to blend and balance these elements depends on the autoethnographer. The result might be an interpretive story with vivid and engaging details, an analytical explanation of how narrative fragments are interconnected, or a socio-cultural interpretation of personal experiences.

Many different modes of writing, ranging from a more literary-artistic style to a more scientific-analytical style, have been successfully adopted by autoethnographers. Adopting Van Maanen's (2011) typology of ethnographic writing, I offer four types of autoethnographic writing styles: "imaginative-creative writing," "confessional-emotive writing," "descriptive-realist writing," and "analytical-interpretive writing" (Chang, 2008, pp. 141–148).

The *imaginative-creative* style represents the most innovative and experimental type of autoethnography and departs most from the conventional scholarly discourse. Published autoethnographies in this style have incorporated poetry and performative dialogues grounded in researchers' autobiographic material (e.g., Gallardo, Furman, & Kulkarni, 2009; Randolph & Weems, 2010).

Confessional-emotive writing also distinguishes itself from the impersonal, conventional, "scientific" writing style. Autoethnographers engaging in this style readily expose personal details that may provoke emotional reactions from readers. Many autoethnographies focusing on personal life and relational issues have engaged in this style (e.g., Adams, 2012; Holman Jones, 2005; Poulos, 2012; Ronai, 1996; Smith, 1999).

Descriptive-realist writing contains detailed accounts of autoethnographers' experiences on their research topic. Since the goal of this writing is to describe reality as accurately as possible, researchers may engage in a story-telling style, integrating rich details to help readers reconstruct in their minds the described reality. Although Van Maanen (1988) stated that this style of writing in the context of ethnographic research could produce boring texts encumbered with heavy details, autoethnographies using this style have shown that the descriptive-realist autoethnographers can produce engaging stories that provoke vivid images of the reality of the writers (e.g., Ellis, 2009; Murakami-Ramalho, Piert, & Militello, 2008; Ngunjiri, 2011; Romo, 2004).

Analytical-interpretive writing tends to engage a more typical academic discourse common to social science research reports and to incorporate theoretical and conceptual literature sources. In this style, narration tends to support researchers' socio-cultural analyses and interpretations (e.g., Hernandez, 2011; Klinker & Todd, 2007; Lucal, 1999; Phillips et al., 2009; Poplin, 2011; Reed-Danahay, 1997).

These autoethnographic writing styles are "ideal types" in a Max Weberian sense. They are conceptually distinct in theory, but their boundaries are blurred in reality. It is common that one autoethnography blends several different writing styles. For example, Gallardo, Furman, and Kulkarni (2009) merged autoethnographic poetry (imaginative-creative style) and personal stories of depression (confessional and evocative style) into a conceptual discussion of depression (analytical-interpretive style). Therefore, the purpose of this discussion is not to limit an autoethnography to one style, but to provide different possibilities for autoethnographic writing.

Up to this point I have explained the process of autoethnography from a social science perspective, in particularly making decisions on a research topic and method, collecting autobiographic data, meaning-making with collected data, and writing. Although these are explained step by step, I cannot overemphasize the iterative nature of the research process. Steps can be blended with each other: for example, while making initial decisions of a research topic, autoethnographers may write about their experiences, which may help them with their decisions about topics. While making meanings with collected data, autoethnographers already begin writing their final product. Also those who do not follow the delineated steps of data collection, analysis, and interpretation are already conducting autoethnography in an iterative process without making it explicit. Just as they can personalize the outcomes of autoethnography, researchers can make the process as personalized as they want. At the end of the process, readers will judge what makes each product "autoethnography." What would be the context within which future autoethnographies are likely to be embraced and judged?

Questions for the Future of Autoethnographic Inquiry

The growing popularity of autoethnography as a research method, process, and product is encouraging. The growth shows that diverse academic disciplines have been touched by this method. Subsequently, the coverage of research topics and agendas has been broadened to address personal, relational, professional, and social issues. Autoethnographic approaches have also been diversified to include "accidental ethnography" (Poulos, 2008), "analytic autoethnography" (Anderson, 2006), "duoethnography" (Norris, Sawyer, & Lund, 2012), "co-constructed autoethnography" (Ellis, 2007), "critical autoethnography inquiry" (Afonso & Taylor, 2009), "evocative autoethnography" (Ellis, 1995, 2004, 2009), "new ethnography" (Goodall, 2000), "performative autoethnography" (Holman Jones, 2005; Spry, 2001), and "collaborative autoethnography" (Chang, Ngunjiri, & Hernandez, 2012; Geist-Martin, Gates, Wiering, Kirby, Houston, Lilly, & Moreno, 2010). I predict that this method will continue to appeal to scholars with postmodern bents, innovative spirits, and strong literary skills. I also predict that praxis-oriented fields that have traditionally valued practitioners' self-reflection, such as education, health, social work, ministry, and management, will embrace autoethnography much more easily than those social science disciplines valuing "scientific" research based on a larger number of research participants.

Given the rising popularity of autoethnography among academics and its significant contribution to the understanding of first-hand human experiences and their relation to the social, one question remains: Does the knowledge that autoethnography produces privilege the perspectives and experiences of academics? If the reaches of academics stop at their own worlds, who will bring out the perspectives of non-academic persons to publications from which all can learn? If scholarly power and scientific knowledge become more concentrated on the members of the academy as a result of increasing autoethnography and diminishing studies of others, I wonder if the voices of ordinary others without such scholarly endowment will be sufficiently present in the literature. Against the unintended hegemony of scholars in social science, I recommend that researchers not only study themselves but also expand their inquiries to include others, especially voiceless others in the academic discourse, whose perspectives need to be studied and documented (as an example, see Tomaselli, Dyll-Myklebust, & van Groothest, this volume). As Adams (2011) shows in his skillfully crafted and provocative individual autoethnography, interviews and conversations with others can widen the reaches of autoethnographic knowledge. In addition, by involving non-academics in a collaborative process, autoethnographers can include the perspectives of common folks as their equals in their academic research. Such a practice of distributed power will match the innovative spirit of autoethnography.

References

Adams, T. E. (2011). *Narrating the closet: An autoethnography of same-sex attraction*. Walnut Creek, CA: Left Coast Press, Inc.

Adams, T. E. (2012). Missing each other. *Qualitative Inquiry, 18*, 193–196.

Afonso, E. Z., & Taylor, P. C. (2009). Critical autoethnographic inquiry for culture-sensitive professional development. *Reflective Practice, 10*, 273–283.

Anderson, L. (2006). Analytic autoethnography. *Journal of Contemporary Ethnography, 35*, 373–395.

Anderson, L. (2010). Book review: Heewon Chang, Autoethnography as method. *Qualitative Research, 10*, 493–494.

Cann, C., & DeMeulenaere, E. (2010). Forged in the crucibles of difference: Building discordant communities. *Penn GSE Perspectives on Urban Education, 7*, 41–53.

Chang, H. (2008). *Autoethnography as method*. Walnut Creek, CA: Left Coast Press, Inc.

Chang, H., Ngunjiri, F. W., & Hernandez, K-A. C. (2012). *Collaborative autoethnography*. Walnut Creek, CA: Left Coast Press, Inc.

Charmaz, K. (2006). *Constructing grounded theory: A practical guide through qualitative analysis*. Thousand Oaks, CA: Sage.

Creswell, J. W. (2012). *Qualitative inquiry and research design: Choosing among five approaches* (3rd ed.). Thousand Oaks, CA: Sage.

Denzin, N. K. (2006). Analytic autoethnography, or déjà vu all over again. *Journal of Contemporary Ethnography, 35*, 419–428.

Ellis, C. (1995). *Final negotiations: A story of love and chronic illness*. Philadelphia: Temple University Press.

Ellis, C. (2004). *The ethnographic I: A methodological novel about autoethnography*. Walnut Creek, CA: AltaMira Press.

Ellis, C. (2007). Telling secrets, revealing lives: Relational ethics in research with intimate others. *Qualitative Inquiry, 13*(1), 3–29.

Ellis, C. (2009). *Revision: Autoethnographic reflections on life and work*. Walnut Creek, CA: Left Coast Press, Inc.

Ellis, C., & Bochner, A. P. (2006). Analyzing analytic autoethnography: An autopsy. *Journal of Contemporary Ethnography, 35*, 429–449.

Ellis, C., Kiesinger, C., & Tillmann-Healy, L. M. (1997). Interactive interviewing: Talking about emotional experience. In R. Hertz (Ed.), *Reflexivity and voice* (pp. 119–149). Thousand Oaks, CA: Sage.

Galman, S. (2011). "Now you see her, now you don't": The integration of mothering, spirituality and work. In H. Chang & D. Boyd (Eds.), *Spirituality in higher education: Autoethnographies* (pp. 33–50). Walnut Creek, CA: Left Coast Press, Inc.

Gallardo, H. L., Furman, R., & Kulkarni, S. (2009). Explorations of depression: Poetry and narrative in autoethnographic qualitative research. *Qualitative Social Work, 8*, 287–304.

Geist-Martin, P., Gates, L., Wiering, L., Kirby, E., Houston, R., Lilly, A., & Moreno, J. (2010). Exemplifying collaborative autoethnographic practice via shared stories of mothering. *Journal of Research Practice, 6*, Article M8. Retrieved from jrp.icaap.org/index.php/jrp/article/view/209/187

Goodall, H. L. (2000). *Writing the new ethnography*, Walnut Creek, CA: AltaMira Press.

Goodall, H. L. (2008). *Writing qualitative inquiry: Self, stories, and academic life*. Walnut Creek, CA: Left Coast Press, Inc.

Hayano, D. (1979). Auto-ethnography: Paradigms, problems, and prospects. *Human Organization, 38*, 99–104.

Hernandez, K-A. C. (2011). Spiritual introspection and praxis in teaching and assessment. In H. Chang & D. Boyd (Eds.), *Spirituality in higher education: Autoethnographies* (pp. 163–180). Walnut Creek, CA: Left Coast Press, Inc.

Holman Jones, S. (2005). (M)othering loss: Telling adoption stories, telling performativity. *Text and Performance Quarterly, 25*, 113–135.

Klinker, J. F., & Todd, R. H. (2007). Two autoethnographies: A search for understanding of gender and age. *The Qualitative Report, 12*, 166–183.

Lietz, C. A., Langer, C. L., & Furman, R. (2006). Establishing trustworthiness in qualitative research in social work: Implications from a study regarding spirituality. *Qualitative Social Work, 5*, 441–458.

Lucal, B. (1999). What it means to be gendered me: Life on the boundaries of a dichotomous gender system. *Gender & Society, 13,* 781–797.

Maxwell, J. A. (2004). *Qualitative research design: An interactive approach* (2nd ed.). Thousand Oaks, CA: Sage.

Muncey, T. (2010). *Creating autoethnographies.* Thousand Oaks, CA: Sage.

Murakami-Ramalho, E., Piert, J., & Militello, M. (2008). The wanderer, the chameleon, and the warrior. *Qualitative Inquiry, 14,* 806–834.

Ngunjiri, F. W. (2011). Studying spirituality and leadership: A personal journey. In H. Chang & D. Boyd (Eds.), *Spirituality in higher education: Autoethnographies* (pp. 183–198). Walnut Creek, CA: Left Coast Press, Inc.

Ngunjiri, F. W., Hernandez, K-A. C., & Chang, H. (2010). Living autoethnography: Connecting life and research [Editorial]. *Journal of Research Practice, 6,* Article E1. Retrieved from jrp.icaap.org/index.php/jrp/article/view/241/186

Norris, J., Sawyer, R. D., & Lund, D. E. (2012). *Duoethnography: Dialogic methods for social, health, and educational research.* Walnut Creek, CA: Left Coast Press, Inc.

Patton, M. Q. (2001). *Qualitative research & evaluation methods.* Thousand Oaks, CA: Sage.

Phillips, D. K., Harris, G., Larson, M. L., & Higgins, K. (2009). Trying on—being in—becoming: Four women's journey(s) in feminist poststructural theory. *Qualitative Inquiry, 15,* 1455–1479.

Poplin, M. (2011). Finding Calcutta: Confronting the secular imperative. In H. Chang & D. Boyd (Eds.), *Spirituality in higher education: Autoethnographies* (pp. 51–68). Walnut Creek, CA: Left Coast Press, Inc.

Poulos, C. N. (2008). *Accidental ethnography: An inquiry into family secrecy.* Walnut Creek, CA: Left Coast Press, Inc.

Poulos, C. N. (2012). Stumbling into relating: Writing a relationship with my father. *Qualitative Inquiry, 18,* 197–202.

Randolph, A. W., & Weems, M. E. (2010). Speak truth and shame the devil: An ethnodrama in response to racism in the academy. *Qualitative Inquiry, 16,* 310–314.

Reed-Danahay, D. (1997). *Auto/ethnography: Rewriting the self and the social.* Oxford, UK: Berg.

Rodriguez, N. M., & Ryave, A. L. (2002). *Systematic self-observation.* Thousand Oaks, CA: Sage.

Romo, J. J. (2004). Experience and context in the making of a Chicano activist. *The High School Journal, 87,* 95–111.

Ronai, C. R. (1996). My mother is mentally retarded. In C. Ellis & A. P. Bochner (Eds.), *Composing ethnography: Alternative forms of qualitative writing* (pp. 109–131). Walnut Creek, CA: AltaMira Press.

Saldaña, J. (2009). *The coding manual for qualitative researchers.* Thousand Oaks, CA: Sage.

Smith, B. (1999). The abyss: Exploring depression through a narrative of the self. *Qualitative Inquiry, 5,* 264–279.

Spry, T (2001). Performing autoethnography: An embodied methodological praxis. *Qualitative Inquiry, 7,* 706–732.

Tillmann, L. M. (2009). Body and bulimia revisited: Reflections on "A Secret Life." *Journal of Applied Communication Research, 37,* 98–112.

Van Maanen, J. (2011). *Tales of the field: On writing ethnography* (2nd ed.). Chicago: University of Chicago Press.

de Vries, P. (2012) Autoethnography. In S. Delamont (Ed.), *Handbook of qualitative research in education* (pp. 354–363). Northampton, MA: Edward Elgar.

Wolcott, H. F. (1992). *Transforming qualitative data: Description, analysis, and interpretation.* Thousand Oaks, CA: Sage.

Chapter 4

Interpretive Autoethnography

Norman K. Denzin

C. Wright Mills (1959) is a good place to start:

> The sociological imagination enables us to grasp history and biography and the relations between the two in society. The challenge is to develop a methodology that allows us to examine how the private troubles of individuals are connected to public issues and to public responses to these troubles. That is its task and its promise. Individuals can understand their own experience and gauge their own fate only by locating themselves within their historical moment period. (pp. 5–6, slight paraphrase)[1]

Or Deborah E. Reed-Danahay (1997):

> Autoethnography is a form of self-narrative that places the self within a social context. It is both a method and a text. (p. 6)

Or Tami Spry (2001):

> Autoethnography is...a self-narrative that critiques the situatedness of self and others in social context. (p. 710; see also Alexander, 2000)

Carolyn Ellis (2009):

> As an autoethnographer, I am both the author and focus of the story, the one who tells and the one who experiences, the observer and the observed....I am the person at the intersection of the personal and the cultural, thinking and observing as an ethnographer and writing and describing as a storyteller. (p. 13)

Handbook of Autoethnography, edited by Stacy Holman Jones, Tony E. Adams, and Carolyn Ellis, 123–142. © 2013 Left Coast Press, Inc. All rights reserved.

Mark Neumann (1996):

> Autoethnographic texts…democratize the representational sphere of culture by locating the particular experiences of individuals in tension with dominant expressions of discursive power. (p. 189)

Leon Anderson (2006):

> Analytic autoethnography has five key features. It is ethnographic work in which the researcher (a) is a full member in a research group or setting; (b) uses analytic reflexivity; (c) has a visible narrative presence in the written text; (d) engages in dialogue with informants beyond the self; (e) is committed to an analytic research agenda focused on improving theoretical understandings of broader social phenomena. (see also Lofland, 1995)

Finally, Holman Jones (2005) herself:

> Autoethnography is a blurred genre… a response to the call… it is setting a scene, telling a story, weaving intricate connections between life and art… making a text present… refusing categorization… believing that words matter and writing toward the moment when the point of creating autoethnographic texts is to change the world. (p. 765)

○

Apples and oranges, are these different tasks, or different sides of the same coin? C. Wright Mills and Holman Jones want to re-write history. Anderson wants to improve autoethnography by using analytic reflexivity. Ellis wants to embed the personal in the social. Spry's (2011) self-narratives critique the social situatedness of identity (see also Adams, 2011). Neumann (1996) wants to "democratize the representational sphere of culture" by writing outward from the self to the social (p. 186). So do I.

I want to turn the autoethnographic project into a critical, performative practice, a practice that begins with the biography of the writer and moves outward to culture, discourse, history, and ideology. Sartre (1971/1981) reminds us that (paraphrasing):

> No individual is just an individual; each person is a *universal singular*, summed up and for this reason universalized by his or her historical epoch, each person in turn reproducing himself or herself in its singularity. Universal by the singular universality of human history, singular by universalizing singularity in his or her projects, the person requires simultaneous examination from both ends. We must find an appropriate method. (pp. ix–x)

Interpretive autoethnography is that method. It allows the researcher to take up each person's life in its immediate particularity and to ground the life in its historical moment. We move back and forth in time, using a critical interpretive method, a version of Sartre's (1963, pp. 85–166) progressive-regressive method. Interpretation works forward to the conclusion of a set of acts taken up by the subject, while working back in time, interrogating the historical, cultural and biographical conditions that moved the person to experience the events being studied (Denzin, 2001, p. 41).

With Sartre, there is a political component to interpretive autoethnography, a commitment to a social justice agenda—to inquiry that explicitly addresses issues of inequity and injustice in particular social moments and places.

In this chapter I want to outline the basic features and concepts of this approach, connecting the dots between lives, performance, representation, epiphany and interpretation. I weave my narrative through family stories. I conclude with thoughts concerning a performance-centered pedagogy, and the directions, concerns and challenges for autoethnography. But first, a genealogy of terms.

Some Terms

Consider the following cartography of terms as they all circulate in the present:

1. *performance* (Conquergood, 1985): to enact; *mimesis* (imitation), *poesis* (construction), *kinesis* (resistance) as transgressive accomplishment;

2. *performance:* to study persons as if they were performers, or to study performers;

3. *ethnography* (Clifford & Marcus, 1986): inscribing culture, writing culture vs. performing culture;

4. *autoethnography:* reflexively writing the self into and through the ethnographic; isolating that space where memory, performance, and meaning intersect;

   4a. *autoethnography as disruptive practice:* inclusive, political, utopian;

5. *ethnodrama* (Saldaña, 2005, 2011): monologues, monologues with dialogue and ethnodramatic extensions, often involving the audience in post-performance feedback;

6. *duoethnography* (Norris, Sawyer, & Lund, 2012): a collaborative research methodology in which two or more researchers juxtapose their life histories in order to provide multiple understandings of a social phenomenon; they use their own biographies as sites of inquiry and engage in dialogic narrative;

7. *collaborative writing* (Diversi & Moreira, 2010; Gale & Wyatt, 2009; Wyatt, Gale, Gannon, & Davies, 2011): the co-production of an autoethnographic text by two or more writers, often separated by time and distance;

8. *performance [auto]ethnography* (Denzin, 2003; Pelias, 2011): the merger of critical pedagogy, performance ethnography, and cultural politics; the creation of texts that move from epiphanies to the sting of memory, the personal to the political, the autobiographical to the cultural, the local to the historical. A response to the successive crises of democracy and capitalism that shape daily life; showing how these formations repressively enter into and shape the stories and performances persons share with one another. Showing. It shows how persons bring dignity and meaning to their lives in and through these performances; it offers kernels of utopian hope of how things might be different, better.

In the beginning there was *ethnography*, an inscriptive practice captured in the phrase writing culture (Clifford & Marcus, 1986). Then there was *performance*, the understanding that people perform culture, through their interpretive practices (Conquergood, 1985). This implied that we could study persons as performers and cultures as performative or ethnodramatic accomplishments (Saldaña, 2011). *Autoethnography* inserted itself in the picture when it was understood that all ethnographers reflexively (or unreflexively) write themselves into their ethnographies. The ethnographer's writing self cannot not be present, there is no objective space outside the text. *Duoethography* and *collaborative writing* move the project into a dialogical space, two or more autoethnographers merge their writing selves into a multi-voiced performance autoethnographic texts, including those that disrupt the status quo.

Clearly this discourse is not standing still. Writing selves are performing new writing practices, blurring fact and fiction, challenging the dividing line between performer and performed, observer and observed.

Epiphanies and the Sting of Memory

The subject matter of interpretive autoethnographic research is meaningful biographical experience (Pelias, 2011; Tamas, 2011). Interpretive studies are organized in terms of a biographically meaningful event or moment in a subject's life (Poulos, 2008; Ulmer, 1989). This event, the epiphany, how it is experienced, how it is defined, and how it is woven through the multiple strands of a person's life, constitutes the focus of critical interpretive inquiry (Denzin, 2001).

The biographical project begins with personal history, with the sting of childhood memory, with an event that lingers and remains in the person's life story (Ulmer, 1989, p. 209). Autoethnography re-tells and re-performs these life experiences. The life story becomes an invention, a re-presentation, an historical object often ripped or torn out of its contexts and recontextualized in the spaces and understandings of the story.

In writing an autoethnographic life story, I create the conditions for rediscovering the meanings of a past sequence of events (Ulmer, 1989, p. 211). In so doing, I create new ways of performing and experiencing the past. To represent the past this way does not mean to "recognize it 'the way it really was.'" It means to seize hold of a memory as it flashes up at a moment of danger" (Benjamin, 1969, p. 257), to see and re-discover the past not as a succession of events, but as a series of scenes, inventions, emotions, images, and stories (Ulmer, 1989, p. 112).

In bringing the past into the autobiographical present, I insert myself into the past and create the conditions for rewriting and hence re-experiencing it. History becomes a montage, moments quoted out of context, "juxtaposed fragments from widely dispersed places and times" (Ulmer, 1989, p. 112). Thus are revealed hidden features of the present as well of the past. I want to invent a new version of the past, a new history. This is what interpretive autoethnography does. Here is an example, an excerpt from an on-going project (Denzin, 2005, 2008, 2011, 2013).

SCENE ONE: *The past: Docile Indians*

Voice 1: Narrator-as-young-boy: When I was little, in the 1940s, living in south central Iowa, my grandmother would tell stories about Indians. She loved to tell the story about the day a tall Indian brave with braided hair came to her mother's kitchen door and asked for some bread to eat. This happened when Grandma was a little girl, probably around 1915.

Voice 2: Grandmother: This Indian was so polite and handsome. Mother said his wife and children stood right behind him in a straight row. The Indian said his name was Mr. Thomas. He was a member of the Fox Indian Nation. He said that he and his wife and his children were traveling to the Mesquaki Reservation near Tama, Iowa, to visit relatives. Mother believed him. He said that they had run out of money and did not like to ask for hand-outs, but this looked like a friendly farm house. Mother said it is a crime in this country to be hungry! I believe that, too!

Voice 3: Grandmother-as-young-daughter: Mother made lunch for Mr. Thomas and his family. They sat under the big oak tree in the front yard and had a picnic. Later, when they were leaving, Mr. Thomas came back to the kitchen and thanked Mother again. He gave her a small handwoven wicker basket as a gift. I treasure to this day this basket. It has become a family heirloom.

SCENE TWO: *Real Indians*

Voice 4: Narrator-as-young-boy: When I was not yet ten one Sunday Mother and Dad took my brother and me to Tama, to the Mesquaki Fox Indian Reservation, to see a Pow Wow. I wondered if we'd see Mr. Thomas, if I would even recognize him if he was there. We walked through the mud, past teepees to the center of a big field. Indians in ceremonial dress with paint on their faces and long braids of hair were singing and dancing. Some were drumming and singing. At the edge of the field tables under canvas tents were set up. Dad bought some Indian fry bread for all of us, and bottles of cold root beer. We took the fry bread and pop back to the dance area and watched the dancers. Then it rained and the dancing stopped, and we got in the car and drove home.

SCENE THREE: *Made-for-movie Indians*

Voice 5: Narrator-as-young-boy: The next time I saw an Indian was the following Saturday night when grandpa took me to a movie at the Strand Theater in Iowa City. We watched *Broken Arrow* with Jay Silverheels, Jimmy Stewart, Debra Paget, Will Geer, and Jeff Chandler, who played Chief Cochise. Those Indians did not look like the Indians on the Tama Reservation. The Tama Indians were less real. They kind of looked like everybody else, except for the dancers in their ceremonial dress.

The Sting of Memory

By revisiting the past through remembered experiences I insert myself in my family's history with Native Americans. This history is part of a deeper set of mid-century memories about Indians, reservations, life on the Midwest plains, and American culture. As I narrate these experiences, I begin to understand that I, along with my family, am a participant in this discourse. I am a player in a larger drama, performing the parts culture gives to young white males. From the vantage of the present I can look back with a critical eye on those family performances, but the fact of my participation in them remains. We turned Native Americans into exotic cultural objects. We helped them perform non-threatening versions of Indian-ness, versions that conformed to those tame Indians I watched on the silver screen.

A "mystory" text begins with those moments that define a crisis, a turning point in the person's life. Ulmer (1989) suggests the following starting point:

> Write a mystory bringing into relation your experience with three levels of discourse—personal (autobiography), popular (community stories, oral history or popular culture), [and] expert (disciplines of knowledge). In each case use the punctum or sting of memory to locate items significant to you. (p. 209)

The sting of memory locates the moment, the beginning. Once located this moment is dramatically described, fashioned into a text to be performed. This moment is then surrounded by those cultural representations and voices that define the experience in question. These representations are contested, challenged.

The sting of the past. A string of childhood and young adulthood memories: My brother and I are watching *The Lone Ranger*. We are playing cowboys and Indians—I'm Tonto. Thanksgiving, fourth grade, Coralville, Iowa: I'm dressed up as Squanto in the Thanksgiving play; my grandparents are in the audience. Summer 1960: I'm older now, drinking and driving fast down country roads, playing loud country music. I'm a cowboy now, not an Indian. I fall in love with June Carter singing "Ring of Fire." Wedding, Winter 1963: I close my eyes and remember Sunday fish fries along the Iowa River, hayrides and football on Friday night, homecoming dances in the University High School gym, pretty girls in blue sweaters and white bobby socks, tall young men with blue suede shoes, flat top haircuts, Elvis singing "Heart Break Hotel."

I wish I could reach back and hold on to all of this, things I loved then. James Lee Burke (2009) reminds me that the secret is "to hold on to the things you loved, and never give them up for any reason" (p. 274). But did I really love them or was I just afraid to act like I didn't love them? Which self was I performing? Have I really talked myself into giving them up?[2]

I've always been performing, even in front of the black and white TV. The dividing line between person and character, performer and actor, stage and setting, script and text, performance and reality has disappeared, if it ever existed. For a moment

I was Tonto, and then I was Squanto. Illusion and make-believe prevail, we are who we are through our performative acts. Nothing more, nothing less.

Process and Performance

The emphasis on self, biography, history and experience must always work back and forth between three concerns: the concerns of performance, of process, and/or of analysis. A focus on performance produces performance texts, the tale and the telling, like the narrative above. A focus on process examines a social form, or event, for example epiphanies. The focus on analysis looks at the specific lives of individuals who live the process that is being studied in order to locate their lives in their historical moment.

Building on Pollock (2006), Madison (2006, 2012), and Thompson (1978), interpretive, biographical materials may be presented in four different ways. First, complex, multi-leveled performance texts may be written, staged and performed; for example, the performance narratives assembled by Pelias (1998, 2004, 2011).

Second, following Spry (2006, 2011), single personal experience narratives may be presented and connected to the life-story of a given individual. Spry (2006) writes that after she lost her son in childbirth,

> Things fell apart. The shadowlands of grief became my unwanted field of study.…After losing our son in childbirth, writing felt like the identification of body parts, as if each described piece of the experience were a cumbersome limb that I could snap off my body and lay upon the ground. (pp. 340–341)

Third, a collection of self and personal experience stories may be collected and grouped around a common theme. Stewart (2005) does this in her essay on cultural poesis. She records and performs episodes from mundane, everyday life, including making trips to daycare, the grocery store and picking the sick dog up at the vet.

> My story, then, is not an exercise in representation…
>
> Rather it is a cabinet of curiosities designed to excite curiosity. (p. 1040)

Fourth, the researcher can offer a cross-case analysis of the materials that have been collected, paying more attention to the process being studied than to the persons whose lives are embedded in those processes. Glaser and Strauss (1964) did this in their famous analysis of the awareness contexts (open, closed, suspicion, pretense) that surround death and dying in the modern hospital.

It is recommended that interpretive autoethnographic studies be sensitive to each of the above modes of presentation. Because any individual can tell multiple stories about his or her life, it must be understood that a life will consist of multiple narratives. No self, or personal experience story will encompass all of the stories that can—or could—be told about a single life, nor will any personal history contain all of the self-stories that could be told about that life's story. Multiple narratives, drawn from the self-stories of many individuals located in different points in the process being interpreted can be secured. This triangulation, or combination of biograph-ical methods, insures that performance, process, analysis, history, and structure receive fair and thorough consideration in any inquiry. The interpreter always works outward from the epiphany to those sites where memory, history, structure, and performance intersect, the spaces of Tami Spry's "performative-I" (2006, p. 340; see also Madison, 2012). These are performances that interrupt and critique hegemonic structures of meaning (Spry, 2011, p. 35).

Interpretive Assumptions

A life refers to the biographical experiences of a named person. A person is a cultural creation. Every culture, for example, has names for different types of per-sons: male, female, husband, wife, daughter, son, professor, student, and so forth. These names are attached to persons. Persons build biographies and identities around the experiences associated with these names (that is, old man, young man, divorced woman, only daughter, only son, and so on).

These experiences have effects at two levels in a person's life. On the *surface level*, effects are unremarkable, barely felt. They are taken for granted and are non-problematic, as when a person buys a newspaper at the corner grocery.

Effects at the *deep level* cut to the inner core of the person's life and leave indel-ible marks on him or her. These are the *epiphanies* of a life. Interpretive researchers attempt to secure self and personal experience stories that deal with events—mundane and remarkable—that have effects at the deep level of a person's life.

Experience can only be studied through performance (Bruner, 1986, p. 6). However, what counts as experience or performance is shaped by a politics of representation, and hence is "neither self-evident nor straight-forward: it is always contested and always therefore political" (Scott, 1993, p. 412), shaped by matters of race, class, gender, sexuality and age. Representations of experience are perfor-mative, symbolic, and material. Anchored in performance events, they include drama, ritual, and storytelling.

This view of experience and the performative makes it difficult to sustain any dis-tinction between "appearances and actualities" (Schechner, 1998, p. 362). Further, if, as Butler (1993, p. 141) reminds us, there are no original performances, then every performance establishes itself performatively as an original, a personal, and locally situated production.

An extended quote from Goffman (1959) summarizes my position.

> The legitimate performances of everyday life
> are not "acted" or "put on" in the sense that the
> performer knows in advance just what he [she]
> is going to do, and does this solely because of the effect
> it is likely to have. The expressions it is felt he [she] is
> giving off will be especially "inaccessible" to him [her]…

but the incapacity of the ordinary individual to formulate

in advance the movements of his [her] eyes and body does not mean that he [she]
will not express him [her] self

through these devices in a way that is dramatized and
pre-formed in his [her] repertoire of actions. In short,
we all act better than we know how. (pp. 73–74)

Liminality, Ritual and the Structure of the Epiphany

Within and through their performances, persons are moral beings, already present in the world, ahead of themselves, occupied and preoccupied with everyday doings and emotional practices (see Denzin, 1984, p. 91). However, the postmodern world stages existential crises. Following Turner (1986) the autoethnographer gravitates to these narratively structured, liminal, existential spaces in the culture. In these dramaturgical sites people take sides, forcing, threatening, inducing, seducing, cajoling, nudging, loving, living, abusing, and killing one another (p. 34). In these sites on-going social dramas occur. These dramas have complex temporal rhythms. They are storied events, narratives that rearrange chronology into multiple and differing forms and layers of meaningful experience (p. 35). They are epiphanies.

The critical autoethnographer enters those strange and familiar situations that connect critical biographical experiences (epiphanies) with culture, history and social structure. He or she seeks out those narratives and stories people tell one another as they attempt to make sense of the epiphanies, or existential turning point moments, in their lives. In such moments persons attempt to take history into their own hands, moving into and through, following Turner's (1986) liminal stages of experience.

Here is an example. Yvonna Lincoln (2002) writes about grieving immediately after the attacks on the World Trade Center Towers and the Pentagon on September 11, 2001, "Grief in an Appalachian Register":

For two weeks now, we have watched the staggering outpouring of grief, shock and horror as a nation struggles to come to terms with the attacks....And I, too, have sat numb with shock, glued to the television screen, struggling with the incomprehensibility of these acts, overwhelmed by the bewildering world view which could have led people to commit such atrocities. But I have been numb for another reason, and it will be important to see my reasons as another part of the phenomenon which has struck so deeply at the heart and soul of the United States. I sat numb because my reactions to grief are always usually private. They are always delayed....

My people—my family (of English and Dutch and Scottish stock) were born and raised, as were their parents before them, in the southern Appalachian mountains....Mountain people...keep their emotions to themselves, especially those of a most private nature....The end result, I have come to realize, is a human being who lives with his or her grief for all their days. The future, like tears, never comes. (p. 147)

Epiphanies, like reactions to September 11, are experienced as social dramas, as dramatic events with beginnings, middles, and endings. Epiphanies represent ruptures in the structure of daily life.[3] Turner (1986) reminds us that the theatre of social life is often structured around a four-fold processual ritual model involving *breach, crisis, redress,* and *reintegration* or *schism* (p. 41). Each of these phases is organized as a ritual; thus there are rituals of breach, crisis, redress, reintegration and schism. Americans sought rituals of reintegration after 9/11, ways of overcoming the shocks of breach, crisis, and disintegration.

Many rituals and epiphanies are associated with life-crisis ceremonies, "particularly those of puberty, marriage, and death" (Turner, 1986, p. 41). Turner contends that redressive and life-crisis rituals "contain within themselves a liminal phase, which provides a stage…for unique structures of experience" (p. 41). The liminal phase of experience is a kind of no-person's land, on the edge of what is possible (Broadhurst, 1999), "betwixt and between the structural past and the structural future" (Turner, 1986, p. 41).[4]

Epiphanies are ritually structured liminal experiences connected to moments of breach, crisis, redress, reintegration and schism, crossing from one space to another.

The storied nature of epiphanic experiences continually raises the following questions: Whose story is being told (and made) here? Who is doing the telling? Who has the authority to make their telling stick (Smith, 1990)? As soon as a chronological event is told in the form of a story it enters a text-mediated system of discourse where larger issues of power and control come into play (Smith, 1990). In this text-mediated system new tellings occur. The interpretations of original experience are now fitted to this larger interpretive structure (Smith, 1990).

The reflexive performance text contests the pull of traditional "realist" theatre and modernist ethnography wherein performers, and ethnographers, re-enact and recreate a "recognizable verisimilitude of setting, character and dialogue" (Cohn, 1988, p. 815), where dramatic action reproduces a linear sequence, a "mimetic representation of cause and effect" (Birringer, 1993, p. 196). An evocative epistemology demands a postmodern performance aesthetic that goes beyond "the already-seen and already-heard" (p. 186). This aesthetic criticizes the ideological and technological requirements of late-capitalist social realism and hyperrealism (p. 175).

Performances must always return to the lived body (Garoian, 1999). The body's dramaturgical presence is "a site and pretext for…debates about representation and gender, about history and postmodern culture" (Birringer, 1993, p. 203). At this level, performance autoethnography answers to Minh-Ha's (1991) call for works that seek the truth of life's fictions, where experiences are evoked, not explained (p. 162). The performer seeks a presentation that, like good fiction, is true in experience, but not necessarily true to experience (Lockford, 1998, p. 216).

The body in performance is blood, bone, muscle, movement. "The performing body constitutes its own interpretive presence. It is the raw material of a critical cultural story. The performed body is a cultural text embedded in discourses of power" (Spry, 2011, pp. 18–19). The performing body disrupts the status quo, uncovers "the understory of hegemonic systems" (p. 20).

Whether the events performed actually occurred is tangential to the larger project (Lockford, 1998, p. 216). As dramatic theater, with connections to Brecht (Epic Theater) and Artaud (Theater of Cruelty), these performance texts turn tales of suffering, loss, pain, and victory into evocative performances that have the ability to move audiences to reflective, critical action, not only emotional catharsis (on Brecht's theatre, see Benjamin, 1968).[5]

The performed text is lived experience, and lived experiences in two senses (Pelias, 1998). The performance doubles back on the experiences previously represented in the writer's text. It then re-presents those experiences as an embodied performance. It thus privileges immediate experience, the evocative moment when another's experiences come alive for performers and audiences alike. One way the performed text is given narrative meaning in interpretive autoethnography is through the mystory.

Mystory as Montage

The mystory—for example, the excerpts from my family story earlier in this chapter—is simultaneously a personal mythology, a public story, a personal narrative, and a performance that critiques.[6] It is an interactive, dramatic performance. It is participatory theatre, a performance, not a text-centered interpretive event; that is, the emphasis is on performance, and improvisation, and not on the reading of a text.

The mystory is a montage text, cinematic and multi-media in shape, filled with sounds, music, poetry, and images taken from the writer's personal history. This personal narrative is grafted into discourses from popular culture. It locates itself against the specialized knowledges that circulate in the larger society. The audience co-performs the text, and the writer, as narrator, functions as a guide, a commentator, a co-performer.

Focusing on epiphanies and liminal moments of experience, the writer imposes a narrative framework on the text. This framework shapes how experience will be represented. It uses the devices of plot, setting, characters, characterization, temporality, dialogue, protagonists, antagonists—showing, not telling. The narration may move through Turner's four-stage dramatic cycle, emphasizing breach, crisis, redress, and reintegration or schism.

Jameson (1990) reminds us that works of popular culture are always already ideological and utopian. Shaped by a dialectic of anxiety and hope, such works revive and manipulate fears and anxieties about the social order. Beginning with a fear, problem, or crisis, these works move characters and audiences through the familiar three-stage dramatic model of conflict, crisis and resolution. In this way they offer kernels of utopian hope. They show how these anxieties and fears can be satisfactorily addressed by the existing social order. Hence, the audience is lulled into believing that the problems of the social have in fact been successfully resolved.

The mystory occupies a similar ideological space, except it functions as critique. The mystory is also ideological and utopian, it begins from a progressive political position stressing the politics of hope. The mystory uses the methods of performance and personal narrative to present its critique and utopian vision. It presumes that the social order has to change if problems are to be successfully resolved in the long run. If the status quo is maintained, if only actors, and not the social order, change, then the systemic processes producing the problem remain in place. We are left then with just our stories.

Staging Lives

In the summer of 1953 I was twelve and my brother Mark was eight.[7] This was the summer my parents divorced for the first time. This was also the summer my father joined Alcoholics Anonymous. Mark and I were spending the summer on the farm with Grandpa and Grandma.

> *This was the summer*
> *of the Joseph McCarthy Hearings*
> *on television, black and white screens.*
> *Eisenhower was president,*
> *Nixon was his vice-president.*
> *This was the summer Grandpa bought the first family TV.*
> *In the afternoons*
> *we watched the McCarthy Hearings,*
> *and each evening*
> *we had a special show to watch:*
> *Ed Sullivan on Sundays,*
> *Milton Berle and Cardinal Sheen on Mondays,*
> *Norman Vincent Peale and Pat Boone on Tuesday.*
> *This was the summer my parents*
> *divorced for the first time.*
> *This was the summer my father's life started to fall apart.*
> *I look today at the face of Joseph McCarthy*
> *in George Clooney's movie,* Good Night and Good Luck,
> *a scared lonely man,*
> *Clooney's movie tells me McCarthy died from alcoholism.*

o

I thought of that summer of 1953, and Clooney's movie as I was going through Dad's scrapbook. The pictures are all from the late 40s and early 50s. Mark and I were little and living with Grandpa and Grandma. Mother and Dad lived in Coralville, just outside Iowa City. Dad was a county agent for the Farm Bureau, and Mother kept house and was ill a lot.

I think this is when Dad's drinking
started to get out of hand.
He'd work late, come home drunk.
Some nights friends from work drove him home.
Mother and Dad had put knotty pine siding
on the walls of the family rec room,
which was in the basement of our new house.
Dad built a bar,
And mother got cocktail glasses, a blender,
shot glasses, glass coasters—
really fancy stuff.
On the weekends men from the insurance agency
brought their wives over,
and the house was filled with smoke, laughter,
and Benny Goodman and Harry James
on a little Philco phonograph.
Fats Domino was on the jukeboxes
Singing "Ain't That a Shame" and "Blueberry Hill."
Mother was drinking pretty heavily.
She liked Manhattans and maraschino cherries.
Dad drank Pabst Blue Ribbon (a "Blue"),
and straight shots of Jim Beam whiskey.

○

Around this time the Communist scare had gotten all the way to Iowa City. World War III was on the horizon. The John Birch Society was gaining strength. *This Is Your FBI*, *The Lone Ranger*, *The Shadow*, and *Inner Sanctum* were popular radio and TV shows. We were all learning how to be imaginary consumers in this new culture: Gillette Blue Blades, Bulova Time, Lava Soap. Life Savers (Dylan, 2004).

Citizen Civil Defense Groups were forming.
People were worried about Communists,
and air attacks at night,
atomic bombs going off in big cities.
People started building bomb shelters.
Dad built a shelter in the back yard.
Every town had a Civilian Civil Defense team.
Dad was a team leader,
gone from midnight
until 6:00 in the morning two times a week.

He stood guard with three other men,
scanning the skies with binoculars and telescopes
looking for low-flying Russian planes.
He would come home drunk.

○

Bob Dylan wrote a song about this post-WWII paranoia: He called it "Talkin' John Birch Paranoid Blues." In it, Eisenhower is a Russian spy.

○

We became an A.A. Family in 1953. The drinking had gone too far. About one year later, Mom and Dad had some A.A. friends out for a cookout on the farm. There was a new couple, Shirley and George. Shirley had black hair like mom, and she was small and petite. She was wearing an orange dress that flowed all around her knees. Dad set up the archery set behind the lilacs in the side-yard. The men gathered with bows and you could hear the twang of the arrows all the way back in the house. But nobody was very good.

Mom had Pete Fountain and his clarinet playing on the portable record player. Everybody came back in the house, and before you knew it the dining room was filled with dancing couples. Men and women in 1950s dress-up clothes, wide collar shirts, pleated slacks, and greased back hair. Women with Mamie Eisenhower bangs, hose, garter belts, and high heels.

All of a sudden, Dad was dancing with Shirley, and Mom was in the kitchen fixing snacks. I thought Dad and Shirley were dancing a little close to just be friends.

○

About a month later our little world changed forever. I came home from high school and found a note from Dad. It was short and read, "I have to leave you. You and Mark are on your own now." I was eighteen and Mark was fourteen.

Civilian Civil Defense teams,
Bomb shelters,
Talking John Birch Society paranoia,
The CIA, the Cold War, Communists, the Axis of Evil,
another war, global terror, an out of control right wing government.

○

My father's life segues into this question, "What went wrong with our generation's and our parent's generation's version of the American Dream?" And like in George Clooney's movie, good luck was no longer enough, even if Mamie Eisenhower did wear bangs, just like my grandmother, and even if my father kept the United States safe from the Communists.

Back to the Beginning

Today I want to write my way out of this history, and this is why I write my version of autoethnography. I want to push back, intervene, be vulnerable, tell another story; I want to contest what happened (Pelias, 2011, p. 12).

I want to return to the memories of my childhood, fish fries along the Iowa River, that Sunday morning when my family visited the Mesquaki Reservation. We were happy that day. Alcoholism had yet not yet hit our little house, but A.A. was not far off. As a family we were slipping. A day on the reservation brought escape from what was coming. Could things have happened differently if my father had stopped drinking on that day? I know my brother and I fought, and we were not grateful. Could my father and mother have recovered a love that day that would have withstood infidelities and drunkenness? Did Indians have anything at all to do with this? Maybe an alternative ending is fruitless, why even try?

○

I think I'm like the narrator in Guy Maddin's 2007 film, *My Winnipeg*.[8] In the film Maddin returns to his family home and rents the house for a month so he can re-do some things that happened in that house when he was twelve years old.[9] He hires actors to play his mother, father, brother and sister. He rents a pet dog. When the month is up, there are still issues that have not been resolved.

○

I could be like Gay Maddin. I'd rent the Iowa farm house for one week, the house where Dad and Shirley danced too close, and I'd have mom tell Shirley to take her hands off of her husband. Or maybe I'd go back to the little house on Coralville and have Dad and Mom pretend that they didn't have to be drinking in order to act as if they loved each other.

Performing the Text: Writing to Change History

The goal is to produce an interruption, a performance text that challenges conventional taken-for granted assumptions about the racialized past. Let's return to Indians, Squanto, Tonto and to my opening scenes with Mr. Thomas and the Fox Reservation. For example, in my current research (Denzin, 2008, 2011, 2013) I criticize the representations of Native Americans by such nineteenth century artists as George Catlin and Charles Bird King. I also critically read William Cody's (aka Buffalo Bill) Wild West Shows, which staged performances by Native Americans in Europe and America from 1882 to 1910.

Recurring figures in my narrative include the voices of marginalized Native Americans, including: Ms. Birdie Berdashe,[10] a two-spirit person, an aboriginal dandy, a man who assumes a female gender identity painted by George Catlin; Miss Chief, the drag-queen alter ego of Cree artist Kent Monkman (2007, 2008a,

2008b, 2009, 2010); Lonesome Rider, a gay cowboy; Virile Dandy, a Mandan warrior, close friend of Birdie Berdashe; and the LGBT Chorus. These figures literally and figuratively "queer" my text (Adams & Holman Jones, 2008, p. 383). These transgressive figures challenge the stereotype of the masculine heterosexual Indian warrior. They refuse to be submissive. Miss Chief and Ms. Birdie bring agency and power to queer Indians who were mocked and ridiculed by Catlin, King and Cody. Imagine these queer Indians dancing on the Fox Reservation.

Here is a sample text. It appears at the end of a four-act play titled "The Traveling Indian Gallery, Part Two." In the play, thirty-five Fox, Iowa, and Ojibwe tribe members, along with the LGBT Chorus, Birdie, Miss Chief, and Lonesome Rider, contest their place in Catlin's Traveling European Indian Gallery (1843–1846). The play culminates in a play-within-the-play on stage outside the Boudoir Berdashe. Fox Indians, perhaps related to the Fox Indians my brother and I saw dance in the Reservation Pow Wow in 1950, perform in Catlin's play. The excerpt begins with Birdie.

> **Birdie:** Before we walk off this stupid stage I want to do a "Dance for the Berdashe." George called it an "unaccountable and ludicrous custom amongst the Sacs and Foxes which admits not of an entire explanation" (Catlin, 1848, p. 286).

> **Virile Dandy:** The dance honors the power of the Berdashe. In his painting, George demeans the Berdashe, contrasting his/her passive femininity with the raw, virile masculinity of the bare-chested male dancers who are wearing loincloths and holding weapons.

> **Narrator:** At this point I try to remember back to the Pow Wow. I wonder if we only saw bare-chested warriors waving weapons. What if a young two-spirited Fox was also one of the dancers? Would we have been able to identify him/her and understand his/her place in the tribe's hierarchy of male/female identities?

> (Off-stage: "The Hot Club of Cow Town," a Cowboy swing band from Austin, Texas, breaks into a slow dance waltz, "Darling You and I Are Through."[11] At the opposite end of the hall, the "All-Star Sac and Fox Drummer and Dance Band" [from IndigeNow][12] begins playing a soft blues ballad led by Clyde Roulette [Ojibway], aka Slidin Clyde Roulette, blues guitarist.[13])

> (Stage Directions: The stage is transformed into a dance floor, the lights dim. The members of the LGBT and Indian Show Choruses pair off as couples, men waltz with men, women with women, men with women, children with children. Off come Berdashe masks. Bodies swirl around the dance floor. Virile Dandy dares to take the Queen by her hand and put his arm around her waist, leading her in a two-step waltz across the stage.)

o

In this excerpt the Native American players mock and queer the concept of the straight Indian performing as an Indian for a white Anglo-European audience. They turn the performance event upside down; in so doing they expose and criticize a racist heterosexualist politics buried deep inside the nineteenth century colonizing imaginary. This performance bleeds into the earlier Native American narratives. Surely there were queer or two-spirited Indians on the reservation, but they were not visible to a young white boy on that Sunday in 1950.

Like Guy Maddin I'd try to go back and re-do that Pow Wow. I'd bring in Birdie, Virile Dandy and the LGBT Chorus. I'd have Indian vendors sell cheap copies of George Catlin's paintings of Fox Indians. I'd write myself into the storyline and tell my parents that I think we should not go to these kinds of performances.

Working to Transgress

The goal with this work is to create a safe space where writers, teachers and students are willing to take risks, to move back and forth between the personal and the political, the biographical and the historical. In these spaces they perform painful personal experiences. Under this framework we teach one another. We push against racial, sexual and class boundaries in order to achieve the gift of freedom; the gift of love, self-caring; the gift of empowerment, teaching and learning to transgress. We talk about painful experiences, those moments where race, class, gender, sexuality intersect. We take these risks because we have created safe space for such performances—from classrooms, to conference sessions, to the pages of journals, and in our books—and the pay-off is so great. We are free in these spaces to explore painful experiences, to move forward into new spaces, into new identities, new relationships, new, radical forms of scholarship, new epiphanies.

This is performance-centered pedagogy that uses performance as a method of investigation, as a way of doing autoethnography, and as a method of understanding. Mystory, performance, ethnodrama, and reality theatre are ways of making visible the oppressive structures of the culture—racism, homophobia, sexism (Saldaña, 2005, 2011). The performance of these autoethnographic dramas becomes a tool for documenting oppression, a method for understanding the meanings of the oppression, and a way of enacting a politics of possibility.

The pedagogical model I offer is collaborative. It is located in a moral community created out of the interactions and experiences that occur inside and outside the walls of the seminar room. In this safe space scholars come together on the terrain of social justice. While this is done in the sacred safe spaces of collaborative discourse, the fear of criticism and misunderstanding is always present. When they occur, we seek pedagogies of forgiveness.

Notes

1. I altered the pronouns in Mills's text, changing from *his* experience, to *their* experience.
2. This paragraph steals from Burke, 2009, p. 274.
3. The next three paragraphs draw from Denzin (2001, pp. 38–39).
4. Clearly Turner offers a traditional Judeo-Christian model of selfhood and change. Non-Western models of self-hood turn this framework upside down.
5. Benjamin (1968) contends that Brecht's Epic Theater is diadatic and participatory because it "facilitates…interchange between audience and actors…and every spectator is enabled to become a participant" (p. 154).
6. The following section re-works Denzin (1997, pp. 115–120; 2003, pp. 42–56).
7. The following passages draw from *Searching for Yellowstone* (Denzin, 2008, pp. 185–191), and *Custer On Canvas* (Denzin, 2011, pp. 225–227).
8. Maddin is a well-known Canadian filmmaker. *My Winnipeg* was awarded the prize for Best Canadian Feature Film in 2007.
9. His pet dog died. His sister had a big fight with his mother. His father may have died.
10. My name. An American or First Nation Indian who assumes the dress, social status, and role of the opposite sex (see Califia, 1997).
11. From the first album (*Swingin' Stampade*) by the Hot Club of Cowtown, the Texas Jazz/Western Swing Trio from Austin, Texas.
12. Compliments of IndigeNOW with Gordon Bronitsky and Associates.
13. Clyde sounds a little like Stevie Ray Vaughn. He recently played with the Neville Brothers in Sioux City, Iowa.

References

Adams, T. E. (2011). *Narrating the closet: An autoethnography of same-sex attraction*. Walnut Creek, CA: Left Coast Press, Inc.

Adams, T. E., & Holman Jones, S. (2008). Autoethnography is queer. In N. K. Denzin, Y. S. Lincoln, & L. T. Smith (Eds.), *Handbook of critical and indigenous methodologies* (pp. 373–390). Thousand Oaks, CA: Sage.

Alexander, B. K. (2000). *Skin flint (or, the garbage man's kid):* A generative autobiographical performance based on Tami Spry's *Tattoo Stories*. Text and Performance Quarterly, 20, 97–114.

Anderson, L. (2006). Analytic autoethnography. *Journal of Contemporary Ethnography, 35,* 373–395.

Benjamin, W. (1969). *Illuminations* (H. Zohn, Trans.). New York: Schocken Books.

Birringer, J. (1993). *Theatre, theory, postmodernism*. Bloomington: Indiana University Press.

Broadhurst, S. (1999). *Liminal acts: A critical overview of contemporary performance and theory*. New York: Cassell.

Bruner, E. M. (1986). Experience and its expressions. In V. M. Turner & E. M. Bruner (Eds.), *The anthropology of experience* (pp. 3–30). Urbana: University of Illinois Press.

Burke, J. L. (2009). *Rain gods*. New York: Simon & Schuster.

Butler, J. (1993). *Bodies that matter: On the discursive limits of "sex."* New York: Routledge.

Califia, P. (1997). *Sex changes: The politics of transgenderism*. San Francisco: Cleis Press.

Catlin, G. (1848). *Catlin's notes of eight years' travels and residence in Europe, with his North American Indian collection, with anecdotes and incidents of the travels and adventures of three different parties of American Indians whom he introduced to the courts of England, France, and Belgium*. In two volumes. Vol, I. London: Published by the author at his Indian collection, No 6, Waterloo Place. Printed by William Clowes and Sons, London: Stamford Street.

Clifford, J., & Marcus, G. E. (Eds.). (1986*). Writing culture: The poetics and politics of ethnography.* Berkeley: University of California Press.

Cohn, R. (1988). Realism. In M. Banham (Ed.), *The Cambridge guide to theatre* (p. 815). Cambridge, UK: Cambridge University Press.

Conquergood, D. (1985). Performing as a moral act: Ethical dimensions of the ethnography of performance. *Literature in Performance, 5,* 1–13.

Denzin, N. K. (1984). *On understanding emotion.* San Francisco: Jossey-Bass.

Denzin, N. K. (1997). *Interpretive ethnography: Ethnographic practices for the 21st century.* Thousand Oaks, CA: Sage.

Denzin, N. K. (2001). *Interpretive interactionism* (2nd ed.). Newbury Park, CA: Sage.

Denzin, N. K. (2003). *Performance ethnography: Critical pedagogy and the politics of culture.* Thousand Oaks, CA: Sage.

Denzin, N. K. (2005). Indians in the park. *Qualitative Research, 3,* 9–33.

Denzin, N. K. (2008). *Searching for Yellowstone: Performing race, nation and nature in the New West.* Walnut Creek, CA: Left Coast Press, Inc.

Denzin, N. K. (2009). *Qualitative inquiry under fire.* Walnut Creek, CA: Left Coast Press, Inc.

Denzin, N. K. (2010). *The qualitative manifesto: A call to arms.* Walnut Creek, CA: Left Coast Press, Inc.

Denzin, N. K. (2011). *Custer on canvas: Representing Indians, memory and violence in the New West.* Walnut Creek, CA: Left Coast Press, Inc.

Denzin, N. K. (2013). *Global Indians: The commodification of Native American in performance, art and museums.* Walnut Creek, CA: Left Coast Press, Inc.

Diversi, M., & Moreira, C. (2010). *Betweener talk: Decolonizing knowledge production, pedagogy, and praxis.* Walnut Creek, CA: Left Coast Press, Inc.

Dylan, B. (2004). *Chronicles* (Vol. 1). New York: Simon & Schuster.

Ellis, C. (2004). *The ethnographic I: A methodological novel about autoethnography.* Walnut Creek, CA: AltaMira Press.

Ellis, C. (2009). *Revision: Autoethnographic reflections on life and work.* Walnut Creek, CA: Left Coast Press, Inc.

Gale, K., & Wyatt, J. (2009). *Between the two: Nomadic inquiry into collaborative writing and subjectivity.* Newcastle upon Tyne, U. K.: Cambridge Scholars.

Garoian, C. R. (1999). *Performing pedagogy: Toward an art of politics.* Albany: State University of New York Press.

Glaser, B., & Strauss, A. (1964). *Awareness of dying.* Chicago: Aldine.

Goffman, E. (1959). *The presentation of self in everyday life.* New York: Doubleday.

Holman Jones, S. (2005). Autoethnography: Making the personal political. In N. K. Denzin & Y. S. Lincoln (Eds.), *Handbook of qualitative research* (3rd ed., pp. 763–791). Thousand Oaks, CA: Sage.

Jameson, F. (1990). *Signatures of the visible.* New York: Routledge.

Lincoln, Y. S. (2002). Grief in an Appalachian register. *Qualitative Inquiry, 8,* 146–149.

Lockford, L. (1998). Emergent issues in the performance of a border-transgressive narrative. In S. J. Dailey (Ed.), *The future of performance studies: Visions and revisions* (pp. 214–220). Washington, DC: National Communication Association.

Lofland, J. (1995). Analytic ethnography. *Journal of Contemporary Ethnography, 24,* 30–67.

Madison, D. S. (2006). The dialogic performative in critical ethnography. *Text and Performance Quarterly, 26*(4), 320–324.

Madison, D. S. (2012). *Critical ethnography: Method, ethics, performance* (2nd ed.). Thousand Oaks, CA: Sage.

Mills, C. W. (1959). *The sociological imagination.* New York: Oxford University Press.

Minh-Ha, T. T. (1991). *When the moon waxes red: Representation, gender and cultural politics.* New York: Routledge.

Monkman, K. (2007). *The Triumph of Mischief.* Acrylic on canvas.

Monkman, K. (2008a). *Mah-To-To-Pa (Four Bears) with Indian Dandy, No. 19, 233.* Acrylic on canvas.

Monkman, K. (2008b). *Dance to the Berdashe.* Video installation.

Monkman, K. (2009, August 18). *Dance of Two Spirits.* Video Installation. Montreal: Museum of Fine Arts.

Monkman, K. (2010, March 9). *Western Art, Colonial Portrayals of First Nations Peoples and the "European Male": The Triumph of Mischief and the Treason of Images.* Glenbow Museum, Calgary, Canada.

Neumann, M. (1996). Collecting ourselves at the end of the century. In C. Ellis & A. P. Bochner (Eds.), *Composing ethnography: Alternative forms of qualitative writing* (pp. 172–198). Walnut Creek, CA: AltaMira Press.

Norris, J., Sawyer, R. D., & Lund, D. E. (2012). *Duoethnography: Dialogic methods for social, health, and educational Research*. Walnut Creek, CA: Left Coast Press, Inc.

Pelias, R. J. (1998). Meditations and mediations. In S. J. Dailey (Ed.), *The future of performance studies: Visions and revisions* (pp. 14–22). Washington, DC: National Communication Association.

Pelias, R. J. (2004). *A methodology of the heart: Evoking academic and daily life*. Walnut Creek, CA: AltaMira Press.

Pelias, R. J. (2011). *Leaning: A poetics of personal relations*. Walnut Creek, CA: Left Coast Press, Inc.

Pollock, D. (2006). Making new directions in performance ethnography. *Text and Performance Quarterly, 26*, 325–329.

Poulos, C. N. (2008). *Accidental ethnography: An inquiry into family secrecy*. Walnut Creek, CA: Left Coast Press, Inc.

Reed-Danahay, D. E. (1997). Introduction. In D. E. Reed-Danahay (Ed.), *Auto/Ethnography: Rewriting the self and the social* (pp. 1–20). New York: Oxford.

Richardson, L. (2000). Writing: A method of inquiry. In N. K. Denzin & Y. S. Lincoln (Eds.), *Handbook of qualitative research* (2nd ed., pp. 923–948). Thousand Oaks, CA: Sage.

Saldaña, J. (2005). An introduction to ethnodrama. In J. Saldaña (Ed.), *Ethnodrama: An anthology of reality theatre* (pp. 1–36). Walnut Creek, CA: Left Coast Press, Inc.

Saldaña, J. (2011). *Ethnotheatre: Research from page to stage*. Walnut Creek, CA: Left Coast Press, Inc.

Sartre, J-P. (1963). *Search for a method*. New York: Knopf.

Sartre, J-P. (1971/1981). *The family idiot: Gustave Flaubert*, Volume 1, 1821–1857. Chicago: University of Chicago Press. (Originally published 1971.)

Schechner, R. (1998). What is performance studies anyway? In P. Phelan & J. Lane (Eds.), *The ends of performance* (pp. 357–362). New York: New York University Press.

Scott, J. W. (1993). The evidence of experience. In H. Abelove, M. A. Barale, & D. M. Halperin (Eds.), *The lesbian and gay studies reader* (pp. 397–415). New York: Routledge.

Smith, D. E. (1990). *The conceptual practices of power: A feminist sociology of knowledge*. Boston: Northeastern University Press.

Spry, T. (2001). Performing autoethnography: An embodied methodological praxis. *Qualitative Inquiry, 7*, 706–732.

Spry, T. (2006). A "Performative-I" co-presence: Embodying the ethnographic turn in performance and the performative turn in ethnography. *Text and Performance Quarterly, 26*, 339–346.

Spry, T. (2011). *Body, paper, stage: Writing and performing autoethnography*. Walnut Creek, CA: Left Coast Press, Inc.

Stewart, K. (2005). Cultural poesis: The generativity of emergent things. In N. K. Denzin & Y. S. Lincoln (Eds.), *Handbook of qualitative research* (3rd ed., pp. 1027–1043). Thousand Oaks, CA: Sage.

Tamas, S. (2011). *Life after leaving: The remains of spousal abuse*. Walnut Creek, CA: Left Coast Press, Inc.

Thompson, P. (1978). *Voices of the past*. Oxford: Oxford University Press.

Turner, V. (1986). Dewey, Dilthey, and drama: An essay in the anthropology of experience. In V. M. Turner & E. M. Bruner (Eds.), *The anthropology of experience* (pp. 33–44). Urbana: University of Illinois Press.

Ulmer, G. (1989). *Teletheory*. New York: Routledge.

Ulmer, G. (1994). *Heuretics: The logic of invention*. Baltimore: Johns Hopkins University Press.

Wyatt, J., Gale, K., Gannon, S., & Davies, B. (2011). *Deleuze and collaborative writing: An immanent plane of composition*. New York: Peter Lang.

Chapter 5

Negotiating Our Postcolonial Selves

From the Ground to the Ivory Tower

Mohan J. Dutta and Ambar Basu

This is a co-script. It is a conversation—face-to-face, over the phone, over email, in our conscious and un/sub-conscious thought. (We lived in the same geographic space for four years, and now meet once or twice a year, sometimes at a conference site and at other times in our field sites in India, besides being in touch over the phone and email almost every week.) This co-script is a renarrativization/re-collection of our conversations over the past nine years. We went back and forth as we wrote about the topics discussed in this chapter, and then consciously organized our co-script to lend sense and salience to our ideas. Our conversation is a reflection—reflections, actually—on our reflexivity, our positionality as humans/scholars who strive to thrive on hope, compassion, and the pragmatic possibilities of solidarity with the margins of civil society that have been and continue to be erased from so-called civil sites of discourse. The stories we share with each other and with you are largely situated in the backdrop of the work that we do as development and health communication scholars engaging in projects of social change in global contexts. Our goal in this chapter is to conceptualize how autoethnography intersects with the idea of positionality in the context of postcolonial scholarship. We begin with an introduction into our (the authors') worlds as academics from the third world trained in and working within a Eurocentric paradigm while being invested in the politics of challenging the absence of marginalized voices in OUR Eurocentric discourse. We follow this up with a section that describes and re-conceptualizes critical ideas we use

Handbook of Autoethnography, edited by Stacy Holman Jones, Tony E. Adams, and Carolyn Ellis, 143–161. © 2013 Left Coast Press, Inc. All rights reserved.

through the chapter. Ultimately, we show and tell—through our critical bodies, postcolonial positionalities, and through a deconstruction of our selves and our co-script—how our work in the field and beyond exemplifies the crucial intersections of autoethnography, reflexivity, and postcolonial studies.

Shuttling Between Worlds—Whose Standards?

Our voices together: Because we do so much of our work on the ground in global margins—spaces that Mohan and Mahuya (see Dutta & Pal, 2010) describe as the erased spaces at sites of neoliberal governmentality—our journeys are intertwined in between our worlds of praxis and the world of academic speak that we inhabit.

Mohan: Ambar, do you remember the time we talked about my fieldwork in the Santali communities of West Bengal, when one of the reviewers of my manuscript had asked me what scales I used and how I mapped out the reliability and validity of the stories I was sharing in the essay? She asked whether the beliefs of health among Santalis could be simply measured by a scale built on the basis of the health belief model (HBM) or the theory of reasoned action (TRA)? Was I really adding anything new to the literature that was not already known? The reviewer assumed, I guess, that measures of reliability followed by means and standard deviations would somehow give her the certainty of mapping the hunger of the fathers and mothers who shared their agony with me at not having enough to feed their children. How could she as the reviewer or I as the author expect to develop just the right methodological tool to capture the feelings and thoughts of Bagaram, who occasionally toyed with the idea of ending the lives of his entire family because of how unbearable the pain of hunger was for his children? This is what I wrote then:

> *When you ask me for your reliability scores*
> *To gauge effectiveness*
> *When you ask me for some meta-level theory*
> *That pushes the discipline forward*
> *I look at you in pain*
> *Remembering the suffering*
> *The unfulfilled wishes*
> *And the empty stomachs.*

Through the poetic response of autoethnography, I found the language to connect my pain in writing the response with the pain I experienced on the ground when listening to the many stories that Santali mothers and fathers recounted of not being able to feed their children because they simply didn't have any money. When this reviewer asked for the measures of reliability and validity, I felt that I could never really bring these stories back and share them in a way that could communicate the pain and the suffering being experienced by the community members. At the same time, in writing about the pain I was experiencing, I *could* perform my self as a participant in the co-creation of the story. What is telling here is the mismatch between the expectations of the reviewers and the standards that are held by community members that ask us to be authentic, to put our own bodies at risk, and to find possibilities of solidarity that lend our voices to their struggles for dignity.

In other instances, reviewers ask for statistical effect sizes; they want to know if the stories of participants from the global South have anything to offer outside their lay theories of health (which are therefore by extrapolation, primitive). I remember one instance when the reviewer wasn't sure if I was making this—the stories, the data—all up, or even more, if the participants were making it all up.

> *Truth, yes.*
> *Truth, you hold the gateway to it.*
> *So I have to partake in*
> *Your silly song and dance*
> *Pretending to go along*
> *In the rhythm*
> *So you could go on with your games.*

So, here we were once again, caught in our need to translate our research findings and the value of our work to the Eurocentric center, far away from the immediacy of the context within which we carry out our work on the ground. We have to sing to the White man to gain our own voice.

Ambar: I hear you, Mohan. But, are we "brown souls," doing "postcolonial work," not held up in this quagmire, too? We, too, are a part of privileged academe, the so-called "experts," who continue to, as Paul Farmer (2005) says, commit violence through our works, research, and our very positions as knowledge creators, as researchers who write about poverty such that the research can be turned against the people we profess to write for/about and with. How, then, can we express/be in solidarity and "bear witness" (p. 28; see also Beverley, 2004), instead, with voices from the margins?

I think we (as in, you and I and several of our colleagues) make a decent effort to understand what Farmer (2005) advocates: to implicate ourselves in our work and to be pained at the pain that we bear witness to on the ground and the pain we bring to bear, as you note earlier, in our attempts to story the pain, the suffering, and the violence experienced at the margins of "civility." I am reminded of Holman Jones's (2005) premise that the personal is the political—as one stories the self, one's culture, into and within the research that one does with the marginalized. And, I do believe that this scripting of the self in one's fieldwork/writing is what we (you and I) would like to conceptualize as autoethnography, a concept

developed and used in varied contexts and under equally varied theoretical and
methodological rubrics (Denzin, 1997; Ellis, 2004; Ellis & Bochner, 2000). I
know we have talked about writing on the processes—the means and methods—
with which we engage in our fieldwork in marginalized settings; to explicate our
positionalities/politics as postcolonial scholars. Let's try to put the pieces together
and make some sense of how we can and do negotiate our postcolonial selves as
we make connections from the ground to the ivory tower. I would love to talk
about autoethnography, postcoloniality and positionality in the context of doing
fieldwork with marginalized communities.

Terms, Contexts, Questions

Mohan: Given the premise(s) and politics of our scholarship, here are two conceptualizations of autoethnography I find myself connecting to. Ellis (2004) states:

> *Autoethnography* refers to writing about the personal and its relationship to
> culture....Back and forth autoethnographers gaze: First they look at the eth-
> nographic wide angle lens, focusing outward on social and cultural aspects of
> their personal experience; then, they look inward, exposing a vulnerable self
> that is moved by and may move through, refract, and resist cultural interpre-
> tations. (p. 37)

Holman Jones (2005), notes:

> Our autoethnographic texts do not stand, speak, or act alone; are not texts alone;
> and do not want to be left alone. I want to create a noisy and fractious dialogue
> on and about personal stories, performance, and social change. I want to stage
> this dialogue in and through the flesh of my own experience....I want to suggest
> how we make our personal accounts count. (p. 783)

Ambar: What is appealing to me in these conceptualizations is the need and
the intention to create a mess, as I would like to call it, between the self and the
non-self (both of which cannot but co-exist), and the art and science of thinking,
working with, and talking about this messy process of co-creation. Further, such
a thought appeals to the politics of the postcolonial lens that scaffolds most of our
(yours and my) research in marginalized settings, particularly this idea of positionality embedded in postcolonial and subaltern studies scholarship.

Mohan: I agree. For you and me, making the personal political lies at the heart
of our legitimacy to participate at the sites of recognition and representation, at
the heart of our attempts to make our voices and the voices of those who are at
the margins be heard, be counted in ways that matter. This is the critical turn in
postcolonial writing on the ground. We have been bred on a culture of denying
our personal identities, being taught to erase the "I" so that we can repeat the
Master's stories, steeped in the language of science. So centering the personal
in our journeys through discourses of change is also imbued with struggle. I

remember making this point at a doctoral dissertation defense where most of the doctoral committee insisted that the student should remove all references to "I" in the dissertation. The legitimacy of my concern was intrinsically connected to the fight for legitimacy of the "I," so that the many voices that stand "othered" by academic discourses have opportunities to be heard.

Ambar: At the heart of postcolonial studies lies this othering of the "other" non-expert (read non-Eurocentered) "I." So, postcolonialism refers to the social, political, economic, and cultural practices which arise in response and resistance to colonialism, where colonialism or the colonial project can be explained as the paradigm of "representing the 'other' as inferior and radically different, and hence incorrigibly inferior" (Chatterjee, 1993, p. 33). Postcolonial studies, according to Shome and Hegde (2002), is concerned not merely with chronicling the facts and the history of colonialism. Its commitment and goals are critical, insurgent, and political in so far as it theorizes "not just the colonial conditions but why those conditions are what they are, and how they can be undone and redone" (p. 250).

Mohan: It is at this precise juncture of the modern and the primitive, where the articulations of the modern are specifically tied to the development of specific programs and policies with material implications, that autoethnography undoes the modernist structures underlying contemporary material inequities. Engaging the postcolonial interrogates the ways in which Eurocentric discourses carry out programs of violent erasure often framed in the name of altruism. I wrote this in graduate school when taking a class on "Global Health":

> *I am a brown man*
> *Primitive, backward, insolent*
> *I have for generations*
> *Hated my brownness*
> *To learn to love*
> *Your interventions, values, and educations*
> *But today, I Refuse…*
> *I Refuse to be the subject*
> *Of your interventions*
> *And programs and education*
> *Directed at me*
> *To change my behaviors*
> *And to teach me to follow*
> *Your ways*
> *So I could be civilized.*

As people like you and me have found our ways into spaces of academic discourse [thanks to the White man's colonial education], we have questioned the values and logics that constitute health communication work on the ground. In re-working our identities as we come from the dirty, backward, non-modern Third World and yet seek our legitimacy among our First World colleagues, I hope that we can return the gaze at the Master and her or his imperial tropes. In both our work and in works of colleagues like Collins Airhihenbuwa (1995, 2007) and Linda Tihuwai Smith (2005), localized health knowledge is fore-grounded and pitted against the colonial impetus of health/education knowledge that seeks to maintain the position of the expert by universalizing the knowledge it creates for those at the margins. Positionality, in other words, the imbrication and/or implication of the researcher self, is of critical import in this political stance of engaging in the (im)possibility of co-creating the narratives from the margins. I find Ellis's (2004) notion of working through a "vulnerable self" (p. 37) incredibly powerful because it empowers me to place my self within discourse and turn the stories that I feel have silenced me into projects of activism based on solidarity on the ground. At the same time, it is my hope that the incomplete, partial, forever displaced accounts of my story, continuously in conversation with the incomplete, partial, and displaced accounts of the people I have journeyed with in the field, forever render impure and indefensible (see Cesaire, 2000) the Eurocentric categories of man that underlie the world of interventions, programs, and policies directed at the margins.

Ambar. I remember us grappling with this notion of positionality and the cen-trality of it in postcolonial studies in the course on "Culture, Marginalization, and Resistance" that you taught at Purdue. In what I described as located at the heart of a culture-centered methodological (Dutta, 2008) stance, I wrote:

> By adopting a culture-centered methodological stance in my engagement with subaltern sex worker participants, my aim is to be a collaborator in the process of co-creating meanings on health and HIV/AIDS that emerge from within the sex worker cultural spaces. I center the politics of positionality in the methods I adopt; I turn back on myself, and make myself accountable for my research paradigms, my position of authority and my responsibility vis-à-vis making judgments and interpretations of locally-made meanings. Through this process, I not only critique the notion of objectivity in research, but also the notion of subjectivity that is shorn of the resistive political ideology of self-reflection (Goodall, 2000; Madison, 2005). Thus, I am critically aware of and reflexive about the dangers of the processes I adopt, and I question the very foundations of my method of engaging with subaltern voices. (Basu, 2008)

I would say, Mohan, that this ideology of positionality offers a meeting point for postcolonial/subaltern studies scholarship and autoethnography.

Mohan: Ambar, let's ponder more over this issue in the rest of this chapter. I am sure we can show, and tell, from our work in the field, how such intersectionality materializes.

Ambar: My evaluation of autoethnographic work related to the idea of positionality seemed to point me more towards the notion of reflexive/critical ethnography merging with contextualizations of autoethnography. A reflexive/critical ethnographer, in this sense, is described as one who is morally and politically self-aware and present in her or his writing. For instance, D'Cruz, Gillingham, and Melendez (2007), in their expansive discussion on reflexivity in social work education and research, conclude that reflexivity could be taken to mean that individual problems are the consequence of poor decisions, or reflexivity is "an individual's self-critical approach that involves him/her in questioning how knowledge is created and he/she may be complicit in relations of knowledge and power that have consequences for inequality, privilege and power" (p. 86).

Mohan: As a health communication scholar, my reading of positionality and autoethnography resounds with the works on communicating grief and loss by Carolyn Ellis (1995, 2000) and Ellis & Bochner (1992). Ellingson (2003) uses autoethnography to emphasize how the researcher's reflexive body and the narratives that emerge from an engagement with the body provide distinctive insights into how meanings of health are framed and reframed in clinical settings. Foster, McAllister, and O'Brien (2006) explain how an exploration of the self should be a place from which to start practice as a mental health nurse. They conclude:

> In revealing through research and evocative writing the humanity that we share, personal insights and understandings may resonate for others so that the private, which has been made public, becomes an opportunity to enhance the lives of others as well as the self. (p. 50)

Then there are Foster's (2006) autoethnographic accounts as a volunteer hospice caregiver, and methodological musings on embodiment of the researcher's emotional and bodily ways of knowing and experiences of difference such as culture, race, and religion and how these experiences influence implications for knowledge generation on health and well being.

Ambar: It seems that autoethnography from the standpoint of a postcolonial subject, and more so, in a postcolonial marginalized context could be a critical addition to this literature. As Reed-Danahay (1997) says, there are but varied emphases on *graphy* (the research process), *ethnos* (culture), or *auto* (self); but whatever the specific focus, authors use their own experiences in a culture reflexively to look more deeply at self-other interactions within structures and institutions of power and knowledge. And that's where, why, and how our work on health communication and marginalization would fit in. I think about our ethnographic work as what Madison (2005) calls a move towards "new" or "postcritical ethnography" imbued with a need to "contextualize our own positionality, thereby making it accessible, transparent, and vulnerable to judgment and evaluation" (p. 8).

Mohan: So Ambar, by returning to the "I" or to the notion of positionality, you and I can disrupt the legitimacy of the Eurocentric structures that justify carrying out epistemic and structural violence on the margins through narratives of universal appeal that "write out" the voice of the other and at the same time "write on" the body of this other.

Postcolonial Positionality

Ambar: Our work in the field is political, and yet when we bring this work back into our academic structures where we must find another kind of legitimacy, there is another level of politics. In revising one of our manuscripts we were asked to "tone down" the violence narrativized by sex workers (who spoke about countering physical violence inflicted on them with violence in equal measure or more) and to craft a narrative of compassion and dialogue, even in moments where I don't feel a whole lot of compassion with the Eurocentric modernist structure—material and discursive—that is ever-present and yet hidden.

Mohan: These battles are almost everyday battles; having to justify and legitimate every single action of mine (with the assumption that my legitimacy is always suspect as an outsider—a questioning "brown soul," right?). So it makes me suspicious of the very structure and its games even as I partake in these games so I can speak; I feel that I enter the field with a politics of suspicion. If I do not publish in the right journals that the White man wishes me to publish in, I am not tenurable. If I do figure out their game and give it back to them in their own language, then I must be doing something weird (the implication is that you must either be plagiarizing from some White man/woman, or getting some other White men/women to write for you)… When they ask me the question about productivity (with the implied assumption that I must be getting it from someplace), I just like to tell them that I worship Kali and have a lot of tantric sex (my recipes of productivity!). Because of having to fight these battles of legitimacy at every step, my response is one of anger and indignation. The suspicion and anger have a history though, a history imbued with politics that has manipulatively erased so much of my cultural knowledge through its program of White privilege couched as altruism (after all, remember that the White man established his colonies in India under the guise of wanting to trade with India). A poem titled "The White Man Cometh" that I wrote during fieldwork in India in 2004 reads:

> *He comes*
> *With his interview protocols*
> *And questions*
> *About cultural practices, magic, and ritual.*
> *He comes*
> *Because he has the tools*
> *Of this thing*

He calls Ethnography.
Through which
He says he can
Figure out our culture
And explain our weird customs.
He comes
To conquer
Disguised as a friend
Lives amidst us, eats our food,
And dances in our pagan dances
Only to write back
To his other White friends
About our primitive stories.

Ambar: It is this looking back and forth in which we situate ourselves—we critically examine the power and the politics imbued in our cultures *and* in our academic work. And it is in our autoethnographic turn that we make sense of our postcolonial subjectivities even as our critical bodies come to the fore, standing in the line of state-sponsored neoliberal policies.

Our Critical Bodies

Mohan: How beautifully put, Ambar! In bearing witness to the implications of these policies and programs on the ground, critical bodies script the stories of pain and suffering borne through state-sponsored policies and programs, and at the same time, refuse to be scripted into these policies and programs by interrogating the logics of power written into them. In my fieldwork with *Santalis* (Dutta-Bergman, 2004a, 2004b) in the Midnapur district of West Bengal, Jibonda shared with me how his wife passed away only a few months after being diagnosed with cancer:

> When my wife was sick with cancer, and the doctor at the state hospital said: go to the hospital in Calcutta. I took her to the hospital in Calcutta and waited there for three days; the doctor said you take her to some other big city, I don't remember the name. I said, how can I pay *babu*? I brought her back here to Kharagpur...went to Biduda [local homeopathic doctor] and he gave medicine for 2 rupees every week. She took that all those months, gave her relief....I also gave *manat* [offerings] at the *Shashan Kali* [Hindu goddess] temple and prayed there every week. (Dutta-Bergman, 2004a, p. 252)

In listening to Jibonda's story, I became very aware of my middle-class privilege, which allowed me a certain level of guaranteed access to health care. I noted:

> What would I have done had I been detected with cancer? For one, my story would have been somewhat different because I could afford [or rather my

University-paid insurance could afford] the preliminary care. This difference is something that I am experiencing in the field. The basic necessities of health that I have access to are the ones that are so fundamentally absent from the lives of the communities where I am doing my work.

This realization of the differences in access then also becomes the rallying point for my organizing work, collaborating in solidarity with community members to secure access to the basic necessities of health such as food, hospital services, and medicine. The absence of these basic necessities of health interrupts the assumptions of the worldview that I grew up amidst and the world I now inhabit; these differences emerge as the very sites of the politics of change. Consider the voice of Lokhon (Dutta-Bergman, 2004a):

> Where do we have anything *babu*? Where do Santalis get to say anything? Work hard for a job, get scolded by the *babus*, go to bed hungry. Even the little children go to bed hungry. They need food. They cry. But they go to bed hungry. (p. 256)

Lokhon struggles every day to secure food for his children. As I read this now, in a world of plenty and the privilege as a father to provide for my child, I often wonder, "How would I respond if my struggles to find food for my child were met with all sorts of challenges? How would I respond if my child cried all night because he did not have any food to eat?"

It is through the autoethnographic lens that I find voice in my body, witnessing the pain of hunger, and performing it as a witness in discursive sites of policy-making and program planning through reports, white papers, policy briefs, poems, performances, and so forth. Here is a poem I penned in the early days of my fieldwork, listening to stories of community members who talked about how useless the state-run programs felt to them:

> *No*
> *I am not going to shut up*
> *And pretend*
> *That I agree with*
> *Whatever it is*
> *That you*
> *Shove down my throat.*
> *No*
> *I am not going to shut up*
> *And sing praises*
> *to your cross*
> *and white coat and*
> *Whatever it is*
> *That you*

Want me to memorize.
No
I am not going to shut up
And sing
Praises for
Whatever it is
That you
Throw at me as aid.

Ambar: My critical body, like yours, Mohan, has wilted and rebounded, carried with me my stories of bearing witness—to violence, love, hope, frailty, complicity, guilt, shame, and humility. I struggled. I was humbled. I learned. Here are a few excerpts from my journal entries at different points in my fieldwork with two poor sex worker communities—Sonagachi and Kalighat—in Kolkata, India, over the past seven years. I believe they document the vulnerability that I grappled with from the standpoint of being a postcolonial subject as well as an instrument of colonization.

Mousumi told me this and did not want to say more: "I was seven years old when I was sold by my uncle to a woman who used to come to the city to sell vegetables. She sold me to a *masi* [madam] in Kidderpore. They used burning wax to make up my breasts. I was forced to have sex with a client..." Their stories are so sapping, it takes all the energy out of me. It's so emotionally draining that by the end of three interviews, I was restless, I needed a break! And I feel drained by just listening to them. What about these people who have been at the heart of these stories, bearing them, living with them?

It's a new world I enter into everyday, a dark world, I would say from my privileged worldview that is not able to cope with sadness, deprivation, and inequity.

But I cannot just do away with my context, my history, my present, who I am. It kills me to do the switch every day, from my family in the morning to "my people" in Kalighat during the day and the evening, and then back to material comforts of family and friends at night. It pains after the initial euphoria of having been successful in mapping "my subjects" of having secured access to their world! I fail to realize that the world I am let into is just their doorsteps.

Every story I heard affected me, implicated me in my guilt, in my engagement with the sex workers; it affected my further conversations with them, in the questions I asked, in the way I approached them. For instance, I was told that the sex workers would not like to discuss the specificities of the services they provide. From a few I gathered that sex workers in Kalighat do not, on principle, give blow jobs!

This is one virtue I have really learned from my research: Be patient. Research in the field, and among members of a highly marginalized community that is absolutely closed to outsiders, needs tons of patience. I learned that I stand obliged every time a sex worker comes forward to talk to me, taking time out of her strict daily routine. I realize that the one hour spent with me is time she could have used to earn for her family.

Today was not a bad day after all. I was apprehensive, yes. And I had reason to be so. I still have reason to be so. But I realized that it is important that I realize I will remain an outsider. The best I can do, as I tried to do today, is lay out my cards, my politics, and my privilege on the table, be as transparent as I can and engage with my collaborators knowing fully well their inhibitions, their rightful indignation for people like me, and their holding themselves, not opening up as I would want them to.

Mohan: Yes, Ambar, these stories of poverty and suffering have often been intertwined with anger at state policies, imagining resistance as a strategy of rupturing the inequities written into these state policies. Over the last five years, I have become particularly aware of this anger as many of the Santali communities in Midnapur and across West Bengal have risen up in resistance. When I returned in the summer of 2008, and in the following years, my access to the field sites became intensely limited. Sitting at home, in the safety of my joint family in Kharagpur, I wrote this excerpt:

> The television stations here are inundated with stories of the uprisings in Lalgarh. Images of people burning homes of political leaders and taking over police stations are interrupted by the images of the police and paramilitary operation being carried out on village after village (Kantaperia, Lalgarh, Belpahari). Sitting in my safe space (being home), I am much more aware of the politics of the body now than ever before; the boundaries between my privileges and the struggles for dignity among the Santali storytellers in my writings are apparent in the risks written on their bodies. Whereas my body, content with its share of rice and food cooked to my tastes every day sits and bears witness to the violence, it is their bodies that must be beaten up, massacred, and hung like loot (the military personnel often would carry the bodies of killed Santali protestors on poles, showing them off like trophies).

As I bear witness to the violence that is now enacted by the state in the name of "Operation Green Hunt" (the name used by the Indian media to describe the Government of India's paramilitary offensive against the Maoist Naxalite rebels starting in 2009), as I look at images of police torture and of women being carried like trophies hung on poles by Central Reserve Police Force personnel, the avenue for the expression of my anger and disbelief becomes my own writing; I write my anger and disbelief on my blogs, on my Facebook posts, on my video accounts on YouTube. Through these spaces of sharing the personal witnessing of the violence, my writing enacts its resistance, joining its voice with the many other voices that bear witness to the violence enacted by the State. In bearing witness, in sharing the stories, the stories of bodies that disrupt the aesthetic of a modern India, my words and their bodies come to stand together, becoming voices in collectivities of protest.

I wrote:

> *Is anyone listening?*
> *Democracy and participation and all the BS*
> *Shining India on a global stage*
> *Decimating its tribal people*
> *As they are not citizens*
> *Threats to security and development*
> *They must be raped and killed*
> *Whenever needed, wherever needed*
> *They must be decimated.*
> *Is anyone listening?*

The same critical body working together with critical enunciations, I found again, in my participation in the politics of hope in the last few months in the United States; in participating in the various Occupy protests across the country to protest the vast inequities in the distribution of resources promoted by the "free market" neoliberal ideology.

Debalina (my wife), Shloke (our three-and-a-half-year old) and Baba (my father), and I have driven to New York to participate in the protests at Liberty Square. Today is our first night, and we are surrounded by the chants calling for equality and for taking our democracy back. It is amazing to feel the sounds of protest reverberating through my body, remembering the promises Baba had made a few years back about the change that was going to come in the United States. Standing with my wife and son, and sharing this bond with my father, I feel as though we as a family are part of this much bigger family standing here today, having taken to the streets because for so long we have been told that our voices do not matter.

Ambar, it is the critical body that must bear the pain or at least attempt to feel the pain of the other; it is also critical body that stores resources of hope and desire and (com)passion—resources that enable us in our activist journeys in the field.

Ambar: But drawing you back again, Mohan, beyond and along with the anger and indignation, the critical bodies and the bearing witness, you and I, because of the privilege [*sic*] of our Euro-centered education in India and in the United States, are implicated in this colonization of the "primitives." Our politics and positionality mean we own up to this privilege—not in a narcissist footnoting about the joys and so-called perils that come with it (Bourgois, 1995), but in an effort to stand in pragmatic solidarity with the marginalized. Farmer (2005) writes:

> If solidarity is among the most noble of human sentiments, then surely its more tangible forms are better still. Adding the material dimension [humans rights

such as medicine, food, shelter, and access to communicative platforms] to the equation—pragmatic solidarity—responds to the needs expressed by the people and communities who are living, and often dying, on the edge. (p. 230)

The least we can do, Farmer notes, is to document the narratives of pain, suffering, resistance, hope and counter-violence that emerge from the margins but are hardly ever heard in a way that matters to the mainstream discourse (Beverley, 2004). Documenting marginal narratives is a political act in itself. Yet, in documenting also lies the accountability of deconstructing the narratives that you and I present on marginalization. They are, after all, OUR narratives.

Reflections: Deconstructing the Self and the Self's Text

Mohan: One of the reviewers of a manuscript I wrote about the dialogues between the Santali life worlds and my own life worlds asked me to take out the personal stories as they got in the way. Yet, in other pieces, reviewers have asked to see more of me in the texts in the spirit of co-construction, asking for my voice to be visible in the texts. To be honest, Ambar, this is something I have struggled with: which stories to tell, which stories to foreground, which stories to keep within me (because their time has not yet arrived), and which stories to background? What is the line between narcissism and the imperative to tell a story because it matters to the other stories being told, and to the politics of change? Where does one step back so that other voices that have historically been marginalized precisely because of the stories we have told find avenues for expression? At what points does my voice become relevant to the politics of change, imbued with its privileges and situated amidst its knowledge of unlearning privilege as our loss (Spivak, 1990)?

Ambar: I think what you are talking about here, Mohan, has a lot to do with our positions as heterosexual men in a culture where we have grown up being taught to trust our voices (albeit in the Master's language). In listening to the voices of sex workers and in working with them as they organize to challenge inherently unequal structures, I have wondered where inserting my voice would make a difference and would have a political impact [*Mohan:* I love that you talk about this moment of wondering about the purpose of inserting our own stories into these journeys of collaboration on the ground]. So when I talk about my own fieldwork in Sonagachi and Kalighat, my personal stories reflect on the privileges that I have inherited as a male member of the middle class, and subsequently, the lens through which I ask questions in the field, collect "data," interpret the data, and write the "findings." Spivak (1990) calls this hyper-reflexivity—a bodily engagement and a distinct enunciation of how our discursive constructions (of the subaltern) are intimately linked to our positioning—socioeconomic, gendered, cultural, geographic, historical, institutional. Spivak never shies from implicating herself in her critique of the above-mentioned historical, geographic, cultural and class positionings, often confessing, for instance, to being a privileged Third World academic working in the West (Kapoor, 2004). By being hyper-reflexive, and this, I believe, one can do through writing the self (autoethnography), the privileged academic (that I am) is showing and telling how I am inescapably positioned in a variety of discourses, and how my personal and institutional desires and interests—contaminations—are unavoidably written into my representations. Autoethnography, in this context, becomes a process of endless reflection, a reflection on reflexivity, to the point of deconstructing the self and the self's text, and opening it up for further scrutiny/interpretation/negation and re-orientation. In that sense, no academic collaboration with the subaltern is collaboration unless one is acutely aware of the contradictory nature and impossibility of such collaboration. What Bourgois (1995) writes on this stance/positionality while doing research with crack dealers in Harlem, New York, is particularly appealing to me. He writes: "Although the literary quality and the emotional force of this book depend entirely on the articulate words of its main characters, I have always had the final say in how—and if—they would be conveyed in the final product" (p. 13). And this stance of not simply being conscious of/reflexive about one's privilege, but scrupulously attending to unravel it at every step of the research with marginalized communities is what I believe a critical contribution postcolonial/subaltern studies brings to autoethnography. Here's a story/example from my work I want to share:

> Suranjan, the HIV/AIDS specialist doctor, who worked with sex workers and their families in Kalighat, had on a number of occasions told me how the lack of education among sex worker mothers makes them incapable of taking care of themselves and their children, how alcohol addiction was ruining the community, how sex workers refused to get themselves tested for HIV/AIDS even though the tests were free and provided by New Light, a local NGO. As I heard his narratives day after day, I really began to think of whether this community needed long-term prescriptive interventions to address the "problems" Suranjan spoke about. He was clearly invested in the community, taking time every day from his flourishing private medical practice to tend to patients in this poor community. But what I believe is my "hyper-reflexive" self somehow kept pushing me to think beyond. Towards the end of my fieldwork in the community in 2007, I think I was able to put it all together, deconstruct the lens that I was using to interpret and judge Suranjan and the sex worker mothers.
>
> In my journal, I wrote: Suranjan constructs health within the auspices of the dominant bio-medical model, as I tend to do, too, wherein experts like him are considered to have the ability to care and cure, and where health is measured with respect to development indices like awareness, sanitation, nourishment, education, and preventive blood tests. Within this logic, education and knowledge structures driven by experts take precedence and indigenous mechanisms of healing and illness negotiation are likely to be delegitimized as superstitions and primitive cultural practices. "It is hard to get them out of

their traditional beliefs in black magic, herbal remedies, and spiritual healers though they have finally realized the need to go to a doctor when they are ill," Suranjan says about members of the sex worker community in Kalighat. But, as I have "learned to learn" (Spivak, 1990) from members of this marginalized community, there is an independent rationality (Basu, 2011) that I and/or Suranjan cannot make sense of, more so because such a rationality challenges our expert logics and premises about what we think is wrong and right for the sex worker mothers. Yes, they go to the doctors, but they also go to the spiritual healers. Their approach to health, an approach that has worked through generations, is indeed polymorphic, depending on available resources (time, money, access to doctors) and the perceived seriousness of the illness. While most sex worker mothers I spoke to wanted to get HIV/AIDS tests done—pointing again to an autonomous rationality that draws from and resists the oppressive logic of care and prevention—almost all of them said they would rather not see the results of the tests because the structural violence that the marker of HIV brings to them deprives them of their only means of sustaining dreams and hoping for a better future—for their children.

I realized that Suranjan's narratives were actually mine, and my efforts to "unlearn my privilege" (Spivak, 1990, p. 6) and "write in reverse" (Beverley, 2004, p. 25) pointed to the intersections of autoethnography and postcolonial studies.

Mohan: I have similar stories to share in my fieldwork among African Americans in inner-city Indianapolis and in Gary, Indiana. The fieldwork is humbling. As we talk about heart health of African Americans in Gary and work collaboratively on social change efforts, I become continually aware of the large gap between my privilege as a Brown heterosexual male employed in a university that holds strong clout in the region and the everyday erasures that are experienced by community members who talk about their struggles with lack of resources and racism. As I have written elsewhere (Dutta-Bergman, 2004a, 2004b; and with Mahuya in Dutta & Pal, 2010), our privileges are our greatest obstacles, and yet, they are our strengths in equipping us to negotiate policies and programs that are directed at fostering structural transformations through participatory dialogues. Even as we talk about discussing our roles in this politics of recognition and representation, we also become aware of the (im)possibilities of representation.

Looking Ahead—(Im)possibilities of Representation

Mohan: What do we do then with such an impossibility? Below is an excerpt from a field note I wrote after back-to-back community workshops with African American community members on actionable steps for fostering heart health in the community (Gary, Indiana). The meeting went really well, and community members, in collaboration with us, came up with a number of powerful advocacy solutions such as developing healthy food resources within the community, building walkways, and advocating for zoning laws in the context of fast food chains. The conversation felt like a spiritual dance, with the moments of convergence choreographed amidst the many divergences through which we traveled. As I drove back home from the meetings, what I carried with me were residuals of this dance:

> As Shaunak and I were driving back from Gary after a meeting with community members, our discussion kept coming back to the impossibilities of representation. We became intensely aware that nothing we do now would embody the moments of dialogue that were generated by the community members in today's discussion. They were spirited today, completely engaged with each other and with us, as we discussed the politics of race, and the role of everyday stressors of racism and inequitable opportunities on the lives of African American community members in Gary. The air was filled with anger and with hope. Community members decided that we needed to explore avenues for shaping research agendas that study the role of racism on stress and the corresponding role on heart disease. The excitement stayed with us the entire car ride, and yet we were all too aware that by the time we went back home and wrote down our journal entries, what we would have with us would be our vague representations of the dialogues and conversations that came about in our community meetings. What then?

Ambar: Mohan, I guess the actionable steps that the community configured at that point provide you with some strategic essentialisms—essentialist positions espoused as debatable yet unitary ideas, particularly among marginalized communities, often to make strategic gains in their struggles against subjugation/colonization—just as your autoethnographic turn subjects you to the inevitable realization of the incompleteness written into a politics of representation (***Mohan:*** Yes, Yes!). As we wrap up this chapter, I want to thank you for this wonderful journey in which we have travelled together, had many arguments, learned to care for each other and to respect each other's perspectives in building our theories, methodologies, and most of all, to solidify our commonly shared and always-agreed-upon political stance of solidarity with the margins. This is a commitment that Spivak (1990) notes comes with the dangers of struggling to redefine the standards of authority and authenticity for the academy and for knowledge creation; and of course, grappling with the (im)possibilities of holding up marginalized voices with the same, if not more, esteem as ours. (***Mohan:*** I want to thank you Ambar, for your friendship and for working with me on this difficult, complex, and most fulfilling journey that seeks to connect activism and advocacy with academic writing.) Kapoor's (2004) take on Spivak's (1988, 1990, 2001) notion of positionality and postcoloniality could help us look ahead to the challenges of connecting our scholarship from the ground to the ivory tower:

> A final and important Spivakian test is being able to work "with no guarantees." This is because we need to recognise that, ultimately, not only is the subaltern heterogeneous...it is "irretrievably heterogeneous" and hence

"non-narrativisable." Coming to terms with the Other's difference is precisely reckoning with the impossibility of knowing it, accepting that it exceeds our understanding or expectations. This includes being open to the "non-speakingness'" of the subaltern, its refusal to answer or submit to the gaze and questioning of the ethnographer....Working without guarantees is thus becoming aware of the vulnerabilities and blind spots of one's power and representational systems. It is accepting failure, or put positively, seeing failure as success. The implication for development is that we need to learn to be open, not just in the short-term, to the limits of our knowledge systems, but also to the long-term logic of our profession: enabling the subaltern while working ourselves out of our jobs. (p. 644)

Our voices together: Learning to learn from the subaltern, and investing in scholarship that seeks to find out the multitude of methods to do so, then becomes a crucial challenge as autoethnography is positioned—away from its seemingly inherent narcissist postmodern politics of identity—as a viable paradigm to unlearn privilege, subvert OUR discourse, and create openings for a discourse that is messily THEIRS and OURS. Postcolonial positionality, marginality, and autoethnography come to create this fractious ideology of imagining the possibilities of listening to the subaltern—her/his silences and interjections, her/his theories and struggles. Our positions in these fractious spaces are rife with contradictions, and the autoethnographic turn engages the politics of these contradictions with the materiality of structural violence, imagining therefore an incomplete and yet hopeful imaginary for the praxis of change.

References

Airhihenbuwa, C. O. (1995). *Health and culture: Beyond the Western Paradigm*. Thousand Oaks, CA: Sage.

Airhihenbuwa, C. O. (2007). *Healing our differences: The crisis of global health and the politics of identity*. Lanham, MD: Rowman & Littlefield.

Basu, A. (2008). *Subalternity and sex work: Re(scripting) contours of health communication in the realm of HIV/AIDS*. Unpublished PhD dissertation. Purdue University, West Lafayette, Indiana.

Basu, A. (2011). HIV/AIDS and subaltern autonomous rationality: A call to re-center health communication in marginalized sex worker spaces. *Communication Monographs, 78*, 391–408.

Beverley, J. (2004). *Subalternity and representation: Arguments in cultural theory*. Durham, NC: Duke University Press.

Bourgois, P. (1995). *In search of respect: Selling crack in El Barrio*. New York: Cambridge University Press.

Cesaire, A. (2000). *Discourses on colonialism*. New York: Monthly Review Press.

Chatterjee, P. (1993). *The nation and its fragments: Colonial and postcolonial histories*. Princeton, NJ: Princeton University Press.

D'Cruz, H., Gillingham, P., & Melendez, S. (2007). Reflexivity, its meanings and relevance for social work: A critical review of the literature. *British Journal of Social Work, 37*, 73–90.

Denzin, N. (1997). *Interpretive ethnography: Ethnographic practices for the 21st century*. Thousand Oaks, CA: Sage.

Dutta, M. (2008). *Communicating health: A culture-centered approach*. Cambridge, UK: Polity.

Dutta, M. J., & Pal, M. (2010). Dialog theory in marginalized settings: A subaltern studies approach. *Communication Theory, 20,* 363–386.

Dutta-Bergman, M. (2004a). Poverty, structural barriers and health: A Santali narrative of health communication. *Qualitative Health Research, 14,* 1–16.

Dutta-Bergman, M. (2004b). The unheard voices of Santalis: Communicating about health from the margins of India. *Communication Theory, 14,* 237–263.

Ellingson, L. L. (2003). Embodied knowledge: Writing researchers' bodies into qualitative health research. *Qualitative Health Research, 16,* 298–310.

Ellis, C. (1995). Final negotiations: A story of love, loss, and chronic illness. Philadelphia: Temple University Press.

Ellis, C. (2000). Negotiating terminal illness: Communication, collusion, and coalition in caregiving. In J. Harvey & E.D. Miller (Eds.), *Loss and trauma: General and close relationship perspectives* (pp. 284–304). Philadelphia: Brunner-Routledge.

Ellis, C. (2004). *The ethnographic I: A methodological novel about autoethnography.* Walnut Creek, CA: AltaMira Press.

Ellis, C., & Bochner, A. P. (1992). Telling and performing personal stories: The constraints of choice in abortion. In C. Ellis & M. Flaherty (Eds.), *Investigating subjectivity: Research on lived experience* (pp. 79–101). Newbury Park, CA: Sage.

Ellis, C., & Bochner, A. P. (2000). Autoethnography, personal narrative, reflexivity: Researcher as subject. In N. K. Denzin & Y. S. Lincoln (Eds.), *Handbook of qualitative research* (2nd ed., pp. 733–768). Thousand Oaks, CA: Sage.

Farmer, P. (2005). *Pathologies of power: Health, human rights, and the new war on the poor.* Berkeley: University of California Press.

Foster, E. (2006). *Communicating at the end of life: Finding magic in the mundane.* Mahwah, NJ: Erlbaum.

Foster, K., McAllister, M., & O'Brien, L. (2006). Extending the boundaries: Autoethnography as an emergent method in mental health nursing research. *International Journal of Mental Health Nursing, 15,* 44–53.

Goodall, H. L. (2000). *Writing the new ethnography.* Boston Way, MD: AltaMira Press.

Holman-Jones, S. (2005). Autoethnography: Making the personal political. In N. K. Denzin & Y. S. Lincoln (Eds.), *Handbook of qualitative research* (3rd ed., pp. 763–791). Thousand Oaks, CA: Sage.

Kapoor, I. (2004). Hyper-self-reflexive development? Spivak on representing the Third World 'Other.' *Third World Quarterly, 25,* 627–647.

Madison, D. S. (2005). *Critical ethnography: Methods, ethics, and performance.* Thousand Oaks, CA: Sage.

Reed-Danahay, D. E. (1997). Introduction. In D. Reed-Danahay (Ed.), *Auto/ethnography: Rewriting the self and the social* (pp. 1–17). Oxford: Berg.

Shome, R., & Hegde, R. (2002). Postcolonial approaches to communication: Charting the terrain, engaging the intersections. *Communication Theory, 12,* 249–270.

Smith, L. T. (2005). On tricky ground: Researching the native in the age of uncertainty. In N. K. Denzin & Y. S. Lincoln (Eds.), *Handbook of qualitative research* (3rd ed., pp. 85–108). Thousand Oaks, CA: Sage.

Spivak, G. C. (1988). Can the subaltern speak? In C. Nelson & L. Grossberg (Eds.), *Marxism and interpretation of culture* (pp. 271–313). Chicago: University of Illinois Press.

Spivak, G. C. (1990). *The post-colonial critic: Interviews, strategies, dialogues* (S. Harasym, Ed.). New York: Routledge.

Spivak, G. C. (2001). A note on the New International. *Parallax, 7,* 12–16.

Chapter 6

Walk, Walking, Talking, Home

Devika Chawla

I have a walking history, if there can be such a thing. It begins when I was seven years old. We lived in a small north Indian town called Moga close to the Pakistan border. My grandfather had recently died, and Biji, my grandma, had come to live with us. She and I shared a room and developed the love-hate relationship that inevitably ensues when a child finds herself rooming with a 75-year-old grandparent. Biji had many rituals—waking up at 4 a.m. to recite portions of the *Gita* and the *Gayatri Mantra*; cleaning her dentures as she whispered "*hai ram*" for the next hour; oiling her hair with coconut oil; eating her *isabgol* —an ayurvedic stomach cleanser which everyone in generations previous to mine swears upon—with warm water. On weekdays, we held a reluctant peace since I needed to wake up for school at 6 a.m., and with Biji around I was never going to be late. But on weekends, the room became a battle zone as I resisted getting out of bed until 8 a.m.—a considerably late wake-up time in Biji's world. For Biji, every day was everyday, and she lovingly nourished her routines.

After the first year we became used to this pattern. Weekend mornings were still unpleasant, but we had discovered a fondness for one another, a fondness that came from my childish realization that Biji's presence was beneficial to me. She had begun to help me tidy my room, and being a devout Hindu, she'd tell me stories from the *Ramayana* and *Mahabharata* before I slept. I have never taken to religion, yet because of Biji, I remain enthralled with the fantastical dimensions of most religious stories. And whatever I know about Hinduism comes from these

Handbook of Autoethnography, edited by Stacy Holman Jones, Tony E. Adams, and Carolyn Ellis, 162–172. © 2013 Left Coast Press, Inc. All rights reserved.

bedtime tales. Biji bathed me before school, braided my hair, and even helped me with my Hindi homework. Born in 1908, Biji was my paternal grandmother. She never attended college, but had passed the highest-level exam on Hindi proficiency that women were allowed to take in the early 1900s. It was called the *Prabhakar*, and my parents tell me that it was then considered equivalent to a Master's degree.

Only now, I realize how radical this education must have been for an Indian woman born in that era. It makes me wish I had met her when I was a grown-up. Alas, grandparents are always presented to us in the autumn of their lives, and we are able to garner mere remnants of their personalities, their experiences, and their histories. In time, I stopped complaining about the morning rituals and would often help Biji oil her long white hair. Even today, almost three decades later, a mere whiff of coconut oil can take me back to my elderly roommate. Much to Amma's chagrin, I keep the product away from my own hair. Amma, my mother, constantly reminds me that the coconut oil was the secret behind my grandmother's hair, which remained thick and long until she died. Out of guilt (for not applying it) or habit (because coconut oil was a permanent fixture in my childhood home), I keep a fresh bottle of coconut oil at home, here in Appalachian Ohio. But I cannot recall the last time I massaged it into my hair.

One summer evening Amma asked me to begin going for walks with Biji. "Why do I have to do that, Amma?" I demanded. Yet another hour of my day was being given to my grandparent. Her only response was a frightening glare. I conceded. What was the other option? I often threatened to leave home because of such incidents, but my parents and Biji would laughingly urge me to stay until the next morning, knowing misery would turn into memory overnight. At breakfast, Papa explained that Biji's evening walks had become unsafe. "How?" I asked. We lived in a compound that was enclosed within the Nestle factory where my father was the personnel manager. Biji walked along the sidewalk adjacent to large Eucalyptus trees that were apparently home to an army of crows. Since she was a diminutive woman, they'd fly close to her head and scare her. A crow had poked a beak in her skull a few evenings ago. When she complained, Papa and Amma thought a companion would help. I was asked to fling around my grandfather's walking stick if the crows came too close. The stick went with Biji wherever she traveled. Biji was a small woman, and I was probably barely four feet at the time; I have never grown over five feet anyway. Stick or no stick, we hardly made a daunting pair.

Her walk began a half hour after our regular afternoon tea, which was taken at 4:30 p.m. Not surprisingly, I was sullen when we started, and Biji humored me by telling me about the time when I was a toddler and fell into a shallow ditch full of water outside the family house in Delhi. "What happened? Did I drown?" I asked. "You would not be here, would you?" she grinned. I was constantly interrogating Biji about my routines as a baby, what I ate, how I spoke, why I cried, and when I crawled. As I have grown older, childhood stories have taken on a mystical and mythical quality. They are a space that I long to know again, but as an adult. I also find this fascination with one's past, whether more immediate—as for a seven-year-old—or further on in time, sustains us as one of the ways we meet our selves in the present and future. We are not our childhood, but that space shadows us, infused with meaning, asking to be recalled. When Biji and I reached the row of Eucalyptus trees I realized that Papa had not been exaggerating. There were at least twenty crows perched on two of the trees, and as soon as they saw Biji, they began crowing angrily. There were some men walking ahead of us, but the crows had their eyes on my tiny grandmother. I thanked my stars that I was carrying the stick and waved it around angrily. Biji continued talking. And so began our daily walks that would last until I was ten and was sent to boarding school.

We were a curious pair—a tiny white-haired lady in a white cotton sari with her head covered, and almost a foot shorter, a small girl in a frock and a pageboy haircut carrying her dead grandfather's walking stick. But we were fearless together. These walks and our room created a bond that would have otherwise never been forged. As the weeks, months, and years went on, we talked of everything. I learned more and more about my family in Pakistan, about my great-grandfather who was given the title of *Rai Sahib* during British rule. Biji told me about the great Quetta earthquake of 1935 that almost killed my grandfather. He was trapped under a large wooden wardrobe and was rescued by his younger brother, Mahinder. This explained why my father's uncle was so dear to Biji and why no trip to Delhi was complete without a visit to his home. She also told me how we lost our land and home in India's Partition in 1947. I think I was the only grandchild who knew early on how we became refugees, moved to Delhi, built homes, and how my father and his siblings came to be educated amidst deep economic hardship. When these stories disturbed and frightened me, I'd naively urge Biji to forget them and not be so unhappy. She would sigh and say, "When you grow old, you are sad; I cannot explain it, there is a word in English for it—melancholy; it does not go away." As I write this, I am gripped with sorrow at my foolish words to this widowed refugee who was also my grandmother. Grief remains an unknown place until one has encountered it.

When my parents decided to send me to Waverly, a Catholic boarding school in Mussoorie, a small hill town nestled by Himalayan ranges, my evening jaunts with Biji ended. My older brother Sameer had left for boarding school a few years before me, and with no grandchild in the house, Biji decided to return to living with her older son. As an adult, I've come to understand how important the moment of my departure was because after it, Biji and I would never again live together in the same house for an extended period of time.

At the beginning, Waverly was a difficult place—an old and strict Catholic convent that opened in 1845. I was afraid of its aging buildings and also of the other girls, some of whom had known each other since nursery school. I'd been sent there in grade six as a ten-year-old. So there was a lot of catching up to do. In those initial months, when finding even one friend was difficult, I walked the corridors of Waverly—the school sat on a hill and was cordoned off from the town, so hiking the hill was not allowed. I made two friends during these walks—Glenda and Ria—and we remained inseparable, like sisters, until we left Waverly. Days in Waverly were so regimented that the only down time was the forty-five minutes of dead time between dinner and bed. On some days, we would saunter down the stairs from the middle school to the baby dormitories—the name given to dorms where the seven- to nine-year-olds slept. The baby dorms were a novelty because the children slept on small beds that were placed together in large hall-like rooms. I think it was so they wouldn't be frightened if they awoke at night. Our beds in the senior dorms, on the other hand, were separated from each other by frilly white curtains, which you could draw to create makeshift cubicles. Ria knew the baby dorms well. She'd been at Waverly since she was seven years old, three years before I was sent there. When we walked past them, she studiously avoided looking inside the large glass windows. She said they reminded her of her first year in Waverly when she was unbearably homesick.

If you have not been to British-style boarding schools in north India, you may be surprised to know that they are spread across vast spaces. While mine took up only one small mountain, my brother's reached across seven hills. The important thing was that because we walked we learned to notice things that we were blind to during the day. I discovered that the head girl sat at a particular spot behind the statue of Mother Mary on the main hard court before dinner and read her mail for the day. The head girl was the student-voted leader of the school student council, which was made up of four captains and four vice-captains who governed one house (a group of students) each. Dividing schools into houses continues to be common practice in British schools; I am unsure of the history of this practice, but it was popularized contemporaneously in the Harry Potter series. Walking, I noticed that this was the spot girls chose when they wanted to read letters from home. It was where I would begin reading Biji's and Amma's letters, and the occasional letter from Papa.

We were not averse to peeping into rooms that we were disallowed from entering. The staff dining room was a particular favorite, mostly because we hated our own dining hall food. The nuns and teachers had a separate kitchen and a different cook, and even though they are supposed to lead ascetic lives, they seemed fond of eating well. We saw fresh meat and delicious-looking dessert at their table, every night. And each nun nursed a routine. Sister Lia, our needle-work instructor, drank red wine with her dinner every night. Sister Lucy, who was also our Chemistry teacher, had a sweet tooth and liked to play music in the nun's dining room—I think it was because she could not bear to talk to the other nuns. Our English teacher, Ms. Diaz, spoke with her mouth full, and our biology teacher, Ms. Pinto, had a penchant for tomato ketchup, pouring it liberally on all foods. The senior dorm matron, Ms. Maria, barely ate anything. She'd confessed to us that she found the food too bland. We knew she hoarded junk food in her bedroom adjoining our dorm—we could hear the crinkling of wrappers late into the night. We were comrades in our dislike for that food, we thought, so we were peeved when she busted a midnight feast we planned one Easter weekend. Ms. Mishra, our art teacher, never ate with the other teachers; we would later come to know that she was a Brahmin and sharing food with the Catholics was a sin for her.

The nuns at Waverly wore habits that revealed just the front circles of their faces. They were part of a conservative French-Catholic order founded by Claudine Thevenet, who was canonized in the early 1990s, a few years after we graduated from Waverly. We were ever-curious about how our wardens looked with their heads uncovered. The closest we ever came to finding out was with our principal, Sister Prudence. We all agreed, from what was visible, that she had the most symmetrical features of all the nuns. One day we'd wandered by her quarters and chanced upon her sitting at her dressing table admiring herself. While we could only see her in silhouette through the frosted glass windows, it was hard to miss her thick, waist-length dark hair. Her quarters became a regular part of our walks, and we soon discovered that Sister Prudence brushed her tresses with great gusto every evening—an after-dinner ritual. It did not take us very long to spread the news about her hair and the hair-brushing ritual. I've always felt that Sister Prudence knew of our peeping, but she humored us; we were never reprimanded for either the spying or the gossip. For many months, we stayed busy speculating why such a beautiful woman would take the habit. Many years after Waverly, I heard from a friend-alum that Sister Prudence was the youngest offspring of a wealthy Anglo-Indian family from Kerela and that she'd taken her vows against her family's wishes. I often wonder what her life might have been without the habit.

We spent innumerable hours contemplating whether the nuns and the teachers ever invited men to eat with them. Waverly was an all-girls convent school, and men were a scarce species. Sometimes brothers from the all-boys Irish Catholic school in the area came to dinner, and we waited in anticipation for a nun to elope with a brother and give up her habit. Surely, the pretty Sister Prudence deserved to be saved from this life? We were so cloistered at Waverly that dreaming about Sister Prudence's escape was the only way we could imagine a way out of our own existence and could envision, albeit in a miniscule way, what our own lives could and would be outside of school. But, we'd become so disciplined that we never dared imagine our own liberation.

Walking the 150-year-old corridors of Waverly was a ritual, a continuity that linked my present to my walking days with Biji. Each foot-step made me feel more at home in this place away from home. Each foot-step returned me to the comfort of our walks and made me less homesick. Walking continued to prepare me, as it had with Biji, to pay attention and to "learn to listen" to the stories my friends told me. I was creating my own rhythm of peripatetic listening, observing, and thinking that would eventually become *my* manner and movement for understanding oral and life histories of Indian women, what became my research focus as an academic. Decades later, I would read Rebecca Solnit's (2000) meditations on walking and need no translation for her musings, "The rhythm of walking generates a kind of rhythm of thinking, and the passage through a landscape echoes or stimulates the passage through a series of thoughts" (pp. 5–6). More necessity than leisure, both movement and thought, walking was (is) my way of comprehending the known and the unknown around me—both an unlikely and an obvious legacy of walks that began because a little girl was asked to guard her grandmother from cawing, ferocious, and unruly crows.

I finished high school and moved home, and then there is a drought in my memory about walking. I must have walked, but I don't remember much. Maybe I did not walk, and so I could not remember much. To some extent the drought can be explained by two absences—Waverly and Biji. After leaving for Waverly, Biji was lost to me. Now we only met each other during crowded family moments. When she was in her early eighties, Biji returned to stay with us temporarily. On a short trip to visit us, she broke her hip in a fall during dinner at a relative's home. I was with her when it happened. We became roommates for the duration of her convalescence. It did not take us long to fall into our old habits. We talked, we argued, we grumbled, we complained about each other. We never spoke of walking. We knew that her walking days were over. She lived to be ninety-two, but in the last ten years of her life, she was instructed to walk only if necessary. I was terrified that she was going to die. I'd taken to waking up with her at 4 a.m., and if she was late in getting up, I would put my index finger to her nose to check if she was still breathing. She'd inevitably pipe up and laughingly declare, *main abhi zinda hoon*, "I'm still alive."

Walking takes on significance with my move to the United States in the late nineties. My experience of the United States begins, like a lot of foreign students', in a small college town. In my first few months here, I was almost afraid of the vast Midwestern spaces of Michigan, and I kept my walking limited to campus sidewalks. The expansive emptiness of the Midwest was frightening, and the absence of human bodies on the road made me almost apologetic for being on foot. After my first semester, I felt braver and began venturing into the quaint downtown area beyond the campus, where a lot of international students happened to also convene. In the summers, I took to walking at six in the morning and came to notice the nuances of small town living in the United States. The people returning from night shifts at local factories, workmen heading to gas stations for their morning coffee, the odd professor jogging, and even the odd student, like me, trying to get a walk in before the day sprang to life.

Later, I would move to northern Indiana to join a doctoral program, in the college town of West Lafayette—a slightly larger city. I could not afford a car, and would not get one until 2009, years after I could afford one. I began walking earnestly in Indiana—the landscape was flat, boring, and dismal, a stark contrast to the lush and familiar greenery of the Himalayas—but putting my feet to the ground somehow made the place less strange, made it almost a part of me. During the winter months, in both Michigan and Indiana, I walked the snow in wonder, not because I had not seen snow before, but because I'd never seen it fall on such leveled topography. Perhaps walking the vastness peeled away some layers of the alienation I associated with the terrain, almost as if by treading upon it I was domesticating it. After being in the United States for three years, I knew that walking was one way to calm the turmoil of exile that raged inside of me. In those early years, walking was like a bridge between the country of my childhood and this new country that I was making my own. A bridge held together by the stories Biji had told me. It was during my daily walks that I made the decision to not return home to India.

I cannot say that there is a specific walk on a special day when I made up my mind; it came gradually as some decisions in life do. I was in my second year in doctoral school, and in any week I was clocking about thirty hours of reading for my graduate seminars, ten hours of actual in-class time, and some twenty hours of teaching as an assistant in public speaking classes. I was also in and out of several sweet, but ultimately unsuccessful, romances. I did not have time for anyone but myself. When I walked, I'd consider how lonely my life was. Here I was, almost thirty, still single, and studying for a doctorate that was only going to make me even more ineligible for marriage to an Indian man.

Still, I did not always feel sorry for myself. Walking helped me to think through some dense readings that I was undertaking in my doctoral seminars. In between ingesting much scholarly jargon and my daily walks, I read innumerable novels. I'd been an aspiring writer for years and had studied literature as an undergraduate. I was getting a doctorate because it seemed the ideal way to do the two things I liked best—reading and writing. I think walking became a different, and in some ways necessary, way for me to encounter these twin worlds. What if a character had done this instead of this? What if the story had been set in New York instead of Caracas? What if the protagonist were a man instead of a woman? I'd imagine answers to these questions as I walked the spare landscape. I took to carrying a pen and a mini-notebook with me—to note ideas about writing, people—I completed unfinished sentences and thoughts and found words for essays and poetry that my dingy attic apartment would certainly never have inspired. This curious dance between writing, reading, and walking convinced me that I was happy, that I was where I needed to be and that home was going to be a place I would find because I had learned how to step inside this medley.

Later, when I set out to write a dissertation on the experiences of Hindu women in arranged marriages, walking remained central to how I listened to the recorded life-histories and wrote them as stories. I spent four months one summer collecting these stories in India, and when I returned, I was able to listen to them, hate them, love them, and finally write them because I carried them with me on my walks. Somewhere along these meanderings, I understood that one rhythm—one foot in front of the other—was becoming my way of deciphering the rhythms of others in other worlds. I was (re)learning and (re)visiting that merging movement to ear was "my" organic way of living with the stories I had gathered from my field. Could my dissertation have been written had I not walked? Of course. Only the stories would not be a part of me as they are even now. Taking them in as I walked had settled them inside of me, a kind of convergence that sedentary listening might or might not have engendered. I walked one hour every day, and still do, and I experience those sixty minutes as both empty and fecund—they take me where I must go—inside the stories I should note and away from the ones that I should let go.

What I know is that Biji, our walks, and her stories were companionable shadows in these trans-continental perambulations. In 2007 it came as no surprise to anyone in my family (or myself) that I initiated a cross-generational oral history study of refugee family stories and India's Partition. And when "home" as—sense, presence, absence—became the central focus that I "chose" to note in the oral histories, I knew that things were coming full circle. I was going home or being taken home, to learn more about refugees of my grandmother's generation—to find more pieces of her and of the life she left behind in Pakistan. Movement and travel had become my metaphors for understanding experience, life, and the world. Perhaps this was fated, as my devoutly Hindu Biji would say, things were going just the way they had always been planned. Our walks were (and are) trailing me, directing me to where I needed to go and what I needed to learn.

For years I associated walking with the company of women—my grandmother, my friends in Waverly, the women in my doctoral research. I cannot say that I have any memories of walking alongside any boyfriend, and my spouse loathes the activity, calling it boring. I return to Delhi at least once, if not twice a year. In the last five years, I realized that I'd overlooked my father and his walking regimen. Of course, I have always known that he walks every day, but I'd never given it much thought—Papa worked long hours, and we were a little bit in awe of him as children; we just didn't know him well. During these return visits, I found that Papa would return from his walk at 6 a.m., just as I was stepping out for mine. He had retired some years ago, so I was puzzled and asked him why he felt it necessary to walk at the crack of dawn—well, almost. He replied,

> "I know all the men in the neighborhood, they want to walk and talk and chat and gossip about this, that, and the other. It's too much chatter too early, so I go before any of them reaches the park."

"Are you running away from your friends?" I giggled.

He glared at me and said, "I don't need them that early in the morning."

True. Of course, once all these Uncles—a title we use to refer to all my father's friends—knew who *I* was, they would take turns to walk one round of the park with me. Indian women who live alone abroad are still curiosities, particularly Punjabi women. The Uncles wanted to know if I lived alone, whether I cooked for myself, if I had any friends, and didn't Americans make bad friends because they are, after all, selfish? Once they warmed up, the questions turned more personal:

"Why are you not thinking of marriage?"

"Why are you living so far away, leaving your brother to take care of your parents? Are you not concerned about them?"

Then when I did eventually get married, the questions shifted:

"Are you not planning children?"

"Do you not want them?"

"Do you not like children?"

I decided that my father's walking dilemmas were very real. Some stories could be sacrificed. I needed to let the Uncles go. Now when I am home my father and I walk together—Uncle-less—at the crack of dawn. We talk of the extended family, my father's cousins and Papa's surviving uncles and aunts. Biji inevitably enters our conversations—she was a central figure in the extended Chawla family, much loved and immensely respected. Sometimes our talks turn a bit morbid; I am given an update on all of the elderly relatives who have died in the months that I have been away—reports that show me that, at seventy-one, my father has begun paying attention to mortality.

Three years ago, when I was approaching my thirty-fifth birthday, my husband and friends insisted that I needed to get a driver's license. They said it was time for me to get independent and taste some freedom. They reminded me that I was an oddity in a culture where driving is associated with becoming an adult. I argued and argued, telling them freedom does not come from knowing how to drive. I feel free, I said. "And besides," I accusingly asked my husband, "didn't we agree that one of the benefits of living in a college town was that one could buy a home close to the campus and walk to work?" No one was having it. I was told to stop waxing philosophical, get practical, and realize that driving was a necessity in the United States. So I took driving lessons and passed my test a few weeks short of my thirty-fifth birthday. I drive to work when I need to carry books and heavy objects. But I avoid long drives. Driving does not come naturally to me, which is sort of inevitable when one learns the skill this late in life. It is also not natural for me because I associate bodily movement with thinking, and when I drive, even though there is movement, I feel imprisoned in the rules that I must follow and the violations I must not commit. I am not a fearless driver, nor an aggressive one. Driving has, in fact, made me less punctual. I overestimate my speed and also find it necessary to stop for every pedestrian attempting to cross the street—they could, after all, be me. I know I anger at least one driver behind me every day. Driving is a complication that I have grudgingly accepted. My only solace is that I still can walk my sacred hour.

I was in the United States when Biji passed away. She died on a cold December day, three days before I was to arrive home for winter break. It was a sad entourage that came to meet me at the Delhi airport. On the thirteenth day after her cremation, as is customary, there was a celebration in our neighborhood temple—a small *havan,* high tea for the extended family, and the singing of *bhajans.* After this we congregated at my parents' home for dinner—we had not been together like this for at least ten years. Not surprisingly, the talk turned to Biji, who I was told had been very worried when I had moved away to the United States. She'd blamed my father for letting me go and told him, "This child is now lost to you, she will not return." My father's older brother, *Bade-Papa,* addressing me by my family nickname, asked, "Gudia, you were her favorite, you know?" I shook my head, "Oh no, she loved Sameer the most, she treated him like a son." Sameer had been almost entirely raised by Biji because when he was born my mother held a full-time job. Biji became his day mother and Amma his night mother. My cousins and I always knew that he was special to her. We did not feel un-loved by her, we just knew.

Uncle walked over to his briefcase, popped it open, and took out a picture of me when I was sixteen, an old modeling shot which a professional photographer friend of the family had taken. I'd mailed Biji that picture because after she moved away we only met once a year, and I wanted her to keep up with how I was changing. I wanted to show off and let her know that I was almost an adult and that I was pretty. She replied with a letter written in her very proper Hindi. In it she admitted that I was turning into a beautiful girl, but she cautioned me to cultivate modesty. Instead of taking pride in my appearance, I was to worry more about school and making something of myself, she instructed. After she died, my uncle and aunt discovered the photograph inside her *Gita;* behind it she had written in Hindi, "Gudia, *meri poti,*" my granddaughter. Uncle said she inevitably displayed the picture to all her visitors, proudly announcing that I was living and studying for a doctorate in the United States. She never failed to mention that I had taken care of her by being her guard during her evening walks and saved her from the wicked crows. The moral of this story, according to my uncle, was simple—if I could fend off Indian crows, I was brave enough to live alone in the United States. There were shouts of laughter around the table, with my older cousins improvising a rhyme, "Gudia can fend off crows, so Gudia is brave, so she can live alone—in the United States." Maybe Biji was right, maybe staving off the crows was brave, maybe it taught me to be unafraid. Our walks were her main memory when she was dying. That day I realized how special those evenings were. I will always feel guilty for not having seen her before she died. There is nothing to be done, no dramas to be staged, no memorials to be written, and no eulogies to be read. But I can walk. And I do.

Glossary

Amma: Mother

Bade-Papa: Older Father. A term used to refer to your father's older brother in some north Indian families.

Gita: One of the most famous and popular of the Hindu religious texts.

Gayatri Mantra: A portion of Hindu scripture. A small two sentence prayer in Sanskrit.

Gudia: Doll. A common nickname given to girls in north India.

Hai Ram: Hail Ram. Ram is a famous Hindu God, who is the central protagonist in the Hindu epic *Ramayana*.

Havan: A prayer ceremony.

Bhajans: Devotional songs.

Reference

Solnit, R. (2000). *Wanderlust: A history of walking.* New York: Penguin.

Chapter 7

"Sit With Your Legs Closed!" and Other Sayin's from My Childhood

Robin M. Boylorn

You are your stories. You are the product of all the stories you have heard and lived—and of many that you have never heard. They have shaped how you see yourself, the world, and your place in it. Your first great storytellers were home, school, popular culture, and perhaps, church. (Taylor, 2001, p. 1)

Blackened Autoethnography

This chapter theorizes the notion of sayin's[1] as performative autoethnography. Sayin's, as a version of what Geneva Smitherman (1994) calls *black talk*, is language that crosses

> boundaries—of sex, age, region, religion, [and] social class—because the language comes from the same source: the African American Experience and the Oral Tradition embedded in that Experience. On one level, there is great diversity among African Americans today, but on a deeper level, race continues to be the defining core of the Black Experience. (p. 2)

By focusing on the language and style of black talk and the popular expressions therein, I focus on the ways that sayin's in the black community are both performative and autoethnographic. This essay is also an attempt to represent the cultural-specificity and feminist epistemology that is grounded in my personal lived experiences as a black woman with rural roots. Through sayin's I analyze how particular cultural performances are influenced and emphasized

Handbook of Autoethnography, edited by Stacy Holman Jones, Tony E. Adams, and Carolyn Ellis, 173–185. © 2013 Left Coast Press, Inc. All rights reserved.

by cultural and family stories. Further, I suggest that autoethnography about black experiences offers an intervention for theorizing these particular, but shared, experiences. I blacken my autoethnography by centering black vernacular and making claims about the ways language informs how stories are told and remembered. Autoethnography, like a two-way mirror, is part reflective and part transparent. This duality is particularly significant for people speaking from the periphery. Autoethnographic stories, like double-image mirrors, offer twofold realities and possibilities, speaking for and with, and reflecting multiple versions of a narrative. Black speak does a similar duet, borrowing from and distinguishing itself from intercultural influences, and playing off of the poetics of language to perform itself narratively.

As a black woman who was raised in the South in a working class and matrifocal family, sayin's were meaningful lessons in my childhood that served as reminders and warnings. It was through sayin's that I learned the politics of my existence and the agency of my voice. I learned ways of resisting discriminatory labels by having myriad ways to talk, tell stories, and make myself visible. Similarly, in what Alice Walker (1983) refers to as "double vision," or the ability to "see [your] own world and its close community while intimately knowing and understanding the people who make up the larger world that surrounds and suppresses [your] own" (p. 19), I use autoethnography to see myself twice, talking back to myself and others at the same time. Autoethnography is particularly helpful because it is a doubled storytelling form and moves from self to culture and back again. In the black community, this strategy and dual awareness has also been referred to as "shifting" (Jones & Shorter-Gooden, 2003) and "double consciousness" (DuBois, 1918); it is the ability of black folks to see themselves through the eyes of others while being fully aware of themselves.

In the following pages, I examine seven sayin's that signal stories from my childhood and the storied contexts in which I learned them. Sayin's are simultaneously a practice of storytelling and a performative accomplishment that theorize both in vernacular ways and in relationship to race/culture/class/geography and its people. Through the use of sayin's and memories, black folk use a dramaturgical approach to storytelling that is performative, situational, and audience-oriented. Embedded in sayin's are lived experiences and cultural influences. Therefore, I attempt here to express how cultural sayin's reflect the homogeneity of black culture while I also express the singularity of my personal experience. Further, while the particular sayin's I focus on are woman-centered and situated within the context of my rural upbringing, they could easily translate across social identities.

I also speculate about the ways in which autoethnographic method allows stories to speak for themselves, and how sayin's are cultural performances of autoethnography. Sayin's, in this context, are intended to mark and theorize about the ways that our memories and cultural inheritances (re)emerge in our work and serve as catalysts of behavior.

Sayin's serve as lessons, warnings, instructions, compliments, and advice. They also reflect and reinforce the ways in which American and African American cultures shaped my identity and feminist politics (my relenting to and resistance of them). The side effects of racism, sexism, classism, and heterosexism affected the ways in which I was taught to be a (strong) black woman in the South. These critical and reflective stories reflect how I was conditioned to see myself as a poor, black girl in my southern, quasi-conservative rural community. The sayin's reflect themes of gendered bodily decorum, the politics of beauty, legislative sexuality and reproduction, class and its treasures, performative resistance, and alms for dignity.

Sayin' One: "Sit with Your Legs Closed!"

I suppose she is selective with her words because she holds on to them like a secret she promised to never tell. Her voice is bigger than her body: massive, impossible, beautiful and terrible, and it falls from her mouth like thunder falls from fair weather cumulus clouds, out of nowhere.

I am sitting, wide legged, on the porch, legs dangling, listening, not for her voice, but for cars passing, shoes pushing against rocks, birds singing in trees, and the drone of flies as they sneak past me into the house through the dilapidated screen door. Dandelion hairs float in the air past my face as I blow breath making wishes, smiling because I am young enough to believe that secret wishes come true.

I am facing the road. Facing the cars that go by and throwing my hands up every time I recognize a car, or a face, or a shouted greeting, out of habit and good home training, waving back at strangers who wave at people who are sitting on their porches when they pass by. This is my way of practicing being grown. This, and pretending to smoke a cigarette with the bubble gum wrapped in white paper that I got from the mini-mart for fifteen cents, inhaling and exhaling every five seconds like the women at the card table. This, and talking loud and throwing my head back when my imaginary company says something foolish. This, and rolling my eyes and neck at the same time. This, and singing off key while wiggling my hips.

I am sitting, solitary on the porch, with my knees separated and my arms folded in my lap, my right hand going up every two minutes, waving.

Her voice is a hum in the background. I hear her without hearing her. I am listening to being outside, and while I often concentrate on her words, I am distracted by the cars, the rocks, the trees, the flies, the wishes, the practicing. My delayed response inspires her anger.

"You hear me talking to you?"

I turn around and meet her focused eyes. I want to say, "Yes, ma'am," but don't. We only say ma'am when we are in trouble or in public. It is not required at home or when there is no company to witness it. I swallow fear and resist the urge to respond, knowing she does not require my words, only my obedience.

"Sit up and close your damn legs. This ain't no peep show!" Her tone and her eyes let me know she means business.

She looks mad. Three vertical lines appear on her forehead, waiting for me to mind. I jump up, pushing my knees tightly together, sorry for not remembering I was not a boy, sorry for acting like I wasn't raised right, like I wasn't taught any better. Good girls don't sit gap legged. Sitting wrong gives the wrong impression. I don't want to be the kind of girl who sits with her legs wide open, grown, fast, hot in the ass. My legs are now together, touching. My obedience pleases her, and she returns to the house without speaking.

I will consistently remember, in her presence and in public, to sit with my ankles touching.

Sayin' Two: "Beauty Is Pain!"

An old wives' tale warns that you should only cut your hair with the growing of the moon, otherwise it won't grow back. I did what I could to follow the rules, but my hair refused to grow long. And *whitegirl* rituals (like brushing your hair one hundred times every night and washing your hair every day) only made my hair fall out. Most black folk don't wash their hair every day, and it is not a matter of cleanliness or good grooming, but rather an issue of hair type. When I attempt to treat my hair like it's white, it dries out, breaks off, and falls out. The edges of my hairline become bald. Having a ponytail that touched my back seemed impossible. My natural hair, even after being straightened with the hot comb, would always stubbornly concede to sweat, water, humidity or time and go back to its original state. I wanted a more permanent solution and begged my mother to let me have a perm, like her and my sister, but she refused, saying I already thought I was "grown." She said she wouldn't be able to do anything with me with straight hair. Chemically-straightened hair was for grown women (and *whitegirls*). She decided I was too young to get a perm and had no business wanting one. She told me that it hurt and burned, worse than the hot comb, which ritualistically would give me the same general effect, only short-lived.

Hair Story

hot torture
hot hands
close to scalp
hot comb
hot air
pushing against nape of neck
Mama's hands
gentle, strong, unrelenting
combing through yesterday's kinks
making them straight
hot
burning

smoking
smelling like
singed and melting
hair
hands on chin
elbows on knees
but Mama is pleased
at the outcome
coming along
and yielding an inch
of new growth
from last time
our hour-long ritual
every few months
when my hair is dirty enough to wash
curly wet
nappy dry
coming together like arms hugging
Mama complains
my hair is just like hers
unruly
hard to comb
not like her Mama's
side
this hot comb is our salvation
transforming texture
from tight around my scalp before
to touching my shoulders after
hot comb magic
making my hair
whitegirl *like*
hot torture
sitting between Mama's legs
trying not to cry
and sitting still
worrying there won't be
enough cocoa butter
to cover the scars
holding ears with loose hands

eyes closed
the metal combs
resting on the hot eye of the stove
taking turns
bringing tears to my brown-black eyes
an embrace like love
legs tightened around my body
"Beestyour head still girl,"
Mama says
careful to not keep it too hot
or let it get too cool
blowing the comb 'til smoke rises
and inhaling the fumes like cigarette smoke
she is in the kitchen
pulling out my kitchen[2]
tight waves
too stubborn to move
and falling out
on some days
Sundays
is when hair must
lay down
and behave
tamed
under bows
and blue pomade
and fancy braids
made with three strands
wrapped around each other
pulled between Mama's greased fingers
caressing my scalp
and wrapping around until my hair is connected like rope
falling
finally
past my ears
near my shoulders
and I smile
knowing
beauty is pain

but loooooooooooooooooooooong hair
is everything
to little black girls.

Sayin' Three: "If Somebody Hits You, Hit 'Em Back—Harder!"

All of the grandchildren got the same "talking to" when it was time to start public school. Entering a space where we would not have the protection of grown kinfolk, my grandmother expected us to learn early. I was not even five years old when I stood between my grandmother's knees and listened to her tell me what to do if somebody hit me at school.

"If somebody hits you, you better hit 'em back—harder!" She emphasized the last word by hitting her own hand with her fist, showing me how to ball my fingers up like hers. "Don't let me hear tell of you letting somebody put their hands on you and you don't hit 'em back. And if you let somebody whoop your ass at school, look for another ass whooping when you get home."

I knew she meant it. But I also knew that the lesson embedded in her words was more about me learning how to take care of myself for the rest of my life, not just in school. She meant that she literally expected me to defend myself physically against attackers, but also to defend myself in the world, because as a black woman, I would get pushed around. She didn't intend for me to get used to it, she intended for me to learn how to fight back.

No one ever talked about how this advice contradicted what we were taught in Sunday school, to "turn the other cheek" when someone strikes you. The biblical teaching and the colloquial practice were incongruous, but my grandmother found it illogical and backwards to not teach her children to fend for themselves. "If God gives you strength," she would say, "you knock the hell out of 'em!"

I listened to her give this same lecture to every other child on the verge of entering school. And they nodded, practiced the fist, and promised to follow her instructions, just like I did. Hoping, though, that it would never come to that and fearing that it inevitably would.

Sayin' Four: "You're a Pretty Ole Dark-Skinned Girl."

My privacy wasn't a secret place to escape to in order to forget my problems, or hide. When I was a child, my privacy was the triangle below my navel, the slight curve on my otherwise flat chest, the soon-to-be-black girl butt that arched when I bent over, begging for maturity. But it was no secret that being dark-skinned was not preferable or privileged. On the playground, children would chant, "If you white, you all right, if you brown, get down, if you black, get back!"

We didn't understand why race mattered but it was clear that it did, especially outside of our homes. We understood the dynamics of colorism at play, even though we didn't have the language. Our conversations were not that sophisticated. We didn't walk around hearing or saying the word racism. But we understood nuance in our small, rural town, and we knew what a redneck was, what a Confederate flag meant, and what to do if/when we were blatantly mistreated.

Racism made my grandmamma mad and my mama tired. But we had ways of loving on each other with our language, and we passed around sarcasm and humor by starting sentences with "Nigga please" and ending them with "with your black ass." In response to some form of self-aggrandizement one would say, "Nigga please... go sit down!" And to punctuate a request or soften a compliment one would say, "C'mere... with your black ass" or "I didn't know your black ass could cook this good." In response to an unwelcome or unreasonable request or comment, one would say "kiss my black ass!" This is how we showed we belonged to each other, and were just alike, and would be all right.

○

"Don't make me slap the black off you"; the threat from my mother doesn't alarm me because I don't believe it is possible, and wouldn't be disappointed if some of the black did come off my skin. She is agitated because I have been crawling on my knees. She is disappointed because now they are turning black, burned from the carpet. She doesn't understand why I don't take better care of myself. She insists that I bathe longer now, to salvage the parts of my skin that are still brown. She gives me special lotion to make it better.

○

To be black with good hair was never quite as bad as just being black. My dark-skinned cousin with long hair says that men like black women who look like white women dipped in chocolate. Black girls with *whitegirl* features were considered beautiful by everybody's standards, and had a face that not only a mama could love. I instinctively understood *whitegirl* beauty was something I would never be able to accomplish because I was dark-skinned. I never asked her why, but I did beg for a black Barbie doll for Christmas.

○

We didn't know sexism, but we paid attention when men walked into rooms and were always happy to see them, bending over backwards and fixing plates and catering to them. We loved them entirely, and since they were more absent than present, they usually disappeared before we could discern that their actions were grounded in privilege. We did not expect them to explain or keep promises.

Class had more to do with how you acted in public than how much money was in your pocket. To have class was to have nice things or to think you were better than everybody else. Some people said it was acting white. Which made whiteness more desirable than being black.

Because everybody in the world wanted to be white-like.

Even other black people.

And in the media white women's lives were often romanticized with fairy tale endings. They are automatically beautiful. Automatically loveable. Love and happy endings were automatically possible. But fairy tales and Prince Charmings only came in white.

○

When I am a teenager I am told that I am pretty. The words come from someone who has known me all of my life but who never said it. She seems surprised, leaning her head and concentrating on my features. "You are a pretty ole dark-skinned girl." I know she means it as a compliment. I say thank you. And smile. And mean it.

Sayin' Five: "Betta Not Get Pregnant!"

At school they are not teaching us about sex; they are teaching us about our bodies. My mother never told me much about my body except that I should not touch it or talk about it in public. She seems uninterested and unconcerned that I am desperate to get the period that the woman at school told us about. She seems ambivalent that this, according to the woman, will mean I am a woman. Mama tells me that I don't know what I'm talking about and that once I get it I'll wish I never had it. I don't believe her. I think that she is trying to keep me from knowing the truth, keep me from growing up. She doesn't want me to know that when I have my period, the changes in my body will stop and I will finally have some rest. Finally be a woman. She doesn't want me to be a woman yet, and she doesn't want me to know about sex because I am only thirteen. She worries about what it will mean when I have a woman's body, what I will do with it. She worries that if I know about sex that I will be sweet talked by boys and be fast. She is ambivalent about the woman at school who is telling me to embrace my body and own my womanhood. She does not offer a counter-narrative.

Sex is unspoken like sin yet ubiquitous in our little community. When my period finally comes, I am warned that I "Betta not get pregnant."

Post menses I am accused of being pregnant every time there is a fish dream. In our family, if anyone dreams of fish or water it means someone (usually someone who has no reasonable relationship or business having sex, and no money, or as my grandmother says, "No pot to piss in, or a window to throw it out of") is pregnant. The questions, "You pregnant?" and "You messing with boys?" feel like accusations. When I say no, they don't believe me. Everyone in our already crowded house is angry until the pregnant person is discovered. No one ever apologizes for thinking it is me.

I hear my grandmother say women don't ever get to go nowhere because they are tied down with babies and no-good husbands. Based on her declaration and mourning plea I decide to not have any babies and never get married because I want to go places, be somebody. They shake their heads at me and say that I will want a baby, because that is what women do. When I say "Not me," they say I will probably get married early and have a house full of youngins.

When I try to prove my disinterest in babies by cutting open dolls, I am accused of being ungrateful. "That damn doll cost money. You don't 'preciate nothin'."

Sayin' Six: "Our House Is the Po' House."

"Come on and go with me to the po' house," my family's favorite phrase, inviting neighbors and friends to follow us home. When I was a child, po' wasn't a derogatory term or an insult, it was the name of our house. I knew we weren't rich, but I didn't know we were poor.

Our modest house wasn't big, but we had enough. Our yard and land were covered with broken glass, plastic soda bottles, trash bags, broken plates... everything but money. The paraphernalia in the dirt was evidence that before we lived there, the land we lived on was covered with whatever one could throw away and leave. Every time it rained a new layer of contraband would emerge from the dirt. The basketball court, a gift for my sister, was beneath trees too tall to cut down and above stumps too stubborn to move.

My uncle's green Thunderbird, with no tires and no hope, sat defeated on cement bricks, surrounded by other junk from our lineage's childhoods—my aunt's white Cutlass, my grandmother's brown sugar Cougar, one of the forty something cars she totaled in her lifetime. She was determined not to sell or give away what she worked so hard to have. Her parked car was filled with things we had no use for: old magazines, clothes long outgrown, pictures and mementos, simple things we couldn't bear to let go of. The car smelled like kerosene and musk, a constant reminder of how far we had come and how far we had to go.

Black country families have an acquired taste. In many ways our cultural heritage is tied to class circumstances. We make do with what other people don't want. We eat the parts of the pig that everyone else throws away. Pig's feet, ears, jaws, snout, brains, and chittlins are fried or boiled and drowned in vinegar and hot sauce, a delicacy only prepared for special occasions. Fixing chittlins was a time-consuming labor of love generally saved for Thanksgiving and Christmas. My grandmother would spend hours "cleaning" the pork intestines before she cooked them. I never understood how with that much meticulous cleaning they still smelled like shit. It only took them about an hour to cook, but it would take all day to the get the smell out of the house. But little or nothing, we never perished for lack of food. If you were hungry, my grandmother was Jesus, feeding the multitude with loaves and fishes. Everyone always left full.

Our furniture never matched, but we were happy. Always something fuchsia or orange, lime green, but never purple. The house always looked the same, clean or dirty. The orangey carpet, dark lace curtains, and brown walls never made me either proud or ashamed. It was home, it was safe, and it was ours.

Sayin' Seven: "Don't Go Beggin' Nobody for Nothin'!"

"Not love. Not money. Not respect! Don't you go beggin' nobody for nothin'!"

I hadn't done anything this time, but this was my warning, for future reference, based on the fact that she heard of somebody else's child, thank God not one of her own, who had been going door to door begging for handouts, cause her own mama wasn't paying her no mind.[3] It wasn't a need, or a necessity that the girl had her hand out for, but a want, something extra, something she probably didn't "need" no way (meaning it was a luxury that her mother could not afford). It could have been anything from candy to shoelaces, but it should have stayed in their own house. But this daughter was a poor, desperate, misguided thing, taking her mama's business all around the neighborhood, telling it from door to door. She was too young to understand the embarrassment she was causing and too poor to be ashamed, even though begging carries both of those words with it wherever it goes. She hadn't been to our house yet, but Grandma had already heard.

"Don't let me hear tell of you going around beggin' nobody for nothing. If they want you to have it, they'll give it to you."

I don't bother asking who "they" are, or how "they" would know I needed something if I didn't ask, because I know better than to ask questions, or talk back, or sass. This was a teachable moment. She was instilling pride. Showing me how to do without something I didn't need in the first place. She was teaching me about having family pride and self-dignity. She was showing me how to avoid embarrassment and remember to only expect help and hand-outs from kinfolk.

Mama's Lessons

The autoethnographies that I write are deeply influenced by my family and history. I adopted this approach so that a) my research is never inaccessible to my family, and b) I always remember, through my scholarship, to value the rich lived experiences I inherited from them. As an ethnographer I was trained to study people in different cultures through the way they live their lives, and through the stories they tell about their lives. As an autoethnographer I was trained to study my self and my culture through my personal narratives.

As Daniel Taylor (2001) states, we are all the products of all of the stories we have ever heard and lived, and those stories are often influenced, filtered, and shared through myriad storytellers. Taken together, the seven sayin's in this essay commemorate important lessons in the life of a rural black girl. The stories offer a commentary on expectations for proper etiquette and lenient, but restrictive, gender scripts; the politics of intra-racial constructions of beauty in the black community; the consequences of racism on the psyche; the nuances of workingclassness; and survival strategies. The sayin's provide a poetic and performative critique of larger hegemonic expectations that I was taught to equally resist and fulfill.

○

my mama taught me everything I ever needed to know
and she never went to any college
or took any night classes
or earned any degrees
or wrote any book
or traveled to any foreign countries
or spoke multiple languages
or saw her name in print
my mama graduated high school
homecoming queen who came back home
and raised two daughters with no help
the weight of it all, enormous
yet she never complained
instead she laughed and inspired laughter
danced without rhythm
taught without picking up a book
and loved without hesitation
my mama
who speaks in tongues, one of which is broken English
and sings salvation songs
with a voice that could set the world on fire
with words and sayin's that said it all
and taught me everything I needed to know

Notes

1. Throughout the text I will use "sayin's" rather than "sayings" to emulate the vernacular of my rural southern community.
2. For black folk with ethnic hair, a "kitchen" refers to the portion of your hair at the nape of the neck that is usually shorter and kinkier than the rest of your hair.
3. "Paying no mind" is a colloquialism for "not paying one any attention."

References

DuBois, W. E. B. (1918). *The souls of black folk: Essays and sketches*. Chicago: A. McClurg.

Jones, C., & Shorter-Gooden, K. (2003). *Shifting: The double lives of black women in America*. New York: HarperCollins.

Smitherman, G. (1994). *Black talk: Words and phrases from the hood to the amen corner*. Boston: Houghton Mifflin.

Taylor, D. (2001). *Tell me a story: The life-shaping power of our stories*. New York: Bog Walk Press.

Walker, A. (1983). *In search of our mothers' gardens: Womanist prose*. San Diego, CA: Harcourt Grace Jovanovich.

Chapter 8

Who's There?
A Week Subject

Sophie Tamas

1. Monday

I am sitting in an office at the university, on the twelfth floor. This room is mine on Mondays. It is the size of an average suburban bedroom, but it sounds like an airplane flying at night, full of sleeping people. Bookshelves line the long walls, filled with someone else's books. One short wall holds a door. The fourth wall is windows, from desk to ceiling. I am in a chair, looking out these windows. I have eaten half a cup of tamari almonds in the past ten minutes, one by one.

I am in the middle of a city, surrounded by one million people, but I am looking out at a farm. The fields of November are patches of umber and ochre. There is a red barn with white shutters and a yellow barn with green doors and, on a good day, a tractor. Last week it plowed the nearest field, pulling curved blades to turn the stubble under waves of earth with a long plume of seagulls swirling behind it. Trees line the seams of the fields and the canal that cuts between the farm and campus. A few have heads of yellow leaves, thin as a blonde baby's hair, but most hold their gray empty hands up to the sky. There are high-rise apartments and office buildings in the distance but most of the view is fields and trees. The clouds are moving toward me, lying flat on the air like the stuffing of a duvet, solid and gray in the middle but thinning at the edges to puffy white clumps. Past the horizon, fifty kilometers west, is home.

Handbook of Autoethnography, edited by Stacy Holman Jones, Tony E. Adams, and Carolyn Ellis, 186–201. © 2013 Left Coast Press, Inc. All rights reserved.

I want to tell you about these things because they matter to the me who is not speaking, the person I purport to represent when I talk about myself. I am supposed to be writing, not watching the sky.

Now the clouds are gone, en route to Montreal. But I am cold, and tired, and there are two red dump trucks driving by. I plug in the heating pad I've brought from my bed, and put it behind my back. I close my eyes. What am I trying to say?

Several months ago, I received an email from the editors, inviting me to write a chapter for this book. This feels like receiving an award for a test on which I've cheated. In autoethnography, we peer into social issues and problems through the lens of our own experience. Our vulnerability and exposure are the price of seeing something insightful or profound. But…

It's almost noon. I wonder what Shawn is up to? A moment later, he calls.

"You're sounding awfully small," he says.

"I'm trying to work on my chapter," I reply. "I thought I might do something about the construction of my subjectivity in my writing and how it feels fraudulent. So far I've got a tightly crafted description of the view."

He snorts. "And that took you all morning?"

"It did!" I say. We are both laughing but I can feel a hot mass of tears, like a bubble in a pot of thick porridge, bulging at the surface somewhere in my chest. Shawn feels it, too. "I know it can take a long time," he says, "and you're really fast. You're doing a good job."

"I just don't know if I have something to say or which I is saying anything." This bleated complaint comes from a small split in my breastbone. "But if I can keep saying it for twenty pages, then maybe I'll have a paper." We laugh again, and the bubble subsides.

2. Tuesday

I have kissed Shawn and the girls goodbye for the day. The dishwasher is gurgling in the kitchen and the washing machine is hissing a few feet away from my desk in an unfinished corner of our old wooden house. In the journal I am holding, Alicia Jackson and Lisa Mazzei (2008) have just called for deconstructive autoethnographies that "disrupt identity, discourage identification, and refuse understanding" (p. 303). Instead of reading further I am watching the wind caress the treetops near my window and considering the kinds of identity and understanding available in *The X-Men*. At crucial junctures in its epic plot, Professor Xavier—a noble, scholarly telepath—stands in a sphere surrounded by thousands of video screens, skimming through the babble of subjectivities like seven billion radio stations. This gives him a headache, but enables him to find out essential facts that inevitably save the world. This is possible because each person has one voice; he or she is a discreet individual, thinking or wanting or feeling one thing at a time, with one face per station.

While autoethnographers may not take such a naïve view of subjectivity, we still imagine that knowing and representing are possible, useful ways of spending our days. If I cannot peer into the minds of others, surely I can eavesdrop on myself and pluck out salient messages from the internal static, fitting my observations into narrative arcs that follow the traces of individual subjects with more-or-less perceptible boundaries. I offer "a coherent, explanatory subject who gathers up meaning and reflexively lays bare the process of knowledge production" and propels her through stories that seek "connection and recognition in the midst of complexity" (Jackson & Mazzei, 2008, p. 303). If I am troubled by the gaps in this cursory self, I might add nuance, asking the Professor to listen more deeply and hear that each of us bears multiple voices. Poor Xavier, imagine the headache now.

Then I add to this cacophony the evidence that I enact, reading it for signs of my buried and emergent selves. My contradictory, ambiguous impulses are compressed into knowable signifiers and rendered as turning points in the intricate, linear plot of my life. In many versions of reality, the moral complexity of my decisions is reduced to clearly marked binaries: desire and duty, reason and passion, self and other, good and bad. I stand with one in each hand, as the hero of my own story, making the choices that define who I am. But what if there's nobody in the middle, choosing?

I get up to pee. The bathroom is next to my workspace; my feet on its floor remind me of shimming and sistering the joists and laying the subfloor and thin four foot by four foot sheets of smooth plywood nailed every six inches and choosing the linoleum and bringing it home and cutting and gluing it down into place. I did not know that I could build a bathroom floor until I did it. What else don't I know I can do? Who else is in there?

I pick up John Wylie (2010), who is sitting by the tub, butting his desire for creative geographies against the romanticism of individual experience in personal narratives. Deleuze, he explains, sees subjectivity as always emergent, never emerged and able to reflect, from a distance, on the "affective swirl" in which it formed. The self is a changeable possibility, continuously arising and folding back. Derrida similarly suggests there is no seamless subject, present to itself. Subjectivity *is* loss, experienced as a sort of yearning for something that will never arrive. Our spaces are haunted, and "*we are the ghosts,* already and necessarily" (p. 108; original italics). As ghosts, we are neither purely present nor entirely absent, but we are absolutely unknowable and thus "each of us, in some ways, *always alone.* There is no world, only islands" (p. 109, italics in original).

I close the book with a sigh, wondering what Derrida would look like if you scrubbed him with feminist relational theory. Neuropsychologist Paul Broks (2003) is watching from under a catalogue. He suggests we all feel that "as well as a brain, something else occupies the interior of our head and the heads of other people—an irreducible mental core, the origin of thought and actions" (p. 61). But where is this ghostly self? If you fiddle with the brain, we flicker and fade out. Our senses, memory, identity, facial expressions, desires, voices, behaviors, bodies, and beliefs can be radically altered by mechanical or chemical intrusions. Probe here, and I experience the immanent presence of the divine. Probe there, and I wet my pants. Scar the gelatinous almond of my amygdala, and I no longer feel. Cut out my hippocampus, and I forget. The halves of my brain structurally mirror each other. Put part of it to sleep, and the person who emerges may be unrecognizable; a shadow self kept secret from my consciousness. "When we see the brain," Broks declares, "we realize that we are, at one level, no more than meat; and, on another, no more than fiction" (p. 63).

I return to my desk, but the dogs have stirred from their baskets and are staring at me, using their Jedi mind powers to move my hands off the keyboard and into their ecstatic fur. Pollywog, who is still a puppy, wriggles with glee; Cricket takes love with more dignity. "C'mon, girls," I say. "D'you want to go out?" I want out, too, but there's no break for me: even this writing is a treat, stealing time from the marking and course prep I ought to be doing.

3. WEDNESDAY

I am considering my non-existence at another university two hours away from home, facing a cement wall, blackened with lichen. I am looking out over rows of peaked glass windows, lighting the hallway below as if the students were hydroponic plants. It is not a view worth looking at, even on this unseasonably warm and sunny day, when every piece of me yearns to be outdoors.

I am here to work with my postdoctoral supervisor—a lovely woman, my age, but with tenure and a baby instead of a new PhD and three teenagers. She is from Glasgow, and her voice rolls out with the thick resilient texture of pulled taffy. We are sitting in the antechamber to her office, a haphazard assemblage of mismatched quasi-functional furnishings and decorative objects. We have just returned from the cafeteria, where I bought sushi and tea and a tub of smoked turkey barley soup, which is surprisingly good and properly hot. I am impressed and grateful and curious about how they mass-produce such tasty soup.

"How is it going?" Joyce asks.

"Okay." I shrug. But this is too mean; she actually wants to know. Oh dear.

"How was the conference?"

"It was good?"

What should I tell her? That my room two weeks ago in Vancouver was well-kept and large, with a thirtieth floor view of skyscrapers sparkling like some futuristic utopia? That I did not go visit the downtown east side, where 2,000 homeless people live in ten square blocks, but I did rent a bike and cruise around the sea wall in Stanley Park, where I saw a woman pushing two dachshunds in a baby stroller, and another woman get pooped on by a cliff full of black cackling birds? ("I'm sorry," I said, as I pedaled past, "I don't even have a Kleenex.") That I saw a little boat towing a barge with two garbage trucks on it, and a floating gas station, and sent home a daily travelogue of annotated photos to blunt the edge of loneliness? That the mountains made me miss the landscapes of my miserable youth? That I walked to the shopping district to replace the ear-buds I forgot in the Toronto airport and smiled at four middle-class, middle-aged white women protesting for a free Palestine, and pierced kids playing devil sticks, and a street vendor wearing a large foam hot dog hat? That the service was excellent in the little shops where I bought my daughters jade rings that I hoped would fit and postcards and, after much deliberation, three kinds of sparkly nail polish? That I had a bowl of terrible noodle soup in one restaurant and a bowl of delicious noodle soup in another?

Or should I focus on the conference, and explain that I could not afford to attend but had to in order to collect an award which then felt bittersweet? That sitting at the book signing table with a conference volunteer gamely making small talk beside me while disinterested scholars trickled by stuffed with their Italian buffet lunch made me feel like a bearded lady sideshow? That they gave away several copies of my book about spousal abuse as cocktail party door prizes on the last night of the conference, and tipsy strangers came up to me waving pens: "Now your book is going to Sweden," one giggled. "This is the first time I've won anything," said a woman from Ghana. "Keep on winning," I wrote in the book. "All the best, Sophie."

Perhaps I should start earlier, and tell her how I phoned Shawn from the Vancouver airport while I waited in the wrong place for the shuttle to the hotel. I asked how their stew was for supper, and he paused and said, "Well…" I made that stew the night before so it could simmer in the crock-pot while I flew across Canada and my girls would come home from school to the savory, sustaining evidence of love. Ruth, my fourteen-year-old, was supposed to take it out of the fridge and plug in the crock-pot that morning. I stopped Shawn from doing it himself as we were leaving. "She can do it," I said. "Let this be a success experience for her." She had done it, all right, but plugged in the blender instead. Shawn unwound this story into my ear as I stood on the curb in the late afternoon sun. He was laughing. "I have to go," I said. "I am so angry I cannot speak."

Once I'd found my shuttle, I called back. "I'm sorry," I said. "For some reason that just made me furious. It shouldn't be such a big deal. I just feel like why the fuck do I even bother trying?" I was crying—over stew—alone in the white twelve-passenger van while the driver chatted with the cabbies out front.

"Are you okay, baby?" Shawn asked. He asked the same thing this morning, as I was leaving again. Both times I shrugged. "I don't know," and he exhaled, shaking his head: "No."

I tell my supervisor that my papers went well but that people always comment on the writing rather than the content, and I find this—I run out of words—kind of strange. I asked a clever question in each plenary session, and if the point was to build my network so I might someday get an academic job, then I did well. She nods, smiling but a little concerned, waiting to hear what accounts for my hesitation.

I start trying to explain. Flying somewhere unfamiliar leaves me feeling disoriented. It is not just that I feel unsafe when I have no mental map of the place I am navigating; my history of being in a space provides mooring points that anchor me into the terrain. I know how to find things, where things belong, and how to escape. If I drive somewhere new, my orientation and mobility get more dicey, but I still have some agency and confidence: I can go places, even reverse the ribbon of road and find my way home. But when I am coughed up by a plane I have no frame of reference. In this new space, I feel insubstantial, unreal. I am a stranger. The feeling is not liberating or joyful, but it is not entirely unpleasant. It is like a negation, erasure. In this space I don't exist.

I can make this make sense. According to Broks (2003), our minds are "distributed beyond biological boundaries" (p. 101). The presence of familiar others provides us with templates for self-definition, drawing out behavioral repertoires and mental structures. This is how he explains brain-injured patients whose behavior and perceptions are stabilized by the proximity of their loved ones, even if they have no discernible capacity to recognize them. It is not just that my particular history of trauma has left me feeling unsafe in the world (Tamas, 2009, 2011); my brain is compromised by isolation from points of connection.

I can also make sense of this by questioning the line we draw around the social. My subjectivity is not just an abstract, theoretical entity determined by extrinsic, symbolic, discursive, and ideological orders; I emerge from a continual weaving of "multiplicities of bits and pieces" (Anderson & Harrison, 2010, p. 8), which change when I am displaced. The dachshunds, birds, barges, mountains, and the scent of seaweed at low-tide represent a more-than-human world of spaces, things, and affects with primary, constitutive meanings that precede and exceed me (p. 44). My various selves are shadows, cast against matter and shaped by its contours, but this world is no "inert backdrop of brute things" on which I project my hopes, desires, and fears (p. 8); it is filled with the "missing masses" of actors and forces, "some of which we know about, some not, and some of which may be just on the edge of awareness" (p. 12). As 153 pounds of quasi-sentient meat, I exist in relation to non-human spaces and beings driven by other kinds of knowing.

Should I tell my supervisor that I maneuvered a puppet of myself through conference sessions and buffet lines and sat at empty tables to eat? When people approached me—and they did—I responded politely. They were often moved or impressed or grateful for things that I had said. I thanked them, but the performance they were responding to feels only loosely connected to me. Even though I ate the chocolate-dipped strawberries that were in my room when I arrived, I was not there.

I could not recognize myself in those spaces. In a similar, troubling way, I cannot recognize myself in my autoethnographic writing, even though I throw myself into the text, again and again, hoping something like a self will leave its imprint on the page.

What I feel primarily—what I recognize as real—is the charm and peculiarity of things around me. I watch an elderly Tibetan couple walk through the airport as if they are a work of art. They appear to be on a journey that began on some ageless steppe and continues, in running shoes and knapsacks, past Gate 22. Her floral headscarf and his cylindrical hat, their matching compact bodies and walnut faces fill me with something like awe, and I gaze at them fondly, from a distance, knowing that I will write them into my collection of memories. I notice a conference delegate who eats alone at every meal, and sits alone in the hall between sessions, always with the same inward expression on her plain face. Is that what I look like?

Before I can explain any of this to my supervisor, a student knocks on the door to speak with her, and we're done. Then my parking has expired, so it's time for me to pack up and go outside, where it is no longer sunny.

4. THURSDAY

I am in an über-pink shrine of girly consumerism. My cousin is seven hours away in first year university but her makeup and laundry are strewn about as though she plans to be right back. I'll teach a class in this city tomorrow morning and have brunch with my supervisor before heading home. She will ask about the post-doctoral research I am not doing because there is nothing left once I am done mothering and teaching and paying the bills and walking the dogs and applying for professor jobs I won't get in places we can't live. She will be supportive and sympathetic, and then we will talk about her toddler—a watchful, tender creature, soft as a slice of freshly baked white bread.

My back hurts. It has hurt every day for almost four years. I cannot remember what it was like to live in my body before it hurt, but I know that I used to do inconceivable things, like emptying a dishwasher without propping an elbow on the counter. I know it is getting worse by the things that are suddenly problems: putting a suitcase in the overhead bins on the plane, shopping for groceries, digging holes. And now, apparently, sitting cross-legged on a bed for several hours, writing.

Chronic pain reveals the banal awfulness and humiliation of how easily we are felled. Its obdurate constancy combines with diagnostic and prognostic uncertainty to "exceed normalized conventions of rationality" (Bissell, 2010, p. 88). Of course I have tried all the treatments, hoarding my hope for each futile attempt. My MRI indicates three different problems, all or none of which may the culprit. This crippled body has nothing to do with me. She is not welcome at conferences or in my classrooms or on the page, where I need to be smooth and persuasive. I want to leave this frightened, defenseless person at home, where Shawn can help me roll over in bed, smoothing my spine into place like you'd straighten a bed sheet. He covers the dead zone in my back with his big warm hand. We are both powerless. It is indecent, unspeakable.

I find my Naproxen, apologize to my stomach lining, take a breath, and keep going. It is like trying to write with a crying baby in the house.

If the self is not tucked into a slippery nook in our cauliflower brain, we may be tempted to place it in the body. Indeed, the many critics of mind-body dualism would argue that I *am* my body. But which parts? Is my subjectivity equally diffused throughout this assemblage of cells, chemicals, microbes, and partially digested toast and jam? If I am 60 percent water, should I experience water pollution as an assault on my person? What parts of my body could you cut off or alter before I stopped being me? Limbs? Fingernails? Hair? Of course not, we say. Don't be silly. But my father shaved his moustache once, and my mother would not sleep with him until it grew back. He did not look like himself.

I recently learned that one of my colleagues—a witty, articulate, admirable woman—has had a stroke. This feels like being robbed but not yet knowing what we've lost. I imagine Broks (2003) describing a blossom of blood, like a red hibiscus blooming in the neural folds—but maybe there was no hemorrhage; just a brain curled over its stem like a sprout in the dark of a skull gone suddenly airless. I hear Deleuze and Guattari (2004) transposing theories of meaning onto flesh, describing the felted tissue, the unfamiliar emerging selves. Who will she be, once she is not herself again?

I do not want to be my body, this broken wheelbarrow of hungers and pains. My therapist tells me this is because my trauma response is disembodiment; I must learn to feel my feelings, mapping their physical traces, so I can notice without judgment the surges and tides of somaticized affect. I struggle to cast a line of comprehension across this chasm. "You mean," I say, slowly, "I need to learn that feelings are not problems that need fixing?" I get a gold star, but I still don't understand.

The scripture I was raised on would say that I am not my body; I am a soul, a little packet of consciousness that gained identity at the moment of conception and will retain it for the rest of eternity. Its primary function is to reflect divine virtues, like a mirror held up to the sun, so long as I polish off the dust of attachment to material things and animalistic desires.

I lost my faith, along with my marriage, shortly before starting my PhD. A peculiar expression; lost. As if these are separable things I can extract and leave on a bench like my ear-buds. Some lessons are indelible. I can hear my mother chanting, her face mournful: "Imperishable glory I have chosen for thee, but boundless shame thou hast chosen for thyself." I can hear him panting in my ear: "You're a filthy whore. Say it."

My body has done astonishing things: it lactated for four years, turning grubs into miniature humans. It can carry a canoe on a two-kilometer portage. It broadcasts emotion, caressing my daughters' faces when I kiss them goodnight.

It knows more about me than I do. But bodies are not to be trusted; they break down and age and betray.

My uncle calls from downstairs; do I want a cup of tea? I look up; my face is haggard in the room's many mirrors. I pause, considering. Should I keep growing out my hair, or am I too old, on the cusp of forty, for long flowing curls? Even the phrase is ridiculous.

When I was on campus Monday, I bumped into a colleague. "The students say they're not learning anything," he grinned. "So I'm telling them all to take your course after Christmas."

"What?" I said, covering my mouth, aghast. "Oh my God, no pressure." It's my first graduate course, and I have no idea what to do with them.

His eyes were full of mischief. "I tell them you're SMART," he said, leaning in, "and HOT."

I smacked my palm against his forehead. "You do NOT," I said. "I'm going back to my office to cry." I walked away, appalled and flattered. Before going back to my desk, I stopped by the bathroom mirror to see what it means to look hot.

I join my uncle and drink my tea, standing for fifteen minutes in their professionally clean and spacious kitchen, discussing the merits of Russian Caravan (Lapsang, Darjeeling, and China black) versus the Number 22 we had yesterday afternoon (Ceylon green and black with a touch of bergamot for pronounced citrus and floral tones). Then I march myself back upstairs. Quiet, child-free time is too precious to waste on rest; I have to wring every possible word from this interlude. When I get home Ruth will have an air cadet parade on Saturday and a spaghetti supper fundraiser Saturday night and biathlon on Sunday and Dora will have a basketball game Saturday and my dad will be freshly back from Afghanistan with my mum in Moncton so I'll be having him over for supper and we've got to switch my van over to snow tires and put the motorcycle away for the winter and wash the two king-sized duvets that one of the dogs peed on yesterday while the girls were forgetting to walk them. I'll have to prep to teach on Monday and—

I need to stop that line of thought right now.

Can I credibly perform "hot and smart"? Other people seem to think so, sometimes. Who am I to say that they're wrong? Is that self any worse than the chronically tired, whiny person I see now? More to the point: is one of these selves more "authentic"? "Hot and smart" seems like an ill-fitting titanium sheath that some autonomic system slips me into whenever I pass into public spaces where I anticipate scrutiny and judgment. I cover the dark circles under my eyes, as if courage can be bought at the MAC counter, and arrange myself in carefully managed poses. Once upon a time, as a figure drawing model, I did this with my flesh. Now, as an autoethnographer, I do this with my words. The images are never seamless; they leak, unpredictably, but we imagine that what you are seeing is me; that I am more than a crust of skin enclosing a void.

My neuropsychology book describes the case of a woman who did not believe she was real. All she had was words: "just a voice, and if that goes, I won't be anything" (Broks, 2003, p. 101). Just a voice. Is that why I write? Her eventual diagnosis was Hashimoto's disease—a neurological complication of a common autoimmune thyroid disorder, one that I have had for over twenty years.

Instead of wondering about degrees of authenticity, it's more interesting to ask why I feel compelled to push an elusive self onto the stage of published text. Clearly, she is ambivalent about appearing; after all, this writing hurts, and, as I am learning with my recently published book, after it is out there in the world it keeps on hurting. I have wanted to be a writer since I was four years old, hooked by the trick of making something from nothing, conjuring fixity from flux. Writing casts spells of connection without the immediate risks of contact. David Mamet (1998) suggests that we write in order to lessen the gap between our conscious and unconscious minds and thus to feel peace, but there is not, so far, any cathartic release or reconciliation to be had. When people tell me that they love my work, I feel a brief flash of hope before my throat tightens with the worry that I've over-shared, fooled them, and created expectations that I can't possibly fulfill. This, my therapist explains, is how people with low self-esteem respond to compliments.

Liz Bondi (2013) describes the subject position that allows us to observe, symbolize, and reflect on experience in psychoanalytic terms as the "third space." It is achieved in infancy by breaking open our primary relational dyad, but it remains a wobbly work in progress. When it becomes inaccessible, we lose our sense of curiosity and our capacity to think and create; instead, we vacillate between defensiveness and despair. Achieving the third space depends on introducing a gap, like the little balloon the surgeon inserts to open a collapsed artery and restore narrative flow. Ordinarily, we can skip easily across the gap from experience to reflection. However, memories of trauma make this difficult; "We are either fully immersed in the raw experience itself or we are very far away from it" (p. 15). The gap may feel so large that "the third position is impossible because it always misses what is most important, most authentic, and that upon which we seek to reflect" (p. 15). Our words slip off the impermeable surface of the events we're trying to make sense of, and land on the qualities that surround it, such as our "sense of alienation from the world" (p. 15).

Self-representation is a promise I cannot keep. There should be a warning sign on my autoethnographies: mind the gap.

Like the doctor who puts half the brain to sleep in order to see what peeks through from the other side, I am waiting to learn what my writing smuggles out into consciousness. But what are you doing here? Perhaps you are my proxy third space, and I am using you, like a mirror, to peer around the corner of myself, in order to "breach, shatter and overflow horizons of expectation" (Caputo, 2007, p.

22). I am staging an event on the page, to release the grip of the present and open up the future "in a way that makes possible…a new invention of ourselves, even as it awakens dangerous memories" (p. 6). The problem is, I can barely look at you, and if you like me, I don't believe what you see.

Instead, I assume you are beguiled by the public persona who appears in class-rooms and at conferences. She is fabulous; smart, witty, and well put together, prone to laughter, flirting and pithy comments. She has excellent posture and seems happily present, but her popularity is unsustainable. She deflates when I come off-stage and re-inhabit my fretful, busy home self, familiar and dull as a pair of slippers; the hard-working woman who is constantly wiping up a thin dust of despair. But who is this, alone at my desk, writing? Neither shiny nor dull; someone outside of my field of vision who sends me letters and is moved primarily by something like beauty. Her determination is frightening and I don't know where she's going. In the novel *Fugitive Pieces,* the narrator is haunted by his missing sister, who whispers on the other side of a "vibrating, gossamer wall"; he eventually realizes that she is calling him close so she can "push him back out into the world" (Michaels, 1996, p. 170). Is this the function of the writing self—that ghostly, isolated, Derridan subject?

None of them is real. I do not believe in the possibility of rescue, but I can't help hoping that this savage writer is coming to save me.

Yesterday I had a chat with my cousin. He is in his early twenties, freshly back from a Master's degree in England. He wants to write science fiction short stories. We walked their perpetually optimistic dog, and then sat in his room. I was curious and pleased to see what Oxford has done to his mind.

"I think writing is my happiest state," I said. I did not say it can also leave me spent, like the sag between contractions; that it reduces my loved ones to inter-rupting irritants; that I leave the text feeling unsteady; and that this post-partum sensation doesn't dissipate but seems to increase with each piece that I publish.

I read one of his stories. It is charming, a child's ball-pit full of bouncing met-aphors and quirky humor. I remember, when I was seventeen, a writer telling me that my poetry was sentimental. I was devastated. I choose my words with care. I talk about what he likes in the story, encouraging him to join a writer's group, discussing character and connection and carrying the narrative forward. I say I'll send him Laurel Richardson's "Writing: A Method of Inquiry" (2003), and recommend Julia Cameron's *The Artist's Way* (2002). He is spending every day at the university library, writing. The sweetness and courage of this breaks my heart.

I say, write for process, more than outcome. When we write we are writing ourselves, trying on identities, writing who we are becoming. He nods and smiles. I say, I write because it scares me. I do not talk about living with fear; he'll have enough of it. Or not. I do not say that you can fall madly in love with the unbear-able selves that you write, even though you can't tell if they're ruining your life or making it worth living or both.

5. Friday

I am sitting in my fifteen-year-old Toyota minivan, in the car park behind the courthouse, which is the cheapest lot near campus. It is Remembrance Day; soldiers and students with red poppies on their lapels are sifting back to their cars from the service.

During the moment of silence at 11:00 I was entertaining my supervisor's daughter in a restaurant booth, putting small dollops of ketchup and butter and jam and peanut butter on a saucer, giving her my home fries one by one, and saying, "dip, dip."

"She likes you," Joyce said. My capacity to make a game instead of a power struggle out of putting on a snowsuit should be on the first page of my CV. I spent eight years at home with babies. I am not a textbook mother, but right now earning a child's willingness to communicate and play feels more real and gratifying than any publication.

It is easy to wax nostalgic. I remember, when my youngest was that age, trying to write a rhapsodic poem about my children with her tugging at my elbow. After a few frustrating minutes I took her urgent face in my two hands and shouted, "Why do you always NEED?" A thousand daily failures, some of them funny. The mother in me may seem solid but she is no more stable and happy than the rest of me. She is, however, most viscerally connected, flooding with love and madness. Writing this makes me want to rush home to whatever mayhem awaits.

The crisp sunny morning has congealed into cold rain and ice pellets; I turn the van on, every few minutes, to warm up my toes. Soon I will set this nonsense aside, start my audiobook, pull out of my parking spot and turn north.

It's coming down harder, now; white pellets are bouncing on the pavement like hopping bugs, then melting, because the ground still holds the memory of sun. I am waiting for Sophie to write, for the inevitable conclusion to appear. Who will come on stage? What will she have to say?

6. Saturday

I am sitting up in bed. My butt is already numb but I am not moving; in less than an hour I'll have to get up to make supper and before then I need to try again. Until a few minutes ago, Shawn was tucked in beside me, reading this paper aloud, holding each line in his mouth.

"When I've got a new paper," I said, "it's like I've got a child in intensive care, and I need your help reading the medical reports. It's like, between us, we're a writer."

"No," he said, "I don't do anything." Then he carried on, patiently going over the sore spots in the text as if he were finding invisible glass slivers in my skin with the tip of his tongue. He paused when we got to Professor Xavier. "It's not just a headache, you know."

"Really?" I said, "Tell me: what happens?" Smiling at his grasp of the comic-sphere.

"Thank you very much," he continued. "Xavier risks losing himself, his own subjectivity. It's like a pressure. He normally works to keep people out of his head. Their voices are like knives."

Earlier today, I spent a long time crying, parked with Shawn by the river. We were in one of his favorite spots: a small barn, recently built, used once a year for livestock at the fair. We discussed its framing and trusses in the lulls between my existential crises.

"I think writing is going to kill me."

He nodded. "You're feeling way over exposed."

"And am I going to have to write this?" I sobbed. "Does there have to be a Sa - Sa - Saturday?"

He shrugged. "You're a writer."

"No I'm not, I'm not, I just pretend and then I have to be this big smart person and I ca- can't DO it; inside I'm a stupid mean narcissistic housewife." Hiding my snot face behind my hair, fumbling around for a tissue.

"Kiss me," he said, "Never mind wiping your nose."

I leaned into his chest. "I should just get a normal job and stop writing."

"You write because you need to."

"It's not worth it."

There was more: a long, brutal emotional hailstorm that left us both dented but melted on contact, soaking the day but leaving no trace of words on the surface.

7. Sunday

I am back at my desk. Shawn has taken Ruth to biathlon and gone to the gym with Dora. My hands are shaking as I type; this morning Shawn went down, cracking in the jaws of his unrelenting post-traumatic stress disorder. We pass hope between us like a badly swaddled baby. Today it was my turn to hold, and comfort, and make pancakes.

Tomorrow I will teach my third-year qualitative research students about personal narrative. I have assigned three readings; my students' questions on them are due now, at noon. My inbox chimes with one sliding in under the wire as the church bells a block away start to ring.

Their first reading is by Ellis and Bochner (2000)—who deftly show and tell what autoethnography is, and suggest that we write in order to produce coherence—"to make a life that sometimes seems to be falling apart come together again, by retelling and restorying the events of one's life" (p. 746). My unruly cast of selves seems to mock the very possibility of coherence. When I last saw my therapist, she asked how I was doing. "Still not okay," I said. "I keep waiting for things to turn, to start coming together." Alas. Susan Brison's (2002) therapist once told her "it's because you're doing so well…that you're feeling so much worse" (p. 111).

Their second reading is Sherene Razack's (1993) analysis of the power and danger of narrative. I have copied her quote from Trinh Minh-ha into my lecture notes:

> What kind of tale will I choose to tell, and in what voice?…[H]ow do you inscribe difference without bursting into a series of euphoric narcissistic accounts of yourself and your own kind? Without indulging in a marketable romanticism or in a naïve whining about your condition? (cited in Razack, 1993, p. 67).

I don't know: I am guilty of all these sins. Razack suggests the remedy of continual critical reflection on "how we hear, how we speak…the choices we make about which voice to use, when" (p. 68). But this seems so feeble and circular, rearranging the furniture instead of breaking down walls. Critical self-reflection may be all we've got, but it's wrestling with shadows; our voices never offer an originary and present platform for choice and critique (St. Pierre, 2009).

Finally, for the first time, I have assigned one of my own pieces—"Writing and Righting Trauma" (2008). I wrote it as a PhD student, in a rush of frustration over the tidy voices we use to tell our messy autoethnographic tales.

My hands have stopped shaking, but in between words I am biting my nails; an old habit that emerges now only when I am writing.

My article wrestles with the ethics of autoethnography, arguing that it uses an internal god-trick (Haraway, 2003) to turn trauma into knowledge. I describe the troublesome nature of testimony, the tension between its performative and representative functions, and our (misplaced?) faith in empathy. My voice is confident and ironic. I critique our urge to redeem and make sense of loss by packing it up in tidy stories and calling it a career. "Clean and reasonable scholarship about messy, unreasonable experiences is an exercise in alienation," (para. 18) I proclaim. The answer is for us "to write both what and how we actually feel" (para. 19), making

> my voice match my words no matter how much my audience and I just want to be reassured and comforted.…If I can find this voice and the courage to use it, my telling might produce its own kind of knowledge and empathy. It might one day be done. (para. 23)

To illustrate this argument, I wrap it around a story: a breezy version of the breakdown of my marriage.

Now my nine students have read this. Their responses range from barbed generalities—"What constitutes scholarship?"—to the oblique safety of the third person: "Considering our relationship with the author, how does this affect our reading of it?" I click through their emails, collecting their questions. I will use them to structure a class discussion—once I have carried my body into the seminar room and arranged my features and limbs as something resembling an instructor.

I open the last student's letter. She asks decent questions of the first two readings, but then splits the frame:

> Sophie! I just wanted to comment on your piece before asking my question. I was shocked when you revealed that you left your husband. I know that…you

have had a few years since writing that to recover from what happened but I would just like to say that I am so sorry for what you went through. I had no idea that as you have been talking to us about your research regarding victims of spousal abuse and other trauma and all of the hurt that those women were going through, that you were also hurting. I was inspired reading about how you moved forward from such a traumatic experience by researching, reading and developing a new identity for yourself as a scholar… that was really brave (I'm sure that I am just one of many people to say that to you).

And now my question… Do you feel like writing academically and critically about your own traumatic experiences has more cost than benefit for the writer? You mentioned that there is a certain degree of alienation that comes by interpreting your own experiences in such a critical, focused manner. (personal communication, November 13, 2011)

Brave? Inspirational? Hurting? The unbearable weight of those attributions squeezes the air out of me. My work is about the impossibility of recovery, and yet this is what she sees. I have turned my class into an encounter group. If they're extra nice to me I'll probably even cry. How can I answer her question?

I keep typing and deleting expletives, then stop, defeated. Marianne Williamson (1992) points out that "playing small does not serve the world" (p. 190). I saw a women's shelter worker, once, receiving compliments. "I accept, I accept," she said, beaming, as she plucked the words from the air with her hands and pulled them in to her chest.

Last night, as we were emptying the dishwasher, I was explaining a social issue to my daughter. "Most people are not very happy," I said.

"But you are," she replied. "I mean, you have your moments, but you're a happy person." I paused, holding a stack of blue bowls, trying to make room for her knowing, to respect it. Why should only shameful things feel true? Who am I inside her?

Writing to push myself back into the world is necessarily the imperfect work of a lonely ghost, tracing the edges of a subject it can't quite touch. Calling this fraudulent reveals my lingering attachment to a naïve understanding of truth and a fear-based desire for the false safety of control. Autistic primatologist Dawn Eddings Price (forthcoming) would say that instead of using language as a web of connection, I am using words to cut and contain. "None of us are normal," she would whisper and smile; "we are all beyond description." I cannot name the mess or mind the gap without trying to tidy it up, to manage and know, to make my self present and useful. I cannot accept. And yet, here we are. I have become an autoethnographer, writing in the voice that I warned me about.

References

Anderson, B., & Harrison, P. (2010). The promise of non-representational theories. In B. Anderson & P. Harrison (Eds.), *Taking-place: Non-representational theories and geography* (pp. 1–36). London: Ashgate.

Bissell, D. (2010). Placing affective relations: Uncertain geographies of pain. In B. Anderson & P. Harrison (Eds.), *Taking-place: Non-representational theories and geography* (pp. 79–98). London: Ashgate.

Bondi, L. (2013). Research and therapy: Generating meaning and feeling gaps. *Qualitative Inquiry, 19*(1), 9–19.

Brison, S. (2002). *Aftermath: Violence and the remaking of self.* Princeton, NJ: Princeton University Press.

Broks, P. (2003). *Into the silent land: Travels in neuropsychology.* New York: Grove Press.

Cameron, J. (2002). *The artist's way: A spiritual path to higher creativity.* New York: Tarcher/Putnam.

Caputo, J. (2007). *The weakness of God.* Bloomington: Indiana University Press.

Deleuze, G., & Guattari, F. (2004). *Ten thousand plateaus: Capitalism and schizophrenia* (B. Massumi, Trans.). London: Continuum.

Eddings Price, D. (forthcoming). Academic writing as a divisive tool: An autoethnographic reflection on stereotypically autistic tendencies. In J. Davidson & M. Orsinin (Eds.), *Critical autism studies.* Minneapolis: University of Minnesota Press.

Ellis, C., & Bochner, A. P. (2000). Autoethnography, personal narrative, reflexivity. In N. K. Denzin & Y. S. Lincoln (Eds.), *Handbook of qualitative research* (2nd ed., pp. 733–768). Thousand Oaks, CA: Sage.

Haraway, D. (2003). Situated knowledges: The science question in feminism and the privilege of partial perspective. In N. K. Denzin & Y. S. Lincoln (Eds.), *Turning points in qualitative research: Tying knots in a handkerchief* (pp. 21–46). Walnut Creek, CA: AltaMira Press.

Jackson, A. Y., & Mazzei, L. A. (2008). Experience and "I" in autoethnography: A deconstruction. *International Review of Qualitative Research, 1,* 299–318.

Mamet, D. (1998). *Three uses of the knife: On the nature and purpose of drama.* New York: Vintage.

Michaels, A. (1996). *Fugitive pieces.* Toronto, ON: McClelland & Stewart.

Razack, S. (1993). Storytelling for social change. *Gender and Education, 5,* 55–70.

Richardson, L. (2003). Writing: A method of inquiry. In N. K. Denzin & Y. S. Lincoln (Eds.), *Turning points in qualitative research: Tying knots in a handkerchief* (pp. 379–396). Walnut Creek, CA: AltaMira Press.

Singer, B. *X-Men.* 20th Century Fox, July 2000.

St. Pierre, E. A. (2009). Afterword: Decentering voice in qualitative inquiry. In A. Jackson & L. Mazzei (Eds.), *Voice in qualitative inquiry* (pp. 221–236). Abingdon, UK: Routledge.

Tamas, S. (2008). Writing and righting trauma: Troubling and autoethnographic voice. *FQS: Forum Qualitative Social Research, 10,* retrieved from www.qualitative-research.net/index.php/fqs/article/view/1211/2642

Tamas, S. (2009). Three ways to lose your epistemology. *International Review of Qualitative Research, 2,* 43–60.

Tamas, S. (2011). *Life after leaving: The remains of spousal abuse.* Walnut Creek, CA: Left Coast Press, Inc.

Williamson, M. (1992). *A return to love: Reflections on the principles of a course in miracles.* New York: Harper Collins.

Wylie, J. (2010) Non-representational subjects? In B. Anderson & P. Harrison (Eds.), *Taking-place: Non-representational theories and geography* (pp. 99–118). London: Ashgate.

Section Two

Making and Relating

Section Two Introduction

Cool Kids on the Quad

H. L. (Bud) Goodall, Jr.

> The tensions that guide the ethnographic writer's hand lie between the felt improbability of what you have lived and the known impossibility of expressing it, which is to say between desire and its unresolvable, often ineffable, end.
>
> – H. L. Goodall, Jr. (2000)

> To be a convincing "I-witness," one must, so it seems, first become a convincing "I."
>
> –Clifford Geertz (1989)

Writing about how autoethnographers "make and relate" their texts is one of the distinguishing features of qualitative theory and research. This bald-faced fact in a research world where facts are rare should not, however, be surprising to anyone familiar with the history of ethnography (Manganaro, 1990). From Malinowski's debt to Joseph Conrad (complicated by his diary's admission of how he really felt about relating to the natives) to Geertz's genre-blurring cockfight (complicated by how he and his wife were ignored "as wind" by the Balinese) to Ellis's text-book-as-novel (complicated by her relationships to the students and their work), ethnographers have always placed a high value on literary style that evokes as well as represents "what happened" while they were in the company of others. It is,

Handbook of Autoethnography, edited by Stacy Holman Jones, Tony E. Adams, and Carolyn Ellis, 204–208. © 2013 Left Coast Press, Inc. All rights reserved.

then, how they/we accomplish those two goals that is worthy of our scholarly and aesthetic attention (Ellis & Bochner, 2002).

Creating and relating in texts of all kinds—from articles and books to poems, performances, and images; and these days from e-books to blogs and websites—regardless of where we write or publish, the issue of *how we represent and evoke the research process and outcomes* must be either stylistically self-evident or in some way discussed (Goodall, 2008). Inquiring minds want *to know.* Students want to learn *how to.* And readers want to feel that the person telling these tales is credible (Geertz, 1989), not just as a trained observer/participant in a social world, but also as a narrator—a writer—who shows us how he or she *"got there,"* or what Ron Pelias calls how we write "to realization" (Pelias, 2011). Choices about the making of texts are therefore intimately bound up with choices about *how we represent* how we relate to those we write about as well as what we learned in the field (Van Maanen, 1988).

For the authors in this section of the *Handbook*, each one offering her or his own style of "making and relating," we see a diverse range of "places" and "practices" for the craft of personal narrative reflection about how they do these acts. These chapters offer us old and new ways to think creatively about an author's articulation of her or his personal and epistemic standpoint in relation to the story or report as well as the communities studied; the deployment of a "voice" to represent the author's character; concern for the often complex and always problematic relational ethics involved in revealing (and concealing) secrets; the always complicated relationship between selves and others, selves and communities; and—this one is relatively new to autoethnographic discourse—the institutional constraints on relating to others and representing that relationship that must be navigated by researchers in their appeal for approval of a research plan.

The exemplars also range widely across forms of showing and telling about selves, histories, relationships, the challenges of collaborative writing, and African-American spirituality. So it is that "making and relating" becomes a special case of textual reflexivity (Ellis & Bochner, 2000). Yet here that rhetorical move to personal reflection about the how and why of it—usually associated in qualitative writing with straightforward claims made from reasoned arguments—becomes more nuanced, messier, and (perhaps) even more likely to inspire critical dialogic engagement with readers through its expression as poetry, story, jointly authored quest, and the personal and community transformations of queer through drag.

I don't have the available space to introduce each piece separately or to treat them as an assemblage of related themes that somehow add up to a coherent whole. They do not add up to a coherent whole. Nor should they. So instead I will use what space I have to frame some general concerns raised in these chapters, albeit in my own way.

Let's put it this way: It's all about being the Cool Kids on the Quad.

○

We have long understood that how a text is written is as important as what is written about. Style is not something novel added to an argument; style *is* the argument in contemporary nonfiction (Anderson, 1987). Or by analogy, as Art Bochner (1994) famously has it, "story *is* theory." Hence, our overt concern with "making and creating" texts—from language and structural considerations (Ellis, 2004; Goodall, 2000, 2008; Richardson, 2000) to how the voice narrating the story "seduces" readers by revealing "what it is like to live this way" (Goodall, 2009; Worth, 2004, 2005, 2008)—is as important as what is written about. That's why, among the otherwise mostly staid prose of the social sciences, we are the cool kids on the quad.

But us cool kids with literary habits of mind are also usually burdened by a hyper-awareness of two things: (1) *the nature of meaning in relation to discovered truths about ourselves and others in our composed social worlds*; and of (2) *ourselves as the "makers" of those social worlds, ourselves as storytellers.*

Our cool is thus partly a chilly realization of the symbolic power of a well-told tale to be read and interpreted as a revealed truth, and with that drop in temperature the sudden loneliness that comes from feeling that the task of truth-telling may be a little bit above our skill level. For no matter how well we write, no matter how deep our local knowledge, no matter how adept we are at collecting and coding data, the proof of our abilities will be words (and maybe images) on a page of our own making.

I'm not usually a fan of the phrase "what it comes down to is," but this time I think the common concern expressed, worried over, elaborated, complicated, and thoroughly explored in the following chapters does, in fact, come down to this "making and relating" theme: *When we write about others, who are we to do that? What gives us the right? What drives us to write in the first place? And is our imposition of self into a context of others for the purpose of inquiry of the most intimate kind itself a questionable act?*

Joan Didion (1976) questions her own writing this way:

> In many ways writing is the act of saying I, of imposing oneself upon other people, of saying *listen to me, see it my way, change your mind*. It's an aggressive, even hostile act. You can disguise its aggressiveness all you want with veils of subordinate clauses and qualifiers and tentative subjunctives, with ellipses and evasions—with the whole manner of intimating rather than claiming, of alluding rather than stating—but there's no getting around the fact that setting words on paper is the tactic of a secret bully, an invasion, an imposition of the writer's sensibility on the reader's most private space. (pp. 17–18)

It's the chain of words at the end of that paragraph that either imprisons us or at least gives us pause. Not only do we not want to think of ourselves and our writing as the work of a bully, we don't want our writing—regardless of how careful/ethical/IRB approved/friendly we are—to be invasive for either our subjects or our readers. We are nice people. We only want to learn and through our writing share what we have discovered. We all believe that our first rule of conduct in the field and in our writing is the qualitative research version of the Hippocratic Oath to "do no harm." Cool kids care. What then, to do?

One result of this hyper-awareness has been a critical and cultural take on an alphabet-soup of influences on our standpoint as researchers, our epistemic and ontic self-reflexivity, and our obsession—for that is what it is—with how we represent and evoke what James Agee (1941, p. 9) calls "the cruel radiance of what is." (1941). One result of that critical cultural take is a furtherance of a "sunny side of the street" evolution in our ethnographic understanding of the relational ethics and institutional constraints that should light and guide our best practices by reflexively showing not just what we did in the field, but how and why we did it.

But there is also a "dark side" to our evolution. It is a dark side that, like the interconnected and interdependent wrap of that well-known black-and-white Tao yin-and-yang image, reminds us that we hold both the good and the bad in our own hands as writers, and that this is a good thing because each one gives rise to the necessity of the other. It is part of our job as scholarly storytellers to reveal both the good and bad—our conflicted selves in the context of conflicted others—sometimes through questions we raise but cannot adequately answer; sometimes through deeds we witness but do not condone; sometimes through our own troubled complicity; and sometimes through the sound of our voices, as we choke or hesitate or stutter or fail to find the right words to deal with not only Agee's "the cruel radiance of what is," but moreover the sometimes crueler radiance of what and how we come to know.

I've run out of space here so I have to go. But no worries. Those influences and how we story, how we imagine, and how we make into poetry that cruel radiance, are explored in detail in the following chapters.

Cool kids. Hard questions. We hang at the quad. Discuss.

References

Agee, J. (1941). *Let us now praise famous men: Three tenant families.* Boston: Houghton Mifflin.

Anderson, C. (1987). *Style as argument: Contemporary American nonfiction.* Carbondale: Southern Illinois University Press.

Bochner, A. P. (1994). Perspectives on inquiry II: Theories and stories. In M. Knapp & G. Miller (Eds.), *Handbook of interpersonal communication* (2nd ed., pp. 21–41). Newbury Park, CA: Sage.

Bochner, A. P., & Ellis, C. (2002). *Ethnographically speaking: Autoethnography, literature, and aesthetics.* Walnut Creek: CA: AltaMira Press.

Didion, J. (1976, December). Why I write. *New York Times Magazine,* 17–18. Retrieved July 5, 2012, at www.idiom.com/~rick/html/why_i_write.htm

Ellis C. (2004). *The ethnographic I: A methodological novel about autoethnography*. Walnut Creek, CA: AltaMira Press.

Ellis, C. (2007). Relational ethics in research with intimate others. *Qualitative Inquiry, 13*, 3–29.

Ellis, C., & Bochner, A. P. (2000). Autoethnography, personal narrative, reflexivity: Researcher as subject. In N. K. Denzin & Y. S. Lincoln (Eds.), *The handbook of qualitative research* (2nd ed., pp. 733–768). Thousand Oaks, CA: Sage.

Geertz, C. (1989). *Works and lives: The anthropologist as author*. Palo Alto, CA: Stanford University Press.

Goodall, Jr., H. L. (2000). *Writing the new ethnography*. Walnut Creek, CA: AltaMira Press.

Goodall, Jr., H. L. (2008). *Writing qualitative inquiry*. Walnut Creek, CA: Left Coast Press, Inc.

Goodall, Jr., H. L. (2009). Writing like a guy in Textville: A personal reflection on narrative seduction. *International Review of Qualitative Research, 2*, 67–88.

Manganaro, M. (1990). *Modernist anthropology: From fieldwork to text*. Princeton, NJ: Princeton University Press.

Pelias, R., (2011). *Leaning: A poetics of personal relations*. Walnut Creek, CA: Left Coast Press, Inc.

Richardson, L. (2000). Writing: A method of inquiry. In N. K. Denzin & Y. S. Lincoln (Eds.), *The handbook of qualitative research* (2nd ed., pp. 923–948). Thousand Oaks, CA: Sage.

Van Maanen, J. (1988). *Tales of the field: On writing ethnography*. Chicago: University of Chicago Press.

Worth, S. E. (2004). Narrative understanding and understanding narrative. *Contemporary Aesthetics*, 2, N.P. Retrieved July 5, 2012, from www.contempaesthetics.org/newvolume/pages/article.php?articleID=237

Worth, S. E. (2005). Narrative knowledge: Knowing through storytelling. MIT 4: Fourth Media in Transition Conference, Cambridge, MA, May 6. Retrieved July 5, 2012, from web.mit.edu/commforum/mit4/subs/mit4_abstracts.html#worth

Worth, S. E. (2008). Story-telling and narrative knowing. *Journal of Aesthetic Education, 42*, 42–55.

Chapter 9

Spinning Autoethnographic Reflexivity, Cultural Critique, and Negotiating Selves

Keith Berry

In 1982, complete with music and wardrobe, I spun like Wonder Woman during fifth grade recess and lived to talk about it. I was an eleven-year-old boy with adult-like seriousness, which meant commitment and planning. Securing the music was easy, as I had just received a double-decker, double-cassette boom box for Christmas. When no one in my family was looking, it only took a few tries of holding its tiny microphone to our 19" Zenith to capture the theme music that opened the hit television show. Acquiring the wardrobe was different. Wonder Woman typically wore star-spangled nylon shorts and cape, a golden Lasso of Truth, bullet-proof bracelets, golden tiara, and bright red knee-high boots. I opted for a tight-fitting pair of shorts, a white clothes hanger rope lasso attached to my belt, gray duct tape bracelets, and a light blue nylon jacket-cape. Imagination filled in the rest of the details. I was a young boy pursuing a mission that would come to shape me personally, culturally, and reflexively.

Wonder Woman was a "princess warrior" transplanted from Paradise Island to Washington, DC, where she lived under the alias of Diana Prince and worked for the government tackling World War II evils. She possessed superhuman strength and a handy invisible airplane. Whenever she needed to transform into Wonder Woman, her secret identity, Diana Prince would extend her arms to her sides and spin. Each spin, each transformation, was accompanied by music and explosions as dynamic as the injustices she confronted.

Handbook of Autoethnography, edited by Stacy Holman Jones, Tony E. Adams, and Carolyn Ellis, 209–227. © 2013 Left Coast Press, Inc. All rights reserved.

I was a young White Chicagoan being reared by loving parents of differing backgrounds (Mom is a retired teacher of German descent; Dad is a retired roofer and Irish), taught to work hard, be kind, and feel grateful for all I had. I was also a chubby and sensitive boy whose secret identity, my own inner princess, remained unacknowledged and under-nurtured. I was someone not comfortable with playing as I saw other boys doing, and often felt I was different than others. I was someone who, at times, would have benefited from becoming invisible.

I remember that spin as if it were yesterday: How I was sure to locate myself on the concrete area of the playground and close to my favorite teacher, Miss Cheek, and a handful of chatting, presumably safe(r), female classmates; how I was happy the boys were playing a robust and distracting game of kickball away on the grass; and how, in that moment, the ways I typically had lived fell away from my being.

I pressed play on the boom box and, as if in slow motion, felt the shifting of how those others around me appeared; how, in that moment, I related to those bodies and beings. I closed my eyes and began to spin, slowly at first, but soon swiftly and more loosely. As the music and wind picked up, my face blushed and smile increased. My cape floated to the ground from the force of my imaginary blast. Although my eyes remained closed, I still could see others. I saw them seeing me, and then me seeing them seeing me, spinning gracefully and happily. I spun in that space of excitement and risk, compelled to continue, and carried by the winds, the energy cultivated from movement, and the theme song's chorus, *"You're a wonder, Wonder Woman!"*

Wonder Woman's story compelled me to perform in ways that unsettled my young cultural being. Through spinning I explored being a particular boy, a counter-normative boy within cultural spaces that lived sex/gender conventionally. I spun unaware of my being attracted to the same sex, yet aware I did not like girls as other boys seemed to like them. Indeed, that spinning displayed my difference and aspects of difference previously unknown or kept invisible. Through spinning I called out to others, seeking change, comfort, and company.

Miss Cheek called Mom, alerting her to my performance. Mom tells me she replied, "If it makes him happy, what does it hurt?" I wrote Lynda Carter, who played Wonder Woman, telling her proudly of the spin and my love for her. Her reply must still be in the mail.

o

I begin with this account, told in this way, because I believe it is a helpful entry point for reflecting on the dual focuses of the chapter: reflexivity and identity negotiation. In what follows, I describe ways researchers have engaged reflexivity in autoethnography that pursues cultural critique. Of particular interest is how reflexivity enables a transformation of selves, or how autoethnography can change autoethnographers. I also convey narrative fragments to illustrate struggles in negotiating LGBTQ identity that have been common, and that, for many, still persist today. I spin to show how reflexivity dynamically serves autoethnography and autoethnographers and contributes to a complex pursuit of hope and joy, amid struggle.

Cultural inquiry begins having already begun, with a confluence of past, present, and anticipated future influences informing any given moment. That is, the selection of intellectual starting points is always in process, and, thus, contingent and uncertain (Schrag, 1997). I "begin" here in ways that draw together hermeneutic phenomenology and autoethnography and assume culture and cultural identity to be the outcomes of situated and (inter)subjectively constituted interaction, processes complexly dwelling in and outside our awareness.

As critical cultural inquiry this chapter suggests how scholarship should be directed to something larger than us. I work to do more uncovering of cultural practices and their meanings, and to amplify possibilities for (re)imagining the complexities inherent to reflexivity and cultural identity. As such, I write

…for persons who, like me, are allured by the ways reflexivity functions in autoethnography, both shaping research and researchers in humane and vital ways;

…to better understand how cultural identities are not just formed but "negotiated" (Jackson, 2002), thus, stressing how becoming and being ourselves can be tenuous;

…frightened by the increased bullying of LGBTQ youth (Kosciw, Greytak, Diaz, & Bartkiewicz, 2010), and hopeful that life writing can help increase awareness and motivate more compassionate and inclusive relating (see Savage & Miller, 2011).

I reflexively explore reflexivity, believing a mindful understanding of its place and power in autoethnography means getting as close to that experience as possible. The processes are too complex, the stakes are too high, to examine from a distance. I offer my story as a voice for others immersed in their own negotiations, and perhaps in need of a story to which to cling. I convey this story, my spin on spinning, knowing that across our lives, some spins are encouraged and others discouraged, and some spinners are deemed more worthy of inclusion and love than others. I spin knowing that we are always already spinning, and sometimes in distressing ways.

Reflexive Autoethnographic Doing and Making

Like all ethnography, autoethnography is a discursive accomplishment, a spinning whose rotations personify a commitment to experimentation, evocation, and scholarly voice. This discourse is situated in processes of production (Fabian, 2002), dynamic and prolific and "historicizing" processes (Berry & Warren, 2009) that call us to examine how our work represents/constructs culture (Clifford & Marcus, 1986) and, consequently, risks "speaking for" others (Alcoff, 1991/1992).

Reflexivity is a contested concept and methodological strategy dwelling at the heart of autoethnography and cultural critique (Berry & Clair, 2011). Understanding and working reflexively often are complex, knotty, and uncomfortable processes (see Finlay, 2002; Pillow, 2003; Spry, 2011). Reflexivity calls us to trouble in our research the relationship between researchers' "selves" and "others," typically non-self others, a focus that has been explored with creative depth and breadth (see Alexander, 2009; Denzin, 1997; Pelias, 2011). It means spinning in the correlative space between the two, insofar as constituting experience entails an interaction between the understanding we bring and the phenomena presenting themselves to us through the spinning. Indeed, autoethnographic conversations are "partial, partisan, and problematic" (Goodall, 2000, p. 55). Thus, reflexivity entails taking seriously the self's location(s) in culture and scholarship, circumspectly exploring our relationship to/in autoethnography, to make research and cultural life *better* and *more meaningful.*

Schrag's (2003) "communicative praxis" is a philosophical and rhetorical way of understanding the constitution of lived experience that I believe is instructive when thinking of reflexivity in autoethnographic discourse. Praxis, for Schrag (2003), is a "holistic space…in which the performances of speech, writing, and action are situated" (p. 137). It entails doing, performing, and accomplishing; in this sense, the constitution of understanding of our interactions, worlds, and persons who come into being through these experiences. "Communicative praxis," he writes, "displays a referential moment (about a world of human concerns and social practices), a moment of self-implicature (by a speaker, author, or actor), and a rhetorical moment (directedness to the other)" (p. viii). Therefore, praxis is a process entailing a convergence of influences by/among topic(s), author(s), and audience(s).

Of particular interest within Schrag's (2003) position are the ways subjects experience communicative praxis, specifically how our "self-implicature" informs how we understand experience and ourselves. Far from innocent or objective bystanders who stand at the margins of experience, presumably as experience constitutes itself, subjects are always "in" praxis, and we have a personal stake in the interpretive processes of experience. We are "held within a web of delivered discourse, social practices, professional requirements, and the daily decisions of everyday life" (p. 4). In turn, subjects emerge from the "human dramas of discourse and social practices" (p. 138) co-constituted by ourselves and others; hence, subjects make and are made by praxis. We emerge as "an event or happening that continues the conversation and social practices of [human kind] and inscribes its contributions on their textures" (p. 121). In this sense, communicative praxis underscores a processual understanding of how subjects are (re)constituted through the situated spaces of doing comprising cultural lives. For better or worse, our emergence is always and already ongoing and subject to reconsideration and revision.

Autoethnography provides a vivid instantiation of how cultural beings are implicated in communicative praxis or, for the purpose of this chapter, the spinning of autoethnographic praxis. Therefore, I next explore how our being embedded in autoethnographic praxis allows for a dynamic immersion into culture and cultural critique, as well as the potential for researchers' transformations of selves—certainly an intriguing and intimate mode of scholarly spinning.

Most autoethnographic praxis entails scholars revealing and prioritizing how we are present in, or move through, culture. In fact, the work tends to be poorly done without the skillful exploration of this presence. Autoethnographic reflexivity is the impassioned process whereby autoethnographers use and play with our implicature to render meaningful accounts. Interestingly, the process of reflexively engaging this presence, in effect, also immerses researchers in the reflexive (and additionally implicating) process of writing. Thus, at once, autoethnography shows how we are in our work and further locates subjects within the complexities of the craft, thereby discursively creating additional ripples of reflexivity (and complexity) to which we must attend.

Attending to our location in culture in these ways entails negotiating social constraints, dimensions to this spinning occurring in at least two ways: At one level, autoethnography requires selecting some stories for use over others, and myriad other decisions about representation. I think here of how including in our scholarship the experiences of cleaning a mother's buttocks because she is no longer able to do so for herself (Ellis, 1996), or seeing smears of a mother's make-up remain on the wall after her husband pushed her face into it (Adams, 2006). These moments aspire to reconcile what feels necessary in representation with others' (e.g., readers') expectations concerning which experiences are appropriate, and at whose expense. Yet, at another level, still today, this research often is talked about as a "novel" path, in part, because of its difference within/from the larger ethnographic community. Moreover, it is commonly marked in relation to what it is not (i.e., objectivist ethnography) (see Alexander, 2011). This social comparison is accentuated by ethical considerations on how autoethnographers are challenged to account for this work with/for others, and by how the heightened transparency and emotion in autoethnography call for the heightened engagement of others (Bochner & Ellis, 2006).

A most compelling aspect of autoethnographic praxis relates to how its reflexive and emotional accomplishments enable a social constitution of the public/cultural fabric and the individual. By its nature, this praxis entails drawing on reflexivity to situate culture and cultural persons as distinctive, dynamic, and fluid, and to engender possibilities for imagining not just what is, but what could be. Indeed, autoethnographic reflexivity "lives for maybe" (Pelias, 2004, p. 12). In what follows, I offer a focused review of autoethnographic scholarship, looking at some of the ways this constitutive process appears through reflexivity.

This reflexive potential appears in autoethnographies tackling difficult issues, such as "coming out," whether as gay (Adams, 2011; Berry, 2013) or atheist (Myers, 2012), insipid pressures of an ambivalent pregnancy (Faulkner, 2012), hardship in a post-recession job market (Herrmann, 2012), and secrecy/shame concerning bulimia (Tillmann, 2009a). Interacting with evocative accounts like these can implicate readers' orientations to the given topic(s), inviting a chance to respecify what we presumed to be true and important about culture and the ways we represent issues. Spinning stories autoethnographically can effectively announce that non-conventional spinners dwell and thrive outside the mainstream and that diverse modes of doing cultural inquiry are alive, thriving, and awaiting our consideration and experimentation.

This constitutive potential also shows in praxis seeking critical ends, in which scholars join reflexivity with the overt and sustained goal of advocating social reform, often by uncovering power imbalances and cultural oppression. The work challenges us to perform by "making the personal political" (Holman Jones, 2005), indeed, a spinning that accentuates possibilities for a critical reflexivity (see Alexander, 2009; Madison, 2011; Spry, 2006).

Dynamic instances of critically oriented autoethnography show a range of issues being interrogated, such as the negotiation of Whiteness (Warren, 2003), marriage equality (Tillmann, this volume), Black female identity (Boylorn, 2013); tensions embedded with getting Latina/o performance heard in academic journals (Calafell & Moreman, 2009), postcolonial discourses of home and exile (Chawla & Rodriguez, 2011), and critical communication pedagogy (Fassett & Warren, 2007). These discourses advocate for a more thorough examination of how we organize and understand ourselves and others, to the benefit of some and disadvantage of others. They call us to (re)imagine ways for building more inclusive spaces and movement for all cultural bodies.

Indeed, reflexivity diversely troubles ways of understanding and investigating culture. By more transparently playing with how we are "in" this praxis, autoethnographers have made available cultural portraits previously unavailable and, at times, unimaginable. Yet within the flurried spinning of this research dwells another dimension that draws us to look at how reflexivity enables a social constitution for autoethnographers at more personal/individual levels.

Making Autoethnographers

Langsdorf's (2002) "communicative poiesis" explores the potential for persons to creatively perform ourselves within the space of Schrag's (2003) praxis. Communicative poiesis occurs through two dimensions of making.

> One dimension is the making of things—spatiotemporally existant entities—which are the intrinsic product of poiesis. The second is the constituting of self in performances that may also produce things. The subjectivity that comes into being in the space of communicative praxis is the extrinsic, or transcendent, result of poiesis. (p. 282)

Hence, in making "things" (buildings, paintings, relationships), we also can come to be different persons. Put differently, as we produce cultural accounts (autoethnographic texts, performances, criticisms, and so forth), we can perform or make ourselves anew.

For example, I am at my first Gay Pride Parade in Chicago, standing at the intersection of Halsted and Belmont, eyes wide open. Cultural discourse envelops me: rainbow flags appearing on windows, t-shirts and body parts; dance beats pumping loudly in ways that stress celebration; and parade goers yelling provocatively and flirtatiously to scantily dressed and dancing go-go boys on floats for nightclubs, or with stirring applause for Parents, Family and Friends of Lesbians and Gays (PFLAG), or with jeers and laughs at drag queens dressed as right-wing Republicans. As I participate in these activities—helping craft the "intrinsic products" in Chicago Gay Pride poiesis—I experiment with cultural practices and meanings and begin appropriating some of them into my life. Over time these experiences allow for related ways of performing as a gay man. I come to understand myself as living with celebratory, frustrated, appreciative, scared, and political selves—complex and reflexive "extrinsic results" of poiesis.

Poiesis extends the position that praxis is about, by, and for someone, suggesting it is also for the persons enacting the praxis themselves, thus evoking a sense of an emerging self-as-other. The performances of poiesis allow the self "to appropriate alternative meanings that were created in his or her own communicative praxis.... The emergent self comes to know itself as capable of more than—and even, as other than—its own history" (p. 285). Therefore, within praxis exists the potential for persons—through rhetorical engagement with others—whether deliberately or tacitly, to create and utilize alternative selves. "Instead of merely 'making do,'" Langsdorf (2002) writes, "the emergent self's praxis can realize those possibilities and thereby engage in the *making* of self, rather than continuing to *do* what the self of past experiences did" (p. 287, emphasis in original). Thus, the experiences of poiesis within praxis offer an opportunity, a potential, to do and be in ways that, without this situated action, would not be possible.

This (re)constituting potential in the spinning of autoethnographic reflexivity tends to work in at least two directions. On the one hand, readers or audience members who engage others' autoethnographic scholarship are often rhetorically implicated through the engagement, presenting a need to reconsider and therein potentially transform how we understand ourselves and our cultural worlds (see Alexander, 2009; Berry, 2006; Goltz, 2011; Tillmann, 2009b).

On the other hand, the potential for autoethnographers to creatively (re)make *ourselves* is also present. It comes alive through the panoply of rhetorical practices often comprising the research: informal/formal conversations and interviews and everyday interaction; reflections on what has been, is now, and might be in the future; complex processes of (co)constructing narratives; working experimentally with ideas and choices for representation; and negotiating complex emotions and thoughts. This potential for change has been described in a number of ways, such as epiphanies (Denzin, 1988), catharsis (Ellis, 2004), healing (DeSalvo, 1999), reinvention (hooks, 1999), and transformative learning (Boyd, 2008). Indeed, as Tomaselli, Dyll, and Francis (2008) tell graduate students prior to fieldwork: "You will be changed" (p. 347). For me it is a more subtle change possible over time and for all spinners. We see through Ellis's (2007) (re)visiting how past choices in her fieldwork inadvertently hurt participants with whom she had personal relationships. She explores how those experiences now help her to understand "relational ethics" in more complex ways, an orientation made possible through reflexive praxis.

Spinning reflexivity can create an opening for how we understand ourselves. For instance, we see changes in "starting points" and the assumptions and expectations informing our spinning that might have felt essential at one time, yet no longer feel familiar; shifts in how we identify as autoethnographers and with the method itself; and variations in who we understand ourselves and others to be—resilient and weak, thriving and suffering, powerful and helpless, encouraged and disheartened, pretty and ugly, and worthy and excluded. The possibility for change, the chance to understand ourselves more closely, and to re-reflect on what was and who we were, in contrast to what is and who we are now, is one of autoethnography's greatest gifts.

○

It has been over thirty years since my spinning as Wonder Woman. I have been aware of my attraction to other men since my late teens; yet, awareness should not necessarily suggest an openness and smooth movement in negotiating identity. I next spin narrative fragments of my experience as a gay man. Each can be read as an individual moment and as contributing to what I hope is a meaningful portrait of LGBTQ culture and identity, and what it might look like to pursue this portrait reflexively.[1] I spin this cultural critique because, while I have yet to perform a formal encore of this performance, the spinning inherent to that moment—the negotiations within its rotations—have persisted in distinct ways across many facets of my life.

○

I am standing in the kitchen with my best friend, Robert, and his brother Michael, on a night in my early twenties. Their family always exudes love toward me as an honorary family member. Having come from work and feeling hungry, I ask them if I may eat one of their bananas. As is often the case, I want to make them laugh. Once I have peeled it, I engulf the banana dramatically, in the most full-throated way possible. This draws loud laughs from them, laughs accompanied by their looking at each other, as if to confirm what they just witnessed.

I had not been "out" to Robert at the time and fear what his response will be when I tell him. I recently agreed to be the best man at his wedding and felt honored and excited. Later that night, as I try to fall asleep, I begin ruminating. I think about what outing myself to Robert might look like, my stumbling through the words, holding back tears, and racing clumsily to the presumed finish line, "I... um, am... well, I'm not straight." I envision him kicking me out of the wedding party and the family, and my sneaking in the back of the church to see the ceremony. It is a vision that would recur persistently that year, powerful viscerally and emotionally.

I had long since been an ardent ruminator (see Berry, 2007). As a child, I would try to sleep, and when I couldn't, I would go to the room where Mom was watching television. "Mom," I would say in a frustrated and sullen voice, "I cannot fall asleep!" Putting down her newspaper, Mom would respond, "Just think of nothing." "It'll be okay, sweetie," she would say, as she returned to her paper and television, and as I returned to my room, frustrated because I figured this would not help. You see, thinking of nothing, for me, entailed thinking about thinking about nothing, and how that felt impossible, only propelling more rumination.

In the middle of the night of the banana incident, I wake up yelling and in pain. I am living in my parents' basement, and my bed is positioned alongside one of the paneled walls. It is the type of paneling that, if you fiddle with it even slightly, sharp splinters of wood become exposed. I soon trace the pain to my left wrist, and, after turning on the light, find blood on my wrist and my sheets and small shreds of paneling on my bed. I sit up groggy and shaken. I am sure nightmares led me to bash my wrist against the wall.

That next day I take Polaroid pictures of my wrist and the visible marks my nightmare had created. Never having contemplated suicide before, I was scared and did not want to forget.

○

It is 1997, and I am a new graduate teaching assistant. I am eager yet green, teaching my first section of the introductory course. As part of an activity exploring self-disclosure, students and I write down on slips of paper our "deepest secret." We'll share them as a group.

As I make my way through the pile of secrets, relaying them to the class one by one, we learn of unusual habits, desires to have a variety of superhuman strengths, and sexual secrets.

When I come to the end of the entries, I quickly skim the next secret's message: "I think all gay people should be put on an island and blown up." I pause in horror, placing the slip of paper to my side. I say, "Let's talk about what we're doing next time." I don't share the secret. I am unequipped and fear announcing it will create a spectacle, rather than a learning moment. Skipping that secret would mean that it does not exist.

○

When I came out as gay more than fifteen years ago I was not jettisoned from my family or a wedding party. The event of coming out was largely met by deep and genuine love.

When I came out, I could no longer pass in the same ways. I could not as easily hide behind the homophobic jokes that once veiled my sexuality, because others knew, thus, rendering those jokes incoherent, contradictory, and hyp-ocritical. I knew who I loved, so the same jokes no longer worked, unless I preferred to continue passing in that way and to battle the self-scrutiny that often would result.

When I came out, I began looking at the world differently. I began seeing the same stereotypical and marginalizing representations of gay folks in television and movies. Yet I no longer could laugh them off as easily as I had in the past, for I would be laughing at myself. I began not knowing how to reconcile a few family members' homophobic jokes that, although far less numerous since my coming out, persisted. I could no longer laugh them off or ignore them in the same ways; because I was out to them, the homophobia, joking or not, felt more personal. I began seeing ways in which I was shifting from passing to covering, the toning down, or making less obtrusive, my sexuality (Yoshino, 2007; see Glave, 2003). I naively believed that being gay is one thing, but not being "too gay" was still important. I was a "straight-acting" gay man who believed the ways I carried myself effectively reinforced this ideal: chest up, no swoosh of the hips when walking, and limited eye contact time with other men I did not know.

Before coming out, I thought a yellow brick road was on the other side of the closet; once out, problems would be alleviated. When I came out, I traded one set of challenges for another.

o

For some time I have been interested in the ways men who love men, or at least men who are sexually attracted to men, orient themselves toward each other through highly aestheticized bodies (Berry, 2007; see Santoro, 2012). In the bathhouse context, a situated cultural space I believe points to a pattern within the larger gay male community, many men tend to privilege and engage hyper-idealized bodies. Tan, tight/thin, and smooth (that is, hairless) bodies. I have accounted for my negotiation in bathhouse praxis as someone with a larger or stocky body, and the ways in which that embodiment might locate and exclude me culturally.

I am currently collaborating on a project examining the relationships compris-ing an online community of men who want to gain weight, doing/performing that contrasts common assumptions about the gay male body, including my own (Berry & Adams, 2011). As part of "gainer culture," these men understand them-selves through expanding, hyper-idealized, bigger bodies. Many eat in excess, and those who do not typically encourage those who do to eat more.

Reflexively maneuvering between these different cultural spaces, I ask myself tough questions on how I perform as a gay man and autoethnographer: How do I make sense of my responses to gainer and bathhouse praxis, those mixed and intuitive impulses of excitement, familiarity, and yet, lack of immediate identifi-cation? What personal questions does encountering this space impress upon me, what sorts of assumptions dwell in this process, and how am I to reconcile them? Similarly, as I continue to delve deeper into the folds of gainer culture, what shifts occur concerning how I understand myself as a gay man, a man with a marked way of relating to cultural bodies and persons?

○

I struggle with the academic call to be "queer." Granted, my work has aimed "queerly" to underscore the multiplicity inherent to culture and the fragmented nature of subjectivity, hopefully in non-normative and non-essentializing ways. I have worked directly with queer projects, and I see beautiful intersections between autoethnography and queer theory as well as the synergistic potential in embodying the tenets of a "queer autoethnography" (Holman Jones & Adams, 2010). Yet, I struggle in some ways with the identity of "queer academic," a process that feels increasingly important today as a gay scholar who works critically.

I struggle with being queer because, with Warner (2012), I worry about the identity politics pervading the ways in which some scholars live out this sensibility. My concerns are grounded in experiences not necessarily located in journal pages and performance stages, but those dwelling in everyday interactional practices of folks with whom I believe I share many of the same critical goals. I have witnessed scholarly identities being hastily questioned, explicitly and implicitly, with respect to "how queer" someone is, or whether or not someone's scholarship is "queer enough," and how these ways of being a queer scholar, in effect, define whether one is "in" or "out" of scholarly relational circles. Indeed, many queer scholars practice the kinds of exclusionary violence they purport to undo. I struggle with being queer because, for this movement to be especially meaningful, we need to be vigilant with respect to inclusivity and multiplicity. We need to make visible and model the heightened sense of openness for which we advocate in scholarship.

○

On Grindr, a smart phone application using Global Positioning System (GPS) technology to bring men seeking other men together more quickly, BlazeStevens' profile reads, "Looking 4 a real man, a man acting like a MAN. Str8 Acting ONLY!" On Scruff, a similar application catering primarily to hairier and larger gay men and men who love them, John's profile includes, "I am masculine, safe, normal and sane, looking for the same." Thanks to GPS, connecting is now more efficient, alluring, and a bit creepy.

Yet, as I engage these applications, I also find myself interested in how many men still pursue other men in highly normative ways. My interpretations create a distance from them. "Don't these guys realize what they are doing?" I ask friends. "They're rooting their desires and attractions in highly polarizing ways, ways that 'other' others, those others who have already been othered enough!" I object to associating same-sex love with mental health, knowing that our love often has been deemed abnormal; to myopic and essentializing notions of masculinity, as they feel more manufactured and reproduced than organic and innate; and to cheap and easy comparisons of same-sex living and loving to heterosexuality.

These ways of reading cultural practices feel as coherent to me as they probably do for those enacting them.

As I begin to reflect more closely on how I am implicated through the engagement of these applications, these practices start to feel not so new or distant. I realize that while the persons performing these practices and their judgmental modes of doing them might be unfortunate, they resonate with many of the ways I related to/with other men as I first explored my sexual identity, and sometimes, ways that still creep into these negotiations. I remember stating on phone chat lines my interest only in "sane gay men," and my profile on gay.com that "I am a masculine man looking for similar." Similarly, while these mediated enactments might be done in the current moments of their postings, they make sense only in relationship to a deep historical context. Thus, these current ways of relating that feel so new are actually quite old. They are well-seasoned performances, ways of othering, informed by normative ideas of what it means to be a man. They are ways of othering ourselves grounded in the sort of violence that has roots in heteronormativity and its ways of sterilizing and marginalizing uniquely gay experiences. Sometimes what feels like new encounters involve the same ole' "tricks."

○

It is 2012 and I am teaching my conflict course, "*It Gets Better*: Communication, Conflict & Difference," which focuses on the international and online movement, the *It Gets Better Project (IGBP)*. This campaign is comprised of videos created by public personae (e.g., celebrities, politicians) and private citizens. Those appearing seek to comfort high school students, primarily LGBTQ persons, facing the violence of bullying. For their final project in the course, students create their own videos, which they can post online with the *IGBP*.

Four hockey players in the class, two women and two men, decide to complete the project as a team. Although each is a competent student, I do not know what to expect, especially from the men, who are new students. I fight stereotypes that prompt me to think the men—hockey playing men—might do the bare minimum amount of work, or won't understand or care. Yet, their outcome could not be further from what I had expected. The team submitted a lovely video, called "Our Promise," in which they, along with numerous other student athletes they recruited, appear and convey their promise to help end bullying and discrimination. One male player enthusiastically proclaims: "Gay Rights in Sports!"

We feature the video in our department's year-end reception. The students beam with pride. I hear one of the guys has been showing it to faculty on campus and to his mother. I also feel proud, because I asked for a lot from the students and many delivered beautifully. Indeed, instead of sentencing gay people to banishment and detonation, we collectively responded with care and attention.

I marvel at how the students open themselves here in nonviolent and reflexive ways, and their willingness to negotiate new philosophies, experiences of hardship, empathizing and ways of doing cultural critique. While issues of homophobia persist, and sometimes horridly so, students' progress here leads me to wonder about how current students might be better equipped to identify with and examine cultural issues, and to speak out against injustice. I am also struck by my opening through this experience, and how my work here contrasts with past ways of negotiating myself. Present now are more moments of direct examination and risk taking and fewer moments of fear and avoidance. Negotiations are far less about *if* I confront issues, and more about *how.* As I continue to learn of more suicides among young LGBTQ youth, and as rights and protections are still kept from LGBTQ citizens, my energy level once reserved for tolerating ignorant and discriminatory spinning and spinners now feels depleted.

○

I emerge from the spinning of these stories still spinning. I move toward and within this complex of linguistic and embodied practices; family, friendship, public, and mediated spaces; physical and emotional pain, pride and joy, worry and relief, assuredness and uncertainty; and issues of authenticity and acceptance, inclusion and exclusion, and clear and foggy ways of looking and feeling. As I do, I come to better terms with processes of heightened and difficult identity negotiations. Indeed, a spin means much more than a twirl for some. It means realizing that our spins overlap in an intersubjective space of social influence and constraint, and being ourselves often entails being others' versions of us. Even amid the palpable change appearing in U.S. culture concerning gay rights, it means looking closely at the extent to which all persons spin "freely."

I leave these stories thinking more about connections between reflexivity and cultural critique. This spinning suggests how drawing out our relationship to culture and cultural issues—and doing so in ways that put experiences, that put us, on the line, as voices who use critical cultural scholarship to advocate for justice—renders doing reflexivity well *essential.* Part of this means appreciating how reflexive inquiry provides more intimate and informed inquiry and how the selves explored autoethnographically, like discourse generally, are always and already situated, contingent, fluid and often contradictory. Indeed, cultural beings tend to be far more complex than we might imagine. Autoethnographies will be richer when we show and emphasize our identities in ways that underscore their dynamic and processual nature. It also means looking at the double meaning of "to spin." A constitutive approach shows how spinning allows ideas and persons to come into being. Still, we also can "spin" in ways that manipulate, conceal and lie. Thus, as ethical spinners we can/should mindfully spin our stories as true as we know them to be, minimizing the extent to which we exclude persons, identities, stories and realities.

I also emerge thinking more about how reflexivity allows the chance to experience and witness personal growth. It feels, to me, to be a precious opportunity rooted in the performance of selves made possible by autoethnographic reflexivity. I next chart some of those general ways of performing, or the spinning of *historical, processing, breaching, contested, unapologetic,* and *hopeful* selves as a tentative way others might find resonance with their own performances, and further contemplate their experience with autoethnography. I end by considering how this insight might inform, and is informed by, a critically-oriented under-standing of ongoing struggle.

Spinning reflexivity entails performing as *historical selves.* We come to our "now's" as "historied" persons. We perform in ways suggestive of, and that neces-sarily are informed by, our histories, indeed, drawing on the virtues of narrative (Bochner, 2001), particularly the clarifying force of hindsight (Freeman, 2010). That we are historical selves is especially important when reflecting on how the production of those histories occurs and how we perform ourselves historically in our research. Whether this work enables selves about which we feel happy and/or distressed, in our own ways we emerge as persons with histories to be considered, molded, and disclosed.

We also perform as *processing selves.* Spinning personalized lived experience in complex ways entails filtering through seemingly endless experiences. The process-ing self often is required to go through tiring self-questioning and self-interrogating: Is my story significant enough to incorporate in my account, and, in effect, does my story matter? What experiences should I include? In turn, these questions implicate us existentially: To what extent am I included, relevant, and essential in this descrip-tion of culture and to the various audiences who engage my work? These selves stress the intensity of our work and the need to remember how our choices in processing shape how we understand ourselves and the hustle and bustle of everyday life. These considerations entail difficult choices which, for me, are rooted in our responses to human anguish. Autoethnographers are processing selves who tend to acknowledge the universality of suffering, the temptation to sugarcoat tough times, and yet, the need to compassionately, though directly, move into the sharp edges of experience (Chödrön, 2002).

Spinning reflexivity also entails performing *breaching selves.* I am thinking here of Garfinkel's (1967) ethnomethodology, which calls researchers to delib-erately perform in ways that contrast with (that is, "breach") social custom, to make available a better understanding of the social rules that guide these experiences and, more generally, constitute social order and us as social actors. Deliberate or not, autoethnographic reflexivity tends to disrupt the status quo. Autoethnographers implicate themselves as cultural critics whose breaches draw attention to possibilities for myopic thinking, complacency and social injustice.

Autoethnographers also spin in multifaceted ways as *contested selves.* This spinning, for many, is rooted in how a critical cultural orientation calls autoeth-nographers to perform in ways that reveal and examine experiences of bigotry, discrimination, and power. Thus, this reflexivity inherently stresses and relies on contestation. Similarly, using reflexivity like this asks for or demands social reform, praxis that amplifies identity negotiation, positioning autoethnographers as critics who call out not only issues but others. We spin against injustice, exclusion, and so on—indeed, contestation that can be as uncomfortable as it is vital.

Yet, spinning reflexivity also entails performing who we feel we are with/for others. It entails negotiating ourselves in ways others may not understand or accept (Ellis, 2004). At the same time, the spinning can require us to work in contradiction to who we feel we are in a current moment or who we have been in the past. Courageously, we try to clearly see who we have been and who we are willing to become. Similarly, we ask through this reflexive spinning a pivotal question: How willing are we to let go of the self we thought we once knew, a self we knew to be "true," to explore and learn about ourselves afresh, indeed, to encounter selves we might not even like? Our brave work will show the answer.

There is also a way in which reflexivity entails spinning *unapologetic selves*. It requires us to "step boldly into the fullness of life, with all of its dangers and all of its promises" (Lesser, 2005, p. xvii). This way of performing is not about infallibility. Instead, the unapologetic self personifies a sense of assuredness, or, at the very least, a confident spirit in foregrounding researchers' selves. Assuredness, in this sense, proudly advances the self; apology makes excuses, gives in to external forces, and stifles the self. We become risk takers and take chances; who we wish to become is worth any fallout that might occur through our becoming.

Spinning also entails performing *hopeful selves*. We comprise a community of many practitioners who perform as survivors. Our work advocates more inclusive ways of understanding how we live with/among each other. It is enacted with hope, even if implicit, that cultural realities might come to be different, and that cultural beings might understand and respond to issues and identities differently. Yet, how we look at this "hope" matters. I use it here believing hope can and should be messy. Hope, and spinning hopeful autoethnographies, rarely occurs without ambiguity, contradictions, and complications.

Extending the attention we spend on how autoethnographic reflexivity shapes its praxis and performers calls us to explore more fully the depths and shades of how we are implicated by cultural critique. To do so is to advocate conscientious and dynamic representation, as well as a means of honoring more fully the persons "in" this difficult work. It is to understand the processes inherent to constituting autoethnographic research, which, to be sure, also entails constituting autoethnographers. Thus, orienting ourselves involves respecting each performance for the experiences that have led to the spin and the particular ways of spinning being displayed; being especially mindful in doing this cultural work, knowing that spinning autoethnographic reflexivity does things, sometimes powerful and transformative things, for cultural life and beings; and being mindful of how each spinner, spin, and way of spinning matters. It means that the palpable feeling often resulting from this praxis comes to be as a consequence of the inevitability that autoethnographers are not only present in this dynamic praxis, and I suspect in greater and more diverse ways than many imagine, but are becoming as a result of our labors.

Epilogue

I end reflecting on tensions that accompany performances of hope and as hopeful cultural critics because the complexities and contradictions inherent to lived experience can often promote a curious mix of promise and frustration. As I write, I am reminded of President Obama's historic announcement of emotional support for marriage equality. While much more work is necessary, I never felt I would hear those words from a sitting U.S. president in my lifetime. Yet, as I write, I also peer at the recent teaching evaluations for one of my courses, in which a student writes, "Did he say he was gay??? If so, he should keep it to himself." While these comments have become more atypical as of late, I still dwell on this discursive violence. I end here, thinking of the challenges and opportunities in autoethnographic reflexivity for working through messy issues and times like these, the sticky experiences of negotiation that might render the relational maneuvering and focusing of reflexivity difficult and tiring.

I dwell in the messiness of hope that shapes the ways we do and become in and across cultural spaces, and as we work to represent and critique those spaces, remembering the reflexive wisdom of the late John T. Warren (2011):

> Looking back on my career so far, I think about how much time I wasted talking about how burdened I was. And although I have been busy and stressed, I have recently become committed to look for the joy, the wonder, and the true generosity my job enables me to experience. Part of my reflexive work lately is to reframe my labor. Rather than lament the amount of my work or the impact of budget cuts, I aim to celebrate the joy; rather than lead with the negative, I want to live in the positive. I work in a magical place, in a wondrous field of study where intellectuals come to engage each other—we do the work of scholarship, activism, and public engagement and we do it well. Personally, I think I happen to teach classes with the best graduate students in the country and I serve on dissertations committees that make me think, make me struggle, make me care about the world in new ways. Part of what I hope to inspire here is more talk of vision, of crafting the kind of academic experience we find fulfilling—building a community through our hopes and desires. (p. 142)

I end confident that what John speaks of here is not a simplistic or flat joy, devoid of an understanding of the hardships of which he speaks. Instead, it is a joy to which we might aspire that also accompanies the difficult work of writing and performing reflexively and being the sort of cultural critics that address tough issues and persist in working to uncover ignorance, hate and inequities within our cultural lives. It is, for me, a mindful joy about which we remind ourselves when the heaviness of everything else feels like it is too much. It is a joy reconciled with suffering, an opportunity in our work to be more aware of all that matters in a given moment, knowing that those moments are always and already fleeting. It means cautiously and bravely spinning, and spinning now, in ways that feel important and needed, and allowing the reverberations of our movements to flow out to others and ourselves.

Note

1. For me, cultural critique calls for an intersectional understanding. Multiple dimensions to our identity (race, ethnicity, class, sex, gender, sexuality, geographic location, and more) simultaneously shape identity. I focus specifically on sexuality, yet hope my ideas serve as an opening for other factors to be considered.

References

Adams, T. E. (2006). Seeking father: Relationally reframing a troubled love story. *Qualitative Inquiry, 12*, 704–723.

Adams, T. E. (2011). *Narrating the closet: An autoethnography of same-sex attraction.* Walnut Creek, CA: Left Coast Press, Inc.

Alcoff, L. (1991/1992). The problem of speaking for others. *Cultural Critique, 20*, 5–23.

Alexander, B. K. (2009). Autoethnography: Exploring modalities and subjectivities that shape social relations. In J. Paul, J. Kleinhammer-Tramill, & K. Fowler (Eds.), *Qualitative research methods in special education* (pp. 277–306). Denver, CO: Love.

Alexander, B. K. (2011). Standing in the wake: A critical auto/ethnographic exercise on reflexivity in three movements. *Cultural Studies ↔ Critical Methodologies, 11*, 98–107.

Berry, K. (2006). Implicated audience member seeks understanding: Reexamining the "gift" of autoethnography. *International Journal of Qualitative Methods, 5* (3). Retrieved on September 1, 2011, from www.ualberta.ca/~iiqm/backissues/5_3/html/berry.htm

Berry, K. (2007). Embracing the catastrophe: Gay body seeks acceptance. *Qualitative Inquiry, 13*, 259–281.

Berry, K. (2013). "Storying mindfulness, (re)imagining burn." In S. Faulkner (Ed.), *Everyday relational challenges: Readings in relational communication.* Walnut Creek, CA: Left Coast Press, Inc.

Berry, K., & Adams, T. E. (2011). Size matters: Unfolding the discursive rolls of gainer culture. Paper presented at the National Communication Association 96th Annual Convention, San Diego, CA.

Berry, K., & Clair, R. P. (2011). Special issue: The call of ethnographic reflexivity: Narrating the self's presence in ethnography. Cultural Studies ↔ Critical Methodologies, 11(2).

Berry, K., & Warren, J. T. (2009). Cultural Studies and the politics of representation: Experience, subjectivity, research. *Cultural Studies ↔ Critical Methodologies, 9* (5), 597–607.

Bochner, A. P. (2001). Narrative's virtues. *Qualitative Inquiry, 7*, 131–157.

Bochner, A., & Ellis, C. (2006). Communication as autoethnography. In G. J. Shepherd, J. St. John, & T. Striphas (Eds.), *Communication as…Perspectives on theory* (pp. 110–122). Thousand Oaks, CA: Sage.

Boyd, D. (2008). Autoethnography as a tool for transformative learning about white privilege. *Journal of Transformative Education, 6*, 212–225.

Boylorn, R. M. (2013). *Sweetwater: Black women and narratives of resilience.* New York: Peter Lang.

Calafell, B. M., & Moreman, S. T. (2009). Envisioning an academic readership: Latina/o performativities per the form of publication. *Text and Performance Quarterly, 29*, 123–130.

Chawla, D., & Rodriguez, A. (2011). *Liminal traces: Storying, performing, and embodying postcoloniality.* Boston: Sense.

Chödrön, P. (2002). *When things fall apart: Heart advice for difficult times.* Boston: Shambhala.

Clifford, J., & Marcus, G. E. (1986). *Writing culture: The poetics and politics of ethnography.* Berkeley: University of California Press.

DeSalvo, L. (1999). *Writing as a way of healing: How telling our stories transforms our lives.* Boston: Beacon Press.

Denzin, N. K. (1988). *Interpretive biography.* Newbury Park, CA: Sage.

Denzin, N. K. (1997). *Interpretive ethnography: Ethnographic practices for the 21ˢᵗ century.* Thousand Oaks, CA: Sage.

Ellis, C. (1996). Maternal connections. In C. Ellis & A. P. Bochner (Eds.), *Composing ethnography: Alternative forms of qualitative writing* (pp. 240–243). Walnut Creek, CA: AltaMira Press.

Ellis, C. (2004). *The ethnographic I: A methodological novel about autoethnography.* Walnut Creek CA: AltaMira Press.

Ellis, C. (2007). Telling secrets, revealing lives: Relational ethics in research with intimate others. *Qualitative Inquiry, 13,* 3–29.

Fabian, J. (2002). *Time and the other: How anthropology makes its object.* New York: Columbia University Press.

Faulkner, S. (2012). That baby will cost you: An intended ambivalent pregnancy. *Qualitative Inquiry, 18,* 333–340.

Fassett, D. L., & Warren, J. T. (2007). *Critical communication pedagogy.* Thousand Oaks, CA: Sage.

Finlay, L. (2002). Negotiating the swamp: The opportunity and challenge of reflexivity in research practice. *Qualitative Research, 2,* 209–230.

Freeman, M. (2010). *Hindsight: The promise and peril of looking backward.* New York: Oxford

Garfinkel, H. (1967). *Studies in ethnomethodology.* Englewood Cliffs, NJ: Prentice-Hall.

Glave, T. (2003). On the difficulty of confiding with complete love and trust, in some heterosexual "friends." *The Massachusetts Review, 44,* 583–595.

Goltz, D. B. (2011). Frustrating the "I": Critical dialogic reflexivity with a personal voice. *Text & Performance Quarterly, 31,* 386–405.

Goodall, H.L. (2000). *Writing the new ethnography.* Lanham, MA: AltaMira Press.

Herrmann, A. F. (2012). "I know I'm unlovable": Desperation, dislocation, despair, and discourse on the academic job hunt. *Qualitative Inquiry, 18,* 247–255.

Holman Jones, S. (2005). Autoethnography: Making the personal political. In N. K. Denzin & Y. S. Lincoln (Eds.), *Handbook of qualitative research* (3rd ed., pp. 763–791). Thousand Oaks, CA: Sage.

Holman Jones, S., & Adams, T. E. (2010). Autoethnography and queer theory: Making possibilities. In N. K. Denzin & M. G. Giardini (Eds.), *Qualitative inquiry and human rights* (pp. 136–157). Walnut Creek, CA: Left Coast Press, Inc.

hooks, b. (1999). *Remembered rapture: The writer at work.* New York: Henry Hold.

Jackson II, R. L. (2002). Introduction: Theorizing and analyzing the nexus between cultural and gendered identities and the body. *Communication Quarterly, 50,* 242–250.

Kosciw, J. G., Greytak, E. A., Diaz, E. M., & Bartkiewicz, M. J. (2010). *The 2009 National School Climate Survey: The experiences of lesbian, gay, bisexual and transgender youth in our nation's schools.* New York: GLSEN.

Langsdorf, L. (2002). In defense of poiesis: The performance of self in communicative praxis. In W. McBride & M. B. Matustik (Eds.), *Calvin O. Schrag and the task of philosophy after postmodernity* (pp. 281–296). Evanston, IL: Northwestern University Press.

Lesser, E. (2005). *Broken open: How difficult times can help us grow.* New York: Villard.

Madison, D. S. (2011). *Critical ethnography: Method, ethics and performance* (2nd ed). Thousand Oaks, CA: Sage.

Myers, W. B. (2012). Joyful moments of sorrow: Autoethnography and atheistic joy. *Qualitative Communication Research, 1,* 195–208.

Pelias, R. J. (2004). *A methodology of the heart: Evoking academic & daily life.* Walnut Creek, CA: AltaMira Press.

Pelias, R. (2011). Writing into position: Strategies for composition and evaluation. In N. K. Denzin & Y. S. Lincoln (Eds.), *The SAGE handbook of qualitative research* (4th ed., pp. 659–668). Thousand Oaks, CA: Sage.

Pillow, W. (2003). Confession, catharsis, or cure? Rethinking the uses of reflexivity as methodological power in qualitative research. *International Journal of Qualitative Studies in Education, 16,* 175–196.

Santoro, P. (2012). Relationally bare/bear: Bodies of loss and love. *Cultural Studies ↔ Critical Methodologies, 12*, 118–131.

Savage, D., & Miller, T. (Eds.). (2011). *It gets better: Coming out, overcoming bullying, and creating a life worth living.* New York: Penguin.

Schrag, C. O. (1997). *The self after postmodernity.* New Haven, CT: Yale University Press.

Schrag, C. O. (2003). *Communicative praxis and the space of subjectivity.* West Lafayette, IN: Purdue University Press.

Spry, T. (2006). A "performative-I" copresence: Embodying the ethnographic turn in performance and the performance turn in ethnography. *Text and Performance Quarterly, 26*, 339–346.

Spry, T. (2011). *Body, paper, stage: Writing and performing autoethnography.* Walnut Creek, CA: Left Coast Press, Inc.

Tillmann, L. M. (2009a). Body and bulimia revisited: Reflections on "A Secret Life." *Journal of Applied Communication Research, 37*, 98–112.

Tillmann, L. M. (2009b). The state of unions: Politics and poetics of performance. *Qualitative Inquiry, 15*, 545–560.

Tomaselli, K. G., Dyll, L., & Francis, M. (2008). "Self" and "other": Auto-reflexive and indigenous ethnography. In N. K. Denzin, Y. S. Lincoln, & L. T. Smith (Eds.), *Handbook of critical indigenous methods* (pp. 347–372). Thousand Oaks, CA: Sage.

Warner, M. (2012). Queer and then? *The Chronicle of Higher Education.* Retrieved on January 3, 2012, from chronicle.com/article/QueerThen-/130161

Warren, J. T. (2003). *Performing purity: Whiteness, pedagogy and the reconsitution of whiteness.* New York: Peter Lang.

Warren, J. T. (2011). Reflexive teaching: Toward critical autoethnographic practices of/in/on pedagogy. *Cultural Studies ↔ Critical Methodologies, 11*, 139–144.

Yoshino, K. (2007). *Covering: The hidden assault on our civil rights.* New York: Random House.

Chapter 10

Sketching Subjectivities

Susanne Gannon

I am hesitant to begin this writing, for many reasons. Most mundanely, it is too late to begin, although perhaps it is too late to stop. I circle around and around because it is difficult to know where to start...

So I start with the academic argument, which is part of what I want to do in this chapter as I work around the problematic of the self—of subjectivity—in autoethnography. I explore the creation of autoethnographic selves and subjectivities, and the construction of self in the field, on the page, and on the various "stages" of the world, and how we might trouble or critique the "I" in autoethnographic work. In particular, I want to argue for a relational autoethnographic subjectivity, a self that is contingent on the recognition of others, and a self who finds voice through that relation. This is not fixed but rather a moment to moment, negotiated, responsive location. The distinction I make between "self" and "subjectivity" draws attention to the constructedness of the voice inside any text, including those that are written in the first person grammatical voice. The self that I lay claim to with "I" or "me" gives the impression of a stable, coherent and bounded humanist individual; however, the poststructurally-inflected term "subjectivity" draws attention to the contingencies of identity and multiplicity of discourses through which we come to recognize ourselves as particular beings.

The questions that are of perennial interest to me as a critical autoethnographer with poststructuralist inclinations are: How might a self be materialized or

Handbook of Autoethnography, edited by Stacy Holman Jones, Tony E. Adams, and Carolyn Ellis, 228–243. © 2013 Left Coast Press, Inc. All rights reserved.

made possible in a text? What are the ethical and material and methodological consequences of the textual choices we make as autoethnographers, and what assumptions lie behind these consequences? What might be entailed in shifting from self to subjectivity? What are the relations negotiated from moment to moment within which the speaking self comes into being? Where are the "others" in our ethnographic texts, besides the subject, and beyond the human? In particular I'm interested in textual work and the performances of subjectivity that might be possible in autoethnography.

My suggestion that the textual self is a performance draws attention to the artfulness of ethnographic writing that is responsive and oriented towards the evocation of emotion and the opening of flows of affect. Such texts invite multiple points of connection and recognize the movements of attraction, repulsion and compulsion between writers, readers and texts. In this chapter I want to write around and about and through autoethnography and the shifts in register and authorial voice. The first section of the chapter surveys theoretical ideas that might be useful for thinking about autoethnographic writing within a poststructural paradigm, in particular the notion of a textual call and response as a way of attending to the relational conditions of autoethnography. The second section of the chapter offers fragments of autoethnography written in response to texts about the loss of a beloved brother (Ellis, 2009a, 2009b). Excerpts of this autoethnography are offered throughout the earlier sections of the chapter. This is a jagged, stuttering sort of writing that starts again and again, and slips away, interrupting itself and finding no place to settle into a credible version of truth. Traces of material artifacts, including photographs, letters and government reports, jostle against memories and imaginings. It suggests but does not resolve the possibilities of alternative accounts, and although it situates an authorial subject with a strong voice at the center of the text, it also tries to destabilize what might be known. It is in part a writing back, responsive to the call of another sister who writes of the loss of a brother, and it is in part the expression of a desiring machine collapsing together thought and affect, self and other, reality and memory.

Situatedness of Self Writing/Situatedness of Writing

I keep approaching this aslant, and again in the almost dark, almost midnight when things like this rush out. Until I read your paper, Carolyn, I didn't know you had a brother, too…

We do not speak from nowhere. Inevitably, always, we bring experiences and dispositions with us—personal, professional and disciplinary—to any text that we read and write, including autoethnography. We bring all of the relationships we have in the world onto the pages and, with them, come unconscious thoughts and desires that are difficult or impossible to articulate. There is no neutral space from which we write, or from which we read. As well as our past experiences, we bring our present locations, and the immanence of futures that are opaque and that offer multiplicitous possibilities. Past experiences shift in and out of focus as we write them, reshaping their contours and significance as we write into them at different writing moments, in different moods and from different lines of sight (Gannon, 2002). We write ourselves into being as we write our texts, but not in a naïve or innocent manner. Instead, we write ourselves into particular subject positions within the texts we write and, in unpredictable ways, we call others into relation—both inside the text and in their readings of our texts.

This is not to set the situated and subjective qualities of autoethnographic writing against the claims to objectivity of other modes of writing. Rather, the objectivity that much social science espouses can be best understood as a posture taken up within a text, with a set of rhetorical conventions that entail suppression and elision of detail in a desire to appear neutral and objective (Ellis, 2009b; Richardson, 1990, 1997). However, writing autoethnography is more complex than merely inserting details that are otherwise suppressed—details such as first person point of view, embodied details of time and space, distinctiveness of voice, and affective and embodied registers—into writing that strives towards objectivity. These details carry ethical consequences, and responsibilities, in terms of the textual performance of self and other in, and around, any text. Nor do I suggest that autoethnography can be achieved when the ethereal abstractions of texts that strive towards an illusion of "scientificity" are replaced by the esoteric abstractions of high cultural theory. I want to move closer to the details of things, whilst not foreclosing on meaning, by striving to keep the text—including the text of the self—open to multiple possible readings.

The text of the self is also, always, simultaneously, a text that brings others into being, too. At the same time as I want to respect the materiality of bodies, places and spaces in my autoethnographic writing, I also want to stay open to other texts. Writing by others about their lived experiences brings me into new relationships with my own experiences, opens a sort of textual call and response, creates a mobile textual and material assemblage within which my self and others are always in circulation.

> *She says I should write what I need to write. It's my story, too, she says. It's his, it's hers, it's ours, each time and for each person a little different as our trajectories and intersections shift.*

The suggestion of "sketching" in the title of the chapter[1] highlights the always tentative and unfinished quality of the autoethnographic project. The "sketch"—as "a hasty or undetailed drawing or painting often made as a preliminary study," or as "a brief, slight or hasty delineation; a rapid or offhand presentation of the essential facts of anything," or as "the first suggestive embodiment of an artist's idea as expressed on canvas or on paper, or in the clay model, upon which his more finished performance is to be elaborated or built up"[2]—draws attention to the always *unfinished* quality of autoethnography. There is no determinate, or definitive, autoethnographic representation of any event, experience, or phenomenon—despite the "auto" implication that this might be a single person's account of a lived experience. Rather, there is a project, an ongoing investigation, always subject to revision and retelling from another angle, via a different lens, within another set of relations, along a different line of sight with the concomitant impossibility of an ending or a resolution (or of a "finished performance") (Ellis, 2009b; Gannon, 2002, 2006). Although the unfinished element signaled in the dictionary definition of sketching is crucial to autoethnography, I would not advocate a "hasty" or "undetailed" or "offhand" approach, and I am left wondering how "the essential facts of anything" might ever be reliably determined. The following section of the chapter reviews some of the philosophical work that underpins this approach to a critical autoethnography that tolerates, even encourages, uncertainty.

Self, Subject, Subjectivity—
Poststructural Approaches to Subjectivity

You open me up unexpectedly, blindside me, sock me in the gut. You can't predict what points of connection a reader might have inside a text, what might rise up demanding to be written...

The idea of narrative material rising up and demanding to be written suggests writers and readers who are not entirely in control. It suggests affective flows between subjects and texts. It implies a degree of instability in the reading and writing subject. In this section I survey some of the approaches to self and subjectivity of poststructural authors who I have found useful in my own struggles with writing the self. This is not a comprehensive overview but rather a more detailed reading of particular provocative ideas around the self and/in writing.

The subject is considered, within poststructural accounts of subjectivity, as an ongoing project—as shifting, contradictory, multiple, fragile, fragmented. Rather than the discrete humanist subject, the individual, poststructural approaches suggest subjects who are "co-implicated" with others and with the world, including other texts in the world (Gannon & Davies, 2012, p. 72). In particular, poststructuralism drew attention to the self as a subject who is constituted in language, within and through discourses that are socially and culturally framed, and that are always in circulation not only within texts but in the multiple stages and pages of our lives (Davies & Gannon, 2011; Gannon & Davies, 2012). Recent theoretical moves have strengthened the imperative to know the self differently by focusing less on the individual self, separate from others and from place, and more on the self in relation to others, including "human, non-human and earth others" (Somerville, Davies, Power, Gannon, & Carteret, 2011, p. 1). In contrast to humanist versions of identity that focus on the coherence of an individual rationalist subject—the subject who knows—poststructuralism proposes a subjectivity that is not the property of any one of us but that is precarious, always in process and reconstituted anew each time we speak or write within constantly shifting circuits of power and knowledge. This is a dynamic and continuous crafting of the self and of experience within particular historical and cultural conditions and within circulating textual assemblages. This position problematizes autoethnographic writing that revolves around the experiences and accounts of a singular knowing subject, the confident author of a particular text. Rather, the self produced in a text is always contingent, tentative, situated, and relational (Gannon, 2006). However, paradoxically, at the same time as the subject is relationally, discursively, and textually constituted, there is a singularity and uniqueness about each subject—that I will return to later in this chapter—that ought not to be foreclosed (Cavarero, 2000).

The concept of the subject comes initially from the Latin "subjectum" meaning broadly "a ground, basis, or what exists independently" (Colebrook, 2004, p. 71). In modernity, Colebrook explains, the human subject came to be seen as fundamentally different from non-human beings, as it became recognized as the one who knows and is "the basis and centre of all inquiry" (p. 71). There is an impossible folding within the text that means there is "always a gap between the subject *who speaks* and the represented subject *spoken about*...the subject is not a thing so much as the process through which things are given, represented or synthesized" (p. 72). This is not meant to apply to any specific "self" so much as to the broader assumption that human subjectivity produces the world and all within it as we know it. In autoethnography, the self that is constituted within the text and that is the subject of the text—regardless of the verifiability of detail or the claims of grammar—is inevitably an installation in the text, an artifact of textual practice and authorial choice. Limits exist as to what can be known in and through a text, and these limitations can be foregrounded in how we write. There is an impossibility and excess in language, an unpredictability and volatility, that, as Colebrook argues, warrants attention through "ironic writing" that "does not pretend to be [a] full and transparent representation" (p. 73). Even texts that are autoethnographic in their intent have their own momentum in language, exceeding intentionality, rationality and the particular contexts of production and reception. This is a performative mode of writing where aspects of style and form can draw attention to the ways that autoethnographic writing can never be enough and is always too much. As well as fragmentation and multiplicity, the inadequacy of language might be suggested by movement away from an autoethnographic register of emotion and embodiment.

Annex E, Enclosure 1, 9:45, 16:00, fifty-five pages of transcripts, ten pages of typed witness accounts, fourteen pages of drawings, a scale, a key, two pages of ambulance records. Amongst the detail, I look for the few sentences that bring comfort.

Autoethnography has at times been criticized for a relentless emotionality. According to Clough (2000), it can risk "melodramatic focus" on tragedy and forget the "unconscious and desire" (p. 16). In overcompensation for the excesses of objectivity in other modes of ethnographic writing, its subtext has been the production of an unproblematized subject identity for the author (p. 16). It is not the singularity of versions of events that are sometimes told in autoethnography that is in question, but the confidence of a speaking voice that may be too full of self-identity, too knowing, too certain, too sure. Clough suggests that, after Derrida, we might query any "presumption of the unity of speech…of an inner presence, an inner voice, so that the subject, when it speaks, is presumed to speak its own voice, to speak its intention and to express its inner being" (p. 17). Broadly, she argues for a shift in attention to the circulation of affect that exceeds the individual. Clough suggests that the truths of experience cannot be chronologically or rationally ordered when temporality is itself disjointed and we are haunted by memories of times, places, and events that "repeatedly pressure the subject with bodily effects" (p. 4). Rather, we might aspire to writing that is embodied, visceral, nonlinear, that shows shifts in thought as they are happening to the writer, that throws the writer "backward and forward to find the self that is turned into parts, turned around parts of a new assemblage" (p. 14). That new textual assemblage will detail memories, matter, subjectivities, technologies, blank spaces, and hesitations that exceed and disrupt the rhetorical intentions and the capacities of the writer.

Contemporary poststructural philosophers have much to say about the self in writing, and they demonstrate textual strategies that are of interest for autoethnographers. Derrida argues for a re-situating of the subject that entails moving from the assumption of an essentialized and unified identity that has substance independent of language towards an understanding of the subject as *inscribed* in language. He stresses that the concept of the subject need not be "dispensed with," rather that it should be "deconstructed." The precise strategy of deconstruction that he advocates means more than just unpacking the assumptions embedded in language or discourse. Rather, it means finding points of contradiction and hierarchies of meaning and pressing at these points and hierarchies until they are at the point of collapse. As Derrida (cited in Kearney, 1995) states,

> To deconstruct the subject does not mean to deny its existence. There are subjects, "operations" or "effects" (*effets*) of subjectivity. This is an incontrovertible fact. To acknowledge this does not mean, however, that the subject is what it *says* it is. The subject is not some meta-linguistic substance or identity, some pure *cogito* of self-presence; it is always inscribed in language. My work does not, therefore, destroy the subject; it simply tries to resituate it. (pp. 174–175)

Thus he argues that the subject must always be precisely situated in its multiple contexts, including the text itself.

If we follow Derrida, insisting simultaneously that the subject exists *and* also that it is inscribed in language, if we recognize that the subject speaks *and* that it is not "what it says it is," and if we direct our endeavors to "situating" the subject, while maintaining suspicion about the transparency of language, then autoethnography might seem to be impossible (Gannon, 2006). Or it might invite the sort of seriously playful textual deconstruction that attempts to problematize the self in writing while at the same time performing a textual and relational self—even through evasion and aside. As Colebrook (2008) notes, Derrida attends to "seemingly irrelevant textual details, such as metaphor, example, excuse, misquotation or sounds, but he makes little mention of biography…a claim to truth takes place in a body of signs that it at once displaces but also fails to master" (p. 117).

Derrida's collaboration with feminist literary scholar Hélène Cixous (Cixous & Derrida, 2001) operates as a sort of call and response, and provides an interesting provocation to autoethnographic writing. The book contains two essays. The first half of it, "Savoir," by Cixous, is a personal reflection on her myopia as a veiling from the world. The second essay in the book, by Derrida, is called "A Silkworm of One's Own" and is a direct response to the first essay. This second essay, by Derrida, is described as offering "points of view stitched on the other veil" (p. 17). Both texts give tantalizing glimpses of approaches to self-writing through which the worldly subject—that is, Jacques or Hélène—slips away almost as fast as it is sighted. While they are relationally inscribed they also retain a certain singularity and uniqueness (Cavarero, 2000). The details are precise and inclined to the poetic. Place and time are written in explicitly, and elusively. Derrida is in Buenos Aires on a certain day in November 1995, and he is writing "from the lower corner of the map, right at the bottom of the world"; he is in sight of Tierra del Fuego, he says, and at the same time he is in sight of Magellan's caravels (Cixous & Derrida, 2001, p. 24). He says he is a boy with a prayer shawl, a tallith, inherited from his Moses, his maternal grandfather, which was left in El Biar with his father and finally brought from Algeria to France at the time of "the exodus" (p. 44), and at the same time he is a man writing in the present, writing his own text in response to the text written by Cixous. The second essay ends with a detailed memory of Derrida as a child with silkworms. In this moment of memory the man closing his eyes in a bed in Sao Paulo in December experiences a "lapse in time" (p. 92). He lets himself "be invaded, as they say, gently, in gentleness, by a childhood memory, a true childhood memory, the opposite of a dream, and here [he says] I embroider no longer" (p. 87).

Both essays utilize material objects and biographical fragments, with the allure of truth about them, as flights into thoughts, and as provocations for reflection on ethics and philosophy rather than as the subjects of the text itself. Although they provide opportunities for textual "embroidery," for displacement of the self as the subject of the text, or perhaps the self as the dominant voice of the text, this sideways treatment does not deny or undermine the credibility of the details of lived experience that are included. The deconstructive moves in the text do not deny the existence of a subject, nor do they remove the capacity of that subject to speak about her- or himself, though they do work against singular or authoritarian claims to knowledge. Most importantly, they respond, each text to the other. Colebrook (2008) describes these dialogues as more literary in style than the combative style of philosophical discourse, as like "love letters" between the texts (p. 7). Cixous takes up the dialogue again in her later essay, "The Flying Manuscript" (2006), wherein she says of Derrida "you have always staged the entry of voices into your interior scene pushing the interior to declare and show itself" (p. 15). Neither Cixous nor Derrida labeled their writing autoethnographic—they may well have been entirely unaware of methodological debates in the Anglophone social sciences—but the strategies they use are provocative and offer potential to autoethnographers to push their work in new directions. Although autoethnographers have written about literary form and the responsive of autoethnography to the "other," there have thus far been few examples of dialogic autoethnography. Direct address to another inside the text, the back and forth of call and response, the collapse of the singular self inside the text, and the use of literary tropes and material referents thus open new possibilities for autoethnography.

The trope of writing "between the two" has also been taken up by Wyatt, Gale, and others including myself (Gale & Wyatt, 2009; Wyatt & Gale, 2011; Wyatt, Gale, Gannon, & Davies, 2011) in "nomadic" and collaborative inquiries into writing and subjectivity. Influenced by the philosophies of Gilles Deleuze and Felix Guattari, Gale and Wyatt (2011) generate a dialogic mode of writing characterized by movements, intensities and flows that envisages the subject as always part of "the *assemblage*, of which—with others, matter, time and space—we are a part" (p. 494). The text of the self becomes an occasion of folding and unfolding selves, tracing selves as continuous becomings in relation. This is not a version of a self that is abstracted from time or space, or that is untethered from the materiality of bodies and lived experiences, but rather a version of a self that is provisional and intensely responsive. Collaborative writing practices are alert to, and try to instantiate within, the text, the "haecceity" or "just this-ness" of the particular moment.

Deleuze and Guattari (2004) describe *haecceities* as assemblages incorporating bodies located at the intersections of longitude and latitude but also "climate, wind, season, hour"; they argue that these elements are "not of another nature than the things, animals or people that populate them, follow them, sleep and awaken within them.…Forms and subjects are not of that world" (p. 290). Rather, they suggest that we are all distributed in a "variable fashion" and that we align temporarily along "dimensions of multiplicities" on an immanent plane of possibilities (p. 290). The self does not come into being only through the material and sensory dimensions of particular spaces and times, but also through ineffable elements, including imagination and memory, that are always in circulation within and amongst subjects. As Wyatt ponders, my "subjectivity" lies beyond the physical boundaries of my body, that I am bound and beholden to, connected and complicit with, amongst others [it includes]: the page onto which I'm writing on a pale autumn Wednesday afternoon; the wooden shelf on which my forearms are resting; the wonderful, inviting smell of coffee; the two young women baristas and their machinery behind me; the cold air outside that, because I am sitting near the door, hits me as the mother and buggy come in; the man at the table next to me who is always here on Wednesdays, and who seems sad each time, an impression I gain, perhaps mistakenly, simply by how he moves; the images I have of each of you as I write, my pictures of what you look like and where you live, and the lives you lead. (Wyatt et al., 2011, p. 36)

This mode of writing the self—even as it yearns towards particular others who write back their own autoethnographic fragments (or "love letters" in Colebrook's terms) in response—is informed and shaped by conventions of both literary writing and philosophy.

The influence of Deleuze also draws attention to the movements of affect in autoethnographic writing and their impact on porous subjectivities. Rather than feelings or emotions, affects are "becomings that spill over beyond whoever lives through them, thereby becoming someone else" (Deleuze, 1995, p. 137). This spilling over and becoming something "other" occurs between people and texts, and affect "contagion" can be provoked by powerful, evocative and engaging writing. Probyn (2010) describes how affects are neither internal to the discrete or bounded body, nor externally imposed on that body, but bodies themselves are defined by "dynamic relations"—"thousand of bits all whizzing around" and in dynamic relation with all sorts of other bodies, including texts we read and write which are "integral to our capacities to affect and to be affected" (p. 77). They operate as "relays that connect word, gesture, memory, sound, rhythm, mobility, image, and thinking" (Connolly, cited in Probyn, 2010, p. 77). They promote the movement of affect within and between subjects.

Thus, for autoethnographic writing to be evocative, it must *move* the reader—affectively, aesthetically, rationally—as well as the writer, and the text itself will move in unpredictable ways. This is well recognized by autoethnographers who argue for evocative and emotional texts (e.g., Ellis, 2004, 2009b). Probyn (2010) talks about "honesty" in writing as being contingent on a combination of passion and precision in language and on awareness of the potential reader. The goal of writing is connection between reader and writer such that "the affects of writing can penetrate the body of the reader and the writer" (p. 82). Strong affect, such as that evoked in powerfully evocative autoethnographic writing, "radically disturbs different relations of proximity: to ourselves, bodies, pasts" (p. 86). Writing is dialogic in terms of the constant movement or flow of affect. Autoethnographic subjectivity is non-unitary and constituted in relation to other human and non-human subjects, spaces, times, surfaces and events, particularly the event of writing.

A final insight and a caveat to keep in mind in a more dialogic approach to autoethnography comes from the work of Adriana Cavarero (2000) on narratives and the self. She theorizes a subject who is always already in constitutive relationships with others, and she sees the desire to be narrated by the other as a condition for recognition as human subjects. Despite this interdependence and despite the desire for recognition through narrative, Cavarero insists on the singularity of the narratable subject. Her project is to recover the uniqueness of the human subject, and of her story—the "who" who is "concrete and insubstitutable" (p. 73)—without abandoning the insights into the contingency of subjectivity of poststructuralism. Even though my story yearns towards and responds to your story, even though there are points of irrevocable contact between our stories, there is no merger or collapse of one into the other, and there is no easy path to empathy. Cavarero argues that, despite similarities,

> your story is never my story. No matter how much the larger traits of our life-stories are similar, I still do not recognize myself *in* you and even less, in the collective *we*. I do not dissolve both into a common identity, nor do I digest your tale in order to construct the meaning of mine. I recognize, on the contrary, that your uniqueness is exposed to my gaze and consists in an unrepeatable story whose tale you desire. (p. 92)

In the final section of this chapter, responding to another's story of the loss of her brother with my own autoethnographic fragments, I cannot claim to know or to feel or to experience in the same register. My keening at the loss of my brother must be in a different key. My obligation is to work with the specificity of the story I have to tell as closely as I can, and to articulate those ambivalences and uncertainties that arise as I write. Nevertheless, I do not claim that this autoethnography exemplifies all of the strategies of deconstructive writing that I have elaborated; rather, it is what I could write at this moment, in this space, with this knowledge and these materials—papers, photographs, conversations, the stuff of memory. As is the way with texts, affective flows between texts and between subjects writing and reading these texts—circling between Carolyn and Susanne and other readers beyond us—moving in unexpected directions, and I am moved beyond myself, and beyond my intentions.

Circling Loss

Dear Carolyn,

I am hesitant to begin this writing for many reasons. Most mundanely it is too late to begin, although perhaps it is too late to stop. I circle around and around also because it is difficult to know where to start. Then suddenly it is eleven PM on Friday night when I begin again, on the sofa, laptop on my knee, squashed behind the coffee table wishing that I could write this section in a rush right through the night but instead I know I'll sleep on it again, circle around it in my dreams, and be back here again, fingers cramping, shoulders tense, wondering where to start. And there'll be some time soon, too, when I will need to take the package from the government out again from the shelf under the coffee table where it has been for more than three years now as I have no other place where I can file away my brother.

○

I keep approaching this aslant, and again in the almost dark, almost midnight when things like this rush out. Until I read your paper I didn't know you had a brother, too. I don't know how I missed this, or didn't register or remember this from your earlier work. Where was I, I wonder, and what was I avoiding? Your mention of a brother who dies, late in your paper (2009a, p. 374), opens me up unexpectedly, blindsides me, socks me in the gut. You can't predict what points of connection a reader might have inside a text, how that text might call to her or him, and what she or he might recall, what might rise up demanding to be written. Perhaps it is the brevity of your mention of his death, that I don't yet know your brother's name, when I read this paper, before I trace back through your other work, that means your story has such an impact on me, as I write the details of my loss into the space in your text.

○

It's more than thirty years ago and you're peering into the TV screen looking for your brother in the Potomac where his plane fell in the water, and it's almost thirty years ago and I'm flying across a million miles of desert, switching from plane to plane to plane and train, going home to my small town, knowing that I'm already and always (and still) too late and too far away.

Mum and Dad sit vigil in another city by his broken fallen body, holding him to life, calling us as often as they can. Mum remembers talking about organ donations when he got his license, almost a year ago when he turned eighteen. Yes, they say to the doctors, give life to someone else if you can, knowing such donation means turning off life support, not knowing it means staying away from home another day, or having to identify 'a body' so many times. Mum talks to me on the phone when I get home. I feel like (I should be) the big sister, the eldest one. The grown up. I think she says some things she can't say to the younger kids, or to Nanna. I feel like the conduit, the calmer, the one to decide what to say and how to say it. We're all so frightened. He's not going to make it, they say. His organs will fail, one by one, the doctors explain. He looks so calm and still and like himself, they say, despite the fall, despite bouncing off the bonnet of a car at the bottom, onto the bitumen. They don't want to let him go.

Déjà vu. We'd just got through this with my other brother a few short years before. He hadn't looked like himself for months, his head shaved and all stitched up again, his face and body all black stitches and bruises and skin off from the gravel that his body had skidded along. He'd already had the last rites from a priest when my parents made it in to that hospital and was in a coma for three months. They thought for a time that he'd lost an eye, but he didn't, and he didn't die.

Until they sold the place, each time I turn the corner of the passageway upstairs I catch a glimpse of long limbs hanging off his little single bed, twisted round with sheets and falling every which way, his head half off the bed, mouth open, door open, light still on. So sound asleep and so at peace like only kids can be. He was a long and lanky golden boy. We didn't know he'd grow so tall. Where did that come from we wondered, and the lightness of his blue eyes. He was a placid little boy, happy to draw for a whole day, or to glue together tiny pieces of plastic to make model aeroplanes and boats. He was a dreamy sweet sort of a kid. He loved cats and bananas and the Beatles, who broke up about the time he started school.

○

We lived in the middle of nowhere, too, like you. No mountains ringing us in but flat dry land stretching in every direction, salt-stunted mallee and acres of wheat, and a string of low grey lakes. In a good season, if the silo was full, my brothers would let themselves in at the top and leap down to moonwalk through the wheat. They'd bring pockets full away to chew like gum. The tallest buildings on our horizon were the silo and our place, the two story red brick pub with agapanthus along the side and dusty casuarinas sighing out the back. The four or five houses, the football field, the railway platform were all more horizontal than vertical. We had a balcony upstairs where we'd watch electrical storms coming across the sky in summer or we'd check the speed of a rolling red dust storm coming from the west and rush to close the louvers and block the gaps beneath the doors.

How did this landlocked boy get from here into the Australian Navy? That we didn't know. Perhaps it was the enchantment of the toy model kits. Perhaps a recruitment officer visited our high school and one kid in the room paid attention. Perhaps it was the lure of Patrol Boat, an Australian TV show that started just before he signed up for the junior recruit program. He didn't make it through to see the second series. I could ask the same of all of us, all of us who peered beyond that low horizon and moved on to other lives and other places.

○

There's a photo Mum sent me, of the two of us. Just one of just us. With five children that's unusual—or it was in those days when we paid one by one for every photo and waited for weeks for them to come back from the lab. I'm in blinding white, long white socks and sleeves, a white gauze veil falling over my shoulders from a circle of white fake flowers, like a sort of halo on my head. I know my nanna made the veil, perhaps the dress, and probably the little round collared blouse that my little brother wears under his buttoned up brown cardigan. I'm seven. He's three. My head is down, looking to the side, showing off my veil and the crown of my head for the camera. We're in front of my nanna's apple tree, in a larger town we left a few years later. My little brother looks straight at the camera. His cheeks are baby fat and the curls on his forehead would be damp, I know, from someone damping and combing them into place. He looks a little worried, his eyes creasing over a smile-for-the-camera sort of a smile. This is a big day. Mass, we used to go back then. Masses of people, parades of children in white, all the rituals of the first holy communion, all the fussing and fandangle. Four children to scrub up ready for the day. Although my body's turned away from him, his right hand is out towards me, and I've got a big-sister-grasp on his wrist. I'm holding him in place.

Sometimes I think there was another version of this photo, one with all of us in the dappled light under the apples. There's a tiny flash of red on one edge, the dress my sister wore that day, and I imagine where my other brother would have been in that other photo in my mind. I think I see his figure in my memory, arms draped around his beloved floppy eared black spaniel. I wonder if I did this myself, if years ago I cropped the photo Mum had scanned and sent to me. If I forgot, in my desire to retrieve my hold, to magnify our point of contact, to emphasize the circle my hand makes around his, that I was not the only one who suffered the loss of a brother.

o

There was no memorial for my brother. There was only a funeral. His mates from the submarine came all the way into our little desert, his commanding officer. In uniform, they played the last post, draped the flag over his coffin, carried it to the hearse and into the ground. We never saw them again. They circled around our questions about the truth. They couldn't talk about the details. They weren't there. They knew nothing. The hard-edged stone in my gut that started then and stays, turns again each time I hear the last post played. My brother, white capped in his summer uniform, smiles still—a looser smile-for-the-camera smile than when he was three, a red spot on his teenage cheek forever—from the frame on the windowsill in the kitchen in my parents' house. Although they can't be seen here, I know he was wearing white trousers creased seven times for the seven seas, and black shoes shiny from a daily polishing with the brush I now have under my kitchen sink, his name written in his own hand on the back of it. This military issued shoe brush with his name printed on it is the only thing I have now of his, the only thing that his hand and mine have both held. In my mother's kitchen, framed on her windowsill, he still smiles his eighteen-year-old smile at anyone who rinses a glass or washes a pot in the sink, anyone who might lift his or her eyes to glance into his, perhaps to ponder mortality and justice for a moment, before they lift their gaze across the top of the photo frame and down towards the lake.

○

In 2008, when I heard on the radio that the new Australian minister for defence had made a formal apology to the parents of young people who had suicided in the armed forces in recent years, I wrote to say there were other families who had been waiting much longer for an explanation. I received a fat package of papers from the government in response a few months later. My parents also received a long overdue letter of condolence.

Some of these documents I'd seen before. An earlier, slimmer, sheaf of papers—extracted with great difficulty by our lawyers from theirs—had been locked in the safe in my parents' house for decades. My parents had walked me in once, when they first got them, sat me down on their bed, left me there alone to read them, perhaps knowing that I would be calm and that I needed to know. Perhaps, at some point, they walked each of us in for our own personal confrontation with the story the Navy chose to tell us then about the death of my brother. We tend to circle around things when we can. I tell my mother when she visits that I want to write this piece about my brother; she says I should write what I need to write. It's my story, too, she says. It's his, it's hers, it's ours, each time and for each person a little different as our trajectories and intersections shift. And here, Carolyn, what comes up for me in reading your story of loss is another point of intersection, perhaps an invocation. This fat new package from Canberra enters into the assemblage telling me more than I want to know. I don't remember what is new in this bundle, but I read it again and again, over a long time, putting it down and taking it up again when I can stand it.

The minister noted that an in-house board of inquiry was held onsite at the Navy Barracks just three days after the fall from a fifth floor window of the accommodation block. It notes that my brother died "as a result of injuries sustained" and that blame "could not reasonably be attributed to any other person." He notes that "it appears your family was not given access of the Board of Inquiry Report" and encloses a copy of the report, excluding "Annex E to Enclosure One, photographs of the scene, due to their potentially disturbing nature." The minister also details how legislation and policies governing Defence inquiries have drastically changed in the years since 1982. Inquiries are now held in public, he assures me, rather than secretly, and families are provided legal representation before the inquiry.

The report details times and numbers—for example "declared 'brain dead' at 9:45" and "mechanical life support measures ceased at 16:00," the license plate number of the car his body fell onto "LWG859," names and multiple accounts. And it builds an elaborate rationale as to why this young man had variously "dived," "leapt," "thrown himself," "flown," "jumped out" through a window after a scuffle in another sailor's cabin and in the presence of three other sailors. The details of the rationale are not credible to us who had known him intimately all his life. Comments such as "Difficulties were experienced in finding details of the next-of-kin of the deceased" are inexplicable.

The fifty-five pages of transcripts of interviews include graphic details of how the medics managed the body, which clothes were cut off and in what order, details of visible and likely injuries, and details of all the running about, confusion, reported conversations and order of events on the ground. There are ten pages of typed witness accounts to the Naval Police, taken on the night. There are fourteen pages of drawings of the car park and the rooms with angles drawn, a scale for distances, and a key to bloodstains and other pertinent details. There are two pages of ambulance records marking up injuries on a template drawing of a body and tick-boxing the various vital medical details of those injuries. In a sociological context, as well as a legal context, all of this might be fieldnotes, triangulating details in search of the truth. For me they offer complex testimony. I don't read these notes often because each time there is a point (this time it is page 20 at the details of the hospital's desperation to find next-of-kin) where my body starts to shake.

Amongst all the detail, what I look for as I read it again are the few sentences that bring me comfort. The duty officer who is quizzed on how many people were there and how quickly they appeared when he was trying to clear his passageways so he could breathe again says: "I can't honestly say. I didn't bother to count. I was just looking after the boy." He says that they gently turned his body and supported his head while they were waiting for the ambulance. They took his wallet from his back pocket and when "we found who he was we started trying to talk to him to see if he would come around at all." I imagine that scene over and over as I want it to be. If I could I would be there, but I am reliant on these others. It's a Pieta of sorts, in my mind's eye, lit by the street lights at the edge of the car park. I imagine it's around midnight on a soft midwinter Sydney night, as quiet as it can ever be on a Saturday night in this part of the city. While people are running this way and that, panicking, and before the ambulance comes with all its lights and noise, I imagine there's a small circle of stillness in the centre. In it there's an older man, kneeling on the concrete, gently holding this young boy's body in his arms, holding him in place, holding him to life, soothing him towards death, and saying his name softly in his ear—David. David. David.

Sincerely
(With love)
Susanne

Notes

1. Initially the title "Sketching Subjectivities" was allocated by the editors, but the notion of the sketch became a useful figure to think through the post-humanist subject.
2. Definitions compiled from various dictionaries at Wordnik: www.wordnik.com/words/sketch.

References

Cavarero, A. (2000) *Relating narratives: Storytelling and selfhood.* London: Routledge.

Cixous, H., & Derrida, J. (2001). *Veils.* Stanford, CA: Stanford University Press.

Cixous, H. (2006): The flying manuscript. *New Literary History, 37,* 15–46.

Clough, P. T. (2000). *Auto-affection: Unconscious thought in the age of technology.* Minneapolis: University of Minnesota Press.

Clough, P. T. (2007) *The affective turn: Theorising the social.* Durham, NC: Duke University Press.

Colebrook, C. (2004). *Irony.* London: Routledge.

Colebrook, C. (2008). Friendship, seduction and text: Cixous and Derrida. *Angelaki: Journal of the Theoretical Humanities. 13,* 109–124.

Davies, B., & Gannon, S. (2011). Feminism/poststructuralism. In C. Lewin & B. Somekh (Eds.), *Theory and methods in social research* (2nd ed., pp. 312–319). London: Sage.

Deleuze, G. (1995). *Negotiations 1972–1990* (M. Joughin, Trans.). New York: Columbia University Press.

Deleuze, G., & Guattari, F. (2004). *A thousand plateaus* (B. Massumi Trans.). London: Continuum.

Ellis, C. (2004) *The autoethnographic I: A methodological novel about autoethnography.* Walnut Creek, CA: AltaMira Press.

Ellis, C. (2009a) Fighting back or moving on: An autoethnographic response to critics. *International Review of Qualitative Research, 2,* 371–378.

Ellis, C. (2009b). *Revision: Autoethnographic reflections on life and work.* Walnut Creek, CA: Left Coast Press, Inc.

Gale, K., & Wyatt, J. (2009). *Between the two: A nomadic inquiry into collaborative writing and subjectivity.* Newcastle upon Tyne, UK: Cambridge Scholars.

Gannon, S. (2002). Picking at the scabs: A poststructuralist/feminist writing project. *Qualitative Inquiry, 8,* 670–682.

Gannon, S. (2004). Out/performing in the academy: Writing "The Breast Project." *International Journal of Qualitative Studies in Education, 17,* 65–81.

Gannon, S. (2006). The (im)possibilities of writing the self: French poststructural theory and autoethnography. *Cultural Studies ↔ Critical Methodologies, 6,* 474–495.

Gannon, S., & Davies, B. (2012). Postmodern, post-structural and critical theories. In S. Hesse-Biber (Ed.), *Handbook of feminist research: Theory and praxis* (2nd ed., pp. 65–91). Thousand Oaks, CA: Sage.

Kearney, R. (1995). Jacques Derrida. Deconstruction and the other. In R. Kearney (Ed.), *States of mind: Dialogues with contemporary thinkers on the European mind* (pp. 156–177). Manchester, UK: Manchester University Press.

Probyn, E. (2010). Writing shame. In M. Gregg & G. Seigworth (Eds.), *The affect theory reader* (pp. 71–90). Durham, NC: Duke University Press.

Richardson, L. (1990). *Writing strategies. Reaching diverse audiences.* Newbury Park, CA: Sage.

Richardson, L. (1997). *Fields of play.* New Brunswick, NJ: Rutgers University Press.

Somerville, M., Davies, B., Power, K., Gannon, S., & Carteret, P. (2011). *Place pedagogy change.* Rotterdam: Sense.

Wyatt, J., & Gale, K. (2011). The textor, the nomads and a labyrinth: A response to Graham Badley. *Qualitative Inquiry, 17,* 493–497.

Wyatt, J., Gale, K., Gannon, S., & Davies, B. (2011) *Deleuze and collaborative writing: An immanent plane of composition.* New York: Peter Lang.

Chapter 11

Self and Others

Ethics in Autoethnographic Research

Jillian A. Tullis

I'll just write an authoethnography. Maybe you've heard your graduate school peers or faculty colleagues utter these words when faced with the frustrations of trying to gain access to a research site, when filling out Institutional Review Board (IRB; also sometimes called Human Subjects Committee) applications or when trying to recruit seemingly elusive study participants. Doing autoethnography sounds like an easy solution to the myriad bureaucratic, social, political, and regulatory hoops through which scholars must jump to conduct human subjects research. And on its face, it may also appear an easy way to side-step the ethics review process to recruit and engage with others. Deciding, however, to write about or perform your own experiences as a way to understand certain aspects of culture does not eliminate or resolve ethical issues. Nor does it erase the need to engage with others. In fact, using the Self as the primary focus of research—as researcher, informant, and author (Clandinin & Connelly, 2004; Tolich, 2010)—may actually lead to more and more complex ethical dilemmas, some of which may or may not undergo the scrutiny and supervision of an IRB review. Many researchers can collect their data and never return to the field or face their participants again. Scholars who decide to perform or write about culture using their personal experiences will find those performances and manuscripts become permanent records of once private feelings and thoughts that, once set in motion, cannot be revised (Adams, 2008). This dynamic research environment, which uniquely

Handbook of Autoethnography, edited by Stacy Holman Jones, Tony E. Adams, and Carolyn Ellis, 244–261. © 2013 Left Coast Press, Inc. All rights reserved.

tethers researchers to their texts, requires a type of ethical engagement that is highly contextual, contingent, and primarily relational.

A Bit about Me

To begin this discussion about ethics and autoethnography, I should start by explaining my own relationship to this method. In 2009, I completed my doctoral studies in Communication at the University of South Florida, known for its specialization in qualitative research methods, especially autoethnography, narrative, and performance. For full disclosure, I think it's also important for readers of this chapter to know that Dr. Carolyn Ellis, a professor of Communication and Sociology, whom many consider foundational to the proliferation of autoethnography, chaired my dissertation committee. I also took four classes with her, including a doctoral seminar in Autoethnography, and more important than any of these facts, I consider her a mentor and a friend.

I'd like to think I was one of Carolyn's favorite students despite the A- grades I regularly earned in her classes—I promise I'm not bitter—but I can say with certainty that any student of Carolyn's understands her commitment to doing all research, but especially autoethnography, *ethically*. I know the readings and class discussions that focused on ethics left an indelible mark on me because I can hear myself channeling Carolyn when advising my own students. In fact, just days ago, one of my advisees came to me to discuss the possibility of changing the topic of her Master's thesis to an autoethnography about a fifteen-year-old family trauma. My primary questions to this student focused on how she would broach the idea of studying this topic with her family, the ethics of turning this experience into research, and her plans for navigating the IRB application process.

My experiences at the University of South Florida, as expected, shaped my understanding of what constitutes autoethnography. Having explored a wide range of autoethnographic texts and performances, I believe autoethnography exists on a continuum from highly fluid and artistic to formulaic and highly analytic. I find I'm most drawn to autoethnographies that explicitly link personal stories to the broader cultural and scholarly literature. I prefer to let the questions I have about a topic drive my methods, but I recognize that most of the questions I have aren't answered using surveys or statistical analysis, so I conduct primarily ethnographic and narrative research. When hard pressed to define my work, I frequently describe myself as a reflexive ethnographer (see Ellis & Bochner, 2000), which for me involves using my thoughts and feelings to inform my analysis and interpretation of interview and observational data. For some, the explicit role of my experiences on a text makes me an autoethnographer, but because my research goals center on the experiences of those I come in contact with and less on self-narration, I don't ascribe to the label of autoethnographer.

The positionality of the researcher is just one of many important issues to consider when doing autoethnograpy ethically. Autoethnography, as a method, can lead to emotionally and intellectually powerful texts that extend out beyond the page or the stage to affect audiences and communities. Autoethnographers must, therefore, consider the personal, social, political, and ethical consequences of using their experiences as the primary source of research data.

Preview of What's To Come

In order to explore the ethical issues and dilemmas of autoethnography, it is necessary to map the terrain already traversed. Tolich (2010; see also Adams, 2006; Chang, 2008; Chatham-Carpenter, 2010; Ellis, 1995a, 2004, 2007, 2009; Ellis, Adams, & Bochner, 2011; Kiesinger, 2002; Rambo, 2007; Snyder-Young, 2011; Tamas, 2011; Trujillo, 2004; Wall, 2008) offers an excellent exploration of these issues, some of which I will also address here. In discussing the ethical dilemmas of autoethnography for this Handbook, I will discuss the ethics of writing about personal, sometimes traumatic, and potentially stigmatizing topics. Next, I will describe the ethical issues autoethnographers have tackled and those that continue to perplex them. I will close with several guidelines for ethical autoethnography. But first, I will offer some context for understanding ethics in scholarship.

Ethical Foundations and Institutional Review Boards

According to Christians (2005), there are four guidelines that comprise the Code of Ethics for research: 1) informed consent, 2) the prohibition of deception, 3) privacy and confidentiality, and 4) accuracy. In other words, participants should know that the details of a study and their participation is voluntary, researchers should not deceive participants without justification, and researchers must take measures to protect participants' identities and personal information. Finally, ethical research should avoid fabricating, omitting or contriving data ("Protection of Human Subjects, 45 C. F. R. pt. 46," 2009). These guidelines raise several questions for autoethnographers about how personal experience or data are collected and reported and how to protect participants' identities and their confidentiality. Yet, questions arise, especially in an academic setting, about whether or not autoethnography is research.

In the United States, the Belmont Report specifically establishes 1) what practices or methods constitute research, as well as any medical/psychological interventions in a research protocol; 2) the basic ethical principles of autonomy, beneficence, and justice; and 3) applications which include informed consent, risk/benefit assessment, and selection of research participants. Together, the Code of Ethics and the Belmont Report establish the guidelines IRBs and other similar ethics committees at universities and hospitals use to review and approve research studies involving human participants.

Because these guidelines were developed in response to unethical medical and psychological experiments (particularly during WWII), many qualitative researchers, but especially autoethnographers, will find many parts of an IRB application do not apply to their endeavors. However, while some IRBs may not define certain autoethnographic methods and data—such as field notes, interviews, stories, memories, constructed dialogue and arts-based works (e.g., dance, performances, music)—as research, this does not mean that autoethnography is exempt from undergoing at least an initial IRB review.

Most IRBs expect to review projects to determine if they constitute research or scholarship and whether they are exempt from further oversight. Researchers cannot make a determination about what is or is not subject to review independent of the IRB without running the risk of sanctions. It is useful, then, for autoethnographers to familiarize themselves with their institution's or organization's guidelines as a starting place to enact ethical research because the questions posed in IRB applications prompt thinking about research practices and also how to successfully navigate an IRB review.

The ethics review process is not impossible—if I can conduct IRB-approved research with hospice patients (considered a vulnerable population) in their homes, anyone with diligence and patience can see their study approved—but IRB approval is potentially more complex for researchers whose projects do not fit neatly into prescribed ethical containers. To illuminate this point, consider an autoethnographer who may choose to write about past relationships using memories or emotional recall (Ellis, 1999) as the basis for narrating experiences. Some IRBs, for example, do not grant retrospective review and approval of previously collected data. If an IRB applicant fails to articulate how she intends to use her memories, or describes them as "previously collected data," the IRB may question this practice and return the application for revisions or reject the project. It is also useful to state in an IRB application what the data are *not*. For example, it is worth stating (if appropriate) that the data do not come from personal journals or existing field notes from a class, which an ethics review committee may interpret as previously collected data.

Whether subject to IRB review or not, or drawing upon memory or engaging field notes or interview data autoethnographically, "writing about yourself always involves writing about others" (Ellis, 2009, p. 13). It is not always clear to autoethnographers or the IRBs responsible for reviewing and approving their research when the persons autoethnographers write about must consent to participate. In the next section, I will address this topic along with common ethical dilemmas that emerge when doing autoethnography. In doing this, I will touch upon the ethical foundations (e.g., autonomy, beneficence, justice) and the issues of risk and benefit.

Who's a Participant? Issues of Consent and Autonomy

Autoethnographers may claim the stories they write or perform are their own (see Tolich, 2010), but they ultimately cannot avoid implicating others (Ellis, 2007) in their writings or performances. The "others" who appear in autoethnographies are partners (Ellis, 1995b, 2001, 2009; Ellis & Bochner, 1992), friends (Richardson, 2007), family (Adams, 2006; Bochner, 2002; Ellis, 2001; Tamas, 2011; Trujillo, 2004; Wyatt, 2006), students (Ellis, 2004, 2009; Rambo, 2007), colleagues (Berry, 2006; Boylorn, 2006), neighbors (Ellis, 2009), clients (Etherington, 2007), community members (Toyosaki, Pensoneau-Conway, Wendt, & Leathers, 2009), and sometimes strangers (Snyder-Young, 2011). The goal of securing informed consent is to ensure that participants are making an informed, voluntary, and autonomous decision to participate or appear in a text or performance. It also helps ensure that participants are not deceived about the purpose of a scholarly endeavor. Some maintain that individuals who appear in a text are participants who must voluntarily consent prior to the start of a research project or scholarly activity. Conversely, Rambo (2007), for example, attempted to argue her autoeth-nography did not constitute research, as defined by the Belmont Report and her university's IRB, because an individual who appeared in a manuscript she wrote did not participate in a systematic research protocol designed to lead to general-ized findings—and thus consent was unnecessary. Rambo's retrospective request for IRB approval was ultimately denied to protect the interests of the participant featured in the text, and she was unable to publish the manuscript, which was already accepted for publication. This example makes a case for the effort and time it takes to seek and obtain IRB approval.

Tolich (2010) asserts that retrospective consent like that described above is any-thing other than coercive because "it creates a natural conflict of interest between an author's publication and the rights of persons mentioned, with the author's interest unfairly favored over another" (p. 1602). Tolich not only questions the judgment of authors who pursue consent in this way, but also journal editors who agree to publish under these circumstances. While retrospective consent is less than ideal, I think calling this practice coercive lacks nuance. The prescriptive nature of informed consent as frequently carried out now is impractical for many research settings. Consider, for example, when I was conducting research with hospice patients, a vulnerable population that requires extra protections by IRBs. There were times when the setting was laden with sadness as family members surrounded their loved one's bed praying or saying their final goodbyes. I found this the least appropriate time to explain my study and ask for consent. When possible, I waited for more suitable opportunities to engage in this process or opted to not do it at all. These individuals were not included as participants in the larger project, but these experiences did inform my analysis. What this example illuminates is that the inductive nature of qualitative research makes it difficult to consistently predict how and when researchers will need to seek permission from those individuals they may want to include in their projects. I believe not pursuing publication on the part of a scholar or editor because an author did not receive informed consent prior to beginning the project is shortsighted, particularly if we understand writing or performing as an emergent method of inquiry (Richardson, 2000) and accept that autoethnography frequently involves investigating past experiences and related memories.

Decisions about how to approach obtaining consent from the others autoethnographers choose to include in their narratives are not easily resolved by employing a single or universal procedure. Researchers and ethics review boards should consider the timing of an autoethnographic project (e.g., writing about the past vs. the present), its content (e.g., is the topic potentially stigmatizing or controversial and for whom?), and how prevalent are others in the text (e.g., is a family member, friend, or community member mentioned just once or does he or she appear frequently in a text and become, therefore, a major character in the narrative?). Most IRB applications will ask autoethnographers to articulate how they will secure consent. Best practices allow participants to consent as early in the process as possible. In some instances, this will occur during the planning phase; for others consent may occur after a text is drafted. This will ensure ethical research and minimize harm to participants while considering the context and the researcher/participant relationship. Seeking consent early in the process is preferred, but researchers who find themselves seeking consent retrospectively (if allowed by their IRBs) should make clear their commitment to follow through only with the permission of those who appear in their texts.

First, Do No Harm

Informed consent may seem cumbersome and a bureaucratic formality, but this is frequently the first opportunity researchers have to discuss the risks and benefits of the study or project. Therefore, autoethnographers should take into account what Etherington (2007) calls the ethics of consequences as well as the beneficence of the project and ensuring justice. In autoethnography, the ethics of consequence include the positive and negative costs of participating in a research study. This practice mirrors what Ellis (2007) calls "process consent" where the scholar checks in with participants during each stage of the project to ensure their continued willingness to take part. Beneficence, or non-maleficence, is the edict to do no harm and calls upon scholars to consider if and how the research or interventions (if there are any) may cause harm to participants. It is important to note that the absence of harm is not necessarily a requirement—emotional responses, which are not by definition harmful, are difficult to predict or prevent in some settings—but researchers should make every effort to minimize harm and maximize the benefits for participants. It is here where researchers should enact the ethical principle of justice, which involves ensuring the distribution of risks and benefits equally among all participants. If an autoethnography only involves a researcher and two participants, for example, a researcher should not expose one participant to more risk than the other. The same standards apply to organizations or community groups.

To draw a sharper distinction between these two related concepts, autoethnographers should understand beneficence as those actions they can take from the conceptualization phase and beyond to minimize harm and maximize benefits (if any should exist) to the others whom they engage. Whereas the ethics of consequences involves conversations between a researcher and participant(s), including communities, to consider the pros and cons of their inclusion in a project, throughout its evolution. It is during this dialogue that researchers, while acknowledging, and in some cases minimizing, the power differentials that exist in research relationships (Etherington, 2007), can help participants make informed choices and prevent deception.

Just as when working with intimate others, autoethnographers should work to enact the ethical principles of autonomy, beneficence, and justice as well with the communities they work with and perform or write about. A major challenge when working with communities frequently involves attempting to appease many individuals with diverging goals and meshing those demands with the scholar's own research plan. Much like conducting research with individuals, it is wise to use these differences as an opportunity to engage in a dialogue with community members and stakeholders. These interactions are often necessary to gain access, but are useful for developing a trusting research relationship that fosters a depth of understanding about a community's experience (Toyosaki et al., 2009). Community members, IRBs, and individuals may pose questions about the risks, costs, and benefits of the end product, the performance, art, or manuscript; this is an excellent time to discuss the possibility and consequences of being identified by readers or audiences and how confidentiality will be protected, which is the focus of the following section.

Protecting Identity and Confidentiality

Protecting participants' identities and keeping their private information confidential is an essential component of ethical research. There are several strategies for protecting the identity and keeping confidential those who appear in autoethnographic research and performances. Often this involves keeping records secure by doing such things as de-identifying data. Giving individuals pseudonyms or changing a person's demographic information (e.g., age, race, sex) is common. Creating composite characters by collapsing several people into one is another technique (Ellis, 2007). Others choose to fictionalize parts of a narrative to disguise time and place, building some distance between the facts of an event and the researcher (Ellis, 2004). Robin Boylorn (2006), Stacy Holman Jones (2005), and Christopher Poulos (2008), all professors of Communication Studies, use a variety of abstract, perhaps postmodern, writing techniques and modes of performance, including poetry and spoken word, that are particularly effective at obscuring and de-identifying the others in their work. Wyatt (2006) discusses the use of the third-person over the first-person to give the reader psychic distance and grant the protagonists respect. According to Wyatt, by not getting *too close* the third person gives space to the unknown and accomplishes writing without power, which involves writing tentatively and with less certainty than found in most scholarship so that readers can come to their own conclusions. Even these efforts may not do enough to protect all who appear in autoethnographic narratives.

There are some instances when there is no way to avoid revealing a person's or community's identity and confidentiality while accomplishing the objectives of the project. This is especially true if an autoethnography is about a family member, partner, or even a professional colleague (see Adams, 2006, 2008; Bochner, 2002; Ellis, 1995b, 2001; Poulos, 2006, 2008; Tamas, 2011; Trujillo, 2004). The techniques designed to obscure a person's identity do almost nothing to keep confidential or private certain information from other family members or from friends, colleagues, or acquaintances who already know the make up of a family or organization or community group (Etherington, 2007; Tolich, 2010). The potential for exposure requires careful deliberation about its consequences. In some cases (see Etherington, 2007), not appearing in a text or performance is the best solution. Sometimes, revealing the contents of a project to others not directly related to but implicated in the scholarship helps mitigate shock, embarrassment, or harm. Potential autoethnographers need to consider the risks of conducting this type of research not only for others, but also for themselves.

Protecting the Self

IRBs are rightly concerned with minimizing risks and protecting research participants from harm, but they are far less concerned with the effects the research process can have on the researcher. The texts and performances produced from autoethnographic methods not only expose others, but can also make autoethnographers themselves vulnerable. Chatham-Carpenter (2010) explores this issue in a meta-autoethnography focusing on her decision to write about her compulsive eating disorder, which reemerged as compulsive writing behavior during the project (see also Tolich, 2010). Her story brings up questions about what harm, if any, autoethnography can have on the writer/performer.[1] The writing process itself can be considered therapeutic (Ellis, Adams, & Bochner, 2011), but tapping into past experiences also involves recalling and in essence reliving them. While reengaging and interrogating past experiences may prove cathartic, it can also generate emotions that require attention, even professional therapy (Chatham-Carpenter, 2010; Tolich, 2010). Once written, autoethnographic work is subjected to the scrutiny of others in the classroom, at conferences, while undergoing peer review, or when presenting findings to community and organization members. Making autoethnography public in this way can be exhilarating and gratifying when others affirm the value of personal experiences and interpretations. Alternatively, having a personal story critiqued, especially publicly, can hurt emotionally, personally, and professionally. The very thought that it could hurt is troubling for some (Wall, 2008). In some cases these critiques feel harsher because the method is so readily challenged. I offer these words of caution to potential autoethnographers, and I repeat them often. I also encourage scholars to anticipate questions and critiques, not only about the choice of method, but also the content, just as any other scholar would. Preparation, however, doesn't always work; I've seen emotions emerge in response to challenges or a well-meaning and valid question from audience members. Emotional reactions are not inherently problematic, but if self-presentation is important, it is worth considering if these risks outweigh the benefits of this method.

While I believe the potential pitfalls of disseminating autoethnographic texts exist for veteran and novice researchers alike, I believe students who write personal narratives require specific direction. As a graduate student I frequently questioned, with the guidance of my professors, if I had the skills and credibility to write effective autoethnography. I also considered what barriers autoethnography might pose to employment and tenure. I contemplated how making certain private details about my life public would alter the way others viewed me and those who might appear in my stories. I was aware that certain disclosures, especially about stigmatizing topics, could perpetuate stigma and prejudice towards me even if my goal was to combat these attitudes. Despite the successes of several of my former professors and three peers who all became successful and gainfully employed autoethnographers, I made choices during graduate school about autoethnography based upon my comfort with making myself personally and professionally vulnerable (see Ellis, 2004).

Autoethnographers may knowingly take on some personal and professional risks to write, perform and present their research. But I think it is wise to consider the ethics, for example, of requiring students to pursue autoethnographic writing in class assignments as well as their research, due to the professional and emotional risks. Rather than avoid autoethnography all together, I make it one option among several others in my classes. If students choose this approach to scholarship, I counsel them about the advantages and disadvantages of making their personal stories public, particularly if those stories involve emotionally or politically charged topics such as abortion. Because I also require peer reviews and public speeches in my classes, I offer strategies for students to modify their papers and presentations so they can maintain their privacy. I also ask students to consider whether or not they can accomplish the same research and writing goals using a different method because autoethnography is rewarding but ethically challenging.

The discussion thus far suggests that writing or appearing in an autoethnography is not inherently problematic. However, doing no harm and knowing when this standard is met is a bit more difficult to discern. With other methods, the research design and data collection techniques are said to mitigate harm. But as I have written elsewhere (Tullis, 2012), even the most sound research protocol vetted and approved by an IRB—autoethnography or not—can raise ethical dilemmas. For autoethnographers doing no harm is sometimes an imagined state rather than a known reality, particularly if the researcher has no direct contact with the intimate others who appear in a text. With that said, doing no harm in the context of autoethnography rests on the notion that every effort was made to protect a person's identity, portray him or her as accurately and with as much nuance as possible, and when feasible and practical, engaging in informed consent and member checks, which I will discuss in the next section. The potential for harm may remain, however, when intimate others or community/organization members disagree with interpretations or are hurt by the ways we depict them, even if those depictions are accurate.

Member Checking, Memories and Interpretations

Some autoethnographers may choose to engage in a process akin to a member check (Lindlof & Taylor, 2002) where individuals are given a chance to read and comment on stories in which they appear to check accuracy and interpretations (Ellis, 1999; Tamas, 2011). Still others will choose not to engage this process out of concern that sharing will do more harm than good to their relationships (Adams, 2006; Kiesinger, 2002). I understand why some authors may choose this approach, but I'm reluctant to recommend pursuing scholarship under these circumstances without careful consideration. If I feel I am unable to share my work, I use this sentiment to engage in additional reflexivity and reevaluate my depictions or interpretations. If I have engaged this process and still cannot reconcile my feelings, I've committed to not present or publish any work I feel uncomfortable showing to those I've written about. Some will disagree with this stance and contend that there are times when the benefits to self and others and related contribution to our knowledge outweigh this hazard. Whether or not intimate others have a chance to respond to what is written about them or discover these texts, autoethnographers run the risk of hurting a person they love or care about (Ellis, 1995a; Tamas, 2011) or damaging a research relationship with a community group or organization.

Issues also arise if the others we write about disagree with our interpretations or recall the details of an experience differently (see Tullis Owen, McRae, Adams & Vitale, 2009). I've experienced challenges to my interpretations and my memories in response to conducting member checks and seeking permission to include others in my work. In a study of a hospice team, I simply made changes based upon a participant's feedback. The revisions did not fundamentally change the point of the narrative, but did improve the accuracy of my recollections. But in another case, a friend and graduate school colleague disagreed with my depiction and interpretations of her. We engaged in a dialogue about how and why I made certain authorial choices, and she ultimately allowed my version to stand—even though she initially found the description of her emotions less than flattering. Her training as a qualitative researcher and autoethnographer may have influenced her decision to let my rendition stand, yet others less familiar with the conventions and goals of research may respond differently or not at all. I worry about how participants (whether they see or hear about findings or not) will receive my interpretations and depictions, and I find the time between sending the manuscripts to participants for review and receiving their responses nerve-wracking. Despite striving for accuracy and offering the most generous, albeit sometimes messy, descriptions of participants (Adams, 2006), I'm aware of the awkwardness others may feel when reading what is written about them. The experience, however, creates space for dialogue, which can lead not only to more accurate descriptions and details, but also to deeper and more nuanced interpretations. Ethics in autoethnography do not stop after considering the risks to self and others and minimizing or preventing harm; scholars must also consider the audiences who come in contact with their work.

Ethically Engaging Audiences

During a performance in 1971, artist Chris Burden was shot in his left arm by an assistant with a rifle from fifteen feet (Schjeldahl, 2007). Thirty-four years later, I learned of Burden during a course co-taught by Stacy Holman Jones and Art Bochner. Stacy's reference to Burden's performance, *Shoot*, haunted me. She challenged us to think of how we leave the audiences we engage and implicate in our performances and presentations. Interestingly, that same year while I sat in my first courses as a doctoral student, Burden and Nancy Rubins, his wife (also an artist), resigned from their professorships at UCLA because they felt administrators were too slow to sanction a student who used a gun during a performance to simulate Russian roulette (Boehm, 2005). While these performance artists were not engaged in autoethnography, the performances were certainly personal since each artist put his body at risk in the presence of audiences. It is not clear if either considered his act ethically responsible to his audience, yet Burden's work took place in an arts context where the audience members placed themselves in a situation in which the "shoot" of the advertised performance would occur. The performance at UCLA was a surprise for classroom audience members and generated a good deal of fear. Both performances illustrate the importance of ethically engaging audiences in context.

Berry (2006) notes that the impact of autoethnography on audiences is under explored and calls upon researchers to consider the "less-planned ways in which audiences are implicated by autoethnography" (p. 96). I want to take this observation a bit further and discuss the ethical issues relevant to presenting or performing autoethnography to audiences.

Researchers present their scholarship for a range of reasons and types of audiences, including academic peers or the very communities previously under investigation. Performance/presentation goals consist of promoting thinking and learning, fostering understanding, and disseminating knowledge (Berry, 2006). Audience analysis—determining what audiences know, need and expect—is key to a successful presentation, yet autoethnographers may also have certain specific objectives for audiences. Ellis and Bochner (2000), for example, call for an evocative form of autoethnography that prompts an emotional response in audiences (including readers). Gingrich-Philbrook (2005) questions this aim and observes that to "compel a response is to compel an experience" (p. 308). Compelling an experience may prove ethically precarious, especially because audiences' reactions can exist on a rather long continuum, even when encountering the same text at the same time.

IRBs and other ethics committees responsible for reviewing and monitoring research rarely consider what happens after data collection ceases and reports or scripts are written and presented. This means that scholars are usually solely responsible for making ethical choices when interacting with audience members. Is it ethical, for instance, to perform or present in a way that fosters tears among audience members, or that encourages them to engage in violent behavior or re-live past traumas? The answers to these questions are not universal and frequently depend upon how audiences come to a text (see Tullis Owen et al., 2009).

While I've not heard of such overtly violent or traumatic performances of autoethnographic texts as the performance art examples just referenced, I do know of performances and presentations that involved profanity, nudity, fake weapons, allusions to suicide attempts, simulated masturbation, and displays of pornography. In these cases, it is worth considering the makeup of audiences and offering an advisory or warning prior to the start of a public presentation with explicit content. Some presenters also offer opportunities for audience members to process what they've witnessed during talk backs, debriefs, or question and answer sessions illustrating an ethic of care. Those who do not engage in these practices should have a justification for leaving audiences to process their experiences on their own. If scholars are compelling a particular response or experience, the goals of an autoethnography must be ethical, especially since we can never fully know audiences and how they will react to performances or print texts.

Existing in (and Answering) the Questions

Exploring ethical autoethnographic practices reveals how much control, power, and responsibility scholars of this method have. This *narrative privilege*, as Adams (2008) calls it, means that life writers (which include autoethnographers) "must consider who is able to tell a story and who has the ability to listen" (p. 180). Adams goes on to say, "Acknowledgment of narrative privilege motivates us to discern who we might hurt or silence in telling stories as well as those stories we do not (and may not ever) hear" (p. 183). Autoethnographers frequently acknowledge these concerns in their writing (see Etherington, 2007), but this is just the first step. Here are several questions autoethnographers should consider and answer before and during the writing process (paraphrased from Ellis, 2009), many of which will not appear in an IRB application:

- Do you have the right to write about others without their consent?

- What effect do these stories have on individuals and your relationship with them?

- How much detail and which difficulties, traumas, or challenges are necessary to include to successfully articulate the story's moral or goal?

- Are you making a case to write (or not to write) because it is more or less convenient for you?

- Should you and will you allow participants to read and approve all of the stories about them? Or just those stories that you think are problematic or potentially hurtful?

Ellis (2009) takes "solace in believing that continuing to be mindful about ethics in research and to ask ethical questions are crucial parts of ethical decision making" (p. 22). These questions and contemplations create ambiguity and can thus lead to endless questioning (Adams, 2008). Not all research, however, can subsist in the questions alone, especially since we frequently look to published literature for answers. Contemplating ethics in research is important, but theories and values should match praxis (Tolich, 2010). Autoethnographers are not only the instruments of data collection, but also the data, as well as the authors of texts, and this makes some audiences leery about the ethos of the method and therefore the knowledge generated from this approach. This skepticism can enable and constrain, but it ultimately creates additional pressures for autoethnographers to explain the sources of their data as well as the way they address ethical issues. If an autoethnography consists of emotional recall, triggers, or critical incidents (Ellis, 1999), it is worth describing this process to readers. Descriptions of what stories were selected over others and how they were crafted (that is, by fictionalizing) can lend credibility to an essay or a performance and, by extension, a scholar's analysis and interpretations. Laying bare a scholar's answers enables ethical practice.

Ethical Guidelines for Autoethnographers

Others before me have created guidelines for conducting ethical autoethnography (Adams, 2008; Ellis, 2004, 2009; Tolich, 2010; Wyatt, 2006), so what I intend to do here is link them together, if possible, and recount many of them while including some strategies to accomplish ethical life writing. The guidelines are as follows:

1. *Do no harm to self and others*. It is important that autoethnographers do not ignore the potential for personal and professional self-harm while minimizing risk and maximizing benefits to others.

2. *Consult your IRB*. While IRBs appear an enemy of the autoethnographer, ask because it is safer to ask for permission than seek forgiveness. IRBs can offer helpful advice about how to proceed with conducting research that protects not only the institution's interests, but also those of researchers and their

participants. The consequences for failing to consult the IRB are great and can result in banning a researcher from conducting any research.

3. *Get informed consent*. This practice is consistent with a commitment to respect participants' autonomy, honors the voluntary nature of participation, and ensures documentation of the informed consent processes that are foundational to qualitative inquiry (*Congress of Qualitative Inquiry*, 2006). Secure informed consent as early in the process as possible to avoid conflicts of interest or consenting under duress (Tolich, 2010). This may occur when contemplating a project, while in the field, during the writing process, or after the project is complete. Remember that it is easier and more ethical to obtain consent and later choose to not include a person in a narrative then it is to ask permission later. Consider from whom, how, and when to obtain consent before starting the project.

4. *Practice process consent* and explore the *ethics of consequence* (Ellis, 2007; Etherington, 2007). This affords others the opportunity to remain autonomous and helps ensure voluntary participation in a project throughout the project.

5. *Do a member check*. A member check is the final stage of process consent procedures and affords those who appear in autoethnographies an opportunity to comment upon and correct interpretations and observations, as well as rescind their participation completely.

6. *Do not present publicly or publish anything you would not show the persons mentioned in the text* (Ellis, 2004; Tolich, 2010). Prudent autoethnographers will use this guideline even if they are reasonably certain those persons will never gain access to or ever see what was written about them (Adams, 2008; Ellis, 1995a). This rule should apply to the living as well as the dead because it will encourage thoughtful consideration of how others are portrayed, even if they never see or hear what is written.

7. *Do not underestimate the afterlife of a published narrative* (Adams, 2008; Ellis, 1995a). While a published narrative may remain static, audiences' responses to it do not. It's worth considering how to write to multiple audiences while considering ways to protect the others who appear in texts.

These seven guidelines are a starting place for creating ethical autoethnography, and those who choose to take up autoethnography may find other ways to ensure autonomy, beneficence and justice for themselves and those they include in their texts. I would encourage autoethnographers to give more consideration to the latter two principles of the Belmont Report—beneficence and justice—as these considerations are often neglected by all types of researchers, qualitative and quantitative. Doing autoethnography well means taking ethics seriously. As Carolyn Ellis (2009) observes:

> It is easier to talk abstractly about ethics than it is to put an ethical stance into practice; it is easier doing a "mea culpa" about what one should have done in former studies than figuring out the right way to proceed in current ones; it's

easier to instruct others who must make ethical decisions in their research than to follow one's own advice; it's easier to embrace relational ethics than it is to figure out whom we owe relational loyalty when our readers and participants differ in values, our hearts and minds are in conflict. (p. 23)

I agree that our hearts and minds will disagree from time to time—the opportunity to publish, for example, is enticing and central to our work as scholars—but to detour from these guiding principles when it solely benefits autoethnographers is risky. At the same time, I recognize that these guidelines are only guidelines, and I encourage autoethnographers to engage in contextual, yet relational, ethics, which take into consideration the personal and professional connection between researcher and participants, to protect themselves and others. And always to keep their eyes trained on the ethical and moral foundations that guide their research agendas in the first place.

The issues described here illustrate the complexities of applying ethical research practices, because what constitutes research, who are participants, and the very techniques used to create autoethnography are fluid. Autoethnographers must consider how they will navigate and address each of these issues before, during, and after the writing process. The edict *do no harm* should serve as an ever-present guiding principle for protecting others while considering if and how doing autoethnography can cause harm to the researcher as well. The flexibility and ambiguity inherent in this method serves as a keen reminder that ethical research is not accomplished by checking boxes, completing forms, creating pseudonyms or drafting an ironclad informed consent form. In fact, autoethnographers should regard ethics as a process that is frequently relational (Adams, 2008; Ellis, 2007, 2009; Ellis, Adams, & Bochner, 2011). Autoethnographers should use, rather than resist, the Code of Ethics (e.g., informed consent, accuracy, deception, confidentiality, and privacy) and the moral standards for research involving human subjects as established by the Belmont Report (e.g., autonomy, beneficence, and justice; see Christians, 2005) to establish and enact practices that focus on and respect the interests of others as well as themselves.

Closing Thoughts

Autoethnographers sometimes receive less oversight from IRBs than other researchers because scholars don't consult them and sometimes because IRBs don't consider autoethnography research, but this does not discharge autoethnographers of their ethical responsibilities. I have suggested here that because of the authorial power autoethnographers have over those individuals who appear in their texts, and in light of the fact that these individuals are frequently intimate others, means that the responsibility to do no harm is even greater (Adams, 2008; Ellis, 2007). I would like to call on all autoethnographers to lay bare and make vulnerable their ethical process. Ethical considerations are frequently addressed at the end of an autoethnography, with authors relegating their ethical concerns and considerations to the last few pages of a manuscript. Readers should not assume that ethics are an afterthought; it behooves writers, performers and artists to address these issues throughout their work when possible. These pages, however, should not only include the ethical questions raised by the writing, but the answers to those questions. There is much to gain from making an autoethnography's ethics more visible. Not only does it boost the ethos of life writing, but makes autoethnography less daunting for those who may want to attempt this scholarship. Moreover, by ethically shoring up autoethnography, it also makes visible the ethical concerns of other methods. In writing this chapter, for example, I've come to question how any researcher could ever know that her or his work has met the standard of doing no harm. For decades, many of us have worked under the assumption that the method and its application, coupled with informed consent, protect against harm. By considering the issues raised by autoethnography and turning them back onto other methods, what constitutes ethical research praxis may require development. While I am confident that ethics are not an afterthought, at least not among the autoethnographers I know, this should be clear to readers and theory should match practice. Most autoethnographers have considered the ethical pitfalls of life writing from the beginning, during, and well after completing their manuscripts. And many of them write their narratives despite the risks to themselves in the interest of challenging canonical narratives that render so many experiences voiceless. If autoethnographers don't take up this charge, especially in the academy, I'm not sure who will. For many scholars this call to self-narration *is* the ethics of autoethnography.

Note

1. In extreme cases where the safety of the writer is at stake or potentially compromised, an editor could require the author to assume a nom de plume, as was the case for one survivor of domestic violence (Morse, 2002).

References

Adams, T. E. (2006). Seeking father: Relationally reframing a troubled love story. *Qualitative Inquiry, 12,* 704–723.

Adams, T. E. (2008). A review of narrative ethics. *Qualitative Inquiry, 14,* 175–194.

Berry, K. (2006). Implicated audience member seeks understanding: Reexamining the "gift" of autoethnography. *International Journal of Qualitative Methods, 5,* 94–108.

Bochner, A. (2002). Love survives. *Qualitative Inquiry, 8,* 161–169.

Boehm, M. (January 22, 2005). 2 Artists quit UCLA over gun incident [Electronic Version]. *The Los Angeles Times,* from articles.latimes.com/2005/jan/22/local/me-profs22

Boylorn, R. M. (2006). E pluribus unum (Out of many, one). *Qualitative Inquiry, 12,* 651–680.

Chang, H. (2008). *Autoethnography as method.* Walnut Creek, CA: Left Coast Press, Inc.

Chatham-Carpenter, A. (2010). "Do thyself no harm": Protecting ourselves as autoethnographers. *Journal of Research Practice, 6,* 1–13.

Christians, C. G. (2005). Ethics and politics in qualitative research. In N. K. Denzin & Y. S. Lincoln (Eds.), *The SAGE handbook of qualitative research* (3rd ed., pp. 139–164). Thousand Oaks, CA: Sage.

Clandinin, D. J., & Connelly, F. M. (2004). *Narrative inquiry: Experience and story in qualitative research.* San Francisco: Jossey-Bass.

Congress of Qualitative Inquiry. (2006). *Position statement on qualitative research on IRBs.* quig.psu.edu/docs/IRB_PositionStatement.pdf [Electronic Version].

Ellis, C. (1995a). Emotional and ethical quagmires in returning to the field. *Journal of Contemporary Ethnography, 24,* 68–98.

Ellis, C. (1995b). *Final negotiations: A story of love, loss, and chronic illness.* Philadelphia: Temple University Press.

Ellis, C. (1999). Heartful autoethnography. *Qualitative Health Research, 9,* 669–683.

Ellis, C. (2001). With mother/with child. *Qualitative Inquiry, 7,* 598–616.

Ellis, C. (2004). *The ethnographic I: A methodological novel about autoethnography.* Walnut Creek, CA: AltaMira Press.

Ellis, C. (2007). Telling secrets, revealing lives: Relational ethics in research with intimate others. *Qualitative Inquiry, 13,* 3–29.

Ellis, C. (2009). Telling tales on neighbors: Ethics in two voices. *International Review of Qualitative Research, 2,* 3–28.

Ellis, C., Adams, T. E., & Bochner, A. (2011). Autoethnography: An overview [40 paragraphs]. *Forum Qualitative Sozialforschung/Forum: Qualitative Social Research, 12*(1), Art. 10, nbn-resolving.de/urn:nbn:de:0144-fqs1101108

Ellis, C., & Bochner, A. (1992). Telling and performing personal stories: The constraints of choice in abortion. In C. Ellis & M. Flaherty (Eds.), *Investigating subjectivity: Research on lived experience* (pp. 79–101). Newbury Park, CA: Sage.

Ellis, C., & Bochner, A. (2000). Autoethnography, personal narrative, reflexivity: Researcher as subject. In N. K. Denzin & Y. S. Lincoln (Eds.), *Handbook of qualitative inquiry* (2nd ed., pp. 733–768). Thousand Oaks, CA: Sage.

Etherington, K. (2007). Ethical research in reflexive relationships. *Qualitative Inquiry, 13,* 599–616.

Gingrich-Philbrook, C. (2005). Autoethnography's family values: Easy access to compulsory experiences. *Text and Performance Quarterly, 25,* 297–314.

Holman Jones, S. (2005). (M)othering loss: Telling adoption stories, telling performativity. *Text and Performance Quarterly, 25,* 113–135.

Kiesinger, C. E. (2002). My father's shoes: The therapeutic value of narrative reframing. In A. Bochner & C. Ellis (Eds.), *Ethnographically speaking: Autoethnography, literature, and aesthetics* (pp. 95–114). Walnut Creek, CA: AltaMira Press.

Lindlof, T., R., & Taylor, B. C. (2002). *Qualitative communication research methods.* Thousand Oaks, CA: Sage.

Morse, J. (2002). Writing my own experience. *Qualitative Health Research, 12,* 1159–1160.

Poulos, C. N. (2006). The ties that bind us, the shadows that separate us: Life and death, shadow and (dream)story. *Qualitative Inquiry, 12,* 96–117.

Poulos, C. N. (2008). Narrative conscience and the autoethnographic adventure: Probing memories, secrets, shadows, and possibilities. *Qualitative Inquiry, 14, 46–66.*

Protection of Human Subjects, 45 C. F. R. pt. 46. (2009).

Rambo, C. (2007). Handing IRB an unloaded gun. *Qualitative Inquiry, 13,* 353–367.

Richardson, L. (2000). Writing: A method of inquiry. In N. K. Denzin & Y. S. Lincoln (Eds.), *Handbook of qualitative inquiry* (2nd ed., pp. 923–949). Thousand Oaks, CA: Sage.

Richardson, L. (2007). *Last writes: A daybook for a dying friend.* Walnut Creek, CA: Left Coast Press, Inc.

Schjeldahl, P. (2007). Chris Burden and the limits of art [Electronic Version]. *The New Yorker.* www.newyorker.com/arts/critics/artworld/2007/05/14/070514craw_artworld_schjeldahl

Snyder-Young, D. (2011). "Here to tell her story": Analyzing the autoethnographic performance of others. *Qualitative Inquiry, 17,* 943–951.

Tamas, S. (2011). Autoethnography, ethics, and making your baby cry. *Cultural Studies ↔ Critical Methodologies, 11*, 258–264.

Tolich, M. (2010). A critique of current practice: Ten foundational guidelines for autoethnographers. *Qualitative Health Research, 20*, 1599–1610.

Toyosaki, S., Pensoneau-Conway, S. L., Wendt, N. A., & Leathers, K. (2009). Community autoethnography: Compiling the personal and resituating whiteness. *Cultural Studies ↔ Critical Methodologies, 9*, 56–83.

Trujillo, N. (2004). *In search of Naunny's grave: Age, class, gender, and ethnicity in an American family.* Walnut Creek, CA: AltaMira Press.

Tullis, J. A. (in press). Participant observation at the end-of-life and the power of tears. *Health Communication.*

Tullis Owen, J. A., McRae, C., Adams, T. E., & Vitale, A. (2009). truth troubles. *Qualitative Inquiry, 15*, 178–200.

Wall, S. (2008). Easier said than done: Writing an autoethnography. *International Journal of Qualitative Methods, 7*, 38–53.

Wyatt, J. (2006). Psychic distance, consent, and other ethical issues: Reflections on the writing of "A Gentle Going?" *Qualitative Inquiry, 12*, 813–818.

Chapter 12

Relationships and Communities in Autoethnography

Kathy-Ann C. Hernandez and
Faith Wambura Ngunjiri

Introduction

We[1] met in Kathy-Ann's office after receiving feedback on the first draft of this chapter to discuss how we could improve it:

Kathy-Ann: *Okay, I think we did a decent job figuring out the conceptual elements of the chapter and highlighting what the literature says. Perhaps now we need to be a bit more transparent about our own experiences.*

Faith: *Yes. Let's draw on our four years of working together to illustrate relational dynamics in autoethnography. Alongside that we could keep a dialogue going to reveal our process working together on this chapter.*

Kathy-Ann: *I like it! My one concern is that our experiences with collaborative autoethnography involve Heewon, yet she is not a co-author in this chapter. We need to make sure that her voice is represented here.*

Faith: *You are right. Let's figure out the storyline. Then we can involve Heewon as the story unfolds.*

As social scientists, we have strong backgrounds in quantitative (Kathy-Ann) and qualitative (Faith) research methods. Our colleague Heewon Chang, author

---

Handbook of Autoethnography, edited by Stacy Holman Jones, Tony E. Adams, and Carolyn Ellis, 262–280. © 2013 Left Coast Press, Inc. All rights reserved.

of *Autoethnography as Method* (2008), was the first to introduce us to autoethnography praxis. For both of us, it was love at *first write*. Finally, here was the opportunity to bring skills from our undergraduate education in language and literature and to position our experiences into our scholarship. Still, it is a struggle. The many years of training and practice in social science research methods have distanced us a bit from that earlier background, and we are prone to lean on the more analytical end of the autoethnography continuum (Ngunjiri, Hernandez, & Chang, 2010). Inserting ourselves more intimately into our scholarship has yet to become "natural" praxis; it is a skill that we are still learning to master.

Since we were introduced to autoethnography we have worked on a number of solo and collaborative projects. Collaborative work is an exercise in the intersubjective nature of human experiences. What you are now reading represents an artifact of our (Kathy-Ann's and Faith's) collaborative efforts to listen to, care for, and represent each other's voices, and be sensitive to the expectations of our peer-reviewers and editors even as we attempt to represent our individual selves. We also [re]present our colleague Heewon because, to an extent, our stories of collaborative writing involve and implicate her as our collaborator. We weave some of our experiences of doing solo and collaborative autoethnography that are illustrative of the relational dynamics in autoethnographic work throughout this chapter.

Autoethnography and Self-Others Connections

Autoethnography, whether solo or collaborative, is a research genre that is dependent on relationships. As we attempt to tell our stories, we inevitably find that these incidents involve others. Thus, autoethnography may be the study of self, but it is the study of self in relation to others within a particular social setting (Chang, 2008; Ellis, 2004). Salient to these stories are two kinds of relationships: intrapersonal and interpersonal. Many authors have published autoethnographies in which the focal relationship is intrapersonal—the researcher is confronting one of his/her marginalized or unexamined selves—for example, dealing with/living with eating disorders such as anorexia (Chatham-Carpenter, 2010) or struggling with one's depression (Jago, 2002). Other autoethnographies have focused primarily on interpersonal relationships. For example, the researcher's experience with an intimate other's life struggles such as a mother-daughter relationship where the mother is sick and the daughter is the caretaker (Ellis, 1996) or watching a close friend die (Richardson, 2007).

Irrespective of the primary focus of an autoethnographic study, intrapersonal and interpersonal relationships remain interconnected. We have written autoethnographies in which we explored the intersection of our spiritual and academic selves in institutions where we have worked. Our relationships with others within these contexts were central to the stories we told. Faith writes of encounters with faculty who, during her graduate studies, discouraged her from undertaking studies on women, spirituality and leadership, suggesting that to do so would be to marginalize herself and her work (Ngunjiri, 2011). Kathy-Ann critiques institutional cultures and academic practices that perpetuate grade inflation by referencing interactions with students at our current university (Hernandez, 2011). Writing those pieces, we each experienced qualms about what to say. Nagging questions surfaced: "Should I write this about myself/others?" "What if my department chair reads this?" "What if my former faculty colleagues read this?" "Have I portrayed others fairly?" When we first began doing autoethnographic work, we had given little thought to such questions. However, as we mature in our understanding of autoethnographic research practice, we are more cognizant of these relational dynamics.

Life stories are by definition "self-and/with-other" or "self-in-relation-to-others." Prus (1996) describes this as the intersubjective nature of our experiences—the notion that human life is the "product of community life" (p. 2). As such, he notes that our individual and collective stories cannot be understood apart from the social context in which they are enacted. The autoethnographic task is then an exploration of "how [we] become social entities, and how [we] attend to one another and the products of human endeavor in the course of day-to-day life" (p. 2). In sum, relational concerns are integral to autoethnographic work.

In this chapter, we discuss the relational dynamics inherent in autoethnographic work. We examine how the process of autoethnographic research impacts relationships and creates unique challenges and opportunities in the context of solo autoethnographic (AE) and collaborative autoethnographic (CAE) work. We end the chapter with suggested questions that autoethnographers should ask in the process of undertaking their projects, and we also provide guidelines for how we can continue to nurture, protect, and sustain relationships in autoethnographic work. Throughout the discourse, we assert that since autoethnographic work inextricably involves relationships with our various selves and/or others, autoethnographers need to be (1) sensitive to these relational dynamics, and (2) intentional in articulating guidelines and implementing strategies that address these concerns.

Researching Our Relationships

When we choose to make *our lives* the subject of study, we have also chosen to make *our relationships with others* the subject of study. In the process of self-study, we insert an additional dimension into our relational encounters—us, as researchers and the theoretical perspectives through which we interpret these interactions. This intrusion into our personal lives can create relational ambiguity and change the very relationships we study in solo and collaborative autoethnographic projects.

Relationships in Solo Autoethnographic Work

Adding dual roles to our relationships with significant others can create ambiguity about how we present ourselves to them and how they come to perceive such intimacies. For example, Ellis (2007) reflects on her interactions with individuals in her first ethnographic study, *Fisher Folk: Two Communities on Chesapeake Bay* (Ellis, 1986). She confronts the challenges of navigating dual roles in her encounters: Should she present herself as a "friend" or "researcher"? She acknowledges that, "my role was unclear to me. Although I was a researcher, I also saw myself as a friend to many people there, and sometimes I felt and acted like family" (p. 8). Reflecting on these experiences years after the study, Ellis (2007) writes of the sense of betrayal some of these individuals felt when she, as researcher, published excerpts from these *friendly* encounters. The person they came to know as a friend had switched roles on them. Indeed, as Miles and Huberman (1984) have asserted: "Fundamentally, field research is an act of betrayal, no matter how well intentioned or well integrated the researcher is" (p. 223). At the end of the project, we as researchers report what we saw and heard, based on our own meaning-making process, selecting what to report and what to leave out. We make the private public, and therein lies the potential for participants to feel betrayed.

Additionally, the process of studying our relationships can change them. We first heard Ellis read excerpts from the piece "Maternal Connections" (1996) at a workshop she was conducting. Several days later we were still talking about it. We wondered how the careful observation and writing about the intimate details of her mother's ill body might have impacted the dynamics of their mother-daughter relationship. What did Ellis observe with the researcher's eye that she might have missed in her role as daughter? How did she balance the call to write what she observed with her filial desire to protect her mother from public exposure? Similarly, after reading Richardson's (2007) work in which she relates her experiences watching her friend die, we wanted to know how studying her friend impacted the kinds of questions she chose to ask, or the frequency of her calls; in effect, how it shaped the relationship. Was there a negotiated balance between calls/visits as elements of their relationship and those made in the pursuit of generating data?

When personal relationships become the subject of study, the publication represents one dimension of a created work—relationships are also crafted through the process. As such, it is important that researchers make space in their scholarship to discuss openly the experiences and processes involved in navigating relational dynamics in AE/CAE. Alternately, a separate reflective piece can be written on the relational tensions experienced in the course of the study (see for example, Ellis, 2007; Lapadat, Mothus, & Fisher, 2005).

Relationships in Collaborative Autoethnographic Work

Kathy-Ann: *Faith, this would be a good place to insert our experiences doing CAE with Heewon. Should we discuss it with her first?*

Faith: *I'm sure she doesn't mind. Isn't that part of our implicit trust assumption?*

Kathy-Ann: *That's what I think. But, just to be sure…*

The relational ambiguities that affect AE studies can be amplified in the context of CAE due to relational layers at work—pre-existing relationship statuses among CAE team members, and evolving relationships as co-researchers and/or friends.

First, as with AE, juggling dual roles of researcher/friend in collaborative work can impact pre-existing relational statuses and may also lead to relational uncertainty. Our experiences as collaborators are illustrative of these dynamics. Since 2008, we have been involved in ongoing CAE projects, including a coauthored book on CAE (Chang, Ngunjiri, & Hernandez, 2013) and a co-edited special issue on autoethnography as research practice for the *Journal of Research Practice* (see Ngunjiri, Hernandez, & Chang, 2010). Before beginning our collaborative work we were distant colleagues at the same institution. Through co-researching we have come to know intimate details about one another involving our spouses, natal families, and experiences in academia. Because the sharing was initially prompted by our researcher roles, it could be described as a sort of pseudo-intimacy and not necessarily real friendship. Confusing pseudo-intimacy for genuine friendship can result in hurt emotions, as expectations are unmet. Below we illustrate this confusion with individual stories.

I (Kathy-Ann) became painfully aware of this in a recent experience that Heewon and I shared. We are colleagues in the same department, where she has served as chair for graduate education. Due to lack of office space, I have been sharing an office with another colleague two doors down from Heewon's office since 2009. The space though adequate is not comfortable. I was therefore surprised and hurt when I learned that Heewon had advocated that a recent hire she recruited get a single office in the same building. "What about me?" I asked as tears welled up in my eyes. "Apart from being colleagues, aren't we friends? Friends look out for each other?" She appeared genuinely baffled and explained that she was simply trying to help the new co-worker. I expected more from her as my friend, based on everything we knew about each other from our co-researcher sharing, did I mistake a research and collegial relationship for a genuine friendship? Or was I betrayed by a friend?

Similarly, I (Faith) experienced a defining moment with another colleague with whom I had done collaborative work. Our collaborative research efforts had so connected us that it spilled over into our private lives—she attended my wedding and visited me after I had surgery. However, after she agreed months in advance to relieve me of the stress of twelve months of teaching by taking over one of my courses, she reneged on her promise because something had "come up." I found out later, the "something" that had come up was a conference, not an emergency. I was hurt beyond belief. After some time passed, we were able to talk about the incident and reconcile our differences. However, residual feelings still linger on both sides. We are still co-researchers, but are we friends?

As our separate incidents illustrate, misunderstandings can arise about relational statuses in the course of doing collaborative work. These kinds of scenarios can arise when you realize that what you presumed to be genuine friendship brought about by sharing vulnerability was in fact merely a research relationship, nothing more.

Second, in CAE, tensions may also arise in the course of fulfilling our roles as co-researchers and writers. As co-researchers, we must work together to accomplish the research task—a relational expectation that is not unique to CAE methods. For example, Lapadat, Mothus, and Fisher (2005) reflect on the shifting roles and relational dynamics as they worked on a classroom study. They write, "What we discovered…was that our perceptions of our own researcher roles and of our role relationships with each other as co-researchers, which had at first seemed invisible and unproblematic, transformed into an elephant" (p. 2). That "elephant" was unvoiced feelings and tensions they experienced interacting with each other in pursuit of the research objective; for example, discomfort in reading what the other had written or hesitancy to edit a co-researcher's contributions. Such tensions are inherent in collaborative work, yet this aspect of our work will remain invisible unless we make space for it in our scholarship (Lapadat, Mothus, & Fisher, 2005). Writing about such tensions is an opportunity to proactively manage our co-researcher relationships; reading about such relational dynamics informs potential co-researchers of the realities of collaborative work.

We confront these tensions every time we work together collaboratively. Our recent work completing a book manuscript was rife with challenges. Writing this chapter gave the two of us a space to talk about some of the internal conflicts we experienced working together and to suggest to Heewon that we write about it in the future—feelings of being held hostage to each other's schedules, of being bullied into meeting last minute deadlines, grieving the loss of our unique voices as the piece went through the editing process, and reluctance to share our candid review of one another's work. When we first began our collaborative work, we were oblivious to some of these issues. Now we are learning to be intentional, for example, about setting guidelines for representing multiple voices, achieving consensus, negotiating authorship, and editing content (see Chang, Ngunjiri, & Hernandez, 2013).

The trust aspect of evolving relationships in CAE can also become problematic if it is not clearly defined. In CAE, we become confidants to each other's secrets and voyeurs into each other's self-described life experiences. This connection amongst co-researchers comes with the attendant expectations of what Ellis (2007) calls an "implicit trust assumption" coined from Freadman (2004). As Freadman explains it, this means that co-researchers trust each other to "act in accordance with the ethos of decency" that we share when it comes to making decisions about how much to expose each other's secrets in our scholarship (p. 123). On another level, we trust that outside of the research context, we will continue to keep each other's confidences as friends do.

We suggest that collaborators discuss relational and trust expectations early in the research process. Make these expectations explicit. That includes having discussions about the boundaries of the CAE relationship, what to do with the personal stories collected as data, and ensuring that whatever is discussed/shared is held in confidence. At the same time, we recognize that some participants in our stories are implicated as opposed to actively involved in the telling. This creates a need to think about the relational dynamics of those who are unwilling or un-consenting participants in our autoethnographic stories.

Implicating Others in Autoethnography

> **Kathy-Ann:** *Remember the graduate student who did an AE dissertation on her experiences as a survivor of incest? I'm wondering if we should include her story here. It still seems so private...*
>
> **Faith:** *Yeah. But she chose to make it public.*

A few years ago, we attended a session at the International Congress of Qualitative Inquiry (ICQI) conference. At that conference, we heard a doctoral student, along with her dissertation chair, present reflections on her autoethnographic study of her experiences as a survivor of incest (Clark & Carter, 2009). At the time, we were relatively new to autoethnographic practice. As she told her story, we were stunned. In the question and answer session that followed the presentation, she discussed the uncertainties and ambiguities she experienced in making heart-wrenching decisions to tell family secrets and the steps she took to protect identities. Listening to her story became a critical moment in our understanding of how autoethnography involves the "outing" of others (that is, exposing their vulnerabilities) and presents researchers with complex relational dilemmas. We highlight some of these dilemmas in writing about others who are alive and those who are dead.

Writers often implicate others who are a part of their immediate community. For example, Jago's (2002) struggle with depression implicates and involves twenty-three other individuals and relationships. Jago had not sought consent from any of those individuals, and only did so when journal reviewers and editors asked her to before agreeing to publish her work. This raises the question: Should we inform others that we are including them in our stories? We address this ethical and relational consideration later in the chapter.

Sometimes these stories implicate others with whom we are not intimately related, but who still might be hurt by how we portray them. For example, communities in Ellis's (1986) and in Stein's (2001) ethnographic studies were offended when they read about themselves in the respective books. Ellis's (1986) work focused on a fishing community in the Chesapeake Bay, and Stein (2001) studied a small town that was engulfed in conflict over sexual values and politics—a place she called Timbertown. Even though both authors used pseudonyms, individuals were able to recognize themselves/the characters in the stories and were hurt by the way they were portrayed. They felt betrayed by people whom they had come to regard as friends, perhaps not fully understanding what they had consented to as participants in ethnographic research.

When autoethnography is done in collaboration with others, we risk exposing our relationships with intimate others to members of the research team and to the public. Geist-Martin, Gates, Wiering, Kirby, Houston, Lilly, and Moreno (2010) wrestled with this dilemma in a CAE project on mothering experiences. Collaborating necessitated the "exposure of significant others as pivotal characters in [our] accounts" (p. 12), first to co-researchers and later to the public. These authors also question whether it is "ethical to share these stories that implicate them [participants], to an extent, without their consent" (p. 12). In the end, the story they tell focuses more on process and less on the details of their mothering and motherhood experiences (that is, a writing story), though they had previously presented their autoethnographies at a conference. However, the question they ask is relevant for autoethnographers thinking about writing, presenting and publishing their stories, because others are invariably involved.

Even when we write about those who are deceased, we face the dilemma of how best to represent them. For example, Spry (2010) and Ellis (1995) focus on their relationships with people who have passed on. These stories celebrate and memorialize and sometimes reveal intimate details about the dead. In both cases, would the loved one have been pleased with their portrayal or disappointed with the public airing of intimate details? Writing about those who are dead still requires navigating relational dynamics—thinking about what they would have felt about their portrayal, but also how the living who are implicated in those stories feel about the portrayal of the deceased loved one.

In sum, unanticipated and unavoidable ethical concerns arise in the course of doing autoethnographic work, and these considerations require us to make critical choices about how to include others in our work. Failing to do so can have implications for our existing relationships, and might even affect whether we are able to publish our work or not.

Protecting Others

Each autoethnographic work must include careful consideration of the ethical issues around how we choose to protect the identities and vulnerabilities of those involved or implicated in our studies. Guillemin and Gillam (2004) make a distinction between two dimensions of ethics in research—"procedural ethics" and "ethics in practice." Procedural ethics involves formal applications to a research ethics committee, such as an Institutional Review Board (IRB) for approval before one can commence a study involving human subjects. However, some IRBs do not require autoethnographic projects to undergo review because they do not consider autoethnography to be *research* (Clark & Carter, 2009). Where IRB approval is required, we view this as a useful step in ensuring that our research adheres to broad ethical principles of our discipline. However, because of the emergent design of qualitative inquiry in general and autoethnography in particular, procedural ethics does not take into account situations that may evolve as we conduct the research.

Ethics in practice is described as those "situations that are unexpected when doing research that can potentially have adverse consequences" (Guillemin & Gillam, 2004, p. 264). This would include what Ellis (2007) calls "relational ethics," our obligations and responsibilities in protecting the identities and vulnerabilities of those involved or implicated in our studies. Relational ethics requires us to be critically reflexive throughout the research process and if at all possible to seek informed consent from those implicated in our study.

Critical Reflexivity

Ellis (2007) argues that *critical reflexivity* is necessary throughout the process of writing autoethnography. As our story unfolds and exposes those connected to us, we should "hold relational concerns as high as research" (p. 25). That, however, is easier said than done. Holding relational concerns involves reflexivity and negotiation with self. The dialogue and internal struggle with self might sound like this:

> Though I have many good things to say about them, I worry about how they will react to my study. Then I worry that my concern is limiting what I'm able to say. How can I write honestly when I am so uneasy about how members [of the community] will react? (Ellis, 2004, p. 95)

Because doing autoethnography involves a back and forth movement between experiencing and examining a vulnerable self and observing and revealing the broader context of that experience (Ellis, 2007), it is critical to recognize that in the writing of our stories, and after we publish our autoethnographies, those relationships can be improved or diminished by the choices we made. Ellis (2007) argues that autoethnographers do have to make choices about *what to tell and what to omit*, understanding that relationships should be protected as much as is feasible—even if that necessitates omitting or changing certain details of the story while retaining the overall "truthfulness" or essence of the story (see also Jago, 2002).

In deciding what and how much to tell, working with a research team or having peers review a manuscript can be helpful. Others might be able to more easily notice the relational quagmires the publication might bring up if there are perhaps too many details that "out" and identify those implicated in our stories. For example, in Jago's (2002) case, peer reviewers recommended retrospective consent from those implicated in her study.

In spite of feedback we may receive, the final decision about what to include lies with the researcher and his or her research purposes. For example, the choices Ellis made about what to include in *Final Negotiations* (1995) were guided by the need to leave the complexity intact. She writes:

Final Negotiations argues for story as analysis, for evocation in addition to representation as a goal for social science research….[R]eaders' responses illuminate similarities and differences in socialization and experience. These insights are important to examine in their own right, not just in relation to my personal feelings about how I am viewed. (Ellis, 2004, p. 22)

Her intent was not only to represent her relationship with her deceased partner, but to also evoke responses in her readers. She chose to tell the story congruent with this purpose and live with the personal repercussions. Autoethnographers can be similarly guided by their research goals; at the same time, we have to be ready to "defend" such decisions if need be. Is it possible to tell the same story without providing every intimate (and maybe hurtful) detail? Can we tell the truth without telling the whole truth? We suggest that yes, this is possible, and it is sometimes desirable in research in order to protect the vulnerability of those implicated/involved in our stories.

Seeking Consent

> To: Heewon Chang (hchang@eastern.edu)
>
> From: Kathy-Ann Hernandez (khernand@eastern.edu);
> Faith Ngunjiri (fngunjir@eastern.edu)
>
> Date: June 8, 2012
>
> *We would like to include more of our experiences with relational tensions in AE and CAE in this chapter. Since it involves you as well, are you okay with this? Please let us know. If you agree, we will write and forward what we have for your review.*

> To: Kathy-Ann Hernandez (khernand@eastern.edu);
> Faith Ngunjiri (fngunjir@eastern.edu)
>
> From: Heewon Chang (hchang@eastern.edu)
>
> Date: June 9, 2012
>
> *Absolutely! You have my blessing.*

Autoethnographers often start projects not knowing who will be implicated in their work. However, as the work unfolds, we face a choice of whether to tell those who will be implicated in the work that we are writing about them. Based on our experiences and the experiences of others, we hold that where feasible, consent should be obtained early in the research process. The email messages above illustrate our exchange with Heewon, once we realized that our stories would implicate and involve her. Once she gave her blessing, we were then free to write our stories (earlier in the chapter) and gave her drafts of the chapter as it evolved.

I (Kathy-Ann) was confronted with my ethical responsibility to those involved in an autoethnographic piece as I was writing a chapter for the book *Spirituality in Higher Education* (2011*).* As I wrote, I found myself including several individuals, but in particular my elementary school teacher and four students with whom I worked at my current university. I was confident that my elementary school teacher would be flattered by my portrayal of him so I quickly sent off a draft for his review. We joked about my perception of him back then, and he wished me the best. However, my remembrances of incidents with students required more finesse. They were difficult encounters involving plagiarism and sub-standard work. Three of the incidents were early in my tenure, and I did not remember the students' names nor was I still in contact with them. Because the encounters occurred between the students and me privately in my office, I felt I could protect their identities by only using pseudonyms. However, the fourth student and I still had an existing relationship. I wanted to use our prior in-class conversations and e-mail exchanges to illustrate a conflict we experienced over her grades. She was a mature student who I felt would be open to such exposure, so I asked for her permission. She agreed. Thus, I was able to seek consent early in the research process.

In some cases the decision to seek consent comes much later in the research process. After publishing her first piece on taking care of her mother, Ellis (1996) admits that "not telling my mother about publishing this story felt ethically suspicious" (p. 18). In a follow up piece (2008), she made a decision to discuss the work with her mother while she was writing it. Ellis read parts of the story to her, but chose to leave out graphic details that might hurt her mother. Similarly, as already illustrated in Jago's (2002) article, she obtained consent retrospectively. We can learn from the experience of these researchers that when others are implicated in our stories, we can actively engage with them as we write. Failing to obtain consent as the story evolves may only delay the inevitability of having to do so before our work can be published. Moreover, retrospective consent can undermine the rights of participants to choose to consent or not without undue influence. Tolich (2010) asserts that obtaining consent after the fact "is problematic and potentially coercive, placing undue obligation on research 'subjects' to volunteer" (p. 1600).

In seeking consent early in the process, we have an opportunity to give others voice in our work. The final piece can then represent a negotiated balance between what we want to write, and what others are comfortable with having others read about them. This negotiation process can enhance our ability to write sensitive to the vulnerabilities of those implicated in our stories. It goes beyond procedural ethics to relational ethics where we place relational concerns at the same level as the desire to tell authentic, evocative stories.

Alternately, others choose not to obtain informed consent. Richardson (2007) admits that she struggled with whether to tell her friend that she was writing about her. In the end, she decided not to tell her. Instead, she relied on her firm belief that her friend would have wanted her (Richardson) to tell her stories; she relied on the *implicit trust* they had in each other as friends. Since Richardson's friend was dying, Richardson did not have to deal with the possible consequences of how her friend would respond to the published piece. In some instances it may be impossible or harmful to the autoethnographer to seek consent of those implicated in the story (see, for example, Carter, 2002). If we do choose to expose others' vulnerabilities without their consent, then we must be ready to deal with any relational strain and personal cost that might accrue.

Protecting Ourselves in Relationships and Communities

As researchers, we may also need to protect ourselves in autoethnographic work. Autoethnographies that address intimate and or sensitive information about our 'selves' expose our vulnerabilities and can threaten our own stability. Likewise, given the intersubjectivity of our various experiences, as we implicate others in our narratives, we can place ourselves at risk for negative reactions from those we have exposed. Thus, we must be mindful to protect ourselves.

Writing personal stories about our internal struggles can place us in the vulnerable position of succumbing to the very pathologies about which we write. Chatham-Carpenter (2010) reflected on how the process of writing about her struggles with anorexia, coupled with her compulsion to publish, triggered unhealthy thinking and behavior patterns. Though she was able to eventually write and publish her autoethnography on anorexia, the writing story elaborates on the actual writing journey, the struggles, the choices she made about what to tell or exclude from her eventual article, ensuring that she told the truth while leaving out what was not necessary for the veracity of her story.

In this case, Chatham-Carpenter's (2010) relationship with her eating disorder and with her role as faculty who needed to publish were in conflict. She writes, "It's like my anorexia and research were having an affair with each other, right under my nose, and are not even concerned about me" (p. 4). When she did eventually write the story, she learned an important lesson: "I realized I was multifaceted in my experiences with anorexia, and now I allowed myself to show the different areas of my life where I have relationship with anorexia, personifying anorexia" (p. 6). Though it was a painful process, the acknowledgement of these "relationships with selves," the multiple shifting identities (Reed-Danahay, 1997), enabled her to look at anorexia in a way that would not elicit unhealthy behavior, and thus protect herself from further harm.

Writing personal stories that criticize those in our social context can have negative repercussions. For example, Lisa William-White (2011) utilized spoken word and performative autoethnography to explicate her experiences after publishing a co-authored book chapter in which she openly criticized and exposed institutional racism (Brown & William-White, 2010). That publication resulted in micro-aggressive behaviors from her department and institution. She defined micro-aggressions as subtle, stunning, verbal and non-verbal exchanges that disconfirm and exert power. She was harassed in the department. Meetings were held in which she was criticized to the point that institutional leaders checked with general counsel to see whether she had in fact crossed ethical boundaries that they could use to fire her. In describing the experiences that she calls a public be-heading, she was left wondering: Was it worth it?

As painful as it was, her publication provoked conversations about institutional racism and the experiences of minorities in the academy and resulted in communal learning in her department. If only for this reason, it could be argued that making herself vulnerable to such negative repercussions may have been a cost worth paying. As a tenured professor, William-White was perhaps better positioned to take this risk than an untenured professor. On the other hand, could she have anticipated the reactions and written in a way to avoid or minimize them? Is there room in autoethnography to "protect thyself" (Chatham-Carpenter, 2010)?

The need to protect ourselves should come from the understanding that "we become the stories we write" (Ellis, 2007, p. 22). Ellis (2007) explains that after writing about her and her partner's abortion (Ellis & Bochner, 1992), they became the couple "who had an abortion and wrote about it" (p. 22). Ellis (2007) later reflected on how an essay like this impacted her teacher-student relationships and familial and communal relationships. In the classroom context, she questions the appropriateness of sharing the essay with her students. How might her students come to view her as a result of that piece? What impact might it have on their relationships with her?

In the context of CAE, researchers need to think about how autoethnographic data sharing can have residual effects on their pre-existing relationship statuses and power differentials that might be part of these statuses. For example, Ellis participated in a collaborative project on bulimia with two other researchers who were still graduate students when the research began (Ellis, Kiesinger, & Tillmann-Healy, 1997). Given the sensitive nature of the topic and the professor-student relationships, Ellis was careful in emphasizing to these students that they should "not reveal anything to me they might regret later because they might be concerned about how I, their professor, saw them" (Ellis, 2007, p 20). Additionally, the team devised strategies to protect the anonymity of the students, such as private writing sessions and occasions where the students could talk together without Ellis being present.

As editor of the *Journal of Qualitative Health Research*, Janice Morse included an autoethnographic piece on spousal abuse in an issue of that journal (see Carter, 2002). However, she insisted that the author use a nom de plume. Another strategy that autoethnographers can use to protect themselves when writing stories that can have negative personal or communal repercussions is to write the story as fiction. This is the approach that Sally McMillan and Margaret Price (2009) took in explicating their experiences of conflict in their institution. They utilized *Alice in Wonderland* and *Through the Looking Glass* as metaphorical constructs through which to recount their experience team-teaching a naturalistic inquiry course. Using the genre of fiction, they were able to describe their experiences of institutional backlash—the criticism, support, imposition and even grievances filed against them for their efforts. This strategy was successful in offering the authors some protection as it enabled them to fictionalize some of their experiences. Protection of self, our relationships, and communities must be a critical concern in autoethnographic work.

Power in Research Relationships and Communities

To: Kathy-Ann Hernandez (khernand@eastern.edu);
Faith Ngunjiri (fngunjiri@eastern.edu)

From: Heewon Chang (hchang@eastern.edu)

Date: June 28, 2012

Overall, I thought your paper was excellent... The portion referring to our friendship caused me to think a lot about myself, our relationship, our possibly different (cultural and individual) concepts of friendship, and the meaning of granting permission in autoethnography. When you sent me the email, I had a moment of hesitation in giving general permission, not knowing what you would write about "us." Then I thought to myself, "This is about autoethnography of collaboration and autoethnographers have the right to tell their story. I need to live the spirit of autoethnography I have been writing about." However, when I first read it, I felt hurt and saddened to know there are still unresolved issues... and that they had to come out in public.

To: Heewon Chang (hchang@eastern.edu); Faith Ngunjiri (fngunjiri@eastern.edu)

From: Kathy-Ann *(khernand@eastern.edu)*

I did feel some qualms about writing our stories, especially since your voice was not represented. I am happy for you to help me write a bit under my paragraph about your perspective on the situation.

The autoethnographies referred to previously (Brown & William-White, 2010; Chatham-Carpenter, 2010) and others also point to power dynamics in thinking about relationships and communities. Ayanna Brown's and Lisa William-White's (2010) approaches to navigating power differentials in a co-authored piece is illustrative of their recognition of these dynamics. As an untenured assistant professor, though she was critical of the issues in her department, Brown was careful about how she framed her critique, recognizing the power differential between herself and those in positions of authority. On the other hand, William-White was openly critical of perceived racism in her department, aware that she was taking a risk, but doing so from the position of a tenured associate professor. In telling our stories, we do have to recognize the power relations at work. In effect, these relational dynamics impact the stories we tell and how we tell them; at the same time, our stories have the potential to transform the power dynamics in our relationships.

Power differentials, where the researcher's telling of the story is privileged over the community/participants' story, are perhaps what necessitates the kind of relational concerns that both Ellis (2007) and Stein (2010) discuss. In both instances, Ellis and Stein did tell participants about their research and seek their consent, but they utilized their authorial power to tell the stories as they wished—from their own perspective and position as researchers. Indeed, their books (Ellis, 1996; Stein, 2001) and the later reflective autoethnographies (Ellis, 2007; Stein, 2010) further illustrate that we can never be completely truthful in our research, and that the participants may be informed, but they are never *fully informed*—especially because we, too, are never fully sure what we will do with the stories until we actually write them (see also Ceglowski, 2000).

However, even in cases where the work is more AE than CAE, we can still utilize multiple voices and perspectives to diffuse our authorial power by inviting others to read and react to our stories in formation. Ceglowski (2000) seems to appreciate that as she talks about "this new journey [of reciprocity] means talking with those we study in different ways" (p. 101). Reciprocity is about inviting dialogue and conversation into our work. Another example of dialogue and reciprocity is Ellis's (2002) piece where as she talks about her experiences after the events of September 11, she invites Bochner to respond to her ideas and her writing. She thanks him for being a character in her story and also thanks several others for reading and making suggestions. We recommend reciprocity as a worthwhile practice that enables us to be more reflexive and to welcome other voices into our stories. Further, Ellis (2007) encourages autoethnographers to share their writing with those involved/implicated in their stories, not so much as consent seeking, but more about inviting other voices, eliciting reactions, and engaging in dialogue.

In engaging our multiple identities as researchers and all of those other roles, familial, communal or otherwise, we need to write with an awareness of power dynamics and keep in balance the power we hold as authors and use it in a relationally responsible manner, in order to build/transform the communities even as we represent ourselves.

Counting the Costs

To: Kathy-Ann Hernandez (khernand@eastern.edu); Faith Ngunjiri (fngunjir@eastern.edu)

From: Heewon Chang (hchang@eastern.edu)

Date: June 28, 2012

After a more careful reading of your chapter, I began to see your story about me in a different light. I thought you framed and couched our incident brilliantly within the discussion of the blurred boundaries between collegial collaboration and friendship. My hurt subsided.

To: Heewon Chang (hchang@eastern.edu); Kathy-Ann Hernandez (khernand@eastern.edu)

From: Faith Ngunjiri (fngunjiri@eastern.edu)

Heewon, both of your reactions arc totally on point. But I am glad you were able to see the deeper issues that we are trying to raise—that autoethnography engenders intimacy amongst the co-researchers, thus the potential for conflict.

To: Heewon Chang (hchang@eastern.edu); Faith Ngunjiri (fngunjiri@eastern.edu)

From: Kathy-Ann Hernandez (khernand@eastern.edu)

Please don't feel any pressure to agree to anything we shared—we want to represent you accurately. In the end, the relationship is far more valuable than any publication.

To: Kathy-Ann Hernandez (khernand@eastern.edu); Faith Ngunjiri (fngunjiri@eastern.edu)

From: Heewon Chang (hchang@eastern.edu)

It's fine. It will make a great contribution to the handbook and readers will learn about us as authors of Collaborative Autoethnography.

In this chapter we have illustrated the inextricable links between our autoethnographic work and the relationships and communities of which we are a part. We urge autoethnographers to demonstrate sensitivity to these concerns by asking and responding to the following questions relevant to each autoethnographic study:

1. What are the various intrapersonal and/or interpersonal relationships at the forefront of this work? How can I attend to these relationships in this study?

2. Who are the individuals likely to be implicated in this story? What, if any, is the scope of my responsibility to seek informed consent?

3. What are my ethical responsibilities to protect the identities and vulnerabilities of those who may be exposed in my story as it unfolds?

4. What are precautions that I can take to protect myself, others, relationships, and communities connected to this work?

5. What are the power differentials to be considered in this work and how can I navigate them in a relationally responsible manner by using my authorial

power to build/transform the communities—even as I authentically represent myself?

Decisions about how to tell our stories authentically while attending to the relational concerns embedded in these questions defy neat answers. However, we have attempted to draw from the insight of others and our own experiences to provide some direction for addressing these concerns in autoethnographic work. Ellis (2007) and Tolich (2010) both offer advice on how autoethnographers can deal with some of the persistent relational challenges we have highlighted. To these, we add our list of strategies that researchers can employ as discussed and illustrated throughout this chapter:

1. Be selective about what to include and what to exclude of your own story as well as the stories of those implicated in your autoethnography. For example, let concerns for protecting the vulnerabilities of others guide you in deciding how to tell an evocative and authentic story without *telling everything* (Jago, 2002). As such, it is important that researchers make space in their writing to discuss openly the relational experiences and processes involved in the research process.

2. Where the relational concerns demand that you protect yourself and others, consider using literary means, such as employing composite characters and fictionalizing your narrative (see, for example, Hernandez, 2008; McMillan & Price, 2010).

3. When your personal safety is at too high a risk, write using a pen name (see Carter, 2002). You can negotiate with editors to ensure that you can still get credit for your work.

4. Seek the consent of those involved/implicated in your stories, where this is feasible, safe, and desirable, using ethics in practice (that is, prior to, during, and/or after the writing process as you realize who is involved/implicated in the telling of your stories).

5. Dialogue with others in the process of your writing. Whenever possible, let your autoethnography embody your voice as well as the voices of the "others" involved/implicated in your story as part of reciprocity (Ellis, 2002). Dialogue can also include asking peers to read your work and comment on it, as well as journal peer reviewers (e.g., Jago, 2002).

6. Engage in co-creation of autoethnographies through collaborative work. This can facilitate dialogue that enables deeper self reflexivity and a higher likelihood of attending to relational concerns within the team. We believe CAE is as yet a largely untapped resource in AE work and that there is much more that can be learned by co-creating knowledge and co-constructing stories (see Chang, Ngunjiri, & Hernandez, 2013).

As examined from the point of view of our responsibility to relational dynamics, autoethnography is both self-focused and other-focused. As Ellis (2004) concludes, "in the same way autoethnography requires you to go inside yourself, it also requires you to understand other people. If you do, then you can't just dismiss their points of view" (p. 318).

Autoethnography has the potential to impact relationships and communities in positive ways. As illustrated in this chapter, it can help us resolve inner struggles with our various selves (Chatham-Carpenter, 2010; Jago, 2002), allow critical and useful examinations of existing relationships (Ellis, 1996; Richardson, 2007), promote communal learning (Brown & William-White, 2010), and, if managed effectively, can lead to meaningful relationships in the context of collaborative work (Lapadat, Mothus, & Fisher, 2005). However, because we as autoethnographers have authorial power to control our stories, we need to be relationally responsive in telling them. The cost of our autoethnographic narratives must never be higher than the benefits to ourselves, others, and the communities we represent.

Note

1. Regardless of the order in which our names are listed, we each contributed equally in writing this chapter.

References

Brown, A. F., & William-White, L. (2010). "We are not the same minority": The narratives of two sisters navigating identity and discource at public and private white institutions. In C. C. Robinson & P. Clardy (Eds.), *Tedious journeys: Autoethnography by women of color in academe* (pp. 149–176). New York: Peter Lang.

Carter, S. (2002). How much subjectivity is needed to understand our lives objectively? *Qualitative Health Research, 12,* 1184–1201.

Ceglowski, D. (2000). Research as relationship. *Qualitative Inquiry, 6,* 88–103.

Chang, H. (2008) *Authoethnography as method.* Walnut Creek, CA: Left Coast Press, Inc.

Chang, H., Ngunjiri, F. W., & Hernandez, K-A. C. (2013). *Collaborative autoethnography.* Walnut Creek, CA: Left Coast Press, Inc.

Chatham-Carpenter, A. (2010). "Do thyself no harm": Protecting ourselves as autoethnographers. *Journal of Research Practice, 6*(1). Retrieved from jrp.icaap.org/index.php/jrp/article/view/213/222

Clark, M. C., & Carter, N. (2009) *Guiding an autoethnographic dissertation: Making the road as we walked it.* Fifth International Congress of Qualitative Inquiry, University of Illinois, Urbana-Champaign, Illinois, May 2009.

Ellis, C. (1986). *Fisher folk: Two communities on Chesapeake Bay.* Lexington: University Press of Kentucky.

Ellis, C. (1995). *Final negotiations: A story of love, loss, and chronic illness.* Philadelphia: Temple University Press.

Ellis, C. (1996). Maternal connections. In C. Ellis & A. Bochner (Eds.), *Composing ethnography: Alternative forms of qualitative writing* (pp. 240–243). Walnut Creek, CA: AltaMira Press.

Ellis, C. (1999). Heartful autoethnography. *Qualitative Health Research, 9,* 669–683.

Ellis, C. (2002). Take no chances. *Qualitative Inquiry, 8*(2), 170–175.

Ellis, C. (2004). *The ethnographic I: A methodological novel about autoethnography.* Walnut Creek, CA: AltaMira Press.

Ellis, C. (2007). Telling secrets, revealing lives: Relational ethics in research with intimate others. *Qualitative Inquiry, 13,* 3–29.

Ellis, C. (2008). Do we need to know? *Qualitative Inquiry, 14*, 1314–1320.

Ellis, C., & Bochner, A. P. (1992). Telling and performing personal stories: The constraints of choice in abortion. In C. Ellis & M. Flaherty (Eds.), *Investigating subjectivity: Research on lived experience* (pp. 79–101). Newbury Park, CA: Sage.

Ellis, C., Kiesinger, C., & Tillmann-Healy, L. (1997). Interactive interviewing: Talking about emotional experience. In R. Hertz (Ed.), *Reflexivity and voice* (pp. 119–149). Thousand Oaks, CA: Sage.

Freadman, R. (2004). Decent and indecent: Writing my father's life. In P. J. Eakin (Ed.), *The ethics of life writing* (pp. 121–146). Ithaca, NY: Cornell University Press.

Geist-Martin, P., Gates, L., Wiering, L., Kirby, E., Houston, R., Lilly, A., & Moreno, J. (2010). Exemplifying collaborative autoethnographic practice via shared stories of mothering. *Journal of Research Practice, 6*(1), Article M8. Retrieved from jrp.icaap.org/index.php/jrp/article/view/209/187

Guillemin, M., & Gillam, L. (2004). Ethics, reflexivity, and "ethically important moments" in research. *Qualitative Inquiry, 10*, 261–280.

Hernandez, K-A. C. (2008). Sometimes. *Callaloo, 31,* 840–843.

Hernandez, K-A. C. (2011). Spiritual introspection and praxis in teaching and assessment. In H. Chang & D. Boyd (Eds.), *Spirituality in higher education* (pp. 163–179). Walnut Creek, CA: Left Coast Press, Inc.

Jago, B. J. (2002). Chronicling an academic depression. *Journal of Contemporary Ethnography, 31*(6), 729–757.

Lapadat, J. C., Mothus, T. G., & Fisher, H. (2005). Role relationships in research: Noticing an elephant. *International Journal of Qualitative Methods, 4*, 1–16.

McMillan, S., & Price, M. A. (2009). Through the looking glass: Our autoethnographic journey through research mind-fields. *Qualitative Inquiry, 15*(December), 1–8.

Miles, M. B., & Huberman, A. M. (1984). *Qualitative data analysis: A sourcebook of new methods.* Thousand Oaks, CA: Sage.

Ngunjiri, F. W. (2011). Studying spirituality and leadership: A personal journey. In H. Chang & D. Boyd (Eds.), *Spirituality in higher education: Autoethnographies* (pp. 183–198). Walnut Creek, CA: Left Coast Press, Inc.

Ngunjiri, F. W., Hernandez, K-A. C., & Chang, H. (2010). Living autoethnography: Connecting life and research. *Journal of Research Practice, 6*(1). Article E1. Retrieved from jrp.icaap.org/index.php/jrp/article/view/241/186

Prus, R. C. (1996). *Symbolic interaction and ethnographic research: Intersubjectivity and the study of human lived experience.* Albany: State University of New York Press.

Reed-Danahay, D. (1997). Introduction. In D. Reed-Dahanay (Ed.), *Auto/ethnography : Rewriting the self and the social* (pp. 1–17). Oxford: Berg.

Richardson, L. (2007). *Last writes: A daybook for a dying friend.* Walnut Creek, CA: Left Coast Press, Inc.

Spry, T. (2010). Call it swing: A jazz blues autoethnography. *Cultural Studies ↔ Critical Methodologies, 10*, 271–282.

Stein, A. (2001). *The stranger next door: The story of a small community's battle over sex, faith, and civil rights.* Boston: Beacon Press.

Stein, A. (2010). Sex, truths, and audiotape: Anonymity and the ethics of exposure in public ethnography. *Journal of Contemporary Ethnography, 39*, 554–568.

Tolich, M. (2010). A critique of current practice: Ten foundational guidelines for autoethnographers. *Qualitative Health Research, 20*, 1599–1610.

William-White, L. (2011). Dare I write about oppression on sacred ground [emphasis mine]. *Cultural Studies ↔ Critical Methodologies, 11*(3), 236–242.

Chapter 13

Autoethnography as the Engagement of Self/Other, Self/Culture, Self/Politics, and Selves/Futures

Jacquelyn Allen-Collinson

Exhaustion clouds my body-mind, cotton woolliness of brain. World dimly perceived through a veil of fatigue. Nearly three weeks solid of marking. Legs and arms heavy from it, neck and shoulders rigid, strained, taut to breaking. Eyes red and gritty. It's going to be a hard run tonight, I guess. But just a few minutes into my stride the navy-dusk wind is cutting away the work smog, sloughing off the grey skin of the working day. I am cleansed. I am back. I am back in-body after yet another day of attempted body denial and enforced focus on the headwork. Quads surge forward, muscles strong and bulking, pushing against tracksters, abs tighten and flatten against the chill wind as I begin to up the pace... Power surges through me, I feel butch, lean, mean and honed, and very much woman. [Extract from field notes]

Introduction

In many ways, autoethnography represents a challenge to some of the very foundations and key tenets of much social science research in its exhortation explicitly to situate and "write in" the researcher as a key player—often *the* key player—within a research project or account, as illustrated by the opening excerpt from my autoethnographic account of being a female distance runner. Despite its burgeoning popularity, increasing sophistication and sustained challenge to more orthodox forms of qualitative research, there are those who view autoethnography's

Handbook of Autoethnography, edited by Stacy Holman Jones, Tony E. Adams, and Carolyn Ellis, 281–299. © 2013 Left Coast Press, Inc. All rights reserved.

focus on "self" with deep suspicion and skepticism, accusing the genre of flirting with indulgent, "navel-gazing" forms of autobiography. For many of us, however, it represents a fresh and innovative variation of ethnography—and more!—where an ethnographic perspective and analysis are brought to bear on our personal, lived experience, directly linking the micro level with the macro cultural and structural levels in exciting ways. For us, too, autoethnography provides rare discursive space for voices too often muted or forcibly silenced within more traditional forms of research, opening up and democratizing the research space to those seeking to contest hegemonic discourses of whatever flavor.

Within autoethnography, the selves of researcher and participant coalesce and our own experiences *qua* member of a social group are subject to analysis, often generating richly textured, powerfully evocative accounts[1] of human lived experience. As autoethnographers, we thus occupy a dual and challenging role as both member of the social world under study and researcher of that same world (Anderson, 2006), requiring acute and sustained reflexivity. Of particular interest to many of us has been a focus on embodiment, our subjective experience of existing as a corporeal being in the physical world. For as Denzin (2012) notes (in relation to sports studies, but certainly applicable more widely): "An embodied (sports studies) project that matters must locate the body within a radically contextual politics. It must focus on the active, agentic flesh-and-blood human body" (p. 298). Thus, as a feminist autoethnographer, one of my concerns has been to explore some of my lived-body experiences as a gendered being, including as a female distance runner (Allen-Collinson, 2011a) often subject to sexist verbal and occasionally physical harassment. There is also in autoethnography a concern to portray self-consciousness, to "open up the realm of the interior and the personal" (Fiske, 1990, p. 90), as well as setting us on a challenging, potentially emotionally painful, voyage of self-investigation.

This chapter considers autoethnography as a relational research approach that offers a variety of modes of engaging with self, or perhaps more accurately with selves, in relation to others, to culture, to politics, and the engagement of selves in relation to future possibilities for research. These domains are also inter-related; engagement with culture often entails engagement with self, others, and politics (see the discussion of Antoniu's [2004] work later, with regard to intersectionalities of gender, sexuality, nationality, politics, and culture). In relation to future directions of autoethnography, I portray two particular variants—collaborative autoethnography and also autophenomenography (Allen-Collinson, 2011b), which I have selected as two contrasting forms that take forward the autoethnographic enterprise in distinctive ways. But first, our attention turns to autoethnography as the engagement of self and/with others.

Autoethnography as the Engagement of Self/Other

In general, autoethnography is a research approach in which we as an author draw upon our own lived experiences, specifically in relation to the culture (and subcultures) of which we are a member. As Reed-Danahay (1997) neatly encapsulates, autoethnography synthesizes postmodern ethnography (where realist conventions and "objectivity" are strongly called into question) and postmodern autobiography (in which the idea of the coherent, individual self is similarly called into question). Autoethnography seeks to connect the personal to the cultural and to locate both "self"— however shifting and fragmentary—and others within a social context. The researcher, in social interaction with others, is thus the subject of the research, traversing and blurring distinctions of the personal and the social, and of self and other (Ellis & Bochner, 1996; Reed-Danahay, 1997) and also of "native" and "non-native" (Motzafi-Haller, 1997) in some writings. Autoethnography thus engages with the dialectics of subjectivity and culture, albeit with different emphases by different authors on the elements of, respectively: the self (*autos*), the "race" or nation—extended to include a cultural, subcultural or social group of some kind (*ethnós*), and the research process and its representation (*graphein*). In addressing autoethnography as the engagement of self and others, we also encounter some thorny ethical issues surrounding the engagement and representation of self in relation to others, and a body of work addressing autoethnographic ethics has recently begun to emerge (see Ellis, 2007; Chatham-Carpenter, 2010; Roth, 2009; Tullis, this collection). Here I focus upon some key ethical issues surrounding representing the "self," representing others, and also the need to acknowledge the dialogical nature of autoethnography.

While writing about our own lives and experiences may at first, superficial glance seem relatively devoid of ethical concerns, compared with other forms of research, some delicate ethical issues and thorny dilemmas can indeed arise, including in relation to the representation of self in autoethnographic accounts. For some writers and researchers, engaging in the autoethnographic process can of itself be a very painful and even potentially self-injurious act. Chatham-Carpenter (2010) reminds us that while we may be accustomed to considering the protection of others from harm within our research, more rarely do autoethnographers consider how to protect ourselves in the autoethnographic process, should this prove necessary. She describes vividly how, during the writing of her autoethnography on anorexia, she felt the compulsion to publish her work become intertwined with the compulsion of her anorexia. Engaging in the analytic self-reflection at the heart of autoethnography made her vulnerable once again to engaging in anorexic thought processes and behavior, which she had determinedly sought to leave behind.

For many autoethnographers, there is the question of how far along the self-disclosure/exposure and vulnerability route we wish or feel compelled to situate ourselves, and how "honest" we decide to be in creating and representing the "auto/biographical I" (Stanley, 1995), or perhaps more accurately, the "autobiographical *we*" given the multiple authorial selves we hold across different contexts. Autoethnography may well confront us with dilemmas regarding self-presentation, and just how much "real" "true" biographical information and "authentic" self/selves to reveal in pursuit of this honesty, particularly as we know that significant others, and also students and employers (current and potential) may read our words and make judgments. Ellis (1999), for example, highlights the vulnerability of the autoethnographer in revealing intimate information, and subsequently being unable to retract what has been written, with no control over how readers interpret such sensitive biographical information. Similarly, Antoniu (2004) describes how: "As I write, I become public, visible, vulnerable" (p. 128). And Chatham-Carpenter (2010) questions: "Is there such a thing as being too vulnerable for one's own good, when doing autoethnography?" (p. 6).

Writing in a personalized and often emotional, open and vulnerable autoethnographic style challenges the orthodoxy of researcher as neutral, "objective," super-rational, and textually absent, leaving us vulnerable to charges of being "irrational, particularistic, private, and subjective, rather than reasonable, universal, public, and objective" (Greenhalgh, 2001, p. 55). Not only might such charges be experienced as personally wounding, but also potentially professionally disastrous within contemporary academia. Anthropologist Ruth Behar (1997) also acknowledges the warnings regarding the over-exposure of the autoethnographic researcher's vulnerable self: "Vulnerability doesn't mean that anything personal goes"; the exposure of the self "has to be essential to the argument, not a decorative flourish, not exposure for its own sake" (pp. 13–14). Self-disclosure should therefore, it is argued, be subject to some degree of self-discipline or self-monitoring, and to careful premeditation.

In terms of autoethnography as the engagement of self and/with others, another key issue is that however "personal" and self-revelatory our autoethnography may be, it is likely to feature other social actors with whom we have some degree of interaction. As Erben (1993) notes in relation to autobiography, it is a very rare account that does not contain many, shorter or longer, biographies of other people who figure in the writer's life, and thus contribute to her or his life story. Wall (2008), for example, highlights some of the dilemmas and difficult judgments arising from recounting her story of parenting an adopted child. These dilemmas are neatly encapsulated in a footnote where she acknowledges that although she speaks of the autoethnography as "my" story, her husband and children are also "authors" of the story (p. 51). I return to such dialogical, relational issues later in this section.

As autoethnographers, then, we must consider carefully *if* and *how* others are represented within our personal narratives. Concerns to guard the anonymity of co-participant others may loom large as, even when made anonymous in terms of remaining formally unnamed, others may nevertheless be identifiable via their social or physical characteristics. Mellick and Fleming (2010) discuss the ethics of disclosure in relation to a personal narrative that included a portrayal of a rugby player with "a rich and therefore identifiable biography." Despite attempts to make this individual anonymous, his biography made him a "unique case study," as Mellick and Fleming admit. The ethical dilemma for the authors was that the biographical information and international reputation of their particular unique case study was essential to the theoretical framing of the narrative; its removal would have rendered the analysis "impotent." Additionally, in relation to the representation of others, as Wall (2008) highlights, there are questions of how exactly to "use" another person's life to tell our own stories (p. 49). In the case of joint or collaborative autoethnographic research (see below) it is standard practice to discuss and agree with one's co-researcher/author what should be included in and excluded from the account, and this may require careful negotiation. In a collaborative autoethnography I undertook some years ago (Allen-Collinson & Hockey, 2001), narratives about and photographs of other people were included in published articles based on the study. Although it would have been difficult to ascertain the identity of individuals, given that the photographs were taken at some distance, identification *may* have been possible for someone familiar with the individuals portrayed. We decided after due consideration that the photographs provided useful contextual information and while not essential to the account were sufficiently informative as to warrant inclusion. The likelihood of anyone being recognized, we surmised, was very remote. Similarly, in the accounts generated from the autoethnographic data, family members, friends, and others could—with some detective work—have been identifiable. In these circumstances, it is incumbent upon us as researchers to weigh up with great care the ethical issues; prescriptive (and indeed proscriptive) statements of what should/should not be included would not be appropriate for a research genre that celebrates its openness, including to a multiplicity of evaluation criteria.

A further point I address here with regard to self/other engagement concerns the wish not to "finalize" the stories of others in the autoethnographic narrative, but to engage in dialogical rather than monological research (Smith, Allen-Collinson, Phoenix, Brown, & Sparkes, 2009), to "converse" with others and indeed with the autoethnographic process itself (see Wall, 2008), rather than seeking to give "the final word." To this purpose, autoethnography often deliberately utilizes relational language (including addressing the reader directly in the second person) to create reader/author dialogue, rather than making monologic pronouncements. To explain, for Bakhtin (1984), monologue is a self-narrative that seems self-sufficient, telling what the author/speaker knows and to what the listener must attend. Monologue is also construed as a self-narrative seeking to *merge* with the other, assimilating the other into the narrator's self, and thus abridging difference. According to Bakhtin (1984), dialogical writing requires abandoning the illusion that we can, even with the best of intentions, merge with another. We should not therefore presume to know exactly how another person feels and speak *for* him or her, an issue to which I return later in discussing the voices of "silenced" and underprivileged groups. We should, rather, acknowledge and respect alterity and seek to preserve some intersubjective distance (for an extended discussion of this, see Smith et al., 2009). It is thus important to acknowledge "difference" and subject it to analytic attention in our autoethnographic writing.

Dialogical research involves critiquing the belief in our own self-sufficiency, and explicitly recognizing our inter-connectedness, so that an individual's "self" narratives are acknowledged to be "structured under the continuous influence of someone else's words about him [*sic*]" (Bakhtin, 1984, p. 207). In this way, analogously to symbolic interactionist theorizations of the self, humans are viewed as fundamentally relational beings, never entirely self-sufficient. An important consequence for autoethnographers is that no individual person's story or self is therefore completely and entirely her or his own; the voices and selves of others intertwine with ourselves and our stories, as Wall (2008) so perceptively recounts in her autoethnographic study of adoptive parenting.

This section has considered some key elements relating to autoethnography as the engagement of self and others in the research process. Next, I consider the engagement of the autoethnographer with and within culture.

Autoethnography as the Engagement of Self/Culture

One of the tenets of "classic" anthropological ethnographic research often undertaken in far away "exotic" locations (e.g., Malinowski's [1935] study of the Trobriand Islanders) was that researchers could somehow "capture" the lived experiences of the cultures and social groups they studied. This assumption was subsequently rendered highly problematic under challenges posed by the "crisis of representation" (Denzin & Lincoln, 2000) when it was raised to analytic attention that the representation of these experiences was formed to a great extent by the text crafted by the researcher. The researcher's own voice rather than those of her or his participants often came to the fore, while couched in a neutral, objective, third-person style. Further problematization of these ethnographic representations focused upon the othering of social groups, of which the (often Western, White, middle-class, male) researcher was usually not a member, but who brought a supposedly neutral analytic eye to bear on the "exotic" social worlds and strange customs that she or he encountered. Such othering occurred not only in relation to non-Western societies and social groups, but also to social groups deemed more exotic or "deviant" within the researcher's own culture; for example, frequenters of taxi-dance halls (Goalby Cressey, 1932/2008) and hobos (N. Anderson, 1923/1967) studied by researchers working within the Chicago School of sociology. It should be remembered that these are works located very much in their epistemological and methodological epoch, and ethnography has moved and changed since those times, autoethnography being one of the more innovative trends to spring from its ethnographic parent.

The degree of focus upon wider ethnographic concerns, and/or the departure (or not) from more established realist and neo-realist writing styles toward more innovative representations, has generated much debate amongst autoethnographic researchers, whose work has been categorized—by some at least (see L. Anderson, 2006)—as either analytic or evocative in nature. For many of us, however, this distinction operates as a continuum rather than a binary categorization, with specific autoethnographic works falling somewhere along this continuum. In terms of the "auto" element, too, as Atkinson (2006) reminds us, "all ethnographic work implies a degree of personal engagement with the field and with the data....Autoethnography is...grounded in an explicit recognition of those biographical and personal foundations" (p. 402). The researcher's own personal narratives are thus "written in," explicitly, upfront, systematically, sometimes poignantly, as a fundamental and integral part of the research process, rather than as a subsidiary, confessional "aside" to the ethnographic account. Autoethnographic researchers whose focus shifts toward the "culture" end of the auto-ethno spectrum usually subject to in-depth analysis their lived experiences *qua* member of a cultural or subcultural group, with the aim of portraying vividly, and illuminating perceptively, wider cultural experiences, practices and processes. As Ellis, Adams, and Bochner (2011) succinctly note, autoethnographers use personal experience to illustrate cultural experience and thus make characteristics of a culture familiar for both insiders and outsiders. Of interest to us as autoethnographers, then, is the notion of the *ethnós*.

But what actually constitutes this elusive *ethnós*? What makes a culture, or a social group? Who is included and who excluded? Ty and Verduyn (2008) caution against essentialist notions of the social group, and in terms of insider status, interactionists would remind us that membership of any social group or category—our group insiderness—is ever shifting, mutable and context-dependent. From an anthropological perspective, Strathern (1987) problematizes the insider status of professional anthropologists who portray themselves as members of the culture they study, but who, she argues, do not necessarily hold the same views as do the "natives." But who are the "authentic" natives? As Motzafi-Haller (1997) argues, the binary categories of "native" and "non-native" can be highly misleading. Indeed, it is debatable whether anyone can ever be deemed a complete member of any culture, subculture or social group, for what criteria would have to be fulfilled in order to ascertain complete membership and for how long? Who would decide and agree upon such criteria? Rather, it might be more accurate to posit that there are degrees of insiderness and outsiderness, which change over time, place and social context. For example, as an academic sociologist and a "veteran" female distance runner (amongst many other things), I hold membership of various social groups, but at any one point, my felt membership may relate to any one or combination of these groups, or indeed to none of them.

In this vein, Ty and Verduyn (2008), writing about Asian-Canadian autoethnography, problematize the notion of according special insider status to group members. As they argue, we may be researching and writing autoethnographically *qua* member of a particular social group or groups, but we cannot represent or "speak for" all members of that group. In the case of the Asian-Canadian writing upon which they focus, Ty and Verduyn (2008) note that while the work of Chinese Canadians, Japanese Canadians, and South Asian Canadians has dominated the field of Asian-Canadian literature, a literature by Cambodian Canadians or Vietnamese Canadians is only just beginning to emerge. The intersectionality of identities is salient, for there are likely to be further specificies beyond membership of the nation-state, relating to gender, age, ethnicity, and so on. The complexities of culture and group membership are rich and intricate, and now I consider some of the tensions between culturally-situated author/researchers and the cultures in which we are situated, and indeed from which we may seek to disassociate.

Our shifting engagement and disengagement as an autoethnographic author with and from our culture makes for fascinating and sometimes emotionally painful writing and reading. Seeking and sustaining membership of different cultures (culture being widely defined) and subcultures simultaneously may prove highly problematic. Antoniu (2004), for example, examines her own situatedness both as a Cypriot woman and as a lesbian. These she posits as two seemingly incompatible cultures and elements of her identity held in uncomfortable tension, the first of which, at the beginning of her tale, she indicates having to marginalize or even at times reject in order to claim the latter. She talks poignantly of her Cypriotness as being a "festering wound...too painful to write" (p. 127). Her autoethnographic writing captures well the interactional and intersectional flux of her cultural identities, for "rejecting my Cypriotness doesn't make it disappear. I'm always Cypriot and lesbian. In the face of racism, I'm undeniably Cypriot" (p. 129). Further along in the text (written in the form of a Cypriot cookbook, where analysis is interspersed with recipes), however, Antoniu begins to challenge the incompatibility of these aspects of her identity, asserting her difference *within* Cypriotness, re-imagining her Cypriotness to allow a lesbian presence to be inscribed into her ethnic identity. Thus, she is engaged in the radical act of "queering Cypriotness" (p. 131) in a challenge to what she argues to be the dominant discourses of heterosexual-Cypriotness. She also problematizes the binary categorization of Black/White in terms of racial identities, for as a working-class Cypriot woman from East London she feels herself to be not entirely "*white* white" nor indeed "*black* black" (p. 137). Other autoethnographic work has similarly and thought-provokingly engaged with issues of whiteness, identity, and privilege (e.g. Motzafi-Haller, 1997; Nicholls, 2011; Spry, 2001; Warren, 2003), including in relation to the politics of race and ethnicity. It is to some of the political dimensions of autoethnography that I now turn.

Autoethnography as the Engagement of Self/Politics

It is important to highlight the many and varied ways in which autoethnography has always engaged, and continues to engage, powerfully and poignantly with politics at all levels, from the micro, through the organizational, to the macro, state level. The personal can indeed be political, as feminists and autoethnographers alike have pointed out (Holman Jones, 2005). Autoethnography has been utilized to provide a trenchant critical perspective on dominant discourses, ranging from those of Western colonizing powers, through male hegemonic discourses, to dictatorships of many political persuasions. It has also been used to critique all manner of other forms of dominant discourse such as the bio-medical, where the autoethnographic narratives of patients themselves challenge powerful medical discourses that can seek to erase lived-body experiences (e.g., Moore, 2013). Academia itself has provided a rich seam for autoethnographers to mine (e.g., Pelias, 2004), and moves toward a much more managerialist approach within universities and the rise of the audit culture have been challenged by a range of autoethnographic writers (e.g., Jones, 2011; Ngunjiri, Hernandez, & Chang, 2010; Sparkes, 2007) within academia. In this section, I focus specifically upon autoethnographic engagement with politics in relation to non-Western peoples, and then move on to the ways in which it has challenged political regimes in need of change.

The politics of representation have been engaged in relation to the portrayal of non-Western, "indigenous" peoples, where the voices of the colonizers often spoke for, or indeed drowned out, the voices of the colonized. As Blodgett, Schinke, Smith, Peltier, and Pheasant (2011) note, for many non-Western peoples, research has actually become a dirty word. This, they argue, stems from "a history of mainstream research being imposed on indigenous peoples in ways that have subverted the knowledge and voices coming from within their communities," thus affirming the dominant, colonizing culture's view of itself as the sole locus of legitimate knowledge and power (p. 522). We should of course be wary of uncritical use of the term "indigenous," particularly as appeals to "indigeneity" can of course be used by racists as much as by those seeking to challenge racist thinking (see Williams & Law, 2012). As Pathak (2010) reminds us, however, autoethnography as a form of scholarship engaged with a critical perspective can create a body of literature that disrupts and challenges a colonial mindset that feels no need to articulate its own roots, assumptions and origins. Even with the best of intentions, relatively privileged researchers can wittingly or unwittingly silence, mute or distort the viewpoints of the relatively underprivileged communities to which they are attempting to give voice. Nicholls (2011), for example, asks from a feminist perspective, "If I speak for my sister, do I amplify her voice or silence it?" In her paper, which includes an autoethnographic commentary, she discusses the debates (often vitriolic) between different groups of Caribbean feminists surrounding the removal from power of Haiti's democratically-elected president, Jean-Bertrand Aristide, in 2004 by a US-backed coup. She raises issues of insiderness/outsiderness in relation to Haitian and Caribbean communities, and considers who is in a position to speak for such communities, feminist or otherwise. Nicholls (2011) argues that the work of politically *engag(e)és* scholars in the privileged "global North," desiring to make judgments in support of feminists in the underprivileged "global South," can itself constitute the kind of colonizing or repressive move that annuls the very solidarity it seeks to enact. Autoethnographic work that adopts a critical postcolonialist stance can provide a potent voice aimed at challenging and disrupting imperialist discourses and practices, however "well-intentioned" these may be.

With reference to politics and repression, autoethnographies can be called upon to generate powerful counter narratives and tales of resistance (see Rivera-Fuentes's [2009] disturbing, visceral account of being tortured). A powerful autoethnographic work that addresses deep political concerns, in this case surrounding nation-state borders, border politics and border-transgressors, is Khosravi's (2010) often harrowing account of being an "illegal" migrant. In this multi-faceted account, he evocatively recounts the liminality, terrors and dreadful vulnerabilities of illegal border-crossings in what is often portrayed as an era of globalization and effortless transnationalism, but where also "violation of the border regime is a violation of ethical and aesthetic norms" (p.2). The border system is portrayed as one governed by criminalization. In his work, Khosravi, drawing upon both his own personal experiences and narratives and those of his co-("illegal")travellers, deploys these personal lived experiences to illustrate vividly and "on the ground" the human-felt and often severe consequences of national and international laws and policies. He argues forcibly that freedom of mobility and permeability of borders for some groups is made possible only via the rigorous and organized policing and exclusion of others. Here, autoethnography is utilized to link, powerfully, evocatively, and analytically, the particular with the general, the personal with the wider socio-political context, to give voice to groups often unheard, and to address those long-standing sociological and anthropological concerns surrounding the structure-agency nexus.

Autoethnography can therefore provide us with a potent methodological means of engaging in a discursive and representational space for voices hitherto unheard or actively silenced, thereby posing a direct challenge to hegemonic discourses. As Neumann (1996) notes, "Autoethnographic texts...democratize the representational sphere of culture by locating the particular experiences of individuals in tension with dominant expressions of discursive power" (p. 189). These texts provide representational space for those with divergent voices actively to contest, and even delegitimate, dominant meaning systems (Langellier, 1989). Autoethnography can also provide a potent means of mounting epistemological challenges, for it offers up space for dissenting voices to question whether supposedly universal, neutral, rational knowledge is in fact highly partial and particularist, merely serving to reinforce dominant discourses.

Autoethnography has the capacity to disrupt and contest these discourses, and to be engaged in powerfully political ways (Pathak, 2010).

Autoethnography as the Engagement of Selves/Futures

In this final section, I have selected from the range of emerging forms of the genre two promising new (or relatively new) directions in autoethnography upon which to focus: 1) collaborative autoethnography (a growing trend perhaps, rather than a "new" perspective as such); and 2) what has been termed "autophenome-nography" (Grupetta, 2004; Allen-Collinson, 2009, 2011a, 2011b), a novel form of automethodology. The first of these, collaborative or joint autoethnography, I have chosen because it is a form of autoethnography that appears to be receiving greater attention amongst contemporary writers (see Ngunjiri & Hernandez, this volume) and is an approach that I have found both stimulating and challenging in undertaking with a close colleague (Allen-Collinson & Hockey, 2001). The second form, autophenomenography, I have selected as it is a new approach that I am seeking to develop, particularly in relation to experiences of embodiment (Allen-Collinson, 2011a, 2011b). In some ways, these two forms might be construed as residing at different ends of an autoethnographic (or at least an automethodolog-ical) spectrum, for collaborative autoethnography extends the "auto" outwards to the dyad and beyond. Autophenomenography, on the other hand, might be construed as extending the "auto" focus further inward to the phenomenal layers of the researcher's lived experience.

First, then, I consider collaborative autoethnography. While Norris has been credited with coining the term "duoethnography" (Sawyer & Norris, 2004, discussed in Ngunjiri, Hernandez, & Chang, 2010), joint or collaborative autoeth-nography has a somewhat longer history (see Bochner & Ellis, 1995). Together with a colleague and co-runner, I first started engaging in collaborative autoeth-nography, with some trepidation, in 1997 (Allen-Collinson & Hockey, 2001). In recent times, however, it has become more widely practiced and is signaled as a key future direction for the genre (Ngunjiri et al., 2010). As I discuss here, these two new directions can be seen to respond in different ways to challenges of rampant subjectivism sometimes leveled at autoethnography by its less informed critics.

Collaborative autoethnography is a wide-ranging form of autoethnography, which may span the involvement of one other researcher/author and/or participant to co-construct the narrative (Bochner & Ellis, 1995; Allen-Collinson & Hockey, 2001) to that of many others to produce a community autoethnography (Toyosaki, Pensoneau-Conway, Wendt, & Leathers, 2009). As Ngunjiri et al. (2010) note, too, collaborative autoethnographers adopt various models of collaboration, ranging from full involvement at all stages of the research process to collaboration at a spe-cific point or points during the research. In their own research they used a parallel or concurrent approach, where several researchers based at the same university gath-ered autobiographical experiential data as immigrant women of color in the university system within the United States. Data were gathered independently but concurrently, and the researchers then came together to share and discuss their findings, subsequently feeding back these discussions into the collaborative autoethnographic narrative. This is an approach similar to one that I and a co-researcher/runner utilized some years ago to examine our lived experience of long-term running injuries and the consequent disruptions to our identities as long-distance runners (Allen-Collinson & Hockey, 2001), a project that I now use for illustrative purposes.

During our collaborative autoethnographic project, as part of the systematic data collection process, we constructed detailed personal logs throughout the two-year, often painful and distressing, identity-challenging, injury and rehabilitative period. Such recording was a habit already familiar to us, not only via our academic research work, but also as a habitual practice amongst "serious" runners who record their daily performance in training logs. Our own data collection was undertaken via field note books and micro tape recorders, the latter accompanying us on training sessions and also throughout the day for "notes to self" when thoughts occurred to us, such as when traveling to work in the car. In addition, we created a joint analytic log in which our discussions and salient themes, theoretical ideas and concepts were recorded. For example, if one of us had documented a particular narrative theme, we would discuss this, asking questions, challenging each other's assumptions, trying to pinpoint the precise composition of that theme, its boundaries and its connections to other themes already generated.

As two qualitative, interactionist sociologists—one female, one male— with strong running identities, we shared many similarities, but inevitably also diverged (sometimes widely!) in relation to our embodiment, experiences, and ideas. In our collaborative log, thematic or conceptual differences between our individual accounts were identified and, if possible, "reconciled." Where no analytical reconciliation proved achievable, we were happy to accept and record the differences. We also discussed the reasons for such divergence and the impact, if any, upon the process of handling our injuries, thus adding to the data collection process in a manner similarly recounted by Ngunjiri et al. (2010). We sought to act as the "primary recipient" (Ochs & Capps, 1996, p. 35) of each other's data, discussing events, experiences and interpretations. Journal entries were analyzed and re-analyzed, employing processes of re-memory (Sanders-Bustle & Oliver, 2001) to send ourselves back in our "time tunnels" to recapture the sometimes wildly oscillating emotions of the injury and rehabilitative journey. At times our injured knees would suddenly deteriorate, often for no discernible reason, and we would confront a deluge of emotions—fear, anger, despondency, despair:

> Cold, rainy evening. Still maintaining the 5-mins (of running) with 5-mins walking in between. Going absolutely fine, then suddenly the knee completely gave way in the second. No rhyme or reason. Too tired/despondent to write much. Just feel grey. Very frightened. Am I back at square 1? Or is this just a temporary set-back. The old fear is back. Feel like giving up right now. Tomorrow I won't? (Individual Log 2)

In this particular form of collaborative autoethnography, in a similar fashion to Ngunjiri et al. (2010), we moved between individual, divergent activities (recording our individual logs) and collaborative, convergent activities (discussions and recording of the joint, analytic log) at multiple points in the research process. For us, undertaking the collaborative autoethnography fulfilled a range of purposes, including at times the cathartic and therapeutic, generating something positive out of what was, for us both, a difficult and painful (psychologically and physically) experience. Both the long-term injury/rehabilitative process and the autoethnographic research process proved to be learning and life-changing experiences, which demonstrated in deeply phenomenological ways both the centrality of shared human lived experience and the limits of intersubjectivity, the times of existential alone-ness which even the most supportive, loving and caring of lifeworld-sharers could not share.

With regard to the phenomenological dimension, the second new direction I consider here is autophenomenography (Gruppetta, 2004; Allen-Collinson, 2009, 2011b). In this form of research, the primary focus is upon the researcher's lived experience of a phenomenon or phenomena rather than upon her or his cultural or subcultural location within a socio-cultural context (more usually the locus of attention in autoethnography), although clearly these are not mutually exclusive categories. For a sociological phenomenologist such as myself, it is impossible to separate phenomenal experience from the social context in which it occurs. For example, Jago's (2002) autoethnographic account of the lived experience of the phenomenon of depression contains potent autophenomenographic elements. In autophenomenography, the self is engaged in a specific way—in relation to phenomena—things as they appear to our conscious mind. The term is derived from the Greek *phainomenon*, taken from *phaino*, from the root *phôs*, or light. *Phainomenon* thus means that which is shown, placed in the light. From this, we derive *phenomenon*: an appearance, observable occurrence, or perceived event or circumstance.

Gruppetta (2004) seems to be the author who first makes reference to the term "autophenomenography," in arguing that if an autoethnographic researcher analyzes her or his own experiences of a phenomenon rather than of a cultural place, then the term autophenomenography is applicable. This is a research approach that I have found interesting but also very challenging in relation to my lived body experiences of distance running. I should explain that I choose to use the term autophenomenography rather than autophenomenology in relation to this particular project for two reasons. First, as with autoethnography, "graphy" is taken as applicable to the research process in general as well as to the written, or representational, product of that process. Second, autophenomenology has specific and highly contested meanings within phenomenology (see Drummond, 2007), and here is not really the forum to engage in such debates, interesting though they are.

Analogous to its autoethnographic sibling, autophenomenography is capable of producing the rich, finely textured "thick descriptions" of first-person experience, so central to the phenomenological quest to bring to life the felt, lived bodily experience. Within the autophenomenographic genre there is scope for a wide spectrum of representational styles, including evocative forms such as poetic representations and performative, audience-interactive presentations, already familiar to those of us working within autoethnography.

To give a flavor of this approach, I portray briefly a recent autophenomenographic project in which I was involved, which focuses upon female embodiment and distance running in public space. To contextualize this research, I should explain that while falling (very) firmly within the non-élite category, I am nevertheless a highly committed, serious runner whose running encompasses two of Bale's (2004) forms: 1) welfare running, pursued for health and fitness aims, and 2) performance running (of a sort), pursued in order hopefully to improve and sustain performance, although nowadays performance is not what it once was!

During the research project, I maintained a research log for a period of three years, recording highly detailed descriptions of my subjective and corporeal experiences during distance-running training sessions. My autophenomenographic research broadly adheres to Giorgi's (1997) descriptive, empirical-phenomenological guidelines, and incorporates the following elements:

1) collection of concrete descriptions of phenomena from an "insider" perspective;

2) the adoption of the phenomenological attitude, an attitude of openness and wonderment toward the world, requiring a degree of bracketing of pre-suppositions (for further details, see Allen-Collinson, 2011b);

3) initial impressionistic readings of the descriptions to gain a feel for the whole;

4) in-depth re-reading (and re-reading!) of these descriptions as part of a process of thorough data-immersion, to identify themes and sub-themes;

5) free imaginative variation, where I search for the most fundamental meanings of a phenomenon, its essential characteristics, via imaginatively varying elements of the phenomenon to ascertain whether it remains identifiable and so to identify and draw out the "essences"—those elements which are, for me, necessary for the phenomenon to be that particular phenomenon; and

6) the production of accounts of the essential structure(s) of experience. Given the *auto*phenomenographic nature of the research, I depart at this juncture from Giorgi's (1997) approach in that rather than constructing *general* descriptions based upon the accounts of a number of participants, the descriptions are based on my own lived experiences of a phenomenon.

My twenty-six-year career in running gives me some confidence of being an insider to the subculture, but the need for familiarity can render problematic a key element in the phenomenological method, *epochē* or "bracketing"—the suspension of the researcher's pre-suppositions and assumptions about a phenomenon. In order to bracket, as far as possible, my own preconceptions about female running in public space, in the project I engaged in two bracketing practices aimed at rendering the familiar strange: 1) discussions with both insiders and non-insiders to the distance-running subculture, female and male; 2) in-depth reading of detailed ethnographic accounts of other sporting activities, to compare and contrast other sports with my own lived experience of running, including the gendered dimension. As a woman who undertakes the vast majority of running in "public space," I am acutely conscious that this is gendered space, and my running is structurally-shaped by various key sociological factors such as gender, age, socio-economic class, and so on.

To give an illustration from within the project, over the years of my running, I have been subjected to varying degrees of both verbal and physical harassment, including being lunged and grabbed at by men and even teenage boys. The embodied consequences of such harassment mean that my corporeal vulnerability is brought forcibly to the forefront of my consciousness when, for example, I run through dark, narrow streets at night. I then run warily, eyes scanning and ears on full alert, in order better to listen for alarm signals and untoward sounds. My body no longer feels like my familiar running "habit-body," at ease with self and comfortable in the environment, but rather it is brought suddenly and vividly to consciousness. My bodily intentionality is also redirected from other important running elements, such as the terrain underfoot and everyday "obstacles" such as pedestrians and cars. In contrast, though, the pleasures of being a running-woman far outweigh the negative elements for me. Experiences of social agency, empowerment, corporeal power, muscularity, strength, and sensory pleasures all coalesce within my lived experience—at least on a good running day! All these feelings emerged from my autophenomenographic data as key elements in my experience of training for distance running, although on any single training occasion one or more elements might be in greater evidence.

Overall, the experience of engaging with the autophenomenographic research was thought-provoking and challenging, particularly in requiring me to stand back and focus a sharp analytic eye on some of my long-held, tacit assumptions about being a female runner. In many of the research methods texts on phenomenological and qualitative research, epoché and bracketing appear as relatively straightforward techniques simply to be applied by the researcher. In practice, however, they are highly problematic, and require hard self-analytic work and sustained, rigorous self-questioning, all part and parcel of the autoethnographer's work. Bracketing was never fully achieved in my research project, and I would argue that full bracketing is not actually achievable, certainly not for a sociologist or anthropologist—for none of us can stand entirely outside of her or his experiential and socio-cultural, interpretive framework to approach the phenomenon completely "fresh" without any presuppositions (see Allen-Collinson, 2011b).

We can, however, seek an open, enquiring, questioning attitude of mind, and be reflexive and self-critical vis-à-vis our own preconceptions. This research attitude also of course accords well with autoethnography, which similarly requires us to adopt a critical, reflexive perspective toward our lived experience, albeit with a greater focus upon our socio-cultural location. As an example of such self-questioning, and the challenges of attempting to be self-critical toward our own preconceptions and prior experience, I include the following fieldnote from the autophenomenographic project, which centers on an alarming experience I had when out running in a relatively isolated location:

> [Running] Out along the river meadows quite some way from the city and approaching the weir. Suddenly out of the blue, a red pick-up truck is hurtling its way across the field towards me down the track toward the river. I had spotted the truck previously careering across the fields, but within sight and earshot of dog-walkers and others, I had paid it little heed. Now there is no one in sight, and the houses bordering the river are some way off on the other bank. Is that a shot gun sticking out of the open passenger window? I catch male voices drifting toward me on the evening air. Heart pounding in my ears now—quiet, quiet, I order—I need to be able to hear and think. Try to steady breathing, better to concentrate. The truck is still approaching down the grassy track, bumping and swaying. I up the pace, pull down my baseball hat firmly and set my jaw sternly. I will my body harder, leaner, tauter, try to look focused and 'don't mess with me.' Not for the first time, I wish my slight, 5'3" runner's body were somewhat more imposing. Suddenly, breath-catchingly, the truck veers off the track a few metres in front of me. I hear loud male voices and a radio blaring. Heart still pounding out time. Just in case… I up the pace to get out of the danger zone…

Now, if I attempt to bracket decades of experience of similar encounters with males when out running, often resulting in verbal and/or physical harassment, my response to the pick-up truck men does appear bizarre, and rather melodramatic, to say the least. I cannot, however, completely bracket and suspend my long experience of running, of being a female runner moving through public space and being accosted by men, particularly during my younger days. My lived and hard-won experience has taught me that these situations harbor danger, and it would be extremely foolish not to pay attention to this experiential and gendered knowledge.

It is this very nexus—of structure and agency, of personal and political, of the phenomenal and the social-structural—that intrigues me and inspires my sociological work. At the heart of autoethnography, for me, is that ever shifting focus between levels: from the macro, wide sociological angle on socio-cultural framework, to the micro, zoom focus on the embodied self.

○

This chapter has considered autoethnography as a potent, challenging, and strongly relational research approach that offers a variety of modes of engaging with self—or perhaps more accurately, selves—in relation to others, to culture, to politics, and the engagement of selves in relation to future possibilities for research. Autoethnography seeks to connect the personal to the social, the cultural, and the political, and locates self/selves, however shifting, transient and fragmentary, and others within a social context. It asks us continually to shift the research lens back and forth from the "auto" to the "ethno" and to recognize that we need fundamentally and analytically to acknowledge the interplay between the two; the link is indissoluble. Autoethnographers thus boldly traverse, blur, and threaten the putative distinctions of the personal and the social, and of self and other. To conclude the chapter, I have suggested two possible directions that for me offer interesting future possibilities for autoethnographic researchers, but there are of course many others. For one of autoethnography's greatest strengths is its openness to new directions and new forms, its wide-ranging, protean nature, refusing to be tied down and constrained by being pigeon-holed into a particular research approach or set of techniques.

Note

1. Here I focus primarily upon written rather than performance autoethnography. For a detailed discussion of performance autoethnography, see Spry (2001).

References

Allen-Collinson, J. (2009). Sporting embodiment: Sports studies and the (continuing) promise of phenomenology. *Qualitative Research in Sport and Exercise, 1*, 279–296.

Allen-Collinson, J. (2011a). Feminist phenomenology and the woman in the running body. *Sport, Ethics & Philosophy, 5*(3), 287 302

Allen-Collinson, J. (2011b). Intention and epochē in tension: Autophenomenography, bracketing and a novel approach to researching sporting embodiment. *Qualitative Research in Sport, Exercise & Health, 3*, 48–62.

Allen-Collinson, J., & Hockey, J. (2001). Runners' tales: Autoethnography, injury and narrative. *Auto/Biography, 9*, 95–106.

Anderson, L. (2006). Analytic autoethnography. *Journal of Contemporary Ethnography, 35*, 373–395.

Anderson, N. (1923/1967). *The hobo: The sociology of the homeless man.* Chicago: University of Chicago Press.

Antoniu, M. (2004). My Cypriot cookbook: Re-imagining my ethnicity. *Auto/Biography, 12*, 126–146.

Atkinson, P. (2006). Rescuing autoethnography. *Journal of Contemporary Ethnography, 35*, 400–404.

Bakhtin, M. (1984). *Problems of Dostoevsky's poetics* (C. Emerson Ed. and Trans.). Minneapolis: University of Minnesota Press.

Bale, J. (2004). *Running cultures.* London: Routledge.

Behar, R. (1997). *The vulnerable observer: Anthropology that breaks your heart.* Boston: Beacon Press.

Blodgett, A. T., Schinke, R. J, Smith, B., Peltier, D., & Pheasant, C. (2011). In indigenous words: Exploring vignettes as a narrative strategy for presenting the research voices of Aboriginal community members. *Qualitative Inquiry, 17*, 522–533.

Bochner, A. P., & Ellis, C. (1995). Telling living: Narrative co-construction practices of interpersonal relationships. In W. Leeds-Hurwitz (Ed.), *Social approaches to communication* (pp. 201–213). New York: Guilford Press.

Chatham-Carpenter, A. (2010). "Do thyself no harm": Protecting ourselves as autoethnographers. *Journal of Research Practice, 6*, Article M1. Retrieved September 9, 2011, from jrp.icaap.org/index.php/jrp/article/view/213/183

Denzin, N. K. (2012). Afterword. Sport and neoliberalism. In D. Andrews & M. Silk (Eds.), *Sport and neoliberalism* (pp. 294–302). Philadelphia: Temple Press.

Denzin, N. K., & Lincoln, Y. S. (2000). The policies and practices of interpretation. In N.K. Denzin & Y. S. Lincoln (Eds.), *Handbook of qualitative research* (2nd ed.; pp. 897–992). Thousand Oaks, CA: Sage.

Drummond, J. J. (2007). Phenomenology: Neither auto- nor hetero- be. *Phenomenology and the Cognitive Sciences, 6*, 57–74.

Ellis, C. (1997). Evocative autoethnography. In W. Tierney & Y. S. Lincoln (Eds.), *Representation and the text* (pp. 115–139). New York: State University of New York Press.

Ellis, C. (1999). He*art*ful autoethnography. *Qualitative Health Research, 9*, 669–683.

Ellis, C. (2007). Telling secrets, revealing lives: Relational ethics in research with intimate others. *Qualitative Inquiry, 13*, 3–29.

Ellis, C., & Bochner, A. P. (Eds.). (1996). *Composing ethnography: Alternative forms of qualitative writing.* Walnut Creek, CA: AltaMira Press.

Ellis, C., & Bochner, A. (2006). Analyzing analytic autoethnography: An autopsy. *Journal of Contemporary Ethnography, 35*, 429–449.

Ellis, C., Adams, T. E., & Bochner, A. (2011). Autoethnography: An overview. *Forum: Qualitative Social Research/Sozialforschung, 12*, Article 10. Retrieved August 19, 2011, from www.qualitative-research.net/index.php/fqs/article/viewArticle/1589/3095

Erben, M. (1993). The problem of other lives: Social perspectives on written biography. *Sociology, 27*, 15–25.

Fiske, J. (1990). Ethnosemiotics: Some personal and theoretical reflections. *Cultural Studies, 4*, 85–99.

Giorgi, A. P. (1997). The theory, practice and evaluation of the phenomenological method as a qualitative research procedure. *Journal of Phenomenological Psychology, 28*, 235–260.

Goalby Cressey, P. (2008). *The taxi-dance hall: A sociological study in commercialized recreation and city life.* Chicago: University of Chicago Press. (Original work published in 1932.)

Greenhalgh, S. (2001). *Under the medical gaze: Facts and fictions of chronic pain.* Berkeley: University of California Press.

Gruppetta, M. (2004). Autophenomenography? Alternative uses of autobiographically based research. In P. L. Jeffery (Ed.), *Association for Active Researchers in Education (AARE) Conference paper abstracts—2004.* Sydney: AARE.

Holman Jones, S. (2005). Autoethnography: making the personal political. In N. K. Denzin & Y. S. Lincoln (Eds.), *Handbook of qualitative research* (3rd ed., pp. 763–792). Thousand Oaks, CA: Sage.

Jago, B. J. (2002). Chronicling an academic depression. *Journal of Contemporary Ethnography, 31*, 729–757.

Jones, R. L. (2011). Leaving. *Qualitative Inquiry, 17*, 631–638.

Khosravi, S. (2010). *"Illegal" traveller: An auto-ethnography of borders.* Basingstoke, UK: Palgrave Macmillan.

Langellier, K. M. (1989). Personal narratives: Perspectives on theory and research. *Text and Performance Quarterly, 9*, 243–276.

Malinowski, B. (1935). *Coral gardens and their magic: A study of the methods of tilling the soil and of agricultural rites in the Trobriand Islands.* London: Routledge.

Mellick, M., & Fleming, S. (2010). Personal narrative and the ethics of disclosure: A case study from élite sport. *Qualitative Research, 10*, 299–314.

Moore, I. (2013). The beast within: Life with an invisible chronic illness. *Qualitative Inquiry, 19*, 201–208.

Motzafi-Haller, P. (1997). Writing birthright: On native anthropologists and the politics of representation. In D. Reed-Danahay (Ed.), *Auto/ethnography: Rewriting the self and the social* (pp.195–222). Oxford: Berg.

Neumann, M. (1996). Collecting ourselves at the end of the century. In C. Ellis & A. P. Bochner (Eds.), *Composing ethnography: Alternative forms of qualitative writing* (pp. 172–198). Walnut Creek, CA: AltaMira Press.

Nicholls, T. (2011). Should I speak for my sister? Solidarity and silence in feminist struggles. *PhaenEx, 6,* 12–41.

Ngunjiri, F. W., Hernandez, K-A. C., & Chang, H. (2010). Living autoethnography: Connecting life and research. *Journal of Research Practice, 6,* Article E1. Retrieved November 9, 2011, from jrp.icaap.org/index.php/jrp/article/viewArticle/241/186

Ochs, E., & Capps, L. (1996). Narrating the self. *Annual Review of Anthropology, 25,* 19–43.

Pathak, A. A. (2010). Opening my voice, claiming my space: Theorizing the possibilities of postcolonial approaches to autoethnography. *Journal of Research Practice, 6,* Article M10. Retrieved November 8, 2011, from jrp.icaap.org/index.php/jrp/article/view/231/191

Pelias, R. J. (2004). *A methodology of the heart: Evoking academic and daily life.* Lanham, MD: AltaMira Press.

Reed-Danahay, D. (Ed.). (1997). *Auto/ethnography: Rewriting the self and the social.* Oxford: Berg.

Rivera-Fuentes, C. (2009). Mosaics of memory: Ellipses and gaps in life narratives of torture. In A.C. Sparkes (Ed.), *Auto/biography yearbook 2008* (pp. 127–137). Nottingham, UK: Russell Press.

Roth, M-W. (2009). Auto/ethnography and the question of ethics. *FORUM: Qualitative Social Research, 10,* Art. 38. Retrieved January 2, 2010, from: www.qualitative-research.net/fqs/

Sanders-Bustle, L., & Oliver, K. L. (2001). The role of physical activity in the lives of researchers: A body-narrative. *Studies in Philosophy and Education, 20,* 507–520.

Smith, B., Allen-Collinson, J., Phoenix, C., Brown, D., & Sparkes, A. (2009). Dialogue, monologue, and boundary crossing within research encounters: A performative narrative analysis. *International Journal of Sport & Exercise Psychology, 7,* 342–359.

Sparkes, A. C. (2007). Embodiment, academics and the audit culture: A story seeking consideration. *Qualitative Research, 7,* 521–550.

Spry, T. (2001). Performing autoethnography: An embodied methodological praxis. *Qualitative Inquiry, 7,* 706–732.

Stanley, L. (1995). *The auto/biographical I: The theory and practice of feminist auto/biography.* Manchester, UK: Manchester University Press.

Strathern, M. (1987). The limits of auto-anthropology. In A. Jackson (Ed.), *Anthropology at home* (pp. 16–37). London: Tavistock.

Toyosaki, S., Pensoneau-Conway, S. L., Wendt, N. A., & Leathers, K. (2009). Community autoethnography: Compiling the personal and resituating whiteness. *Cultural Studies ↔ Critical Methodologies, 9,* 56–83.

Ty, E., & Verduyn, C. (2008). *Asian Canadian writing beyond autoethnography.* Waterloo, Canada: Wilfrid Laurier Press.

Wall, S. (2008). Easier said than done: Writing an autoethnography. *International Journal of Qualitative Methods, 7,* 38–53.

Warren, J. T. (2003). *Performing purity: Whiteness, pedagogy, and the reconstitution of power.* New York: Peter Lang.

Williams, S., & Law, I. (2012). Legitimising racism: An exploration of the challenges posed by the use of indigeneity discourses by the far right. *Sociological Research Online, 17.* Retrieved May 31, 2012, from www.socresonline.org.uk/17/2/2

Chapter 14

Getting Out of Selves

An Assemblage/ethnography?

Jonathan Wyatt and Ken Gale

With Ken (1st August, La Viala-du-Tarn, Languedoc, France, 5:45 pm)

I am on a stony river beach in the Tarn valley, twenty minutes down from the plateau and the family house at Montjaux we visit each summer, writing to you at a battered wooden picnic table, its stolid legs buried in the ground. It's been a year since we were last at the house, with its view over jagged landscape, its space to write, and its sheep (Wyatt, Gale, Gannon, & Davies, 2011; Gale, Pelias, Russell, Spry, & Wyatt, 2012).

I swung the car fast round the familiar rolling bends, alone, The King Blues turned up loud, the centrifugal forces holding me into the sides of the hills on the left turns, and throwing me outwards to the steep edges on the right.

It's early evening; a wind has picked up—I can hear it in the lush leaves of the branches above me. French families are gathering their bags, towels and empty bottles and retreating to their cars. A teenage boy juggles a scruffy gray leather ball between feet, thighs, chest, shoulders, head. I curse his nonchalance.

I taste dusty water. I swam beyond the rectangular safety barrier and the small children playing, but did not cross to the opposite bank. I was feeling conservative, my resources and boldness depleted by recent weeks. At the quiet center of the river, I lay gazing at the steep sides of the valley with their stark limestone outcrops, the sun beginning to dip behind the western ridge.

Handbook of Autoethnography, edited by Stacy Holman Jones, Tony E. Adams, and Carolyn Ellis, 300–312, Inc. © 2013 Left Coast Press. All rights reserved.

I think of Deleuze's conceptualization of the fold: "this"—life's current difficulties—feels a visceral process of folding and unfolding. The folds, at times, are not soft but jagged, their edges sharp against my skin.

With Jonathan (8ᵗʰ August, at home, Millbrook, UK, 9:30 pm)

I taste dusty water.

The affective sensation of your presence energizes my writing. We are never simply lone ethnographers; we are bound up in changing, complex, multiple interconnections. As I read of you at the river in France, I, too, am alone, in my house, uneasy, with the quietness that the temporary absence of my children brings. I also sense others with me; Spry, Foucault, Pineau, Deleuze: their words, and the images they bring, impress themselves upon me, indent my thinking. This seems to be a form of autoethnographic practice that functions on a plane of immanence. There is no enunciation or utterance that exists as an individual entity, and as Deleuze and Guattari (1988) claim, "the social character of enunciation is intrinsically founded if only one succeeds in demonstrating how enunciation in itself implies collective assemblages" (p. 80).

A teenage boy juggles a scruffy gray leather ball between feet, thighs, chest, shoulders, head.

I have been reading Tami Spry's (2011) chapter in the new edition of *The SAGE Handbook of Qualitative Research* and with the rememberings that make up the complexity of our articulations, I have been thinking of our writing both as a form and a critique of autoethnography. I am fascinated when she makes "a bid for autoethnographic ensemble" (p. 497), a plea for autoethnography as "co-presence with others" (p. 497). I like the shift this offers away from the individualism of the "auto" towards the felted dynamism of Deleuze and Guattari's (1988) notion of "assemblage" (p. 306), with its flows of affect, time, space and place, human and non-human bodies, and… and… and… (Deleuze and Parnet, 2002).

In this I love the way that the various translations[1] of Deleuze and Guattari's assemblage both work and don't work. So that "assemblage" in its original form of *agencement*, while being suggestive of agency and intention, actually owes more to energy and force; it is not about the psychological sense of agency that with intent fights against structure, it is more about the collective multiplicity that creates new vectors of becoming into the not yet known. The more recently translated "arrangement" seems to suggest organization and, perhaps, some kind of systemic sociological ordering of selves with function in mind and, of course, it is not! We know that as soon as we talk of our experience, our genealogies and our histories, as soon as we align our relational ontologies in particular ways, something shifts; our assemblage, a "body-without-organs" (Deleuze & Guattari, 1988), disassembles and in so doing, follows a new and different line of flight, is part of a new affect, striating space differently, and is always becoming.

The Two of Us With You, the Reader, at This Page, Now

In these becomings, detecting and tracing troubled lines and forces during a few months in the second half of 2011, we became aware of an emergent "assemblage/ ethnography," with its collective, multiple forces of becoming.

We have been writing, as the two of us and with others, especially Deleuze, for many years now, exchanging writing via email as we explore the intersecting, overlapping, felted, themes of subjectivity and collaborative writing (see, for example, Gale & Wyatt, 2009; Wyatt et al., 2011). At this "node" (Hilton, 2012) in our lives, our writing together had been stagnant for over a year, and what we might refer to as "Jonathan-as-assemblage" had been unravelling. Also, that which began to emerge in our writing was a sense of getting out of (our)selves.

Spaces

With Ken (10th June, Combibos Café, Oxford, 10:40 am)

As we align our relational ontologies in particular ways…

I wrote recently about hitting fifty (Wyatt, in press). The essay finishes as one character in the story, the bargirl, at the end of her shift searches the pub for another character, the middle-aged writer, whom she has come to view with a concerned pity. She can't find him:

> He's gone. Good. She had intended to tell him it was time to stop writing, and mischievously imagined taking his book from him, pretending to tear it up and ordering him to get out and live.

At the time of writing this I felt, through her eyes, as if getting out there and living might bring relief. That's what she (I) imagined, as if, by doing so, the writer would shatter the carapace that he was trapped within and fly, like her. Free.

But it's not like that.

Getting out there and living is like walking on shards of glass, the splinters wounding and marking me as I pick a way through. Meanwhile, I'm also holding on, not letting go, thinking, processing, trying to understand. I feel on the verge of blowing it all up.

A plea for autoethnography as a "co-presence with others."

A woman walked behind me just now, in this café near my office. I saw her approach as I wrote. I did not turn. I imagined that she was arriving to meet with me. I longed for her to place her hand on my shoulder as she passed.

Writing has never seemed more difficult. It has never seemed more dangerous. Writing *does*. It changes how things are, how I see the world. I am doubting the narrative of writing as healing and therapeutic, of writing as finding a way through the difficulties, of writing as making something good. I fear writing as tearing a line through stability.

A new vector of becoming.

With Jonathan (19th June, Millbrook, 12:30 pm)

On Sunday morning I woke with my head spinning, my body seeming beaten, and a growing sense of remorse. I pieced together the portions of my day that had made up my night, and I remembered drinking wine and staying up late. Perhaps my memory wasn't serving me well but I couldn't remember being too excessive. As I groaned, revealing my displeasure, Viv woke up beside me, chuckled and said, "What's with you? You really like getting out of it don't you?"

I longed for her to place her hand on my shoulder as she passed.

We laughed together, and then as I lapsed into temporary silence I repeated to myself that phrase, "getting out of it," realizing the commonplace and the habitual in its usage in relation to my pleasure-seeking propensities. What does getting out of it mean? Or rather, what can it mean?

When we use the phrase, "get a life" there seems to be a strong propositional prescriptivism about that usage and a thinly-veiled pejorative connotation. I remember thinking once about describing my writing as my work. I think my father might have thought it odd to term writing as working. He would have seen a funny side to that; his laughter would have been gentle, perhaps teasing. The barmaid seems to care for you. She thinks your behavior unusual and she wants you to get a life. If she were to throw your notebook away it would not have been malicious.

"Getting out of it," "Getting out there and living," is something that offers great challenge. As I think of my youthful tendencies and proclivities to enjoy getting out of it, something my physical body increasingly works to disallow because of the subsequent discomfort it brings, I sense that it was and is, for me, very Deleuzian: "The only way to get outside the dualisms is to be-between, to pass between, the intermezzo" (Deleuze & Guattari, 1988, p. 277). It's necessary to move toward the way in which Patti Lather (2007) uses the phrase "getting lost" because I think that getting lost can be used in the Foucauldian sense of "get(ting) free of one self" (Foucault, 1992, p. 8), where the self that we work to gain freedom from is the one that has been discursively constructed, the one that resists reflexivity, and the one that traps itself within the conventions and familiarities of foundational knowledge and a unitary self. While working with what is, for me, Pitt & Britzman's (2003) problematic binary between "lovely" and "difficult" knowledge, Lather (2007) uses the phrase "rich in loss" to describe the benefits and the risks involved in getting lost:

> The former reinforces what we think we want from what we find, and the latter is knowledge that induces breakdowns in representing experience. Here, accepting loss becomes the very force of learning, and what one loves when lovely knowledge is lost is the promise of thinking and doing otherwise. (p. 13)

So the getting out of it cannot simply be a moving from one to the other, from the inner to the outer, from the mindful to the sensual, from the rational to the irrational: why does it have to be one or the other, or the one in relation to the other? Life seems to be full of tropes that constrain us to exist in relation to this "one or the other." Meaning is enticingly constructed around this, providing convenience, compartmentalization and a basis for normatively regulated, organized living. In the valorizing of the one and the queering of the other, a discursive hierarchizing takes place that works to stratify our knowings and to dislocate them from their own potency.

Getting out there and living is like walking on shards of glass, the splinters wounding and marking me as I pick a way through.

It is unusual to find you working with such violent metaphors. I wonder about the black-and-whiteness, the either/or, of what your writing seems to represent. I want to shout out to you as you engage in these struggles, "It is not like that," "It doesn't have to be like that." In your writing there is something of the inside and the outside, the one or the other, that troubles me, and it is not just you, my friend, it is the us, it is the everything, it is the technologies of self, it is the constraints of neo-liberalism, it is what fuels my delight at the humiliation of Murdoch,[2] it is an awareness of those powerful forces that make it so difficult to work, to live, in ways, always, to make the familiar strange. I am with you in this: I understand.

This is the problem. As you say, writing is action, but perhaps there comes a time when digging with the pen is not enough.

With Ken (9th September, Freshwater Bay, Isle of Wight, 5:00 pm)

This afternoon, an hour ago, I walked along the sands of the long beach east of Freshwater Bay, a place we visit with, and that carries poignant memories for, my eighty-something mother. I thought of you. As the onshore wind blew the tops off ragged waves, a lone surfer looked with longing, and in vain, out to sea. As I stepped into the water to walk along its edges, shoes in hand, I thought of you: how you would by then have been in the water, immersed, diving into the irregular gray-white caps.

So the getting out of it cannot simply be a moving from one to the other, from the inner to the outer, from the mindful to the sensual, from the rational to the irrational.

With Tess to one side, pausing, her camera directed at a piece of washed-up seaweed, and with my brother and sister marching ahead, I noticed this thought: I will write "this"—I will dig again with the pen—to Ken. The Ken who at that moment was: Ken-who-dives-into-cold-seawater-and-lives-by-the-sea-and-writes-about-flows-and-waves-and-tides-and-currents-all-the-time.

With Jonathan (12th September, Millbrook, 7:15 pm)

I was amused by your living re/cognition of "Ken-who-dives-into-cold-seawater-and-lives-by-the-sea-and-writes-about-flows-and-waves-and-tides-and-currents-all-the-time." I quite like being known and re/known in this way although I hope I don't go on about it all the time: there are other tunes that I can play!

In thinking about "haecceities"[3] (Deleuze & Guattari, 1988) and how they are often associated with place, it occurred to me this morning that there are so many "places" here in Cornwall that fill me with emotion, not just through memory or the power of evocation but through immersion—again and again. I never tire of scrambling down the cliffs at Whitsands, being alone on Happy Valley beach and swimming, swimming until my heart is content and my body is tired. There are many other places in Cornwall, particularly up on the north coast—Perranporth, Porthcothan, Trebarwith come to mind—that I could describe in similar ways.

With Ken (25th September, Coffee Republic, Abingdon, 10:50 am)

Space and place. This place today, my regular Wednesday workplace, a short bike ride from home: its red walls, black doors. A baby on her mother's lap to my left; close, too close, the café busy. She stands, looking over her mother's shoulder at my red and black laptop, a pink plastic spoon in her hand. The baby's name is Mia. "Where's Mia? Where's Mia?" her mother sings.

My heart meanwhile is with you, hearing the singing place names.

Perranporth, Porthcothan, Trebarwith.

I love their sounds, their Cornishness. I hear your voice when I say those names. Places bring our bodies into material presence, holding themselves/ourselves onto the ground, taking us through them, moving, always moving; still and moving. Flows.

Mia leans over to offer me her pink spoon, which I take and offer back.

I am yearning for a different place than this. A desire is pulling at/in my body, a desire I do not understand. It says: "Not this. Something else. Somewhere else. You have to try. There is not much time." My body is disorganized, unruly. It is not of itself, but a hyphen (Bergson, 1991), "a connecting link between action and reaction" (Hughes, 2011, p. 75); part of the flux, not even mine. Ragged, gray-white waves of longing and sadness, hope and love.

With Jonathan (8th October, Millbrook, 7:45 pm)

This "assemblage/ethnography" not only talks about the spaces in between selves and others but also the spaces we are a part of and create. You and I write so much about and within space, and we cannot think of "assemblage/ethnography" without sensing the intangible, shifting and folding nature of haecceities or Virginia Woolf's (1985) "moments of being." Haecceities are, for Deleuze, timeless moments of becoming in which pure events take place in material existence beyond figuration, imitation and representation. There is something intuitive, something alchemical, and something sensate to do with this: space is integral to these becomings. We think of Bachelard's (1969) "poetics of space" as if the singularity of a particular place becomes through our connectedness with it; we sense relationality in an assemblage that is becoming in terms of intangible forces, energies and senses, a becoming in relation to place.

However, place does not displace space.

In place there is a suspension, a holding in space that becomes through temporality; in Massey's (2005) words we might think of space as "the dimension of a multiplicity of durations" (p. 24). Woolf's "*moment* of being" becomes through the sensing of the place and the cognition, the awareness and the articulation of it, and it seems to me that this inevitable temporal suspension or gap is what we call space. The haecceity of touch, sound, taste, sight and smell that becomes, say, my love of swimming and surfing in the sea is that *momentary* coming together in which time and space fuse. Perhaps this is something akin to what Badiou (2004) calls "splace." In this suspension of time there is an in-between where we have a sense of space; and that sense is enhanced by the kinds of qualities, essences and spirits that we have been playing with here, another kind of in-between, an in-between space and place.

Not Yet Known

With Ken (16th October, at home, Abingdon, 4:05 pm)

I am alone this weekend. This morning, I woke to silence and an empty bed. It was earlier than I had hoped, still dark in this early autumn dullness. Opening my eyes to the vacant mattress beside me, I recalled the horror of what might have become, that morning after the night before, back in July, when we tore open. She sat on the side of the bed, her back to me, her tears beginning again; I, prone, faced away from her familiarity, my body overcome with its own undoing; noticing with surprise that the noise that I could hear, the uncontrollable convulsing of stomach and chest, the water in my eyes and on my face—it felt like, and utterly unlike, the convulsion of laughter.

Another kind of in-between, an in-between space and place.

Getting out of bed in an attempt to put that memory aside, I stepped from our bedroom onto the stairs and saw the open doors of Holly's and Joe's unoccupied rooms. Joe's was dark, his curtains drawn as they always are, clothes and an unfolded tent on his floor; Holly's room was clear and light, her wooden floor visible and uncluttered.

They have gone. They have all gone. I know they will come back but they have gone.

With Jonathan (21st October, Millbrook, 1:30 pm)

This afternoon I have been working with the chilling nihilism of the thought that living life is done in the becoming of memory. Repeating this over and over again in my head has had its imprinting effect upon my body, and as the words have begun to solidify meaning in its unruliness I start to find myself referring back to your last message to me.

They have gone.

Phoebe has been studying the work of Georgia O'Keefe in her art classes at school, and I have been drawn by the images of skulls and bones that O'Keefe painted and the beautiful flower heads that reek in their musty, silent perfume of sex. The skulls and bones lie dry in the desert land of her home, storing in fine display their shining anonymity for infinity.

I know they will come back but they have gone.

The bones of the dead, whether lying in the desert or preserved in her work, seem to bring memory alive. Life's becoming, becoming death; this involves becoming memory and with this more and more bones in the desert.

I stepped from our bedroom onto the stairs and saw the open doors of Holly's and Joe's unoccupied rooms.

This morning in my waking dream I saw Deleuze step from a train speeding madly on its rails into the seething darkness of the night, a night that had become, presumably, increasingly empty for him. The dream was so vividly filmic, as dreams so often are; I saw his mournful face carrying for the last time the hint of a mischievous smile, his unruly hair blowing wildly in the wind that was rushing into the racing carriage. One step and then he was gone. I awoke with the thought, "Why did he choose that way of ending his life?" and followed that thought with another, "Of all the things I could think, why did I think that?"

I am yearning for a different place than this. A desire is pulling at/in my body, a desire I do not understand.

I think of all the times that my children have appeared in the pages that I have sent to you. I see them preserved there like O'Keefe's bones, always shining and bright. I also think about how I was when I wrote those words; I can feel those tears, I can sense the pathos. I always have a knowing of my love for them and each time it comes out differently. As they grow older, they begin to move away and I sense a growing horror. I wonder where my train is taking me. I sense my *délire* taking me out of it again, my train careering off the rails. Am I too frightened to deal with the loss? In visualizing my wave goodbye, can I see the image of my own collapse?

Not this. Something else. Somewhere else. You have to try. There is not much time.

We have talked of "good-byes" before (Gale & Wyatt, 2008). In the grim sadness of those stories, we focused upon the departing of trains, of you and me, the sadness of the children themselves. There is a new presence here. It is one that has been growing in me like an infesting worm for a long time now, it is the presence of their impending departure and the great sense of absence that will inevitably bring. I read back over your writing and the account of Joe's and Holly's recent departure from your house, and it makes me reel with sadness.

Noticing with surprise that the noise that I could hear, the uncontrollable convulsing of stomach and chest, the water in my eyes and on my face—it felt like, and utterly unlike, the convulsion of laughter.

I sit with my eye to the western sky. These inclinations are common: I lean my body toward the sea and the pull is inexorable. You have heard these words and felt the surge of these emotions many times before; my writing is awash with them.

I can't stand it. It's time to run…

Within minutes I am at the top of the cliff, the wind is blowing strong and fresh from the west; my brief hesitation is no resistance to the sound of the waves in my ears and the sharp tangy taste of salt already on my tongue.

In the water I am at my best; I am lost and my madness goes untrammelled. I can shout, scream, and laugh with the wickedness of a satyr and I carry no fear of restraint. The wind is energizing and churning up the waves, and their ceaseless rolling barely allows me time to breathe; ducking deeply under one is coming face to face with the next. This is my ecstasy.

Back on the beach the autumn heat of the rocks warms my body and energizes irresistible thermals that lift the chill wind up and over the top of the cliff. I share my peace with a dozen oyster catchers that I had earlier disturbed in my race to reach the water and with the lonely buzzard that drifts high overhead, resting with intent on the lift of the thermals that had warmed me seconds earlier.

This is a "getting out of it"…

When it was time to run, it didn't occur to the troubled mind that was trying to connect with you that this is what had to be done and now. As I rest in the beauty of these moments, I real/ize, I make real, the getting out of it that is of course a getting into it. So often for me "getting out of it" has been taking part in my own race to oblivion, where the mad driving off the rails has no direction known and is a living toward death; a journey in racing, abandoned, driverless carriages. And yet here in this moment I find myself clicking to Foucault's reflexive prescription and becoming so sharply aware of the need to get free of one self, the need to become something other than the self that is snared on the hooks of tradition, custom and order, riding on the train that passes through the same stations every day. Staying on these rails sometimes seems so easy and yet it is often and increasingly so hard. Why do I forget that with the folding in there is always an unfolding and that without the folding in there can never be a folding out?

With Ken (25th October, Abingdon, 2:15 pm)

Joe (temporarily) and Tessa are back this weekend so the house feels lived in once more. Tessa and I saw Holly at university in London on Friday: I was in her room for a few minutes before we parked the car and walked along the Thames near the Tate Modern in the searing and confusing late autumn heat. I imagine everyone, like the plants, feeling confused, our bodies, readied against an oncoming chill, shocked by exposure to summer sunshine. Walking should have felt easy but, dressed for autumn, I found myself tetchy. I maintained attention to my breathing as much as I could, but it was a struggle.

My body, a multiplicity of bodies (Rothfield, 2011), is confused much of the time. I notice hope, somewhere in my belly, and pleasure, a little higher up, alongside a quiet, relentless despair in my heart. Tess asks, kindly, if I might be depressed. Whatever the clinical diagnosis might be, I am reluctant to seek one and loathe to give "this" a label. It would, I fear, serve to close down possibilities, to stifle my awareness of my body as a mobile state of affairs (Rothfield, 2011).

With Jonathan (26th October, Millbrook, 8:30 am)

Hey, my man, these are the bodies that we need to talk about, whose experiences we need to share. The words are important; stuttering in the language is what comes out as we articulate between feelings and the words and back again. I agree with you about the stifling effects of the labeling and the clinical diagnoses; the power and ultra-negative of the categorical imperative that ensues gives no space for opportunity, no space for the regular reorganization of the becoming "body-with/out-organs" (Deleuze & Guattari, 1988) that seems so necessary for our sanity/insanity to prevail. It almost feels like giving in if we accept rigid extensitis and the delineations and demarcation zones of categorical difference. Living with intensity is hard; in veering off the rails I find myself bumping along in madness and confusion, but I don't think that I could live the life of closure that correlates with avoiding *délire*.

I see you walking along Millbank, uncomfortable in the heat and your unready clothes. I remember dancing by the Thames in the 60s after I had seen exhibitions and shows there that had filled me with excitement and joy and sent me back to my drawing books and sketch pads. Place and space! How conspicuous are the forces of our bodies! How we become challenged by the way in which their organization creeps up on us and we find our/selves constrained, restrained, strained, unable to find the refrain and the rhythm of the dance that will lift us crunching through autumn leaves, spinning from the rigors of one tightening to the unsettling disassembling of another.

Take just a little chance, my friend; something small. Think of all the steps that you have taken. Think of all the rhizo/schizo/opportunities that you have followed through. I know they are messing with your head and your heart right now, and that is inevitable really: your body organizes, reorganizes, it shows you truths and it shows you lies even though it is often telling you the same thing.

What does the man say?

What we're interested in, you see, are modes of individuation beyond those of things, persons, or subjects: the individuation, say, of a time of day, of a region, a climate, a river or a wind, of an event. (Deleuze, 1995, p. 26)

These individuations are not fixing us; they are morphing us in flows: we can be in their play, we can do openings and closings, we can test a current, we can look out beyond the swell and see the next set forming, we can decide to dive under the wave or to crash with total mad exuberance right through it, or we can heave our body in its direction, take three, maybe four strong powerful strokes and be lifted, be there with it, in its flow, mad rushing into shore and in landing in the shore break it is always a new exciting place to be.

With Ken (2nd November, Berkeley, California, 7:00 am)

I am responding to you at breakfast in the high-ceilinged dining room of the Shattuck Plaza hotel in downtown Berkeley. I arrived yesterday evening, having caught the train from the airport. It crept its way into San Francisco, then under the bay before emerging into the suburbs to the northeast. I'm running a workshop here tomorrow and Friday.

(Later in the week, on a journey on another of the Bay Area's variety of public transport systems, I will catch a streetcar. Underground, the train will halt between Folsom and Embarcadero, standing still in the darkness. "We have experienced a slight earthquake," the driver will announce. "We will be moving slowly." None of my fellow passengers will seem perturbed. The man in the Vans and black felt jacket will keep reading his magazine. The student in the charcoal greatcoat and peaked cap will close her eyes and lean her head against the window. I will turn off my iPad, place it in my bag, and concentrate on breathing. Later, when we emerge onto the road and daylight, the floor within the carriage dropping near the doors to form steps, we will get to Cole/Carl station, and I will feel the solidity of the ridged plastic steps through the soles of my scuffed brown shoes as I alight and ingest the cool air of an overcast California day. And I will think of Deleuze stepping from his apartment window, and of your dream of his stepping from a train, and I will wonder about his suicide being a stepping into something, a becoming, rather than a way to "get out of it" whatever "it" was to him at the time. A stepping into, a stepping through, a creating of different assemblages.)

I left home early yesterday morning, Tuesday, November first. Tess drove me in the darkness to catch the airport bus. As we drew away from the house I looked up at Joe's window. His curtains will be closed on Monday when I return, only he will no longer be asleep behind them but in Korea.

You envision the prospect of your two leaving home: for me, there has been a kind of collapse. Not one that brings me to a halt, but one that leads me to pause in my step, to catch breath, to touch the walls of the utility room the night before I left, a clutch of clothes in my hands, in order to not lose balance. I wouldn't want Joe to know that his leaving causes me to sway. He has his own instability to handle.

I went away three days before Joe travels to Korea on Friday. It means that I can feel as if it were I, not he, who left. When I return, I will have to face the implications of his departure, live them. I got out of it but will be required to get into it.

There's a woman on the next table, by the window, looking out onto the darkness of Shattuck Avenue, writing left-handed in the margins of a paper. Is it her paper, I wonder? A lecture she is about to give? Or is it a student's? She pauses to remove her glasses and take a mouthful of breakfast, pausing in between to hook strands of auburn hair behind an ear. I want to tell her that I'm left-handed. I want to ask her about the paper that she's looking at. I say nothing. Our eyes catch but neither of us acknowledges the other, a choice made, perhaps, to not get out of it or ourselves, or a choice not to get into it: life, and the mess it brings.

Two lives all but intersect over breakfast in a strange hotel, their trajectories air kissing. *Life lived in the becoming of memory.*

Both of Us With You, the Reader, Now, on This Page

So how do we learn, how do we become in our living with the Deleuzian notion of *agencement* with its vibrancy of multiple vectors, intersecting forces and lines of flight? How can we craft the becomings of this "assemblage/ethnography"? Is it as if we need to grow a new *leitmotif* for practice and style, a way of getting lost, of getting out of it, of getting free of one self?

In such becomings there is a certain loss of a sense of self and the enforced separations of this self and others; form and content, place and space, begin to dissolve into mixtures and hybridizations. It is not that the name or the classification, the binary or the dualism is done away with; rather it is that it becomes other within the active and fluid and transmutating life force of the assemblage.

Getting Out of Selves

With Jonathan (8th November, Millbrook, 10:40 am)

The sunflower that seeded itself and grew to stand proud all summer in the middle of my vegetable garden bends this morning to the pressures of the wind in late autumn's first storm. I look at the darkening sky and sense the lashing of the rain through the opacity of my window, and I allow this image to symbolize my journey into a new winter.

I write these words in the immediate afterglow of their formation; I wonder at the absence of presence that always allows a gap between the idea and the word forming on the page. I am both excited and chilled by that impenetrable space; it motivates and diminishes me as a person who writes. In this "assemblage/ethnography," as we perform ourselves to one then another, as we write to both unravel and to complexify this shared space of meaning that we create and stand back to look at, I ask this self what it is that writing does. I ask this self why this writing is also forming itself in relation to you. I ask this self, in this space between thought and the action of writing, why did the words about the sunflower gradually morph into writing to and with you? I sense as this writing flows in this here and now, with the rain still lashing against my window, with the sense of last night's life still in my body, that meaning emerges in these words as my sense of writing to/with you becomes present in my always dissolving sense of self. This is not air-kissing, not a tangential brushing of lives. This is an autoethnography of other that performs itself in the shadows and clouds that are formed by the relational spaces that we inhabit outside of our writing space and yet which is so much a part of what we do.

The westerly squall is losing its force and I see the sunflower's battered face easing up, just slightly, to the tentative warmth of the newly lightening sky.

Notes

1. In the translator's introduction to *A Thousand Plateaus*, Massumi uses "assemblage," which has become the more well-known translation of the original *agencement*. However, in his recent biography of Deleuze and Guattari, Dosse uses the less well-known form of "arrangement." We have chosen the former because of its more familiar usage.
2. The Leveson inquiry into phone-hacking by Rupert Murdoch and News International.
3. "Haecceity is based upon the coming together of elements into some kind of assemblage" (Gale & Wyatt, 2009, p. 91).

References

Bachelard, G. (1969). *The poetics of space* (M. Jolas, Trans.). Boston: Beacon.

Badiou, A. (2004). *Theoretical writings* (R. Brassier & A. Toscano, Trans.). London: Continuum.

Bergson, H. (1991). *Matter and memory* (N. M. Paul & W. S. Palmer, Ed., Trans.). New York: Zone.

Deleuze, G. (1995). *Negotiations* (M. Joughin, Trans.). New York: Columbia University Press.

Deleuze, G., & Guattari, F. (1988) *A thousand plateaus* (B. Massumi, Trans.). London: Athlone.

Deleuze, G., & Parnet, C. (2002). *Dialogues II*. London: Continuum.

Dosse, F. (2011). *Gilles Deleuze and Felix Guattari: Intersecting lives*. New York: Columbia University Press.

Foucault, M. (1992) *The history of sexuality: 2: The use of pleasure* (R. Hurley, Trans.). London: Penguin.

Gale, K., & Wyatt, J. (2008). Becoming men, becoming-men? A collective biography. *International Review of Qualitative Research, 1*, 235–255.

Gale, K., & Wyatt, J. (2009). *Between the two: A nomadic inquiry into collaborative writing and subjectivity*. Newcastle-upon-Tyne, UK: Cambridge Scholars.

Gale, K., Pelias, R., Russell, L., Spry, T., & Wyatt, J. (2012). *How writing touches: An intimate scholarly collaboration*. Newcastle-upon-Tyne, UK: Cambridge Scholars.

Hilton, K. (2102). A nodal ethnography: Intersecting lines of a novice researcher. *International Review of Qualitative Research, 4*, 353–363.

Hughes, J. (2011). Believing in the world: Toward an ethic of form. In L. Guillaume & J. Hughes (Eds.), *Deleuze and the body* (pp. 73–95). Edinburgh, Scotland: Edinburgh University Press.

Lather, P. (2007). *Getting lost: Feminist efforts toward a double(d) science*. New York: State University of New York Press.

Massey, D. (2005). *For space*. London: Sage.

Pitt, A., & Britzman, D. (2003) Speculations on qualities of difficult knowledge in teaching and learning: An experiment in psychoanalytic research. *International Journal of Qualitative Studies in Education, 16*, 755–776.

Rothfield, P. (2011). Dance and the passing moment. In L. Guillaumne & J. Hughes (Eds.), *Deleuze and the body* (pp. 203–223). Edinburgh, Scotland: Edinburgh University Press

Spry, T. (2011). Performative autoethnography: Critical embodiments and possibilities. In N. K. Denzin & Y. S. Lincoln (Eds.), *The SAGE handbook of qualitative research* (4th ed., pp. 497–513). London: Sage.

Woolf, V. (1985). *Moments of being*. New York: Harcourt Brace.

Wyatt, J. (in press). In trouble: Deleuze, desire and the middle-aged man. In M. Weems (Ed.), *Writings of healing and resistance: Empathy and the imagination intellect*. New York: Peter Lang.

Wyatt J., Gale K., Gannon S., & Davies B. (2011). *Deleuze and collaborative writing: Writing on an immanent plane of composition*. New York: Peter Lang.

Chapter 15

Fire

A Year in Poems

Mary Weems

I'm never alone. My life is part of a much larger collective of Black people here today, Black people here before, Black people I know, Black people I've never met. Here I use Black specifically to represent my spiritual connection to people of African descent everywhere. This sacred spirituality is steeped in loss and joy: loss of African ancestors, loss of freedom, loss of human rights, coupled with the joy of being Black and proud. Following Laurel Richardson's (1994) call to use writing as my method, I write auto/ethnography, the slash between auto and ethnography symbolic of the fact that I'm never writing from an individual cultural perspective, but rather a collective one. While I write across several genres since I'm first and foremost a poet, these are auto/ethnographic poems. The following pieces represent important moments in my life between January and December 2011. In terms of order, I started with the "Fire" poem and continued placing them based upon what felt right in that moment in terms of flow, but since they weren't written "together," each poem can also stand alone. As with all of my work what each piece means is open to the interpretation of each reader who engages the work.

Fire

I spent my 20s and 30s underwater
in the backyard.

Handbook of Autoethnography, edited by Stacy Holman Jones, Tony E. Adams, and Carolyn Ellis, 313–320. © 2013 Left Coast Press, Inc. All rights reserved.

Family walked, talked, loved
my duplicate like it was me.
Never searched
for the small mole on my neck,

Never looked
to see that my feet, always pointed straight
ahead like the future, were turned out on this
mannequin, that she walked slew footed as a penguin,
that her eyes were too dark,
that she didn't cast a shadow,
that she stayed up all day,
walked the house at night
like a ghost.

Meanwhile, I'm trying to drown in a hole
Mama made day I was born, but
my head keeps bobbing up and down
like a buoy in Lake Erie.

One morning I turned 40, woke up
swimming in blood so red, I thought
I was dead and then, like a match,
like a lighter, like the sun rising in August,
I burst into flame singing for my life,
for what I could be, for what I
suddenly knew I wanted
more than anything.

Declining Figure

Henry Moore's Reclining Figure
Lincoln Center Institute Installation

These days I watch Mama
stooped like a stump, writ small
in a world she used to occupy
like a giant, a smile and a hug
instead of a shrug, asking if it's okay
instead of commands, still not crying,
still lying.

I'm struck by light, by time, how it passes
as days and nights make years, how grief
comes and goes more often, how she says Death
is no big thing, yet clings to life like a newborn.

I wonder how much longer I have to come
close to her as an infant's breath on a cheek,
to understand her, complex problem
I can't reach, wrap love around her like sheets,
to say goodbye when I can't speak.

Ilona's Boutique

Raised red letters
whisper stepmother's name
a space she used to disappear
into, caress fabric, take
her clothes off, change
into disguise after disguise.

The shopkeeper made
her feel like Cinderella
before the Ball, the whole
world ahead, and at midnight
a lost slipper for the Prince.

Today I ride by the shop
the sign leads to nowhere,
Ilona's left the building,
like Elvis she's taken her voice,
the music of giving. The shop's
window dressing stripped
like a woman in a night club
replaced by an "Available"
sign searching for paying
customers.

The Fashion Show

As teenagers we three were close
as shoestrings, our conversations

about being young in love, untrusting
of grown folks who'd forgotten
whatever they knew about being 16.

My friends grew up as sister and brother
learned when we came of age they were
uncle and niece. We were 70s children
caught in her web of pastels, big
bell bottoms, pink apple caps and mini
skirts. One day their aunt invited us to be
models in a fashion show she was taking
on the long road to Columbus, Ohio.

Excited, we practiced for weeks, picking
our best from meager wardrobes,
strutting around pool she'd been told
would be waiting on the estate where
show would take place. Back then we
were cute/handsome/quick to laugh/hope
as much a part of our vocabulary as my nickname.

Cookie, Cookie lend me your comb sorry baby
I left it at home. Thanks to an old television
show most of my relatives don't know my first
name and neither do my two friends,
disappointed in our finest dress by a back yard
no bigger than any of ours, a free standing pool
made for advanced wading on a hot day, and a no-show
promoter.

Today mama told me about my friend, wearer
of the pink apple cap that tilted on its side with an air of grace
and confidence. She described a bald, middle-aged man
missing an index finger and most of his teeth.

Her voice fades as I'm taken back to those rehearsals
at his aunt's house, the lightning bugs in the back yard,
and our laughter, enough to make night pause,
as we signified between practice steps down the runway.

Dictionary

When my daughter started talking
she learned all of my words
and made up some of her own.
When I taught her to read by two,
the lesson included the dictionary
for fun. Since puberty happened
like a sudden summer storm, our
lexicons bump between us like rain
clouds, and I have days I look in each
book in my collection, to find a new
word for love.

Heartbop

* A 'bop' is an African American blues form created by Afaa M. Weaver.

Holding heart in hand is a good way to catch the blues,
defined different by each person who catches what they can't
get rid of. No medicine for bad luck, for heart stuck in one place
like a gearshift on truck going downhill. Once caught, blues
gets in everything like salt. Leaves small wounds in blues notes
everywhere but where you're looking at the moment.

I'll hold out my hand and my heart will be in it[1]

Worst way to try and get rid of the blues
is to fall in love. Moment you think
you've found man who has the answer
you find out he don't know shit either and what two of you
don't know put together can kill. Whoever said
what don't kill you makes you stronger lied. Don't do
no good to repeat clichés when man you love just put
your heart back in hand and left.

I'll hold out my hand and my heart will be in it

After a while blood begins to dry on palm,
you miss the beat, take a chance, put heart
back where it belongs, make up a new blues
song that rhymes, contact every man you ever
thought you loved, sweet talk to get his attention,
tell him story about you with a happy ending.

I'll hold out my hand and my heart will be in it

Two Black Girls

School's let out
high school students collect
like bees around bus stops
on sidewalks, sharing space
with adults puzzled by this energy shot
that bounces like handballs into air too still
to be held down

I'm road bound, car moves toward yet another
full day rendezvous, middle 50s marks my face
in laugh lines that stay. I catch a glimpse of me
as a teen in contemporary clothes, shoes, purses,
eyes so identical for a moment I'm lost
in a hand mirror.

I almost look away till they catch me, catch
this moment—two girls casual as their clothes
say goodbye, lean forward natural as two
people shaking hands in public and kiss,
kiss on the lips.

Blue Heron Sonnet

He arrived suddenly like jazz, like a
bopped Bird song, like love—naked as verse.
Raised between the North and South, at war
with himself and every shade of white pow(d)er.
Tracked truth where it lived in disguise.
Music a Valentine, Black bullets, drums.
Government hatred a constant refrain.
His life a short road map, no rainbows.
Revolution elusive as one love,
Hip hop, chance of Black life on white moon.
Sixty-two the number for solitude,
bold face aged too soon, mouth, eyes glisten.
He left yesterday on a Black sunrise.
Took twenty-eight minutes to arrive.

Rex (2-22-42)

Tombstone is sturdier than a person's.
Set in concrete, surrounded by weedless
grass, its shape the Washington Memorial,
an arrow to his owner's heart, a bullet
piercing spirit of every dog who's lost
a loved one.

I'm stopped by this grave quiet,
private under a broad-branched tree
blessed with shade in 90 degree weather
humid enough to fill his water bowl.

I feel a boy's cap cover my head
so I can take it off, a moment
of bowed respect, as the sudden smell
of Star, the first dog I ever loved comes back
on the lap of air sitting around knees in dirt.

I remember where Star's buried. A pit bull
who loved us more than killing the little dogs
who occasionally trespassed on sacred ground
that was our yard.

How she'd wait silent as shade while a stranger
entered, sniff the air around him, then stay close
enough to sink her sharp teeth
at first sign of trouble.

Removing my shoes I stand where his loved ones
must have stood, say a prayer for Rex, for Star,
for the owner who gave me this gift of memory
and another kind of love.

Daniel's Way

I feel Daniel's presence at the Library reading
and his puppet tips my heart like a pale.
I know it's time to exit stage left, taking
what I hold of his life, a special gift
I keep in the world where he belongs.

Faces in this room, this moment turn
me back in time. I am one key on a piano.
My friend, a guest oblivious to a connection
that covers me like a loud shroud.
Daniel, poet, brother, activist, resister of hate
and bullshit risked his life to bring Black,
White, poor together. Yet here in this place
where we celebrate, it's like it was in '63,
'73, '83, 1993 when I met him—white room,
my one Black face—plus one.

Non-Colored Paper

*Observed on a box of paper in an art museum office

Just underneath its brittle surface
America uses the favorite-flavor
of-the-day the N-word that's really

a quick
white chorus pelting the air
in a private, denied in public

nigger, nigger, niggerrrrrrr

Haiku

Mama's voice a full moon
mysterious as world peace.
All I want for Christmas.

Note

1. The refrain is from "For All We Know" by Donny Hathaway and Roberta Flack (1990).

References

Hathaway, D., & Flack, R. (1990). For all we know. On *A Donny Hathaway Collection* [CD] Burbank, CA: Atlantic.

Richardson, L. (1994). Writing: A method of inquiry. In N. K. Denzin & Y. S. Lincoln (Eds.), *The handbook of qualitative research* (pp. 516–529). Thousand Oaks, CA: Sage.

Chapter 16

How Global is Queer?

A Co-autoethnography of Politics, Pedagogy, and Theory in Drag

Sara L. Crawley and
Nadzeya Husakouskaya

Crossing Borders

(*In an American voice*[1]): I'm sitting in a large, white conference room, rather non-descript like most conference rooms, but this one is different primarily because it is in Ukraine, a place I have never been and where I do not speak the language. The space is charged with apprehension and energy. The thirty people within it are scholars from all over the world and most have not met. The Ukrainian organizers have invited me and other Western[2] scholars (from Finland, Britain, the United States, and Sweden) to spend the next two weeks presenting feminist and queer theory to twenty-five scholars from post-Soviet countries (including Ukraine, Russia, Belarus, Kazakhstan, Kyrgyzstan, Albania, Armenia, and Moldova) who have had restricted access to Western theory owing to capitalism and the cost of acquiring scholarship held hostage under expensive copyright laws. I strain my seventh grade brain to recall the long-ago geography quiz that helps me visualize where these places fall on the globe. Later I reference the internet to place them all. After fifteen years in academia and having acquired tenure, I should feel well versed in the material I am about to present, but I am feeling slightly out of sorts. As a transgender-identified lesbian scholar, I write and teach about gender and the body in the United States (Crawley, 2002, 2008a, 2008b, 2009; Crawley & Broad 2008; Crawley, Foley, & Shehan, 2008). Do my identity, Western theory, and/or my understanding of gender performance make sense here? Will my arguments hold up in a non-Western context?

Handbook of Autoethnography, edited by Stacy Holman Jones, Tony E. Adams, and Carolyn Ellis, 321–338. © 2013 Left Coast Press, Inc. All rights reserved.

We begin introductions around the long conference table. I struggle to hear and scribble each name. I can't visualize many names; the Cyrillic-based, Russian characters completely escape me as my language skills are restricted to English with minimal knowledge of German and Spanish. As I struggle to compare names to my scribbling, I notice several participants endearingly indicate they are "students" of one participant in particular. The participant they indicate begins her introduction: "My name is Nadya. I am from Belarus but I teach gender studies at a university in exile in Lithuania." A what? In exile? That sounds so thirty years ago. This can't be; I must have heard her wrong. She looks so young to be faculty. I make a note to ask about this later.

(In a Belarusian voice[3]): I am entering a conference room in Hotel "Druzhba" (which coincidentally and ironically means friendship both in Russian and Ukrainian) in a small town near the border of Ukraine. I have many friends in Ukraine—people who are close to me in terms of language, common history, and critical mindset. Mostly, I've been in big cities like Kyiv, Kharkiv, Sevastopol; never in a small town like this one. This time, I feel comfortable being on the border. It corresponds with my past five years of experience living in-between Minsk and Vilnius while teaching at the European Humanities University, Belarusian university in exile, in Lithuania.

European Humanities University (EHU), where I got my MA in Gender Studies in 2003, was forcibly closed in Belarus in 2004 due to political reasons. All of twenty-four, I had just about started my career as a teacher. All of us—students, lecturers, administrators—were asked to vacate the university building within five days in late July. Can you imagine? We packed in a rush—books, computers, chairs, papers—everything we could carry and store in our apartments. And in five days, the building was empty. Small demonstrations had no effect on the authorities. The university opened in 1992, shortly after the breakdown of the USSR, with a mission to educate a new generation of young people who in the future would be able to bring Belarus to Europe. Alexander Lukashenko, the president, was precise in commenting on the closure of our university (later all private universities in Belarus would be closed): the Belarusian intellectual elite must be educated in Belarusian state universities governed by the state.

My university was re-established in 2005 in Vilnius, the Lithuanian capital, and became known as "Belarusian university in exile." The mission of the university remained the same—to offer for Belarusian students European education in their languages (Belarusian and Russian). There was little geopolitical change, except now we were residing outside Belarus. In March 2006, Alexander Lukashenko was re-elected for his third presidential term. Opposition claimed that Lukashenko had rigged the election results, and large-scale protests in the October Square in Minsk, the Belarusian capital, followed the election. I was protesting on the Square, like almost all my colleagues from EHU. "Have you been on *Ploshcha* [the Square]?"[4] became the question that identified one's political and ideological position against the regime. We were standing for basic human rights—for more open borders (geographically, politically, and intellectually). That was a revolutionary experience in a time and place where we believed that everything was possible. Perhaps it is comparable with Occupy Wall Street for people in the United States.

We were not as successful as our Ukrainian friends were with the Orange Revolution two years earlier. The bloody repression of March 2006 made me realize that the return of the university to Belarus would not happen in the near future. This was not a temporary lack of freedom; this was the beginning of wider repressions. I've always been an academic person rather than a politician. Thus I moved to Vilnius (only 173 km from Minsk but a city in the European Union), following the university and driven by the need and desire to be part of the newly born institution. There I started teaching gender courses. I was twenty-six, and I had only an MA degree because the closure of the university had interrupted my PhD studies; the university re-established in Lithuania didn't offer PhD programs. Since then, I've been living in-between, like almost all my other Belarusian colleagues, moving between Belarus and Lithuania, spending more and more time in Vilnius until finally I settled there in 2008. I got a residence permit, and thereby accepted myself as a Belarusian migrant.

Now, five years later, in this Ukrainian program I represent the post-Soviet region as a lecturer of gender studies (though only "post-Soviet" faculty can be sponsored by our donors, EHU affiliates are the only exception). All twenty-five participants of the project received scholarships for three years to share experiences in dealing with gender and queer issues in post-Soviet classrooms and to learn from Western colleagues. I am curious about how Western queer theory can conceptualize my experience of being displaced, of being a lesbian, of being a teacher of gender theory in an exiled Belarusian university where the very term "gender" is queer enough to scare my students and colleagues.

In the Ukrainian classroom, participants are mapping places where they have come from with pins on the map hand-drawn by one of our resource faculty from Finland. I hover above the map. I put two points on the map—Vilnius and Minsk.

The introductions begin. There are three people in the classroom who speak English, not Russian—our colleagues from the West. One of them draws my attention. I already know her name is Sara and that she is from the University of South Florida. I find myself in a gender trap trying to figure out her gender, and it makes me feel uncomfortable. Finally, it's her turn. She introduces herself as a transgender scholar. She expresses it easily and openly. I try to apply this strategy to me, and I have to admit I see no way to be so open in my university. What does it mean to identify oneself as a transgender person in academia? Does it affect teaching or career positioning at the university? I have to ask her. But can I ask all these questions? Are they polite? Too personal? Should I keep a distance from our resource faculty, even though I don't feel traditional hierarchy in this queer space?

Whose Queer?

Against a backdrop of various international, political and economic systems creating material differences in our lives, is queer theory globally useful? Whose notion of queer counts? Does it matter that "the canon" of queer theory (if, indeed, that is not an oxymoron) and most academic work is written in English? We undertake these questions as we begin a project funded by a Western philanthropic organization whose mission is to democratize former communist, post-Soviet countries. As such, thirty people from many post-Soviet countries, the United States, and Western Europe converge in one place to debate, learn and question feminist and queer theory. As we begin, some things become very clear: the funding agency has bureaucratic control over what we do (or we lose funding); hence, all coursework is conducted in English; and, given that what is most commonly recognized as the core of queer theory is written by Western scholars, there is an implied hierarchy of American/Western European presenters as more knowledgeable than post-Soviet participants (who are faculty or graduate students at universities in post-Soviet countries). We want to interrogate the implications of privilege inherent in queer theory, including its production and expression in English for its usefulness around the globe. Ultimately, in setting up this conversation between colleagues across continents, we wish to trouble simple notions of "the West" as freedom and all other places as constraint and to think in particular about how gender performance and the teaching of drag performance are tools for activism across cultures.

As a very brief outline, queer theory connects, extends and critiques feminist and critical theories by offering at least four concepts: 1) power is not (Marxist notions of) power over another, but rather (Foucauldian) deployments of discourse, which in turn produce sexual and gendered subjectivities; 2) sexuality is always practiced through and should be interpreted via historical and cultural contexts; 3) the heterosexual binary is a pervasively defining and controlling discourse today; and 4) gender performativity causes the belief in discrete biological sexes, rather than a reverse causal relationship (see Crawley & Broad, 2008, for a detailed discussion). In this way, queer theory deconstructs or queers traditionally received knowledges. Similarly, we see autoethnography as a method that connects feminist theory and queer theory by way of critiquing traditional forms of scholarship. An autoethnography based in Black feminist thought (such as this one) connects modernist interviewing to postmodernist theorizing about bodily experience by valorizing non-traditional concepts such as multivocality and the deconstruction of hierarchal knowledge systems through methodological hybridity (Crawley, 2012). As such, it can address (as well as complicate) the Schutzian problem of consciousness (that is, can we ever know what another is thinking?) and consider epistemological critiques of whose knowledge matters in social research. Further, we agree that autoethnography utilizes the notion of queer at its best—as a verb—in that it participates in queering methods (Adams & Holman Jones, 2008).

In this essay we offer a further twist of feminist and queer autoethnography. Similar to Lugones and Spelman's (1983) interrogation of voice in feminist theory, we want to investigate the imperialism of voice (via writing in the English language) in queer theory and the imperialism of Western drag in drag performance. Here we propose a *co-autoethnography*[5]—an autoethnography written by two authors, in which we strive to maintain our own voices separately as well as maintaining a very tentative use of the concept of "we." Consistent with Lugones and Spelman, we agree that it is a falsehood of consciousness to imply that we have authored this chapter in one, unified voice, especially given our different native languages and life experiences in vastly different geographic locations and political/economic systems. As such, we strive to make it clear throughout who is speaking/experiencing each event and follow Lugones and Spelman's example of speaking from experiences of place—for Nadya (in a Belarusian voice), and for Sara (in an American voice). We do not offer these as authentic or generic voices for all people from these places but rather by way of comparison between us. Co-autoethnography, as method, allows us to maintain our separate voices and express our experiences through our bodies/cultures/identities (Adams & Holman Jones, 2008; Crawley, 2012; Ellis, 1997). We question the implications of imperialism in voice itself in the practice and teaching of queer theory. Ultimately, we see tensions of (sometimes striking) likeness and difference across cultures and several manifestations of privilege in the deployment of academia. We offer this conversation as a fascination with the similarity of effects that heteronormativity has across the globe as well as an interrogation of the imperialism of Western culture and capitalism on the production of academic discourse and the academy itself.

"Let's Do Drag!": Practicing What We Teach

(In a Belarusian voice): I say, "Let's do drag king." Because we all eat every meal together, there is plenty of time to talk about sessions and to make suggestions. I say it jokingly at the very first dinner. However, drag is more than serious for me. My passion for drag is impetuous. Since my first experience in Hungary in winter 2010 with two drag king trainers from Berlin, I have been dreaming about turning an academic environment into a space for political transformation and body experimentation. Why waste so much time and effort explaining that gender is a performative act, or ask what "doing gender" means (West & Zimmerman, 1987; Butler, 1990, 1993) when you can do drag and embody this experience yourself—with profound personal effects in politicizing the body?

When I first did drag it was a new concept for me. That year I included texts on drag and trans identity (Halberstam, 1998; Green, 2004) in my seminars for MA students, but I've never done what I really wanted—drag kinging in a classroom. In this session in our Ukrainian program, Jack Halberstam[6] is our guest lecturer. He helps me purchase a really masculine outfit in a Ukrainian market:

we buy hair gel, ties, and boxers and rob pharmacies of all the Ace bandages they have. I am nervous. Jack says there is no "right" way of doing drag. Is it true? How will Jack and Sara perceive our post-Soviet drag? How will the participants—who are doing drag for the first time—experience it?

There are fifteen daredevils in our drag group in the Hotel Druzhba conference room. They are going to transform themselves into men, and I am going to facilitate. I am doing what I've always craved, though it's happening in a classroom with my colleagues, not students! We establish some rules: no observers, only participants; no previous identities, only new personas; no former narratives, only new names and stories.

We start with the basics: the breast and the bulge. People are laughing and giggling while making the bulge with socks and binding their breasts with bandages. Some participants are easily transforming in front of the others; some find the classroom too public a space and attempt their transformation in the corridor. We continue with the beards and mustaches. Most of them take it playfully—snipping hair and plastering it on faces—but I can see that two or three of them are somewhat confused and surprised. I need to keep an eye on them. I can work with only one participant at a time. I notice that people are mostly working by themselves; those who are done and feel comfortable enough help others. There is much less giggling.

As I work on the Finnish man before me, I hear many comments: "My breasts are too big." "My face is too feminine." "Wow, that's me!" "I look like a loser as a guy." "I feel like my brother." "I thought I would be cooler." "It won't work with my body." "This *thing* disturbs me, it's *so* uncomfortable." "What to do now?" Their remarks, and my latent reactions to them, take me back to my state in a classroom while teaching gender studies. Often the first several lectures are about giggling and challenging the lecturer—me. The students are very playful, just as the reactions to the drag king seminar start out. Then the performative nature of gender begins to emerge through our essentialist presumptions of who we are and how gender works. In the middle of a seminar or lecture, I often catch this specter of "gender trouble" beginning to haunt the students. They usually bring it up openly as disturbing questions and notes. Their reactions range from a questioning of gender theory—"How does gender theory work for me?" "How can I live after I learn all of this?" "It doesn't correspond with my life and my image of myself." "Why should I believe you?"—to a hesitant appraisal of one's own being—"This is precisely how I've been feeling, now I know how it works." It is a very intimate moment. That is exactly what lectures on gender theory must do. That is exactly what drag does.

There are not enough mirrors in the conference room. Maybe it is now time to mirror these new identities in life outside of the conference room—to let the world interact, react and re-socialize with these newly born boys. I am the last one to "become" a man. I feel awkward as Rico, a twenty-three-year-old bar owner in Spain. He emerges from my experience of performance because I want to envision

Figure 16.1 *(left)* Nadya.
16.2 *(right)* Jack Halberstam
with "Rico."
Photos by participants of the
Gender, Sexuality, and Power
Project of Higher Education
Support Program, Open Society
Foundation (HESP).

myself out of academia and Belarus. Something does not work. Perhaps Nadya is still around, evaluating, reflecting, analyzing. Rico, on the other hand, has never had an obsession with "analysis." I find myself torn between the two personae—Nadya and Rico (Figures 16.1 and 16.2).

One other person also seems to be out of sorts: Sara. She doesn't do drag and though engaged, appears distant. Does she feel too masculine to do drag? What does a post-Soviet drag space look like to a Western critical scholar? Nadya wants to discuss all these issues immediately, but Rico wants to go and hang out with the boys and flirt with the girls waiting outside. Rico wins. And the whole crowd of those-who-used-to-be-female-lecturers present their drag king selves to those-who-used-to-be-their-colleagues. Roles shift. Tables turn. Tomorrow Sara will lead a critical discussion on being in drag.

(*In an American voice*): Drag night is an amazing, brave and inspired idea. I am impressed that the participants wish to take on evening group activities that they rightfully organize for themselves. My interest is piqued, but I am unsure if I should participate. Am I invited or is this only for the participants? I don't know what etiquette calls for, and I don't want to be seen as an overbearing American. What is my role in this? I go to my room and don the shirt and tie that I planned to wear at tomorrow's lecture—my everyday drag (Frye, 1983) to signal my

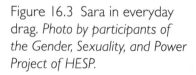
Figure 16.3 Sara in everyday drag. *Photo by participants of the Gender, Sexuality, and Power Project of HESP.*

support (Figure 16.3). At this moment the paradox of my privilege becomes clear to me: Sara is my Rico. This is what I actually wear in my everyday in the United States (which my colleagues tell me is impossible in post-Soviet space); I don't feel a particular need to experience performative moments of becoming a man. My masculinity constantly feels open to scrutiny. So, am I not really participating or am I always in the drag I find most comfortable?

On my way downstairs, I pass several program participants scattered throughout the hotel hallways with laptops and iPods accessing the hotel WiFi—Skyping with family or Facebooking while listening to iTunes. The world has gotten smaller. All of the advertisements, popular music, software programs, and TV shows are familiar—though presented in a language I can't understand. I enter the conference room, which has been transformed to the backstage of a performance space. Nadya is teaching several seminar participants in Russian how to become drag kings. Participants take turns translating quietly into my ear so I can understand what is being said. Nadya is careful to create a safe space—only participants, no voyeurs (am I a voyeur?)—but in that space she is boisterous, funny, engaging, and daring. She is animated and excited about the transformation. She is becoming Rico.

The instruction ends and each participant begins to transform. Tuula, who is also a resource faculty member, asks, "Sara, will you help me bind my breasts?" "Well, we certainly have gotten to know each other," I remark playfully as I help her work the Ace bandage behind her back. Anna is looking pleased and relaxed in her newly masculine look. Several soon-to-be-drag-kings are stepping outside the conference room to look in the mirrors on the wall just outside. Olga is finishing her beard and staring intently. I notice that most stop to stare at themselves with a very serious look. I watch with pleasure, as all of the participants become men right before my eyes. As the drag kings complete their affectations, the whole crowd makes their way upstairs to the other half of the project participants awaiting their arrival. Merita/Mel and Rico begin to flirt mercilessly with those who did not transition. Interesting.

The next day, participants—both drag kings and the observers for whom they performed—are interested in discussing the experience. Our organizers ask if I will facilitate a discussion session. How did it feel to do drag? What was difficult or uncomfortable? Easy? Fun? Several drag kings say that seeing themselves *in a mirror* as a man was transformative. We talk about the way that consciousness comprises reflection on images of self and others (Crawley, Foley, & Shehan, 2008; Mead, 1962). I see me as an image/object reflected through you and your response to me. I adjust this object—me—to meet our belief in realities. This is me; see the image, reflection, performance, adjustment. This is you; see the image, reflection, performance, adjustment. I come to think of this performance as the concrete and persistent reality of this object—me; nonetheless, it is only a carefully crafted veneer.

The drag kings and observers claim many emotions—discomfort, fun, excitement, critique, surprise. I feel compelled to share my own experience. "I was also feeling a bit disconcerted last night. Lately I am feeling a little different when I wear my usual clothing—this shirt, this tie—because I am right now more than five months pregnant and my everyday performance of masculinity feels odd." Side conversations end. Something in the room has shifted. This conversation will last throughout the two-week summer session. Jack approaches me after the discussion ends. "Nice job, dude!" This makes me smile for so many reasons. I had considered hiding the fact of my pregnancy to introduce to my new colleagues the Sara who I imagine myself to be. Now the topic of butch pregnancy opens yet another queer topic.

(In a Belarusian voice): The day after the drag king seminar one of the participants asks me: Why not have a drag queen disco? Why shouldn't we indeed? I go through the "pro" arguments: 1) it is fair to balance drag king with drag queen, to transgress in both directions, not prioritize one of them; 2) it sounds like a great idea for my thirty-first birthday party because 3) it would be the queerest experience of my life—to become a woman voluntarily and playfully rather than being forced into it by social pressure. Here the only constraint appears: I recall my last failure to become a "real" woman and I am frightened of failure again.

Looking in the mirror of my hotel room I ask myself: what am I afraid of? I reconstruct. As a child, and particularly during my late teens, I was constantly confused for a boy. I remember being subjected to makeup by a friend who thought I must necessarily engage with it to become a "beautiful" woman. Notwithstanding my own reluctance, even her best attempts to make me appear more of a "woman" failed. I feel hesitant to undertake one more attempt to meet social expectations.

When I was twenty-two I turned my gender trouble into academic inquiry. I entered an MA program in Gender Studies at EHU. At that time it was (and still is) the only degree program in gender studies in post-Soviet space. Gender theory gave me tools to deconstruct realities and build my identity as a researcher, lecturer, and queer person. Now I am (almost) thirty-one. And I am wondering, could a drag queen experience done in a classroom add something new to our gender and pedagogical experience?

Today there is no hierarchy in our classroom—all of us are participants and facilitators at the same time. One of my colleagues from Ukraine helps Nora to be born as my feminine persona (Figure 16.4). I try to sense, feel and remember every step of the transformation to become Nora so that I might use it later: how does it feel to wear a dress, eye shadow, and nail polish? How do makeup and clothing affect the way I behave, move, and express myself? I feel surprisingly comfortable as a drag queen. I overcome my fear of being feminine the "wrong" way (as Jack put it before, there is no "right" way to do drag).

I notice that this playful gender drag freedom is shaped by national constraints. I imagine Nora is living in Sweden; Rico was born in Spain and is traveling now. As a drag queen or a drag king, I can be from any Western place, but not from Belarus. Being Belarusian means being in national drag—national identity is so overpowering that it excludes gender as performative space. I should talk to Sara about it.

(*In an American voice*): We are in the conference room again, only the transformation is different this time. No one needs to go shopping for the effects, although some are borrowing clothing from others. Very few participants are asking how to do femininity—except Lyosha, the only man brave enough to participate and one of only three in the program. He is bashfully trying on femininity. He begins

Figure 16.4 "Nora." *Photo by participants of the Gender, Sexuality, and Power Project of HESP.*

with a dress over his jeans and works his way to a full face of makeup. As he purses his lips and tries on a bra, I approach him and pull one bra strap off his shoulder and let it fall. "I like the slutty look on you." We giggle about this together. Tuula is sitting quietly allowing someone to apply her makeup. I notice she is sitting up straight, has crossed her legs at the knee and has relaxed her hands, one in the other, palms up; all masculinity is absent.

The transformation takes much less time and this evening we proceed to a drag queen disco that the group has created out of the project's break room. What a party! The night culminates with everyone doing the Macarena—in English and later in Russian—under the gleaming disco ball. No one is working hard at displaying femininity. Several participants look as though they planned to dress for just such an occasion. Again, I am impressed with Nadya. I wouldn't do feminine drag but Nadya did. This is my constraint. It's too real for me—too painful. I have had to do feminine drag before in my life, and I cannot play with it performatively (see Crawley, 2002). Again, I am focused on my everyday reality—and I cannot bring myself to do femininity even playfully. I hate the feeling of it too much. I have had the privilege to live openly as a trans person, and I don't want to relive the coercion of femininity, especially now that this little body growing inside me threatens to discredit my hard-won masculinity.

Languages That Matter: On the Discursive Limits of Translation

(In an American voice): We will begin our discussion today by reading the assigned article, "Часть I Конструируя гендерные идентичности." Can you read this? Neither can I, which is odd since I wrote it—sort of. I wrote the original in English, which was translated and republished in a language (Russian) that I cannot read. I wonder what it says. I can copy and paste into Google Translate to get a rough idea, but I wonder what it conveys to Russian-speaking readers. Do you wonder what the article is about? Frustrating, isn't it? (See endnote for translation.[7])

I wrote this article to track the development of the literature on the construction of sex and sexuality in social science, especially to explain the concepts and contributions of queer theory. I'm a gender scholar and a trans-identified person. It has never occurred to me whether queer theory concepts are American concepts that do not translate outside the United States, though I have always wondered if I could travel safely to certain areas of the world. When Maria, one of the organizers, asked if I would like to participate in the project, the first thing I did was look up whether one can be arrested in Ukraine for being gay/lesbian/trans. You can't be too careful when you look like me. I began to wonder if lesbian or trans looks similar in other countries. How different are performances of masculinity and femininity? This internationalizes the Schutzian problem of consciousness: can we ever know others across cultures?

When I walk into the downtown area of the small town where our program meets, I am surprised at my frustration and helplessness. I've been to countries where I don't speak the language, but never where I cannot read signs. Which is a laundry? Which is a convenience store? Unlike places in Western Europe where I can readily distinguish a *boulangerie* from a *pharmacia*, I have trouble reading characters that are not from the Roman alphabet. When I need stamps, I have to ask Nadya to accompany me to the post office (which I have trouble finding) just to put stamps on my postcards. This puts language difference in perspective for me—as well as tipping the scales of hierarchy between me and the program participants. When we are in town, they are the experts.

One day during the two-week program, we schedule a fun trip for the whole group to see the local sights—castles, cathedrals, historic towns, and the like. I shadow Nadya for the day, and she and Dasha take turns translating for me. At day's end, Dasha says, "I'm tired. It's been a long day." "Me, too," I answer, "that last hill up to this castle was steep and high." Nadya redirects, "Yes, and our tour guide is speaking Ukrainian. It is harder to translate. It's not the same as Russian and I don't recognize all of it." Dasha agrees, then apologizes for not knowing the word for the water that surrounds a castle. An apology? I can't even seem to learn please and thank you in Russian. I can't recognize the difference between Russian and Ukrainian. Nadya and Dasha have been translating between two languages for which neither is native. "A moat," I say. (Seriously, how many times in every-day language does one need to know the word moat?) Without their hard work, I would have been lost all day.

The evening festivities of our two-week program culminate in poetry night during which each of us reads a poem from an author of our own nationality. (It also offers an excuse to have a vodka party.) Some offer translations. Others don't. I choose to read Maya Angelou's "Still I Rise." "It occurs to me that I need to explain something about American racism and what it means to grow up not just black but very black-skinned in Arkansas," I explain to a round of giggles. I'm not sure if they think I am joking. I'm not. I explain where Arkansas is located and the time period when Angelou grew up there and that I love how Angelou's work is hopeful and defiant, not sad. I imagine that experiencing homophobia in post-Soviet countries will give meaning to Angelou's poem. I attempt to read the poem in Angelou's voice and wonder how that will translate for post-Soviet listeners. "I rise. I rise. I rise" (Angelou, 1978, p. 42). As I finish the poem, I notice that Anna has teared up. Something translates.

Because poetry night is a parting event, all of the project's guest presenters have departed except me and Tuula, my Finnish counterpart; we are the project's core resource faculty. As the evening concludes, I look around the room and realize I am the only person in the room who knows only one language. I recall trying to learn German as an undergraduate and how impossible it feels to access communities of non-English speakers in the United States. Being a native English speaker may be a privilege but is it also my constraint?

(In a Belarusian voice): Through this two-week program, we all speak English in our conference settings, despite the fact that all participants from different post-Soviet countries speak and understand Russian. Our Soviet past unites, but the capitalist presence of our program sponsor and restricted language regulations unify us even more. We have different levels of proficiency in English, and I expect a linguistic divide. However, I am pleasantly surprised that here in this program everyone feels comfortable enough to express herself or himself without having to feel the "shame" associated with language constraints. I notice that this freedom to speak (even when "wrong" English is used) is inspired by the participants, but also by our resource faculty, who are mostly native English speakers. I see how easily people can access Sara. I don't feel any reluctance to ask questions, to comment or share experience in and outside of the classroom with Sara or Jack. I have often wondered if linguistic snobbery with respect to English—which I have constantly been warned about and subject to in post-Soviet academia—is a part of Western academic culture. But if so, then why do I not feel this so-called linguistic arrogance in this space? How is it so easy to talk to Western colleagues here in a small Ukrainian town? Does it have to do with the subjects we teach and study? With our/their personalities? With queer settings?

I've thought all my professional academic life that proficiency in English is "a must" to compete in global academia. Does it count that I am also proficient in Belarusian, Polish, Lithuanian, and Ukrainian? How do these language skills compete in the "world market" as opposed to, say, my knowledge of French and German? Inversely, is it possible that English is not only a privilege, but also a constraint of sorts?

All of us in the Ukrainian program joyfully play with the terms "gender," "trans," "intersex," and "queer," and we experience the joy of speaking the same language as and with Sara, Jack, Stevi, and Tuula. When Sara and I discuss our drag transformations, I suddenly realize why I feel more free here in the program than in my classroom teaching gender theory. I cannot play with "gender" in a Russian-speaking classroom. First of all, there is no such word in Russian, so "gender" has been translated as "гендер," a foreign, alien word in Russian, Belarusian, and Ukrainian without any playful connection to "sex." Secondly, "sex" in Russian, Belarusian, and Ukrainian refers to an actual sexual act. Sex as a set of biological characteristics in Russian sounds like "пол" ("pol"), a word that has an ambiguous connotation (actually the first meaning is "the floor"). "Queer," "trans," and "intersex" in Russian sound very odd, with no reference to any idea. So, usually I have a hard time at the very beginning, trying to explain to my students how, where and why all these English-derived concepts and Western-articulated differences can be useful in their lives in a post-Soviet context.

On the first day, I presented myself as Nadya. Usually I refer to myself as Nadya Gusakovskaya. But as a formal name, for example, as a participant of the program or as an author of this article, I am Nadzeya Husakouskaya. In my passport my name is printed in Cyrillic Russian—Надежда Гусаковская.

On the same passport page you find the Belarusian spelling in Latin alphabet—Nadzeya Husakouskaya. Nadezhda and Nadzeya are full versions of my name Nadya—both words mean "hope" in Russian and Belarusian. Each time I have to clarify and translate my name to my (usually Western) colleagues I feel awkward, though I find that it can be a convenient occasion to start queering (not only) language in post-Soviet space. I have one name with two correct spellings (neither of them is "wrong"—funny, isn't it?) I feel excited, as if I am a spy or that I have drag potential inscribed in my name.

Finding Freedom and Constraint in a Ukrainian Bar

(*In an American voice*): As we sit in a Ukrainian bar, Nadya tells me the story of her academic life in detail—recognizing her own gender non-conformity, beginning a PhD program in Women's and Gender studies, having the university closed and reopened in another country where she instantly becomes faculty. As she is talking, I realize Nadya is me fifteen years ago—except for the fascist dictator who controls her country. We are so alike—outgoing, hardworking, diligently pursuing a fierce commitment to teaching feminist and queer theory. Her students talk caringly about her during our summer session and give her an award for her teaching. These things ring familiar to me. This similarity across our very different backgrounds seems so unlikely. Our similar orientation to gender non-conformity and the likeness of our interpretations of various feminist authors amazes me. I am in awe of the consistency of heteronormativity across disparate cultures, although we will have future conversations about minute variations of performances of femininity and masculinity between our cultures.

As she unfolds the tale of post-communist Belarus under a current-day autocrat, I understand my privilege at a US university. Then I feel the constraint of a tenured position under capitalism. Supposedly I have all the privilege. Certainly I do have the privilege of living in a country that is more democratic than a fascist dictatorship (although we can debate how democratic the United States is). Yet, (paradoxically) in the everyday, I do not feel free. Even with tenure, I feel I must compete to keep my job (by continuing to publish aggressively). I feel I cannot move. I cannot leave the country to begin studying at a new university, as Nadya is. Competing to advance my career keeps me from experiencing mobility and enjoyment. Capitalism. Freedom?

I begin to notice some constraints of capitalism throughout the remainder of the summer session. On break from our theory sessions, I show Tim (whose real name is Timur but who shortens it to accommodate Western ears) a picture of my quarter-acre, suburban three-bedroom, two-bath house. He says, "Wow. It is big. It must take a lot of work." I realize I do work for my house; it does not always work for me. My privilege has become my constraint.

On the day we toured the local historical sites, I notice most participants have large, expensive SLR digital cameras. Privilege. I, too, have brought a nice quality digital camera but it is small and convenient—it fits in my pocket. Later we share pictures. I notice Nadya and Tim each have a good eye for framing scenes and faces. They take the time to look. I repeatedly forget to use my camera and can't seem to take the time to focus on capturing images. Lots of freedom, no time. Capitalism.

(In a Belarusian voice): At the end of the first week of our school, I am going with Sara to a local traditional Ukrainian bar, "Kolyba" to talk about life in the US and the post-Soviet academy. Do our academic systems—particularly within gender studies—differ from each other? Sara asks me about my university and I tell her the story. I don't notice any hierarchy (neither academic nor age/gender/status) in our communication. That seems odd to me. She says she got tenure, which means she has a stable job for now. I answer that I am going to quit working full time at EHU. I want to resume studying and am due to start an MA program in Migration and Intercultural Relations in September 2011.

I am constantly struck by how similar and close we are to each other in terms of our understanding of queerness and academia. Yet our historical and geographical backgrounds seem far apart. Sara cannot quit everything she has (career, professorship, house, dogs, wife, the soon-to-be-born baby)—at least not without consequences. I have none of that. The Ukrainian Hotel "Druzhba" is my first nomadic home after I left my gorgeous apartment of two years in Vilnius. Together with my apartment, I left behind my job as a director of a large social and educational project at EHU and reduced my lecturer duties to one on-line course on gender studies. I handed out most of my things (except books and my diaries and some clothes), and I am going to sell my car (which hurts). I know I will lose the Lithuanian residence permit I have had for three years. Two more years of stable life in Lithuania working at my university and I could have applied for Lithuanian citizenship. But I choose to live without a stable "home" for two years, moving according to my new MA program from Germany to Norway and then to Johannesburg in South Africa.

I have never thought about movement as facilitating agency, particularly in a case where you have nothing to lose, nothing behind you, only what is in front of you. I have to admit that this "nothing" encompasses everything I gained from my experience as a teacher and a project director at EHU. It is probably considered a great success to become a lecturer at the tender age of twenty-five, equipped with only a MA degree, and to be leading a huge project having no management experience by the age of twenty-six. But these opportunities emerged at a particular juncture, when the university was literally in a refugee situation with a severe scarcity of human resources. Six years hence, the situation has stabilized and commercialization has taken hold. There is now a rising demand for professors holding PhD degrees. Ironically, almost none of us who took part in the urgent re-establishment of the university—we who became young lecturers having just graduated with a master's—holds a PhD degree. Including me. So I felt the freedom to move ahead. I left with mixed feelings—gratitude to the liberating experience of the first few years of exile at the university and betrayal following its orientation towards a more capitalistic institution. On the other hand, freedom from stability means freedom of mobility.

Jouissance of Writing Co-autoethography

(In a Belarusian voice): When Sara offered to be a co-author and write an autoethnographic article with me, I had no doubts that I would love to do it. My very first thought was this is what I've always wanted to do in academia. It wasn't about gaining a higher status or being in a handbook published in the United States. It has been about creating and supporting our friendship through the writing practice on feminist/queer topics. Writing co-autoethnography has been a dream come true: a space where being an academic and a lecturer does not preclude you from becoming a human and claiming your emotional attachments, your stories, your body, your doubts, and your pain (Ellis, 1999).

During the course and later in our correspondence we discussed a lot of challenging questions that have helped create this dialogue: If/how/does/should queer theory work in global context? Does knowledge from the West become necessarily applicable to all other geopolitical locations? Can we reconsider the meanings of freedom attributed to Western societies and repression attributed to the rest of the world? How can we use drag and gender performance as pedagogical tools? To what extent can we question the imperialism of English as a pedagogical tool while at the same time using it as the common language of communication with each other and for the purposes of this article?

As we proceeded, language (English) became the main concern for me. It was quite unexpected, though we were critically investigating precisely the power of English for East-European scholars. I really appreciate that Sara has been taking care about keeping my voice unaltered. In one of the letters that we exchanged during our work I wrote to Sara (and I still feel this way): "I feel anyway in drag writing in English. I mean it IS my voice (because I am speaking to you) and it IS NOT (because I've been writing in Russian all my life and I will never be able to feel English like I feel Russian—I will never be able to feel the male body the same way I feel the female one). The issue for me is that I trust you."

Nevertheless, I did find my voice. Before Sara introduced me to autoethnography, I struggled with presumptions that a proper academic text should be a well-structured, alienated piece of knowledge with a disembodied neutral author (Ellis & Bochner, 2000). I have never felt it work for me. I always wanted to give more room for literature and art to breathe normally in academia, particularly when exploring and explaining queer theory. This writing and research experience in our co-autoethnographic journey brought my body and identity back to academia, though I am still convinced that this style of writing would not be recognized as an academic one in post-Soviet space.

The writing of the article has been a pleasure, pure jouissance, when "we" is recreated from not melding two separate voices but with each of them having its own room, flow, and nuance. I have always felt it was a conversation about queer theory, feminism, and pedagogy; a dialogue with a colleague and friend of mine; a dance with an excellent partner. I am not sure one can explain how it feels to write a co-autoethnography; it is better to experience it.

(In an American voice): What has this conversation helped me learn so far? I am amazed at how similar some of our experiences seem to have been, suggesting heteronormativity is crosscultural in many ways and that performing drag can be informative and powerful across many cultures. And yet we come from such different places that constrain our travel, thoughts, experiences, choices, and embodiments. I learn new things about Nadya and myself each time we talk. Nothing can be assumed. Is queer theory globally useful? It is impossible to know if we share moments of consciousness. But it is clear that, to the extent that we do communicate, a requirement to speak in English creates an imperial hierarchy whereby non-native English speakers are, by definition, placed at a disadvantage. On what basis can scholars move forward then? In this co-autoethnography, we have borrowed the premise laid out by Lugones and Spelman: that friendship (*druzhba*) is the most honest basis for investigations into imperialism and the control of voice in feminist/queer writing. Rather than falsely assuming we can or wish to become alike via this dialogue, I offer deep respect for my colleague and friend—and a big lesbian hug—as we investigate queer topics, feminism, pedagogies, and our experiences of self and Other.

Authors' Note

Although we are at times critical of geopolitics, we are nonetheless very grateful to the International Higher Education Support Program of the Open Society Foundation for funding the project we describe here. Also, we would like to dedicate this chapter to Olga Plakhotnik and Maria Mayerchyk whose vision, courage, and persistence provide a model for social justice work everywhere.

Notes

1. We realize that "Americans" may come from anywhere in North or South America. Nonetheless, the (primarily) European participants from our project commonly referred to Sara as "American" and so we follow this convention.

2. The concepts Western vs. non-Western are both constructed and made real by global economics. Most of the participants in this project are European; however, the delineation of Western vs. Eastern Europe follows almost entirely down the border of the European economic zone (that is., the EU), creating a kind of "first world"/"second world" economic and political relationship between Western European (and US-based) scholars and post-Soviet scholars. We use all these concepts tentatively and sparingly but in order to outline some very significant issues that arise in everyday life as a result of global capitalism and a history of geo-political distrust. The academic

project described here-in that we all undertake the study of queer and feminist theories with each other pushes beyond this history with tentative trust and hopeful engagement.

3. (Nadya) want to thank those who added some overtones into my voice—my Belarusian colleague Alena Minchenia and Indian comrade Bani Gill—for their strong support, thoughtful comments, and firm belief in me.

4. 'Ploshcha' means 'the Square' in Belarusian. On March 19, 2006, after the results of the Belarusian presidential election were announced, protesters gathered in the October Square in Minsk. The opposition's tent camp was erected on the October Square and stayed there until March 24 when the police smashed the camp and detained hundreds of demonstrators.

5. The authors would like to thank an anonymous reviewer for suggesting this term.

6. Judith Halberstam, author of *Female Masculinity*, goes by the nickname "Jack" in person and in later publications.

7. The article referenced is the Russian translation of Crawley and Broad (2008).

References

Adams, T. E., & Holman Jones, S. (2008). Autoethnography is queer. In N. K. Denzin, Y. S. Lincoln, & L. T. Smith (Eds.), *Handbook of critical and indigenous methodologies* (pp. 373–390). Thousand Oaks, CA: Sage.

Angelou, M. (1978). *And still I rise*. New York: Random House.

Butler, J. (1990). *Gender trouble: Feminism and the subversion of identity*. New York: Routledge.

Butler, J. (1993). *Bodies that matter: On the discursive limits of "sex."* New York: Routledge.

Crawley, S. L. (2002). "They still don't understand why I hate wearing dresses": An autoethnographic rant on dresses, boats and butchness. *Cultural Studies ↔ Critical Methodologies, 2,* 69–92.

Crawley, S. L. (2008a). The clothes make the trans: Region and geography in experiences of the body. *Journal of Lesbian Studies, 12,* 365–379.

Crawley, S. L. (2008b). Full-contact pedagogy: Lecturing with questions and student-centered assignments as methods for inciting self-reflexivity for faculty and students. *Feminist Teacher, 19,* 13–30.

Crawley, S. L. (2009). When coming out is redundant: On the difficulties of remaining queer and a theorist after coming out in the classroom. *Feminism and Psychology, 19,* 210–215.

Crawley, S. L. (2012). Autoethnography as feminist self-interview. In J.A. Holstein, J. F. Gubrium, K. McKinney, & A. Marvasti (Eds.), *The SAGE handbook of interview research* (2nd ed., pp. 143–159). Los Angeles: Sage.

Crawley, S. L., & Broad, K. L. (2008). The construction of sex and sexualities. In J. A. Holstein & J. F. Gubrium (Eds.), *Handbook of constructionist research* (pp. 545–566). New York: The Guilford Press.

Crawley, S. L., Foley, L. J., & Shehan, C. L. (2008). *Gendering bodies*. Lanham, MA: Rowman & Littlefield Press.

Ellis, C. (1997). Evocative ethnography: Writing emotionally about our lives. In W. G. Tierney & Y. S. Lincoln (Eds.), *Representation and the text: Reframing the narrative voice* (pp. 115–139). New York: State University of New York Press.

Ellis, C. (1999). Heartful autoethnography. *Qualitative Health Research, 9,* 669–683.

Ellis, C., & Bochner, A. P. (2000). Autoethnography, personal narrative, reflexivity: Researcher as subject. In N. K. Denzin & Y. S. Lincoln (Eds.), *Handbook of qualitative research* (2nd ed., pp. 733–768). Thousand Oaks, CA: Sage.

Frye, M. (1983). *The politics of reality: Essays in feminist theory*. Freedom, CA: Crossing Press.

Green, J. (2004). *Becoming a visible man*. Nashville, TN: Vanderbilt University Press.

Halberstam, J. (1998). *Female masculinity*. Durham, NC: Duke University Press.

Lugones, M. C., & Spelman, E. V. (1983.) Have we got a theory for you! Feminist theory, cultural imperialism and the demand for 'the woman's voice.' In W. Kolmar & F. Bartkowski (Eds.), *Feminist theory: A reader* (2nd ed., pp. 17–27). New York: McGraw-Hill.

Mead, G. H. (1962). *Mind, self, and society from the standpoint of a social behaviorist*. Chicago: University of Chicago Press. (Original work published 1934.)

West, C., & Zimmerman, D. H. (1987). Doing gender. *Gender & Society, 1,* 125–151.

Chapter 17

Sentimental Journey

Laurel Richardson

The cab driver drives down Skokie Avenue, past the Old Orchard Shopping Center, an upscale megamall. "BRANDEIS BOOK SALE" flashes from signboards. All I know about Skokie is that the Ku Klux Klan called Skokie "Jewtown" and held a rally here in 1978. Skokie's Jewish community, including several thousand Holocaust survivors, sought an injunction against the rally, but the ACLU's defense of the rights of the KKK prevailed. Years ago, I wrote a poem about it:

Accounts

From Moscow to Dachau
There are cemeteries
For Jews.

Jews in parallel rows.
Columns. Regular as
Crosses in Arlington.
Just as many. No.
More.

Regular as a tax
Ledger. Fifty years'
Entries. No. More.

Handbook of Autoethnography, edited by Stacy Holman Jones, Tony E. Adams, and Carolyn Ellis, 339–356. © 2013 Left Coast Press, Inc. All rights reserved.

Debits: Heads,
Arms, Legs.

Tombstones,
Regular as
Sidesteps in
Skokie. Sun
Day's Funnies.

"We are Everywhere."

Now, I get my bags, tip the cabbie, and enter the Skokie Doubletree Inn and Conference Center. It is mid-June, and the showpiece fireplace is ablaze. "Sentimental Journey, Ltd." had tracked me down and here I am in Skokie at the fiftieth reunion of Chicago's Senn High School's 1956 graduating class. I didn't actually graduate with the reunion class, and I haven't seen any of them in fifty-two years. I left high school after my sophomore year to go to college, mostly because my older brother Barrie was graduating, and I would keep up with him academically, as I always had. Plus, I did depend on him for a "high-status" social life. But as I think about it now, the idea of being the only child living at home did not appeal to me. My father's expectations for me were astronomical, and we argued a great deal about the literary merits of different authors. My mother was dysphoric and distant. I hadn't trusted her with my feelings and thoughts since I was eight years old when she punished me for publicly sticking up for my beliefs.

So, why I am at the reunion, I really do not know. To set my heart at ease? About what?

○

"Why are we meeting in Skokie?" I half-heartedly ask the ebullient clerk as I hand him my "Gold Reunion Guest" reservation. I don't expect an answer.

"Ah," he half-smiles, answering me. "You're having your fiftieth reunion here."

"Why?"

"We're the nearest hotel to Senn High School."

"What about the Edgewater Beach?" I ask. "Where we held our proms."

"Torn down."

"The Sovereign?"

"The *what*... oh, all the hotels are gone. Torn down."

Behind me the lobby is bustling with boys and men wearing yarmulkes and girls and women in designer dresses.

"A Bat Mitzvah?" I ask a girl dressed in blue and white. *Bright eyed and bushy tailed*, like a busy squirrel, we would have called her.

"*Bar* Mitzvah," she answers, unsmiling. "My brother's."

"L'Chaim!" I say, as she scurries back to her pack. I feel embarrassed about being chummy and trotting out my elementary Hebrew. For fifty-five years after my Anshe Emet confirmation, I had lived in extreme synagogue aversion. But four years ago I joined Beth Tikvah, started Hebrew lessons, and began considering being Bat Mitzvah'ed, although it feels a little silly to do so at my age. What would I say? *Today I am a crone?*

○

"You look pretty good," I say to my reflection in my hotel room's full-length mirror. I've put on my new blue and black sheer top, black capris, and dressy sandals. My face is made-up—moisturizer, pink blush and brown mascara—and my hair is scrunched into waves. A coat of clear polish helps disguise the wavy furrows in my nails. The "fully insured coordinator" of Senn's "Golden Reunion Celebration" has scheduled a Friday night cocktail party, a Saturday night dinner/dance, and a Sunday morning brunch. It is Friday night. Seven o'clock.

○

"Laurie!" Miriam Levy calls out to me with my LeMoyne grade-school nickname abandoned decades ago. She gives me a hug. "I'd recognize you anywhere. That little chin. You haven't changed at all."

LeMoyne enrolled the rich kids from Lake Shore Drive, upper-middle class kids, like myself, who lived between the Drive and Broadway, and poorer kids who lived next to and south of the "L." All of us walked to and from school, and most of us walked home for lunch.

Each year, I would count the number of Jewish and Gentile kids in my class. Always even, with me being the tie-keeper: half-Jewish and half-Gentile. I was the leader of all the girls, organizing relay races at recess, paper doll shows after school, scavenger hunts, and a club with sailor hats, innocently marked with our name, "JUGS"—an acronym for "Just Us Girls." After eighth grade, some of us went to Lakeview High school, and some went to Senn. Senn was my older brother's choice and mine. My father was in Senn's first graduating class, a top athlete, scholar, and ladies' man, judging from his photo album. Odd to think, now, of my high-school as a seat of family continuity. What else has continued?

My familial narrative has. My mother is still a mystery to me, and my brother still a challenge. At this reunion, my childhood is revivified. Perhaps this is why I have come—to demystify my mother and to understand my brother's place in my life.

Miriam was one of the Lake Shore Drive kids. She had been a plain child, lank haired, square faced, awkward, the last chosen during gym. Now, she looks beautiful. I wouldn't have recognized her. She's had cosmetic surgery, perhaps a tummy-tuck, hours at the spa. Her make-up and highlighted hair are perfection; her manicured nails are blazing magenta. She's wearing a silk three-piece Armani pantsuit, silver and black, and sculpted silver and black jewelry. Until recently, she tells me, she's been hostessing at the Neiman-Marcus restaurant.

"Your mother was warm and kind," she says in her smoker's voice. I am glad that Miriam has raised the topic of my mother. She was a "room-mother" much of my elementary school career. She brought treats to school, visited other children's homes, and "represented" the class in the P.T.A.

"I came to your house a lot," Miriam continues. "Remember the rummage sale we held in your basement?"

"Oh, yes."

"We raised $81.00 for poor children. Our pictures were on the front page of the Sun-Times."

"And we were in Kup's column." Irving Kupicent was Chicago's "King of Gossip." My father, a Chicago attorney, drank scotch with Kup at the men's bar at Berghoff's.

"How's your brother Barrie?" asks Miriam.

"He's a retired professor."

"Tell me more about Barrie," she says. I am less willing to talk about Barrie, I realize, than I am happy to talk about my mother. A poem I wrote about him, disguised by the trope of the third person, comes into my mind:

Mesmery

She remembers—

The times he used the clock's
steady rhythm to still her time,
and the constancy of focused light,
and his voice,
most of all his voice,
saying saying saying, "My sister,
fall into timeless sleep."

The dreams when he called her
to join him on the precipice,
reached by way of magic stairs,
step-riser riser-step step-riser,
like climbing a child's tumble toy.

Sometimes some dreams
he laughs as he leaves her yoked.
Some dreams they lie side by side.
Sometimes he offers her to a friend—

Once he made her vanish.

"Barrie lives in Shreveport, Louisiana," I say. "Four kids. Second marriage." *Enough already. It's my reunion.*

Miriam says, "I told my mother that your father was Irish and your mother was Jewish, but that it was a good marriage—they got on well."

Why would she remember that?

"Their names were 'Tyrrell' and 'Rose'..."

...and their names, too?

Miriam takes a breath and is interrupted by a heavyset, coiffed, face-lifted woman wearing a gold Jewish star. I don't recognize her or the name on her nametag.

Miriam gives Coiffed a big hug. "I'm remarrying my husband," Miriam tells her.

"Oy!"

"We've stayed good friends."

"During your fifteen years apart, already?"

"Yes. It makes financial sense. We're buying a new home together in Winnetka."

"Mazel Tov!"

Coiffed glances at my nametag. Moves on.

Miriam greets a spiffed-up woman with a hug, laugh and "Gut Shabbos." And another woman. "Gut Shabbos." And another. "Gut Shabbos." Miriam does not introduce me to the women, nor do I recognize them.

"We'll catch up later," Miriam says to me, moving on in her disjointed walk.

"That'll be nice."

I look around this room. Nearly all of the women have had plastic surgery. Maybe that's the reason I don't recognize anyone. Hugs, laughs. Shouts, screeches. Yiddish. It's noisy and congested. My head hurts. *Why am I here?*

"Esther Weiss," I say, reading a nametag. I have no idea who she is but I decide to play my "Jewish card," to claim a Jewish identity. "Weren't we in the same confirmation class at Anshe Emet?"

"Laurel *Richardson?*" She raises her eyebrows.

"Rabbi Solomon Goldman officiated," I say. "I was always afraid of him."

"What?" Esther looks shocked. "He was our neighbor. Why would anyone be afraid of him?" She turns and walks away.

I remember the only time I talked to the rabbi. We were alone in his study, behind the bema. "Baruch Ata Adonai..." I recited from memory, pretending to read the Hebrew required of me for confirmation.

"Tov," he said, his blind eyes looking past me. He could not see that I could not read the Hebrew. He asked me some questions about my "faith," and I must have lied because I had none. I was only fulfilling the promise my Gentile father had made to my Jewish mother's mother that the children be raised Jewish, a promise my mother wished had not been made, desiring instead that her children be enfolded in Father's Gentile world, safely removed from the pogroms that had brought her as a child from Russia to America. At least that is the story I have told myself. Mother refused to ever talk about the "horrible things."

Forty-five years would pass before I found entry into a Jewish faith. I was exploring that faith, now. When my husband and I first came to Beth Tikvah, the congregants already knew one of us was not Jewish. "Shabbat Shalom," said one person after another to my husband. "Welcome," they said to me. I felt shadowy. "Why do they think you're the Jewish one?" I asked Ernest. He didn't say a word, but stroked his beard.

"Laurel…?"

"Susan Schwartz," I say, reading a nametag. "Were we in the same confirmation class at Anshe Emet?"

"I went to Temple Sholom!" she retorts. Temple Sholom was the Reform Temple where the upwardly mobile parents sent their kids. It had an organ. Susan Schwartz has turned away, "Rachel! Hi, Rachel! It's me! Susan!"

"I remember *you*." A dark haired, hunched over woman who has not had a face-lift or taken off her coat stares at me. "Do you remember me?" She studies me through rectangular black-framed glasses. Her voice and manner are familiar, but not her face or name on her nametag. "You were good in math!"

"So, what are you doing now, Shoshana?"

"I live with my mother like I always have. I substitute teach like I always have."

"I'm a sociologist."

"A *sociologist*! Why? You were good at math. You went away to school."

"The University of Chicago."

"That explains it."

"Not socialism," I say, not sure what's in her mind.

"I know *that*."

"My dissertation was about the production of pure mathematics."

She peers at me as though I'm crazy. "*What?*"

"I was even married to a mathematician."

"*What?*" She hisses. "We saw the original *Titanic* at the Sheraton Theater together. Don't you remember?"

I remember my mother making me go to the movies with a dark-haired, mechanical-like girl because she had no friends. Was Shoshana that girl?

"Did we get cherry cokes, French fries and ketchup afterwards?" I ask.

"You don't remember me, do you?"

"Did you go to Anshe Emet? I was confirmed there."

"You're lying," she spits out, menacing. "*Richardson!*"

"No, I am not lying," I stand my ground. "I went to Anshe Emet."

"No, you didn't. You're lying." Hunched over, she takes mincing steps away from me and goes out the door.

Witch!

○

I sit down in the main-room next to Miriam and her "dearest friend," Carol Cohen from California. Carol, looking like spun platinum, is a "color consultant."

"Hi, Carol," I say, acting like I know her. *Maybe I am a liar.*

Carol offers me a limp hand. She is thin, thin as a wand; she could be someone's tired fairy godmother. Cancer?

"Things are not good," Carol says in a hoarse voice.

"My mother just died," Miriam says, "and—well my brother mismanaged her money. So I'm not talking to him."

"My brother and I had a falling out about thirty years ago," I say. "I had been in a serious car accident—head trauma, coma, and all—and I needed help for my children, but then when…"

"Hi, Eddie," Miriam jumps up and gives Eddie Edleson a big hug. He still has the bug-eyes he had when he copied my spelling tests in grade school.

"Hi, Eddie," I say. He can't seem to place me. "Do you remember me?" He was the first boy I had ever kissed.

He slaps his forehead, "Oh… Laurie! You even look the same."

"What do you do?" I ask, curious about Speller-Cheater's career.

"I'm a lawyer,"

"Do you remember my mother?" Eddie's family and mine were neighbors.

"Such a nice woman!"

○

"A dry vermouth over ice, please," I say to the bartender.

"There you are! Laurie!" I turn around and see a tall, gray-haired, smiling woman darting across the room. She is wearing a cotton/poly pantsuit, a silver cross and comfortable shoes. "I was so excited to see your name on the roster," she says.

"Mary Anne McCoy," I say. Her teeth are slightly bucked as they were when she was a child and she speaks with the Chicago nasal "a" accent I associate with my Gentile cousins. She gives me a gentle hug.

"I'd recognize you anywhere," she says. "You've got that same face shape."

She takes my arm. "Everyone knew you'd be a professor. No one was surprised." We walk towards a leather sofa in the anteroom. When we were kids we would sit on Mary Anne's greenish sleeper sofa and address envelopes, a money making venture for her family that they had learned about in the back pages of the *Reader's Digest*. I felt useful, important, and grown-up helping this family.

"I remember your mother as so kind to me," Mary Anne says. "She always gave me extra milk when I ate at your house."

"I remember Mother saying to my friends, 'Eat good. Have more.'" One friend ate the entire serving dish of rhubarb and Mother didn't say a word.

"She always sent food home with me, too," Mary Anne continues. "She knew I was an orphan."

"What? Then who was that woman living in your apartment?" I feel confused.

"She was my sister. My guardian."

"And the baby?"

"My sister's."

"And my mother knew?"

"Yes, and she even hand-knitted the baby a blue sweater."

Mary Anne and I talk about JUGS, and we talk about Alpha, our Senn High School Club. Alpha was the only girls' club that accepted both Gentiles and Jews. Its members were the school leaders—twirlers, cheerleaders, student government officers, and editors of *The Forum* and *The Senn-Times*. We were paired with the boys' Alpha, also composed of the school leaders—football and basketball players, especially. Because my older brother Barrie was an Alpha boy and basketball star, I was pledged to Alpha as a freshman, the only freshman to be so honored. I was elected Freshman Class Treasurer, too. At the time, I thought that was due to my personality, but more likely it was due to reflected "heavenly" light from my brother and, of course, because I was "good at math."

Mary Anne and I talk about our families as if we are distant relations at a family reunion, chatting without intimacy. She has lived for fifty-two years with her husband in a two-bedroom house where they raised four children. Now, three granddaughters are at the University of Illinois on volleyball scholarships.

"Too bad they didn't have girls' inter-mural volleyball when we were in high school," I say, remembering Mary Anne setting the ball up high for me and me tipping it over the net. "We were a great team!"

Mary Anne smiles. Then says "Oh, look… There's Linda. C'mon." Linda was one of our fellow Alpha Girls. She is wearing a blue chambray skirt and top. She gives me a big hug. We barely knew each other, but she was like me, sort of. Her father was Jewish, her mother was "nothing." She was raised "nothing."

"Laurie was the resident genius," Linda turns to introduce me to her husband, Kurt. They live in California. Kurt has an uncanny resemblance to my Norwegian ex-husband's father. *Can we all be that old?*

"Join us for dinner, Laurie."

"Thanks, but I am not hungry." *That's a lie.* The truth is sadness has enveloped me, a sorrow I cannot identify, and I want to be alone.

"Join us tomorrow, if you want. We're going to drive into the old neighborhoods."

"Thanks."

What I really want to do tomorrow is to visit my Jewish grandparents' graves, and place a small rock on their headstone. I never saw them dead, have never been to their cemetery. *Maybe there isn't a headstone.*

"Call us! Room 715."

I do not respond, "Or call me. Room 713."

"You were my first love," a graying Jerry Fitch says, walking over and pecking me on the cheek. I remember going with my mother on a pre-kindergarten visit to Jerry's apartment above a drugstore.

"You were mine, too," I say. "Kindergarten."

We look at each other, both of us totally bewildered by how that could have been.

"What do you do now, Jerry?"

"I'm in sales. Copy-machines."

"That must be interesting."

"Demanding. Very demanding."

"Do you remember my mother?"

"Somewhat. You had a seven-inch Admiral television set. No one else had one."

"Yeah."

"See 'ya."

"You haven't changed at all," Ellyn Goldman says to me. "Your little… nose." Her voice, smile, stance still as hesitant as I remembered them. She no longer has brunette curls, though, but strawberry blonde straight locks around her lifted brow. Her Jewish star is set with diamonds.

"Your mother was always so nice to me," she says. "When I was going home from your house, she'd always say, 'Don't talk to strangers.'"

"I remember your maid," I say, envisioning the small dark-skinned woman who called me "Miz Laurie," and set the table for our after school snack with china and sterling. "What was her name?"

"We didn't have her long."

"And I remember dressing in your mother's furs and gowns," I say. I think of how Ellyn's maid, retreating to her bedroom off the kitchen, didn't snitch.

"I don't remember that," Ellyn says, turning away to greet Esther Weiss. Ellyn's father manufactured jackets for the World War II army. I wonder, now, if he was one of those dishonored for producing shoddy goods. I wonder if Ellyn's mother lost her furs and gowns along with her maid.

"I remember you," Alan Greenberg says. "We were in Latin together."

"Miss Cobb," I say. "I loved Latin."

"I did, too. And geometry, too. We were in geometry together."

"I left Senn early," I declare. "I went to the University of Chicago and became a college professor."

"I didn't leave early," Alan says, "but I did become Valedictorian. I went on to Harvard *College* and Yale Medical School." He pauses. "I'm researching early onset Alzheimer's and trying to hold onto the labs I've built—but the university wants me gone—cheaper to hire new flesh." He looks angry as he explains that the graduate students, smelling his fried carcass, are shunning his lab. Without graduate students and labs he cannot survive in academia. "I still want to win The Big One," he declares. I think he's thinking of the Nobel Prize.

Time for me to brag about myself. I tell Alan that my husband went to Yale, taught there for eight years, and that we have a new co-authored book. I tell him the sociology department at The Ohio State University, where I teach *only* graduate students, is top-ranked. My vocabulary enlarges; my speech speeds up; my eyes shine with intelligence—or so I imagine. "I've just retired!" I tell him, bragging, really, that I—unlike he—have gotten past the adolescent need for external reassurance of my worth. *But here I am, again, competing with the boys. Just shut up, Laurel.*

Miriam joins us.

"Let's be sure and catch-up tomorrow, Laurie," she says. "Call me. Room 303. Promise?"

"That's easy to remember. It was our eighth-grade home-room number at LeMoyne."

"Call at any time," she says, giving me a good-bye peck on the cheek.

The effusiveness, squeals, laughs and speech levels crescendo in what has become an overpopulated Jewish sector. A few nasal Chicago voices punctuate the anteroom, where the Gentiles congregate. I am exhausted.

○

"Please leave your phone message," says the hotel's computerized phone voice.

"Miriam, I'm going to breakfast now," I say, "but here's my cell-phone number."

○

"May I join you?" I ask two Orthodox-appearing Jewish women. Their dark dresses cover their arms and legs. *I'll forgo bacon this morning.* By my request, we talk about Jewish funerals, cemeteries, immigrants' burial boxes, and the preparation of the deceased. They tell me there are three possible Orthodox cemeteries where my grandparents might be buried, but finding out which one and getting to it, particularly on Shabbat, would be difficult, maybe even impossible.

"Toda... Shalom." I leave their table, feeling refreshed from having immersed myself in their Orthodox world, where they did me a Mitzvah: They accepted me. *I feel queasy.*

"Join us," Linda says. She and Kurt are in the lobby.

"I need to phone my husband," I say, equivocating.

I go to my room, phone home. Talk. Phone Miriam. Get the same recorded message. Phone my friend Betty. Talk. Phone Miriam. Same message. Free write. Phone Miriam. Same message. I am not sure why I keep phoning Miriam. I stop it. Go down to the lobby. Linda, Mary Anne, and Kurt are still there.

"Why don't you join us?" Linda asks. "See old Senn High."

"Okay... Sure... Thanks," I say, my other two options—Miriam and the cemetery—having vanished. Gratefully, I squeeze into the backseat of Kurt and Linda's two-door car, happy to get out of Skokie.

○

Senn High School's exterior is spotless, the grass tended, trees and shrubs pruned. But the high school hangouts—Eli's frequented by the Jewish crowd and The Penguin by the Gentiles—have been demolished.

"Where do the kids go for lunch?" I ask.

"Maybe they're not allowed out for lunch," Linda suggests.

"I loved the Friday night dances," I say, looking into a gym window. I was on the social committee. I helped create publicity, find sponsors, decorate the gym. Wearing circle pins on our white Ship'n Shore blouse collars, circle-skirts, and bobby-sox, the girls would congregate on one side of the room, the boys on the other, except for those boys and girls who came as "couples." Between dance numbers the couples would retreat to the darkened corners of the room, where the chaperones du jour would scorch them out. Mr. Peabody, the audio-visual manager, controlled the 45's stacked on the phonograph attached to the loud speaker system. Fast numbers—"Come On-A My House," "Rag Mop," "Bibiddi Bobbidi Boo"—were interspersed with the slow-dance ones—"Because of You," "Be My Love," "Unforgettable," and two different renditions of "Sentimental Journey," the warmish Doris Day's and the jazzier Ames Brothers'. I was—and still am—very good at following because my mother insisted I have ballroom dancing lessons when I was a preteen, not for my benefit, but so Barrie would have a practice partner. He and I would dance up our thirty-foot-plus living room, and down its adjoining hall. A slight pressure on my shoulder or hip is all I ever need.

At one Friday night dance, when the Ames Brothers' rendition of "Sentimental Journey" blared over the loud speaker, and it was "Girls' Choice," I asked a boy I hadn't seen before to dance with me. He spun me, dipped me, and tossed me around: Be-bop! A dance not yet danced at Senn. An audience encircled us. I was a star. Then, the music stopped and a pair of chaperones broke through the circle around us.

"This dance is only for Senn students," the male chaperone said to the boy. "You'll have to leave."

"That boy is a colored boy," the female chaperone said to me. "We can't have you dancing with him. What might happen next! What would your mother say?"

I felt bad for the boy, embarrassed about the public scolding, and bewildered. My father had told me to respect all people, regardless of skin color. He patted the shoulders of the parking attendant, the newspaper vendor, and the shoe-shiner, tucking a few extra dollars in their hands, saying, "Enjoy"—"son" or "uncle"—depending on the man's age. So why would "mixed-race" dancing be wrong? *Would my mother—a Jew married to a Gentile—say I was "wrong"?*

Now, Linda's husband drives us south on Broadway, into what had been our old neighborhoods. Our haunts are gone. In their place are Vietnamese, Chinese, Korean, Somalian, Latvian, Russian, Cuban, Dominican, Indian, and Iraqi stores and restaurants. A block or so co-opted by each country, each country separated from others by a four-way stop light. Young men, young women with babies, and young children hang out in their country's cemented terrain. There is barely enough room for all of the people congregated on the sidewalks on this muggy Chicago afternoon.

"Looks like they're fixing the Sheridan Theater," Linda says.

The marquee is in Spanish.

"And the Riviera, too," I say.

Its marquee features Bollywood movies.

We drive through the congested neighborhoods, past the buildings where my female car-mates lived in three-room apartments, children sharing the bedroom, parents sleeping in the living room on sofa-beds. When I was three, we moved from Chicago's south side to the fourth floor of one of those buildings, where I shared a room with my brother. He coaxed me to climb out the closet window to the fire-escape steps and on up to the roof. From the roof-top I saw the entire world. He encouraged me to walk from roof to roof, following the roof edges. He showed me how to get into the basement, where wire cages held all manner of stuff. Once, I got lost in the maze.

We drive further south into what is now called "Wrigleyville." Larger apartments in which some LeMoyne students lived are now six-figure condos. Street sculptures mark the corners. Nobody is on the sidewalks. LeMoyne is still a school, but the play equipment is gone, the playground cemented over and turned into a "Six Dollar a Spot" parking lot. When I was five years old, I ice skated, here, arms behind my back, like Barrie did. I fell, broke my arm. I cried relentlessly. Tears froze on my face. Barrie refused to help me take off my skates, climb over the iron fence, and cross Addison Avenue to the stone three-flat where we lived, and where, when I got there, I got punished for walking up the wood-steps with my skates on. Now, I rub my left-wrist, as I always do, to comfort myself.

"My parents owned the building," I say. Kurt stops the car. The building is for sale—for seven figures. I take a picture.

"You *owned* the building?" Linda asks. "You must have been rich."

"Oh—in the middle," I say. "My father was a lawyer."

We drive up Cornelia. The six-flat we lived in and owned has been demolished, replaced by a contemporary glass and steel eye-catcher. We drive east to Lake Shore Drive, and turn back north towards Skokie. Temple Sholom is to the south and Ellyn's high-rise to the north. I look up and shudder. My brother Barrie had cajoled the seven-year-old me to walk atop the narrow brick barrier atop the twenty-story building. He charged his friends to watch me. One windy day, I looked down. I still have a fear of heights.

"That's where Ellyn lived," I say pointing to the top-floor. "And that's where Miriam lived," I say pointing to the top floor of the next high-rise." "And Suzanne, there… And Esther Weiss must have lived there…" And to myself, I say, "And Rabbi Solomon Goldman." He must have been rich, I think, for these were the places the rich kids lived. I suddenly realize the rich kids were all *Jewish*. I can see myself in the huge, high ceiling apartments of my grade school friends who lived facing the park, windows on the lake. At Ellyn's we would sneak up to the penthouse ballroom dressed in her mother's finery and pretend we were movie stars. At Suzanne's we published and sold a one-page newspaper and "taught" pre-school—fifty cents an afternoon per toddler. Miriam's apartment is vague in my memory, but the feeling is slightly nauseating.

As we continue north, I do not ask to be driven past Anshe Emet. By not playing my Jewish card, am I, by default, playing my Gentile one?

○

Saturday night I arrive at the bar for the dinner/dance wearing my teal blue antique silk dress, in which I always feel elegantly comfortable.

"Hi," I say to Alan Greenberg. "I've been thinking about Latin. You know I placed out of Latin when I went to college. So I never took it again."

"The same with me," he says.

"That changed my life. I was going to be a Latin teacher."

"Changed mine, too… But now I'm reading Homer."

"My husband is, too," I say. "A new translation. I think he's read every translation there is. Probably even those in French, German, and Old English." *I am on a roll here.* Then, I say, "I've been thinking about your laboratory. It's a shame that the East is so retrograde."

Alan offers to buy me a glass of wine. I decline.

In parting, he says, "Of course, I'm reading Homer in the Greek."

"There she is," someone named "Lee Weinstein" says to his hefty wife. "Didn't I tell you?"

"You were always the cutest little thing," he says to me.

I don't know who this man is, but I am embarrassed for his wife.

"How's your brother Barrie?" Lee asks.

"Fine."

"I was in his class. I'm just visiting your reunion. With my sister. And my wife."

"Were you in the Boy Scouts with Barrie?" I ask, following a glimmer of a memory.

He smiles his "Yes."

My mind sees me—maybe eight or nine—bandaged up, hands and feet tied down, wrapped in a sheet, mouth sealed shut, my mother gone. Was he one of the boys Barrie had to the house so the Boy Scout troop could work on their first-aid merit badge? To this day, I cannot stand sheets that are tucked in, restricting my freedom to kick. When my first son was born, I refused to have my hands cuffed to the delivery table, the practice at that time.

"So how's Barrie doing?" Lee asks.

I want to tell him I visited Barrie recently at his lake house in Texas, where he had bagged a "bothersome" raccoon, added rocks to the bag and drowned the critter, live. Barrie said he was finding the squirrels "bothersome," too.

"Fine," I repeat.

"Isn't she just the cutest thing?" he repeats to his wife.

"You should greet David Schwartzbaum," Linda says, tugging on my sleeve. "He's president of Ohio State University."

"Ah. Well… He's not," I say. "I teach there. It's the flagship university. I think he's president of one of our regional campuses." *I am scratching my competitive itch.*

"Aren't you a sociologist?" I ask. *How old he looks.*

"Yes." He looks at my nametag. He doesn't recognize my name from Senn or sociology.

"I am, too. I teach at OSU."

"I've been president of two universities," he says, simultaneously trumping and glad handing me. A slight scowl crosses his face, reminding me of a found poem of mine:

Academia

(Found Poem, Felix Neck Wildlife Sanctuary)

> *The Raptor Barn houses*
> *Various Birds of Prey*
> *That are being Rehabilitated*
> *for release. Those that*
> *cannot be released*
> *successfully*
> *are kept*
> *as Educational Birds.*
>
> *We turn away from each other.*

○

Jews and Gentiles are sitting in different parts of the dining room. *Where should I sit?*

"I'm sorry our table is full," Mary Anne says. "But I've saved you a seat at the next table."

Do I want to sit with complete strangers? Miriam saunters over in her killer heels. She's wearing a black cut-silk blouse over a black camie and black silk pants.

"Sorry about the phone," she says. "I… blah, blah, blah… But I've got your cell-phone now, Laurie," I hear her say as she turns away. "So I can reach you." Sitting there is her friend, Carol, dressed in shimmery silver velvet, Esther Copeland and her Israeli accountant husband, three botoxed Jewish women I don't know, and Miriam's soon-to-be-remarried-ex-husband flashing a flashy pinky ring. Two chairs have been removed from the table.

"Can I buy you a glass of wine, you cute little thing?" Lee Weinstein asks.

"No, and not so little anymore," I respond. "I am 5'10"."

"Be proud of being tall," he says, looking me up and down.

"I am."

"You should be," he smiles.

"Here comes your wife," I say.

"Last call," a tenor voice squeaks over the P.A. system. I join the 442 other alumni standing on the risers for our official picture.

"Linda is not sitting with us after all," Mary Anne says, shepherding me to her table. Others have moved so that Mary Anne and I can sit next to each other. My mind ruminates on the idea of the "Righteous Gentile"—Noah, Joseph, Tamar, Ruth. I add Mary Anne to the list.

Mary Anne and I talk of this and that during dinner; share photos. Mary Anne wants to come to Columbus for a visit. I can't say "No." The banquet's chicken is inedible; I can't swallow it. The young DJ plays hard rock.

"Welcome everyone," says the class president from the bandstand. "Let me tell you how much Senn has changed from our days." The litany begins. Ninety-eight percent of the students are on welfare. They come from seventy different countries and speak fifty-five different languages. Class rolls are not taken until the fourth week because there is a 60 percent drop-out rate. Twenty percent of those who graduate make it to college.

As I listen, I think that Senn no longer has the "Jewish/Gentile" split; now it is splintered.

"There is only one door that opens, and that is fitted with a metal detector," the class president continues. "Freshmen are kept in a separate, locked wing of the school to protect them from the gangs."

An ex-cheerleader sashays up to the bandstand. "You can buy a Senn jacket like the one I'm wearing for seventy-five dollars a throw," she exclaims, spinning around in the green and white jacket, smiling, eyes-aglow, raising her arms in a cheerleaderly way. "Thirty-five dollars goes for Senn's library!"

I definitely do not want one of those jackets. And library? What difference will that make? A band-aid in a neutral skin-tone.

"I'm passing around the microphone, and I want everyone to tell us their names, where they are from, and something about themselves," the class president announces over the post-dinner bedlam.

I groan. When the mic gets to me, I say in my most theatrical, well-articulated voice, "Hello. I'm Audrey Shoshana Hepburn. I live in your memory." No one seems to notice.

"LeMoyne Grade School picture now being taken," the photographer announces.

"Wait," I say. "Where's Ellyn?" I get her. And then, I say, "Wait. We need Miriam." And I get her, too. And I round-up Esther and Jerry and Mary Anne. I am twelve again, the leader of my grade school classmates, organizing them, nicely ordering them around, taking charge of their lives, integrating them, Jew and Gentile, posing them together. Keeping it in balance, that was my purpose in life. My destiny.

○

Photos are spit out of a printer as I watch. "Do you want the Senn High School picture? Seventeen dollars," says the photographer's assistant. In that picture, an unsmiling me is on the third riser, on the edge, next to the boys, but not with them, my body leaning away, distanced. Has the photograph recorded both my present and my past? Was being "near the boys" my strategy for avoiding the Jewish/Gentile split? Or just another way of perpetuating competition with my brother?

"No, thanks," I say. "But let me look at the LeMoyne photo."

"It's seven dollars, five-by-eight," the hawker says, handing me one in a black mat.

There are fourteen of us in the photo, but only three are Gentiles. I am on the edge in this picture, too, but I am sitting with the girls, leaning in. I buy this one.

"Goodnight, Mary Anne," I say.

"Goodnight, Laurie."

"Goodnight, Linda," I say.

"See you at brunch," she says.

"I don't think I'll come," I say. "I'm exhausted."

○

Sunday morning I convince myself to join the others for brunch. A corner of the restaurant has been designated "Senn 50th Reunion."

"Here's a seat, Laurie," Linda says.

"Sit here, Laurie," Miriam says, pointing to a chair at her table. She's wearing a magenta silk blouse. "Do you know Betta?"

Betta's hair is long, gray, curly and unhampered by pins. She's wearing a hand-crafted copper mezuzah and a purple "Outrageous Old Woman" T-shirt.

"Happy to meet you, Betta," I say.

Sitting next to Betta is Ruth. She is blind.

"I'm going to talk to Miriam some this morning," I say to Linda.

"Oh, there you are," Miriam says to someone, getting up and leaving the table.

Betta remembers me from Anshe Emet, but we were in two different confirmation years. And she remembers me from LeMoyne, but we were in different tracks. "I wasn't as smart as you," she says laughing. We talk as if we had been old friends or could be new friends. One of her daughters is an Evangelical fundamentalist, another is a lesbian in a committed kosher-keeping relationship, and the third, manic depressive, was recently diagnosed with an inoperable brain tumor. She invites me to visit her in Marin County where she has an apartment with a moon view. I do not invite her to Worthington, where I have a house, a husband, two sons, three step-daughters, and two cats.

Miriam rejoins us. She has brought Carol, a sliver in silver.

I cannot stand it another minute. I decide to take a risk, and say, "This Jewish/Gentile split is driving me crazy. I'm about to explode."

"Now that *you* raised it," Miriam says, "we were talking about you last night."

And just who is "We"?

"*We* went out after the dinner. And we were talking about you," Miriam repeats.

I am not going to ask her what "We" were talking about about me. I am not.

"I know you belonged to that club. What was it? Alpha?"

What? Alpha was The club. Maybe there were no Jews in Alpha. Maybe it had elite status only among the Gentiles.

"Did you go to the Friday social dances?" I ask.

"No. No. I was in temple," she says.

So, those dances were Gentile dances. I thought I was straddling the two worlds, but I wasn't. By not being all Jewish, I was living in the Gentile world.

"I always felt sorry for you," Miriam continues.

What? No one has ever said that to me. I've never felt pitied.

"I always felt sorry for you because you looked so Gentile."

What? To myself, I say, *and look at your nose-job,* but to her I volunteer, "Yeah… One of the Anshe Emet mothers called my mother to uninvite me to her son's Bar Mitzvah party." Anger from the past is rising in me.

"But you came to the Junior Bat Mitzvah girls' parties at my house, didn't you?" Miriam asks.

I have a vague memory of one all-girl party, once, and of the girls whose names I don't remember who are here at this reunion with bleached hair, perked noses, and face peels. I remember feeling queasy, uneasy at the party, the way I feel now.

"I wasn't Bat Mitzvah'ed," I say. "I didn't think Anshe Emet had them for girls back then."

"We were the first group," Miriam says.

This is news to me. My parents must have chosen to Bar Mitzvah Barrie, but not to Bat Mitzvah me. It was not Anshe Emet's Conservative policy, as I have always believed, but my parents' decision. *Stop thinking about Barrie,* I order myself.

"Last night," Miriam continues, "we talked about how you being half-Jewish is like how being half-Black is now. Back then, the Jews couldn't accept you and the Gentiles couldn't either—but look how you rose above it!"

Breathe, Laurel, Breathe.

"I told *them,*" Miriam says. "Look how she's pulled herself up… rose above it."

Did "they" need convincing? Am I feeling searing anger? Or searing pain?

"I didn't know any of that about you," Betta says, "until just now."

I wonder if she would have talked to me, invited me to her home, had she known.

"It's been wonderful talking to you," says silver-tongued Carol.

To myself I say, *But we haven't talked at all.*

"Be sure and call me when you're in Chicago," Miriam says to me.

She's moving to a new house. I don't have her cell-phone number, address, or email. *Why would I call her, anyway?* Why would I allow myself to be dismissed yet again? Then, it occurs to me that Miriam and the other Jews at the Golden Reunion had been thrown back into the world we inhabited as teenagers—a post-Holocaust world where a survival strategy of the American Jewish people was to close ranks, diminish intimate encounters with outsiders, and to distrust Gentiles. To keep a Jewish world alive meant keeping out from that world progeny of mixed-marriages lest *"Got in Himmel"* one's own child was seduced into marrying a *goy.* Not only were my "friends" thrown back into the 1950s, they were enacting these survival strategies now, just as I was re-enacting mine, reliving the tensions of my childhood, entanglements with my brother, and the interlacing of the cultural, the familial, and my elusive mother.

A sentimental journey? No. A journey of discovery.

Acknowledgments

I thank Ernest Lockridge for his frequent readings of this manuscript, and I thank Maggie Kast and my memoir writing group for their comments. An earlier version of this essay appeared in the *International Review of Qualitative Research* (Vol. 5, No. 2) and is reproduced here with permission from the publisher, Left Coast Press, Inc.

Section Three

Representing, Breaking, and Remaking

Section Three Introduction

Braiding Evocative with Analytic Autoethnography

Barbara Tedlock

Today, the enterprise of doing and writing ethnography consists of the narrative shaping and analysis of human experience and vulnerability. As the essays in this section reveal, autoethnography, or the use of personal knowledge and membership to explore cultural practice (Goodall, 2000; Ellis, 2004), combines participation with memory using artfully embodied qualitative methods. Here the gaze turns inward toward the self while maintaining the outward gaze and responsibility of ethnography.

Over the past twenty years, this mixed form of qualitative research has rapidly expanded, creating the new genre of autoethnography. Working successfully in this space requires the orchestration of various writing strategies—personal narrative, poetic inquiry, lyric essay, ethnodrama and analysis. Such techniques may be woven together with arts-based practices, including photography, music, drawing, and the construction of multimedia collages. Combining evocative methods can help us bear witness to and offer support for vulnerable selves within cultural and social worlds (Behar, 1997; Pelias, 2004; Stoller, 1997). Because the knower and the known are intricately linked, the narrative positioning of the self within the body is a key element in this new endeavor.

In the opening essay, "Reflections on Writing and Autoethnography," Julia Colyar sets the scene of her writing practice, "This is how I write: I am up early with a cup of coffee. The house is quiet as I lace up my running shoes. I leave a note on the kitchen counter—'out for a run, usual loop'—step outside, and pull

---

Handbook of Autoethnography, edited by Stacy Holman Jones, Tony E. Adams, and Carolyn Ellis, 358–362. © 2013 Left Coast Press, Inc. All rights reserved.

my toque down over my ears." She brings us outside with her as she struggles to embody her thoughts, then returns to the comfort of her computer and surrounding books. One by one she considers expressive, transactional, and poetic modes of writing: expressive writing foregrounds energy and emotion; transactional writing emphasizes analysis and theorizing; while poetic writing creates literary texts. Twisting these strands together, she produces an evocative analytic text.

Ronald Pelias, in his essay "Writing Autoethnography: The Personal, Poetic, and Performative as Compositional Strategies," speaks from his body. "I write wanting to *lean in*... writing the labor of obligation, of compassion." He uses evocative autoethnography to describe how bodies lean together, placing themselves in relationship to other bodies. In his most recent book, *Leaning: A Poetics of Personal Relations* (2011), he reveals feeling trapped by labels such as race, class, sexuality, and gender. "I am a man doing the best I know how," then adds, apologetically, "I keep that claim as my excuse" (p. 28). In both works Pelias poetically invokes and analytically describes how writing becomes a space for an embodied examination of the spiritual and ethical aspects of human relationships.

Grace Giorgio opens her essay, "Reflections on Writing Through Memory in Autoethnography," by saying, "When I sit down to write, I find the story behind the memories; I then begin to make sense of those memories, their meaning for me and for others." Memory is an investigative tool for writing that allows Giorgio to bear witness and enact memorials to lives lived. Her autoethnography takes the form of short stories that attend to each person respectfully, a balancing act centering on cultural and political tensions between lived experiences and their meanings and reminds us that our job is not to discredit an antagonist but to reveal his or her feelings and perspectives. Autoethnography allows us to write stories as cultural memories consisting of wars, genocides, and uprisings that bear witness to memories that we may never have had within ourselves but have come to know indirectly through others.

Performing ethnography creates a mimetic parallel or alternate instance through which subjectivity is made available to witnesses. Such work uses dialogue, narrative, performative writing, kinesis, and staging, which directly involve the arrangement of internal and external embodied landscapes, performers, and audience members. Jeanine Mingé, who works in this tradition, is an ethnographer who, like several others in this section of the Handbook, expands upon the impressionistic and confessional fieldwork tradition to produce works of analytic autoethnography that also delight the senses. Her essay "Mindful Autoethnography" combines personal narrative with photographs and collages, creating a dynamic and evocative intersection among linguistic, tactile, and visual fields that adds layer and nuance to her audiences' experiences of the family stories she tells.

When Brydie-Leigh Bartleet asked herself what a "musical autoethnography" might look like, she discovered that a few composers and performers had used this method to uncover the ways in which their personal lives and cultural experiences intertwined during the creation and performance of musical works (Bartleet, 2009; Holman Jones, 2002, 2007). In the context of guiding a young male graduate student in producing a multimedia doctoral submission about the impact of Asperger's syndrome on his musical life, Bartleet notes that the multimedia autoethnographic methods he employed intertwined his research and creative processes in a powerful way. Using a variety of lifewriting and other artistic techniques, he mixed his "black evocative pages with white analytical pages" in such a way as to become an "instigator of personal, disciplinary and broader social change."

Christopher Poulos expands on the project of intertwining autoethnographic methods by foregrounding the therapeutic power of storytelling. In his essay, "Writing My Way Through: Memory, Autoethnography, Identity, Hope," he suggests that writing autoethnography is not only a "method of inquiry" but also, and perhaps more importantly, "a method of relating." It is also *spirited* writing," by which he means that when we write autoethnographies, "we write spirit into being." As he puts it, "the human spirit, shared in communication, gives birth to Hope"—which helps "to piece together the shards of memory into story." "Writing is a lifeline, a way into and through the questions and mysteries that hover at the edge of his consciousness." It is also "a quest for meaning, for truth, for discovery. It is a way to move toward evoking, describing, invoking, transcribing, inscribing, representing, and playing with or building on our life worlds."

Lisa Tillmann's essay, "Wedding Album: An Anti-heterosexist Performance Text," relates the underlying rhetorical strategies used today by opponents of same-sex marriage to those used more than fifty years ago by the opponents of interracial marriage. In each case the rhetoric involves the notion of "God's Plan" and the "protection of children." The judge in *Loving v. Virginia* (1967) proclaimed, "Almighty God created the races white, black, yellow, Malay and red, and he placed them on separate continents. And but for the interference with his arrangement there would be no cause for such marriages." Tillmann reveals that opponents to interracial and same-sex marriage, then and now, wrongly argue that growing up in a family headed by a mixed-race or same-sex partner damages children, an assertion rejected by every major medical, psychological, and child welfare association in the nation. In this essay, she adds an "analytic perspective" (Anderson, 2006; Ellis & Bochner, 2006) to autoethnography by way of her detailed footnotes and coda, which carefully trace the legalization of same-sex marriage in the United States. Her essay is powerful because she braids an evocative and highly personal narrative into a nuanced description and theoretical understanding of the ironic history of racism and homophobia in the United States. By mixing evocative with analytic modes of writing she provides a vision of autoethnography consistent with the practice of "realist ethnography" (Van Maanen, 1988, p. 53).

A similar, profoundly powerful braiding of evocative with analytic autoethnography closes this section of the Handbook. Marilyn Metta incorporates narrative and art therapies with lifewriting in "Putting the Body on the Line: Embodied Writing and Recovery through Domestic Violence." This deeply personal contribution centers on sexual abuse within her marriage. She opens her narrative by starkly revealing herself in drawings and poetic writing as the wife of a monstrous husband; she "shivers in shame as / a feast of porn feeds the beast / merely a piece of red meat / upon which his selfish desires feast." Next she uncovers the public betrayal she suffered from her husband, "on the Web, he spun his web / around her sacred body / offered her to the eyes of strange men / like a prized possession to win envy" (Metta, 2010, p. 120). After speaking and drawing her terror and shame, Metta reveals how she found the practice of mindfulness and training in psychotherapy as central to her physical and psychic recovery.

Metta places herself at the epicenter of her investigation by evocatively intertwining poetry with drawing, portraying herself as both an embodied subject and a silenced object. By the end of the essay she opens outward to others, explaining that the labels "battered women" and "victims of domestic violence" are dangerous because they risk the further silencing and marginalizing of women like her (Metta, 2010, p. 285). She suggests using alternative descriptions such as "women who have experienced domestic violence" (Metta, 2010, p. 285), a phrase that honors how these "deeply personal and embodied narratives of knowing, surviving, and living with, against, and beyond domestic violence form critical bodies of knowledge." By adding these policy suggestions Metta enters the realm of "analytic autoethnography" that informs the conceptual and scholarly understanding of theorists, psychotherapists, and scholars working in the field of domestic/family abuse. Her essay demonstrates how the combining of evocative with analytic forms of autoethnography produces powerful writing about the self in the world in order to help change the world.

Taken together, these essays reveal that writing and performing vulnerably from the heart with passion and analytic accuracy allows one to emerge from a flat soulless representation of social worlds outside the self into sensuous, evocative research that encourages and supports both personal development and social justice within the world.

References

Anderson, L. (2006). Analytic autoethnography. *Journal of Contemporary Ethnography, 35*(4), 373–395.

Bartleet, B-L. (2009). Behind the baton: Exploring autoethnographic writing in a musical context. *Journal of Contemporary Ethnography, 36*, 713–733.

Behar, R. (1997). *The vulnerable observer: Anthropology that breaks your heart.* Boston: Beacon.

Ellis, C. (2004). *The ethnographic I: A methodological novel about autoethnography.* Walnut Creek, CA: AltaMira Press.

Ellis, C. S., & Bochner, A. P. (2006). Analyzing analytic autoethnography: An autopsy. *Journal of Contemporary Ethnography, 35*(4), 429–449.

Goodall, H. L. (2000). *Writing the new ethnography*. Walnut Creek, CA: AltaMira Press.

Holman Jones, S. (2002). The way we were, are, and might be: Torch singing as autoethnography. In A. P. Bochner & C. Ellis (Eds.), *Ethnographically speaking: Autoethnography, literature, and aesthetics* (pp. 44–56). Walnut Creek, CA: AltaMira Press.

Holman Jones, S. (2007). *Torch singing: Performing resistance and desire from Billie Holiday to Edith Piaf.* Lanham, MD; AltaMira Press.

Metta, M. (2010). *Writing against, alongside and beyond memory: Lifewriting a reflexive poststructuralist feminist research practice.* Bern, Switzerland: Peter Lang.

Pelias, R. J. (2004). *A methodology of the heart: Evoking academic and daily life.* Walnut Creek, CA: AltaMira Press.

Pelias, R. J. (2011). *Leaning: A poetics of personal relations.* Walnut Creek, CA: Left Coast Press, Inc.

Stoller, P (1997). *Sensuous scholarship.* Philadelphia: University of Pennsylvania Press.

Van Maanen, J. (1988). *Tales of the field: On writing ethnography.* Chicago: University of Chicago Press.

Chapter 18

Reflections on Writing and Autoethnography

Julia E. Colyar

> Writing is a strange invention.
>
> Claude Levi-Strauss (1955, p. 298)

Expressive

This is how I write: I am up early with a cup of coffee. The house is quiet as I lace up my running shoes. I leave a note on the kitchen counter—"out for a run, usual loop"—step outside, and pull my toque down over my ears. It's a cold spring morning in Toronto. I set off along Islington with a recent *This American Life* playing on my iPod. I know I will come back to this episode later because I am not listening; I am writing. A right turn onto Royal York, south toward the lake. I keep puzzling over this chapter.

It has taken me the better part of a week to write the nine sentences included above. I made the final edit just moments ago when I deleted the word "episode" after "recent." Since I use "episode" in the next sentence, I decided it was repetitive. There's a good chance I will read my paragraph this afternoon and make another change. So it probably isn't my *final* edit. And you can't see it but I have written and re-written the first five sentences of this paragraph several times. My goal is daunting: I am hoping to communicate the complexity of the writing process—the many drafts and decisions—but I am also looking for exactly the right

Handbook of Autoethnography, edited by Stacy Holman Jones, Tony E. Adams, and Carolyn Ellis, 363–383. © 2013 Left Coast Press, Inc. All rights reserved.

words right now, the polished final version. Both process and product are central to my writing life, each satisfying in different ways. Process is particularly import ant—process makes finished products possible—but it's difficult to present; it's a bit like pulling out the ingredients of a cake that has already been baked. How I write is, indeed, a lot less tidy than the nine sentences above. As I step out the front door and onto Islington, my thoughts are cluttered:

> *If I make this light, I will wait to cross to the south side of the street until Royal York. Good, I'll make it. How to start? I'm definitely procrastinating. But I need a beginning. This is how I write. Hmmm. I am up early with a cup of coffee. The house is quiet; I watch the clouds form— gather?— over Lake Ontario. I'll leave out the weather report. This is how I write: I am up early with a cup of coffee. The house is quiet as I lace up my sneakers. Running shoes. Sneakers is a funny word. Maybe I don't want to talk about running. That introduces a whole other metaphor. I don't want to get stuck there. Training, pacing, and so forth. I'm getting distracted. Back to the beginning.*

At the international market, I turn left and run past Sandy and Mary's house. My watch beeps as I cross Lakeshore Drive and I run into the park around Humber Bay. I feel my head clear, ever so slightly, as I practice my text over and over again, adding words, editing. I am relieved. This is how I write.

> *I set off along Islington, or south on Islington? Do I want the structure of urban geography? Don't get stuck on structure. Wait. First I need to get out the front door. I lace up my running shoes. I leave a note on the kitchen counter and step outside. I should add what my note says. Out for a run, normal loop. Usual loop. Smiley face. No smiley face. A detail about the cold so I can situate myself in time. As I step outside, I pull my hat down. As I step outside, I pull my toque down over my ears. Toque is a more interesting word. It's a cold spring morning. In Toronto. It's a cold spring morning in Toronto. This is how I write: I am up early with a cup of coffee. Hmmm. I like how I say I am writing, but actually I am drinking coffee, then running. Mostly I write by not writing?*

Back at home, I sit at the computer and type the lines I have crafted on my morning run. Hours drift by as I write and delete, first the opening sentences, then their generation, these words. I drink more coffee, break for a cheese sandwich, and review a set of student assignments. All the while, I rehearse my first sentences like a mantra, imagining the letters, the semicolon, quote marks. I change a contraction into two words—it is—then back again. A week passes as I turn the sentences over in my mind. Annoyingly, I find myself composing and editing while I drive, stand in line at the Tim Horton's for coffee, and rinse dinner dishes. Anxiety creeps in—I don't know what this paper will look like, I'm starting too many sentences with the pronoun "I," will any of this be useful in the final draft?—but I push against my worries with words: This is how I write.

There is something terribly comforting in that sentence. "This is how I write" strikes me as an apology and a warning, an exhaustive summary and extreme understatement. When the words run through my mind, I hear them as an offering. I am a game show hostess displaying fabulous prizes, my arms spreading wide. I offer you this. Here. It's my writing, as simple as that. And if you look under the surface, you'll see my feet madly paddling. The "this" I point toward is inelegant and unnerving. This is beautiful, and it is a muddle. Most importantly, it is a beginning.

Writing is, of course, a complicated endeavor. For me, it includes running, driving, sitting at the computer and standing in line for coffee. Writing occupies me; words and ideas settle in and pitch a tent. I worry about words and reviewers and deadlines. Perhaps as a response to my anxiety, I read about writing—style guides, empirical research, and a dictionary of composition theory (Kennedy, 1998). An article about comma mis-use in the *New York Times* catches my eye, and I am newly anxious. Punctuation errors feel like personal failures. I have read and re-read multiple versions of my own first paragraphs and the sections I am building about theoretical foundations and best practices in autoethnography. Strangely, none of my reading makes this assignment easier, even the texts that explicitly offer advice. I need a pep-talk. And so I get up early and head out for a run, assuring myself that I will find a beginning.

My reading also reminds me that writing has multiple forms and functions. Writing is a process through which I come to understand myself and my research; writing is also a product, a record of my work and a form of capital I exchange in the academic marketplace. I write formally (letters of recommendation, reports, articles) and informally (emails to distant friends, notes on the kitchen counter explaining my whereabouts). My writing has physical presence, a satisfying thirty-three double-spaced typed pages. And it is words I compose on a morning run, many of which I forget before I get home. James Britton (1971), a scholar interested in language and learning, offers a useful framework which has helped me think about these varied forms of writing (see also Britton, Burgess, Martin, McLeod, & Rosen, 1975). The framework identifies three modes of writing: expressive, transactional, and poetic. I stumbled upon this taxonomy one afternoon last summer as I was leafing through a textbook called *Thinking/Writing* (Olson, 1992). I held my breath a long time, staring at the words. An idea formed slowly—three functions of writing, three sections of this paper. I saw an organizational structure that might work. Another kind of beginning.

My goal in this first section is to describe and enact expressive writing. Britton et al.'s (1975) remaining functions—transactional and poetic—will be described and illustrated in the next sections.[1] According to Britton et al. (1975), expressive writing allows us to explore and reflect upon ideas; it foregrounds the personal and supports the building blocks of our arguments and our sense of confidence as writers. The expressive function may be exercised in journal entries or letters; it may be found in conversation with friends or in the ruminations that occupy writers as they run, drive, or clean the dishes. Freewriting activities may be the most well-known version of expressive writing. For Elbow (2000, 2007), freewriting is active, energetic, and emotional. It encourages authors to locate their voices and their writerly selves. The "rules," Britton (1971) explains, are relaxed; expression is "close to the speaker: what engages his attention is freely verbalized, and as he presents his view of things, his loaded commentary upon the world, so he also presents himself" (p. 207). Though I am distracted by Britton's male pronouns, I am drawn to the idea of proximity: expressive writing is close to me. "This is how I write" is information, but also introduction. This is who I am.

In preparing this chapter, I have used "expressive" writing to brainstorm the sections, to think through the various points I want to make, and to map the ebb and flow of my anxiety. Sometimes my expressive writing is literal, physically on a page; sometimes I carry it around with me in my head. There are six files on my computer with freewriting exercises and initial (mostly discarded) outlines, and I have a notebook full of handwritten thoughts and quotes from my reading. One page of my notebook provides transcriptions of all the posted signs I see one morning in the public library—"please watch your belongings"—followed by the obvious: "writing is everywhere." On another page, I have written a "to do" list, starting with "look up autoethnography." When I search online for definitions of autoethnography, I am comforted with key words: personal, cultural, reflexivity, insight, subjectivity, context. These words are written all over my notebook.

Elbow (2000) and Kinneavy (1971) argue that expressive writing leads to purposeful action. This is certainly true in my writing process. I run, I think, I am consumed with words, I write. The pathway is not smooth or without frustrations, but I work out a route nonetheless. These scholars, however, also discuss action in the social world. For O'Donnell (1996), the "unguardedness" of expressive writing provides space for developing a social and political consciousness, as well as a sense of purpose. "Learning a word," O'Donnell notes, "is learning how to do something" (1996, p. 430). Writing a word is doing something, too—an idea that keeps me inspired even after long hours at the computer, even when I delete more than I type. Most of my expressive writing will serve as backdrop rather than focus for this paper, despite Britton's (1971) assurances that it is our principal means of self-understanding and social connection. But it is always present in my texts, because it is how I write.

In the second section, I will think about why writing is important as a scholarly topic. This section will primarily use the "transactional" mode, a more formal approach with the goal of communicating particular information. Transaction may include summary, analysis, or theorizing. This mode is likely familiar to us, though perhaps we haven't used Britton's term to describe it. In particular, I focus on scholarship related to the writing process—a topic which concerns all writers, no matter the specific steps we take toward a completed text.

In the third section, I present the gifts of writing. The poetic. Such texts, according to Britton (1971), have "import" (p. 212). They are highly ordered verbal artifacts; form and content are interrelated. Such texts allow for—inspire, and demand—contemplation and learning. The poetic represents the most sophisticated form of writing, a kind of textual cognac: words are distilled, ideas are so present you can't stop seeing them. In this section, I discuss three autoethnographies which have inspired and challenged me.

Writing undoubtedly has other functions. In the following sections, some of these will be evident—for example, writing as a means of discovery, as a reflection of community and social structures, as a tool of empowerment and enslavement, as the trope which distinguishes between barbarism and civilization, as an instrument of clarity. Writing is also deeply personal, hidden among crowded notebooks full of scribbled ideas and fleeting electronic drafts, slow steps toward self-understanding. I sit at my computer and will myself to relax, to begin, to find the right words. This is how I write.

Transactional

In his 1955 essay, "A Writing Lesson," Claude Levi-Strauss describes the function of writing in the Nambikwara community of the Brazilian Amazon. Levi-Strauss witnessed writing as a symbol used for the sociological purpose of "increasing the authority and prestige" of one individual over another (p. 298). Likewise, the anthropologist describes the role of the scribe in Pakistani villages: he is "rarely a functionary or employee of the group: his knowledge is accompanied by power" (p. 298). Following this introduction, Levi-Strauss continues with a description of writing not often presented. In short, the function of writing—this "strange invention"—is to exploit and enslave rather than to enlighten and empower. Levi-Strauss correlates the emergence of writing with the expansion of civilizations and empires, and the subsequent development of political systems, classes and castes. Writing's function, in this view, is to facilitate the exercise of power. The intellectual and aesthetic functions of writing were secondary consequences, though Levi-Strauss also connects the aesthetic to nefarious purposes: "more often than not [artistic writing] may even be turned into a means of strengthening, justifying or concealing" the exercise of power (p. 299). Writing may thus provide the criterion to distinguish civilization from barbarism, though it might actually be associated with barbarism.

Whether or not scholars would agree with Levi-Strauss's contentions related to exploitation and enslavement, most would support the idea that writing functions as an exercise of power. Writing, for example, can express individual authority. Elbow (1994) offers the connection between "voice" and "power," a connection familiar to qualitative researchers. In her essay, "Why I Write," Joan Didion (1976) locates "I" as the heart of writing work: "writing is the act of saying *I*, of imposing oneself upon other people, of saying *listen to me, see it my way, change your mind*" (emphasis in original, p. 270). Didion's goals may be best described as persuasion or engagement, but she is also asserting her worldview. Didion's "I" is the central voice; indeed, as the author notes, "I" is the phoneme which underlies each word of "Why I Write." Hers is the privileged perspective, imposed upon the reader.

Writing as an instrument of power has also been explored in contemporary scholarship, particularly as researchers have responded to positivist views of "science" (Agger, 1990; Richardson, 2000). Recent poststructural scholarship, for example, has problematized universal truth claims and the role of language/writing/research in the creation and maintenance of power relationships. Richardson (2000), for example, describes the ways language and authority are exercised at the individual and social levels. She notes: "language is how social organization and power are defined and contested and the place where our sense of self, our subjectivity, is constructed" (p. 8). Critiques of traditional research practices have led to new methodologies such as autoethnography, as writers have sought a more productive engagement in culture. The "I" pronoun is used purposefully and with great care to illustrate the subjectivity present in all scholarship, and to situate understandings as developing out of personal experience.

Writing is central to all scholarly activity. Autoethnography is no exception; "writing" is explicitly indicated in the term used to describe the methodology/product. "Graphy" is a Greek suffix used to denote processes, styles of writing, or graphic representation; photography and calligraphy are useful examples. The suffix has more commonly been used to indicate a particular scientific emphasis such as geography or bibliography. Reed-Danahay's (1997) definition of autoethnography utilizes this approach. In her description, "graphy" in autoethnography points toward the application of the research process. It is useful, however, to spotlight the writing aspect inherent in the word. In autoethnography, writing is not a separate act, but a process that supports, or perhaps constitutes, the self and the sociocultural connection. According to the *Oxford English Dictionary*, Greek nouns modified with "graph" and "graphy" are also nouns of action or function, two concepts that are important in thinking about autoethnography, and about writing more generally. Autoethnography is a methodology, a textual product, an evocative expression of research understandings, and a means of acting in the world.

Given the centrality of composition in the autoethnographic project, it is important to discuss the scholarship related to writing. Writing is not simply an artifact used to express scholarly understandings and authority; it has also been the subject of scholarly attention for more than forty years (Kennedy, 1998). In this section, I present two theoretical approaches that have been used to understand the writing process: the cognitive and social views of composition. A discussion of the writing process, however, should begin with product, the first focus of composition research.

Before I jump into this section, I should pause. I've put this section together as an example of Britton's (1971) transactional writing, a mode of writing which is formal and expository. You may have already noticed that transactional writing sounds different from expressive. One reader suggested that this section is a bit dry.

I don't disagree. Even this paragraph is more interesting than the one above. Take a quick look; you'll see what I mean. My initial response to this observation is to own it entirely, to explain that I am writing in/about transactional mode, which is businesslike. If this section is dull, I have succeeded according to Britton's (1971) definition. I'm actually further emphasizing the qualities of the expressive by showing you the transactional. But here's something else about transactional writing: it's a lot safer than expressive. I can synthesize other people's ideas and present arguments that don't require a lot of interpretation; what I believe or feel can stand in the background. I worry over style and clarity, but not about revealing too much about myself. I'm particularly reluctant to admit how difficult the writing process is for me; I'd much rather be a person for whom writing comes easily. I don't want to admit the number of hours I spend typing and deleting, typing and deleting, or the ways writing consumes me when I am running, driving, and washing dishes. Transactional writing may be somewhat dry, but it is straightforward. Perhaps it won't surprise you to learn that I drafted the "transaction" section much more quickly than the others. After all, this is how I have been trained to write.

By the time you are reading this, I will have edited the following paragraphs so that the text is more engaging and personal. I'm still working toward transaction—there are ideas here I want to communicate clearly—but I also want this section to have life. And these two goals are not mutually exclusive. My revised approach also suits my topic; I am intrigued by composition theory because I want to know more about my own writing process. I read and think about these models using my experiences as an example.

Early studies of writing offered the kinds of procedural models I learned in junior high (see Braddock, Lloyd-Jones, & Schoer, 1963; Britton et al., 1975; Rohman, 1965). Rohman (1965), for example, proposed a sequential three-stage model, including prewriting, writing and editing. With a focus on product, researchers were interested in form and grammatical correctness, criteria used to differentiate between "good" and "bad" writing (Rohman, 1965). In Mr. Thatch's eighth grade English classroom, good essays were five paragraphs, and all sentences had a subject and a verb. Form and correctness. Scholars such as Murray (1980), however, decried the focus on product as a means of understanding the complexities of writing. He noted that "the process of making meaning with written language can not be understood by looking backward from a finished page. Process can not be inferred from a product any more than a pig can be inferred from a sausage" (p. 3). In fact, a finished text—a product—hides its own process, which is often a very good thing for text and sausage alike. Writing is therefore *mis*understood when it is considered only in terms of products. Researchers were inspired to look more closely at the work that produces text, and they began to talk about the epistemic function of writing: writing as "a search for meaning" (Bereiter, 1980, p. 88). The first efforts in composition research related to process were grounded in cognitive developmental theory.

The Cognitive View

Cognitive processing models emphasize the inventive power of the writer, the ways in which writing is more than the simple transcription of complete ideas, more than form and correctness. Emig (1971), for example, proposed an alternative to the traditional three-step model of composing; she looked at what writers "do" when they compose, and she argued that composing is "recursive" rather than linear (p. 84). Flower and Hayes (1981) similarly created a model of composing in which the writing process is presented as not linear, but circular.[2] Definitely not tidy. Flower and Hayes's model (1981) includes three major units: the Task Environment, the Writer's Long-Term Memory, and the Writing Process (located in the writer's mind). Each of these has identifiable sub-processes. An earlier version of this paragraph included examples of the major units and sub-processes, but I have edited them out. To be honest, I included that level of detail in order to show, literally in my paragraph, how complicated their model is. Lots of words on a page, especially if many of them are "and," can be more bewildering than not—description doesn't always clarify. Instead of a simple linear expression of how writing works—three stages—Flower and Hayes offer a set of boxes, and boxes within boxes, with double sided arrows connecting them. Instead of straightforward movement from planning to writing, Flower and Hayes argue that planning not only precedes writing, but also follows it. This absolutely reminds me of my own habits. I don't usually make useful plans until I have written an entire draft. How can I know what my paper is about, and therefore how it should unfold, until I have written it? Flower and Hayes's model is perfectly confusing, much like my writing habits.

For Flowers and Hayes (1981), composition involves a series of decisions, each guided by environmental, cultural and personal elements (these elements are represented by the major units in the model). For example, writers must make decisions based on disciplinary and formal conventions, as well as the expectations of readers. You already know that I wrestled with big questions as I started this project—how to begin? How to structure the chapter? What are the central points of my argument? Some guidelines were given to me by the editors of this volume, like page length, citation style, and the purposes of the chapter within the Handbook. I learned some expectations—things like using section headings or drawing on existing scholarship—as part of my graduate school socialization. When I began this chapter, I had a general sense of what it would look like, even though I didn't know what it would say.

Writing becomes more complicated, and more constrained, as texts unfold: paragraph and sentence structure, and mechanics like spelling and grammar, always guide writers (Collins & Gentner, 1980). As my sentences emerge on the computer screen or in my notebook, the available words—words that are grammatically correct, or logical—are increasingly limited. A sentence cannot be just a collection of gerunds. (Running thinking writing.) Mr. Thatch's correctness, it seems, still haunts my writing despite the many years since grade eight. In this essay, process is also constrained by questions of style and clarity. Though "writing" is the subject of the chapter, I try not to use it too often in the text; repetition is inelegant. So I utilize words like "composition" and "text" to ensure that my prose is not too cluttered with "writing." Indeed, I replaced "use" with "utilize" in the previous sentence to avoid further repetition. And now I am worried that I have repeated "repetition" too often in this paragraph. It's exhausting. For scholars, writing is also constrained by disciplinary conventions that create and sustain a particular version of "knowledge" (Richardson, 2000, p. 7). All of these issues occupy me, endlessly. The details matter. At the end of a long day of writing, when John asks me "what do you want to do for dinner?" I can only answer: "I don't know. I can't make any more decisions today." And I feel that indecision in my body, weighing me down.

According to Flower and Hayes (1981), a writer's decisions are also shaped by individual goals. Such goals, however, are not static. Flower and Hayes reflect the epistemic function of writing with this explanation: "In the act of writing, people regenerate or recreate their own goals in the light of what they learn" (p. 281). This point gets to the heart of the cognitive view, and it offers a compelling rationale for engaging in writing projects: writing provides opportunities for learning and discovery (Murray, 1980; Zamel, 1982). Or even more boldly: writing is learning. This, for me, is the heart of the matter, the reason to persist even when I am exhausted by unfinished texts.

The Social View

Though the work of scholars such as Emig (1971) and Flower and Hayes (1981) has often been praised, many critics voiced concerns about the methodologies used to study the writing process as well as the models that were proposed to describe it (see Berlin, 1988; Bizzell, 1982; Dobrin, 1986; Odell & Goswami, 1984; Reither, 1985; Voss, 1983). Gorrell (1983), for example, was concerned about the loss of the "product" in the enthusiasm over process. Process, he noted, is "the attempt to achieve the product" and is to some extent defined by the product itself (p. 276). After all, sausage does suggest something about the pig more than, say, a meat grinder. Some critics were concerned about the essentializing qualities of the models, that such models codify all writing processes for all individuals in singular ways (Bizzell, 1982; Bruffee, 1981, 1986; Cooper, 1986).

Most critics of the cognitive view did not disagree with the idea that writing is a learning process. Rather, they argued that the cognitive process models obscure another important aspect of writing: the socio-cultural context (Bizzell, 1982; Bruffee, 1981). In the cognitive view, writers work in isolation, in the privacy of their own minds. As I sit in my quiet office, or in a library carrel, I feel this isolation acutely. Some days, I turn on a radio so that I can feel engaged in the world. Writing is lonely. Bizzell (1982) describes the cognitive model as "inner-directed," an idea dramatically elaborated by Cooper (1986): "writing becomes a form of parthenogenesis, the author producing propositional and pragmatic structures, Athena-like, full grown and complete out of his brow" (p. 366). If only, I think to myself; texts never spring from my mind fully formed. I even write drafts of birthday greetings. The social view moved scholars from thinking about the autonomous writer, abstracted from the larger context, to a situated, "outer-directed" writer (Bizzell, 1982). In this shift, researchers moved from *how* a writer makes choices in the composing process—a procedural emphasis—to *why* such choices are made (Bizzell, 1982, p. 222).

As with the cognitive view, the social view is best understood as a family of ideas rather than a singular model (Greene, 1990). Faigley (1986), however, identifies a central assumption of the social view: "human language (including writing) can be understood only from the perspective of a society rather than a single individual" (p. 535). This view highlights writing as a social activity, often collaborative. The individual writer is "a constituent of culture" (p. 535), producing the very culture in response to which the writer then writes. A writer is therefore never isolated; even in my quiet office, I am immersed in conversations, I am part of a discursive community (Bizzell, 1982). This idea is both terrifying and amazing—terrifying because creating culture seems a big responsibility, and amazing because I want to be a voice in that endeavor.

The arc of writing's narrative may sound vaguely familiar. I see a parallel in the story of qualitative scholarship. Chase (1988) describes the development of composition research as a shift from product to process, then to an emphasis on discourse communities—a development echoed in the brief description included earlier in this chapter. This shift, and the "turf wars" surrounding the cognitive and social view of writing, mirrors another paradigmatic disagreement in social science research: the debate between quantitative and qualitative research, and between "empirical" studies and sociocultural studies associated with ethnographic/naturalistic research (Berkenkotter, 1991). Cognitive models such as Flower and Hayes (1981) proposed were accused of reflecting "positivistic" norms developed through scientific methods; advocates of the social view argued that knowledge is provisional and socially constructed. Cognitive process scholars relied on research drawn from psychology and other social sciences; proponents of the social view adopted literature from the humanities, including literary criticism. Interestingly, that composition studies can be—and have been—mapped as a reflection of larger philosophical, epistemological, and methodological debates can be seen as an example of the social view proving its point. Composition studies are shaped by discourse communities just as individual writing is shaped by discourse communities.

A careful examination of Flower and Hayes's (1981) cognitive model, however, indicates that the sharp distinctions drawn between the cognitive and social views are not nearly as dramatic as one might think. Flower and Hayes's model, though focused on individual problem solving in the service of writing, also situates the writer in a larger context (Flower, 1989). This is clear as I write about the decisions that exhaust me as I work on a text. The guidelines offered by Mr. Thatch, my graduate school instructors and mentors, and the field of educational research are examples of the larger cultural context and the ways it shapes my text. I cannot make decisions in a vacuum, and I cannot write in a vacuum. These days, I never write a paper without including a roadmap somewhere in the introduction, a remnant of the advice my dissertation advisor offered. Several researchers have called for a truce in the turf wars, recognizing that an ecumenical approach can lead to greater understandings of writing experiences (Berkenkotter, 1991; Bizzell, 1982; Brandt, 1992). In her revised cognitive model, Flower (1989) calls for an integrated theoretical vision "which can explain how context cues cognition, which in turn mediates and interprets the particular world that context provides" (p. 282). She continues:

> Context is a powerful force. However, it does not produce a text through immaculate conception. It is a semiotic source of signs, not a program for action. Context in its many forms is mediated—at all levels of awareness—by the cognition of the individual writer. (p. 289)

Greene (1990) offers a new phrase to describe a more integrated approach to understanding writing—a social-epistemic rhetoric: an approach that "acknowledges and explains the role of individual cognition in constructing meaning within culturally organized practices" (p. 163). Such an approach should not be unified—indeed, likely could not be, given the long history of disagreement and the complexity of the composing process itself, not to mention the fact that everyone approaches writing differently. Rather, Flower (1989) calls for reflective practice, for scholarly habits that examine our tacit theories and assumptions as we also explore new theoretical options.

A call for reflective practice is a useful place to end a section related to theories of composition. Whatever happens in the writing process, reflective practice should be prioritized. The author, by definition, is never entirely separate from the text, is never entirely separate from the reflection and construction of sociocultural meanings. Writing is not innocent, nor is it passive. Rather, it is interested, an action in the world, an exercise of power. Though writing often feels isolating, the writer never acts in isolation. These are indeed important writing lessons.

◉

I worked on the "Transaction" section with as much discipline as I could muster. That is, I tried to figure out an outline before I sat in front of the computer. In truth, it was a rather sketchy outline, and I scribbled it into my notebook knowing I would be unfaithful. When I look back at that outline now, I can't even decipher half of the words. Talk about a lack of commitment. I really didn't even have good intentions; I know I don't write that way, in the perfect three-step model Mr. Thatch advised. To be perfectly honest, I didn't understand the "social view" very well before I started that section. Sure, I had an idea that it reflected a social constructionist view, and I knew that it insists on a situated, contextually located writer. It seemed easy enough. But then I started reading more. I'd write a sentence, delete it, and start again. Stop again. The sun set outside my window. Half of the time I was "writing," I was actually perusing online issues of *College English* and *College Composition and Communication* from the 1980s. Open any volume from that decade, and you'll find something related to the great cognitive/ social debate. Those theorists were not great friends back in the day. Once I started reading more, I realized I didn't understand the cognitive view that well either. So I went back to those paragraphs and tried to write for my own understanding. To specify. To make it clearer that the cognitive view was expressing a positivist paradigm. I still feel uneasy about that point, but not because I don't see it. I am attracted to the cognitive view because writing is, for me, about learning what I think. I hate to see it sullied by the suggestion of positivism. I need to keep reminding myself that in a social-epistemic rhetoric, learning is also part of the bargain. When I really think about it, this version of writing and learning fits better with my worldview. I can be happy about that.

Now I am looking forward to the last section. Though I'll still be talking about writing, I will let go of theory and focus on poetry. Just typing that sentence offers me some relief. But I'm stuck on an important question: What does any of this have to do with autoethnography? On one of my morning runs, I take up this question and ponder the connections. Perhaps autoethnography is an example of the social-epistemic practice, the work of an individual writer constructing and articulating meaning within a culturally organized space. Perhaps autoethnography—the process and product—exemplifies the connection between individual cognition and cultural situations. Autoethnography manifests, in process and on the page, a writer's reflective practice. Perhaps composition theorists should write autoethnographies. Maybe they already have. Some theorist talked about how one means of writing about the composing process is to talk about his own. Isn't that, at least marginally, using individual experiences to describe shared meanings? Isn't that mingling identity with practice? It's a goal I have set for myself here. But who was that theorist? I've found the scribble in my notebook—Dobrin (1986): "In almost every article I've written, I must confess, I base my accounts of what happens when one writes on what happens to me when I write" (p. 724). I'm thankful for my notebook; though it is mostly indecipherable (on one page, I've written "*agitates, Foucault"), this is how I write.

Poetic

Let me start by saying that the three texts I will present in this section do not need my endorsement. They are well known and well respected, written by established researchers who have helped energize new methods in qualitative research. I offer them here as examples of Britton et al.'s (1975) poetic writing function—sophisticated, literary texts; texts that exemplify the marriage of form and content. For Britton (1971), beautiful words are only the beginning of the poetic text. Such texts also bring context to the foreground and invite us to see ourselves in that space. As you will notice, what I see in these texts is not always comfortable. These examples actually inspire a great deal of discomfort for me, followed by a quiet moment when I notice how skillfully the authors have led me into thoughtfulness.

Similarly, I will not offer a specific definition of autoethnograpic processes or methods in this section. Other scholars included in this Handbook will no doubt provide definition and description, and anything I might add would be repetitive at best. This section takes me back to products, the first focus of composition theorists. Though scholarship has evolved over the years, and though process has become a center of attention, products—the fruits of academic labor—are essential. An appreciation of process would be impossible without products.

My discussion will utilize an evaluative framework offered by Pelias (2011) in his article "Writing into Position." In preparing to outline his framework, Pelias considers what makes a text seductive rather than simply readable, engaging rather than flat. "Seductive" is an interesting word choice, one that rolls around in my mind. A step past "persuasive," seductive is a word that suggests, however subtly, that we are not always in control. When I am seduced by a text, I surrender to its pleasures. I bargain with myself: one more chapter or section, then I will get back to work. At times, seduction means that I read it even though I don't think I want to. I read in spite of myself. Pelias describes a handful of characteristics that offer seduction and engagement. Rather than outline them all, I advise you to read Pelias's article for the full list. It's seductive. It's poetic. It's how I want to write. Instead, I'll summarize his evaluative criteria briefly.

Engaging texts offer thick description and beautiful writing; the text is a "mouthful worthy of comment, encourages lingering, savoring, remembering" (Pelias, 2011, p. 666). Thick description, however, is not over-written. Engaging texts are precise. The details don't weigh it down. Pelias describes the precise text this way: "it puts leaves on bare limbs, but never bowling balls or toasters" (p. 666). Put another way, the engaging text uses a "highly selective camera, aimed carefully to capture the most arresting angles" (Pelias, 2005, p. 418).

The engaging text is also contextualized, in conversation with other writers and situated in the world. The author does not speak from a vacuum, and does not speak without presence—as if the voice is separate from the body and from experiences. In an earlier essay, Pelias (2005) describes the function of performative writing and asserts the complexity of lived experience. "Human experience," he argues, "does not reduce to numbers, to arguments, to abstractions" (p. 418). As people are contextualized, so should be the text.

Sartorial elements are also important in the engaging text. Such texts are dressed for the right audience and weather—a characteristic that requires that writers understand their readers. Instead of a flamboyant display concealing impoverished ideas, an engaging text is a "vibrant presence," adorned but not ostentatious (Pelias, 2005, p. 421). In terms of form, the engaging text is "guided by the necessity of its subject" rather than old structures and familiar models. In this way, Pelias asserts a poetic ideal—an assertion of the relationship between form and content (2011, p. 666). Banks and Banks (2000) also suggest a focus on constructing beautiful, intentional texts. They remind autoethnographers that they might "write to practice and improve our craft for its own sake" (p. 236).

These efforts at craft and costume are not simply in the service of delivering content, though that is important; rather, engaging texts also expand what constitutes disciplinary knowledge (Pelias, 2005). The status quo is not enough. Pelias (2011) offers images of discovery: "the engaging piece plays, opens closed doors, discovers hidden passageways, creates new spaces. It is mischievous, utopian, saying the unsayable" (p. 666). It is worth noting that "unsayable," according to the grammarian that informs my computer, is not a "real" word. Then again, "autoethnography" itself is not a word my computer acknowledges. Unsayable, indeed.

Pelias (2011) also describes the engaging text as unembarrassed by the struggle of writing. Instead of claims to Truth, sticky with smugness, such texts provide "a small, nervous solution, offered with humility" (p. 666). Words are free, paper and pencils are plentiful, but the right words are hard to find. Engaging texts don't pretend to be perfect. Instead, engaging texts are honest. Rather than burying passion, these texts speak "from the heart," centralizing the subjective and constructing a space in which "others might see themselves" (Pelias, 2005, p. 419).

No doubt there are numerous examples of engaging autoethnographic texts; perhaps you had one or two in mind as you were reading my summary of Pelias's work. I will discuss only three here as a means of operationalizing Pelias's evaluative elements. I have chosen these three because I admire them. They are different from one another in terms of style and voice, they are grounded in different disciplines, and they explore very different topics. But variety was not part of my selection process. These are the articles and books I recommend when someone wants an example of autoethnography. As I apply Pelias's evaluative characteristics, I understand better why these texts have stayed with me.

It took me a long time to understand John Warren's (2001) article "Absence for Whom? An Autoethnography of White Subjectivity." And I wasn't immediately seduced by this essay; in fact, my first response was puzzlement. I really didn't understand what Warren was getting at, and the personal reflections he includes seemed disconnected. I was, in fact, a bit annoyed. I now understand that Warren's essay illustrates my own sometimes disconnected, often confused understanding of Whiteness. As a White woman, I'm in Warren's essay, and my annoyance should make me think.

Warren starts, literally, with absence. Something is being anticipated in the first paragraphs, but it is not immediately clear what that something is. Like the author,

I can't see it. I only feel the tension building. In the second paragraph, with the words "May the force be with you," the subject is finally revealed. Warren is waiting for the latest release in the *Star Wars* franchise. He then reveals his own position, his saturation in the world of *Star Wars*: the toys, coloring books, action figures, board games, and secret photos of the set. Understated, Warren confesses: "I was, to say the least, a bit obsessed" (p. 37). The essay, however, is not about an upcoming movie. The essay is about White identity and the ways in which our social system "hides its tracks, covers its beginning, and [eludes] detection by relying on a rhetoric of normality that makes [racist] images flow over us without suspicion" (p. 38). In four episodes, Warren reveals blindness and seeing—and sometimes blindness *in* seeing. The vignettes he constructs (the anticipation of *Star Wars*, a reflection on the shootings at Columbine, an evening at a small-town festival, and a meditation on list-making) work best in concert rather than as isolated discussions. Together, they reveal the various ways blindness, and the absence of White subjectivity, are present in everyday life. This point is made more powerful by the fact that Warren is a student of White subjectivity; his reading and his scholarship are explorations of race, class, and privilege. As readers, we know this because Warren admits to being bewildered by a bell hooks essay. Despite his scholarly work, he isn't necessarily seeing Whiteness. His experiences powerfully illustrate the protections awarded to Whiteness—protections I recognize are part of my own experiences as a White woman. These are the protections that make it possible for me to be annoyed when the fact of White privilege is placed in front of me.

Warren's context is clearly presented in the essay. He situates himself with external markers like the opening of the *Star Wars* movie and the Columbine shootings; he then locates himself more personally, with his description of Herrinfesta, a yearly gathering in rural Southern Illinois. His context is important as an unnamed character in the drama, the ideas and images and norms that work to distract us from racism, and from understanding ourselves. And he draws this context in striking images. For example, Warren calls on the image of a gated community to describe Herrinfesta—a compelling but economical description signaling exclusion and protection, insider and outsider-ness. In doing so, he enacts Pelias's (2011) call for precision, context, and beautiful writing. Perhaps what Pelias might find most seductive in Warren's text, however, is the author's emotional, embodied presentation. Warren speaks from a White body, at once blind to and recognizing his own Whiteness. Ultimately, Warren sees because he feels; when he is suddenly angry, he understands the hooks essay that had been troubling him. Warren doesn't end his essay with a grand announcement of understanding. Such a rhetorical move would be putting on a too-flamboyant costume. Instead, he notes the various ways he has sought comfort in blindness. Then he returns to making a to-do list. Seeing his context, recognizing absence, is on the list.

Warren's essay reminds me to put "seeing" on my to-do list, too. It's advice which troubles as much as it inspires me. After all, I teach a course called "Cultural

Diversity in Higher Education," and I work to write against the theoretical frameworks and methodologies that re-center "traditional" students and student experiences. Shouldn't I already see all this? Or am I, in fact, blind to Whiteness even as I work to uncover it? Warren's essay reminds me that understanding Whiteness is complicated, risky, and a process that requires continuous engagement. I read Warren's essay often, and I see, again, as if for the first time.

Andrew Sparkes (1996) uses a fragmented presentation to reflect the postmodern body in his article "The Fatal Flaw: A Narrative of the Fragile Body." I was drawn to this article because of the title, on which I projected my own interests in bodies and fragility, and narrative. As a recreational runner, I am too often concerned with how my body works, as well as how it doesn't work. I have only lately come to realize how my identity includes being a runner—an admission I avoided for a long time, as I worried over what a "real" runner looks like. Sparkes begins his article with a warning and a promise: "new biotechnologies are currently redefining the nature of the body-self relationships and posing numerous dilemmas as to how they might develop in the future" (p. 465). In some ways, Sparkes's text is an answer to this dilemma, but not a biomedical one. He offers a narrative instead. In a dis-unified text—one that moves between theoretical discussion, journal entry, medical reports, newspaper articles, and personal narrative—Sparkes asserts coherence despite fragmentation. He aligns his subject and his structure. He does not rely on traditional models of scholarship, but opens new doors and says the unsayable.

Like Warren (2001), Sparkes (1996) is also concerned with embodiment. Sparkes, of course, is literally consumed by it. He is preoccupied by a chronic lower back pain, one which marks him as "failed" in comparison to his younger, able-bodied self. His presentation illustrates the centrality of the subjective, as he notes his writing purpose:

> I draw upon moments from my narrative of self to explore the emotional dimensions and consequences of an interrupted body project in terms of what this means for who I thought I was, who I think I am, and who I think I might be in the future. (p. 466)

At the same time, Sparkes invites the reader "to think with [his] story" (p. 466). Sparkes never succumbs to self-indulgence, to a laundry list of complaints or a de-contextualized story of injury. The story is never exclusively "about" the writer, even as it is his story. He is careful to situate his narrative in the "series of dominant scripts made available within [his] Western culture in relation to gender, age, ableness, social class, race, ethnicity, and sexuality" (p. 86). "No Conclusion," one of Sparkes's final sections, can be anticipated by the reader long before the essay comes to an end. Sparkes is not simply talking about chronic pain, however. He also labels the reflexive project in which he is engaged. He notes: "Reflecting upon my own writing-story enables me to avoid an ending and accentuate myself as a multiple reader of my own narrative of self" (p. 485). He then ends the article with a discussion of the challenge of ending. He spends several paragraphs outlining his revision process, and in particular, the ways in which he came to de-emphasize theory as he prepared the text for publication. Indeed, as earlier paragraphs indicate, his discussion about the role of theory is one I recognize, and wrestled with, in writing/revising this text.

When writers de-emphasize theory, Sparkes (1996) notes, they relinquish control over their texts and allow readers to interpret freely (p. 86). As I write these sentences, I see a different kind of fragility in Sparkes's text, and I think about my own narrative insecurities. Writing is bringing the self onto a page, presented for all to see. It is a public personal act. My anxieties, as I have noted occasionally in this chapter, are many: commas always trouble me, clear arguments are a constant preoccupation, the right words consume me even when I am otherwise occupied. I appreciate the ways Sparkes writes into and against this anxiety. I see in his text that such writing is possible, that being a writer and being uncertain can poetically co-exist.

In Pelias's (2011) evaluative framework, Sparkes's (1996) confession offers much to admire. Perhaps most importantly, Sparkes invites the reader into the writing process, a place where autoethnographers can likely see themselves, and a space in which writers can see process unfolding before them. Like Warren (2001), Sparkes ends with a kind of longing. He seeks "new narratives" of the body that can replace the earlier versions. But revision, of texts, of bodies, is difficult. Sparkes concludes with a literal non-conclusion: "I remain unsure as to where that leaves me" (p. 490). In my reading of Sparkes's article, this last sentence is terribly brave. The poetry is not only in the words themselves, but in their honesty, and in a kind of stubborn refusal to conclude. My eyes jumped down the page, looking for explanation, but all I found were the footnotes. Like Sparkes, I eagerly await resolution.

The final text I will briefly discuss does not call itself autoethnography. Gelya Frank describes her book *Venus on Wheels* (2000) as a cultural biography, a method she defines as "a cultural analysis focusing on a biographical subject that makes use of ethnographic methods, along with life history and life story, and that critically reflects on its methodology in action as a source of primary data" (p. 22). The subject of Frank's book is Diane DeVries, a woman born without arms or legs. The text examines DeVries's experiences and the ways her consciousness is shaped by the larger culture. In addition, Frank focuses on the ways in which individual experiences and consciousness contribute to cultural processes. Ultimately, DeVries challenges the cultural norms associated with disability and femininity even as she is shaped by them.

Frank (2000) is primarily concerned with images: images DeVries projects into the world through her life story, interpretations constructed by those who observe and engage with DeVries, and public records like photographs and newspaper stories. But while DeVries is the center of the text, Frank is equally important in the analysis and presentation; as a cultural biographer, Frank describes her role as a "proxy for future readers" (p. 23). Readers witness Frank's emotional and analytic responses throughout the text as she analyzes what she sees and comes to terms with her own assumptions about disability. Like an autoethnographer, Frank is explicitly present in the text, working to understand sociocultural constructs through personal and scholarly experiences. She "enact[s] the world" she studies (Denzin, 2006, p. 422). She also provides a compelling example of Pelias's (2011) engaging research voice: "It understands how it is fettered. It speaks from the body to those who wish to listen" (p. 666).

My copy of Frank's (2000) book is replete with colorful post-it tabs marking interesting passages and beautiful writing. What I admire most about this book is Frank's careful presentation of DeVries's life—a presentation that might have become voyeuristic or sensationalized. As in all research contexts, power is not distributed equally in their relationship, a point Frank acknowledges as she notes: "Diane has struggled to keep her life story distinct from my life history of her" (p. 116). In this struggle, DeVries works to maintain authorship, and Frank works to recognize it. The author keeps this struggle present in her discussion, often describing the ways DeVries resists her interpretations. Ultimately, Frank's book succeeds because she does not overpower DeVries's story. Or, more precisely, Frank does not simply tell the story of DeVries's life. Her thick description in the text is composed of leaves (or perhaps images, as Frank might say), instead of bowling balls or toasters. She invites readers, throughout the text, to engage with the images she presents and consider our negotiations of sameness and difference.

The subtlety of Frank's (2000) text, the ways she resists the "easy" story of disability, troubled me for a long time. I expected a story that includes a description of difference—indeed, I wondered about how DeVries accomplishes daily tasks like brushing her teeth and getting to work on time. This is how I thought I would understand disability, an understanding rooted in tasks and struggle, daily distress navigated by those different from me, in some way always thinking about me. When I realized that these were my expectations, I was chagrined— why should I automatically assume struggle, why should Diane be defined in this way? Indeed, why should it be about me?—and then I read the book again. Frank invites me to look closely at the ways I automatically imagine disability, the ways I assume that DeVries's experiences must be so different from my own. Frank comes to an elegant, simple question near the end of her book: "What differences do Diane's differences make?" (p. 168). I am still thinking about this question.

As I look over these paragraphs and think about these three texts, I am inspired. These texts have much to teach me about the exploration of White subjectivity, narratives of the body, and disability. They also inspire me to write poetic texts, and to claim the insecurities which are part of my writing identity. They remind me that writing can be exactly this powerful.

Reflections on Writing's Functions

This is how I write: with expression, toward transaction, seeking the poetic. Britton (1971) offers these writing functions as separate and cumulative, starting with expressive and building toward poetry. But I'm not sure expressive writing must be transformed into transactional, as if expressive writing just needs a haircut and a freshly ironed shirt. Or that poetic writing isn't also personal, close to the writer. These writing modes seem more alike than different as I look back on the sections of this chapter. Like the cognitive and social theories of the composition process, the functions of writing may be best understood in an integrated way—the cake rather than the list of ingredients, the whole much more than a sum of its parts. Distinctions may be useful for understanding the elements of the writing process, or for providing structure in a paper. But in the end, writing is complicated. It shouldn't be easy to describe.

I believe the functions of writing are often used by researchers, both in early drafts and in final, completed texts. Autoethnography, it strikes me, is a research practice that utilizes all three, all of the time. Researchers also use writing in the expression and maintenance of power, a function that underlies other writing functions. This is evident in multiple ways; I am not announcing anything surprising here. Questions of power are at the heart of postmodern and poststructural approaches to research, questions that autoethnographers have addressed directly and indirectly, with unguarded expression and poetry. That writing is powerful should terrify and inspire us. This understanding should motivate us toward reflective practice, toward intentional texts, to deeper understandings of how writing works and how we work as writers.

Notes

1. I offer Britton et al.'s functions of writing with some caution. They offer them cautiously as well: They start their 1975 report with "We classify at our peril." There is a great deal of overlap across the functions of writing. That said, their outline of functions provides a useful scheme for exploring different ways writers use writing.
2. Numerous scholars developed cognitive models for understanding the writing process (cf. D'Angelo, 1975; Braddock et al., 1963; Bereiter & Scardamalia, 1987). Because of the centrality of Flowers and Hayes's (1981) work, I focus on their scholarship here.

References

Agger, B. (1990). *The decline of discourse: Reading, writing, and resistance in post-modern capitalism.* Lewes, UK: Falmer.

Banks, S. P., & Banks, A. (2000). Reading "The Critical Life": Autoethnography as pedagogy. *Communication Education, 49*, 233–238.

Bereiter, C. (1980). Development in writing. In L. Gregg & E. Steinberg (Eds.), *Cognitive processes in writing* (pp. 73–93). Hillsdale, NJ: Lawrence Erlbaum.

Bereiter, C., & Scardamalia, M. (1987). *The psychology of written composition*. Hillsdale, NJ: Lawrence Erlbaum.

Berkenkotter, C. (1991). Paradigm debates, turf wars, and the conduct of sociocognitive inquiry in composition. *College Composition and Communication, 42*, 151–169.

Berlin, J. (1988). Rhetoric and ideology in the writing class. *College English, 50*, 477–494.

Bizzell, P. (1982). Cognition, convention, and certainty: What we need to know about writing. *PRE/TEXT 3*, 213–243.

Braddock, R., Lloyd-Jones, R., & Schoer, L. (1963). *Research in written composition*. Champaign, IL: National Council of Teachers of English.

Brandt, D. (1992). The cognitive as social. *Written Communication, 9*, 315–355.

Britton, J. (1971). What's the use? A schematic account of language functions. *Educational Review, 23*, 205–219.

Britton, J., Burgess, T., Martin, N., McLeod, A., & Rosen, H. (1975). *The development of writing abilities (11–18)*. London: Macmillan.

Bruffee, K (1981). Collaborative learning. *College English, 43*, 745–747.

Bruffee, K. (1986). Social construction, language, and the authority of knowledge: A bibliographic essay. *College English, 48*, 773–790.

Chase, G. (1988). Accommodation, resistance, and the politics of teaching student writing. *College Composition and Communication, 39*, 13–22.

Collins, A., & Gentner, D. (1980). A framework for a cognitive theory of writing. In L. Gregg & E. Steinberg (Eds.), *Cognitive processes in writing* (pp. 51–72). Hillsdale, NJ: Lawrence Erlbaum.

Cooper, M. (1986). The ecology of writing. *College English, 48*, 364–375.

D'Angelo, F. (1975). *A conceptual theory of rhetoric*. Cambridge, MA: Winthrop.

Denzin, N. K. (2006). Analytic autoethnography, or déjà vu all over again. *Journal of Contemporary Ethnography, 35*, 419–428.

Didion, J. (1976, December 5). Why I write. *The New York Times Book Review*, 270.

Dobrin, D.N. (1986). Protocols no more. *College English 48*, 713–725.

Elbow, P. (1994). Introduction: About voice in writing. In P. Elbow (Ed.), *Landmark essays on voice and writing* (pp. xi–xlvii). Davis, CA: Hermagoras Press.

Elbow, P. (2000). *Everyone can write*. New York: Oxford University Press.

Elbow, P. (2007). Voice in wring again: Embracing contraries. *College English, 70*, 168–188.

Emig, J. (1964). The uses of the unconscious in composing. *College Composition and Communication, 15*, 6–11.

Emig, J. (1971). *The composing process of twelfth graders*. NCTE Research Report No. 13. Urbana, IL: National Council of Teachers of English.

Faigley, L. (1986). Competing theories of process: A critique and a proposal. *College English, 48*, 527–542.

Flower, L. (1989). Cognition, context, and theory building. *College Composition and Communication, 40*, 282–311.

Flower, L. S., & Hayes, J. R. (1981). A cognitive process theory of writing. *College Composition and Communication, 32*, 365–387.

Frank, G. (2000). *Venus on wheels*. Berkeley: University of California Press.

Gorrell, R. M. (1983). How to make mulligan stew: Process and product again. *College Composition and Communication, 34*, 272–277.

Greene, S. (1990). Toward a dialectical theory of composing. *Rhetoric Review, 9*, 149–172.

Kennedy, M. L. (Ed.). (1998). *Theorizing composition*. Westport, CT: Greenwood Press.

Kinneavy, J. L. (1971). *A theory of discourse*. Englewood Cliffs, NJ: Prentice-Hall.

Levi-Strauss, C. (1955). *Tristes Tropiques* (Trans. J. & D. Weightman). London: Johanthan Cape.

Murray, D. (1980). Writing as process: How writing finds its own meaning. In T. R. Donovan & B. W. McClelland (Eds.), *Eight approaches to teaching composition* (pp. 3–20). Urbana, IL: National Council of Teachers of English.

Odell, L., & Goswami, D. (1984). Writing in a nonacademic setting. In R. Beach & L. S. Bridwell (Eds.), *New directions in composition research* (pp. 233–258). New York: Guilford.

O'Donnell, T. G. (1996). Politics and ordinary language: A defense of expressivist rhetorics. *College English, 58*, 423–439.

Olson, C. B. (Ed.). (1992). *Thinking/writing: Fostering critical thinking through writing.* New York: Harper Collins.

Pelias, R. J. (2005). Performative writing as scholarship: An apology, an argument, an anecdote. *Cultural Studies ↔ Critical Methodologies, 5*, 415–424.

Pelias, R. J. (2011). Writing into position: Strategies for composing and evaluation. In N. K. Denzin & Y. S. Lincoln (Eds.), *The SAGE handbook of qualitative research* (4th ed., pp. 659–668). Los Angeles: Sage.

Reed-Danahay, D. E. (1997). *Auto/ethnography: Rewriting the self and the social.* Oxford: Berg.

Reither, J. A. (1985). Writing and knowing: Redefining the writing process. *College English, 47*, 620–628.

Richardson, L. (2000). New writing practices in qualitative research. *Sociology of Sport Journal, 17*, 5–20.

Rohman, G. (1965). Pre-writing: The stage of discovery in the writing process. *College Composition and Communication 16*, 106–112.

Sparkes, A.C. (1996). The fatal flaw: A narrative of the fragile body-self. *Qualitative Inquiry, 2*, 463–494.

Voss, R. F. (1983). Janet Emig's "The composing process of twelfth graders": A reassessment. *College Composition and Communication, 34*, 278–283.

Warren, J. T. (2001). Absence for whom? An autoethnography of White subjectivity. *Cultural Studies ↔ Critical Methodologies, 1*, 36–49.

Zamel, V. (1982). Writing: The process of discovering meaning. *TESOL Quarterly, 16*, 195–209.

Chapter 19

Writing Autoethnography

The Personal, Poetic, and Performative as Compositional Strategies

Ronald J. Pelias

This is a story about writing autoethnography, about how autoethnographic texts might be constructed. Like any tale, it reflects its teller. I offer a narrative that reflects my own sense-making, my own biases and interests, and my own limitations. I move forward by reaching toward a number of qualitative methods (e.g., personal narrative, autobiography, lyric essay, poetic inquiry, ethnodrama, performative writing) that carry their own genre status and nuances, positioned around the headings of the personal, the poetic, and the performative, to show how autoethnography orchestrates the writing strategies of a number of other associated methods to create its texts. My aim in this rendering, then, is to provide some insights into how an autoethnography might find its form, might meet its demands.

Autoethnography, defined as the use of personal experience to explore cultural practices (Ellis, 2005; Goodall, 2000), serves as my organizing term. I could have just as easily in this telling grabbed a label other than autoethnography as the dominant term. I might have argued that autoethnography can be a productive writing strategy for writing personal narratives or doing poetic inquiry. This seemingly easy exchange gains force for me when I remember the commonalities across the various methods I call forward in this essay. Researchers using these methods have as a central concern the positioning of the self. Based in the belief that the knower and known are intricately linked, how the researcher situates the "self" becomes a rhetorical and open question, always demanding reflexivity and always carrying consequences. Researchers working with these methods also believe in the power of

Handbook of Autoethnography, edited by Stacy Holman Jones, Tony E. Adams, and Carolyn Ellis, 384–405. © 2013 Left Coast Press, Inc. All rights reserved.

the literary rendering. The literary, they trust, has the potential for putting flesh on the skeleton of abstraction, for bringing the affective into shared space with the cognitive, for revealing the human heart. Researchers operating with these methods, to list just one more shared belief, understand their efforts to be pedagogical, performative utterances that stand as lessons, available for personal, community, cultural, and scholarly use. Such commonalities make genres blur, become suspicious and difficult to nail down. Yet, schemes can have their use. I allow autoethnography to serve as my overriding frame, not only because of its current academic muscle, but also because I want to show how autoethnography might be written, in part, by borrowing from associated practices.

As my tale pushes on, my desire is to deploy the strategies I describe. In the first section, "Positioning the Personal," I share my story of coming to autoethnography, point to a few of the scholars who have influenced my thinking and the professional organizations where autoethnographic work is celebrated, and finish the section by discussing how the personal might figure into writing autoethnographic texts. In the second section, "Positioning the Poetic," I strive for a poetic voice to demonstrate the power of the lyric utterance for constructing autoethnography. I also include a series of poems based upon newspaper accounts under the title, "Our Children," to provide a picture of damaged children and their relationship to the adult world within U.S. culture. In the last major section, "Positioning the Performative," I write performatively, best when read aloud without the citational reference markings, to show how performance practices might be tapped for doing autoethnographic work. The essay completes its argument with a series of personal claims that point toward good autoethnographic writing.

Positioning the Personal: Personal Narrative, Autobiography, Personal Ethnography, Memoir, Personal Essay, Autoperformance, Mystory, Testimonio

I found autoethnography as I was searching for a way to write better performance criticism. I was disappointed that the performance criticism I encountered stripped performance of its power, failed to write into its emotional life. It offered thematic insights, historical positioning, and considerations of artistic craft, but it left out what pulled me to performance—its ability to put on display human affect, to allow audience members to enter a given world and to witness how actions carry consequences, to permit those willing to avail themselves to the lessons of an empathic encounter. I wanted to write criticism that would find its way into the heart of performance. I sought a criticism that would reveal how performance might enter into the emotional lives of audiences.

While I was on this quest, a quest that seemed far from any satisfactory completion, a colleague, Bryan Crow, came into my office with a book in his hand.

"Here," he said, offering me the book. "I know this book isn't in your area, but I thought you might like it."

I looked down and read: *Casing a Promised Land: The Autobiography of an Organizational Detective as Cultural Ethnographer* by H. L. Goodall, Jr. (1989).

"Thanks, Bryan," I said, still trying to put together why he thought I'd like this book.

"I think you'll like how it's written," Bryan added. Indeed, Bryan was right.

What I came to see was not only how an organization might be productively viewed as a culture, but also how the literary could enrich a scholarly account. Goodall's detective revealed for me how I might write performance criticism and, more generally, how I might bring affect into scholarly work. As a performance studies scholar, this insight had been right in front of me all along. I had been arguing for years that performance is a method for explicating literary texts and had been involved in the creation of personal narratives for performance. I knew, too, that performance ethnography was a powerful tool for engaging another culture. But I had not realized that the strategies familiar to me for the stage might translate to the page, might make a scholarly bid in written form. Now, this seems overly obvious and I report it with some embarrassment. I remain, however, grateful that Goodall's book was put in my hands. It changed how I did my research, and it led me to others who were doing autoethnographic work.

I remember finding Ellis's (1995) *Final Negotiations: A Story of Love, Loss, and Chronic Illness* and her edited volumes with Flaherty (1992) and Bochner (1996, 2002). I remember reading many other compelling texts: Bochner's (1997) "It's about Time: Narrative and the Divided Self," Richardson's (1997) *Fields of Play: Constructing an Academic Life*, Holman Jones's (1998) *Kaleidoscope Notes*, Tillmann-Healy's (2001) *Between Gay and Straight: Understanding Friendship Across Sexual Orientation*, Denzin's (1997) *Interpretive Ethnography: Ethnographic Practices for the 21st Century*, and more Goodall (1991, 1996, 2000)—*Living in the Rock n Roll Mystery: Reading Context, Self, and Others as Clues, Divine Signs: Connecting Spirit to Community*, and *Writing the New Ethnography*. I remember Ellis's welcoming spirit when I attended her workshop on autoethnography at the 1995 National Communication Association Convention and the excitement I felt at the First International Congress of Qualitative Inquiry (2005), hosted by Norman Denzin at the University of Illinois. I remember feeling that I wanted to be a member of this community, feeling the power of their work, feeling myself becoming increasingly committed to writing autoethnography.

Influenced by those early years of introduction, I began to see the work of my performance studies colleagues who were theorizing and staging personal narratives (e.g., Corey, 1993; Gingrich-Philbrook, 1998; Langellier, 1989, 1998, 1999; Langellier & Peterson, 2004; Lockford, 2004; Miller, Taylor, & Carver, 2003; Park-Fuller, 1995; Pineau, 2000; Spry, 2001a, 2001b) as carrying an autoethnographic impulse. The echoes between autoethnography and personal narrative are, at times, so loud that differences are drowned out. The same can be said of all the labels identified in this section's heading. What consistently comes forward with these forms is the evocative and productive appeal of calling upon the personal. Those who turn to the personal in their work are my writing guides, and they create space for how I wish to render myself on the page.

Writing the personal, I want to offer a detailed account of my human experience, stripped of pretense and equivocation. I strive for an open and raw presentation as I turn remembered fragments into narratives. I struggle, wrestling with memories, images, and glimpses of the past, hoping that they may come together, become momentarily set for my own and others' consideration. I seek to reveal the human in humanity, to show how one human life might or might not find resonance with others. As I proceed, Lockford's (2001) words stay with me:

> It is often dirty work, this digging into the rich soil of humanity. Digging into our humanity, we cannot keep the soil out from under our nails, the clay off our faces, and the sand away from the folds of our skin. We write with humility about that which makes us remember our humanity, that which makes us human. (p. 118)

This digging into the personal is what lets the self unfold, discover itself, and put itself on display. With luck and labor, the archeological effort exposes what was previously hidden and elusive and makes public the unspoken and forbidden. In such uncoverings, I begin to see myself as named, ready for inspection, as a case study calling for further inquiry. I come to understand myself in my human condition, humble, hurrying to make sense of it all.

Writing the personal demands a self available for a reflexive turn. I write examining myself in the desire to lay bare the intricacies of my experience. I endeavor to show one individual's cognitive and affective stance, to demonstrate how one individual, culturally situated, comes to some understanding. In my sense-making search, I acknowledge how I might be complicit in whatever I critique, always wanting to accept responsibility for my problematic actions and always hoping to construct alternative possibilities. This is no act of self-indulgence, narcissism, or navel-gazing, as some (e.g., Buzard, 2003; Hammersley, 2008; Hantzis, 1998; Parks, 1998; Shields, 2000; Terry, 2006) would suggest. Instead, it is, as Goodall (2000) claims, "the process of personally and academically reflecting on lived experience in ways that reveal the deep connection between the writer and her or his subject" (p. 137). The reflexive requires careful and rigorous thought, rhetorically constructed to present a personal narrative in all its emotional and intellectual capacities. Such introspection offers an intimate knowledge based upon lived experience with others.

Writing the personal, I work for an honest account, recognizing that all narratives are "partial and partisan" (Goodall, 2000). Language and experience share a slippery relationship, and no account of any experience is innocent. Even so, my task requires a personal truth, demands that whatever I say is true to my experience. I may have a different story from others. I may lack information. I may be blind to any number of things, but I always know if I am presenting claims that I know to be deceptive, corrupt, or fabricated, if I am lying. I must, if I want my personal narrative to participate in the scholarly conversation, have confidence that I am telling the truth as I understand it. Failing to do so, I become the researcher who is fudging data. I am also aware that my truth implicates others. Some tales I elect not to tell. With some tales, I try to take into account others' perspectives. With some tales, I do my best to protect the identity of those that I bring into my telling. Some tales I license others to revise or veto. All tales must be accountable to their inhabitants. Honesty and ethics are intertwined, knotted together, an imbroglio of obligations.

Writing the personal places me at risk. To share personal aspects of my life leaves me open to the evaluations of others. I am available to whatever constructions others may make of my disclosures. I remind myself, however, that I wish to be accepted or rejected on the basis of who I understand myself to be. I do not want to live a hidden life. I also tell myself that sharing intimate details of my life offers the possibility that others might find themselves in my public confessions or might discover alternative scripts, perhaps in sympathy or perhaps in opposition, for their own behavior. I recognize, too, that social and cultural rules regulating disclosive acts often serve unproductive ends. Such licensing of what can and cannot be told may keep normative practices in place, practices that may limit or harm individual agency. So, I try to write without fear. In doing so, I may in my reporting invite traumatic experiences to return, as Zingaro (2009) suggests, but I persist, believing in the power of allowing a vulnerable self to emerge. Such telling is always a personal choice, one demanding considerable reflection. Once told, it cannot be retracted.

Writing the personal, I speak from the body. I seek a "sensuous scholarship" (Stoller, 1997), a scholarship attuned to the visceral and somatic. I want affect to mark any account I might offer because the personal finds itself most fully in what it does and does not feel. My body and mind work in concert, sensing the wisdom of Gingrich-Philbrook's (2001) poetic insight: "My body makes language. It makes language like hair" (p. 3). As Spry (2011) suggests, my body functions "as a site from which the story is generated by turning the internally *somatic* into the externally *semantic*" (p. 63, italics in the original). I am my body speaking. I am a mind/body fully engaged. I am a thinking and feeling agent trying to assemble some sense of it all, trying to let the cognitive and affective guide my way.

Writing the personal carries material consequences. I recognize that words matter. They matter to me as I construct my sense of self and they matter as potential utterances in the world. I seek words that function productively, that build better human relationships, that work in behalf of social justice. I write wanting to lean in (Pelias, 2011), wanting the labor of obligation, of compassion. This positioning of the personal creates dialogic space, opens possibilities, and offers to others occasions for consideration. When successful, sharing the personal stands as a pedagogical lesson, a performative act that makes a positive difference.

I end this section in the belief that I have put forward not only my own desires when I write the personal in my autoethnographic endeavors, but that I have also articulated familiar expectations for a community of autoethnographic writers who recognize the power of the personal. Write from the heart of your humanity, be honest and self-reflexive, recognize the risks for yourself and others in your constructions, allow your body to have a speaking presence, and create a better, more ethical world. Personal narrative, autobiography, personal ethnography, memoir, personal essay, and testimonio are resonant possibilities in constructing autoethnographic accounts. The self, always situated culturally, becomes an exploratory tool, an affective and cognitive opening for cultural and critical inquiry. I stand as a member of a community of autoethnographic scholars to offer an autoperformance, a "mystory" (Ulmer, 1989, 1994), a testimony on behalf of the personal, on behalf of what marks our humanity.

Positioning the Poetic:
Lyric Essay, Investigative Poetry, Poetic Inquiry

I begin this section with a warning: The poems that follow are hard, not in the sense of difficult to comprehend what the poems are describing, but difficult to take in, to understand how such things could occur. As noted earlier, I base the poems on newspaper accounts of children and, disturbingly, most of them chronicle a horrific act done by an adult to a child. Taken together, they offer a sociological account, rendered poetically, into the world of damaged children. They unfold from multiple perspectives, including at times from the points of view of individuals who inflicted considerable harm. My intent is not to exploit or sensationalize these children's experiences. Instead, I seek a poetic inquiry that reveals the emotional cost of such events, that presents an ethnographic feel, that pushes forward the ethical responsibility that adults must carry.

Prior to each poem is a poetic fragment that can stand as an entry into the following poem and as a comment on how the poetic might work in an autoethnographic essay. This section, then, argues that the poetic and the autoethnographic can come together to speak from the heart, from the body's joys and sorrows, from the most exalted to the most tragic. They can join together to name, to write into the commonality of the human condition, to note the differences that matter.

◦

The poetic gives to the autoethnographic:

A way in, an entry into a lush labyrinth, turning and twisting on a line, curving into the center, into the heart, beating, beating its way, in anticipation, into its seductive surprises, into its delightful and disturbing displays, insisting that more be carried on the way out.

OUR CHILDREN

1.   Front Page Children

○

Caught in the midweek heat of August 15th,
seven-year-old Robby, smiling, soaks his feet
in a creek that runs through Giant City Park.
Tennis shoes and socks wait by his side
as the sun pours color into the cool stream.
He sits in the shade on a smooth rock.

Posed to announce her music scholarship to Julliard,
sixteen-year-old Michelle, master flutist,
blond hair pulled back into a no-nonsense bun,
tailored blue shirt buttoned to the top,
holds her instrument to her lips and plays.
Her hands delicate as a winter whisper.

Pictured, too, in black and white, is eleven-year-old
Ryan, ribbon falling from her hair, hands
on her hips as if ready to begin a cheer,
looking forward, looking straight ahead,
victim of first-degree murder by two boys,
ages 7 and 8, unnamed, who wanted her bike.

The boys, who hit her on the head with a rock,
who molested her with a stick, who suffocated her
by shoving her panties in her mouth, by
stuffing leaves and grass up her small nose,
who, some say, should be tried as adults, sat
in juvenile court drawing pictures and eating Skittles.

Section C, Page 9

○

It seems
it wasn't them.
It seems
the boys were
forced
to confess.
It seems
it was police

work
that made
those two black boys
front page
news.

A sensuousness, through the image into the imagination, through heard into the felt, through the touched into the known. Through and through, the body is called, caressed, claimed—body by body, body to body, a lean in, a taking on.

2.   *Her Baby*

When I put the knife
to her belly,
I almost started to cry,
knowing the baby
was so close and all.
I was wanting to hold it
so bad. So
I pulled that knife
across her,
just like I saw
on that television show,
and there it was,
dark and beautiful,
moving its little hands
into little fists.
I was glad I had
shot that girl twice
in the head,
glad she couldn't see
her with all that talk
about how she was only
seventeen and woman enough
and how I was twice
her age and didn't have none.
I took that baby,
cut it loose,
cleaned it up,
made that baby mine.
I'm a good mother,
much better than her
sassy dead self.

A language, slanted—an apple tumbling at the sight of the knife, a horse graz-
ing with a herd of cows, glass cutting into the palm of a hand—calling for a
pause, a noticing, a gathering.

3. Fix-it Man

I've seen just about everything
around here get broken.
I've been fixing things
for over thirty-eight years—
toilets, those old stairs,
falling plaster, bashed in doors,
holes punched in walls.
You learn to know people
by what they break.
6C can't keep a dish in her place
fighting with that man all the time.
12A can't control her boys
(knocked over a fridge once).
"Henry," they say, "Could you come up
and take care of a little problem?"
They know I won't report
what I don't have to.
So I fix this and I fix that.
I even try to fix them
when they start in on each other.
I patch their wounds,
wipe up their blood.
I know this is a hard place.
I've come to accept that.
But when I stood in front of that
broken window, knowing
8C's baby went flying through it,
I couldn't fix it. Oh, I know how
but I couldn't make myself move.
I just stared at those broken edges
not wanting to see what that child saw
when she came through.
I don't know who is going
to make that pane right.

A piece of evidence, visceral data supporting a case, growing in the gut, weighted, knotted, burning, insisting the rose only finds its true beauty when in company with the thorn.

4.   *Lt. Ashley's Report*

I've been on the force for twenty-three years,
worked the toughest neighborhoods,
seen things I'd rather not talk about,
seen fourteen-fifteen-year-olds
inflict unimaginable harm on each other,
but six- and seven-year-olds, girls. Seems
they were just playing with their Barbie dolls
and got into a name-calling, hair-pulling fight
over a missing Barbie shoe. I'm not sure
who was supposed to be looking after the kids—
we're looking into that—but it seems
the six-year-old told her friend she was
going to kill her, went home, returned
to her friend's apartment with a knife,
stabbed her in the back. The victim,
hospitalized with a three inch wound,
is in serious condition. We questioned
the six-year-old but because of her age,
there is little that can be done.
We released her to her parents.
At the crime scene, we found the missing shoe.
We do not know who was responsible for the loss.

A realizing, a coming together, a fighting against confusion, found by what language figures, forged with fading ink. A moment's truth, a moment's prayer, made as a present answer.

5.   *Ice Breaks*

It could have been Robbie
trapped under
with the other four
who didn't make it out.
It could just as easily have been him
frantic, under ice,
searching for the light.
He said they were taking

a short cut.
I've told him what could happen.
I watched them coming
under that winter's sun
from my kitchen window.
I was making cookies,
covering them with icing.
I saw them laughing
before they fell from sight.
By the time I got there,
Robbie was out, screaming
for the others.
We did what we could.
When help came,
it was too late.
You could feel the current
under the shining, thin ice.
It took them,
turned them greenish, gray,
too cold to call back.
I took Robbie home,
wrapped him in blankets,
threw the cookies out.
We rocked,
waiting for the ice
to break.

A perspective, an "I" standing in for an "I," a reach for the words, for the other: an owl, head cocked, listening; the moment before a gazelle's frightened run; an alligator's pretend sleep; a parrot, perched on your shoulder, saying your words.

6.   Ten-Year-Old Stops School Bus

○

No doubt about it.
He saved us,
saved me.
He's a smart kid
to stop the bus
when I went out.
It was so noisy
that morning

it's a wonder he noticed.
I had yelled at them
a couple of times,
but they were wound up—
Yap, yap, yap.
It's always that way on Fridays.
If we had crashed,
that would have shut them up.
You know what they call me—
Gus the Bus.
I know it's only kids
being kids,
but they don't need
to tell me I'm fat.
Anyway, I can't move
my left side now
and, as you can hear,
I can't speak without slurring.
He saved me alright,
but for what?
I can't even drive
those little yappers.

○

I didn't do much of anything.
Just put my foot on the brake
and pulled it to the side of the road.
I knew how from driving
my grandfather's lawnmower last summer.
The hard part was being by Mr. Graves.
His face seemed frozen, set stiff,
stuck, with those staring eyes.
I was scared about the bus,
but Gus really scared me.
I knew what to do for the bus
but not for him. I kept waiting for him
to yell at me to get off him.
Momma says he can't yell anymore.

An ethical investigation, a questioning, a balancing of one hand against another, and in that search for right and wrong, perhaps marching orders, an action that must be taken, that places one body next to another.

7. Child Molester Beaten

○

When they put him in the same cell with me
I just snapped, remembering how
he made me bend over, his strong hands
holding my hips, pulling me to him, hard,
and me in tears, pleading for him to stop,
but he wouldn't, until he was done. Then,
he took Sal, made me watch as he greased
himself and did to Sal what he did to me.
We'd be dead if he hadn't been scared off
by a noise coming from next door. He left
us naked, two ten-year-old boys, afraid
to look anywhere but down. We wiped
ourselves on the dirty sheet and used it
to cover what young boys should not know.
So, when he came in and smiled at me
like I was some friend he hadn't seen for years,
my fists tightened and I was on him, pounding
him, my flesh against his, until the bones
of his body turned soft, and blood ran.
They say it will cost me some serious time
but the way I see it, I got time back.

A tear, a joy, feelings that matter, taken in, held, guiding our lives, like a closed mouth, like a fist made, like a hand resting on another's heart, vulnerable as flesh.

8. Gwen

○

Shit, man, I didn't know.
Said he was Gwen, wearing
that dress and make-up and all.
So yeah, I was coming on to him
when I thought he was a she.
Then, I saw these guys laughing
and they told me, started
saying I was gay, a faggot.
So me and my buddies took him,
pulled that dress off his skinny ass,
showed him we're not perverts.

I got the longest time.
They say it was my kick
that cracked his naked back.
Been in this hole too long—
done four of fourteen.
Too bad he isn't in here—
we'd use him like those other fags.

○

I still can't believe what they did
to my Eddie, my sweet Eddie
trapped in that chair, unable
to move, unable to feed himself.
It always frightened me,
him dressing like that,
going out, his father yelling
as the door would close behind
his back. Now, he just sits,
waiting, hardly ever smiling,
except when his father is out.
I know what he wants:

I put him in his red silk dress,
leading one dead limb
through at a time, placing
his shoulder-length blond wig,
then, roll him to the mirror.
"Look how beautiful," I say,
rubbing rouge on his cheeks,
coloring his lips with gloss.
"Look, Gwen. Look at you."

Positioning the Performative: Performance, Ethnodrama, Performance Ethnography, Performative Pedagogy, Performative Writing

Performance, that "essentially contested concept" whose essence is found in its disagreements about its nature (Strine, Long, & HopKins, 1990, p. 183) is a "caravan: a heterogeneous ensemble of ideas and methods on the move" (Conquergood, 1995, p. 141), an "opening" (Pelias, 2010), a "placebo" (Myers, 2010), "freedom" (Ellison, 2010), "sex" (Lockford, 2010), "dissolution" (MacDonald, 2010), a "promiscuous lover" (Madison, 2010), a "hurricane burrito" (Hanley-Tejeda, 2010), always on a "collision course" (Pollock, 2010); demanding "artistry, analysis, activism," or, if you prefer, "creativity, critique, citizenship" or, if you wish another alliterative three, "imagination, inquiry, intervention" (Conquergood, 2002, p. 152) that "privileges particular, participatory, dynamic, intimate, precarious, embodied experience grounded in historical process, contingency, and ideology" (Conquergood, 1991, p. 187); located in everyday and aesthetic frames, including a "broad spectrum of entertainments, arts, rituals, politics, economics, and person-to-person interactions" (Schechner, 1992, p. 9); organized in a handbook under the headings "Performance and Literature," "Performance and Pedagogy," "Performance and Politics," "Performance and Ethnography," "Performance and History," and "Performance and Theory" (Madison & Hamera, 2006); positioned as an object of study, examined by an unending series of theoretical stances; as an explanatory metaphor for understanding, including but not limited to, utterances (Burke, 1945; Searle, 1969), human interaction (Goffman, 1959), identity (Alexander, 2006; Butler, 1990, 1993; Johnson, 2003), social dramas (Turner, 1982); and as a method of inquiry based in embodiment (Conquergood, 1991; Park-Fuller, 1983; Pelias, 2008; Pineau, 1995, 2011); all working from the fundamental assumption that bodies performing, in both everyday and aesthetic frames, carry material consequences; which reminds autoethnographic writers that their words are expressive performative acts, framed and available for others' consideration; that their artistic renderings generate imaginative possibilities; that giving themselves permission to bodily enact another may provide them with profound insights into how others move through the world; and that their accounts, when spoken from the body, truly matter:

> *or so it appears: an artistic inquiry, an intimate, somatic analysis offering the imaginable, the achievable, carried by and in the body for the contemplation of others.*

Ethnodrama and performance ethnography—this orchestrated move from field notes to theatrical presentation, this "radical act of translation" (Madison, 2006, p. 397), this "strategic method of inciting culture" (Alexander, 2005, p. 411)—insists that the aesthetic staging of ethnographic findings is a mode of scholarly representation, designed to dialogically engage audiences, or as Saldaña (2005) puts it, "to entertain—to entertain ideas as it entertains its spectators" (p. 14); assumes that "If people are genuinely interested in understanding culture, they must put aspects of that culture on and into their bodies" (Jones, 2002, p. 7), must "put experimental flesh on...cognitive bones" (Turner, 1986, p. 146); recognizes that social life, "even its apparently quietest moments, is characteristically 'pregnant' with social dramas" (Turner, 1982, p. 11); establishes this "body, paper, stage" (Spry, 2011) process laden with demands: it requires the research expertise of the ethnographer as well as the artistic skills of the playwright, director, and actor; a sensitivity to the conflictual and dramatic nature of everyday experiences or, as Denzin (2003) notes, a consciousness that "We inhabit a performance-based, dramaturgical culture" (p. x); an ethical awareness and care, a moral map (Conquergood, 1985), for the representation of one's own and others' lives; a reach beyond one's own cultural positioning to the worlds of others, a "vehicle by which we travel to the worlds of Subjects and enter domains of inter-subjectivity that problematize how we categorize who is 'us' and who is 'them,' and how we see ourselves with 'other' and different eyes" (Madison, 1998, p. 282), to name just a few requirements; which reminds autoethnographic writers of the care that must be taken as they move from the field experiences of their own lives with others to representations on the page; that writing others is always a cultural act and a cultural reach; that the aesthetic staging of their discoveries might find their fullest form in their theatrical articulation; that writing an autoethnographic account might best be conceived, not simply as act of accurate reporting, but as a task of creating an aesthetic script, of locating the drama in everyday experience, of turning autoethnographic accounts into tales that carry theatrical power:

> *or so it appears: a body facing another body, words intertwined, a jazzy waltz, a step forward, a becoming.*

Performative pedagogy, in the classroom and on the stage, is an interventionist lesson designed to critically scrutinize ongoing cultural practices, to interrupt structures of power, and to offer alternative visions for being (Alexander, Anderson, & Gallegos, 2005; Denzin, 2003, 2006, 2010; Fassett & Warren, 2007; Freire, 1992; Giroux & Shannon, 1997; Pineau, 2002; Stucky & Wimmer, 2002), is "an active intervention to break through unfair closures, remake the possibility for new openings, and bring the margins to a shared center" (Madison, 2005, p. 178), where the performing body serves "as raw data of a critical cultural story" that "reveals the *understory* of hegemonic systems" (Spry, 2011, pp. 19–20, italics in the original) to create a "politics of possibilities, a politics that mobilizes people's memories, fantasies, and desires" (Madison, 1998, p. 277) and to offer "performances of resistance" that "claim a positive utopian space where a politics of hope is imagined" (Denzin, 2003, p. 17); where performance functions "simultaneously as a form of inquiry and as a form of activism, as critique, as critical citizenship" (Denzin, 2010, p. 18); where "Pedagogical practices are always moral and political. The political is always performative. The performative is always pedagogical" (Denzin, 2006, p. 326); where "the use of emotion and the personal strives to illuminate the roots of how activism comes to life in the context of a pedagogy, my pedagogy, of love and hope" (Warren, 2011, p. 22); where students will be enabled "to construct meanings that are lived in the body, felt in the bones, and situated within the larger body politics" (Pineau, 2002, p. 53); which reminds autoethnographic writers that their accounts presented on the page or on the stage are a doing, a doing with consequences, that requires a vigilant attentiveness to the work they accomplish; that autoethnographic writing always carries pedagogical instruction, sometimes creating possibilities for social justice and sometimes not; that communicative acts, for better or worse, are constitutive of cultural logics; that autoethnographic writing guided by an ethic of care and hope moves the world, inch by inch, toward new possibilities, new visions, new structures of justice:

> *or so it appears: bodies leaning in, eyes alert, alive, learning how words matter, reassembling the assembled, loosening the glue.*

Performative writing, a writing that unfolds with an insistent fear of its own representations, often takes away what it gives, moves "nervously" on the page, slips around, indebted to its cousins the language poets and the metafictionists who playfully create spaces for play, "evocatively" leaving open the final claim, the set meaning, the question of truth; even with its ongoing troubled dance with language, in its "metonymic" relationship to experience, in its "citational" limitations, it is "consequential," material, as it keeps step with the "subjective" (Pollock, 1998); or, to use Madison's (2005) listing, performative writing is relational, evocative, embodied, and consequential; or, to tap into Spry's (2011) naming, performative writing is embodied, coperformed, evocative, and consequential; or, to share my own labeling, performative writing is embodied, evocative, partial, and material (Pelias, 1999, 2007) which, together, gather resonance, sound a clear citational reverberation, but lack the feel of performative writing, a feel poetically expressed by several performative writers in the preface to *The Green Window: Proceedings of the Giant City Conference on Performative Writing* (Miller & Pelias, 2001), a few of whom I cite here:

> Work involving wanting, asking, offering something unguaranteed, banking on the strategy or profusion to get at least one thing rooted in the future. The one thing called an image. (Gingrich-Philbrook)

> ...giving to do—to make words perform, to make texts into gifts. (Holman Jones)

> ...a blend of genres and a rupturing of boundaries; a carnival through the streets that borrows from everything it meets. (Gray)

> Performative writing composes the body into being. (Spry)

> Language is a summons. An incantation. A performative *nommo* or magical naming that call-into-being each living sensibility according to its nature. (Pineau)

> ...performative writing dances into new territory. (Carver)

> Like Pinocchio, this language refuses to be what it is, refuses to accept itself as mere wood, mere substance. It leaps forth, moves its limbs, opens its eyes, claims to live. (Stucky)

which reminds autoethnographic writers that language is nothing more than water leaking through the fingers of our cupped hands and nothing less than the best way to hold what we value; that the page is a performance, positioning its readers to decide if they are pleased with how they spent their time; that language carefully and aesthetically articulated is evocative as a literary construction and as a tactic for material change in ongoing social practices; and that to make words perform is an invitational call inviting other performative acts:

> *or so it appears: a determined doing, done and undone, daring, defying what language holds steady, a construction deconstructed, poetically rendered.*

A Final Personal Comment

I have listened as students and colleagues use many of the labels identified in this essay interchangeably, wondering if the clear genre expectancies I held for each were stable, commonly shared. I have called upon these various forms in my own work, sometimes beginning to write one thing, only to realize at the end that I had written something else. I have written pieces that I wasn't sure how best to classify. Despite this slipperiness, I remain convinced that autoethnography benefits from its acquaintance with the personal, poetic, and performative as it goes about the business of creating its accounts. Each form stands as a reminder to the others of what might be done, what slant or tactics might serve to most fully enter a subject. In short, familiarity with such practices makes available to autoethnographic writers a repertoire of writing strategies. In the end, though, the question of how a particular essay might be defined is significantly less important than what work it accomplishes. As a writer, I am most satisfied when I know what work each word, each sentence, each paragraph, each section, and each essay does.

I am most satisfied when my autoethnographic accounts are personal, exposed as a jellyfish on the hot sand, become a microscopic and telescopic pause, telling all that it can see. I'm most satisfied when I can trust what I have written, can feel its truth deep in my gut, in my heart. I'm most satisfied when I recognize the times my body deserves blame, when it needs to shake its finger at itself. I'm most satisfied when my personal life is deployed, like a weapon, on behalf of others.

I am most satisfied when my autoethnographic accounts are touched by the poetic, language their way, sentence by sentence, line by line, to the image that summons like a black hole. I'm most satisfied when I work with the rhythm of the steady traveler, always moving forward, always knowing my destination. I'm most satisfied when my lines know when to turn, when to repeat themselves, when to stand alone. I'm most satisfied when I have a firm hand on the literary as I go, as I move through logical arguments, as I make summary claims and theoretical speculations.

I am most satisfied when my autoethnographic accounts are performative, a performance on the page that plots the drama of living. I'm most satisfied when my personal experiences, my notes from the field, become poetic scripts, ready for the page or the stage, when they write others with the care I would hope they might write me. I am most satisfied when my performative acts turn my learning into instruction, clear paths of bramble that snag personal freedom and slow social justice. I am most satisfied when my words work, personally, poetically, politically.

References

Alexander, B. K. (2005). Performance ethnography: The reenacting and inciting of culture. In N. K. Denzin & Y. S. Lincoln (Eds.), *Handbook of qualitative research* (3rd ed., pp. 411–442). Thousand Oaks, CA: Sage.

Alexander, B. K. (2006). *Performing black masculinity: Race, culture, and queer identity*. Lanham, MD: AltaMira Press.

Alexander, B. K., Anderson, G. L., & Gallegos, B. P. (Eds.). (2005). *Performance theories in education: Power, pedagogy, and the politics of identity*. Mahwah, NJ: Lawrence Erlbaum.

Bochner, A. P. (1997). It's about time: narrative and the divided self. *Qualitative Inquiry 3*, 418–438.

Bochner, A. P., & Ellis, C. (Eds.). (2002). *Ethnographically speaking: Autoethnography, literature, and aesthetics*. Walnut Creek, CA: AltaMira Press.

Burke, K. (1945). *A grammar of motives*. Englewood Cliffs, NJ: Prentice Hall.

Butler, J. (1990). *Gender trouble: Feminism and the subversion of identity*. New York: Routledge.

Butler, J. (1993). *Bodies that matter: On the discursive limits of 'sex.'* New York: Routledge.

Buzard, J. (2003). On auto-ethnographic authority. *The Yale Journal of Criticism 16*, 61–91.

Conquergood, D. (1985). Performing as a moral act: Ethical dimensions of the ethnography of performance. *Literature in Performance, 5*, 1–13.

Conquergood, D. (1991). Rethinking ethnography: Towards a critical cultural politics. *Communication Monographs, 58*, 179–194.

Conquergood, D. (1995). Of caravans and carnivals. *The Drama Review 39*, 137–141.

Conquergood, D. (2002). Performance studies: Inventions and radical research. *The Drama Review 46*, 145–156.

Corey, F. C. (Ed.). (1993). *HIV education: Performing personal narratives*. Tempe: Arizona State University.

Denzin, N. K. (1997). *Interpretive ethnography: Ethnographic practices for the 21st century*. Thousand Oaks, CA: Sage.

Denzin, N. K. (2003). *Performance ethnography: Critical pedagogy and the politics of culture*. Thousand Oaks, CA: Sage.

Denzin, N. K. (2006). The politics and ethics of performative pedagogy: Toward a pedagogy of hope. In D. S. Madison & J. Hamera (Eds.), *The SAGE handbook of performance studies* (pp. 325–338). Thousand Oaks, CA: Sage.

Denzin, N. K. (2010). *The qualitative manifesto: A call to arms*. Walnut Creek, CA: Left Coast Press, Inc.

Ellis, C. (1995). *Final negotiations: A story of love, loss, and chronic illness*. Philadelphia: Temple University Press.

Ellis, C. (2005). *The ethnographic I: A methodological novel about autoethnography*. Walnut Creek, CA: AltaMira Press.

Ellis, C., & Bochner, A. P. (1996). *Composing ethnography: Alternative forms of qualitative inquiry*. Walnut Creek, CA: AltaMira Press.

Ellis, C. & Flaherty, M. (Eds.). (1992). *Investigating subjectivity: Research on lived experience*. Newbury Park, CA: Sage.

Ellison, S. (2010). Performance is…freedom. *International Review of Qualitative Research, 3*, 187–188.

Fassett, D. L., & Warren, J. T. (2007). *Critical communication pedagogy*. Thousand Oaks, CA: Sage.

Freire, P. (1992). *Pedagogy of hope: Reliving pedagogy of the oppressed*. New York: Continuum.

Gingrich-Philbrook, C. (1998). What I 'know' about the story (for those about to tell personal narratives on stage). In S. J. Dailey (Ed.), *The future of performance studies: Visions and revisions* (pp. 298–300). Annandale, VA: National Communication Association.

Gingrich-Philbrook, C. (2001). Bite your tongue: Four songs of body and language. In L. C. Miller & R. J. Pelias (Eds.), *The green window: Proceeding of the Giant City Conference on Performative Writing* (pp. 1–7). Carbondale: Southern Illinois University.

Giroux, H. A., & Shannon, P. (Eds.). (1997). *Education and cultural studies: Toward a performative practice*. New York: Routledge.

Goffman, E. (1959). *The presentation of self in everyday life*. Garden City, NY: Doubleday.

Goodall, Jr., H. L. (1989). *Casing a promised land: The autobiography of an organizational detective as cultural ethnographer*. Carbondale: Southern Illinois University Press.

Goodall, Jr., H. L. (1991). *Living in the rock n roll mystery: Reading context, self, and others as clues.* Carbondale: Southern Illinois University Press.

Goodall, Jr., H. L. (1996). *Divine signs: Connecting spirit to community.* Carbondale: Southern Illinois University Press.

Goodall, Jr., H. L. (2000). *Writing the new ethnography.* Walnut Creek, CA: AltaMira Press.

Hammersley, M. (2008). *Questioning qualitative inquiry: Critical essays.* London: Sage.

Hanley-Tejeda, D. (2010). Performance is a hurricanado burrito: An experiment with a performative mixed metaphor. *International Review of Qualitative Research, 3,* 175–182.

Hantzis, D. M. (1998). Reflections on "A dialogue with friends: 'Performing' the 'other'/ 'self' OJA 1995." In S. J. Dailey (Ed.), *The future of performance studies: Visions and revisions* (pp. 203–206). Annandale, VA: National Communication Association.

Holman Jones, S. (1998). *Kaleidoscope notes: Writing women's music and organizational culture.* Walnut Creek, CA: AltaMira Press.

Johnson, E. P. (2003). *Appropriating blackness: Performance and the politics of authenticity.* Durham, NC: Duke University Press.

Jones, J. L. (2002). Performance ethnography: The role of embodiment in cultural authenticity. *Theatre Topics, 12,* 1–15.

Langellier, K. M. (1989). Personal narratives: Perspectives on theory and research. *Text and Performance Quarterly, 9,* 243–276.

Langellier, K. M. (1998). Voiceless bodies, bodiless voices: The future of personal narrative performance. In S. J. Dailey (Ed.), *The future of performance studies: Visions and revisions* (pp. 207–213). Annandale, VA: National Communication Association.

Langellier, K. M. (1999). Personal narrative, performance, performativity: Two or three things I know for sure. *Text and Performance Quarterly, 19,* 125–144.

Langellier, K. M, & Peterson, E. E. (2004). *Storytelling in daily life.* Philadelphia: Temple University Press.

Lockford, L. (2001). Talking dirty and laying low: A humble homage to humanity. In L. C. Miller & R. J. Pelias (Eds.), *The green window: Proceedings of the Giant City Conference on Performative Writing* (pp. 113–121). Carbondale: Southern Illinois University.

Lockford, L. (2004). *Performing femininity: Rewriting gender identity.* Walnut Creek, CA: AltaMira Press.

Lockford, L. (2010). Performance is sex. *International Review of Qualitative Research, 3,* 189–192.

MacDonald, S. (2010). Performance is dissolution: (Or, the merits of Kool-Aid). *International Review of Qualitative Research, 3,* 193–198.

Madison, D. S. (1998). Performance, personal narratives, and the politics of possibilities. In S. J. Dailey (Ed.), *The future of performance studies: Visions and revisions* (pp. 276–286). Annandale, VA: National Communication Association.

Madison, D. S. (2005). *Critical ethnography: Methods, ethics, and performance.* Thousand Oaks, CA: Sage.

Madison, D. S. (2006). Staging fieldwork/performing human rights. In D. S. Madison & J. Hamera (Eds.), *The SAGE handbook of performance studies* (pp. 397–418). Thousand Oaks, CA: Sage.

Madison, D. S. (2010). Performance is a promiscuous lover. *International Review of Qualitative Research 3,* 199–202.

Madison, D. S., & Hamera, J. (Eds.). (2006). *The SAGE handbook of performance studies.* Thousand Oaks, CA: Sage.

Miller, L. C., & Pelias, R. J. (Eds.). (2001). *The green window: Proceedings of the Giant City conference on performative writing.* Carbondale: Southern Illinois University.

Miller, L. C., Taylor, J., & Carver, M. H. (Eds.). (2003). *Voices made flesh: Performing women's autobiography.* Madison: University of Wisconsin Press.

Myers, W. B. (2010). Performance is a placebo: Symbolic healing on material bodies. *International Review of Qualitative Research, 3,* 183–186.

Park-Fuller, L. (1983). Understanding what we know: *Yonnondio: From the thirties. Literature in Performance, 4,* 65–74.

Park-Fuller, L. (1995). Narration and narratization of a cancer story: Composing and performing *A Clean Breast of It. Text and Performance Quarterly, 15,* 60–67.

Parks, M. R. (1998). Where does scholarship begin? *American Communication Journal, 1*. Retrieved October 1, 2002, from acjounal.org/holdings/vol1/Iss2/ special/parks.htm.zz

Pelias, R. J. (1999). *Writing performance: Poeticizing the researcher's body*. Carbondale: Southern Illinois University Press.

Pelias, R. J. (2007). Performative writing: The ethics of representation in form and body. In N. K. Denzin & M. D. Giardina (Eds.), *Ethical futures in qualitative research* (pp. 181–196). Walnut Creek, CA: Left Coast Press, Inc.

Pelias, R. J. (2008). Performative inquiry: Embodiment and its challenges. In J. G. Knowles & A. L. Coles (Eds.), *Handbook of the arts in qualitative inquiry: Perspectives, methodologies, examples, and issues* (pp. 185–193). Los Angeles: Sage.

Pelias, R. J. (2010). Performance is an opening. *International Review of Qualitative Research, 3*, 173–174.

Pelias, R. J. (2011). *Leaning: A poetics of personal relations*. Walnut Creek, CA: Left Coast Press, Inc.

Pineau, E. L. (1995). Re-casting rehearsals: Making a case for production as research. *Journal of the Illinois Speech and Theatre Association, 46*, 43–52.

Pineau, E. L. (2000). Nursing mother and articulating absence. *Text and Performance Quarterly, 20*, 1–19.

Pineau, E. L. (2002). Critical performative pedagogy. In N. Stucky & C. Wimmer (Eds.), *Teaching performance studies* (pp. 41–54). Carbondale: Southern Illinois University Press.

Pineau, E. L. (2011). Intimacy, empathy, activism: A performative engagement with children's wartime art. In N. K. Denzin & M. D. Giardina (Eds.), *Qualitative inquiry and global crises* (pp.199–217). Walnut Creek, CA: Left Coast Press, Inc.

Pollock, D. (1998). Performative writing. In P. Phelan & J. Lane (Eds.), *The ends of performance* (pp. 73–103). New York: New York University Press.

Pollock, D. (2010). Performance is a collision course. *International Review of Qualitative Research, 3*, 203–206.

Richardson, L. (1997). *Fields of play: Constructing an academic life*. New Brunswick, NJ: Rutgers University Press.

Saldaña, J. (2005). *Ethnodrama: An anthology of reality theatre*. Walnut Creek, CA: AltaMira Press.

Schechner, R. (1992). A new paradigm for theatre in the academy. *TDR: A Journal of Performance Studies, 36*, 7–10.

Searle, J. R. (1969). *Speech acts: An essay in the philosophy of language*. Cambridge, UK: Cambridge University Press.

Shields, D. C. (2000). Symbolic convergence and special communication theories: Sensing and examining dis/enchantment with the theoretical robustness of critical autoethnography. *Communication Monographs, 67*, 392–421.

Spry, T. (2001a). From Goldilocks to dreadlocks: Hair-raising tales of racializing bodies. In L. C. Miller & R. J. Pelias (Eds.), *The green window: Proceedings of the Giant City Conference on Performative Writing* (pp. 52–65). Carbondale: Southern Illinois University Press.

Spry, T. (2001b). Performing autoethnography: An embodied methodological practice. *Qualitative Inquiry, 7*, 706–732.

Spry, T. (2011). *Body, paper, stage: Writing and performing autoethnography*. Walnut Creek, CA: Left Coast Press, Inc.

Stoller, P. (1997). *Sensuous scholarship*. Philadelphia: University of Pennsylvania Press.

Strine, M. S., Long, B. W., & HopKins, M. F. (1990). Research in interpretation and performance studies. In G. M. Phillips & J. T. Wood (Eds.), *Speech communication: Essays to commemorate the 75th anniversary of the Speech Communication Association* (pp. 181–204). Carbondale: Southern Illinois University Press.

Stucky, N., & Wimmer, C. (Eds.). (2002). *Teaching performance studies*. Carbondale: Southern Illinois University Press.

Terry, D. P. (2006). Once blind, now seeing: Problematics of confessional performance. *Text and Performance Quarterly, 26*, 209–228.

Tillmann-Healy, L. M. (2001). *Between gay and straight: Understanding friendship across sexual orientation*. Walnut Creek, CA: AltaMira Press.

Turner, V. (1982). *From ritual to theatre: The human seriousness of play.* New York: Performing Arts Press.

Turner, V. (1986). *The anthropology of performance.* New York: Performing Arts Press.

Ulmer, G. (1989). *Teletheory: Grammatology in the Age of Video.* New York: Routledge.

Ulmer, G. (1994). *Heuretics: The logic of invention.* Baltimore, MD: Johns Hopkins University Press.

Warren, J. T. (2011). Social justice and critical/performative communicative pedagogy: A storied account of research, teaching, love, identity, desire, and loss. *International Review of Qualitative Inquiry, 4,* 21–33.

Zingaro, L. (2009). *Speaking out: Storytelling for social change.* Walnut Creek, CA: Left Coast Press, Inc.

Chapter 20

Reflections on Writing through Memory in Autoethnography

Grace A. Giorgio

Memory: the act or instance of remembering or recalling; the mental faculty for retaining and recalling a past event; something remembered.

Bear witness: to show by your existence that something is true; to provide evidence for.

Memorial: an object which serves as a focus for the memory of something, someone or an event; something such as a monument or holiday intended to celebrate or honor the memory of a person or event.

I Remember

I remember. I bear witness. I memorialize. When I write. As autoethnographers, we use memory for much of our data; through memory we ground our analyses; our memories inform our epistemologies and methodologies. Memories are stored and showcased in our stories, bearing witness to life's experiences—our losses, sufferings, and sacrifices; our conflicts, healings and transformations. Our stories memorialize lives lived by keeping the past alive and imagining a better future. When I sit down to write, I remember scenes, exchanged words, rolled eyes; a smile. I remember an event from my perspective and in conversation with others, in flashes and snippets, rarely in a narrative continuum. When I sit down to write, I find the story behind the memories; I then begin to make sense of those memories, their meaning for me and for others. When I write from memory, I re-live and re-imagine, shaping my

Handbook of Autoethnography, edited by Stacy Holman Jones, Tony E. Adams, and Carolyn Ellis, 406–424. © 2013 Left Coast Press, Inc. All rights reserved.

memories into autoethnography, a suturing of lived experience with theory, memory with the forgotten, the critique of self with those of others and of culture. When we write autoethnography, we retell stories, our own as well as others'.

In many ways, we come to define and know ourselves and the world we inhabit through storytelling. Poulos (2008) reminds us that we humans "are fundamentally *homo narrans*, driven by the very roots of our co-being in telling our stories" (p. 64). Our cultures are created and transmitted through our collective memories, captured in our numerous modes of narration, of which writing is one. "Writing," as Laurel Richardson (1994) argues, is "a method of inquiry, a method of discovery and analysis," and "a way of finding out about yourself and your topic" (p. 516). Autoethnography, a form of storytelling, is a mode of inquiry that relies significantly on the author's memories of his or her lived experiences.

My autoethnographies are mostly short stories. I use my memory and imagination to create characters, settings, drama. My autoethnographies present "*traces* of the *whole* story" (Poulos, 2008, p. 64, italics in original); my memories of the lived experience build the narration in short scenes, composite characters, and truncated dialogue that represent the event without getting lost in its minutiae. The short story format confines the narration to its barest meaning—a concise rendering of lives lived and remembered. My stories capture the tension of an experience and aim to release the conflict for individual and social healing (Giorgio, 2008).

We write autoethnographies to make sense of the seemingly senseless, to deepen our understanding of self and other, to witness lived experience so others can see it, too. We bring the political and critical home through words, expressions, descriptions, remembering. Autoethnography places the author in the center of the text; the author's memory and voice, not to be parsed, not omniscient, create the story. Nevertheless, autoethnography is not memoir writing, nor is it autobiographical writing (Giorgio, 2009). Autoethnographic writing attends to the cultural and political tensions between lived experiences and their meanings and ethical concerns about representation of self and others. Autoethnographic writing (and the reading of it) challenges us to question cultural truths and institutional structures. Our writing can be therapeutic—healing (Giorgio, 2008); it can be unruly and enact change (Holman Jones, 2005). Our writing goes beyond storytelling: It enacts stories, all in need of witnessing and remembrance.

In this chapter, I explore memory as an investigative tool in the creation of our autoethnographic story making. I suggest that when writing through memory we find and create meanings and experiences of ourselves and others; we also bear witness to the lives and struggles of those who came before us. Writing from memory, we memorialize the past and present, creating new spaces for community and collective memory. As memorials, our texts keep the past alive and create hope for a better future. You may ask: How do we begin to write autoethnography? To which I reply: By closing our eyes and remembering.

An Autoethnographic Gift

May 2011

I open my email and find an invitation to write about autoethnography and memory, bearing witness, and memorial. How did the editors know I had been writing an autoethnography that was working with these three concepts? A gift, an autoethnographic gift! For two years I had been writing a short story about the house my life partner "Jake" and I rebuilt. Drawing from memories lived and told, letters and photographs given and shared, I wrote "In His Own Time: An Autoethnographic Memorial" (forthcoming)[1] to bear witness to Jake's suffering and healing and to memorialize his place in the re-building of a home and family heritage. In choosing to write this story, I enacted the possibility for creating healing and resolution from old and new family wounds; the autoethnography shows love for those who came before us and those who will follow.

When asked to write this chapter, I hesitated to use this autoethnography. Certainly, the themes were there, but could a story written from another's perspective work as a clear example of memory in autoethnography? I was working with memories, but very few were my own. And yet, the story is just as much mine as it is Jake's. Our home represents his family's history and heritage, its rebuilding, the family's survival. And yet, as an outsider to the family, the house never quite felt like it belonged to me, until I wrote the story. Although my entry into Jake's life became a part of his rehabilitation, telling his story with my voice allowed me to also heal from family wounds. Upon researching memory, witness bearing and memorial, I found several autoethnographies that helped me make sense of how these themes are explored in my authoethnography. Thus, after much deliberation, I came to the conclusion: Yes, a resounding yes! I gratefully accepted the editors' autoethnographic gift and hope you as readers will accept my gift of testimony on autoethnography and memory, bearing witness and memorial.

Memory: The Bricks and Mortar of Autoethnography

Ruins

Ruins, crumpled piles of brick, wood shards and shingles, the remains of a once grand old mansion, greeted Jake as he approached his newly purchased property. Fifteen acres long ago cut and divided, inherited and sold, from the 1,000 acres amassed by his great, great, great, grandfather, "Uncle Bert." From 40 to 1,000 in half a lifetime, homesteaded, built upon and up into productive farm ground that fed and brought prosperity to his children and his children's children. Upon Uncle Bert's death in 1893, his will divided the land evenly among his four children, his daughters included. Justice of the peace, founder and pastor of the Nackville Christian Church, a man known for his sense of fairness, Uncle Bert told all who sought his advice, "Do right no matter the consequences."

Driving his truck onto the traces of a gravel driveway, Jake noticed the yellow tape wrapped around the remains of the brick house. The house stood roofless when Jake closed on the land. His seller asking him, "What you gonna do with it? Rebuild or tear down?"

"First, I'll have to see if it can stand on its own," Jake answered.

○

"In His Own Time" tells the story of a man rebuilding a brick house, the bricks themselves holding memories of the land from which they were made and the family that inhabited the house for seven generations. The story opens with Jake finding the house already in disrepair, charred to a crisp by a fire in his absence. From these ruins he begins his journey, a journey explored in close third person, his story a tapestry of his life and family memories. Memory is the brick and mortar of autoethnography; we build the narration of lived events with what we can recall and what we forget or choose to forget. We create scenes, characters and dialogue from our memories. Chang (2008) suggests that autoethnographers "openly acknowledge your memory as a primary source of information in your research" since "personal memory is a building block of autoethnography because the past gives context to the present self and memory opens a door to the richness of the past" (p. 71). As the building blocks (or bricks) of autoethnography, memory becomes our primary data, yet memory as data is more than recall. Our mind at work, our memory, is triggered and stored in various forms. As autoethnographers, we record observations of events and conversations, we review written and visual materials; we close our eyes and remember. Our data are as varied as our stories.

A list of potential memory-data

Stories: Narrations we tell one another often of the past;

Secrets: What is known by a few but not by all to protect knowers from shame or embarrassment;

Artifacts: Photographs, letters, objects;

Transcripts: Interviews, formal and informal, written down with permission to record and transcribe, of course;

Observations: Witnessing events and taking notes (permission granted, of course);

Journals: What writer has not kept a journal of some kind at least once?

Conversations: Recalling words said, voices, tones, facial expressions.

We reference many of these forms of data as we craft our stories. To illustrate I again share a section of "In His Own Time," which provides back-story to the house and the land it sits on:

Immigrating from the German mountain tops to the new promised land, Uncle Burt's father, Christian, kept his family heading west until they settled on the Indiana plains, a cross of hardwoods and prairie grasses so tall you had to machete your way through them. In the spirit of his father, once with a family of his own, Uncle Burt moved further west to Central Illinois in 1834, seeking the prosperity Andrew Jackson's and later Martin Van Buren's expansionist policies offered white immigrants at the expense of the Indians. Uncle Burt, his wife Alice, and their four children at first joined his brother's family of five in a log cabin for two years while Burt built his family home and amassed more farm ground. Cramped quarters and only a Bible to read gave Uncle Burt extra incentive to build quickly, but not quickly enough. Tensions in the shared cabin grew by the season. The men's wives worked dutifully to get along, but still jealousies and different approaches to homemaking and childrearing made the effort stressful, especially in the second winter so cold that you only went outside for firewood. The brothers didn't do too much better. There could only be one man in the house, and age, according to Uncle Dan, the younger, could not be the deciding factor. He and his family settled in Nackville first; thus he considered himself be the household patriarch. Uncle Burt, the elder, could not wait the ten or so years it would take to build his family's home, and in the spring of 1837, he built his own cabin north of his brother's.

Jake never found the cabins; he only read about them in the family letters that rolled in from neighbors and interested parties over the years. Photographs came in periodically—the first one of the house before the east addition had been built. Shutters covered the windows and a back porch served as the summer kitchen; Uncle Burt, his family, and their belongings, a chair and two horses, on display. Despite the formality of the photograph, the family looked happy, relieved even. Home at last, the photograph seemed to say. In another photograph, most likely taken twenty years later, Uncle Burt sat in a rocking chair—his hat blown off his head just as the camera operator took the shot. Still, his family, children all grown and with children of their own, stood in front of the house now in its mansion formation; the east extension encased the kitchen where two servant girls (they looked Native American) stood. Jake wondered if they got in trouble for their intrusion—or were they like family members, like the servants his grandparents once had in their rural home—the one five miles from Nackville, an oversized farmhouse that sheltered Jake's family when hard times hit.

"Building it up or tearing it down?"

"Not sure yet, need to clean it out first."

o

This section of the story interweaves the "bricks and mortar" of memory-data on the list. I learned of the family's history through stories told to me by Jake and his family, reading through family documents, including a genealogy book, and examining the photographs and letters that family and friends shared with us over the years as we rebuilt the house. Together, Jake and I sat and read the letters and studied the photographs seeking a glimpse into the past. Each artifact indicated the import of Jake's family in the rural community it settled in the 1830s. A prominent family with wealth and stature could afford a professional photographer and servants, but as the narration indicates, the stature was squandered over the generations—a legacy that still haunts Jake and his family. Allow me to share another list of what we use memory for in our autoethnographies as I did in writing "In His Own Time."

We use memory to:

Understand who we are, our identity, how lived experiences change us;

Delve into social dynamics such as family; we discover and uncover family stories and secrets, keep the social world alive with meaning;

Help us relive traumas for healing, both individual and social;

Bear witness to events and persons so that others can view them, can understand them, can find community with others;

Memorialize a person, community or event deserving to be remembered for individual or social healing; a coming together to honor lives lived.

We come full circle while writing our texts; from memory we begin, creating meaning for others' witnessing; we enact remembering, memorializing stories not to be forgotten. As the building blocks of autoethnography, "the mortar between all events, a veritable *glutinum mundi*" (McGlashan, 1986, p. 6, italics in original), memory provides coherence between past and present, self and others, self and culture.

An Ethical Balancing Act: Unruly Memories, Forgetting and Care

Although we all have the capacity to remember, memory as an investigative tool is complex and at times unruly. It is elusive, changeable, interruptive, selective; we can choose to forget as well as choose to remember. Memory, too, can be shared and contested. Memory exists in the consciousness of the writer and the subjects, and each subject has differing vantage points framing his or her memories of the event recorded. Muncey (2005) writes, "Memory is selective and shaped, as it is retold in the continuum of one's experience, (although) this does not necessarily constitute lying" (p. 2). Memory censors and distorts past experiences, thus in autoethnography the "validity of data can be questioned" especially "when it comes from a single tool of the researcher's unbridled subjectivity" (Chang, 2008, p. 55). In autoethnography, we begin with memory but end with a story—memory and story are not the same things. We remember details of an event as moments; when we write, we thread those remembered moments together to make sense of the meaning of the experience. Bochner (2000) writes,

The purpose of self-narrative is to extract meaning from experience rather than to depict experience exactly as it was lived. These narratives are not so much academic as they are existential, reflecting a desire to grasp or seize the possibilities of meaning, which is what gives life its imaginative and poetic qualities. The call of narrative is the inspiration to find language that is adequate to the obscurity and darkness of experience. We narrate to make sense of experience over the course of time. (p. 270)

Making sense of our experiences through our memories involves acknowledging and working with the gaps, or our forgetting, of the past. Forgetting is also a part of the story making—not only do we not include moments we find irrelevant to the story's meaning, we as writers cannot recall them all. As McGlashan (1986) suggests, forgetting the past and its injuries is a form of healing and release, an essential component to sanity (p. 6). Thus, here we find some tension in working with memory as autoethnographic data: Do we aim to remember or to forget? I suggest that the dialectic between remembering and forgetting is a formal function of writing autoethnography as working with memory also involves attending to the gaps, the forgotten as well as those one wants to forget.

Straddling the dialectic of remembering and forgetting, we record our memories. As we write stories, we release memories. According to Poulos (2008), memory "holds us in a coherent life narrative" and forgetting "allows us to go on in the face of pain and loss and trauma" (p. 51). Writing of self and culture, autoethnography creates an indelible deposit for one's impressions and memories, while the act of writing is itself a form of release, not quite forgetting but a letting go. Stories shared weave "intricate connections among life and art, experience and theory, evocation and explanation... *and then let... go*, hoping for readers who will bring the same careful attention to your words in the context of their own lives" (Holman Jones, 2005, p. 765, italics mine). To let go through the act of writing, we must remember first.

And memories are unruly—sometimes ungovernable. Poulos (2008) writes,

The problem with memories is that no matter how much you try to ignore or bury them, they won't stay put. They show up in the strangest places, at the oddest times. Triggered by seemingly random events in our everyday world, the in-breaking of memory can be faint as a whisper, as nagging as an itch, as blinding as a flash of lightening [*sic*], as chilling as the Arctic wind, as breathtaking as a plunge into icy water. Or it can just sort of seep into our consciousness, like too much rain seeping through saturated ground into the edges of a basement. When memory is trauma, there is often an insistent human urge to bury it. (p. 50)

Poulos's autoethnography explores how family secrets take on life forms of their own, won't stay put, emerge and interrupt the everyday flow of living. He understands the complexity of working with memory as a tool of autoethnography. He argues for narrative and dialogic methodologies for working with such data, suggesting that "an ethics of care" (Ellis, 2007) must be applied to unearth family secrets, which hold and complicate family memory/legacies.

Certainly, writing autoethnography requires an ethical approach, one that honors and respects those we write about, while staying true to the meaning of the story. Ellis (2007) suggests, "Relational ethics recognizes and values mutual respect, dignity, and connectedness between researcher and researched and between researchers and the communities in which they live and work" (p. 4). Writing "In His Own Time" brought such concerns to the forefront for me, as my story describes a family heritage filled with successes and failures, secrets and disappointments. Much of the back-story is crafted from other family members' memories told to me and Jake. I needed to carefully attend to the past events' meanings while protecting family members' identities. Writing the story in close third person, which allows the writer and reader to observe the main character's thoughts and actions, while still being able to witness the thoughts and actions of others from their own points of view, allowed me to include "multiple reflections" (Holman Jones, 2005, p. 764) of the family events and to handle them with an ethics of care. For instance, while the narration follows Jake's life story, the story also includes the stories of the people who shaped his life, such as his mother.

The man in the family

"Your father's gone, Jake," his mother informed him with her usual matter-of-fact tone perfected in bitterness towards her marriage.

She had married well, or so she thought, when she met up with Henry in her last year of high school. Henry came from a family with money. His father owned the only department store in the midsized metropolitan area thirty miles from Nackville, where his family had settled several generations ago. Marla, Jake's mother, had never been to Nackville, but on their dates, Henry would tell her about the old mansion that his distant family still lived in, though he doubted for much longer. It had been added onto three or four times since its inception in 1848 and belonged to a tract of farmland good for raising cattle. Henry had plans of taking over the family business when his father, Oscar, retired. Not long into their marriage, when Marla had two children and another on the way, the business folded. Oscar had gambled it away and moved in with his paramour. Marla could not believe the shame she felt; but as a young mother and wife, she vowed to support Henry in his endeavors whatever they be. Unfortunately, Henry had little vision beyond the department store and the family name. Unable to secure gainful employment in the business world, he took to the road as a truck driver for a large family farm outside of town.

Marla's past didn't offer her much to stand on her own. Her mother died of alcoholism when she was three. At first, her stepfather (her mother had married twice since having Marla out of wedlock) dragged her to rodeos, but a little girl cramped his style with the ladies and soon he dropped her off with his mother, a mean spirited old woman who needed the help around the house. Escaping that house proved Marla's early life goal, and if she could do it by marrying into wealth, well then all the better. When Henry proved unable to support his growing family, Marla grew impatient and embittered. A marriage that began with bursts of affection and trust ended badly when a hen-pecked Henry packed his bags and took to the road permanently. He promised to send money and mostly he did over the years, but the large house Marla had wanted so badly only became reality when she begged her wayward husband's mother, another woman wronged by the family men, to take her and her kids in.

"You're the man in the family now, Jake. That means you have to get a job."

o

Interweaving stories from Marla's upbringing and Henry's poor choices, this scene reveals the tensions Jake grew up with without exposing his family's literal history. In working through this scene I enacted what could be called an ethical balancing act of autoethnographic writing, one that mediates and re-imagines what is remembered and told and that which is forgotten or left out with Ellis's (2007) "relational ethics of care." This balancing act attends to each person in the story with gentle yet honest treatment, keeping the meaning of the story intact, while protecting those we write about. The ethical autoethnographer attends to others carefully, respectfully, and fairly. When we use memory as our data, we must take special care to work with it critically and responsibly. Memory-work is a method that can guide our efforts.

In the 1980s, German feminist scholar Frigga Haug defined "memory-work" as a social and feminist constructivist method that bridges the gap between theory and experience. Much feminist scholarship emphasizes "everyday experience" as "the basis for knowledge" (Onyx & Small, 2001, p. 775). Onyx and Small (2001) suggest, "the very notion of our own past experience may offer some insight into ways in which individuals construct themselves into existing relations, thereby themselves reproducing social formation" (p. 774). Memory-work has been adopted by feminist researchers as a way to break down the barriers between subject and researcher by making the researcher a subject through memory-work's three phases: writing down as much as can be remembered into transcripts; collectively examining and discussing with one's subjects the recorded memories, looking for and filling gaps; and analyzing the transcripts.

I used this approach when working "In His Own Time." I listed each character from the past and present and spoke with family members about the family's history, recording and then reviewing their memories together. I then wrote the story and shared it with Jake and others in the family who wanted to read it. Sometimes, though, in my writing I have not been able to speak with my subjects, and instead I speak with others who know them and the experience to verify my impressions. In assembling the story arc, I review my notes and transcripts alone and with my subjects to maintain the ethical balance between what is remembered and recorded and written and thus read. The task of autoethnography is not to discredit the antagonist (if there is one) but to understand and elucidate his or her perspective and feelings—such an approach deepens the value of the story for writer and reader, especially if and when the reader is someone in the story.

As social and cultural critique, autoethnography investigates multiple reflections; to write the self one must be able to write others, for the self, as most critical theorists posit, is a composite of experiences and others, culture. Crawford, Kippax, Gault and Benton (1992) explain, "The underlying theory is that subjectively significant events, events which are remembered, and the way they are subsequently constructed, play an important role in the construction of the self" (p. 37). When we write from the bricks and mortar of memory, and adapt the narration for ethical balance, attending to our subjects as composites of selves and experiences, we begin to make sense of how we got here and where we might want to go next. Writing from memory also concerns how elusive our memories of our experiences truly are, for we know that our memories are inaccurate pixels shared by others who may fairly contest their accuracy. Memories are intangibles, not static as we are not static, taking shape over time and hence reshaped by following circumstances and conversations. Yet as the brick and mortar of autoethnography, when handled carefully and ethically through memory-work, our memories reflect the lived experience as a shared experience with multiple meanings and its multiple reflections.

Memory, Bearing Witness and Enacting Memorial through Bakhtin's "Eloquent I"

Thus far I have attended to memory as an essential investigative tool for the act of writing autoethnography. I have explored how memory is the brick and mortar of our stories and complicated the tensions involved in its use. Now, I would like to draw connections between memory as our data to the cultural concepts and expressions of bearing witness and enacting memorial through Bakhtin's "Eloquent I." In "Bakhtin's Others and Writing as Bearing Witness to the Eloquent 'I,'" Chikako Kumamoto (2002) reminds us of the traditional Western conception of the self: "as the unitary 'I'; the self as an essence, coherent, autonomous, fixed, unified, and normative standard" (p. 67), which autoethnography, along with poststructuralist, postmodernism, post positivist research, contests (see Denzin, 2000; Richardson, 1994). A stable, unified and knowing subject can, at times, be present in autoethnographic writing; however, autoethnographic texts themselves challenge many of our assumptions about autonomous selves in culture. For instance, "In His Own Time" presents Jake as the tale's protagonist, who confronts his demons, past and present, as he rebuilds a family home rendered as devastated as he finds himself in mid-life. Hence, Jake's journey appears solely his own, and yet, it is not, for his and the house's rehabilitation represent an entire family heritage in need of repair and hope. This is how and why I wrote the story—to find repair and enact hope—though doing so required Jake to re-establish his place in the family lineage, a long line of ancestors who expressed expectations for the family heritage as represented by the family house. In writing and reading authoethnographies, we find ourselves in others: "We can never claim the totality of one's self unless submitting to someone else's gaze and that human knowledge depends on trusting the witness of others" (Kumamoto, 2002, pp. 73–74). Hence, a multi-vocal, multi-subjective, and multi-temporal narration is less like the Western "unitary-I" and more in line with Bakhtin's "Eloquent I," which creates "an inner discourse, observing a special psychic grammar predicated on the unique writerly self-consciousness made up by numerous I's who potentially become other I's" (p. 74). Kumamoto's essay provides three I's for the writer to work with (another list):

> *I-for-myself*: My interior mind and heart; my values, needs, hopes and possibilities;

> *I and the other*: How I see myself in relation to others and how I see them; finding myself in empathy for others;

> *Other-for-me*: Sharing lived experience with another, like me or not, knowing the other sees me as also sharing the experience. (p. 72)

Through autoethnographic memory re-narration, we bring forth our awareness of the three eloquent I's: *I-for-myself, I and the other* and *Other-for-me*. Working with memory in autoethnography acknowledges the witness—the view we take of ourselves; the view others take of ourselves; and how others see us and how that vision shapes how we see ourselves and our culture, ourselves in culture, and culture in ourselves. Enacting autoethnography allows us to express Bakhtin's three eloquent I's in action. We can find ways to bear witness and enact memorial through autoethnography and Bakhtin's "Eloquent I." As bearing witness is to be present, to bear, to carry, to hold, to be physically present, writing autoethnography is to carry and hold lived experience for others to witness. As in enacting memorial, creating an object or event to help us all remember that which we do not want to forget, our autoethnographic texts as objects and events keep lived experience alive. In the next few pages, I explore several autoethnographies that take up these themes along with excerpts from "In His Own Time" to illustrate my argument. Each text, I believe, demonstrates the power of the memory-text to take the act of remembering into the social and cultural and political worlds of bearing witness and enacting memorials for others and ourselves.

I-for-Myself: Emotional Memory

We find ourselves when we use memory in our autoethnographic texts; we find our own sense of *I-for-myself*, our "inner makeup or possibility," our values, needs, hopes and possibilities (p. 72). For instance, Pelias (2008) reflects on a pastiche of memories to juxtapose cultural masculine norms with his understanding of his own body:

"White, middle-class, middle-aged, heterosexual male, a member of United States citizenry" (p. 65), the male norm. Yet, his past renders him suspect, at least in his own eyes. Pelias explores his inner make up through memories of his relationships with others and the cultural and sexual expectations of normative masculinity. He writes, "memories from family and friends, from women I have known, from the culture I participate in day in and day out have guided me into my role, led me to act in just the right way and sometimes, made me question how I've been asked to behave" (p. 72). His resistance, expressed through emotional language: *I won't tell*, meaning I know but won't share, "I won't tell how my large body may look strong but isn't" (p. 66); *I carry* the burden of the cultural and gender expectations: "I carry all those cultural images, images that say what a real man should be" (p. 71). I *see* the culture and its distortions. It hurts me as a witness:

> I see all those ads: the hairless models, their six-pack muscles rippling, sprawled on the leather sofa in their boxer shorts, surrounded by two beautiful women who are offering another a beer; the silent man, groomed to perfection, taking it all in before making just the right purchase with his American Express card; and the smiling man, alive again, after taking Viagra. I do not identify with any of these men. (p. 71)

Pelias bears witness to culture's gender making, and the distortions and disappointments they bring, opening up discursive spaces for the male struggle with body image and masculine performance. Through his memories, Pelias critiques a culture that demands the impossible, that he challenges through autoethnographic writing. Making peace with himself, he writes *I-for-myself* to bear witness to injustice to men and to self in culture.

I-for-myself can also be found in Joyce Hocker's (2010) "It's All Come Down to Me: Meaning Making with Family Artifacts," which explores the process of going through family boxes filled with letters by and photographs of forgotten ancestors, after the death of her mother, the family memory keeper. As Hocker digs into the boxes, reflecting on each artifact's relation to the present and herself, she discovers new aspects of her identity, an *I-for-myself* moment. "In making meaning for the deceased family members, I simultaneously make meaning for myself" (p. 865), she writes. She bonds with her family heritage, making peace with her place in the family. Through the process of purging and writing about the purge, a sorting through and editing of captured memories, Hocker bears witness to and memorializes her ancestors' lives. The process is a struggle for her. That which she cannot identify as meaningful must be tossed, yet she questions her arbitration of an ancestor's value to others in the family. Existentially, she asks, how else do we know where we come from? Hocker finds she can keep the memories alive for family and the future, contained in boxes for others to read and add to, including photographs of her. Further, in writing the autoethnography she keeps the memory alive, memorializing the family's past for the present and future generations.

Finding peace within herself, she writes, "I have learned more about where the streams came from that now flow through me" (p. 869), an *I-for-myself* moment.

Like Pelias (2008) and Hocker (2010), I, too, experienced *I-for-myself* when writing "In His Own Time," which while bearing witness to Jake's overcoming his own past struggles, helped me find peace with some of my own. I married Jake with the hope of being accepted as a member of the family, but as I have written elsewhere (Giorgio, 2008), this was not to be the case. Within a year of marrying Jake I began to question my decision to marry him as his siblings rejected me and he felt unable to defend me. My inner turmoil brought me back to my childhood when "mean girls" bullied me everywhere I went. Writing autoethnography has freed me to explore my "inner makeup," my values, needs, hopes and possibilities (Kumamoto, p. 72) through explorations of my memories, which have shaped my values, needs and hopes. Writing respectfully and candidly about Jake's family helped me find and nurture an inner peace necessary for well-being in a context of conflict. Although I tell the story through Jake's experiences, it is my voice that shapes the narrative and configures the characters, and I interweave my values, needs and possibilities into the text. In writing "In His Own Time" I found my voice in the family as a writer who records the family history and as a life partner who decided to choose love and joy over conflict and struggle.

I and the Other: Absent Memory

Autoethnography allows one to bear witness to memories that one may not even have within oneself but through others one knows of through family stories, memories, artifacts, even memories housed in remaining family members' bodies. Absent memory, according to Ellen Fine (1988), is a memory that one knows exists but that "is repeatedly met with the silence" of those "who transmit the wounds of suffering but not the memory" (p. 44). Margaret McNay (2009) explores how children grow up witnessing past traumas mapped on their parents' lives, their bodies, their choices and behaviors in silence and denial, the imprint of the past felt but not seen, felt but not heard, felt like a ghost's presence that leads the offspring to question what happened and how and why they escaped the trauma. In her case, McNay learns of her father's trauma of being a "home child" (p. 1182). As a home child, he along with tens of thousands of other destitute Scottish children in the late nineteenth and early twentieth centuries were placed in orphanages in Great Britain and then sent to Canada to work on farms. In her reflections on discovering the truth to her father's tragic past, never discussed, only felt and witnessed on his worn body, McNay's work with absent memory reads like Bakhtin's *I and the other*: How I see myself in relation to others and how I see them; finding myself in *empathy* with others. We observe others' silent suffering, absorbing it in our own quiet, making sense of ourselves in relation to another's emotional wear and tear. We sense the traumatic event when we are with the other, and know we can never fully understand it and should not re-create it by experiencing it. Yet re-creating it through writing many of us do. For instance, many holocaust writers, according to Fine (1988), "have inherited the anguish, yet at the same time feel excluded from a universe they can never know" (p. 41). Thus, these writers "imagine an event they have not lived through, and...reconstitute and integrate it into their writing—to create a story out of History" (p. 41). Like these holocaust texts, autoethnographies can "present memory as absent" (p. 50), bearing witness to others' pain as a way of saying that one "will never know and, at the same time, must not forget" (p. 56).

When writing from absent memory, we inhabit the space of another's past. In doing so, we can make sense of the past and its effects on the present. Certainly, I wrote "In His Own Time" from absent memory. I first noticed traces of Jake's family's difficulty when I met him. A handsome man in his late forties, sometimes his visage suddenly turned from light to dark. As I came to know him and his family, I noticed each person carried the heavy weight of their ancestors through shadowy faces, burrowed frown lines, slumped shoulders. Over time I learned how each family member feels an obligation to maintain the family heritage and reputation, but struggles to do so, given modern life's complexities. The following scene, drawn from family letters sent to each other, shows how desperate the family has been to keep up with its heritage. Set several generations ago, we witness a family member's call to keep the family and house intact:

Do not destroy this house

Of the fifth generation to have lived in the old house, Jake's Great Aunt Carrie was preparing to die in it like her ancestors before her. She had witnessed the family's growth into prosperity and was now seeing the chimera of such success: Oscar had disgraced the family; Henry hit the road leaving his family behind, and Abby, the big man of the family, was turning out to be a real ne'er-do-well. The house still stood tall in the farming community, but the land had been divided up so many times that there was nothing left for it to compete with the burgeoning industrial farms taking over the countryside. The New Deal had been meant to help family farms, but over time, the need for price controls for affordable food and affordable farming led to a concentration of resources, dependence on tractors and other expensive machinery, and government subsidies. Carrie's family was no longer in the farming business; it was scattered among the smaller and large towns of Central Illinois. The automobile allowed for this—it brought the far away closer and yet kept the far away just that out of range. Carrie could remember Uncle Burt, though she was quite young when he died. She could remember his death—in the east room, he was confined to bed for weeks on end, still chatting with those who would visit, offering advice and helping to settle disputes. She, like her siblings and parents, wondered how the house and community would fare without Uncle Burt to guide them. In his lifetime Burt had founded and built a church, become the local pastor, and married just about every young couple in town. He was the glue of the community—holding it together with his kindness and joviality. With his death, Carrie feared that should the house go, the family would also go.

"Barbara," Carrie begged her child, "while I'm alive do not destroy this house."

Upon Carrie's death, the house was sold to a farmer related to the family through marriage. The sixth generation to live in the house eventually left it for a nursing home in the late 1960s.

○

Writing the story from absent memory allowed me to experience Bakhtin's *I and the other,* as I related my witnessing of and relationship to Jake and his family's history by looking "to those others, projecting my self into him and experiencing his life from within him, [and] come to see myself and to know what he experiences" (Bakhtin, cited in Kumamoto, 2002, p.72). I projected myself into Jake's experience, his losses and successes, understanding better his life and my place in the family. As the excerpt above suggests, for Aunt Carrie the house represents the family's survival. Hence, when the house deteriorates, the family does as well.

In helping Jake rebuild the house and then writing about the experience, I claimed a place for myself in the family heritage.

Other-for-Me: Cultural Memory and Enacting Memorial

Ellis and Bochner (2000) describe autoethnography as connecting the personal to the cultural; in many ways we write our stories as cultural memories. Cultural memories are shared reflections of events past; wars, genocide, mass rapes, uprisings, occupations, for instance, are cultural memories societies may bear. Cultural memories also hold our collective triumphs such as the extension of rights, the expulsion of tyrants, the celebration of heroes and heroines. We often pay tribute to such persons and events through enacting memorial. Memorial is generally defined as an event, display, holiday or shrine that pays tribute to those who served and sacrificed for others, those who suffered for us so we can live better lives. Memorial insists that we don't forget the past while helping us understand our own present place and time in relation to that past.

As autoethnographers working with our own memories, we can conjure up the collective memory, the cultural memory of an event or time past, to enact memorial collectively. In doing so we experience Bakhtin's *Other-for-me* through sharing lived experience with another; like me or not, knowing other sees me as also sharing the experience. Autoethnographic writing can enact memorial by creating texts that imprint our collective experience and memories for the present and future. Such texts allow us to see how sharing a lived experience shapes who we are, as individuals and as a culture, creating sites for cultural memory to be witnessed and remembered.

For instance, Cynthia Dillard (2008) writes her autoethnography from memories recorded in her journals written while in El Salvador in 1987. While "personal journal writing provides a way to capture life at a given moment in time" (p. 85), it also allows her to reflect on the past, a time when she joined others from her church to travel to the war zone. Dillard's autoethnography pays tribute to and keeps alive the cultural memories of the El Salvadoran War. Her journals and her reflections describe the suffering endured and sacrifices made by Salvadorans during the war: "Heard stories yesterday all day that were heartening and disheartening at the same time. *'Prison is the reality of this country.'* That's from a father whose son had been tortured and killed" (p. 91, italics in original). Dillard's journals also capture the spiritual and communal strength of the Salvadorans and her connection to them. During a march, she finds herself singing a momentous song with her Salvadorian friends, "How powerful of a connection this was for me, having sung this song all of my life in English in the U.S. Now, in Spanish, I sing along my Salvadoran sisters, bearing witness to their losses, our losses" (p. 93). In bearing witness as an activist, a journal writer and twenty years later as an autoethnographer, Dillard enacts memorial of a time and struggle not to be forgotten, so as to create and extend community understanding and respect.

Her journals also show her journey as coming to witness how others perceive her and, thus, how she comes to know herself better in the context of another country. After the march, Dillard reflects on her presence in the Salvadoran struggle as an African American woman traveling in a country where Black people are not allowed to live. "I suppose it's okay for us to visit???" (p. 90, question marks in original), she sarcastically questions the country's entrenched institutional racism. Becoming aware of how others in her group as well as her Salvadoran sisters and brothers see her, she further writes, "Now I understand why I am the 'star attraction' amongst the group since we arrived! Black folks are absent on purpose. My pelo (hair) is a big deal" (p. 90). Her indignation, however, eventually makes way for encouraging thoughts on how African Americans have laid the path for others to overcome tyranny. "Black people have been influential in changing the world in revolutionary ways" (p. 93), she writes, expressing pride in being who she is in relation to the others around her at that moment. Reading as Bakhtin's Eloquent I *Other-for-me*, her thoughts reflect "the lived experience of this particular and unique other human being, a way of others seeing my self and my self theirs" (as cited in Kumamoto, p. 72). She witnesses herself in others as they also see her. Through her connection with the people in a time not to be forgotten, Dillard discovers aspects of herself while honoring the lives lived and sacrificed by others. Her journals and her analysis of them capture a self in formation in the context of other, of culture unfamiliar, culture under attack, a culture and past not to be forgotten.

Although I am not featured in the story until its close, I, too, experienced self in formation in the context of other, *Other-for-me*, as I wrote "In His Own Time." *Other-for-me* is the new family I became a part of, a rural family whose roots are vastly different from my own; other-for-me is also the ancestors I came to know through the artifacts I sifted through and the memories told to me by Jake and his family. I witness myself in the shared experience of rebuilding a family home and heritage with others, through sharing lived experience with another, like me or not, knowing other sees me as also sharing the experience. As the story comes to a close, I include a scene that introduces me as a contributing member of Jake's and the house's repair:

Let the house decide

In mid-March, with the promise of spring right around the corner, Jake returned to his property ready to work. This year he would enlist the help of his children, his sisters and brothers-in-law, and friends. He also had a new friend of his own, Gigi, a younger woman who taught yoga at a local studio in town. Intrepid by nature, she was ready to learn to cling to scaffolding like a monkey and use her yogic concentration to steady wood sheets as Jake hammered and sawed. By late spring, after most of the exterior tuck-pointing and the east wall reinforcement had been placed, the house was ready for load-bearing walls to support the second story and then the roof. The summer was hot—but nothing that turned the work crews away. Often they camped; sometimes they rented rooms from the bed and breakfast down the road.

By fall, the house was ready for trusses for the roof. That weekend offered crystal clear skies for seeking falling stars to make more wishes upon. The group gathered around a fire, roasting dogs and drinking beer in the fashion of days long gone by the pool. Gigi asked Jake to walk with her to the house.

Once inside, she looked up and said, "It's a shame we'll have to cover the sky with a roof. Wouldn't it be nice if it could have a glass roof? Like a skylight?

Jake reached his arms for her tiny waist; Gigi fell into his arms like a cat into a basket—seeking warmth and security all at once.

"Once the roof goes, the house follows," he told her.

As they emerged from the house holding hands, faces alit by the fire, Kelsey asked her dad, "After we get the roof on, what're you going to do with it, Dad?"

"Yeah, what comes next, Jake?" his sisters and friends asked.

Jake looked back at the house, and then to the gathering, "Donno. I guess we'll have to let the house decide."

The story closes with the promise of new possibilities for the house and the family legacy; I find myself and my place in that promise, for in writing the story I hoped to enact a renewal for home and family. Since finishing and moving into the house, Jake and I have flourished and the next generation is beginning to take interest in the land; the family heritage, like the house, restoring in its own time.

Beginning to Remember

This chapter has offered reflections on memory as an investigative tool for writing autoethnography as well as how autoethnographic writing allows us to bear witness to and enact memorial of lives lived and events not to be forgotten. I have explored the tensions involved in such endeavors, our need to forget, along with the unruliness of our memories, and the ethical balance we as autoethnographers must bring to our stories. I have examined several autoethnographies that attend to such concerns through Bakhtin's "Eloquent I," which I believe is well suited for the complex work of autoethnography with its focus on how we perceive ourselves through self and culture, self and other, and as other sees us. I have drawn from my autoethnography "In His Own Time" to also illustrate how memory, bearing witness, and enacting memorial are all possible in autoethnographic writing. Autoethnography, like restoring an old house, offers us the chance to re-imagine and re-invent lived experiences of our own and others.

Note

1.   Excerpts from "In His Own Time: An Autoethnographic Memorial," to be published in *Qualitative Inquiry* 19.2, reprinted with permission.

References

Bochner, A. P. (2000). Criteria against ourselves. *Qualitative Inquiry, 6,* 266–272.

Chang, H. (2008). *Authoethnography as method*. Walnut Creek, CA: Left Coast Press, Inc.

Crawford, J., Kippax, S., Gault, U., & Benton, P. (1992). *Emotion and gender: Constructing meaning from memory*. London: Sage.

Denzin, N. K. (2000). Aesthetics and the practices of qualitative inquiry. *Qualitative Inquiry, 6, 256–263.*

Dillard, C. (2008). A whole sense of self, a whole sense of the world: The blessings of spirituality in qualitative research and teaching. *International Review of Qualitative Research, 1,* 81–102.

Ellis, C. (2007). Telling secrets, revealing lives: Relational ethnics in research with intimate others. *Qualitative Inquiry, 13*(1), 3–29.

Ellis, C., & Bochner, A. P. (2000). Autoethnography, personal narrative, reflexivity: Researcher as subject. In N. Denzin and Y. Lincoln (Eds.), *The handbook of qualitative research* (2nd ed., pp. 733–768). Thousand Oaks, CA: Sage.

Fine, E. (1988). The absent memory: The act of writing in post holocaust French literature. In B. Lang (Ed.), *Writing and the Holocaust* (pp. 41–57). New York: Holmes and Meier.

Giorgio, G. (2008). The wedding dress. *Qualitative Inquiry, 15,* 397–408.

Giorgio, G. (2009). Traumatic truths and the gift of telling. *Qualitative Inquiry, 15,* 149–167.

Giorgio, G. (forthcoming). In his own time: An autoethnographic memorial. *Qualitative Inquiry.*

Haug, F. (1987). *Female sexualization: A collective work of memory* (E. Carter, Trans.). London: Verso.

Hocker, J. (2010). It's all come down to me: Meaning making with family artifacts. *Qualitative Inquiry 16,* 863–870.

Holman Jones, S. (2005). Autoethnography: Making the personal political. In N. K. Denzin & Y. S. Lincoln (Eds.), *Handbook of qualitative research* (3rd ed., pp. 763–791). Thousand Oaks: Sage.

Kumamoto, C. (2002). Bakhtin's others and writing as bearing witness to the eloquent "I." *College Composition and Communication, 54,* 66–87.

McGlashan, A. (1986). The translucence of memory. *Parabola: Myth and the Quest for Meaning, 11,* 6–11.

McNay, M. (2009). Absent memory, family secrets, narrative inheritance. *Qualitative Inquiry, 15,* 1178–1188.

Muncey, T. (2005). Doing autoethnography. *International Journal of Qualitative Methods, 4,* 2–12.

Onyx, J., & Small, J. (2001). Memory-work: The method. *Qualitative Inquiry, 7*, 773–786.

Pelias, R. (2008). Making my masculine body behave. *International Review of Qualitative Research, 1,* 65–74.

Poulos, C. N. (2008). Narrative conscience and the autoethnographic adventure: Probing memories, secrets shadows and possibilities. *Qualitative Inquiry, 14,* 46–66.

Richardson, L. (1994). Writing: A method of inquiry. In N. K. Denzin & Y. S. Lincoln (Eds.), *Handbook of qualitative research* (pp. 516–529). Thousand Oaks, CA: Sage.

Chapter 21

Mindful Autoethnography, Local Knowledges

Lessons from Family

Jeanine M. Mingé

It is a triple crisis, a triple threat, a triple crown of thorns: representation, legitimation, and praxis. These crises, which mark and coincide with a turn toward interpretive, qualitative, narrative and critical inquiry in the human disciplines, are summoned in an oft-recited line in a familiar play: How much does a scholar know, how does she know it, and what can she do with this knowledge in the world? (Holman Jones, 2005, p. 766)

Holiday Season, 2011: In Pennsylvania

I am at the long brown kitchen table in my older sister's house in the middle of Pennsylvania. The cold and dreary clouds release steady drops of rain. My nephews fixate on the origami set and the newly downloaded game on the iPhone. My sister rests on the couch after three long days of preparation for our arrival. My brother-in-law types an email on his computer. My mother laughs and hugs my baby niece. My family members, here—in the middle of dreary Pennsylvania—*are* my home.

As I listen to the two boys banter, I am pulled into the tug-of-war of childhood demands: for stimulation, for imaginative dreaming, for careful attention without overindulgence. I am pulled into the movement of family, of our family values.

It's been a while. I live on the West Coast, alone.

My nephew Owen asks me, "When are you moving closer Aunt NiNi?" I kiss him on his tiny cheek and say, "I'm not sure my darling. It depends on work." I know it isn't enough of a response, but to be honest, I don't know if I am ever moving back to

Handbook of Autoethnography, edited by Stacy Holman Jones, Tony E. Adams, and Carolyn Ellis, 425–442. © 2013 Left Coast Press, Inc. All rights reserved.

the East Coast. Out of the corner of my eye I can see Ryan, my other nephew, lift his head from his Gameboy to listen to my response. He drops it, sullen and quiet. It is, for me, a bittersweet reunion. Another year will pass before I see them again.

I walk over to Ryan and put my hand on his ten-year-old head. I kiss his light brown hair and say, "I love you. You are the best nephew ever." He smiles and says, "I love you, too." I know my family is lucky. We have parents who are still together after forty-six years and who actually still love each other.

This holiday time spent with my biological family reminds me of the interlocking and interwoven make-up of academic families. As academics, we are part of a disciplinary kinship, a chosen family. And within these chosen families we are raised within belief systems. We are also acculturated into a system of understanding, family values, and methodological approaches. And even though we may physically live across the world, we speak to each other almost daily, challenging systems of thought, methods of approaching understanding or capturing the truth. Some families focus on the objective, some the subjective, and some seek to balance the objective and subjective in mixed marriages. Some families are nurtured to have a critical eye, others to focus on uncovering or discovering the Truth. In my academic family, we realize that the truth is messy, subjective and slippery; that there are as many truths as there are beliefs. In my family, we know some kinds of knowledge are more privileged in the academy than others. We also believe this inequity has a detrimental effect on historical perspective as well as on cultivating or crafting futures. This inequity silences some voices while it privileges others. This silencing leaves too many stories untold. Because of this silence, lives are ignored, histories are not told from a balanced perspective, and too many people are voiceless.

My nephews begin to argue over whose turn it is on the iPhone. I am reminded of academic squabbles over method and our approaches to generating knowledge. I hear my niece call in a high-pitched plea, "Mama. Mama. Mama," until my sister turns from her pot of turkey soup and picks her up. I think about academic legitimacy. I look at my father resting with arms folded on the green couch. My mother crosses the carpet floor and hands him a cup of coffee. He thanks her and she kisses him on the cheek. I think about family values.

I pad on slippered feet into the living room, and my father, a clinical psychologist and professor, asks me about my research. My mother urges, "Oh yes, please tell us. We are all just so curious." Over the cacophony of child voices and parental negotiations, I begin to speak about my current research—the book, this article, my collage art, and the beginning stages of a performance script. I hear myself narrate my work and my passions, the fusion of arts-based research, performance, and autoethnographic texts. I watch as my father's lips purse, but not too tightly. I hear echoes of the critique that autoethnographers are constantly trying to please the academic patriarch; that we want daddy's approval (Gingrich-Philbrook, 2005). I want both of my parents to be proud. I smile and respond to my actual mother and father, "My work is coming along. The book is in final round of reviews. I'm also working on a handbook chapter on autoethnography."

Ellis (2004) defines autoethnography as "writing about the personal and its relationship to culture. It is an autobiographical genre of writing and research that displays multiple layers of consciousness" (p. 37). According to Wolcott (2004) the term autoethnography was first used to describe a method of ethnographically studying a group of which you are a part. Today, autoethnography encompasses a multitude of approaches and writing forms, such as Crawford's (1996) personal ethnography, Ellis and Bochner's (1996) reflexive ethnography, Ellis's (1996) emotional sociology, Wolcott's (2004) ethnographic autobiography, Ronai's (1995) layered account, Denzin's (2000) experiential texts, Fox's (2010) Autoarcheology, and Reed-Danahay's (1997) autobiographical ethnography. Each of these approaches, while it may not be characterized as solely autoethnographic, implements elements of the autoethnographic method. These methods focus on the self-narrative, or autobiographical voice, within social context.

My father is a dedicated quantitative researcher and applied behavioral psychologist. He insists, "I am sick of the postmodern. How many more stories do we need to tell?"

In a huff of defiance, I almost begin to defend my position through the immature slander of the other forms of research. But I stop and think about it. There is no reason to slander or point fingers. I will not use this opportunity to seek my father's approval but instead use this moment to clarify my own connections to this method of research and to my own academic family. Perhaps my biological and chosen families outside of the institutions of higher education can help me sketch what I understand to be both important and troubling work. My father's questions ask me to articulate the qualities of and concerns about the autoethnographic methods, epistemologies, products and processes, the aesthetic and the textual, the loss of the literary that has tainted the ability for autoethnographic research to flourish (Gingrich-Philbrook, 2005).

I visit my families—biological, academic, and chosen—to explicate how autoethnographic writing attends to, is, and creates knowledge. Autoethnography creates knowledge through relational—familial—connections, focuses on local action, and attends to sensory details. I frame this writing during the *Holiday Season of December 2011* to mark the celebratory, everyday of interpersonal relationships (Pelias, 2011), the mundane (Holman Jones, 2005), or ordinary affects (Stewart, 2007) in autoethnographic research. As I write from the *Holiday Season,* I also move back and forward in time to moments in my past with my biological, academic, and chosen families that help to explicate the complex nature of co-constructing knowledge in and through autoethnography.

My father asks, "So, what did you learn while writing about Los Angeles?"

I smile and say, "Methodologically, my work on the sexual terrains of Los

Angeles taught me about the intersection of arts-based processes, products, and autoethnographically writing down the bones of the complexity of an embodied community experience (Mingé & Zimmerman, 2012). Like our family interactions, writing about Los Angeles taught and continues to teach me about the importance of local action—actions that take place where we live and exist daily—and the ways in which we cultivate or possibly destroy relationships in and through minute daily interactions. It taught me that place, where the communicative act is happening, is as important as the act itself."

And here, in this autoethnographic text—away from my biological family and living in Los Angeles—I revisit family stories about a research practice that attends to sensory discourses, local concerns and mindful action. Arts-based practices ask us to focus on the visual, aural, the written and the tactile in autoethnography. It is the practice of attending to the performance of the body in the making and doing of community art that contributes to the cultivation of and is mindful of action. Our mindful actions cultivate, take apart, and refigure kinship systems and familial ties. Our mindful actions in both our academic and daily life families are what create and perpetuate our relationships and our understandings of knowledge, of truth and value. In the act and art of *doing* in context we make sense of ourselves and others in the world.

Focusing on the varying forms of family highlights important conundrums and dissonances between theory and practice, the collaborative nature of community building, and the seemingly solitary practice of writing autoethnographically. I tell my family—tell you—that as autoethnographers we should experiment in our research processes, expand our methodological breadth, open ourselves to tactile and action-based research, and engage in arts-based research experiences. Autoethnography is a method for creating change in the world through community building and local action, through focused attention on the present moment in the contexts closest to us. And as a family member, I offer these six epistemological lessons so we, as a family, can learn and grow—together.

A Familial Approach to Autoethnography: Six Epistemological Lessons

Each of my families has taught me a few epistemological lessons.

- First, realities and knowledges are messy, complex, and multiple.

- Second, as part of a whole, we construct these knowledges from a particular point of view within a particular context.

- Third, as we experience the world with our senses, we should also share worlds with sensory—aural, aesthetic, visual, and verbal—discourses.

- Fourth, knowledge construction is rooted in local contexts and actions.

- Fifth, we enact change and create knowledge through mindful action. We do create change, each and every day; with every decision, each movement, each action, we are impacting one another. We are and should be mindfully acting, in community (Holman Jones, 2005).

- Finally, the future challenge for autoethnographers is to expand our methodological processes, to do more in our research processes, to expand our knowledges from our personal stories to creating and making knowledges, and to expand not only our research process, but ourselves, in the doing of research.

Each of these lessons begins with the storied, local moment from each of my families. From these autoethnographic moments, I move into how each moment is an epistemological lesson. From these lessons, I learn, transform, change, and learn again.

1. Realities and knowledges are messy, complex, and multiple.

My sister turns on a sing-along song. I watch as my sweet niece dances in her rainbow tutu. She smiles and claps her hands. I smile at her and she giggles back. My sister walks over and hugs me and says, "I am so happy you were able to get here. We miss Aunt NiNi." I am overjoyed, grateful for our family. I am thankful that our strained past has shifted and changed. I think back to a time when my sister and I did not agree about… well, anything.

○

In the middle of Disney World, the happiest place on earth, I'm not happy. I want to get outta here, away from the oversaturated consumption, away from children screaming for empty pleasures. And my sister is criticizing me, again, for my choices in life, for my new serious relationship with a woman, for the big tip I wanted my mother to leave at the table for the waiter. She pushes her stroller towards me with anger on her lips and she fires out the words, "I don't want you to go with her. I don't think she is right for you, OK? Who are you right now? Who are you? I don't think you should go with her."

"Whatever. You just don't want me in a lesbian relationship." I dismiss her far too easily and try to walk away.

She follows and continues, "Are you serious right now? I'm just asking you to not walk away from me. Don't leave with her."

"Whatever you think, Sis. Tell me what you really think," I challenge her with snide despondency and then slowly turn from her. I know this is going to piss her off. It does. She pounces.

"Fine. You want me to say it? You are going to hell. And as your sister, I just want you to go to heaven with me."

I storm towards her, "Are you serious right now? I'm going to hell? Great. Yes, leave me there burning."

With years of sibling rivalry on her breath she says, "You never supported me. You were always too busy. Too cool. Whatever. Do you remember when Oreo died? And I came to tell you? I looked for support and all you did was laugh at me and tell me I was stupid for caring about our dog. You always act this way. Aren't you my sister? Why can't you treat me like family?"

Figure 21.1 Sisters.
Photo courtesy of author.

I listen to her truth, her reality, her pain, and I realize I wasn't the best sister. We are only one year apart and throughout our childhood we lived like twins (see Figure 21.1). We loved and fought like two close siblings would. I know I could have been better at… well, everything.

○

She is a devout Christian. I am a queer woman. She did not feel quite right about my sexual orientation or my past serious relationship with a woman. I felt hurt by that. I assumed our realities were/are not aligned. However, over time and collision, confrontation and permutation, we have come to a place of mutual respect and admiration. Our family values are stressed and distinct, and yet our messy and complex realities have shifted. As part of this family, as we intersect lives, we change.

Being a part of a family that is complex and complicated taught me about the messy and multiple intersections of knowledges and truths. I have learned that the individual is a de-centered subject, culturally inscribed/constructed, contradictory, and relational (Arber, 2000; Lather, 1991). Experiences create and co-create knowledges that aren't so cut and dry (Gale & Wyatt, 2006). My sister's truth about heaven and hell, God's will and punishments is not my truth. My truth rests in the spirit and nature and being part of an ecological whole, with love, light, and kindness as guiding principles. Similarly, love and grace are certainly part of her truth. She is the kindest woman I know. The elements of our truths, when mixed together, shift—what each element is and can become. Autoethnography allows these truths to be articulated and changed, told and retold, shifting and mutable. As we experience the world, we change. As we change, we change our worlds. Autoethnography leaves room for these multiple, changing and shifting truths. And point of view is everything.

2. We construct knowledges from a particular point of view within a particular context.

I call her on the phone to ask about this story. I can feel my voice get scratchy and my nerves jump a bit. I ask, "I wanted to ask you about the story. I wrote a little bit about the kids. It's a sweet story about them, about our car rides. You know that ride we took when CeCe pointed to the moon?"

"Sure, I don't mind about that."

"What about us? I wrote about how your religion and my sexual orientation did not quite line up. I wrote about Disney World."

"It was never about that, Jeanine. It was about the fact that she bossed you around. And it was about the drinking. Remember, her driving drunk with you in the car? None of the family wanted to say anything but I did. That's why we had that blow up at Disney World. You just weren't yourself anymore."

"Oh. I thought you didn't want me to be in a lesbian relationship."

"Well, I'm not going to say I'm 100 percent comfortable with that, but I was always nice to her. Matt and I both were. We just didn't like the way she treated you. You weren't yourself anymore. You shrunk."

I hang up the phone and my reality shifts; I am grateful for our blow-up at Disney World.

Context and point of view play an ever-important role in the knowledges shared in the autoethnographic story. As an autoethnographer, I work in context, focusing in on how place, products, and people create and cultivate knowledges in relational experiences. The personal here is in conversation with and is situated within social, political, and cultural contexts (Holman Jones, 2005). Context is place, space and time, local detail, moment-to-moment interaction situated within the personal and the cultural. I thought my sister was persecuting the relationship for being homosexual. I thought she was criticizing me for not following Christian beliefs. I thought she was yelling at me for being me—queer and in love. My sister thought she was trying to save me from a bad relationship. She didn't want me to get in the car with someone who had been drinking. She didn't want me to be in a relationship that wasn't healthy. She watched my relationship from the outside and wanted to protect me from it.

Knowledge is subjective, deeply connected to the knower, and is known in context. And my reaction as writer to this argument is also situated in context, in time, and through my point of view. I recognize that the complex relationship I have with my sister frames the moment and how I write about it. Autoethnography turns the "ethnographic gaze inward on the self (auto), while maintaining the outward gaze of ethnography, looking at the larger context where self experiences occur" (Denzin, 1997, p. 217). Like Denzin, I am aware of how my point of view as autoethnographer frames and articulates this story, how I make sense of and am impacted by my sister's and her husband's religious beliefs.

If I had written this story of my sister and me in the middle of Disney World without asking her about it, my point of view would have been different. I would not have been as understanding, or viewed this act of her yelling at me in the middle of park with such gratitude. I would have been and would have continued to be dismissive, angry, dejected. Our strained relationship, at that time, would have influenced how I view our relationship now. Over time our relationship has grown in love and understanding. And as I write this story I know it isn't the only way this story could and can be written. Understanding perspective, taking on a point of view, unpacking complicated commitments—for both ourselves and with others—is essential in autoethnographic work. Each of us is embedded in multiple realities that are shifting and changing. Our story, however real to us at the moment, will change over time, memory, and distance.

I am only one part of my academic family, one person out of many, writing "highly personalized, revealing texts in which authors tell stories about their own lived experiences, *relating the personal to the cultural*" (Richardson, 2000, p. 931, italics mine). I am embedded within the politics, the people, and the moments of day-to-day interaction of my own personal and political life. I cannot separate my self from the research project but also know the important value and worth of each individual, each particular point of view that makes up this family. And as part of our family, each of us is changed as we listen and grow, make choices, and take on or dismiss beliefs as we intersect and co-create knowledge.

Autoethnography creates space for the messiness of multiple truths; the seemingly incompatible coexist, together. For my sister and me, there are things that supersede our ideologies and principles—things like love and family connection. These principles are what hold us together today. And as part of a family, I want to share my world with her and with all of you. I want to share my world, this shifting point of view, in the moment, in ways that engage you fully—with all of your senses—so that you hear, feel, smell, and touch the things that hold us together. I want to write these stories in and through sensory discourses.

3. As we experience the world through and with our senses, we should also share worlds with sensory—aural, aesthetic, visual and verbal—discourses.

I type on this laptop, sitting on a red Adirondack chair above dusty ground. I sip my sparkling wine and inhale. I watch as the neighborhood peacock struts across the land. His long plume of feathers drags behind his bright blue body. He stops and cocks his head to the side, weighing whether or not my gentleman of a dog, Miles, will lift his. Miles doesn't. The heat seems to have slowed his body, and the dust is way too cool to be left for this bird. Mr. P. walks onto my landlord's front porch (see Figure 21.2). He squawks his arrival and waits for the shower of seeds to be released by her hand.

Miles is up with a growl, then a bark. Shelby, his wolf-breed girlfriend, runs up the drive, past Miles and into my house to search for the scraps of food and laps

Figure 21.2 Mr. P.
Photo by author.

of water in Miles's half-full bowls. I follow her into the house, knowing that her run up the drive is much faster than the saunter of Steven and Johnny.

I pour another glass of wine and smile out the kitchen window. Miles is on the edge of the property, watching with his tail in full wag. He knows not to leave this land, so he waits for them, tense with joy. My friend Steven, Shelby's owner, and my boyfriend Johnny walk side-by-side. A joke or observation finishes with laughter. Johnny holds up one of Mr. P.'s hearty wing feathers. He moves his fingers down the edges then holds it up to show me from afar. Johnny grins. I know he is proud of this medicinal find. I turn on the faucet, fill a glass with tap water.

They enter through the sliding glass door. I smile and kiss Johnny on the lips. I hug Steven, then turn back to the kitchen to fill the water bowl. I ask, "Are you hungry?"

"Yea, what can we make?" Johnny looks in the half-size fridge.

"I was thinking about a vegetable stir-fry or soup. Whataya think?" I grab the wine glass and lean against the kitchen counter.

"Either sounds great," Steven says gratefully. He pets Miles, who seems content now to lie down on his dog bed. Johnny grabs the garlic, carrot, kale, zucchini, celery, and leeks. He wants to make soup, so I pull out the large pot. The metal hits the chopping board, the rhythm—music.

I've been writing a lot about family, as if the writing might manifest my own family. I've been writing about manifesting family and home in a city that is not my city. After my painful break-up with my ex-girlfriend, I've been writing to find home in Los Angeles. And I have. In our own way, my community/family in Topanga has become my chosen family, and the Santa Monica Mountains have become home.

I want to draw you, my academic family, and my biological family across the country into my new home, into this family. I welcome you into my home with sensory discourses. I want you to know me, to know this journey, to feel my heart expand and release. One of the goals of autoethnography is to "practice an artful, poetic, and empathetic social science in which readers can keep in their minds and feel in their bodies the complexities of concrete moments of lived experience" (Ellis, 2002, p. 30). In the sharing of this lived experience, I attend to sensory discourses; I must make myself and you aware of embodiment and engaged knowledge (Spry, 2001). Sensory discourses focus on tactile experiences in the world, with the engagement of stimuli that impact our senses. And our bodies experientially interact with environments and stimuli—the things, people, places, sounds, sights, and tastes that engage us.

I want your hands to feel the way my hands feel when I turn on the faucet. I want you to see the brilliance of the peacock feather, the rumble then squawk of its warning call. I want you to feel the love I feel when Johnny kisses my lips and hugs me close. I want you to sit at our table and taste the soup we made together. I want to share the sounds, scents, voices, noises, and kinesthetic moments I encounter and co-create here in Topanga. I want you to feel these movements, too—of the wind, of the dust, of the dog's tail against summer skin.

I want my family to feel, know, and experience through sensory engagement. The question becomes: How do I engage *you*, here, in this text, after a seemingly simple moment and movements at my home (Cancienne & Snowber, 2003; Taylor, 1998). Negus and Pickering (2004) state, "What matters is how artistic creativity and cultural production relate to experience, what an art product does with and in experience, how experience becomes aesthetically founded and so resonant with expressive meaning" (p. 42). My goal is to offer you a collage of texts so you can engage the sensory pleasures of experience and nature. The photographs and the collages create layers of texture and add a visual story to this text; these textures and stories engage your senses differently. This engagement of the senses allows the reader—allows you—to experience context and to know the intimate interaction of relationships and communities in motion (Irwin, 2004; Irwin & de Cosson, 2004; Saarnivaara, 2003).

Figure 21.3 Found object collage of Topanga Canyon. *Collage and photo by author.*

Though knowing through the intersection of textual and visual elements is no more truthful or encompassing than any other form of knowing.

Referring to the photograph in ethnographic research, Pink (2001) states, "It does not claim to produce an objective or 'truthful' account of reality but should offer versions of the ethnographer's experiences of reality that are as loyal as possible to the context, negotiations and intersubjectivities through which knowledge is produced" (p. 18). The photographs and collages are not meant to substitute for written experience but rather to add layers to your experience of the family stories I'm telling here.

This found object collage (see Figure 21.3) was created from elements collected in Topanga—a hawk feather, the map of the mountains, flowers and seeds, foxtail and twig. Geographically, Topanga Canyon is nestled between the San Fernando Valley and Malibu. It is an exquisite landscape, with high peaks and jagged rocks. A creek runs through it. After years of living in Burbank and exploring other locations in Los Angeles, I moved to the canyon for respite, retreat, and reflection. Topanga welcomes scavengers, squatters, and people searching through demons. Musicians and artists like Woodie Guthrie and Neil Young found and find respite in the canyon. Using found-object collage juxtaposed with autoethnograhic stories and photographs, I want to welcome you into my new home. The intersection of linguistic, artistic, tactile, and visual texts creates a hybrid arts-based autoethnography, as well as a hybrid epistemological position that represents an ecologically diverse range of discourses, ideologies, subject positions, and possibilities (Scott-Hoy, 2003). Using sensory discourses and arts-based methods to constitute and reconstitute hybrid knowledges also helps us learn what home can mean when we look to and learn from local actions within local contexts.

4. Knowledge construction is rooted in everyday, local contexts and local actions.

"Jeanine, what time is Johnny going to get here?" Haddie asks as a flash of seagulls rise from the shore and twist their voices across the sea (see Figure 21.4).

"I just texted him so he should be here soon," I say as I stuff my phone back in my soft blue fabric bag. I sink into the blue and white striped blanket but promptly rise to grab half of an organic peanut butter, jelly, and coconut butter sandwich.

"There's Johnny," she says. I turn my head around to look behind me. I see a tall, thin woman dragging a young boy behind her. "Oh, no. Not him. That's a girl," Haddie says and scrapes the sand beside her.

Stacy laughs and says, "She was asking this about you… until you got here. She actually saw one girl who looked a lot like you. She was carrying two surfboards, one on her head and one under her arm."

"Yea, she had long, blonde hair too. Is your hair actually brown?" Haddie asks innocently, and I think about how I haven't had time or money to get my hair colored.

Then, "Jeanine, look at my foot."

I look down and see her foot carved perfectly, buried sideways in the sand, as if her foot had become part of the landscape.

Figure 21.4 Lesson.
Photo by author.

"There's Johnny." And this time he is there, carrying two surfboards. I kiss his sweet lips and feel the tickle of his soft, gray beard. He hugs Stacy and Haddie. Joy rushes over me. Haddie and Johnny pull on their wetsuits, and off they go into the ocean. I grin at his generous and loving qualities.

We watch from afar. Haddie lies on her stomach on the bright yellow foam board. I can see Stacy's body tense as they paddle closer to the other surfers catching baby waves. We watch as Johnny moves a bit away from her. He catches a wave and is close to the shore. Haddie's novice arms paddle in the water to get closer to him. The current pushes her further back.

"Do you want me to go tell him to stay closer to her?" I ask Stacy, who sits knees up, watching every move.

"Well, is she ok?"

"Yea. I think so. She is pretty far away from the other surfers. And there aren't any waves right now," I say preemptively as a swell moves in. Johnny moves closer to her. He is off his board now, hanging on the edge, talking to her. He lightly pushes her into the baby wave, and she rides it in, her belly never leaving the top of the board. She holds on, and as the wave dies, then rumbles softly on shore, she paddles back to meet him. His soft voice praises her movement. The waves lightly curl onto the shore. The water recedes and opens air pockets in the sand. A low rumble bubbles up, then pops as the water reenters.

He waves at her. Her board has drifted too far from him once more. He wants her close. He also doesn't want to miss the wave. He sits on top of his board, shakes water from his ear, then shows her, with a loving gesture, about the tide, the movement of waves, about the proper way to be in the water, how to keep paddling.

From shore, we watch, on guard, wrapped in towels and California sunshine. Another wave, larger now. She is in position. He pushes her board towards the shore. I hear, "Paddle, paddle, paddle." And she moves with the wave. Then as fear takes over, she turns to the side. Her horizontal board is almost flipped by the crest of the wave.

"Whoa," she calls, then pulls back.

"Uh oh," Mama Stacy warns. We lose her as the wave grows and covers her from sight.

"She's alright. She is still on her board," I say as she reappears.

A crow follows another on the sand, his beak in the other's ear, obnoxiously cawing. He shadows his partner, scolding him. Haddie paddles in toward the shore, and Johnny moves to where the more seasoned surfers are waiting for waves. A wave barrels over her head as she tries to stand up at the edge of the ocean. Stacy and I move fast to help carry the board in. "We are just so proud of you! Great job!"

She grins and asks, "Did you see me? I almost got one. But then I turned my board sideways. Johnny said that's why it pushed me over."

"Well, that's how you learn, right? By and through the 'almost made it' moments. Now, next time you will know how to position the board, right?"

"Yea. I was so scared. But it was really fun," she says and hugs Stacy in close.

In autoethnographic research, it is important to examine local action—the minutiae, the details, the in-the-moment interaction between people, the vivid description of contexts. Autoethnography is an intimate method of speaking about the everyday and local process of creating knowledge—the way the ocean feels against the surfboard, and the board against her belly; our hands against the sand, and against each other in joyful hugs. The power of trial and error, the moments of triumph and pride, of tragedy and error, all deserve a form of writing that showcases "concrete action, dialogue, emotion, embodiment, spirituality and self-consciousness" (Ellis, 2004, p. 38). The stories are located and localized in the small gestures, the intimate interactions that occur in the seemingly non-story, the moment of Haddie on the surfboard, next to more seasoned surfers, leaning into and back from the wave. Lived experience happens in places where bodies collide, learn and relearn, try and try again (Berger & Luckmann, 1966; Boal, 1992). And these lived experiences create and constitute our knowledges. The local, the seemingly ordinary moment and sequence of moments are part of the construction and creation of our knowledges (Adams & Holman Jones, 2011; Noy, 2009; Pelias, 2011; Stewart, 2007). And it is here, in the local, that we can create knowledges that in turn make change. This making and changing happens with and through our mindful action.

5. We enact change and create knowledge through mindful action.

I lay my purple mat down on the smooth, wooden floor close to the back door and push my flip flops next to the white walls. I sigh out deeply. It has been a rough month—university life stress, a few bumps in my new relationship fueled by monetary stresses, and my desire to start our own family. I've been struggling to find my breath, my strength and grounding in the possibility that we might not

Figure 21.5
Buddha and the lizard.
Photo by author.

have children, but I hold on to the hope that, one day, we might. My yoga practice calms and centers me, lessens my anxieties. The teacher opens the back door. A steady pulse of wind moves through the studio. I push my hands down on the mat and push back into down dog.

Lydia calls for us to move, shift from position to position. I move out of my breath and raise my head. I see a lizard on the concrete wall. I imagine it watching us, connected to our breath. I laugh to myself and focus back on the movement. Time passes. I look up. The lizard has moved onto the Buddha statue, onto its third eye (see Figure 21.5).

For me, a believer, someone connected to nature the spiritual world connecting and communicating, this moment is a reminder to be one with stillness. Lizard energy is a reminder to watch in connection to the earth, in camouflage, to be ready at any moment to move away from what and who isn't connected to your life's path and talents. To be mindful in your actions.

I say to myself, in mantra, "Be still, at one with the environment and creative talents, in stillness and spirit." I am reminded that my families, my biological, chosen, and academic families, are part of this environment. As a family, we can enact change. We do create change, each and every day; with every decision, with each movement and action, we are impacting one another. And because of our connection, we are and should be mindfully acting.

Moments like this, connecting to spirit, to nature, to awareness, are reminders to be mindful. As a writing and artistic practice, autoethnography is much like my yoga practice, is mindful action. Cultivating mindful action happens in three cyclical steps. First, I act. Next, I reconsider. I have reconsidered how to move in the world through personal conflict, through anxiety and fear, and with each movement, push to keep trying. Through these re-considerings, I take new—mindful—action that allows me to reflect more broadly on actions in the world. Of mindful action Augusto Boal (1979) writes, "Humans are capable of seeing themselves in the act of seeing, of thinking their emotions, of being moved by their thoughts. They can see themselves here and imagine themselves there. They can see themselves today and imagine themselves tomorrow" (p. 12). This imagining and reimagining allows autoethnographers to be mindful of local actions as they occur in context. This text has allowed me to be mindful of family, to act, reconsider, and act anew in and with each developing relationship and to write and know how my actions have an effect on the rest of the process.

And from local, mindful action we, too, can create change. In a call for social and political change, Sandoval (2000) asks us to work within local sites of political oppression. According to Sandoval, one creates social change by living in it and learning to navigate that terrain effectively. Autoethnographic stories allow us to focus in on the local terrains and actions, to consider the ways in which we respond to these actions, and to reconsider how these actions create and constitute knowledge, values, realities. Autoethnographers recognize that perception and colliding sensemaking create a relationship to the world that is not simple or direct but complex in its negotiation. Each action we take impacts another. Strategies for local, mindful action within autoethnographic research are contextual and contingent. For example, autoethnography informs our research by shifting political and social consciousness towards local and everyday experiences. Like the meditating lizard, I listen in stillness to how my actions have impacted my families. I write and create autoethnographically to make sense of these actions, these impacts.

I imagine how my actions as a young girl impacted my sister. My despondent reactions to her in our past impact how she understands our relationship today. And now, I work to repair the damage I inflicted as an inconsiderate teenager and squabbling child. I work to be a better sister. We work to be there for each other, no matter how our ideologies conflict. Autoethnographic mindful action creates localized and discursive spaces of social change. I see how my actions and relationship with my best friend's daughter Haddie can help her to grow as a strong and confident person. I work mindfully to be there for her, with all I can offer. I work to be the best friend and colleague I can be to Stacy. I know that our relationship bridges all of my families. And we can create social change, together. Autoethnographic knowledge is created from the embodiment of and reflection upon and through action. I make choices to cultivate strong relationships with my Topanga family, to be generous with my time, my material goods, and my love; to offer to them the space to grow as a family and leave room for growth and possible and eventual separation. In and through these relationships, social change happens locally. Working for social change in the spaces in which we live and move (in contrast to out there/elsewhere) is what I can do here and now; it is what I can do to make the context around me more positive, loving, giving, mindful, and fruitful.

Autoethnography informs and materializes our understandings of each other through artistic and communal practices. I act mindfully with my academic family to write and create arts-based autoethnographic scholarship from my heart, connected spiritually to nature, and expressed honestly, even if it marks me as utopic, grotesque, and/or lofty. I write, create and act mindful autoethnography for change, for love, for the utopic possible. I write, create, and act because my families, all of my families, are so very important to me. I write, create, and act because my families *move* me.

6. Expanding and localizing knowledges are future challenges for autoethnography.

My nephews laugh in the back of the mini van. Owen's laugh is contagious. Its sweet trill jumps and moves. Ryan repeats the words "Rubber Baby Bumper," and Owen laughs out loud. I do not know when I will see them again. Their lives move quickly. They change and grow every day. Owen snaps into tears and then snaps right back out after my sister asks him a question. CC, their two-year-old sister, listens and copies their words from her car seat. She points at the moon and says, "moooon." Her tiny child finger in her mouth, she smiles wetly when I repeat her word. I listened to her and she is pleased.

My nephews begin in singsong, "Cancel California. Cancel California." Then Ryan sweetly asks, "Why do you have to go back to California? I miss you. Why can't you just stay here?"

"I know. I miss you, too. If I could, I would."

"Why can't you?" Ultimately he is right. If I made a complete life change, I could in fact, "Cancel California."

In the mini-van on the way to dinner, I attend to the day-to-day action, the local. And I wish more than anything I could remain local, with them. The challenge here is connecting to my family across the country, staying local in and through autoethnographic writing and arts-based practice. My families have taught me epistemological lessons, and I pass them on to you. I want to stay local with all of my families, drawing connections through and across multiple, messy and complex realities. Autoethnographic practice allows for the complexity of difference while forging community and familial relationships. Through autoethnographic practice we can make sense of how we perpetuate the inequities in our reactions, creation, and cultivations of self in communicative acts and our day-to-day actions. I see the value and worth in the ways we create and re-create knowledge through sensuous discourse and arts-based practices. As we write and create autoethnographic texts we should focus in on how local action moves and moves us. These movements are ever-important and ever-impactful on the creation of and communication of knowledge. And knowing how important local communicative acts are, we should be mindful with and through our movements.

I also understand that, as autoethnographers, one of our future challenges is to expand our research methodologies and possibilities. This is my challenge to you, as autoethnographer: experiment in your research process, expand your methodological breath, open to the tactile, and embrace action and arts-based experiences. I think back to my dissertation research on community art practices and natural building (Mingé, 2008). Through the trial and error of new actions and new tactile processes during that summer-long intensive project, I learned an enormous amount about myself, about others, the environment, and community building. I think forward to the arts-based autoethnography of place my colleague and friend Amber Zimmerman and I co-wrote about the sexual terrains of Los Angeles (Mingé & Zimmerman, 2012). From new actions and breaking old patterns, using a collage of arts-based methods to talk sensually about new surroundings, we discovered that new embodiments and new practices expanded our consciousness. That is, of course, if we practice mindfully. If we bridge autoethnography, community art, performance, and artistic practices, we also make new knowledges. We can expand our experiential and methodological consciousness. Mindful autoethnographic epistemology is in the doing, in the writing, in the detailed and localized exploration of the complexity of relationships and communities. And as a family, we can learn and grow and move and change in possibilities and practices. We can cultivate, mindfully and creatively, new families and communities, together.

Acknowledgments

The author wishes to thank Stacy Holman Jones, Tony Adams, Carolyn Ellis and the anonymous reviewers for their gracious and thoughtful feedback. She would also like to thank her families—all of them.

References

Adams, T. E., & Holman Jones, S. (2011). Telling stories: Reflexivity, queer theory, and autoethnography. *Cultural Studies-Critical Methodologies 11*, 108–116.

Arber, R. (2000). Defining positioning within politics of difference: Negotiating spaces 'in between.' *Race, Ethnicity and Education 3*, 45–63.

Berger, P. L., & Luckmann, T. (1966). *The social construction of reality: A treatise in the sociology of knowledge*. New York: Doubleday.

Boal, A. (1979). *Theatre of the oppressed*. London: Pluto.

Boal, A. (1992). *Games for actors and non-actors*. New York: Routledge.

Bochner, A. P. (2005). Perspective 4: Interpretive and narrative. In J. L. Paul (Ed.), *Introduction to the philosophies of research and criticism in education and the social sciences* (pp. 65–68). Columbus, OH: Pearson.

Bochner, A. P., & Ellis, C. (2003). An introduction to the arts and narrative research. *Qualitative Inquiry, 9*, 506–514.

Cancienne, M., & Snowber, C. N. (2003). Writing rhythm: Movement as method. *Qualitative Inquiry, 9*, 237–253.

Crawford, L. (1996). Personal ethnography. *Communication Monographs, 63*, 158–170.

Denzin, N. K. (1997). *Interpretive ethnography: Interpretive practices for the 21st century.* New York: Sage.

Denzin, N. K. (2000). Aesthetics and the practices of qualitative inquiry. *Qualitative Inquiry, 6*, 256–265.

Ellis, C. (1991). Emotional Sociology. *Studies in Symbolic Interaction,* Vol. 12, 123–145.

Ellis, C. (2002). Being real: Moving inward toward social change. *International Journal of Qualitative Studies in Education, 15*(4), 399–406.

Ellis, C. (2004). *The ethnographic I: A methodological novel about autoethnography.* Walnut Creek, CA: AltaMira Press.

Ellis, C., & Bochner, A. P. (Eds.). (1996). Special issue: Taking ethnography into the twenty-first century. *Journal of Contemporary Ethnography, 21*(1).

Fox, R. (2010). Tales of a fighting bobcat: An 'auto-archaeology' of gay identity formation and maintenance. *Text and Performance Quarterly, 30*, 122–142.

Gale, K., & Wyatt, J. (2006). Inquiring into writing. *Qualitative Inquiry, 12*, 1117–1134.

Gingrich-Philbrook, C. (2005). Autoethnography's family values: Easy access to compulsory experiences. *Text and Performance Quarterly, 25*, 297–314.

Holman Jones, S. (2005). Autoethnography: Making the personal political. In N. K. Denzin & Y. S. Lincoln. (Eds.), *Handbook of qualitative research* (3rd ed., pp. 763–791). Thousand Oaks, CA: Sage.

Irwin, R. L. (2004). A/r/t/ography as metonymic metissage. In R. L. Irwin & A. de Cosson (Eds.), *A/r/t/ography as living inquiry: An introduction to arts-based research in education* (pp. 22–30). Vancouver, BC: Pacific Educational Press.

Irwin, R. L., & de Cosson, A. (Eds.). (2004). *A/r/tography: Rendering self through arts-based living inquiry.* Vancouver, BC: Pacific Educational Press.

Lather, P. A. (1991). *Getting smart: Feminist research and pedagogy with/in the postmodern.* New York: Routledge.

Mingé, J. M. (2008). *Cob building: Movements and moments of survival.* (Unpublished doctoral dissertation). University of South Florida, Tampa, FL.

Mingé, J. M., & Zimmerman, A. L. (2012). *Concrete and dust: Mapping the sexual terrains of Los Angeles.* New York: Routledge.

Negus, K., & Pickering, M. (2004). *Creativity, communication and cultural value.* Thousand Oaks, CA: Sage.

Noy, C. (2009). On driving a car and being a family. In P. Vaninni (Ed.), *Material culture and technology in everyday life: Ethnographic approaches* (pp. 101–113). New York: Peter Lang.

Pelias, R. J. (2011). *Leaning: A poetics of personal relations.* Walnut Creek, CA: Left Coast Press, Inc.

Pink, S. (2001). *Doing visual ethnography.* London: Sage.

Reed-Danahay, D. (Ed.). (1997). *Auto/ethnography: Rewriting the self and the social.* Oxford, UK: Berg.

Richardson, L. (2000). Writing: A method of inquiry. In N. K. Denzin & Y. S. Lincoln (Eds.), *Handbook of qualitative research* (2nd ed., pp. 923–948) Thousand Oaks, CA: Sage.

Ronai, C. R. (1995). Multiple reflections of child sex abuse: An argument for a layered account. *Journal of Contemporary Ethnography, 23*, 395–436.

Saarnivaara, M. (2003). Art as inquiry: The autopsy of an [art] experience. *Qualitative Inquiry, 9*, 580–602.

Sandoval, C. (2000). *A methodology of the oppressed.* Minneapolis: University of Minnesota Press.

Scott-Hoy, K. (2003). Form carries experience: A story of the art and form of knowledge. *Qualitative Inquiry, 9*, 268–280.

Spry, T. (2001). Performing autoethnography: An embodied methodological praxis. *Qualitative Inquiry, 7*, 706–732.

Stewart, K. (2007). *Ordinary affects.* Durham, NC: Duke University Press.

Taylor, J. (1998). *Paper tangos.* Durham, NC: Duke University Press.

Wolcott, H. F. (2004). The ethnographic autobiography. *Auto/Biography, 12*, 93–106.

Chapter 22

Artful and Embodied Methods, Modes of Inquiry, and Forms of Representation

Brydie-Leigh Bartleet

Introduction

I give a quick reassuring smile to the musicians before reaching down and taking my baton in my hand. As I lift my arms they swing their instruments to their mouths. My breathing is slow, but I can feel blood pumping through my body at a rapid pace. This performance is the culmination of twelve months of autoethnographic study into the world of conducting (Bartleet, 2009). It represents my attempt to come to terms with the male-dominated history of the profession and my experiences as a young woman working within it. This autoethnographic process has made me wonder whether I should even be in this line of work, but in this performative moment, I know that I belong on this podium. I am no longer only in my mind, but also deep within my body. As my arms move in an upbeat I breathe with the musicians. Our eyes connect in that moment and we are living and breathing together. I cue entries and catch the players' eyes during split-second interactions. I feel my arms tiring, but I keep going and ignore the painful lactic acid building up. I feel the musicians' sounds on my chest and hum in unison with them. I give everything of myself. My body is tingling. As we near the end of the piece, I draw them in with my eyes. They watch me intensely, knowing that we need to be at one again. I hold the last chord in my hands and it settles on my palms. I leave my arms in the air for a second. There is silence. As I drop them to my side, the audience erupts in applause. I can barely

Handbook of Autoethnography, edited by Stacy Holman Jones, Tony E. Adams, and Carolyn Ellis, 443–464. © 2013 Left Coast Press, Inc. All rights reserved.

remember what just happened. In that fleeting moment, music allowed me to make a human connection with the musicians like never before.

Reflecting on this experience in my dressing room afterwards, I remember the words of renowned conductor Leonard Bernstein (1959): "When one hundred men share [a conductor's] feelings, exactly, simultaneously, responding as one to each rise and fall of the music...there is a human identity of feeling that has no equal elsewhere" (pp. 150–151). During my year of autoethnographic exploration and this culminating performance, I came to realize that despite my profession's male-dominated history, and the gendered overtones Bernstein's comment reflects, it is that sense of human connection that still draws me to it.

Artists often find themselves in the midst of performances or creative moments like the one I have just described and face the challenging task of understanding and communicating the personal, creative, embodied, and cultural processes at play in such an experience.[1] Over the past few decades, many artists have turned towards the deeply reflexive, creative, and embodied genre of autoethnography to meet such challenges (Bartleet & Ellis, 2009). In disciplines such as visual art, drama, performance studies, music, dance, and film, autoethnography has provided artists with a means to understand, contextualize and communicate the personal stories behind their artistic experiences. Autoethnography has brought to the arts an embodied mode of inquiry that is sensuous, emotional, and intimate and a form of representation that is imaginative, evocative, and heartfelt (Bochner & Ellis, 2003). In this exchange, artists and those engaging in arts-based research have also brought to the field of autoethnography new and artistic modes of inquiry and creative forms of expression that move beyond the literal and explicit (see Bresler, 2009). These artful autoethnographies[2] have provided rich and powerful models for perception and conceptualization, which not only engage audiences in an emotional and sensory way and develop deeper relationships between those involved, but also cultivate dynamic processes and products of qualitative research (see Jenoure, 2002; Leavy, 2009).

In this chapter I describe some of the methods, modes of inquiry, and forms of representation that allow artful autoethnographies and artist autoethnographers to reach such aims. In the following section I draw on a wide range of literature and examples from visual art, drama, performance studies, music, dance, and film to illustrate the kinds of contexts in which artful autoethnography is taking place. I explore how autoethnographers are pushing the boundaries of what artful autoethnography can be, using this approach to address a range of complex questions concerning their creative lives and the lives of others. While there isn't the space to detail how these projects have been conceptualized, created, and communicated, these descriptions are intended to foreground the methodological questions that are tackled in the latter parts of this chapter and to inspire readers to seek out the creative work referenced.

In the second and third sections, I draw on literature from arts-based research to focus on a handful of key creative and methodological issues facing those working in this field. Rather than giving a prescriptive formula for how to conduct such work, using literary autoethnographic devices I *show* examples from my doctoral students' work to illustrate how these ideas translate into practice (Ellis, 2004).[3] The collage text was constructed from excerpts from my students' journals, musical practice, dissertations, conference presentations, as well as my notes taken throughout the supervisory process (Goodall, 2000). In the final section I conclude with a discussion of some of the issues surrounding future work in the field of artful autoethnography.

Artful Examples of Autoethnography
Visual Autoethnography

The visual arts have taken a leading role in bringing together autoethnography and the creative arts. Within the genre of autoethnography, visual art has been used as a method for producing cultural knowledge, a mode of inquiry for evoking self-understanding, and a form of representation for research findings (Bochner & Ellis, 2003). For instance, autoethnographers have collaboratively used drawings and words to explore experimental and "troubling" modes of inquiry, which confront issues of the self, art, and method (Sava & Nuutinen, 2003). The resulting "texts" could be described as performative in nature, in that they visually communicate a sense of expressive action and encourage an active engagement with their audiences. Other researchers have used drawing as a research method to explore the multiplicity and complexity of human experiences (Guillemin & Westall, 2008). In other cases, autoethnographers have drawn on the medium of photography to examine and represent a range of social and cultural interactions between people (Ellis, 2008; Thoutenhoofd, 1998). In such examples, photographic images have been used to communicate personal stories, the embodiment of memory and symbolic significance, and a means by which people can come to understand the broader social significance of their personal experiences (Harrison, 2002, p. 109). Both drawing and photography have often provided creative modes of expression for those who are vulnerable and marginalized and who have not customarily been heard through traditional channels of social research (Liamputtong & Rumbold, 2008).

Other works have focused on how autoethnographic paintings can be used to teach, incite, inspire, or provoke responses in a viewer (Scott-Hoy & Ellis, 2008). In these artful explorations, ideas have been considered as important as forms, the viewer's perceptions as important as the artist's intention, and the language and emotions of art as important as its aesthetic qualities. As such, these visual autoethnographies have been designed for use by viewers rather than for passive reception, and created to provoke conversations and questions rather than closed-statements and conclusions (Bochner & Ellis, 2003).

Autoethnodrama and Performance Autoethnography

Alongside the visual arts, a substantial amount of autoethnographic work has been done in the fields of drama and performance. Within the genre of autoethnography, drama has been used as a creative method, an embodied mode of inquiry, and an evocative means to represent research findings (Donmoyer & Yennie-Donmoyer, 1995; Norris, 2000). Oftentimes referred to as autoethnodrama, this work commonly situates the researcher as playwright/dramatist, and uses the conventions of theater to present auto/ethnographic data through scripted performances (Ellis & Bochner, 1992; Finley & Knowles, 1995; Paget, 1990; Richardson & Lockridge, 1991; Saldaña, 2011). Reflections on this work have suggested that a credible, vivid, and persuasive rendering of a researcher and participant's story as a dramatic performance creates insights for the researcher, participant, and audience not possible through conventional qualitative methods (Ackroyd & O'Toole, 2010). This is because theatrical performances can communicate autoethnographic research findings "viscerally, beyond or below the usual cognitive filtering mechanisms similar to academic discourse" (Gray, Ivonoffski, & Sinding, 2002, p. 57). This representational power comes from the dramatic enactment of an autoethnographic script or improvisation with actors and scenery, which bring a story to life for audiences in a deeply embodied way (Diamond & Mullen, 2000; Mienczakowski, Smith, & Morgan, 2002; Norris, 2000).

Closely connected to autoethnodrama is the field of performance studies, which contains a rich body of autoethnographic work. Spry (2001) describes autoethnographic performance as "the convergence of the 'autobiographic impulse' and the 'ethnographic moment' represented through movement and critical self-reflexive discourse in performance" (p. 706). She goes on to suggest that autoethnographic performance makes us acutely conscious of how we "I-witness" our own reality constructions. Examples of this can be seen in the work of Pelias (2011) where he uses autoethnography, poetic inquiry, performative writing, and narrative to describe how bodies lean together, placing themselves "in relationship to other bodies" (p. 9). Interpreting culture through such self-reflections and cultural refractions of identity is a defining feature of autoethnographic performance (Spry, 2001, p. 706). In these performance texts, voices are brought together in singular and plural narratives for a personal scrutiny that is both private and public, and individual and communal (Alexander, Moreira, & Kumar, 2012). Such performance autoethnographies challenge authors to dialogically look back upon self as other, interrogating and embracing a sense of critical agency in the stories of their lives (Gingrich-Philbrook, 1997; Spry, 2001).

Music Autoethnography

In comparison to the visual arts, drama, and performance studies, autoethnographic explorations in the discipline of music have been modest, until relatively recently. Leavy (2009) suggests that music, along with dance, still remains one of the least-explored art forms in this field, more frequently serving as a subject of social and cultural inquiry than as an actual mode of inquiry or method through which to conduct social research. However, she does acknowledge that in recent years promising methodological innovations have begun to emerge. These innovations have begun to look at the expressive qualities of music in particular, and how these can be used to present qualitative research in new and innovative ways; for example, through musical structures, forms, improvisatory processes, song lyrics, and so on (Bresler, 2008, 2009; Daykin, 2008; Jenoure, 2002). Recently, composers and performers have used autoethnography to uncover the ways in which their personal lives and cultural experiences intertwine in the creation and interpretation of musical works (Bartleet, 2009; Knight, 2011; Mio, 2005; Webber, 2011). In musicology and ethnomusicology, researchers have explored the interconnectedness between their lives and their areas of study, and the relationships they share with those in their fields of inquiry (Cottrell, 2004; Mackinlay & Bartleet, 2012). Music teachers have used autoethnography to reflect on the values and relationships they embody in the classroom, and musicians have used autoethnographic methods to reflexively explore the ways in which they learn musical skills (Bartleet & Hultgren, 2008; Mackinlay & Bartleet, 2008; Sudnow, 2001).

In other examples, music has been examined as a cultural text to be analyzed autoethnographically, for example in Holman Jones's (2002a, 2002b, 2010) extensive work on torch singing as a complex social phenomenon and Spry's (2010) work on swing as a method to inspire critical processes in qualitative research. In a recent book I edited with Ellis, a diverse range of chapters also showcases the ways in which autoethnography can expand musicians' awareness of their practice, and how musicians can expand the creative possibilities of autoethnography (Bartleet & Ellis, 2009). In such cases, the focus is on how engaging and personal tales can be told through both music and words, which inspire audiences to react, reflect, and reciprocate in response to the musical story being told.

Dance Autoethnography

While autoethnographic work in the area of dance has been somewhat limited, there are still a number of examples that show how movement can be used to represent and reflect on research in new and innovative ways (Cancienne & Bagley, 2008). Dancers in this area have used movement methods to pose critical questions, connect with the emotions of participants, explore theoretical concepts, treat the self as a place of discovery, and represent research through performance for an audience (Bagley & Cancienne, 2002). Other examples show how the *performative* nature of dance can allow people to simultaneously address the visceral, emotional, and visual aspects of their research, which are frequently invisible in traditional text-based forms of scholarship (Boydell, 2011). This is captured in a photograph taken of Boydell's project, which explores first episode psychosis through the medium of dance (see Figure 22.1).

Figure 22.1 "Anguished Interaction," from Boydell's dance project (Boydell, 2011). *Photo by Ashley Hutcheson.*

Work in the area of improvisatory dance has also shown how movement can extend, energize, and bring previously unseen aspects of the research process to light (see Blumenfeld-Jones, 1995, 2008). In other examples, choreography has been used to explore dance as a place of inquiry and the body as a site for knowledge (Cancienne & Snowber, 2003). Writers argue that the integration of dance/movement within qualitative research, including autoethnography, provides a place for researchers to teach, perceive, and transform education in new ways that acknowledge bodily-based theoretical frameworks (p. 250). Those working in the fields of autoethnography and arts-based research have also noted how choreographed performances can be multi-vocal and dialogical and work to cultivate multiple meanings, interpretations, and perspectives for audiences making the performances evocative rather than literal and explicit (Bagley & Cancienne, 2002; Eisner, 1997).

Film and Autoethnographic Documentary

Autoethnography has also made some inroads in the area of documentary film. Such explorations represent quite a significant shift away from traditional documentary films, where a sense of "objectivity" is strongly upheld (Nichols, 2001). In contrast, autoethnographic documentaries typically reflect the life experiences and ideas and beliefs of the filmmaker or present a topic through a filmmaker's point of view, making the films highly subjective. Filmmakers in this field have noted that autoethnographic films have become important teaching tools (Barone, 2003) as well as significant research instruments (Gertridge, 2008). This is because film and video contain dialogue and plot, display images, and can use sound, particularly music, to augment the image and word, giving them the ability not only to teach, but to also actively engage audiences in the communication of the autoethnographic tale being told (Eisner, 1997). For instance, writers have looked at the ways in which autoethnographic documentaries can allow those who have been traditionally marginalized in films to reclaim their images and rewrite their own stories (Williams, 2011). Those working in this field have suggested that film allows autoethnographers to enhance the "tellability" of their stories and paint vivid pictures in ways that are not possible using traditional research methods (Gertridge, 2008). In particular, given film's rich allegoric possibilities (Russell, 1999), autoethnographic documentaries have the ability to tell several layers of a story simultaneously (Harper, 2005).

Artful Autoethnography in Other Fields

Such artful explorations have not been limited to those who would call themselves "artists." Increasingly, qualitative researchers from a range of disciplines, including anthropology, the social sciences, education, and health, have turned towards artful modes of inquiry and methods of expression. Brady (1991) uses the term "artful scientists" to represent anthropologists who delve into this area and use poetic and literary modes of expression for their research. Likewise, a number of scholars in the field of critical arts-based education have explored the aesthetics and politics of educational inquiry through literary forms of nonfiction writing, screenplay, and painting (Barone, 2000; Finley, 2011). In particular, they have examined the ways in which artistic modes of inquiry, such as observing, interacting, and performing, can be used to effect change in teaching, learning, and the overall school environment (Barone & Eisner, 2006; Eisner, 2002; Leavy 2009). In other examples, those working in the health sciences have explored the ways in which qualitative research findings relating to health issues, such as HIV, can be translated into scripts and DVDs for use in clinical practice (Sandelowski, Trimble, Woodard, & Barroso, 2006).

The wide range of contexts and approaches I have described in this section points to the fact that artful autoethnographies can be representational and also evocative, embodied, sensual, and emotional. Through a range of artistic modes of inquiry, which I touch on in the following section, artful autoethnographers can provide audiences with access to multiple meanings, interpretations, and voices associated with lived experience (Bagley, 2008; Denzin 2003). They also challenge audiences to not only engage with the artist's perceptions and feelings, but to also recognize their own in the artistic work (Bochner & Ellis, 2003). As such, these artful autoethnographies have the potential to speak and engender understanding amongst a wide and diversified audience beyond the confines of the academy (Behar, 1999).

Non-linear, Improvisatory, and Embodied Methods and Modes of Inquiry

I watch Peter intently. The seminar room is still while he sets up his trumpet and laptop. He is undertaking an autoethnographic inquiry into the relationship between composition and improvisation in his musical practice. He has to justify his research approach to his coursework examiners today. Not a word is uttered. He begins to play. We listen.[4] *We watch. Peter's tone is mellow. Rich. Resonant. He manipulates the sounds through his laptop, transforming them into something unrecognizable. They pop, crackle and gurgle. He records layer upon layer on the laptop, and then improvises over the top of it. Moving and shifting perspectives, he zooms out and listens to the loop he has just played, and then zooms back in to respond. Back and forth he goes in an inherently reflexive and improvisatory process. After some time he stops playing. The small audience applauds. He smiles in acknowledgement and puts his trumpet back in the case. "One of my primary motivations as a musician," Peter reveals, "is to find ways of making my music relevant to the time and place in which I live. Creating music that draws on my background in jazz without being bound by the idiom, music that embodies the personal." He pauses for a moment. "I want to create music which unfolds with the inevitability and inner-logic of composed music but with the energy, immediacy, and spontaneous complexity of improvised music."*

Many autoethnographers straddle similar worlds in the creation of their evocative "texts." Thinking of these resonances, I start to wonder where the "ethno" in this autoethnography is. I decide to speak up. "Peter, could you possibly talk a little more about how you're going to contextualize this artistic practice in terms of the time and place you mentioned a moment ago?" He smiles. "George E. Lewis (2004) says, 'the development of the improviser in improvised music is regarded as encompassing not only the formation of individual music personality but the harmonization of one's musical personality with social environments' (p. 150). In this sense a musician's development as an improviser is about gradually allowing one's personality and culture to speak through the music" (Knight, 2011). He pauses. I interrupt, "So in this search for your own voice and sense of social connection, music is your mode of inquiry, your method for contextualizing your work, and your form of representing this process?" He thinks for a moment. "Exactly!" he replies.

The dynamics of Peter's autoethnographic work strongly resonate with those of other artful autoethnographers, particularly those who use art as their *primary* mode of inquiry. In this section, I draw on Peter's work, and examples from other artist autoethnographers, to explore the sorts of non-linear, improvisatory, and embodied methods that arise when using artful modes of inquiry.

Non-linear Methods and Modes of Inquiry

As Peter's work demonstrates, when the arts are used as a mode of inquiry in autoethnography, the research does not always follow a linear sequence or pre-scribed method as much social-scientific research does, but rather an ongoing inquiry committed to continuously asking questions. This involves a quest for understanding that is emergent, generative, and responsive, thus resulting in a reversal of the conventional research sequence. As in Peter's case, questions emerged towards the end of the study rather than at the beginning, the literature (in the broadest sense of the word—for him it included many sound recordings) he used to contextualize his work accompanied the creative activity rather than preceding it (Ritterman, 2004). At the heart of this process is the desire to interrupt taken-for-granted ways of knowing about music performance. The resulting story—whether it is presented in words, musical notes, movement, brush stokes, or filmic images—itself creates a new kind of reality, a revealing and dismantling of one's creative practice so that the new knowledge comes to the fore (Ylönen, 2003). These processes can be somewhat "unruly, dangerous, vulnerable, rebellious, and creative," and are certainly not under the sole control of reason or instrumental logic (Ellis & Bochner, 2006, p. 431). However, the unpredictable nature of this non-linear approach is often what gives the resulting autoethnographies the "unique ability to convey complexity" in the creative process (Bresler, 2008, p. 229).

This non-linear approach characteristically involves cycles of creation, reflection, refinement, and, ultimately, performance for an audience. Artists sort, sift, edit, form, make, and remake in a process of reflection and discovery (Cancienne & Snowber, 2003). These cycles often occur in communion with a wide range of sources, such as recordings, paintings, scores, and so on, that inspire, inform, and contextualize the creation of the work. This inherently non-linear process allows the artists to draw on a range of creative experiences and reference points, so that distinctions between the personal, artistic, and social become entangled (for a visual autoethnographic depiction, see Sava & Nuutinen, 2003, p. 530).

Improvisatory Methods and Modes of Inquiry

When the focus is no longer on predictability, artful modes of autoethnographic inquiry, such as improvisation, can emerge. Improvisatory modes of inquiry allow autoethnographers to explore open spaces where the unplanned and unexpected emerge as central to the research process. Such an approach requires skills and knowledge of the basic structures of the process, imagination, a connection among those involved in the exploration, and a shift away from "automatic pilot" mode (Bresler, 2009). This doesn't mean a free-for-all kind of approach. While many would suggest that improvisation is the embodiment of artistic freedom, Bendrups and Burns (2011) remind us that it needs to be grounded in a kind of "common practice" for both artistic coherence and effective communication with audiences (p. 69). Likewise, as Peter's project suggests, improvisation is not about complete freedom, but is rather based on pre-existing structures that guide an improvisational moment (Becker, 2000; Nettl, 1974). As Peter went on to explain during the seminar, his work would not exist without preconceived frameworks and equally would not exist without the spontaneous gesture within those frameworks. The term he used for this sense of fluidity is "comprovisation" (Hannan, 2006), meaning "the practice of making new compositions from recordings of improvised material" in a kind of collage or montage approach. Applied more generally to an autoethnographic context, the improvised material might entail a first rendering of an autoethnographic tale, and the composition might entail a creative art form that reflects a much broader cultural perspective. Similarly, Bresler (2009) notes that improvisation involves moving back-and-forth between script and exploration, tradition and innovation, as well as working with existing materials, such as texts, scores, images, instruments, as well as creating new ones.

This improvisatory mode of inquiry also entails interplay between a self and others. This is both intuitive and based on shared understandings of artistic language, contexts, and relationships. As Bendrups and Burn (2011) suggest, balancing individual spontaneity with group cohesion and various distinct performance practices and creative ideas is necessary in improvisation. As they describe, their jazz-fusion ensemble is "analogous to a group of seven poets, each with different language (musical) backgrounds, all trying to simultaneously collaborate on a poem, which is recited in real time, with no opportunity for editing or revision" (pp. 76–77). As they discovered, this interplay between artists allowed the ensemble to maintain a musical conversation not only with each other, but also with broader musical influences and cultural contexts.

Such an interplay between people, musical ideas, and cultural contexts resonates with autoethnography, which also involves a shifting of perspectives between the personal and contextual, the intuitive and structured, the evocative and analytical, and the descriptive and theoretical (Burnier, 2006). This moving back and forth results in a blurring of perspectives and genres. As Picart and Gergen (2004) explain from a dance perspective, "like jazz improvisation, which has some 'logic' to it, we have used a 'blurred genre' that aims to be conceptual but aesthetic, explicative but evocative, clear but porous" (p. 837). By embracing this blurriness and fluidity in our autoethnographic work, we can also make our audience sensitive to the fluidity of the personal and cultural experiences explored (Bartleet & Ellis, 2009). Such improvisatory processes thus move us away from a world of order and clearly defined things whose individual permanence is taken for granted, to a world where our certainty breaks down and new insights can emerge (Saarnivaara, 2003).

Embodied Methods and Modes of Inquiry

As Peter's project suggests, when non-linear and improvisatory modes of inquiry are used, the body is often the epistemological and ontological nexus from which these new insights emerge (Spry, 2001). As anthropologist Kirsten Hastrup (1995) reminds us, "The body is the nodal point in our attention to the world. The body is the zero-point of perception, the center from which the senses project themselves out into the world, and defines the horizon of the self" (p. 95; see also Merleau-Ponty, 2001). Just as the work of a musician is corporeal, an autoethnographer also draws on and works from embodied knowledge and experiences. This focus frees the voice and body from the conventional and restrictive mind-body split that continues to pervade traditional academic research and, indeed, writing. Spry (2001) concurs, suggesting that in the autoethnographic process, "text and body are redefined, their boundaries blurring dialectically" (p. 711).

This centrality of the body in artful autoethnography is even more pronounced in the area of dance, where the body is the instrument for communication. Fundamental to integrating dance as part of the autoethnographic research process is the premise that the body is a site of knowledge. An example of this can be seen in Taylor's (1998) performative text, which examines the poetics of the tango while describing her own quest to dance this form. While published as a book, its experimental design includes photographs on every page, forming a flip-book sequence of a tango. By using an embodied mode of inquiry such as the tango, Taylor offers a revealing insight into broader social insights, such as the ways in which personal, political, and historical violence operate in our lives. As Cancienne and Snowber (2003) explain, this kind of combination of dance, a kinesthetic form, and writing, a cognitive form, can forge relationships between body and mind, cognitive and affective knowing, and the intellect with physical vigor, allowing new autoethnographic perspectives to emerge.

As this review of artful autoethnographies implies, these embodied, non-linear, and improvisatory approaches to autoethnography can offer new and artistic modes of inquiry and creative forms of expression that move beyond the literal and explicit. Such approaches allow us to work within research paradigms that respond to the dynamics of the artistic process and the ebb and flow of creative life, rather than pre-ordained, linear prescriptions that are modeled on social-scientific research approaches. As I describe in the following section, the challenge then becomes how to best represent and communicate the insights and understandings that emerge from such creative modes of inquiry.

Representing Autoethnographic Work through Compositions, Scripts, and Performances

I sit down next to Carolyn after introducing my colleague and doctoral student, Ralph. I am nervous for him; I know what he's about to reveal. The small audience is silent in anticipation. Ralph lets the moment linger for a while before saying, "Good morning ladies and gentlemen. My name is Ralph Hultgren and I'm a composer." Taking a deep breath, he continues, "The work I'd like to play for you this morning is an autoethnographic response to suicide." Silence. "My sister Heather's suicide." Deathly silence. "If it's okay with you, I'd like to let the work speak for itself. We can talk about it afterwards." He slowly walks to the edge of the stage and presses "play" on the music system. The hall is awash with choruses of wind and brass.[5] The sounds resonate through the floorboards and up through my feet. As the flute part twists and turns, images of Heather flash on and off the projector screen. Slides with quotes about death, grief, and faith intersect with the music being played. A brass chorale then enters, bringing a sense of warmth and comfort to the room. "Memorial services are for old people and the dead in war, not for Heather Jane—not for my little sister" the accompanying slide says in bold. Goose bumps begin to form on my arms. The words "memorial services," ring in my head. My eyes glaze over and I see the outline of my cousin-in-law Sarah's face. She was my age when she was killed last year. "Memorial services are for old people." Indeed. Not people my age. A lump starts to develop in my throat. The chorale makes it grow bigger and more acidic. I wouldn't say this music is sad. Actually, if you hadn't heard Ralph's introduction or seen the text and images on his slides, you'd say it sounded rather joyful. My eyes come back into focus and fall on Ralph sitting at the side of the stage. He is poised, deeply still. He doesn't look joyful. I see the anguish on his face. As the last chords ring in my ears, Ralph walks to the center of the stage. "Thank you," he whispers vulnerably. I hear a few sniffles coming from audience members behind me.

That vulnerability continued to plague him as he wrote the twin narrative to this musical work. This inter-textual twin narrative took the form of words, with characters, scenes, and a plot, as well as sketches from his composition, quotes from the literature on grief, and photographs of Heather, all working vividly to recount Ralph's interpretation of the events as they unfolded and the meanings he ascribed to them. It reached a final resolution of sorts after his sister came to him in a chorale in D (see Figure 22.2).

Figure 22.2 Music sketch from Ralph Hultgren's *My Sister's Tears*, 2004 (Hultgren, 2012). *Sketch by Ralph Hultgren. Courtesy of the composer.*

The resolution that came from writing the musical sketch shown here became the foundation for his autoethnographic work, My Sister's Tears, *a major case study in his doctorate. This deeply personal and creative process took Ralph to a new place with his grief, as he was finally able to reconcile his relationship with Heather and her death.*

As Ralph's composition shows, an artful form of representation allows autoethnographic work to go straight to the senses and emotions of the author/composer and audience (Barone & Eisner, 2006). As Ellis (2004) explains, you "want to tell a story that readers could enter and feel a part of." You want to "evoke readers to feel and think about your life and theirs in relation to yours…to experience your experience as if it were happening to them" (p. 116). Holman Jones (2002a) concurs, suggesting that through performance, the meanings and stories behind the autoethnography gain further significance, as the audience is challenged to actively engage with them on a number of different levels, from the intellectual to the embodied to the emotional. In this section, I touch on Ralph's work, in addition to examples from other artist autoethnographers, to explore issues relating to the representation of autoethnographic work through such means. In particular, I focus on the temporal nature of performing autoethnographies, the construction of accompanying twin narratives, the vulnerability of subjecting one's creative practice to scrutiny, and balancing artistic and aesthetic concerns with research processes.

Performing Autoethnographic Work and Writing Accompanying Narratives

When the form of representation is a performance, unlike a published research report, the moment is temporal and ephemeral. As Saldaña (2011) reminds us, what remains after a performance might be a recording, slides, photographs, or written artifacts such as a musical score or theatrical script, but these do not constitute the event itself. To use an example from his work, one can read the script for his autoethnodramatic one-man play, *Second Chair*, which explores the feelings of a marginalized individual in a competitive mainstream society, but this does not capture the evocative experience of seeing it performed (Saldaña, 2008). As Bowman (2008) concurs, there is a big "difference between reading a dramatic script (devoid of dramatic nuance, except for what my non-dramatist's imagination succeeded in creating) and seeing it performed" (p. 192). In much the same way, I could read the score to Ralph's composition, but this isn't the same as hearing it performed and seeing the twin narrative working alongside it. This is not to say that artful autoethnographies are in opposition to scores, scripts, and text-based forms of representation: in fact, the twin narrative to Ralph's composition allowed the reader to glimpse new insights and contextual understandings he or she might not have had by listening to the composition on its own. The challenge is to make sure these twin narratives speak *to* the creative work, rather than for it or about it.

As our experiences are always dynamic, relational, embodied, and highly subjective, they are difficult to express, particularly from an artistic perspective where text-based and language-driven forms are not the primary vehicles of communication (Cobussen, 2007). However, as Ellis and I have argued before, autoethnographic approaches offer a way of working through this complex situation (Bartleet & Ellis, 2009). Autoethnography frees artists from writing dry accompanying narratives; rather, it encourages them to convey the *meanings* of their vibrant musical experiences in an evocative (Pelias, 2004) and embodied way (Pollock, 1998). Hence, our goal is to write in such a way that our creative identity can be fulfilled through the autoethnographic writing process rather than be restrained by it (Jenoure, 2002; Leavy, 2009). The resulting artful autoethnographies—in the form of creative outputs and accompanying narratives—can embody the artist's unique voice, colloquialisms, and emotional responses, and provide "a means of inviting others to consider what I (or they) could become" (Bochner & Ellis, 2003, p. 507).

Thinking of Ralph's story, I should also acknowledge that when these forms of representation become public, autoethnographers oftentimes experience a real sense of vulnerability. As Ritterman (2004) explains from a musical perspective, for many musicians, the thought of subjecting one's own musical practice to deep critical reflection and then writing and speaking about it publicly is disconcerting. Similarly, Mienczakowski, Smith, and Morgan (2002) note that the "reality-based" mounting of human life on the dramatic stage is a risky enterprise. Unlike the distancing one may experience when reading a journal article in private, the live performance with live actors before a live audience intensifies the representation. Like autoethnographers, artists grapple with exposing their secrets to the world, knowing that once they are out there, these secrets cannot be taken back. Moreover, as Cobussen (2007) suggests, many artists fear that consciously monitoring what they are doing can lead to a loss of inspiration and freedom. However, as Ellis and I have argued (2009), although revealing the personal and vulnerable parts of their creative lives may feel risky to artists, it also can be highly inspiring and rewarding, especially when the autoethnography is itself lyrical and artful and done well.

Balancing Artistic and Aesthetic Concerns in Artful Autoethnographies

When it comes to representing autoethnographic work through artful means, tensions can arise when balancing artistic and aesthetic concerns with research processes, particularly when autoethnographers are not well versed in the artistic medium they are attempting to use (Finley, 2011). Speaking from a dance perspective, Blumenfeld-Jones (2008) notes: "dance is, first and foremost, an art form.... Insights developed through the practice of dance as an art form are only available through that practice, and the practice focuses on making that art" (p. 184).

He goes on to claim that "there are not many social scientists who are also well-educated dance artists, and without such grounding, the concern is that the emerging art will be poor and nothing significant can be gained from it" (p. 184). Speaking from a drama perspective, Saldaña (2003, 2011) also suggests a researcher's criteria for excellent autoethnography in article or book format don't always harmonize with an artist's criteria for excellent theatre. Others have suggested that when the demands of research are blended with the aesthetics of theatre and other agendas like education or therapy, there are inevitable compromises and trade-offs (see Ackroyd & O'Toole, 2010). Likewise, Gingrich-Philbrook (2005) has raised similar concerns in the writing of poetry and other literary forms, in relation to the epistemic and aesthetic demands of autoethnographic performance.

One possible solution to this situation is posed by Eisner (2008), who encourages the formation of teams of autoethnographers and social scientists who work with practitioners of the arts. He suggests that this artful and collaborative mode of inquiry "might provide a way to combine both theoretically sophisticated understandings and artistically inspired images" (p. 9). Bagley and Castro-Salazar (2012) concur, saying there is much to be gained from arts-based researchers or autoethnographers working across disciplinary boundaries in collaboration with colleagues skilled in a particular artistic craft. There are many examples of this happening (in dance, see Davenport & Forbes, 1997; in visual art, see Scott-Hoy & Ellis, 2008, and Sava & Nuutinen, 2003; in theatre, see Gray, Ivonoffski, & Sinding, 2002). Through such collaborations we end up not only with a quality artistic work, but also with a blurring of genres and a fluid field of hybrid autoethnographies that can't be easily categorized and that nurture the telling of stories based on lived experience (Behar, 1999).

As I have suggested in this section, autoethnographers face a raft of challenges when presenting their work through such creative media. Temporal and aesthetic considerations need to be considered alongside the complicated interplay that can arise between the creative work and words. As I suggest in the following section, finding appropriate ways of addressing these challenges through new multi-modal formats could certainly be a central feature of future work in this area.

Future Directions in Artful Autoethnography

Colin pops his head through my office door. "You got a minute?" he asks. "Yeah sure," I reply. He plunks himself down on my spare chair and flips open his laptop. His autoethnographic project is looking at the impact of Asperger's Syndrome on his musical life. Colin calls himself the Other.[6] It is this feeling of Otherness that he wants to evoke in his audience. He wants to take them into his so-called "defective mind." Colin's doctoral submission is a multimedia document based in web technologies. It is an inter-textual, inter-subjective document that incorporates evocative and analytical text, music, audio, video, images, and photographs.[7] His methods and modes of inquiry are musical, visual, cognitive, intellectual, and embodied.

"So, what did you think?" he asks pulling up the title screen. "Well," I take in a deep breath. "It's amazing. The music forms such an integral part, and as I read the pages and listened at the same time, I found I got so much more out of the text." He looks pleased. "I loved the evocative pages and the analytical pages. You've interwoven these really meaningfully—they now talk to one another and really heighten the inter-subjective nature of your thought-processes." I pause. Colin waits. He knows I always begin with something positive. "But," I begin slowly, "the more I delved into the pages and the links you provided, the more lost I became. It felt like I was entangled in a web that had no direction at times." Silence. Oh dear have I upset him? Colin looks at me with a wry smile. "Welcome to my world! You now know what it's like to be in the head of a person with Asperger's. Those disturbances in trains of thought and obsessive transgressions from the topic are exactly the sorts of things I face all the time." In this moment I realize the potential of this format to not only provide Colin with a mode of inquiry that suits his project and a form of presentation that allows all of his creative subjectivities to be present, but also to provide a means for me as an audience member to enter his life and feel a part of it, and to know the experience by embodying it myself. But it goes further than that. "Yeah, it also made me think differently about how I relate to music," I reveal. "There were so many moments when you blew my mind and challenged everything I take for granted about music and its ability to move me. Like, for example," I turn to my screen and start clicking on some of the links trying to find a good illustration, "your evocative page on the virtual heart." I start reading from the screen:

> Dear Reader,
> the Brain of my Heart, is broken.
> Cognitive empathy is impaired—pretty significantly it turns out....
> This defines my relationship with the social world, and with music.
> Funny to talk about music as a relationship, a two-way thing, a sharing. What is music for you? Does it speak to you? Does it complement your sense of self? Does it stir your heart and soul? Do you love it and fear its loss?
> I love it and I fear its loss.
> Music does not speak to me, but it enables me to speak.
> It does not complement self, but it is a vehicle for self.
> It does not stir my heart and soul, but I can use it to stir others.
> My heart doesn't stir so well on its own.
> So I create my Virtual Heart from the stories I am told and the memories of my experience... My Virtual Heart is the user-interface for the real one.
> It tells me what to feel. (Webber, 2011)

"Wow," I add, looking up at Colin. He looks at the floor, almost a little embar-
rassed, and says, "With posts like that, hopefully you, and my other readers, will
understand a little more about my music and what it's like to walk in an Aspie's shoes."

Colin's project points towards the future potential of inter-textual and inter-subjective autoethnographies in the arts. Taking inspiration from Colin's work, in
this section I briefly explore how multi-modal presentation formats might extend
the future possibilities of artful autoethnographies, and also touch on some of the
broader social and artistic agendas future work in this field might address.

As Webber (2011) argues, in artful autoethnographies "it is entirely relevant
to use a format that directly reflects these research and creative processes." While
he concedes that it is not possible to give the reader the *same* experience, the
multi-modal format offered by his website enables the audience to have input into
the manner in which they engage with the material, the pathways they take, and
the order in which they discover its meanings and experiences. As he explains,
the hypertext format, the inclusion of images, sound, and video, and the multiple
links between pages create a more "writerly text, allowing for the reader to define
significant aspects of the their own experience. The writer and the reader can
make meaning together through these pathways" (Webber, 2011).

Another useful case in point is the book *Dancing the Data* (Bagley &
Cancienne, 2002), and the companion CD-ROM *Dancing the Data, Too*
(Cancienne & Bagley, 2002), where both written text and the multimedia format
provide a way for such artful explorations to be expressed more fully. The emergence of online journals might also make a cross-fertilization of representational
forms that encompass these sorts of combinations of text as print, image, voice,
music, film, and movement more increasingly possible. For instance, *Liminalities:
A Journal of Performance Studies* and Routledge's *Innovative Ethnographies* book
series, which publishes accompanying material online, all have the capacity for
such multi-modal autoethnographies to be presented. However, the future availability of alternative forms of publication will nevertheless need to be matched by
changes in the culture of the academy in the ways in which unbounded forms of
inter-textual representation are perceived and judged.

Speaking of future directions, as the examples in this chapter have shown,
there are ambitious creative and social agendas behind many of these ventures. As
I have intimated, some artists engaging in autoethnography have been driven by
disciplinary agendas, such as the desire to find viable models for demonstrating
the legitimacy of art as a basis for inquiry—a means of producing knowledge and
contributing to human understanding (Bochner & Ellis, 2003). As Colin's example illustrates, others have been driven by broader political and social justice aims,
where artful autoethnographies have been used to enhance access to and engagement with research, promote the voices of the marginalized and dispossessed and
evoke their experiential worlds, and facilitate broader social change (Bagley &
Castro-Salazar, 2012). As artful autoethnography becomes more commonplace,

my suspicion is that we will see the inclusion of many voices that have not customarily been heard before. This is because the critically reflective, empathetic,
and evocative capacity of the arts allows us to transpose autoethnographers, artists, and audiences "into new, critical political spaces" (Denzin, 2003, p. 19) of
cultural awareness and resistance through the performance, representation, and
embodiment of ideas, relationships, and issues. As Cobussen (2007) concurs,
"Art not only lets us experience beings differently; in or through art (an other)
reality is created." He further suggests that, "Whenever art happens, it presents
the instigation of the strife between the unfamiliar and the familiar, between
the extraordinary and the ordinary" (p. 26). Through its different forms of representation, which often go beyond realist realms into the abstract and highly
symbolic, art challenges us to critically engage with the subject matter. Add to
this autoethnography's ability to inspire audiences to reflect critically upon their
own life experience, their constructions of self, and their interactions with others
within socio-historical contexts (Spry, 2001). Herein lies the future potential of
artful autoethnography, not only as a method, mode of inquiry, and multi-modal
and inter-subjective form of representation, but also as an instigator of personal,
disciplinary, and broader social change.

Notes

1. I use the term "artist" to broadly refer to those engaging in creative disciplines, such as visual art,
   drama, music, dance, film, and so on. These artists confront their experiential world by means
   of a craft and draw on their lived experiences to create or interpret something new (Saarnivaara,
   2003).
2. I use the term "artful autoethnography" to refer to autoethnographic works that employ artistic
   methods, modes of inquiry and forms of representation (Ellis, 2004, p. 184).
3. The students gave permission for me to use this work, and were given the opportunity to comment on chapter drafts.
4. To access Peter's music, visit www.peterknightmusic.com/.
5. To listen to this work, visit www.arkivmusic.com/classical/Name/Ralph-Hultgren/Composer/
   160554-1.
6. For a discussion of how autoethnographers are somewhat relieved of the problem of speaking for
   the "Other," because they are the "Other" in their texts, see Richardson (2000).
7. To view/listen/read Colin's work, visit http://www.colinwebber.com.

References

Ackroyd, J., & O'Toole, J. (Eds.). (2010). *Performing research: Tensions, triumphs and trade-offs of
ethnodrama*. Stoke-on-Trent, UK: Trentham Books.

Alexander, B. K., Moreira, C., & kumar, H. S. (2012). Resisting (resistance) stories: A tri-autoethnographic exploration of father narratives across shades of difference. *Qualitative Inquiry, 18*,
121–133.

Bagley, C. (2008). Educational ethnography as performance art: Towards a sensuous feeling and
knowing. *Qualitative Research, 8*, 53–72.

Bagley, C., & Cancienne, M. B. (Eds.). (2002). *Dancing the data*. New York: Peter Lang.

Bagley, C., & Castro-Salazar, R. (2012). Critical arts-based research in education: Performing undocumented historias. *British Educational Research Journal, 38*, 239–260.

Barone, T. (2000). *Aesthetics, politics, educational inquiries: Essays and examples.* New York: Peter Lang.

Barone, T. (2003). Challenging the educational imaginary: Issues of form, substance and quality in film-based research. *Qualitative Inquiry, 9*, 202–217.

Barone, T., & Eisner, E. (2006) Arts-based educational research. In J. Green, G. Camilli, & P. Elmore (Eds.), *Complementary methods in research in education* (pp. 95–109). Mahwah, NJ: Lawrence Erlbaum.

Bartleet, B. L. (2009). Behind the baton: Exploring autoethnographic writing in a musical context. *Journal of Contemporary Ethnography, 38*, 713–733.

Bartleet, B. L., & Ellis, C. (Eds.). (2009). *Music autoethnographies: Making autoethnography sing/ Making music personal.* Brisbane: Australian Academic Press.

Bartleet, B. L., & Hultgren, R. (2008). Sharing the podium: Peer learning in professional conducting. *British Journal of Music Education, 25*, 193–206.

Becker, H. (2000). Examples and generalization. *Mind, Culture and Activity, 7*, 197–200.

Behar, R. (1999). Ethnography: Cherishing our second-fiddle genre. *Journal of Contemporary Ethnography, 28*, 472–484.

Bendrups, D., & Burns, R. G. H. (2011). Subject2Change: Musical reassemblage in the jazz diaspora. In D. Bendrups & G. Downes (Eds.), *Dunedin soundings: Place and performance* (pp. 67–79). Otago, New Zealand: Otago University Press.

Bernstein, L. 1959. *The joy of music.* New York: Simon and Schuster.

Blumenfeld-Jones, D. S. (1995). Dance as a mode of research representation. *Qualitative Inquiry, 1*, 391–401.

Blumenfeld-Jones, D. S. (2008). Dance, choreography, and social science research. In A. Cole & G. Knowles (Eds.), *Handbook of the arts in qualitative research: Perspectives, methodologies, examples, and issues* (pp. 175–184). Thousand Oaks, CA: Sage.

Bochner, A., & Ellis, C. (2003). An introduction to the arts and narrative research: Art as inquiry. *Qualitative Inquiry, 9*, 506–514.

Bowman, W. (2008). Dancing about architecture: A commentary on *Second Chair. Research Studies in Music Education, 30*, 192–196.

Boydell, K. M. (2011). Making sense of collective events: The co-creation of a research-based dance. *Forum: Qualitative Social Research, 12*, Art. 5, nbn-resolving.de/urn:nbn:de:0114-fqs110155

Brady, I. (Ed.). (1991). *Anthropological poetics.* Savage, MD: Rowman & Littlefield.

Bresler, L. (2008). The music lesson. In J. G. Knowles and A. L. Cole (Eds.), *Handbook of the arts in qualitative research* (pp. 225–237). Thousand Oaks, CA: Sage.

Bresler, L. (2009). Research education shaped by musical sensibilities. *British Journal of Music Education, 26*, 7–25.

Burnier, D. (2006). Encounters with the self in social science research: A political scientist looks at autoethnography. *Journal of Contemporary Ethnography, 35*, 410–418.

Cancienne, M. B., & Bagley, C. (2008). Dance as method: The process and product of movement in educational research. In P. Liamputtong & J. Rumbold (Eds.), *Knowing differently: Arts-based and collaborative research methods* (pp. 169–187). New York: Nova Science.

Cancienne, M. B., & Snowber, C. (2003). Writing rhythm: Movement as method. *Qualitative Inquiry, 9*, 237–253.

Cobussen, M. (2007). The Trojan horse: Epistemological explorations concerning practice-based research. *Dutch Journal of Music Theory, 12*, 18–33.

Cottrell, S. (2004). *Professional music-making in London: Ethnography and experience.* Aldershot, UK: Ashgate.

Davenport, D. R., & Forbes, C. A. (1997). Writing movement/dancing words: A collaborative pedagogy. *Education, 118*, 293–303.

Daykin, N. (2008). Knowing through music: Implications for research. In P. Liamputtong & J. Rumbold (Eds.), *Knowing differently: Arts-based and collaborative research methods* (pp. 229–243). New York: Nova Science.

Denzin, N. K. (2003) *Performance ethnography: Critical pedagogy and the politics of culture*. Thousand Oaks, CA: Sage

Diamond, C. T. P., & Mullen, C. A. (2000, October 5). Rescripting the script and rewriting the paper: Taking research to the "edge of the exploratory." *International Journal of Education & the Arts, 1*, ijea.asu.edu/v1n4

Donmoyer, R., & Yennie-Donmoyer, J. (1995). Data as drama: Reflections on the use of reader's theater as a mode of qualitative data display. *Qualitative Inquiry, 1*, 402–428.

Eisner, E. W. (1997). The promise and perils of alternative forms of data representation. *Educational Researcher, 26*, 4–10.

Eisner, E. W. (2002). *The arts and the creation of mind*. New Haven, CT: Yale University Press.

Eisner, E. W. (2008). Persistent tensions in arts-based research. In M. Cahnmann-Taylor & R. Siegesmund (Eds.), *Arts-based research in education: Foundations for practice* (pp. 16–27). New York: Routledge.

Ellis, C. (2004). *The ethnographic I: A methodological novel about autoethnography*. Walnut Creek, CA: AltaMira Press.

Ellis, C. (2008). Homeless in New York City. *Visualizing social science: Photos by Rachel Tanur*. New York: Social Science Research Council.

Ellis, C., & Bochner, A. (1992). Telling and performing personal stories: The constraints of choice in abortion. In C. Ellis & M. G. Flaherty (Eds.), *Investigating subjectivity: Research on lived experience* (pp. 79–101). Newbury Park, CA: Sage.

Ellis, C., & Bochner, A. (2006). Analyzing analytic autoethnography: An autopsy. *Journal of Contemporary Ethnography, 35*, 429–449.

Finley, S. (2011). Critical arts-based inquiry: The pedagogy and performance of a radical ethical aesthetic. In N. K. Denzin & Y. S. Lincoln (Eds.), *The SAGE handbook of qualitative research* (4th ed., pp. 435–450). Thousand Oaks, CA: Sage.

Finley, S., & Knowles, J. G. (1995). Researcher as artist/artist as researcher. *Qualitative Inquiry, 1*, 110–142.

Gertridge, C. J. (2008). *Dilemmas of duality and the dominant voice of progress: A critical performance autoethnography by means of documentary film*. Unpublished master's dissertation. Washington State University.

Gingrich-Philbrook, C. (1997). Refreshment. *Text and Performance Quarterly, 17*, 352–360.

Gingrich-Philbrook, C. (2005). Autoethnography's family values: Easy access to compulsory experiences. *Text and Performance Quarterly, 25*, 297–314.

Goodall, H. L. (2000). *Writing the new ethnography*. Walnut Creek, CA: AltaMira Press.

Gray, R. E., Ivonoffski, V., & Sinding, C. (2002). Making a mess and spreading it around: Articulation of an approach to research-based theater. In A. P. Bochner & C. Ellis (Eds.), *Ethnographically speaking: Autoethnography, literature, and aesthetics* (pp. 57–75). Walnut Creek, CA: AltaMira Press.

Guillemin, M., & Westall, C. (2008). Gaining insight into women's knowing of postnatal depression using drawings. In P. Liamputtong & J. Rumbold (Eds.), *Knowing differently: Arts-based and collaborative research methods* (pp. 121–139). New York: Nova Science.

Hannan, M. F. (2006, April 5). Interrogating comprovisation as practice-led research. Paper presented at *Speculation and innovation: Applying practice led research in the creative industries*. Queensland University of Technology. Brisbane, Australia.

Harper, D. (2005). What's new visually. In N. K. Denzin & Y. S. Lincoln (Eds.), *The SAGE handbook of qualitative inquiry* (3rd ed., pp. 747–762). Thousand Oaks, CA: Sage.

Harrison, B. (2002). Photographic visions and narrative inquiry. *Narrative Inquiry, 12*, 87–111.

Hastrup, K. (1995). *A passage to anthropology: Between experience and theory*. London: Routledge.

Holman Jones, S. (2002a). The way we were, are, and might be: Torch singing as autoethnography. In C. Ellis & A. Bochner (Eds.), *Ethnographically speaking: Autoethnography, literature, and aesthetics* (pp. 44–56). Walnut Creek, CA: AltaMira Press.

Holman Jones, S. (2002b). Emotional space: Performing the resistive possibilities of torch singing. *Qualitative Inquiry, 8*, 738-759.

Holman Jones, S. (2010). Singing it the way she hears it. *Cultural Studies ↔ Critical Methodologies, 10*, 267–270.

Hultgren, R. (2012). *Why do I compose? An autoethnographic examination of a composer's composition process*. Doctoral portfolio and dissertation. Brisbane, Austalia: Queensland Conservatorium Griffith University.

Jenoure, T. (2002). Sweeping the temple: A performance collage. In C. Bagley & M. B. Cancienne (Eds.), *Dancing the data* (pp. 73–89). New York: Peter Lang.

Knight, P. (2011). *The intersection of improvisation and composition: A music practice in flux*. Doctoral portfolio and dissertation. Brisbane, Australia: Queensland Conservatorium Griffith University.

Leavy, P. (2009). *Method meets art: Arts-based research practice*. New York: Guilford Press.

Lewis, G. E. (2004). Improvised music after 1950: Afrological and Eurological perspectives. In D. Fischlin & A. Heble (Eds.), *The other side of nowhere* (pp. 131–162). Middletown, CT: Wesleyan University Press.

Liamputtong, P., & Rumbold, J. (Eds). (2008). *Knowing differently: Arts-based and collaborative research methods*. New York: Nova Science.

Mackinlay, E., & Bartleet, B. L. (2008). Reflections on teaching and learning feminism in musicological classrooms: An autoethnographic conversation. *Outskirts: feminisms along the edge, 18*, www.chloe.uwa.edu.au/outskirts

Mackinlay, E., & Bartleet, B. L. (2012). Friendship as research: Exploring the potential of sisterhood and personal relationships as the foundations of musicological and ethnographic fieldwork. *Qualitative Research Journal, 12*(1), 75–87.

Merleau-Ponty, M. (2001). *Phenomenology of perception*. C. Smith (Trans.). London: Routledge.

Mienczakowski, J., Smith, L., & Morgan, S. (2002). Seeing words—hearing feelings: Ethnodrama and the performance of data. In C. Bagley & B. Cancienne (Eds.), *Dancing the data* (pp. 34–52). New York: Peter Lang.

Mio, V. (2005). *Concerto in two paradigms: An autoethnography in words and music*. Toronto: University of Toronto Press.

Nettl, B. (1974). Thoughts on improvisation: A comparative approach. *Musical Quarterly, 60*, 1–19.

Nichols, B. (2001). *Introduction to documentary*. Bloomington: University of Indiana Press.

Norris, J. (2000). Drama as research: Realizing the potential of drama in education as a research methodology. *Youth Theatre Journal, 14*, 40–51.

Paget, M. (1990). Performing the text. *Journal of Contemporary Ethnography, 19*, 136–155.

Pelias, R. (2004). *A methodology of the heart: Evoking academic and daily life*. Walnut Creek, CA: AltaMira Press.

Pelias, R. J. (2011). *Leaning: A poetics of personal relations*. Walnut Creek, CA: Left Coast Press, Inc.

Picart, C. J. K. S., & Gergen, K. (2004). Dharma dancing: Ballroom dancing and the relational order. *Qualitative Inquiry, 10*, 836–868.

Pollock, D. (1998). Performing writing. In P. Phelan & J. Lane (Eds.), *The ends of performance* (pp. 73–103). New York: New York University Press.

Richardson, L. (2000). Writing: A method of inquiry. In N. K. Denzin & Y. S. Lincoln (Eds.), *Handbook of qualitative research* (2nd ed., pp. 923–948). Thousand Oaks, CA: Sage.

Richardson, L., & Lockridge, E. (1991). The sea monster: An ethnographic drama. *Symbolic Interaction, 13*, 77–83.

Ritterman, J. (2004). Knowing more than we can tell: Artistic practice and integrity. Public Lecture. Queensland Conservatorium Griffith University.

Russell, C. (1999). *Experimental ethnography: The work of film in the age of video*. Durham, NC: Duke University Press.

Saarnivaara, M. (2003). Art as inquiry: The autopsy of an [art] experience. *Qualitative Inquiry, 9*(4), 580–602.

Saldaña, J. (2003). Dramatizing data: A primer. *Qualitative Inquiry, 9*, 218–236.

Saldaña, J. (2008). *Second chair*: An autoethnodrama. *Research Studies in Music Education, 30*, 177–191.

Saldaña, J. (2011). *Ethnotheatre: Research from page to stage*. Walnut Creek, CA: Left Coast Press, Inc.

Sandelowski, M., Trimble, F., Woodard, E. K., & Barroso, J. (2006). From synthesis to script: Transforming qualitative research findings for use in practice. *Qualitative Health Research, 16,* 1350–1370.

Sava, I., & Nuutinen, K. (2003). At the meeting place of word and picture: Between art and inquiry. *Qualitative Inquiry, 9,* 515–534

Scott-Hoy, K., & Ellis, C. (2008). Wording pictures: Discovering heartful autoethnography. In J. G. Knowles & A. Cole (Eds.), *Handbook of the arts in qualitative research* (pp. 127–140). Thousand Oaks, CA: Sage.

Spry, T. (2001). Performing autoethnography: An embodied methodological praxis. *Journal of Contemporary Ethnography, 7,* 706–732.

Spry, T. (2010). Call it Swing: A jazz blues autoethnography. *Cultural Studies ↔ Critical Methodologies, 10,* 271-282.

Spry, T. (2011). *Body, paper, stage: Writing and performing autoethnography.* Walnut Creek, CA: Left Coast Press, Inc.

Sudnow, D. (2001). *Ways of the hand: A rewritten account.* Cambridge, MA: MIT Press.

Taylor, J. (1998). *Paper tangos.* Durham, NC: Duke University Press.

Thoutenhoofd, E. (1998). Method in photographic enquiry of being deaf. *Sociological Research Online, 3.* Retrieved December 23, 2011, from www.socresonline.org.uk/3/2/2.html

Webber, C. (2011). *Creating a virtual heart: Arts practice with a defective mind.* Doctoral dissertation. Brisbane, Australia: Queensland Conservatorium Griffith University.

Williams, C. (2011). *Capturing Southern identities: Auto-ethnographic documentaries of the Southern United States.* Unpublished MA Thesis. Georgetown University.

Ylönen, M. E. (2003). Bodily flashes of dancing women: Dance as a method of inquiry. *Qualitative Inquiry, 9,* 554–568.

Chapter 23

Writing My Way Through

Memory, Autoethnography, Identity, Hope

Christopher N. Poulos

Beginnings

It begins in little shards, fragments of memory that linger like shattered glass in the corner of a kitchen.

Of course, we thought we got it all swept up, tossed in the rubbish bin of history.

We were always so very thorough.

We became very good at stowing away all our darker memories. We learned to ignore them, or silence them, or perhaps just avoid them.

We were always so very thorough.

We just soldiered on, as if nothing had ever happened.

In my family, our narrative inheritance (Goodall, 2006) is an inheritance of secrets, of stories we never dared to utter (Poulos, 2009).

But the memories remain, hovering in the shadowy corners of my consciousness.

And one day, I step on a little shard, feel the tiny fragment work its way through the layers of skin.

I search for it, but it is invisible to me.

I wonder where this will lead...

Handbook of Autoethnography, edited by Stacy Holman Jones, Tony E. Adams, and Carolyn Ellis, 465–477. © 2013 Left Coast Press, Inc. All rights reserved.

Here and Now

Today begins like any other, which is to say that it is nearly exquisite in its ordinariness. Nothing special. Sure, the coffee is good: I buy good beans, grind them myself. The half and half is organic, smooth, tasty. But the day itself is just another day.

Which is not to say that there wasn't a pretty spectacular sunrise (there was), or that the air isn't that clear, crisp, golden autumn air I love so much (it is). It's just that the day, like most others, has a routine about it.

Like I said, nothing special, at least ethnographically speaking.

Or so I think, at first.

But then I find myself, after my shower, staring out my bedroom window. My dog, Jessie, is out in the back yard, staring upward. I follow her gaze, and realize I am perfectly aligned with her.

And something hits me. A little shard makes its way into the top layers of skin. I feel a nagging, insistent, sharp little pain.

Memory pain.

And I realize that, once again, I am on a search.[1]

At first, nothing is apparent, other than the fact that I am, like my dog, staring at an open, blue sky. But then it occurs to me that the sky is, after all, an opening… to the universe.

The universe of possibility…

The search is on.

Eventually, I go on about my business, senses heightened, search engaged. I am onto something, though it hovers just beyond my reach. As the day wears on much like any other day, I begin to feel a little dry tickle at the back of my throat.

Oh no, I find myself thinking. *Please. No.*

The next morning, I wake in a sweat, fever raging, chills surging, throat on fire. A dry, hacking cough catches me off guard, sends me into what seem like endless paroxysms of choking, then catching gasps of breath, then choking some more. All followed by a strong, surging headache—the kind that feels like a cement truck is parked on your temple, then backs off a bit, then surges forward.

Nice touch, I think, in my usual sarcastic, sick humor. I laugh a little, but that just sends me into another coughing spasm.

Five days later, I call the doctor, beg for some antibiotics. I am not getting better. I have no energy. And I cannot sleep. I am at my wit's end.

He prescribes a Z-pack.[2] Two days later, I wake up, feeling a bit better.

Two miles from my home, on this day, somewhere near 1,000 people are marching in the streets of this sleepy Southern burg, protesting the profligacy of our financial wizards, the inhabitants of Wall Street, and the bankers of America, whose recklessness has brought our nation's economy to the brink of ruin.

Meanwhile, inside me, a legion of protestors, armed with fresh Z-packed weaponry, have amassed, fighting off the reckless frenzy of bacteria bent on destroying their host.

You know, being sick gets you to thinking… how can something so small invade something so large and take it down to the level of a whimpering, sweating, feverish, hacking, shivering heap? And then you feel better… and then worse… and then better… and then… And you fight… and you cough… and you wonder… *will it all end?*

And then you wake up one day and you've forgotten all about it.

What a strange war…

I'm hoping for that day of forgetting, soon…

Meanwhile, I have some serious coughing to do.

It is during one of these coughing fits that I am hit with vertigo. Now, I may be onto something. The vertigo triggers a hint… of a memory. Little fragments, or flashes—like rays of sunlight glinting off a shard of glass—catch my attention for a moment.

Flash: Lying in a little bed, wet, uncomfortable.

Hmmm… What's this?

Flash: Crying out for help.

Flash: Wet? It's blood, isn't it? Yes.

Flash: Where is everyone? Why won't anyone help me?

I don't have a grip on these little flashes, these little shards of memory. Memory is like that sometimes; it comes in little fragments, so small as to be unrecognizable. Can't piece it together… like shards of glass, these fragments are not easy to grasp. Sometimes, they cut. Sometimes you reach gingerly, not quite willing to pick them up. It's as if you don't *want* to remember.

But sometimes the memories are insistent. Still, in this case, I don't have a context, or any way to make meaning of them. So I shake my head to shake off that feeling.

But this particular shard sticks me, and sticks with me. It has drawn blood.

Still, right now, I am sick. I must sleep—if I can get a break between coughing fits.

After several days of this, I just *have* to go back to work. After all, I have responsibilities. I am chair of my department. I have to go to work. I have some catching up to do, after having been sick. There are meetings to run, budgets to prepare. I have NCA[3] papers to write, for God's sake… and then, there's this book chapter…

So, I go to work, and get down to it. This is what I do. And, indeed, there *is* much to be done. Deadlines won't wait.

Turning Points

Late one afternoon, I am at my regularly scheduled therapy session. As I begin to talk, I feel a surge of raw pain bubbling up inside me. I am talking about how, throughout my life, I have always felt alone, even—maybe *especially*—in a crowd. I am talking about how, even among friends, I sometimes feel adrift. I am talking about how I have always wondered why some people—notably my father—won't just accept me for who I am, won't just accept each other. I am talking about how some people seem hell-bent on controlling or changing others. I am talking about how at some point, because of all this, I decided that I could do it all on my own anyway, that I didn't need anybody, really.

And suddenly, I start to choke on my words. I feel a wash of memory surging up through me. I don't quite have it yet, but I know it's coming. I've been here before.

And, I start to think: It's that little shard, isn't it? It's that little shard of memory-glass. It has, finally, worked its way up through my body and into my throat.

And I feel a rumble in my voice, and I begin to actually lose my voice. At first, it cracks. Then it just falls apart. My lips move, but there is no sound.

Surely, these are the last vestiges of that evil illness that knocked me to my knees last week.

Or is there something more going on here?

Either way, my voice, which is usually strong, fails me.

So my therapist says, "Focus your attention on your throat, on your voice. See what comes up…"

> *And there I am. I am a small child, very small. A year old? Maybe. Maybe a little older? Maybe two?*
>
> *I am lying in bed, but something is not right. I am sobbing.*
>
> *What comes, at first, is a little vestige of a feeling. No fully formed thought. Just a feeling—fear? Or maybe it's pain… or sadness… or… loneliness. All of these surge up… but fear takes over at first…*
>
> *I am scared.*
>
> *I cry and cry and cry.*
>
> *NOOOOOOOOOOOOOOOOOOOO! Make it stop! Why won't it stop? Please help me!*
>
> *Please—please—please—make… it… stop!*
>
> *Please…*
>
> *And I sob, and sob, and sob…*
>
> *Blood gushing, gushing out my nose, down my throat. I am choking! Please help me! Please make it stop!*
>
> *It's my nose, right? It's bleeding. It won't stop. Where is everyone? Why will nobody help me? I can't breathe.*
>
> *I cry and sob and cry some more.*
>
> *And my voice cracks, and starts to give out.*

I can't breathe.
Tired, so tired.
NOOOOOOOOOOOOOOOOOOOOO!
Make it stop!
Please help me!
Please...
I can't breathe.
I can't make a sound.
Tired, so tired.
And a wave of loneliness overtakes the fear.
Alone, so alone.
I am so alone.

As I come out of the memory, I realize I already knew this story.

In one sense, I had the pieces of "memory" before this moment, this upsurge, in therapy—or, at least, I had the story that constructed the frame for the memory. My parents' memories, rendered in story form, helped me construct a sense of my early childhood.

Isn't it like that for all of us?

Here is the story I was told, growing up.

"One morning, just a regular morning, I went into your room to check on you," Mom says.

"And she let out a blood-curdling, roof-raising scream!" chimes in Dad.

"Well, I was scared, really scared. I stopped at the door, saw you, and just screamed."

"Yes. She did. I ran to see what was the matter. As I got to the door, I saw you, too, lying motionless in your crib, in a pool of blood. Your whole sheet was soaked with blood. Blood was dripping on the floor."

"And you were lying face down, so... I was so scared. I thought you had drowned in your own blood. The plastic sheet on your crib made the blood pool around your face. I thought you were dead."

"We rushed over to wake you, and you just shook your head, kind of shivered awake. You seemed fine, but we rushed you to the doctor anyway. It seemed like an awful lot of blood," Dad says.

"Turns out you just had a bloody nose. But apparently it was a bad one."

That's it. The whole story.

But now, today, *as I write these words*, I am left to make meaning of the memory-cum-story.

As for *this* story, drawn from memory, with a little help from my significant others, it signals a sea change—an early turning point—in my life. You see, for me, something big, something important, started that bloody night long ago. At that moment, I believe I decided—perhaps viscerally, perhaps consciously—that I am *alone* in this world, that I will live, and die... alone.

Or, at least, I began to formulate that impression.

Alone.

In my young mind, I felt I had been left to my own devices, abandoned to my fate. When I was bleeding in my crib, nobody came to help. It was all on me. At first, this was an unconscious impression, if that. But, as my life progressed, it became an overarching sense of how the world worked. As my childhood unfolded, I began to feel I was alone in this world. I was on my own. Sure, I knew people, but there weren't many I could count on, really.

And somewhere along the way, I decided I didn't need them—these other humans who hovered around the edges of my life, who came and went.

So I vowed to go it alone.

Of course, that presented a different kind of problem—one of avoidance. I found I had to work hard to avoid engaging with others. I don't know why I thought I could strike out on my own, make it without help, move through this world barely touching—and certainly not relying on—others. At one point in my early adolescence, I almost struck off into the wild, like young Christopher "Alexander Supertramp" McCandless—a quest that probably would have ended tragically, as did his (Krakauer, 2007).

I didn't go that far, however. And yet, it is that moment, in my little crib, that started me on a path I walked for many years—a path of early and ongoing silence, a path of independence, a path of a loner, a path of self-reliance.

Of course, *that* idea—the dream of solitary self-reliance—is, really, patently absurd. *Nobody* makes it in this world without the help of others. If humans are anything, they are *interdependent*. We are, after all, *social* creatures. Nobody is ever truly alone.

We only *think* we are alone.

And, as I'm thinking all this, I say to my therapist, "I am alone. That is the tragedy of it all. I've always felt alone."

And she says, "You are not alone. You only think you are."

"Yes," I say. "Yes, I do."

And just as suddenly as before, another memory surges up.

Flash: CRASH! BOOM! Shattering glass and twisting metal. Loud. Blood. My blood. This time, it's pouring off my forehead. What happened? And then I realize: I am sitting in the middle of an intersection. Cars are swerving around me to avoid me, horns blaring. I gotta get out of here. What happened? I shove the car into drive, shoot across the busy intersection, narrowly missing a car as the driver swerves left to avoid me. I pull over, see a phone booth by the gas station on the corner. I don't know why I notice this. I think maybe I should call someone. I am feeling woozy.

What happened? I turn back toward the intersection for a moment, and see it— garbage truck. A very big garbage truck! I glance at my car. It's mangled. Badly. What was once a small station wagon is now pretty much a hatchback. Totaled, I think. It's totaled. Ow! I realize I am in pain, all over my body. Am I totaled, too? Blood trickles into my eye. I reach up with my sleeve, wipe. I am cut. I think my head hit the windshield. I walk to the curb and sit, resting my head in my hands. Surely, somebody will help me.

I find myself staring at the road. And I notice, glinting in the sunlight, thousands of little tiny shards of glass, scattered everywhere. They capture my attention, and I wonder what they mean.

And I begin to think I am losing my grip. Surely, somebody will help me.

For a very long while, nobody seems to. I keep thinking, "Help me. Somebody. Please. Help. Me."

But I do not think they will.

The memory ends with that thought.

I cry quietly for a while, then slowly compose myself. I say to my therapist, "Well, that was intense."

And she says, "Yes. But look at what you've learned here. People were there, you just didn't think they were."

"How do you know they were?"

"They always are. You knew you needed help. And somewhere in there, you knew it would come, must come. Why else would you notice the telephone?"

And I realize quickly that my self-declared path of self-reliance actually just magnified my need for others, my desperate need for attention, my need for acceptance, my need to be loved. I was *performing* the loner. There was an aspect to this that was purely "impression management" (Goffman, 1959). I needed you to *see* that I was alone. But what I really needed was acknowledgement (Hyde, 2006). I needed love.

Because, of course, we all need to be loved.

To put it another way, all writers need readers; all teachers need students; all humans need... other humans.

Now, it also occurs to me, with the help of my therapist, of course, why, every time I get sick, it happens in my throat—why every time I get sick, I lose my voice.

My voice requires air in order to work.

Breath.

Flash: He is on top of me, sitting on my chest, holding me down. He outweighs me by 50 pounds, is older and stronger.

Flash: His right hand covers my mouth, his other pinches my nose.

Flash: I struggle, he laughs. I can't breathe. At the last minute, just before I pass out, he lets go. I gasp for air. He laughs again. I am speechless. I am afraid. I am enraged.

In my family, early in my life, a nameless fear crept into our home, in ways and for reasons that I'm only now beginning to remember, only now beginning to understand.

The significant others in my life were troubled, my family was troubled, I was troubled… by the dark, painful, unspoken, and unspeakable fear that lived in us all. And for some, fear turns into anger, anger flies into rage, rage morphs into violence. So much of my childhood was punctuated by violence, by turmoil, by this fear turned into anger bubbling over into rage.

I felt it.

We all felt it.

But we did not know what to do.

Just when we needed to speak, the dark veil of secrecy and shame overtook us (Poulos, 2009).

Violence has a way of silencing us.

Violence in a family is unspeakable.

Violent trauma, of all kinds, is a shattering experience.

Flash: I say something sharp, I don't recall what, but whatever it is enrages him. His fist slams directly into the bridge of my nose, shattering my glasses. I fall to the floor, reach to hold my nose as the blood gushes forth. And I feel the blood pouring out, and at the same time, flowing down my throat. And I begin to gag on it, as I sob, and sob, and sob. He walks away, sneering.

And a shard of that glass lodges itself in my memory.

Communication and Identity

Violence in a family is unspeakable.

So we fell into silence.

My one way to get their attention—those significant others in my life, the ones I needed in that moment, the ones I *still* need, the ones I want, not just to help me, but to love me, love me unconditionally—or at least *mightily*—was through my voice.

And now it was gone.

Voice is the connector of humans—voice and its friend, listening.

As my late friend Bud Goodall (2006) wrote, "Communication is best understood as a spirit in transit made manifest through voice" (p. 37).

Wow.

Right.

But we—my family and I—were bereft.

Our voices were muted, choked off.

Our voices only seemed to emerge when the rage bubbled up, but the words, at this stage, are incomprehensible.

When you are yelling, nobody hears you.

Silence seems preferable.

Along the way, I adapted to this regime of silence.

But it made me sick.

So, naturally, at every big turning point in my life, I get sick—and lose my voice.

Sometimes, it is physical illness.

Mostly, it is spiritual.

As a friend—a scholar of religion—reminded me when I got pneumonia *and* laryngitis after my long, painful tenure battle, the Latin/Greek roots of pneumonia, *pneumon* or *pneumos*, mean "breath" (Poulos, 2010). Nearly losing that battle almost took my breath away.

But this ancient concept of *pneumos* encompasses far more than just the intake of oxygen. In the ancient mind, the in-breath is the taking in of... *spirit*. And the out-breath, including the act of speaking, is the sharing of... spirit.

Breath and the voice that it gives rise to are purveyors of spirit.

Somewhere along the line, I stopped breathing—or, perhaps, it is better to say that I started *holding* my breath. I suspect that trajectory began that bloody night long ago in my crib.

And it was nurtured by the nameless, breathless fear that came to be so central to my family's shared experience.

And as I lived in the shadow of fear and silence and secrecy, I came, gradually, to a decision.

The decision—if you can call it that—to be alone, to stand on my own, to hold my breath, had consequences.

Holding my breath meant holding my voice.

And holding my voice meant that the significant others in my life could never truly *know* me, my spirit.

Sadly, violence is so much easier to perpetrate upon those we don't know.

I was alone, in a self-imposed exile, living in my own interior world.

I rarely ventured out into the world with words; I *thought* about it, but almost never spoke.

I wrote, often.

But I rarely spoke.

When I did, it disrupted things. There were repercussions for breathing spirit, for speaking out of the silence, for lighting the spark between us (Hyde, 2006).

The problem with speaking is it isn't always pretty.

The problem with listening is that we don't always hear what we want to hear.

Taking voice seriously, really *exercising* it, following the insistent need to give voice to my memories, to my stories, to my experiences, to my trials, to my emotions, to my people, means that sometimes I will say challenging things.

Sometimes words cause dissonance.

Sometimes words cause disruption.

Sometimes disruption is a *good* thing.

Sometimes disruption is risky.

Sometimes risk is a good thing: "Communication with the other can only be transcendent as a dangerous life—a fine risk to be run" (Levinas, 1981, p. 120).

Still, it must be acknowledged that a single word can cause a host of problems. In my case, the word "why"—invoked as a question—created a stir more often than not.

"Do as I say, son."

"But why?"

"Because I said so."

"But why did you say so?"

Anger rising, face reddening: "Don't question me! Just do it!"

"Yes sir."

This was a common exchange between my father and me. Over time, it became a pattern. The remarkable thing about a pattern like this is that it is not really communication—at least, not in the sense of communication as mutual acknowledgement, respectful engagement, and collaborative meaning making.

Sure, we both understood the meaning of this exchange, but... this was *power* at work, not genuine dialogue. It was implemented as a regime of control, not a sharing of breath, not a lighting of a "holy spark" (Hyde, 2006). Because of the way it was engaged, it became a pattern of control-resistance. And, as control intensified, so did resistance. When it escalated to yelling, which happened often, it just became noise. Nobody heard a single word. Thus, I could, later in adulthood, reflect back on the many years during which this communication pattern was the norm, and realize that I don't really know my father, any more than he knows me.

We simply did not share much in the way of real meaning, or mutual understanding, other than the notion that he wanted to assert his authority, and I did not want him to.

And then one day, as a fight between us escalated to the brink of violence, it hit me: Seek first to understand, then to be understood (Fisher, Ury, & Patton, 2011). What I needed to do, rather than resist, was to seek to *know* my father. I needed to listen deeply, dialogically, with empathy and compassion (Hanh, 2005).

So I ask him to tell me a story. And a new world opens up to us. We begin to share meaning, through story. The story he tells me—seemingly a random choice—is the story of my car wreck. He says, "I was home having lunch. You were out running errands, I think—no, you were going to the dentist. The phone rings, and it's you. Your voice sounds shaky. You say, 'Dad? Is that you?' I say, 'Yes, son, it's me. What's going on?' And you reply, 'I think I just died.' And I say, 'I don't think so. You're talking on a phone to me, and I'm not dead. Besides, you know, I do a lot of funerals. And the dead ones never talk.' And you say, 'Oh. Well, can you come and get me? The car is ruined.' 'Where are you?'"

"So I came to get you, and the car was, in fact, a total mess. I looked at it, and frankly wondered how you did survive. And there you were, sitting alone on the curb, your head in your hands. You seemed out of it. But the paramedics had checked you and determined that you didn't need to go to the hospital. I was surprised, so I took you to the doctor. He checked you over pretty good, and found nothing wrong. You don't remember any of this, do you?"

"No, sir."

"Well, you just kind of hung around for the next few days, sleeping a lot, and lying around the house. You didn't seem to want to go anywhere. We were very concerned. I kept asking how you were, and you kept saying, 'Fine. I'm fine.' But you didn't seem fine. Your mom and I didn't sleep well for several days. We were so worried. And then you woke up—I think it was the fourth day—and you seemed your old self again, energetic and ready to face the world."

As I listen to my dad telling this story, I find a way to go with him into his side of the experience. Being a dad myself now, I know how awful he must have felt, watching me spiral down like that.

Honestly, so much anger has passed between us, for so long, that it has never really occurred to me how upset he might have been when his son almost died in a car wreck. As this thought occurs to me, I begin to feel a glimmer of compassion for him. And, as I begin to write my way through this trauma and pain and memory, through all the silence and anguish and hurt, I begin to find my way through to the other side…

Writing My Way Through

The meaning we share in our stories is, it turns out, a core part of my sense of who I am in this world, how I became who I am.

Identity—a collage of meanings—comes to me, with others, through the sharing of stories (Eisenberg, 2001).

For that sense of identity—for putting flesh on the bones of the "who" that I am—I turn to autoethnography. It is in writing *this* paper, here and now, after my therapy session, that I begin to discover a dimension of my identity that I was only dimly aware of before I started. Autoethnography is like that, for me. When I write it, when I read it… I find myself in a process of discovery about the "who's" that inhabit this world.

Writing, for me, is a method of inquiry (Richardson, 2000), but it is much more than that. Writing is a lifeline, a way into and through the questions and mysteries that hover at the edges of my consciousness (Poulos, 2009). Writing autoethnography is a quest for meaning, for truth, for discovery. Writing autoethnography is search, and research. It is a way to move toward evoking, describing, invoking, transcribing, inscribing, representing, playing with, building on, enjoining, and enjoying the "who's" of our life worlds.

Naturally, one of those "who's" is me.

As the rock band by that name (*The Who*) put it in their famous anthem of angst falling toward despair: *"Who are you—who? Who?"*

Indeed.

This is a central question of the autoethnographic life.

Who are you?

Who am I?

Who are *we*?

Autoethnography has been criticized as too focused on the self, as "navel gazing." But autoethnography is not really *my* story. When it works, it is the story of us all. It is the story of the people who inhabit my life world, it is the story of *us*, together, navigating this world (Ellis, 2004). And, for me, it is more particularly the story of the communicative praxis (or avoidance thereof) and the memory-and-story urgings of these significant life characters.

You see, autoethnography is the writing of relationships (Gergen & Gergen, 2002).

And thus, writing autoethnography is a method of inquiry, to be sure, but it is simultaneously a method of *relating*.

And this relating pushes me back to writing, pushes me relentlessly, urges me on, draws me out, takes hold of me, *inspires* me. And I find that I simply *must* write, even as I must breathe.

So, for me, autoethnography is *spirited* writing. I am inspired by the possibility that is evoked in this process.

Which brings me back to the beginning, to my dog Jessie and me, staring up at the sky, searching for possibility. And it hits me: I may not always be able to speak, but my fingers have never failed me, even when my voice has.

As I write my life, through these words, and through the words of all the stories I have written and will write, I write new ways of being for myself, and for others.

In the writing of autoethnography, I find possibility.

And as we write our autoethnographies, so we write spirit into being.

And so, in the end, I find meaning in tiny memory-shards… and a way to bring them together to form something worth holding onto: The human spirit, shared in communication, gives birth to Hope, which, for me, comes from piecing together the shards of memory into story.

Later in the day, I return to my window, only to find that Jessie has—after a long day of dogged wandering, sniffing, searching—returned to her spot on the lawn. And she greets the night sky in much the same way as she greeted the morning, looking upward. I imagine she is lost in wonder, looking toward the possible.

And I sit down to write this story.

And in the sharing of this writing, I find Hope.

And I know… I am *not* alone.

Notes

1. See Walker Percy's 1960 novel *The Moviegoer* for a full explication of the meaning and practices of "the search." For our purposes, I will define it, simply, as "poking around the neighborhood to see what's up" and "turning one's gaze on the ordinary, in order to discover the extraordinary."
2. Azithromycin, a powerful antibiotic elixir.
3. The National Communication Association holds its annual conference every November.

References

Eisenberg, E. (2001). Building a mystery: Toward a new theory of communication and identity. *Journal of Communication, 51,* 534–552.

Ellis, C. (2004). *The ethnographic I: A methodological novel about autoethnography.* Walnut Creek, CA: AltaMira Press.

Fisher, R., Ury, W., & Patton, B. M. (2011). *Getting to yes: Negotiating agreement without giving in.* New York: Penguin.

Gergen, K., & Gergen, M. (2002). Ethnographic representation as relationship. In A. Bochner & C. Ellis (Eds.), *Ethnographically speaking: Autoethnography, literature, and aesthetics* (pp. 11–33). Walnut Creek, CA: AltaMira Press.

Goffman, E. (1959). *The presentation of self in everyday life.* New York: Doubleday.

Goodall, H. L., Jr. (2006). *A need to know: The clandestine history of a CIA family.* Walnut Creek, CA: Left Coast Press, Inc.

Hanh, T. (2005). *Being peace.* Berkeley, CA: Parallax Press.

Hyde, M.J. (2006). *The life-giving gift of acknowledgement.* Lafayette, IN: Purdue University Press.

Krakauer, J. (2007). *Into the wild.* New York: Anchor.

Levinas, E. (1981). *Otherwise than being: Or beyond essence* (A. Lingis, Trans.). Pittsburgh: Duquesne University Press.

Percy, W. (1960). *The moviegoer.* New York: Vintage.

Poulos, C (2009). *Accidental ethnography: An inquiry into family secrecy.* Walnut Creek, CA: Left Coast Press, Inc.

Poulos, C. (2010). Transgressions. *International Review of Qualitative Research, 3,* 67–88.

Richardson, L. (2000). Writing: A method of inquiry. In N. K. Denzin & Y. S. Lincoln (Eds.), *Handbook of qualitative research* (2nd ed., pp. 923–948). Thousand Oaks, CA: Sage.

Chapter 24

Wedding Album
An Anti-heterosexist Performance Text

Lisa M. Tillmann

June the twelfth, 1967,
the Supreme Court renders a unanimous decision.
Hear ye,
say they, we find the state of Virginia guilty.
We indict discrimination and segregation in this co-conspiracy
and hereby set free
our Loving citizens:
husband Richard Loving, white, wife Mildred, African- and Native-American.
Justices White and Black—no fabrication—
join Clark, Fortas, Douglas, Stewart, Brennan, Harlan, and Warren
to strike down prohibitions to miscegenation
as violations of fourteenth amendment protections.[1]
Hear ye.

1969, June the twenty-first,
my parents wed in a small-town church.
The longest day,
think they, as summer solstice stretches
further than budgets for reception or dress.
A bride of nineteen, four months pregnant;

Handbook of Autoethnography, edited by Stacy Holman Jones, Tony E. Adams, and Carolyn Ellis, 478–485. © 2013 Left Coast Press, Inc. All rights reserved.

a groom of twenty-one, soon to be drafted.
The longest day.

To mark my wedding, New Year's Eve, 1995,
bullets of water fire from the sky.
Signs of luck,
say they, as wind whips, thunder thwacks, and lightning strikes.
White-lighted, braided-trunk fichus laid waste,
star-patterned luminaries shoot up in flames.
Signs of luck.

Educations, graduations,
professional-level income.
Adventure, laughter, conversation,
a shared network of friends.
Without children to tend,
we are able to mend
a divorcing couple's dream home
half renovated, then abandoned.
Good years,
think we,
our parents young and healthy.
A tenure-track job, savings, security.
Not perfectly enchanted.
We lose Jennifer, our maid of honor, and my dear aunt Patsy to cancer.
Elders fall to stroke, cardiac arrest, pneumonia.
Still, good years.

The twenty-first of September, 1996:
the sixteenth International Day of Peace.
The irony,
think we, as, of all presidents, Clinton
signs DOMA, Defense of Marriage legislation,
fortifying the institution
against subversion of suburban
families headed by two mothers or fathers
and insurrection of tax-paying same-sex couples.
As for perils posed by cum-stained-dress-saving interns and narcissistic grandiosity,
simply repeat after me, "I did not have sex with that woman, Miss Lewinsky."
The irony.

Out of proportion to our privilege and circumstance,
we become Responsible, Sedate, and Serious.
Good enough,
think I, such is the maturation compromise,
the relational pentameter's rise, fall, rise, fall, rise.
Academic vampires suck, veins bleed out, passion cools.
Projects seep into every room.
A summer suspended on scaffolding, he at fifteen feet, I at ten,
double coating our exterior to weather the elements,
while inside the climate
lies dry and silent.
We fight rarely and fairly, so I choose to believe.
We have friendship, respect, mutuality.
Good enough.

Neither proposes disengagement, dropped to one knee,
offering a box of ambivalence, a loneliness ring.
Nothing,
says he, while in the cellar of his conscience
he constructs Betrothed and Beyond compartments.
I misread signs of relational miscarriage.
No legislation passes to defend my marriage.
Nothing.

The eleventh of April, 411, 2006,
seated in our marital therapist's office,
husband looks at his feet, at our counselor, then at me.
"I am leaving,"
says he.
He departs that night; I pack for the next life in June.
How to divide thirteen years' signifiers of two?
Wedding gifts, letters, cards, what do you choose?
What to do with gown and veil of ivory satin and beads,
shrink wrapped, boxed, preserved, and steam cleaned,
saved for a daughter I would not have?
Photos taken from frames, some discarded as trash.
The narrative of albums loses its threads.
Leaving.

The law that once undergirded my marriage
blasts the foundation and scatters the wreckage.
In preparation to attend a post-apocalypse wedding,
I bear arms of a date, dapper, dashing, and handsome.
"Stunning,"
say I with a playful tug to his tie.
This old friend, a gay man,
barred from the institution
I just escaped.
We make quite a pair:
a divorcee with a sensibility queer
and a man who will fall for an international partner,
a legal stranger.
In the incense-perfumed, flower-festooned chapel
we go catty, sarcastic, and cynical,
until we see her,
my beloved student, Laura.
A bride full of light, hope, promise, and faith,
optimism, openness, caring, and grace.
Stunning.

A profile photo, a short story, a test of personality,
thirty dollars a month to sing in eHarmony.
Virtual prospects, perhaps two hundred, in the flesh, sixteen men
and then, in March 2008, John.
Winter turns to spring.
"Marry me,"
says he, an invitation to reenter a structure of inequity,
a fraternity excluding so many of my friends.
Marry me.

June the twelfth, 2011: an anniversary, number forty-three.
For Virginia, a beautiful defeat;
for Loving, for justice, a sweet victory.
This June the twelfth, after seventeen years together,
a Boston marriage joins what no pseudo-defender legislator can tear asunder.
Neither tuxedo nor bustle, neither groom nor bride,
partners, lovers, friends stand side-by-side.
"We do,"
say the two,

"take you Deena, take you Kathryn."
As woman joins with woman,
John, my fiancé, and I rise to defend the sanctity of this union
against heterosexism, homophobia, heteronormativity,
prejudice, discrimination, inequality.
We do.

Coda

To date, the District of Columbia, where Richard and Mildred Loving wed, and nine states—Massachusetts,[2] Connecticut,[3] Iowa,[4] Vermont,[5] New Hampshire,[6] New York,[7] Washington,[8] Maryland, [9] and Maine[10]—have legalized same-sex marriage. As indicated, my friends Kathryn Norsworthy and Deena Flamm, to whom this piece is dedicated, legally wed in Massachusetts in 2011. However, we reside in Florida, where a constitutional amendment bars the state from recognizing their union. As of January 2013, forty-one states have laws or amendments prohibiting same-sex marriage (Human Rights Campaign, 2012). Among them are all sixteen states that had anti-miscegenation laws struck down by the U.S. Supreme Court in 1967 (Wikipedia, 2009).[11]

Even a state-sanctioned marriage does not grant same-sex couples access to federal marriage rights and benefits, such as the right to collect a deceased spouse's social security and immigration rights for an international partner. The gay male friend I brought as a guest to my first post-divorce wedding now lives in England with his Scottish husband, in no small part due to marriage inequality in the United States.

The primary rhetorical strategies of opponents to same-sex marriage mirror those used by opponents to interracial marriage. One strategy involves the notion of "God's plan." The trial judge in *Loving v. Virginia*, Leon M. Bazile, proclaimed, "Almighty God created the races white, black, yellow, malay and red, and he placed them on separate continents. And but for the interference with his arrangement there would be no cause for such marriages" (Loving v. Virginia, 1967).[12] His honor's "logic" matches the intellectual heft of "God created Adam and Eve, not Adam and Steve." A second strategy involves the alleged protection of children. Opponents of both interracial and same-sex marriage have argued that growing up in a family headed by a mixed-race or same-sex couple damages children, a claim rejected by every major medical (American Academy of Pediatrics, 2002), psychological (American Psychological Association, 2004), and child welfare association. The relevant damaging factors are, of course, *racism* and *homophobia*.

In 2007, a year before her death, Mildred Loving issued a statement marking the fortieth anniversary of *Loving v. Virginia*. The conclusion reads:

Surrounded as I am now by wonderful children and grandchildren, not a day goes by that I don't think of Richard and our love, our right to marry, and how much it meant to me to have that freedom to marry the person precious to me, even if others thought he was the "wrong kind of person" for me to marry. I believe all Americans, no matter their race, no matter their sex, no matter their sexual orientation, should have that same freedom to marry. Government has no business imposing some people's religious beliefs over others. Especially if it denies people's civil rights.

I am still not a political person,[13] but I am proud that Richard's and my [names are] on a court case that can help reinforce the love, the commitment, the fairness, and the family that so many people, black or white, young or old, gay or straight seek in life. I support the freedom to marry for all. That's what Loving, and loving, are all about. (Loving, 2007).

My own relationship to marriage remains more ambivalent than Mrs. Loving's. On one hand, I love my partner and am committed to our bond. I also appreciate the forty-three-year stability of my parents' union and have experienced and witnessed how extending and withholding social support shores up and undermines relationships. I worry about preceding John in death. He would lose health coverage obtained through my employer, and the taxes on my estate, which he would not pay as my spouse, would be substantial (admittedly a peril of the privileged). On the other, I question marriage on both personal and political grounds. I endured a complex and painful divorce. Perhaps by delaying marriage, I am postponing the risk of living through another dissolution. In a larger sense, marriage inequality reflects and reinforces other structural inequities, including those associated with class and gender. Doesn't every person, married or not, deserve emotional and economic security? Knowing what I do now, can I be both a heterosexual ally and married? Is participating in heterosexual marriage in its current form any more ethical than joining an all-White social club?

On February 17, 2012, John and I and Kathryn and Deena became the 265th and 266th couples to sign up for Orlando's domestic partner registry, something Kathryn and I campaigned for as members of the Orlando Anti-Discrimination Ordinance Committee. On May 22, 2012, Orange County, Florida (our home county), adopted a parallel registry. While the seven rights granted by these registries are essential (City of Orlando, 2012), such as the right to visit John in a hospital or hospice, they represent a tiny fraction of the more than 1,100 federal rights and protections that come with marriage (Human Rights Campaign, n.d.). Kathryn and I are fortunate to work for a college that provides domestic partner benefits to both same- and different-sex couples, though under federal law, we pay taxes on those benefits (married couples do not).

Over the past ten years, I have engaged in LGBT civil rights activism as a heterosexual woman, both married and divorced, both partnered and single. In some ways, I felt more effective when I had both heterosexual and marital privilege

(I also am rather conventionally feminine in gender presentation, White, comfortably middle-class, educated, and able-bodied). While married, I could speak "purely" as an ally, as someone with nothing immediately personal to gain. In advocating for city and county domestic partner registries over the past year, I felt more "in the trenches," fighting for rights I might need to exercise, and as an unmarried woman cohabitating with her partner, I was subject to the same rhetoric of "living in sin" as were my LGBT friends and fellow citizens.

Marriage equality will come. In 2012, a Pew poll found that more Americans now support than oppose same-sex marriage (Pew Forum, 2012); Vice president Biden and President Obama expressed their support; and a federal appeals court, consisting of justices appointed by Presidents Reagan, H. W. Bush, and Clinton, ruled the denial of federal benefits to married same-sex couples unconstitutional (Seelye & Bronner, 2012). The U.S. Supreme Court is expected to consider the constitutionality of the Defense of Marriage Act in 2013. In the meantime and thereafter, I hope that LGBT communities and their allies will pursue a parallel equality agenda, one that seeks to uphold each person's basic human rights—the right to safe, nutritious food; to clean air and water; to secure housing; to meaningful work; to health care; to freedom from discrimination and violence; and to loving relationships—regardless of marital (or any other) status.

Dedication

Dedicated to Kathryn Norsworthy and Deena Flamm.

Notes

1. Mildred Delores Jeter and Richard Perry Loving married in the District of Columbia on June 2, 1958. Police arrested the couple upon return to their home in Virginia, where marriage between whites and blacks was a felony carrying up to a five-year prison term. The Lovings pled guilty and received a one-year jail sentence, suspended if they left the state. The 1967 Supreme Court ruling in Loving v. Virginia invalidated anti-miscegenation statues in sixteen states.
2. Enacted in 2004 via the Supreme Judicial Court of Massachusetts ruling in Goodridge v. Department of Public Health (Freedomtomarry.org).
3. Enacted in 2008 via the Connecticut Supreme Court ruling in Kerrigan and Mock v. The CT Department of Public Health. In 2009, the legislature and governor reaffirmed the ruling (Freedomtomarry.org).
4. Enacted in 2009 via the Iowa Supreme Court ruling in Varnum v. Brien (Freedomtomarry.org).
5. Enacted legislatively in 2009 with the Vermont House and Senate overriding a veto by Governor Jim Douglas (Gram, 2009).
6. Enacted legislatively in 2010; survived an attempt to repeal in 2012 (Freedomtomarry.org).
7. Enacted legislatively in 2011 (Kaplan, 2011).
8. Enacted legislatively in 2012; survived a voter referendum the same year (Freedomtomarry.org).
9. Enacted legislatively in 2012; survived a voter referendum the same year (Freedomtomarry.org)
10. Enacted by popular vote in 2012.

11. Those states are: Alabama, Arkansas, Delaware, Florida, Georgia, Kentucky, Louisiana, Mississippi, Missouri, North Carolina, Oklahoma, South Carolina, Tennessee, Texas, Virginia, and West Virginia.

12. Bazile died in 1967, the year of the landmark ruling in Loving v. Virginia. How disconcerting it would have been for him to study genetic anthropology and to learn that all modern humans share a common female African ancestor.

13. Indeed neither Richard nor Mildred Loving attended the U.S. Supreme Court hearing. When asked by his attorney what he should convey to the justices on his behalf, Richard Loving said only, "Tell the Court I love my wife" (Buirski, 2012).

References

American Academy of Pediatrics. (2002). Coparent or second-parent adoption by same-sex couples. Retrieved from pediatrics.aappublications.org/content/109/2/339.full

American Psychological Association. (2004). Sexual orientation, parents, & children. Retrieved from www.apa.org/about/policy/parenting.aspx

Buirski, N. (2012). *The Loving story* [motion picture]. United States: HBO Documentaries.

City of Orlando. (2012). Frequently asked questions. Retrieved from www.cityoforlando.net/city-clerk/domestic_partnership/dp_faq[2].pdf

FreedomtoMarry.org. (n.d.) Retrieved from www.freedomtomarry.org

Gram, D. (2009, April 7). Vermont legalizes gay marriage, overrides governor's veto. *Huffington Post.* Retrieved from www.huffingtonpost.com/2009/04/07/vermont-legalizes-gay-mar_n_184034.html

Human Rights Campaign. (n.d.) Issue: Marriage. (n.d.). Retrieved from www.hrc.org/issues/pages/marriage

Human Rights Campaign. (2012). Statewide marriage prohibitions [Graph illustration]. Retrieved from www.hrc.org/files/assets/resources/US_Marriage_Prohibition.pdf

Kaplan, T. (2011, July 23). After long wait, gay couples marry in New York. *The New York Times.* Retrieved from www.nytimes.com/2011/07/24/nyregion/across-new-york-hundreds-of-gay-couples-to-marry-on-sunday.html?_r=1

Loving v. Virginia. (1967). 388 U.S. 1. Loving, M. (2007). Loving for all. Freedom to marry. Retrieved from www.freedomtomarry.org/page/-/files/pdfs/mildred_loving-statement.pdf

Pew Forum on Religion & Public Life. (2012, February 7). Religion and attitudes toward same-sex marriage. Retrieved from www.pewforum.org/Gay-Marriage-and-Homosexuality/Religion-and-Attitudes-Toward-Same-Sex-Marriage.aspx

Seelye, K.Q., & Bronner, E. (2012, May 31). Appeals court rules against Defense of Marriage Act. *The New York Times.* Retrieved from www.nytimes.com/2012/06/01/us/appeals-court-rules-against-federal-marriage-act.html?_r=1&hp&pagewanted=print

Wikipedia. (2009). US miscegenation. [Graph illustration]. Retrieved from en.wikipedia.org/wiki/File:US_miscegenation.svg

Chapter 25

Putting the Body on the Line

Embodied Writing and Recovery through Domestic Violence

Marilyn Metta

A young woman becomes suddenly homeless, without her two young children with her. She has just fled her home where she was imprisoned for twelve years. She has suffered physical, psychological, emotional, sexual, and economic abuse. She finds herself embarking on the scariest journey of her life. She has to stay alive. She has to fight to get her children back. She faces what seems to be an insurmountable and overwhelming task. Her body is deeply wounded, brutalized, absent. She bears the wounds of the feminine condition and masquerade, caught up in a cycle of violence and control that she now lives to tell. She has many stories to tell. Her body becomes both the chasm and the link to her recovery.

There are many layers to her story, and many ways to tell her story. As Denzin (2011) reminds us, "We can only write from the space of the personal, about our own bodies, feelings, hungers, desires, hopes, dreams, fears" (p. 11). This is my story.

> **An Intimate Beast**
>
> She shivers in shame as
> A feast of porn feeds the beast
> Merely a piece of red meat
> Upon which his selfish desires feast

Handbook of Autoethnography, edited by Stacy Holman Jones, Tony E. Adams, and Carolyn Ellis, 486–509. © 2013 Left Coast Press, Inc. All rights reserved.

His secret fantasies rule his world
They fuel his bile and creed
Relentless and cruel while
A woman's heart bleeds

His charms and smooth tongue merely mask
A shaky character beneath
His glib words and sly eyes cleverly hide
An unfaithful heart underneath

Figure 25.1
"The Beast."
*Painting by
Sarah Jayne
McKay and
the author.*[1]

His beastly hunger
Insatiable and vain
No sooner are his desires met
Out he preys again

On the Web, he spun his web
Around her sacred body
Offered her to the eyes of strange men
Like a priced possession to win envy

Figure 25.2
"Caught in
His Own
Web."
*Painting by
Sarah Jayne
McKay and
the author.*

> She is now free
> She no longer fears
> He who gets caught in his own web
> Beware, my dear.
>
> (Metta, 2010, p. 120)

This chapter is an autoethnographic invitation into my journey of embodied writing and recovery. I will explore some of my personal, embodied, and therapeutic journeys as a woman and mother who experienced domestic and family violence, and as a psychotherapist who works with mothers and children who have experienced and/or witnessed domestic violence. This chapter draws on my research in autoethnography, lifewriting, and narratives of resistance in women's lives, and is framed within contemporary feminist and poststructuralist reflexive thinking. I draw from the works of contemporary feminist scholars and the practice of mindfulness to explore different ways of thinking about embodied writing, mothering, and recovery, and the delicate act and art of love for self and other through the therapeutic journey.

Buddhist philosophy and the practice of mindfulness have been central to my journey of recovery and in developing a different kind of relationship with my body, my mind, and my writing. Over the past decade, I have incorporated a regular meditation and mindfulness practice in my everyday life. The meditative spaces of silence have been critical in my embodied writing process as well as in the process of recovery. I will explore how my meditation practice has also been critical in sustaining mindfulness and presence in my psychotherapeutic practice later in the essay. Through meditation and mindfulness practice, I learn to sit with the layers of pain and aches through my body with kindness and acceptance. Through mindfulness, I learn to still my mind enough to attend to my body, to really listen to her, even when she refuses to speak. These embodied shifts in the relational ways of being with my body occur alongside a conceptual and philosophical shift. Tomm's (1995) concept of "the permeable self" provides a useful metaphor. Tomm describes "the permeable self" as "a unique individual without being disconnected from others, yet is connected without experiencing self-loss" (p. 51). Drawing from Tomm's idea of the permeable self, I began working with the idea of the *permeable body*. The permeable body becomes the site of the "connectedness of differences" within one's body and between one's body and others' as well as the reciprocal and inter-relational movement between self and other (Tomm, 1995). I will explore the notion of permeability, reciprocity, and relational ethics of autoethnographic writing later in the essay.

> Thirty spokes share the wheel's hub;
> It is the centre hole that makes it useful.
> Shape clay into a vessel;
> It is the space within that makes it useful.
> Cut doors and windows for a room;
> It is the holes which makes it useful.
> Therefore profit comes from what is there;
> Usefulness from what is not there.
>
> (Lao Tzu, Verse 11)

If words are productive, then the spaces in between are useful. The dotted lined text boxes act as *permeable membranes* that frame different bodies of knowledge and writing throughout this essay, demonstrating their usefulness in reminding us of the inter-exchangeability and reciprocity of knowledge, embodied knowing, and writing. This is an important methodological strategy in creating a text that invites readers as "reciprocal and dialogic respondents to the text" (Metta, 2010, p. 212). Denzin (1997) writes that texts need to demonstrate "interpretive sufficiency," that is, to "possess that amount of depth, detail, emotionality, nuance, and coherence that will permit a critical consciousness to be formed by the reader" (p. 283). The permeable bodies of text also act as necessary and intended interruptions and pauses to the flow of the narrative to suggest the complex and multiple layers of storymaking as well as the reciprocal relationship between different ways of embodied knowing and writing and scholarly research/writing.

The *permeable membranes* serve as a useful metaphor for the fluid, shifting and "uncontainable" nature of the stories and bodies themselves, and problematize the notion that knowledge is fixed, constant, and timeless. The stories, once written, run the risk of being frozen on the page, captured in a specific time and place. Hence, the permeable membranes that hold the stories serve to remind readers of the fluidity, permeability, and uncertainty of the stories, bodies, and the lives in them. I offer these stories to be read imaginatively and to remind readers that the lives and bodies in the stories cannot be frozen on the page. Each telling, writing, and reading changes the narrative and the lives, real and imagined, irrevocably.

The First Rape

Naked on cheap cotton sheets
Exposed, unable to move
Smell of stale alcohol
Thick and dense in the air
I could not breathe

Head spinning
My body screamed out
Stop! Stop! Stop!
No! No! No!
But no voice

Dark shadows looming
Forcing his way into me
A sharp pain
Darkness overcame
That pain that never left my body

Red hot rash left evidence
Of the forced entry

Into the temple of my sacredness
After which this body was no longer mine
Never the same again

My body open and exposed
Assaulted by a man I trusted

A body I rejected
And left behind that day
The split of body from soul

Dispossessed of voice
A body ripped apart and stripped
Of its pleasures and sacredness
Ownership claimed
The bird was caged

(Metta, 2010, p. 215)

As contemporary feminist scholars, we are constantly wrestling with how we create knowledges in an era where personal stories collide with the cultural, the historical, the political, the embodied, and the imaginary; where the meanings we create out of stories are contested, re-invented, revised, and continually re-written to align and realign with emerging life scripts of our selves and our place in the world. Women's autoethnographic writings provide critical spaces for women's silenced experiences, voices, and stories to be told, mapped, and shared, and hence, contribute to the ways in which we make knowledge about the world and our senses of place in it. My own autoethnographic writings can be read as a response to contemporary feminist calls for women's writings to challenge the continuing colonization in the writing and reading practices of texts by women at the margins. By creating new knowledges of women's lives and experiences that have been marginalized based on gender, race, ethnicity, class, sexuality, and nationality as well as their lived experiences of trauma and violence, feminist autoethnographers can reclaim their authority and sovereignty over their own narratives and knowledge-making.

Embodied autoethnography can also be read as a response to contemporary feminist and poststructuralist calls for ways of representation that move beyond essentialist and masculinist frameworks of knowledge-making to ways of reconceptualizing women's writing across difference. As Hopkins (2009) writes:

The possibility of thinking beyond binary oppositions into the field of possibilities where contradictions and similarities coexist, allows one to be released into new conceptual territory. In this territory…one can shed the imperative to think *either/or*, and move more freely to thinking *both-and*. (p. 28, italics in original)

Cixous (1991a) urges that women must

write through their bodies, they must invent the impregnable language that will wreak partitions, classes and rhetorics, regulations and codes, they must submerge, cut through, get beyond the ultimate reserve—discourse. (p. 229, italics in original)

In this text, the writing embodies *both* prose *and* poetry, *both* voice *and* silence, *both* self *and* other, *both* masculine *and* feminist modes of writing, and *both* mind *and* body.

DV

A bird with her wings
Clipped everyday
So she couldn't fly away
Freedom, o freedom

Freedom so sweet
Out of my reach
Love measured by how much
Shit I took

Her loyalty is silent performance
As she watches her wings clipped everyday
So she couldn't fly
Freedom so sweet

She chirped and whistled
Under the sun
While she cried into the
Dark, dark nights

She soon stopped singing as
Life drained out of her
Slowly but surely
She cried but no one heard

Her mask hides
A damaged smile
A brave face that
Nobody guessed

A beautiful bird who can never fly
He who clipped her wings
In the name of love
Blinds himself in fear

His words pierced,
Bit deep into her heart
Tore her spirit apart
Yet she braved day after day

Voiceless and numbed
With guilt and shame
Caught in a hell hole
She could not escape

Cycle of violence
He who controls her
Clipped her wings everyday
So she can never fly away

Torn by a love
So cruel and brutal
With her soft young feathers
She knew no better

A voiceless soul
Trapped in the body
Of a beautiful bird
Who could not fly

She dreams of flying
She dreams of freedom
A little bird who could not fly
Until the time is right

(Metta, 2010, p. 118–120)

My autoethnographic writings become "a tool to speak out of the many layers of silence and oppression associated with racism, sexism and domestic violence" (Metta, 2010, p. 32).

> Writing women's lives and women's self-writings challenge the fundamental hegemonic discourses and assumptions of selfhood, identity and gender by positioning women at the centre of the narratives and knowledge-making. In doing so, women's lifewriting has many socio-cultural and political implications for the ways we read history, construct knowledges, and imagine future generations....Women's lifewriting occupies an important and pivotal place within contemporary feminist scholarship and contemporary scholarly knowledge-making. (Metta, 2010, p. 29)

Autoethnography aims to re-establish "the centrality of personal experience and identity in the social construction of knowledge" and has been characterized as

> a way of writing what feminist theorists call standpoint theories, which...is all about using the material of our personal backgrounds and lived experiences to explain why and how we see and interpret the meanings of persons and things the way we do. (Goodall, 2004, p. 187)

Women's autoethnographic writings place women *at the center* of scholarly texts, critical analysis, and knowledge-making, and as a result, they become important sites for the intervention and resistance of the masculinist discourses within academia as well as wider social, cultural, and political discourses.

Autoethnographic writing creates critical spaces for dialogical, inter-relational, and intersectional exchanges to be made between the storyteller/story*maker*, her lived and embodied experiences, and the readers/viewers. These exchanges transform both the writer and the reader/viewer simultaneously.

> When I identify with you, I am reconstituting a new "we": a new identity, through travelling to your world: through coming to know you, by listening to, witnessing your experience. I am expanding my self to include my relation to you. But rather than assimilating you into myself, assuming sameness, or simply incorporating difference without change to myself, I am opening my self to learning about and recognizing you: I cannot do this without changing who I am. And because this process changes our relationship to each other, it also changes you—more so, of course, if the process of identification goes both ways. (Weir, 2008, p. 125)

The notion of mindfulness is central to this dialogical exchange between writer and reader/viewer as well as between researcher and subject. From a position of mindfulness, I am able to engage with my own embodied stories as well as others' in a kind of "mutual reciprocity that allows for spaciousness of the imagination, softening of the mind and rigorous engagement with the present moment" (Metta, 2010, p. 220).

Autoethnographic texts are personal texts that demand that we pay attention and listen; they invite us into narratives of lived and living experiences outside of ourselves and yet draw on our human and imaginative capacities to bridge across and beyond difference.

These autoethnographic texts are also often *messy* texts. This chapter is a *messy* chapter where the embodied and reflexive narrative impulses create writing that necessarily disrupts, disorders, and unsettles. Denzin (1997) writes:

> The reflexive, epiphany, messy text redefines the ethnographic project. The writer-as-scribe for the other also becomes a cultural critic: a person who voices interpretations about the events recorded and observed. At the same time, as the scribe of a messy text the writer shapes the poetic narrative representations that are brought to the people studied. (p. 225)

Some of my most powerful autoethnographic writings take the poetic form which allows the kind of freedom and spaciousness that prose does not. These poetic forms of writing allow me the space and the permission to immerse in the organic, juicy, and embodied ways of thinking, knowing, writing, and being.

The Aftermath

9 April 2005 was the day
> *She found her freedom*
>> *She saw the narrow chance to slip*

Out of her cage

Purse and keys I grabbed and ran to the car
> *Had no choice but to leave my babies behind*
I will come back for you, I promise!

> *I drove aimlessly for hours*

Paralysed with fear and trepidation
> *My mind threatened to explode*
>> *Into a million pieces*

> *My life hung perilously on a thin rope*
Threatening to snap any moment
> *As I continue to face daily and hourly torments*
>> *I hung on for my children*

As he pushed and shoved me
                              Restrained for hours in my car
                    Snatched my keys and phone
Pummelling at my door at nights
                                        As I crouched in fear

          Pick-up and drop-off times
                              Became my weekly nightmares
As I struggled to breathe through that choking sensation
                    I felt the world closing in on me

                              I never felt more alone in my life
All I could hang onto was my wings
                    They grew stronger every day I was out of that cage
I kept faith as I face the aftermath of leaving him

                    Fear for my life, I wrote my will
And began a long and painful process
                              Restraining orders   Police   000
          Family Court   Lawyers

                    But each day, my wings grew stronger
I could fly longer and farther
                    And dream of the day I would soar through the skies
With my babies tucked under their mother's wings

(Metta, 2010, pp. 121–122)

The moments of silence, gaps and pauses in poetic writing give voice to the embodied experiences that struggle to fit into the confined structures of prose. These embodied experiences are often non-linear, chaotic, unruly, and full of silences, gaps, pauses, and pulses of energy that break the conventions of prose. These poetic forms and language are also reflected in the visual narratives. As Laurel Richardson and Elizabeth St. Pierre (2005) argue, the writing *becomes* the method of inquiry, the research.

> Language is not simply "transparent," reflecting a social reality that is objectively out there. Rather, language is a *constitutive* force, creating a particular view of reality. All language has grammatical, narrative, and rhetorical structures that construct the subjects and objects of our research, bestow meaning,

and create value. This is as true for writing as it is for speaking, and as true of science as it is of poetry. (Richardson, 1990, p. 12, italics in original)

Richardson (2000) also reminds us that:

> Unlike prose, poetry writes in the pauses through the conventions of line breaks, spaces between lines and between stanzas and sections, and for sounds of silence. (p. 879)

Embodied autoethnography also foregrounds the argument that meanings and hence knowledge can be made through bodies. My body becomes a text embodying what I have lived through, witnessed, and experienced. Audre Lorde, a feminist poet and writer, leads us into ways of thinking and writing that embrace the body as multiple texts. Perrault writes that Lorde creates "a writing of self that makes the female body a site and source of written subjectivity, yet inhabits that body with the ethics of a deeply and precisely historical, political, sexual, and racial consciousness" (cited in Morris, 2002, p. 168).

By immersing myself in raw, messy forms of writing, I am tapping into embodied ways of writing that French feminist philosopher Cixous (1986) calls the feminine writing and the feminine imaginary. It is important to note here that the term "feminine" is used by Cixous as a metaphorical signifier of the politics of sexual difference rather than as being tied to biologically sexed bodies. Cixous writes: "Write yourself; your body must make itself heard. Then the huge resources of the unconscious will burst out. Finally the inexhaustible feminine Imaginary is going to be deployed" (p. 97). To Cixous, feminine writing is "open and multiple, varied and rhythmic, full of pleasures and more importantly, full of possibilities" (cited in Tong, 1998, p. 201).

My *uncontainable, permeable*[3] body speaks,

But only in her own terms

She is unbound, unfixed.

My permeable body changes shape, form and texture.

My *rhizome*[4] body

Sheds her old bark, stripping away

Re-sprouting, re-shooting

Re-aligning

My body is silent but she is no longer silenced.

She is in solitary confinement but she is not alone.

In *stillness*, she breathes

Through the membranes *between* herself.

Embodied knowledge-making requires risks, and I would argue perhaps more risks than simply telling the story. This is dangerous work not simply because it disrupts and challenges patriarchal and masculinist ways of making knowledge about women's experiences, but more importantly, it requires the body to be *present*. It requires *putting the body on the line*.

> *The body is present.*
>
> *The body bears witness.*
>
> *The body hears everything.*
>
> *She sees everything.*

Creating knowledge about women's bodies and embodied experiences in these ways exposes the very structures of power, surveillance, and control. For many women and children who have lived with domestic violence, their bodies become *docile bodies* (Foucault, 1979) trained to exist on the edge of the abyss. Foucault's concept of "docile bodies" is useful here in understanding both the implicit and explicit forms of power and control perpetrated on the bodies of women and children who have experienced and/or witnessed family and domestic violence. Many of these women and children survived by modifying and self-regulating their bodies, behaviors, and thoughts in daily attempts to keep themselves safe and sane. Many of the acts of control, regulation, and surveillance become internalized by these women and children as ways of keeping themselves safe. More importantly, these "docile bodies" are not simply the targets of acts of violence and control, they are also sites of resistance and subversion. By *putting the body on the line* in these autoethnographic writings around violence, I am foregrounding the body as a powerful site for resistance and subversion of the very forces of violence and control aimed at containing it.

The conceptual shifts in feminist understandings of the female body are important in working with the bodies of women and children who have lived with domestic violence and how we make knowledge from the body. Adrienne Rich's (1976) call for women to "repossess" their bodies is a timely reminder here:

> In arguing that we have by no means yet explored or understood our biological grounding, the miracle and paradox of the female body and its spiritual and political meanings, I am really asking whether women cannot begin, at last, to *think through the body*, to connect what has been so cruelly disorganised—our great mental capacities, hardly used; our highly developed tactile sense; our genius for close observation; our complicated, pain-enduring, multi-pleasured physicality. (p. 284, italics in original)

My body sits at the center of how I tell my story, how I make my story, and how I create knowledge. My body, my voice, and hence my writing are inextricably linked in a *triple braid*. The *triple braid* is a philosophical and methodological metaphor I have created to represent the reflexive and embodied narratives as well as the writing process. In my own writing, the storytelling and story*making* of my embodied experiences of domestic violence create a braiding of *body/voice/text* and *memory/imagination/experience*.

> Like the image of braided long hair, if we follow the strands of hair in a braid, we can see that the three strands of hair interweave in a beautiful pattern—left strand, the middle strand and the right strand alternate and weave into each other whilst maintaining their separateness and individuality. (Metta, 2010, pp. 187–188)

In this way, my body, my voice and my writing are braided into an *art* of storytelling and storymaking. In the process of writing, all the three faculties are present, and they sit alongside one another in "triple reciprocity" (Metta, 2010, p. 189).

In performing embodied writing about my experiences of domestic violence, my body is also *put on the line* through the process of recovery. Through the journey of embodied writing and healing, my relationship with my body (the somatic) is often raw, mostly messy, almost always beyond language (the semantic). The act (the performative doing) and art (the braiding) of writing through the body uncover many layers of knowing, healing, living, and being. The weaving of visual and written narratives in this text is a deliberate methodology to perform the different layers of storytelling and storymaking. The interweaving of the visual, poetic, and prose narratives is a creative, intuitive, and imaginative process that evolved through the autoethnographic act. The visual representations of narratives are something completely new to me as a non-visual artist, and have emerged as an experimental and experiential layer of the storymaking created in collaboration with a student artist. The experience of collaboration and co-storymaking has been a powerful process both personally and politically. The intensely private and intimate narratives were shifted from the personal autoethnographical written text to a more "public" and collaborative space where different media and textures and layers of representation could be explored. I wanted to tell the silent layers of stories that were beyond words, and I felt that these visual narratives did just that.

Allowing the body to speak in her *own* terms is facing the abyss and moving beyond the abyss. The body bears witness in ways that are not the same as story on paper.

> *Body-ink is mother's milk,*
>
> Blood stains in men's ways
>
> Outside of his language

Inside the insides of the interior

Piercing through olds ways
Like sharpened tongue upon your skin
We cannot ignore the body like we can with paper
This is madness of a different kind

A touch on my skin

Stings like salt on wounds
Yet your delicate touch remains the key
The membrane that binds you and I

Two years after leaving, my body began to shut down. She finally surrendered.

Figure 25.3 "Body and Mind." *Painting by Sarah Jayne McKay and the author.*

My body is weak
She now carries the evidence of the brutality of my past,
my hidden secrets, my darkest moments
She aches…

> She screams at me…
>
> She wants all the brutality to stop.
>
> Yet she is patient.
>
> We have time, she says to me.
>
> She has carried me at her own expense all these years
>
> She is ill, fatigued, drained and weary, she's shutting down.
>
> She refuses to get out of bed some days.
>
> She wants to stay in her darkened cave.
>
> And wait.   And wait.
>
> Until…
>
> (Metta, 2010, p. 231)

Writing the female body is risky work. Holman Jones (2005) writes:

Autoethnographic texts seek to invoke the corporeal, sensuous, and political nature of experience rather than collapse text into embodiment or politics into language play. (p. 767)

If we really listen and pay attention to the body, we can hear her loud protests against the many layers of oppression, silencing, regulations, and surveillance.

> *I lived in the cycle of violence and control that seemed so foreign and yet so familiar in its secrecy. I became this man's possession—my thoughts, my feelings, my experiences and my body were no longer mine. The control, like a disease that penetrated every cell, tissue and organ in your body, penetrated every aspect of my life, systematically isolating and alienating me from my family and friends and ultimately, me from myself….I cried but there were no tears. I was shouting but there was no voice. The contradictions and alienation between my body and my mind were excruciating. I knew exactly what it felt like to be silenced to the point of "madness."[5] I felt like a senseless, irrational, and volatile madwoman who could not live in her own skin. The reality of my life was incomprehensible to me, and the "truths" that were screaming out from deep within were silenced to the point of incomprehensibility.* (Metta, 2010, pp. 116–117)

If autoethnography is, as Spry (2011) describes, "messy, bloody, and unruly" (p. 15), then it is no surprise that embodied autoethnography can be unsettling, challenging, and provocative.

> Unleashed and raging, she belongs to the race of waves. She arises, she approaches, she lifts up. She reaches, covers over, washes a shore, flows embracing the cliff's least undulation, already she is another, arising again, throwing the fringed vastness of her body up high....She has never "held still"; explosion, diffusion, effervescence, abundance, she takes pleasure in being boundless, outside self, outside same, far from a "center." (Cixous, 1986, p. 90)

Embodied writing often emerges through the struggle between experience and language, between body and words, between presence and absence, and between life and story. This struggle is necessary, creative, and productive. Words are sometimes jerked onto the page, and at other times, gently coaxed and stroked onto the page.

Below is a story of how I discovered embodied writing:

> *Much of the creative and imaginative lifewriting has emerged out of what I call the mess of writings that emerged from the dark phase that took place in the early stages of the research. It was through this dark space of messy writing that I tapped into embodied memory. During this period, I had my first experiences of writing from the body....I wrote freely, organically and sporadically. The journal writings were uncensored, messy, raw and organic. I wrote to stay alive. I wrote to feel and to release the pain. I wrote to immerse myself in the moment. I wrote to set free the senselessness, chaos and silence. I wrote from the body. I wrote in and through silence. I wrote to find voice. I wrote in ways that made no sense to me....I wrote because the writing took over....I wrote because I had to. The urge was overwhelming. I simply surrendered to the senselessness of the process. I wrote into floodgates, the drought and the heat waves. I wrote past myself. I wrote past walls, genres, borders, boundaries, censorship and the familiar. I wrote into unfamiliar and unknown territories. In entering the dark phase, I entered into myself. I wrote the hidden and silenced passage into myself.* (Metta, 2010, p. 185)

Writing about my experience with domestic violence was one of the most challenging narratives that I have written, but also one of the most powerful.

> The twelve-month writing block I experienced in the early stages of this research occurred around the same time that I left the relationship in 2005 and the *dark space* I described was like a

kind of speechlessness and shock that I had experienced *coming out*. It was the first time that I had allowed myself to feel the full brunt and extent of what had happened to me in the past twelve years. I was beyond words and beyond feelings. I took two years' refuge in my cave, spending much of the time when my children were not with me in solitary confinement. I needed time to heal, to make sense of what had happened and to slowly bring myself back to life. (Metta, 2010, p. 111)

Another important consideration in autoethnography is the notion of reciprocity and relational ethics. By engaging in feminist autoethnography, I am foregrounding the poststructuralist and feminist thinking that the self can only "exist in fluid, shifting and contextual reciprocity with other selves" (Metta, 2010, p. 31). Embedded within this fluid, ever-changing, and reciprocal self is the notion of *the permeable self*. As a result of our inherent reciprocity as subjects, researchers, writers, and autoethnographers, we cannot begin to write without being mindful of the relational ethics that are implicated in the research and writing process. In my autoethnographic writings, I have had to negotiate the ethical dilemmas involving the breaking of many silences.

In breaking my silence about my experiences of domestic violence, I inevitably have to disclose my ex-partner as a person who has perpetrated domestic abuse. This has always been a huge risk that many women who have experienced domestic violence face in any disclosure about their perpetrator. While I have taken the necessary steps to protect my ex-partner's identity in this research, it is impossible to conceal his identity to people who knew of our relationship. This is one of the many relational ethics that I have had to negotiate between duty of care as a writer/researcher and my relationships with the people involved in this research. (Metta, 2010, p. 59)

The practice of relational ethics must come with "an ever-vigilant and rigorous self-reflexivity and mindfulness of the everyday interaction and conversation as well as an ethical relational engagement with the past, with memory and with the stories" (Metta, 2010, p. 59).

The notion of *embodied mindfulness* becomes central in my work with my self and with the women and children I work with. In my psychotherapeutic practice, I am mindful of the importance of making spaces for women and children to occupy the centers of their own stories and be the authors of their own storytelling and story*making*. By *embodied mindfulness*, I mean being present, being *in tune with* and *attending* to the different and often subtle ways in which my own body speaks, as well as how women and children tell their stories through their *bodies*. I incorporate body movement, body mindfulness, and narrative and art therapies in my work with women and children to offer different media and languages with which to tell their stories. "Andy," a seven-year old boy who witnessed horrific family violence, loved to play with puppets and would only tell his stories about his experiences through his favorite puppets. Our work together involved many hours of puppet storytelling and storymaking, sand-play, drawing, paper-cutting, and simple meditation to re-create a different world in which Andy felt safe to thrive and grow.

One of the more silenced areas of women's narratives of domestic violence is their experiences of mothering. The physical, emotional, and psychological impacts of domestic violence on mothering are complex. Some mothers interviewed have described detrimental effects of domestic violence on their mothering, such as "losing their confidence as mothers, being emotionally drained and with little to give their children, taking out their frustrations on their children, and experiencing an emotional distance between themselves and their children" (Hester, Pearson, Harwin, & Abrahams, 2000, pp. 29–30).

For many of these women, their mothering has been the target of attacks, denigration, and undermining by the violent or controlling partner. Children have often been used in the abuse of women where the abusive partner had "deliberately and systematically" forced children "to witness the abuse and/or compelling them to listen to accusations about, and the demeaning of, their mothers" (Mullender, Hague, Iman, Kelly, Malos, & Regan, 2002, p. 162). Children have also been used by the abusive partner in post-separation custody arrangements to continue to exert control and abuse on the women.

McGee (2000) also found that "most mothers felt that they had in fact become closer to their children because of everything that they had been through together" (p. 48). Embodied mothering, for me and for many of the women I work with, is multi-layered and is often an extraordinary journey. The mundane daily embodied rituals of a mother feeding, bathing, clothing, attending to and caring for herself and for her children become central to the recovery process. The act of combing my children's hair every morning before school became a mindful and deliberate process of connection, soothing, and healing. Embodied mothering is about dealing with the confusion, trauma, fears, and sometimes anger embodied by her children. It is also about the delicate tender and intimate exchanges that are vital in keeping the woman and her children alive and in hope. Motherhood and mothering, for many of these women, become a key source of hope, courage, strength, and resilience for survival and recovery.

The embodied experiences of domestic violence on mothers are critical to both the storying of their experiences as well as their recovery. For many of these women, their wounded, shamed, and silenced bodies are hidden from themselves and their children. Touch is often dangerous territory. Yet, touch and feeling safe while being touched is critical to the body's recovery. My experience of healing the body was a weekly ritual that my children and I created. Each week, we would settle in bed at night and take turns massaging one another. We would often take long warm baths together—it was like returning to the womb together. Looking back now, I realize that it was a critical space we had intuitively created to connect, to attend to and to slowly heal our bodies, and most importantly, to learn to trust deeply again. Touch allows the body to be a powerful site for love, connection, intimacy, tenderness, and healing.

Alongside women's stories are often the silenced stories of the children who survived as victims and witnesses of acts of violence. These stories are vital to how we understand the narratives of domestic violence and the mother-child relationship during, after, and beyond domestic violence.

Figure 25.4 "Monsters in the Night." *Painting by Sarah Jayne McKay and the author.*

The door slams hard. The force of the vibration shakes her little body. She feels the slap on her mother's face. She closes her eyes shut and covers her ears. The monster in her tummy is back again. The monster—He—punches her tummy. It hurts. But she can't make a sound. Tears are stinging her eyes. She looks up at the closed door. She knocks on the door. She sees dark shadows.

When we meet, Sam draws little monsters, ugly dark shadows, skulls with bright red, sometimes black crayons. The red monsters are eating her tummy. They keep growing inside her. They make her sick. They scare her. Another session, she draws colorful rainbows. Caves and caves of rainbows. Rainbows of butterflies. She lies inside the safe cocoons.

We draw butterflies together. Butterflies that eat little monsters. Some butterflies get eaten, too. We keep drawing. We play with sand. We cut out paper butterflies. We placed the butterflies on her skin. On her tummy. She feels better knowing the butterflies are eating the little monsters.

Figure 25.5
"Sail Away."
*Painting by
Sarah Jayne
McKay and
the author.*

We meet again. She tells me stories about fairies and butterflies and the evil monster. We create the stories on the sand. She takes us on an adventure where the princess was captured but was protected by her special fairy and her army of butterflies. The evil monster was defeated; the fairy used her magic wand to turn the monster into a man. He was an old man who died.

We meet yet again. This time we paint pictures together. She draws a boat—her lifeboat—and the people she takes on her boat. She takes her mother, her best friend, her special fairy, and her army of butterflies.

Children's stories are vital to how we understand the impacts of the acts of violence on children and the mother-child relationships during, after, and beyond domestic violence. Many of these children are "aware of, and affected by, violence within their homes from a very young age, even when mothers feel that they have concealed what is happening" (Abrahams, 2010, p. 126).

> They are distressed and bewildered, not only by the physical and sexual abuse directed at their mother, but also the inherent emotional violence and the tension and anxiety that permeates the atmosphere in the home....Children and young people living with domestic violence and abuse inhabit an unsafe and unpredictable world, with feelings and experiences that can be hard to process at any age. (Abrahams, 2010, pp. 126–128)

Recovery...

Recovery can take place in and through the body and the writing. If every aspect of these women's and children's lives and bodies has been invaded and controlled by the brutal forms of power and control, then recovery-work has to be equally invasive in tenderness and freedom. I am deeply inspired and guided, in my own recovery, as a mother and as a feminist scholar and therapist, by Trinh Minh-ha's (1989) words:

> In her maternal love, she is neither possessed nor possessive; neither binding nor detached nor neutral. For a life to maintain another life, the touch has to be infinitely delicate: precise, attentive and swift, so as not to pull, track, rush, crush or smother. (p. 38)

Recovering from experiences of domestic violence and abuse must move beyond the binaries of "victim" and "survivor" to a place of *flourishing*; a place where the woman and her children can live in a place and space of peace, tenderness, and infinite growth that reaches far beyond the trauma. The story must continue beyond the story of violence, tragedy, and survival to one where love, hope, joy, and taking risks sit alongside the past. My hope is to create the spaces to tell different kinds of stories and narratives that will embrace the fullness of life and being for these women and children. I am inspired by the stories of many women and children in their creative and courageous attempts to live with, through, and beyond family and domestic violence. I want to also stress here that the language we use to tell these stories is profoundly important.

> I argue that the use of labels such as "battered women" and "victims of domestic violence" is dangerous and risks further silencing and marginalising these women. These women cannot be defined merely by their experiences of domestic violence, but rather, their experiences of domestic violence and abuse form a part of their experiences, identity, and lives. We need to be ever vigilant and mindful of the effects of labels such as "battered," "abused," or "victims" on these women. I suggest alternative descriptions, such as women who have experienced domestic violence, as a more useful approach of representing these women in ways that do not diminish their experiences of abuse or violence but also do not define them only in terms of their experiences of abuse and violence. (Metta, 2010, p. 285)

Embodied feminist autoethnography surrounding the issues of domestic and family violence has important implications and relevance for researchers and practitioners across different disciplines, such as social work, women and gender studies, social science, cultural studies, health sciences, psychology, and psychotherapy. The deeply personal and embodied narratives of knowing, surviving, and living with, against, and beyond domestic violence form critical bodies of knowledges that inform the philosophical, conceptual, and scholarly understandings as well as the practices of practitioners, theorists, and scholars working the field of domestic/family abuse. I urge scholars and writers of autoethnography to investigate and engage with embodied ways of writing and knowledge making that demand our attention and action. I leave you with Cixous's (1991b) words which aptly sum up my own sentiment:

> Writing: a way of leaving no space for death, of pushing back forgetfulness, of never letting oneself be surprised by the abyss. Of never becoming resigned, consoled; never turning over in bed to face the wall and drift asleep again as if nothing had happened; as if nothing could happen. (p. 3)

Notes

1. The images used in this chapter have been co-created by the author in collaboration with Sarah McKay. These visual narratives sit alongside the poetic/prose narratives to create different layers of storytelling and storymaking.
2. Permission to reprint excerpts from Metta (2010) granted by Peter Lang.
3. I return here to the metaphor of the permeable body which suggests a kind of "uncontainable" body, a rhizome-like body that is organic, resilient, fluid, changing, and capable of self-regeneration and self-renewal. The notions of permeability and fluidity are also useful in thinking through different ways of working with and through the body and embodied experiences.
4. See Deleuze and Guattari's idea of the *rhizome*, a philosophical concept used to describe systems and bodies of knowledge that operate with the principles of connection, heterogeneity, and multiplicities. In *A Thousand Plateaus* (1987).
5. See Phyllis Chesler's *Women and Madness* (2005). The widespread psychiatric labeling of "madness" of many women in the nineteenth and early twentieth centuries that led to their institutionalization has been attributed to layers of social, cultural, ideological, and institutional oppression acting upon entirely sane women. The historical association of madness and hysteria with the "symptoms" of women's acts of rebellion and protests has long been challenged by feminists like Chesler.

References

Abrahams, H. (2010). *Rebuilding lives after domestic violence: Understanding long-term outcomes*. London: Jessica Kingsley.

Chesler, P. (2005). *Women and madness*. New York. Palgrave MacMillan.

Cixous, H. (1986). *The newly born woman*. Minneapolis: University of Minnesota Press.

Cixous, H. (1991a). The laugh of the Medusa. In S. Gunew (Ed.), *Feminist knowledge: A reader*. London: Routledge.

Cixous, H. (1991b). *Coming to writing and other essays*. Cambridge, MA: Harvard University Press.

Deleuze, G., & Guattari, F. (1987). *A thousand plateaus: Capitalism and schizophrenia*. Minneapolis: University of Minnesota Press.

Denzin, N. (1997). *Interpretive ethnography: Ethnographic practices for the 21st century*. Thousand Oaks, CA: Sage.

Denzin, N. (2011). Foreword: Performing autoethnography: Making the personal political. In T. Spry, *Body, Paper, Stage: Writing and performing autoethnography* (pp. 11–13). Walnut Creek, CA: Left Coast Press, Inc.

Foucault, M. (1979). *Discipline and punish: The birth of the prison*. New York: Vintage Books.

Goodall, H. L., Jr. (2004). Commentary. *Journal of Applied Communication Research, 32*, 185–194.

Hester, M., Pearson, C., Harwin, N., & Abrahams, H. (2000). *Making an impact: Children and domestic violence: A Reader* (2nd ed.). London: Jessica Kingsley.

Holman Jones, S. (2005). Autoethnography: Making the personal political. In N.K. Denzin & Y.S. Lincoln (Eds.), *The SAGE handbook of qualitative research* (3rd ed., pp. 763–791). Thousand Oaks, CA: Sage.

Hopkins, L. (2009). *On voice and silence: Giving life to a story and story to a life.* Berlin, Germany: VDM Verlag Dr. Muller.

McGee, C. (2000). *Childhood experiences of domestic violence.* London: Jessica Kingsley.

Metta, M. (2010). *Writing against, alongside and beyond memory: Lifewriting as reflexive poststructuralist feminist research practice.* Bern, Switzerland: Peter Lang.

Minh-Ha, T. T. (1989). *Woman, native, other: Writing postcoloniality and feminism.* Indianapolis: Indiana University Press.

Morris, M. K. (2002). Audre Lorde: Textual authority and the embodied self. *Frontiers: A Journal of Women Studies, 23,* 168–188.

Mullender, A., Hague, G., Iman, U., Kelly, L., Malos, E., & Regan, L. (2002). *Children's perspectives on domestic violence.* Thousand Oaks, CA: Sage.

Rich, A. (1976). *Of woman born.* London: Virago.

Richardson, L. (1990). *Writing strategies: Reaching diverse audiences.* Qualitative Research Methods Series 21. Thousand Oaks, CA: Sage.

Richardson, L. (2000). Writing: A method of inquiry. In N. K. Denzin & Y. S. Lincoln (Eds.), *Handbook of qualitative research* (2nd ed., pp. 923–948). Thousand Oaks, CA: Sage.

Richardson, L., & St. Pierre, E. A. (2005). Writing: A method of inquiry. In N. K. Denzin & Y. S. Lincoln (Eds.), *The SAGE handbook of qualitative research* (3rd ed., pp. 959–978). Thousand Oaks, CA: Sage.

Spry, T. (2011). *Body, paper, stage: Writing and performing autoethnography.* Walnut Creek, CA: Left Coast Press, Inc.

Tomm, W. (1995). *Bodied mindfulness: Women's spirits, bodies and places.* Ontario: Wilfred Laurier University Press.

Tong, R. P. (1998). *Feminist thought: A more comprehensive introduction.* Sydney: Allen & Unwin.

Weir, A. (2008). Global feminism and transformative identity politics. *Hypatia, 23,* 110–133.

Section Four

Moving and Changing

Section Four Introduction

Autoethnography as a Mode of Knowing and a Way of Being

Andrew C. Sparkes

In an audit culture framed by neo-liberalism and scientific imperialism poisonous darts are aimed at autoethnographers by those who wish, at best, to demean this form of inquiry as a mode of scholarship and, at worst, to erase it from the academy. The poison stings the flesh with accusations of self-indulgence and lack of rigor, to name but a couple. Autoethnographers require antidotes and these are provided by the authors in the chapters that follow. Their antidotes not only soothe but also cause discomfort. Good autoethnography does this for both its producers and consumers.

Talking of "good" autoethnography evokes a process of evaluation. Rejecting static criteriological approaches the authors, in different ways, contribute to this debate. For example, Archana Pathak, reflecting on what it means for her to be a child of the Indian diaspora, illustrates how engaging in autoethnography through a postcolonial frame can enhance the vibrant rigor that is a characteristic of well done autoethnography. Likewise, having laid out a series of variables that inform teaching autoethnography and autoethnographic pedagogy that recognizes how these processes are always grounded in compassion and care, Bryant Keith Alexander ponders the evaluative criteria that might be appropriately applied to these processes.

More directly, unpacking the multi-layered case of a Catholic institution controversially withdrawing its invitation for a queer performance artist to give a workshop to students, Craig Gingrich-Philbrook grapples with the problems of

Handbook of Autoethnography, edited by Stacy Holman Jones, Tony E. Adams, and Carolyn Ellis, 512–516. © 2013 Left Coast Press, Inc. All rights reserved.

what orienting story to tell about evaluation when it so often provides the occasions for disorientating experiences. He makes it clear that what we think of as evaluation never stands above autoethnography. Rather, it always occurs alongside it, on the same plane and in the same world as the autoethnographic work under consideration, whether it contests or reaches out to that work in coalition. Gingrich-Philbrook recognizes that budding autoethnographers may seek the reassurance of a checklist outlining things that a "good" autoethnography does and what its qualities are. But, he warns, checklists only make sense as something developed over time and experience, something that changes and grows, adapts to different writers, writing different projects, for different purposes, at different times. A checklist is not to be confused with a metalanguage, something universally endorsed, as this can too easily get converted into a magic contract of power relationships that can operate insidiously as part of a brutal evaluation politics to extinguish the autoethnographic enterprise.

The authors in this section also provide the antidote to another poisonous barb that breaks the skin with the claim that autoethnographic work has no impact beyond the self of the storyteller. Contradicting this, they illustrate how autoethnography can be used to change not only the self but also communities and societies. Thus, Satoshi Toyosaki and Sandra L. Pensoneau-Conway consider the doing of autoethnography as a praxis of social justice. They wonder how different the world would be, and how differently we would move through the landscape, if autoethnography were an ethical way of being *in* the world, being *with* others, and being there *for* others. Toyosaki and Pensoneau-Conway invite the reader to move with them as they situate the ontological and praxiological commitments of autoethnography. In so doing, they set up ways that might privilege autoethnography not merely as a way to know, but also as a way to critically act in the world, and a way to understand the construction of the self. For them, since social justice is a collective journey to actualize the possible rather than simply accept the actual as finished, the autoethnographic project provides a fertile ground for individual and social transformation.

Questions of transformation and postcolonial critique, as raised by Pathak, are embedded in the chapter by Keyan G. Tomaselli, Lauren Dyll–Myklebust, and Sjoerd van Grootheest, who consider personal/political interventions via autoethnography. They examine issues of subjectivity, identity, and methodology in a Eurocentric Cartesian-based institution by focusing on the contradictions resulting from them working with student and research teams that are simultaneously multiracial, multilinguistic, multiethnic, multigendered, and multidisciplinary. Tomaselli, Dyll–Myklebust, and van Grootheest open their chapter by defining and briefly outlining the epistemological procedures that, for them, illustrate autoethnography. The authors show how these autoethnographic procedures operate via a number of case studies that stress their practice as a relationship between Self and Other, researchers and researched, and observer and observed in encounters that are often framed by the debilitating dualisms of inclusion/exclusion, facilitation/obstruction, and acquiescence/resistance.

The performative dimensions of autoethnography echoed by all authors in this section are foregrounded by Deanna Shoemaker in her autoethnographic journey into performing possibilities, utopias, and futures. As part of this journey, autoethnographic performance (AEP) offers Shoemaker critical and cultural spaces in which to theorize the racism, classism, sexism, heterosexism, and homophobia that she grew up with as a white working class girl in West Texas. Later, AEP became a means of survival in graduate school and as she navigated her newly emerging identities of middle-class professor, scholar, performance artist/activist, feminist, partner, and mother. Shoemaker closes her chapter by considering how AEP, both on the page and on the stage, might be utilized to carve out new possibilities for achieving cultural understandings, create situated knowledges, develop more just social relationships, and envision change through performance.

In her chapter, Shoemaker provides an important service for the reader by outlining a topographical map that aspires to gather, distill, and begin to see the complex relationships between many of the foundational concepts currently at play in AEP. This mapping of autoethnographic writing/performance invites readers to seek entry points for their own journeys by giving attention to the ethical values that need to be considered, the possible forms and characteristics of the venture, and the socio-political goals that guide the process. Shoemaker reminds us that these journeys toward utopian possibilities and transformative change are far from easy, involving as they do a self-reflexive and often uncomfortable commitment to dialogue and deep listening in order to understand and transverse in/visible borders, discover buried histories and contexts, evoke revelations and potential transformations, mark identities-in-motion, and excavate meaningful gaps in personal and cultural knowledge.

Various possibilities and futures are also proposed by Bryant Keith Alexander in his reflections on teaching autoethnography and autoethnographic pedagogy. He begins by presenting a performance piece one of his students, Danielle, offered as a response to a two-voiced assignment that requires students to have an intimate engagement with scholarly texts through an embodied, experiential, and expressive mode. According to Alexander, this assignment enables students to filter their lived experience through scholarly texts (and back) as a form a rehydration. As such, his students attempt to use their own senses and critical reflection on experience as the hydrating liquid of both embodied and scholarly knowing. Building on this example, Alexander develops a philosophy of teaching autoethnography/autoethnographic pedagogy that acknowledges the importance of critical (communicative) pedagogy, border pedagogy, public pedagogy, and the performance of possibilities. He then shares with the reader a number of methodological considerations in teaching autoethnography to undergraduate and postgraduate classes. These considerations are clearly outlined and provide fascinating insights into the multi-layered nature of the process along with the possibilities and dilemmas for all involved.

The issues raised by the authors cited above are played out vividly and evocatively in the exemplars that follow provided by Carol Rambo, Eve Tuck and C. Ree, and Kathleen Stewart. These exemplars, which are superbly crafted, do not make for "easy" reading and will affect readers in deep and visceral ways. Telling a tale that is in the active process of being "worked on" as an incest survivor, Rambo decides that it is okay that she does not know what is "really" going on and that she may never know. She also decides that autoethnography and a layered account format is an excellent platform from which to explore the nature of Twitch and the experience of living with chronic liminality or "not knowing." Just who and what Twitch is, and the significance of the roles she plays in Rambo's life, is left open for interpretation as the story unfolds. Here, Rambo skilfully performs chronic liminality while struggling with various psychological narratives that are on offer and her own embodied story line. There is no happy ending, no resolution, just an acknowledgement that trauma touches most of our lives at one time or another. Rambo does not pretend to generalize her experiences to all trauma survivors. However, she is willing to speculate that many people have aspects of themselves like Twitch that are disowned most of the time but surface in their daily lives as extreme aversive reactions or more subtle unconscious biases.

The glossary of haunting in its many forms offered by Tuck and Ree seeks to explore what this phenomenon might mean for understanding settler colonialism, ceremony, revenge, and decolonization. Thus, under [A] the reader is introduced to American horror as depicted in film as well as American anxieties and settler colonial horrors. A comparison of American horror films with their Japanese counterparts illustrates how the latter disrupt the former's logic of righting past injustice or reconciliation by invoking instead a strategy more akin to wronging, or revenge. These themes are developed as the reader is taken though [B] Beloved, [C] Cyclops, and all the way to [W], which deals with righting and wronging Wrongs. Tuck and Ree note that this is the last entry for now, but it is only a temporary stay. More entries wait to be written, and not always patiently. They leave readers with the disturbing thought that they will have to find someone to pull on their ears to bring them out of their nightmares, to call them home and help them remember who they are, and to hope that the ghost will be willing to let them go.

Stewart's "An Autoethnography of What Happens" provides another form of haunting in the story she writes of a death that disturbs but also activates the self-world relation. For her, autoethnography is one route into a broader-ranging, more supple and subtle exploration of what happens to people, how forces hit bodies, and how sensibilities circulate and become collective in different ways. That is, it describes the qualities of connection and impact in recognizable situations while composing a world perturbed by the singularity of events in ways that can be generative. In her reflections on the story, Stewart considers the compositional complicity of subject-world which, for her, is the first question of autoethnography. She also hopes that her offering suggests how autoethnography can be a way to forge a linkage between self and world, the abstract and the concrete, the massive and the minute, and the fuzzy or smudged yet precise. I am certain readers will agree that it does just this.

In closing this section introduction I would simply thank the authors for the honesty and courage they have shown in providing antidotes to the poisons that are so often directed at autoethnographers. I thank them also for the challenges they have presented regarding the future development of autoethnography as a mode of knowing and a way of being.

Chapter 26

Autoethnographic Journeys

Performing Possibilities/Utopias/Futures

Deanna B. Shoemaker

Here. Now. (A Beginning of Sorts)

(Two performers occupy separate spaces onstage. They suddenly look at one another for the first time. They slowly cross to each other, reach out, and tentatively touch. The performers begin to speak a poetic dialogue.)

We don't always recognize ourselves.

We are haunted…

by other voices,

other bodies,

other selves,

other experiences.

We are haunted…

by those who are no longer with us

and who we were

or could have been with them.

You and I are in transition.

Handbook of Autoethnography, edited by Stacy Holman Jones, Tony E. Adams, and Carolyn Ellis, 517–537. © 2013 Left Coast Press, Inc. All rights reserved.

We are liminal beings,

Witnessing time passing, circling back,

Feeling the pull of history

and the weight of culture,

Experiencing the shock,

surprise,

wonder,

confusion of releasing,

Re-imagining pieces of

identity,

abilities,

old/new anxieties,

priorities,

ways of thinking,

ways of working,

ways of creating,

ways of engaging/resisting/intervening,

Transforming relationships with friends,

family,

lovers,

communities,

and others we have not yet met...

(Both voices):
There are urgent new desires and needs TAKING HOLD OF US!

(adapted from Carr & Shoemaker, 2011)[1]

In the midst of generating this autoethnographic performance (AEP) about decay, loss, desire, and transformative discovery through the aging female body with longtime collaborator Tessa Carr, another version of my life, as I know it, is falling apart in slow motion. Or rather, transforming. Each day brings new jolts of pleasure and pain or simply more dull realizations about a shared past. The future looms as an unknown landscape, full of possibilities and pitfalls. Despite the seeming hurdles ahead, I am somehow hopeful... In this uncomfortable moment of flux, I long to speak with you, my readers, to hear your stories, to ask you questions, to better understand.

Where do you hold your sorrows?

Your losses? Your loneliness?

Where do you carry your joy? Your desire?

Where do you lodge your anxieties, your fears?

How do you carry your unspeakable secrets?

Your heartbreaks?

Your wildest laughter?

Can you feel it? (Carr & Shoemaker, 2011)

For days I sit alone at my dining room table, in a house that is suddenly too big. I quietly gaze at words on the computer screen, trying mightily to conjure this chapter on the future possibilities of AEP practices. I nervously bite the skin around my fingernails, drink strong coffee, and attempt to clean my permanently scratched glasses one more time. I yearn for the buzz of a text message, the ding of an e-mail, or a knock on the door to save me from this sense of loss, uncertainty, and nascent excitement I feel about my/our future(s) as well as future journeys for autoethnographic writing and performance. Who am I to prognosticate in this time of chaos and confusion? As usual, I don't have that crystal ball I've always secretly hoped would show me the way. It occurs to me that I am seriously directionally challenged; in fact, being lost has become a defining metaphor in my life. I can never find the right map or set of directions scrawled onto the many small pieces of paper I tend to carry with me. While technology increasingly helps me to find my way, I crave more human-to-human navigation. Perhaps this is precisely the moment to get lost in a rich terrain of possibility, with the past, present, and future pressing down on all of us. Perhaps we can bear witness together to the tears that spontaneously well up as fingers touch the keyboard or another's face, or as we breathe in and out together in a performance space. Perhaps we can take a collective leap into the performative tangle of creative, embodied, and highly interrelational AEP practices to discover our way(s) into new realms of cultural study.

Does this leap represent at least part of what one aspires to when engaging in autoethnographic (AE) work? As a white working class girl raised in the harsh landscape of West Texas, AE writing/performance has offered me critical and cultural spaces in which to theorize the racism, classism, sexism, heterosexism, and homophobia I grew up with. AEP became a means of survival as I navigated my way through the rigors of graduate school and my newly emerging identities of middle-class professor, scholar, performance artist/activist, feminist, partner, and mother. AEP has also provided me with an ethical roadmap for how I strive to move with others through the world.

Like Gingrich-Philbrook (2005), I suspect I am falling into a "midlife crisis, writer's block, or depression" as I struggle to define and argue for the value of AE methods (p. 297). In my own AEP work, heavily inspired by feminist performance art and performance ethnography, I fret over the dominance of my voice and experience as a white woman who now enjoys the privileges of tenure and middle class status. Does my perspective carry unearned currency when a proliferation of other marginalized voices within and beyond the academy is urgently needed? Gingrich-Philbrook's words offer some measure of comfort: "In the wake of this appreciative distrust [of AE], I hope to survive our times and my own image of death by recommitting myself to a queer aesthetic for meaning, one more interested in textualities of livable difference than knowledge as a weapon of mass reproduction" (p. 298). This queer aesthetic makes room for a wide spectrum of lived experiences and aesthetic approaches as a means of disrupting hegemonic "norms" and ideologies that implicitly or explicitly distort, silence, and marginalize difference in its many articulations.[2]

In the spirit of a queer aesthetic that troubles broad Truth claims and investments in normativity, I find myself resisting urges to create clarity or agreement over definitions of AEP or legitimize this vexed and potentially subversive, aesthetic, and performative approach to studying culture. AE/AEP spirals outward from a reflexive, partial, and tentative claim of self to critically dialogue with larger discourses, other subjects, and various socio-political-cultural practices. Gingrich-Philbrook (2005) usefully asserts that AE may be less a method than a "broad orientation" to scholarship that is realized through a dizzying array of textual [and performative] practices, and that the most compelling AE traffics in issues of "representation, power, and subjectivity" (p. 299). This chapter will consider how AEP (on the page and the stage) might be utilized to carve out new possibilities for achieving cultural understandings, creating situated knowledges, developing more just social relationships, and envisioning change through performance. My hope in the face of various odds springs from the promise of collectively evoking potential futures through a broad spectrum of AEP practices and points of view that span and blur the realms of academic and popular cultures.

So where might this AEP journey begin? For me, everything always circles back to the dry, desolate terrain of West Texas:

> I come from a land of two colors
>
> Red dirt blue sky
>
> White skin Brown skin
>
> A land of wide, open spaces where I can roam freely
>
> *(Shatter my heart, bury me there. Sprinkle me over the cotton fields, bury me there.)*

This stark minimalism satisfies me deeply

I panic in small spaces

Drown in overstuffed chairs.

Walking down farm roads between San Angelo and Mertzon, Texas

Between Plains and Lubbock, Texas

(Frying in the Panhandle)

My yellow brick road is dry caliche crunching beneath my feet

A dirt road in the middle of nowhere

(You could scream real loud out there, and no one would hear you…)

Walking, dizzy from the crushing heat

Locusts humming a mad song in my ear

I imagine, shimmering on the steaming, lonely road

Just a ways beyond the dusty rainbow…

A candy store!?

I WANT CANDY, AND LOTS OF IT.

I crave lemonheadstwizzlersjawbreakerspoprocksjollyrancherstootsierolls

pinkbubblegumspreessweettartschocolatekissesspicygumdropsredhots

candycorntwixtwinkiesfriedblueberrypies…

Anything to rot my teeth and fill me up!

Anything at all to carry me away and heal me up…

Anything at all to Fill. Me. (Shoemaker, 1998)[3]

In this early AEP, I look to my own backyard, so to speak, to theorize my white, working class roots by sifting through memories of a striking(ly familiar) physical and cultural landscape steeped in racial inequalities and recurring dreams full of inchoate desires and longings to escape this beloved home space.[4] Where might your AE journey begin? Where do you come from? What do your physical and psychic landscapes look like? Feel like? If you had to draw up a map of this space, what would it look like? Who populates these spaces (and who doesn't)? What does "home" mean to you? How have your familiar landscapes shaped your experiences of self and Other in cultural contexts? What stories of "home" do you share? Why? How? What are the stories you cannot tell, and why?

Traveling Through Liminal Zones

"So, so sorry about all the heartache. It's going to be hard, no doubt… It may sound masochistic, but times like these—that really test you, that force you to live with your feelings so near the surface—are the stuff of real living. There's something wonderful about being present to yourself and others (and not being able to pull the covers of work, daily function, etc. over yourself). Hang in there. Keep your feet on the ground. And dream a little too!" (personal communication, January 5, 2012)

This recent e-mail from a dear friend captures something intrinsic about not only the complexity of our daily lives but also AEP practices, which demand researcher vulnerability, rigor, hope, and a grounded presence that flies in the face of much social scientific research invested in objectivity as the criterion of academic rigor. AEP, as a hybrid scholarly/artistic practice, aspires to situate human experience within larger discourses, troubles power imbalances in our everyday lives, and offers a lens by which to illuminate culture through the shifting prisms of self/other in-and-of the world through enactment. AE/AEP typically resists neat closure, master narratives, and whole, fully knowable selves. Bell and Holman Jones (2008) posit that AE is the "underground" or fringe of scholarly writing [and performance] that becomes a creative space and public forum by which to imagine and enact possibilities for social change (p. 212). Perhaps this is the liminal space where the tangle of our collective desires, dreams, difficult dialogues, and complex relationships across differences can live and transform within academic research as well as popular cultural performance practices.

Contexts and (Some Possible) Definitions: A Map of Sorts

Nov. 26, 2011

Dear Advancement Director,

Please remove us from ALL correspondence from Monmouth University especially Monmouth University Magazine [sic]. Due to your political infusion in the articles of your magazine, especially Brian Greenberg and Deanne [sic] Shoemaker, we neither want to contribute or be associated with Monmouth anymore. It is a sad day in higher education when bias [sic] opinions intrude and distort knowledge.

I recently received a copy of this missive as well as several other negative letters written in response to an article for which I was invited to contribute for my university's Fall 2011 glossy alumni magazine. Six faculty members from different disciplines across campus were asked to reflect on the meaning of the Occupy Wall Street (OWS) movement in nearby Manhattan; we each shared our perspectives in a constructed dialogue of sorts. The cover of this issue of the magazine was supposed to feature a photo of our students taking part in an OWS protest, but the image was cut from the cover right before the magazine went to print. I am struck by the widely held assumption in the letters of complaint as well as in critiques of AEP that knowledge is, or even could be, neutral in educational institutions and beyond. A persistent valorization of objectivity over "bias" (that is, situated knowledges constituted within particular political and cultural contexts) and outright denial of the ways that bias, when masked as objectivity, intrudes upon and distorts knowledge in oppressive ways, reflects the palpably conservative academic climate many scholars work in. Another outraged letter to the editor ended with this barb: "Maybe you should be teaching your students that personal responsibility and hard work are the elements that make success possible—not collective whining about what they think they are entitled to!" The explicit embrace of a capitalist-inspired rugged individualism here dangerously erases deeply institutionalized inequalities and functions to silence those of us who gather together across our differences in public squares, in performance spaces, in university classrooms, and in digital realms to collectively risk performative and sometimes contentious battles for sustainable social change.

Clearly, the professional and personal stakes in adopting experimental research practices such as AEP in academia are (still) high.[5] After carefully considering whether to contribute to this article, I decided to use my privileged status as a newly tenured professor to join the dialogue, albeit in a mostly measured way that framed OWS within the realm of a performance studies-based analysis. Several junior faculty members declined to contribute to the article, which speaks to the real risks academics may or may not be able to take when situating their teaching, scholarship, and/or service as resistant forms of advocacy and activism.

AEP practices, while still taboo for and to many in the academy, are squarely situated within postmodern ideas of subjectivity as local, contingent, historical, and, yes, political. The use of first person, or the "performative-I," in AEP reflects a useful "rupture and fragmentation" of researcher positionality as a subjective claim rather than an assumption of a stable or fully knowable self (Spry, 2006, p. 340). The performative-I in AEP speaks to a parallel troubling of meaning-making within studies of culture as a linear, disembodied process. Clifford (1986) writes of culture:

> There is no whole picture that can be 'filled in,' since the perception and filling in of a gap leads to the awareness of other gaps....Culture is contested, temporal, emergent. Representation and explanation—both by insiders and outsiders—is implicated in this emergence. (pp. 18–19)

Clifford's words signaled a paradigmatic shift in qualitative research with human subjects toward more experimental forms of writing (and performance-based scholarship) that has led to "the full accounting for and utilization of the researcher's personal body and felt experience as research instrument" (Banks & Banks, 2000, p. 234). This move opened the way for AE methods as a self-reflexive praxis that circumvents the "hubris" of "the colonizing and exoticizing action of ethnographer upon the cultural other" (p. 234). Thus, AEP becomes a highly situated (and contested) perspective that gazes inward (auto) and outward (ethno) simultaneously in order to performatively enact complex intersectionalities of identity, place, and power.

At the risk of contradicting the partial and emergent nature of AEP, what follows is my attempt at a topographical map of sorts that aspires to gather, distill, and begin to see the complex relationships between many, but certainly not all, of the foundational concepts currently at play in AEP. This "map" (of course all maps are incomplete and skewed) is also intended as a dialogic, shorthand representation of many scholarly voices who have contributed to the field of AEP. You can read top to bottom in each column, left to right across the three columns, or simply let your eyes wander, connecting the "dots" as you chart your own course. While a number of the concepts included are not unpacked here, you can locate

---

Mapping Autoethnographic Writing/Performance (Possible Journeys)

Ethical Values to Consider ⇨	Possible Forms/ Characteristics ⇨	Socio-Political Goals ⇨
Vulnerability (risks empathy & deep listening over distance)	*Gazes in/out (auto-ethno)*	*Disrupt objectivity, hegemonic discourses, & imperialist modes of representation*
(Self)Reflexivity	*Hybrid, collage, open texts*	*Inspire new forms of & standards for qualitative research*
Positionality (I/We/You/ Them)	*Experimental/creative/ provocative*	
Self ↔ Other Interrelationality	*Dialogic*	*Collective, accessible, critical public forums (third spaces)*
Embodied/Subjugated Knowledges	*Poetic*	*Shared sense-making*
Pomo subjectivities	*Co-performative witnessing*	*Engage borderlands/ margins*
Process driven, temporal	*Participatory*	*Research for/as social justice, change, advocacy*
Situated cultural/ experiential knowledges	*Collaborative*	
Queer resistance	*Emergent*	*Equitable redistributions of power*
Performative transformations	*Liminal/Uncertain/Fluid*	
Marginalized/subaltern voices & performances	*Performative (constitutive)*	*Performative utopias/ pedagogies evoked as politics of hope*
Grounded historical/ cultural contexts	*Epiphanies/fragments of heightened experience*	*Spaces for (silenced) stories that need to be told/heard*
Aesthetic/Emotional/ Ethical/Political	*Breaks and remakes*	
Relational, Evocative,	*Proliferation of voices & bodies*	
Embodied, Consequential, Generative	*Culturally specific forms*	

discussions about these ideas and practices elsewhere in this Handbook. I invite you to redesign this map, fill in the gaps, add to my overlapping lists, and/or stuff it in your pocket as you search for an entry point into your own AEP journey.

This rudimentary "map" is not really a map after all, is it? However, I have learned through years of being lost that there is value in uncertainty; you never know quite where you will end up. As I gaze up at the moon shining outside my window, I hope these partial and tentative lists of complex practices, ideals, and goals will dance off the page, commingle, and re-emerge as possible routes or small beacons of light that somehow inspire you on your journey. AE journeys often circle back around again with new layers of meaning and fluid ways of be/coming. I opened this section with excerpts from letters of complaint about the OWS article I contributed to; while writing this chapter, I received a message from our alumni magazine editor letting the six authors know that the article had won a 2012 gold Hermes award for creative journalism. Perhaps there is some sweetness in taking what may feel like precarious leaps into our work without a clear map. Knowledge is never neutral, culture is always contested, and this kind of research is emergent; hopefully AEP's performative movements toward utopian possibilities open up new public forums for recognizing, engaging with, and enacting some measure of transformative change.

Performing Process (Mapping "What" and "How")

Denzin's "Call to Performance" (2003) is a manifesto that advocates for a performance-based cultural studies as a means of enacting radical social change. This call, which includes AE, invokes Conquergood's (1992) foundational ideas about performance as kinesis, an embodied and interventionary movement of breaking and remaking of discourses (Denzin, 2003, pp. 187–188). Building upon this idea, Denzin argues that if we perform culture as we write (and stage) it, and the lines between performativity (a doing) and performance (the thing done) have dissolved, we are (re)writing culture as we (re)perform it, which potentially can generate social change (p. 188). Framing AEP as both a political and pedagogical practice, Denzin's call to "write and perform culture in new ways" (p. 189) evokes Giroux's utopian performative as a pedagogical politics of hope: "This utopianism and [AE] vision of hope moves from private to public, from biographical to institutional, and views personal troubles as public issues. This utopianism tells and performs stories of resistance, compassion, justice, joy, community, and love" (cited in Denzin, 2003, p. 192).

Conquergood's notion of performance as kinesis sees its potential in AE interventions into discursive constructs and material practices. Because all performance is essentially re-performance (Butler, 1993; Schechner, 1998), AEP offers critical ways to mark, critique, deconstruct, and re-envision hegemonic and often oppressive performances of self/other. Pollock ("Response," 1998) notes that performativity is "what happens when history/textuality sees itself in the mirror—and suddenly sees double; it is the disorienting, disruptive" (p. 44). This heightened, kaleidoscopic effect speaks to how performed experiences can become "sites where... emotion, memory, desire, and understanding come together (Denzin, 2003, p. 192). These sites also reflect Conquergood's (2002) claim that performance can produce liminal realms of cultural/political resistance, deep engagement with the ethics of scholarly (re) presentation, and critical reconfigurations of power.

Turning to some of my own AEP work to trace moments of performance as kinesis and possible enactments of a utopian politics of hope, I am struck by the grace of Warren's (2006) statement: "I turned to performance ethnography (PE) because it gives life to people in context, makes embodied practices meaningful, and generates analysis for seeing the conditions that make the socially taken-for-granted visible as a process" (p. 318). In this way AEP potentially shows us "what is" and what is possible via performative interventions. Dolan (2001) sees the "utopian performative" in theatre and performance studies as sites "of progressive social and cultural practice" that can "articulate a common future, one that's more just and equitable" (p. 455). To reach toward this utopian performative, my AEP journeys out into the world started with "what is" by looking back to West Texas and the powerful women who raised me. Ellis, Adams, and Bochner (2011) note that autoethnographic scholars typically write (and perform) about the past and its weight on the present moment. As Matsuda (1993) reminds, "It is often only upon backward reflection that some kind of beginning is acknowledged.... It is not until one engages in a conscious reconstruction, asking what led to what else, that a history is revealed, or perhaps...chosen" (pp. 3–4).

In the following excerpt from my performance "Speaking Unspeakables: There's No Place Like Home,"[6] I attempt to mark my vexed positionality as both (auto)ethnographer and one of numerous familial subjects within this particular historical and cultural study of whiteness and how it shapes my own and family members' identities. In re-animating the past, I struggle to both re-map a cultural space-in-progress and re/tell "unspeakable" stories to enact a hopeful politics of AE change:

> That's me on my wedding day, in between my mother and granny. I was born in San Angelo, Texas, the year Black Power exploded within the civil rights movement. I've been raised by a circle of strong white women, and their stories of poverty, their dreams of a pot of gold at the end of the rainbow, and the blood bonds of family have been drummed into me. But I keep telling them that this [AEP] isn't a celebration of family, and they might not like it. Because I'm re-reading those familiar stories and listening for the silences, for what has been buried beneath this white skin and these blue eyes. (Shoemaker, 1998)

AEP demands a self-reflexive and often uncomfortable commitment to dialogue and deep listening in order to understand and traverse in/visible borders, discover buried histories and contexts, evoke revelations and potential transformations, mark identities-in-motion, and excavate meaningful gaps in personal and cultural knowledge:

I remember going to a big fish fry with my little brother in Ella Mae's [African American] neighborhood, off Randolph Street.…Her grandmother "Big Ella" was cooking, and crazy sister Barbara and son little Jay were there. Maybe I'm making this part up *(Sly and the Family Stone's "Thank you Falletinme Be Mice Elf Agin" song begins to play)*, but I remember the sounds of many voices bursting into laughter, good food smells, a feeling of warmth and comfort here. Does this memory rise up out of my bones stewed in slavery, where black women raised white children? Is this my Gauguin-esque fantasy of the "exotic other"…having more "spirit" than white folks? I don't know, but I've held on to this memory, and this childhood yearning to shed my skin…*(Music fades out)*. Now I'm grown, and I know better than to say I once wanted to be black. I'm colored too, and I have a history to claim, however hard that might be. (Shoemaker, 1998)[7]

In this AEP, my fieldwork consisted of digging through boxed up artifacts such as childhood journals and family photographs; studying maps of my hometown; revisiting old neighborhoods; deep "hanging out" with family members as co-performative witnessing; conducting formal and informal oral history interviews with women in my family across three generations, and arranging a long overdue visit with Ella Mae, who had established close bonds not only with my immediate family but also with my aunt and uncle as she went off to college. Including highly subjective, impressionistic experiences along with more traditional cultural data, I was able to performatively investigate the knotty intersections between racial identity, racism, sexism, and class-consciousness within familial contexts. This AEP attempts to "show" (collapse distance) as well as "tell" (increase critical distance), include multiple and shifting perspectives, deploy thick descriptions of culture to discern patterns, and reach out to audiences within and beyond academia for more broad-based participation and public dialogue.

Dolan (2001) considers why people still gather to see live performances when there are so many other mediums competing for our attention today (p. 455), and admits,

I go to theatre and performance to hear stories that order, for a moment, my incoherent longings, that engage the complexity of personal and cultural relationships, and that critique the assumptions of a social system I find sorely lacking. I want a lot from theatre and performance. (p. 466)

She reminds us of the value of hope in the research and rehearsal process, in the gathering of people in "special times and special places," and in the resonances that remain after audiences disperse (p. 459). Through performances of "Speaking Unspeakables" followed by talkbacks at The University of Texas and at Kansas State University, I realized that while this AEP aspired to function as "a tool for making the world better" by marking and troubling whiteness in critical ways and to "incite people to profound responses that shake their consciousness of themselves in the world" (p. 466), it also fell short. My mother was troubled by my representations of the women in our family, and I overrelied on scholars of color to do my theoretical work for me at times. However, this AEP sparked sometimes difficult and generative dialogue about race in classrooms, workshops, conferences, and public performance spaces among various groups of students, professors, and community members who engaged with and supported this work over extended periods of time. In this way, the arduous AEP process itself was transformative and reached toward a fleeting, affective horizon of possibility where performers and spectators gathered as witnesses to exercise mutual agency and offer possible meanings that may continue to resonate in tangible and intangible ways (p. 468).

"Speaking Unspeakables" (Shoemaker, 1998) ends by troubling our ideas of "home" (within one's body, within race/gender/class identifications, within oppressive ideologies) and offering an alternative vision of "home-less-ness" that invites a "vagabond life of shifting, moving, banding, disbanding, of risk and discomfort....We can never sleep in one place for too long. Because there is no safe place." In this way, the work imagines an AE-inspired ethos of uncertainty and kinetic movement between multiple, divergent, and typically "unspeakable" perspectives as a means of collectively imagining change.

The following excerpt is from the ending of "Mamafesto (Why Superheroes Wear Capes)," an AEP I developed to explore discourses of "work/life balance" for mothers on the tenure track. Presented to students, faculty, and staff at my university in 2009, "Mamafesto" attempts to make visible the intensely personal and gendered labor of mothering in the domestic sphere while also spiraling outward to critique gendered labor in the academy as well as the lack of clear, consistent family-friendly and paid family leave policies on many university campuses. Relying on a recurring children's song as a framing device, everyday life soundscapes, field samples of unsolicited advice and typical exchanges with my son, logs of daily labor at home and work, an "insomnia" journal, research and statistical data about mothers in and beyond academia, as well as public and private "scenes" with shifting modes of address, this performance ends with an attempt to envision/manifest utopian social change for all current and future caregivers:

[My son begins to fire off more questions. He is six years old.]

Mom, why do I have to go to school everyday?

Mom, why can't I stay home from school today?

Mom, why do I have to go to 'Project Extend' after school? It's boring!

Mom, why can't you make me something I LIKE to eat?

Mom, why can't I play more video games?

Mom, why can't I have a Playstation or a D.S.?

Mom, why do you kiss me so much?

Mom, why are you writing down what I'm saying?

MOM, WHAT DOES 'MAMAFESTO' MEAN? WHAT'S YOUR MAMAFESTO?

[I struggle to come up with an answer.] What's my mamafesto?... I guess it's... what I want...?

I simply want... time.

I simply want and need some time to rest and think. We all need this, don't we?

[Sounds and slides from the show slowly begin to replay and then build in intensity under the following text. Amidst this aural cacophony and visual chaos, I struggle to be heard.]

I simply want to work full-time, to contribute my talents and knowledge, AND have a healthy family life—without sacrificing one over the other.

I simply want workplaces to value quality over quantity.

I simply want a work culture that promotes community and success rather than burnout, competition, and unremitting stress.

I simply want equal pay for equal work, and equal respect for my work, both professional AND domestic.

I simply want families to co-parent, to fully share caregiving responsibilities.

I simply want access to affordable and excellent childcare, public education, and after school care for all children.

I simply want NATIONWIDE policies on family rights and PAID family leave.

I simply want to be a sane mother and a successful professional.

[Son's voice suddenly interjects:] "MOM, WHY DO SUPERHEROES WEAR CAPES?"

[Performer yells "STOP!" In the abrupt silence that follows, lights dim to a spotlight, and the performer slowly responds:]

...I don't know why superheroes wear capes, but I do know that none of us should have to be a superhero. *[Performer turns and walks offstage humming Woody Guthrie's opening children's song "I'll eat you, I'll drink you..." as lights fade slowly to black.]* (Shoemaker, 2011)

This ending, which is also a new beginning of sorts, attempts to re-imagine "simple [and not so simple] wants" as realistic and mutually beneficial change for all caregivers. It also aspires to proliferate "oppositional utopian spaces, discourses, and experiences" (Denzin, 2003, p. 193) via AEP practices that give voice to mothers in academia and beyond so they can speak openly about the impossibility of "work/life balance" within the very workplaces that expect women to hide their maternal identities.

Madison (1998) reminds that AE's "politics of possibility" and pedagogical performances have artistic, moral, political, and material consequences. There is an ethical call here to reach beyond the self to engage with and reveal unfair practices and to open up public discourse to previously denied voices, identities, points of view, experiences, and untold stories. Thus, AEP can/should function as shared epiphany, redress, bearing witness, political theatre, polyphony and/ or liminality in order to carve out more democratic spheres (Denzin, 2003, p. 198). This AEP ethic seeks "external grounding" (a kind of movement inside/ outside) "to understand power and ideology through and across systems of discourse" (p. 198). The performative-I positionality employed in the final moments of "Mamafesto" emphasizes the "critical potential of interrupting dominant cultural narratives deployed upon bodies by retelling those narratives from the body itself subjected/assigned to those narratives" (Spry, 2006, p. 344). This reflexive and tentative claim to "I" spirals outward to include/implicate all of "us" as we imagine a utopic realm where our labor is re-valued and where no one has to be a "superhero."

Madison (2011) argues that AE reflexivity (as the critical, self-conscious performative-I) is a particular act of labor that should matter, that is life force, that "works to leave something behind" when it is shared. This reflexivity critically "contemplates its own contemplations within past and future contingencies of self and Other that are boundlessly committed to an enlivening present" (p. 129). Labor as reflexivity moves away from the authorial "I" to travel with and through Others to new and vast territories of difference constituted by materiality (particular material conditions), futurity (hope for a better future), and performative temporality (an ability to occupy multiple time zones) (pp. 129, 135). In essence, the rigorous shared labor of reflexivity becomes a demand for researcher accountability, transparency, and intervention.

I have attempted to chart an AEP journey that reflexively travels back to past versions of self and Others in West Texas as both home and not-home, travels forward to mark and re-imagine a present moment heavily determined by gendered identities as both mother and feminist professor/scholar, and finally dreams up possible past/present/future journeys through aging female-marked bodies that are simultaneously decaying and transforming. Each of these locations on my AEP map contemplates and hopefully enlivens this present moment we occupy together, but differently. This journey has led me from solo AEP that utilized mostly first-person narratives into collaborative, participatory, and more fragmented AEP work in "Hauntings." This shift in my work springs from what Madison describes as a desire "for a generative and embodied reciprocity," for the creation of something wholly different and something more rich because of the meeting of two bodies on a stage shot through with a history of past and future bodies that we carry with us in particular contexts (Madison, 2006, p. 320).

> Deanna: "We are…very much alive, right here, right now, in this performance, with each other.
>
> Tessa: *(softly)* But we are haunted…
>
> Deanna: *(we slowly move into audience)* Can you feel it? The muscular BEAT BEAT BEAT of your heart thrumming blood through your bodies? *(We all breathe deeply together).*

(Carr & Shoemaker, 2011)

AEP has radically transformed my own understandings of, commitment to, and love of performance work that moved me away from the traditional conservatory theatre practices and mostly stereotypical roles I was trained to disappear into. AEP offered me new maps for creating performances that matter in the world. Perhaps the connective tissue that inherently binds AE to performance on both the page and stage becomes a bridge into future directions and possibilities. In "Hauntings," Carr and I open and close the performance by silently hula hooping. Our slow and then more intense spinning is eventually punctuated by evoking familiar and intimate sounds from our everyday lives or through the display of gothic photographs of our bodies draped, elegiacally, in lush green fields, cemeteries, and snowy woods. We are all living, dying, and breathing together in this quiet space of precarious possibility. There is something mysterious and promising about the circular pelvic motion required to keep heavy hula hoops in motion. The swing and return, swing and return, swing and return becomes a hopeful prayer, a kinetic means of soothing sorrows and conjuring desire and possibility. As we move fluidly, back and forth, together inside our hoops, I begin to appreciate Gingrich-Philbrook's call to "recover the aesthetic impulse currently constrained by desperate allegiances to the academy.…The academy seems poised to crush the life out of us" (2005, p. 302). As an antidote to the pursuit of AE's legitimacy within the academy, he offers an image of the universe forever in motion and a "rhizomatically spreading architecture of multiple possibilities" (p. 306). Embodying principles of nonhierarchical connection and heterogeneity, the rhizome recalls a queer aesthetic that conjures various horizons for AEP. Like the physics of the hula hoop in motion, this queer aesthetic is expansive, playful, and full of risk as it seeks to redefine our centers of gravity.

Challenges and Future Utopic Possibilities (Charting "What If")

When searching "autoethnography" in multidisciplinary databases, you will find that AE appears in a diverse range of academic journals across at least forty fields of study, ranging from archeology to occupational therapy, from social work to tourism studies, from geography to education. The circles of AE influence seem to be expanding and bridging into new territories. I see AEP impulses of critically locating self within larger cultural contexts proliferating out beyond the academy in a multitude of popular cultural practices such as activist performance art; autobiographical graphic novels and alternative comix; poetry slams and Def Jam poetry; in the music of progressive rap and singer/songwriters; experimental films and auto-documentaries; collaborative site-specific/public performance art; visual essays; the use of social media in the Occupy movement to collaborate, dialogue, and document activism; citizen journalism; digital storytelling; activist blogs; National Public Radio's StoryCorps project; Anna Deveare Smith's ongoing study of "American Character"; Robbie McCauley's historically situated autobiographical and community-based performances; Guillermo Gomez-Pena's *La Pocha Nostra* collective for hybrid art, multidisciplinary performance art culture jams, etc. Readers, where do you see the AEP pulse, and what would you add to these expansive lists of academic and popular AEP practices?

My intent with these unruly lists is to consider the value of conceptualizing ever-widening circles of AEP practices and influences in order to inspire new directions and bring more voices into the conversation. These lists that swing (out) and return (in) reflect the rhizomatic influence of critical and cultural performative practices that seek to gather, articulate, analyze, and embody experiences of self and other with/in culture. Mapping an AEP spectrum could include both more and less explicit AEP work conducted by artists, citizens, and scholars who variously deploy self-reflexivity, grounded cultural theory, and socio-cultural critique. Risking greater inclusion of aesthetic/cultural/performative practices may also encourage a progressive trend toward making room for more situated and subjugated knowledges, expanding networks and communities via new media, and more collaborative and inclusive art-making devoted to social change.

There is, perhaps, a utopian impulse in charting the influence of AEP broadly across overlapping spheres of academia and popular culture. "Autoethnography... expands and opens up a wider lens on the world, eschewing rigid definitions of what constitutes meaningful and useful research" (Ellis, Adams, & Bochner, 2011, par. 4). While many bemoan the exploding numbers of people sharing intimate, mundane details via social media and reality shows that bombard us with highly produced, spectacularized performances of self, this sometimes disturbing proliferation of performances and testimonies of self may indicate a growing hunger to be heard, to connect, to perform a multiplicity of selves, and to dialogue across cultural differences and spatial distances. What can we learn from these trends, and how can AEP help us to understand, complicate, and contribute to these popular culture practices?

Muñoz (2006) offers some possible directions for AEP in his vision of the "utopian performative" as a "politics of hope" and "potentially productive modality of knowing and belonging" (p. 10). He explains:

> Utopia is an ideal, something that should mobilize us, push us forward. Utopia is not prescriptive; it renders potential blueprints of a world not quite here, a horizon of possibility, not a fixed schema. It is…flux, a temporal disorganization…a moment when the here and now is transcended by a then and a there that could be and indeed should be. (Muñoz, 2006, p. 9)

Inherent in this moment of flux is a critique of the present moment. We need new ways to conjure more stories and different ways of telling stories that bring past, present, and future together in uneasy and shifting ways. We must continue to revisit, articulate, theorize, and analyze "on the pulses" what we know, what we think we know, and what we don't know at all. Autoethnographers must also keep asking those hard questions: who is speaking, who is listening, and who, if anyone, is emancipated in this work? How can we provoke real-time dialogues, collaborative and participatory explorations in physical and virtual spaces, diverse articulations of mutual needs and desires, multiple modes of survival, and grounded theories as possible maps for living, engaging, and creating social change? What are the epistemological and institutional silences we still need to speak into? How can we make room for humor, pleasure, chance, and improvisation in AEP? Might we consider other languages that bind us together/set us apart such as texting, found texts, everyday life talk, and the often heated and expletive-riddled strings of comments that follow so many online texts and images? Finally, while AEP offers powerfully evocative ways to write/perform ourselves into and out of particular histories, landscapes, mythologies and deeply engrained ideologies that can teach us about ourselves, our cultures, and our possible futures, we must remember, as Behar (1996) urges, that "the exposure of the self who is also a spectator has to take us somewhere we couldn't otherwise get to" (pp. 13–14).

I opened this chapter by marking my own struggle to find a place to start, "an idea or an experience that pulls you into the river of story, into a beginning," as a vehicle for "turning back on and to language, thought, self, culture, and power" (Adams & Holman Jones, 2011, p. 108). A map of sorts slowly coalesced, marked by shards of stories that "speak unspeakables" and that evoke intimate landscapes filled with "other voices, other bodies, other selves, other experiences" ("Hauntings," 2011) both shaped and distorted by larger discourses. As I find myself circling back to my own sense of pain, chaos, and loss (again) in this ending that always charts possible beginnings, I realize that the terror I felt in writing this chapter partly reflects my journey with AEP through the early days of discovering performance studies, activist performance art, and new ways of making theatre that means something in real people's lives. Rather than finally arriving at a destination here, now, I'm instead grappling with my own (im)possible, unknown, terrifying futures in this moment of past-present-future liminality. This is the place of writing/performing without any certainty, without firm conclusions, without an ending (Adams & Holman Jones, 2011, p. 113). AEP here becomes a tenuous means of surviving and hopefully thriving as we move together through uncharted waters. AEP stories can make a difference, give sustenance, and become "insurrectionary acts" when we are courageous enough to share them and make room for more stories (p. 114).

"Hauntings" ends as Carr and I slowly, carefully, cross over an invisible border into the audience and enact a ritualistic communion of sorts where we give away acorns, river rocks, shells, and seed pods from our personal landscapes that memorialize the terrifying loss of self/other and discovery of self in/through others. These bits of ephemera, these pieces of selves are both held and released, like the poised and endless swing and return of a hula hoop back and forth, back and forth. AEP here feels like a transformative, interrelational love in-the-making between co-performative witnesses in this moment of collective possibility:

(Performers speak in alternating voices)

Can you feel it? Beat, beat, beat.

(Pause. Deanna rises, helps Tessa up off the floor, and asks:)

Are you ok?

(Performers turn to audience) Will you hold this for me? *(Performers begin a quiet ritual of passing out artifacts in baskets—shells, rocks, feathers, acorns, etc.—to individual audience members as they ask:)*

Will you take care of this for me?

Will you catch me?

Am I making you uncomfortable?

What would your life be like without me?

What would my life be like without you?

Who are we without our memories?

I don't always recognize myself.

I'm haunted by you.

You've killed me! I'll die without you.

You're already gone.

No, I'm right here.

I'm falling, into something new, something very, very old.

(together) I'm terrified.

I'm swimming, breaking apart, reconstituting, with and through you,

you,

you,

you,

you. *(Performers set baskets down and return to stage:)*

Here.

Now.

Notes

1. "Hauntings: Marking Flesh, Time, Memory" is an ongoing AEP collaboration with Dr. Tessa Carr. Moving away from fully fleshed narratives, we explore texts that offer only partial stories, bits of aural ephemera, or physical rituals that invite audiences to fill in the gaps with their own stories. First, second, and third person fragments of experiences, spoken in shared sentences or given away to one another, disrupt the authenticity of personal narrative and reflect an "other-ing" within the self. "Hauntings" also employs photographic tableaus of us disguised as various female archetypes within intensely personal natural landscapes as a means of mis/recognizing and dis/identifying with our discursive selves. Fashioning stories through constructed tableaus allows us to theorize a range of gendered and working class experiences through critiques of white privilege and a consumer culture that fetishizes youth and beauty. "Hauntings" has been performed at the National Communication Association (New Orleans, 2011), the Patti Pace Performance Festival (Southern Illinois University Carbondale, 2012), at Monmouth University (October 2012), and at California State University, Northridge (February 2013).

2. See also Adams, T. E. & Holman Jones, S. (2011). Telling stories: Reflexivity, queer theory, and autoethnography. *Cultural Studies ↔ Critical Methodologies 11*(2), 108–116.

3. "Speaking Unspeakables: There's No Place Like Home" is an autoethnographic performance that was part of my Master's thesis at the University of Texas at Austin. An autoethnographic study of racism embedded in constructions of whiteness among white working class women in my family, it includes personal narratives; oral history interviews with my mother, grandmother, aunts, and longtime African American babysitter Ella Mae; recurring childhood dreams; and artifacts such as family photos, letters, cards, and girlhood diary entries that I performed to discover how unmarked norms of white privilege, racism, sexism, and class consciousness are deeply intertwined within stock family stories and familial identifications.

4. See Pollock (2006) for vivid examples of student performances of oral narratives about race. Pollock claims, "Oral histories…write the past into the present on the promise of an as yet unimagined, even unimaginable future. They *dream* the past—performing *what happened* as an image of *what might happen*….Oral histories tell the past in order to tell the future" (p. 88).

5. Assumptions about the value of "objectivity" are the result of centuries of binaristic discourses about knowledge as either of the body (experiential/anecdotal) or of the mind (intellectual/abstract/theoretical), as well as the imperialist belief that knowledge can and should be apolitical.

"We are unable to consider the ways in which it is possible to have both embodied and intellectual knowledge in equitable and meaningful ways. And we are taught to see the political positioning of colonial, bourgeoisie, white male scholarship as apolitical" (Pathak, 2010, pp. 3–4).

6. This performance was inspired by Omi Osun Joni L. Jones's courses at The University of Texas as well as her scholarship exploring her AEP of *Sista Docta* (1997), which locates her experience as an African American professor in a predominately white academy structured by histories of institutionalized racism.

7. During my AEP research, I revisited this neighborhood I once knew as a child. I was stunned by the intense poverty and segregation that had been "erased" from my memory. When I interviewed Ella Mae for my thesis project, she told me several of her family members who were at the fish fry before her wedding night were now in prison. While living in the same hometown, as our lives intertwined over a number of years, we simultaneously occupied distinctly different and unequal worlds demarcated by the dialectical tensions between racial privilege and racial injustice.

References

Adams, T. E., & Holman Jones, S. (2011). Telling stories: Reflexivity, queer theory, and autoethnography. *Cultural Studies ↔ Critical Methodologies, 11*, 108–116.

Banks, S. P., & Banks, A. (2000). Reading "The Critical Life: Autoethnography as Pedagogy." *Communication Education, 49*, 233–238.

Behar, R. (1996). *The vulnerable observer: Anthropology that breaks your heart.* Boston: Beacon Press.

Bell, E., & Holman Jones, S. (2008). Performing resistance. In E. Bell's *Theories of performance* (pp. 199–232). Thousand Oaks, CA: Sage.

Butler, J. (1993). *Bodies that matter: On the discursive limits of sex.* New York: Routledge.

Carr, T., & Shoemaker, D. (2011). Hauntings: Marking flesh, time, memory. Unpublished manuscript.

Clifford, J., Ed. (1986). *Writing culture: The poetics and politics of ethnography.* Berkeley: University of California Press.

Conquergood, D. (1992). Ethnography, rhetoric, and performance. *Quarterly Journal of Speech, 78*, 80–123.

Conquergood, D. (2002). Performance studies: Interventions and radical research. *The Drama Review, 46*, 145–156.

Denzin, N. K. (2003). The call to performance. *Symbolic Interaction, 26*, 187–207.

Dolan, J. (2001). Performance, utopia, and the "utopian performative. *Theatre Journal, 53*, 455–479.

Ellis, C., Adams, T., & Bochner, A. P. (2011). Autoethnography: An overview. *Forum: Qualitative Social Research, 12*(1), Art. 10. Retrieved from www.qualitative-research.net/index.php/fqs/article/view/1589/3095

Gingrich-Philbrook, C. (2005). Autoethnography's family values: Easy access to compulsory experiences. *Text and Performance Quarterly, 23*, 297–314.

Jones, J. L. (1997). Sista Docta: Performance as critique of the academy. *The Drama Review, 41*, 51–67.

Madison, S. (1998). Performances, personal narratives, and the politics of possibility. In S. J. Dailey (Ed.), *The future of performance studies: Visions and revisions* (pp. 276–286). Washington, DC: National Communication Association.

Madison, D. S. (2006). The dialogic performative in critical ethnography. *Text and Performance Quarterly, 26*, 320–324.

Madison, D. S. (2011). The labor of reflexivity. *Cultural Studies ↔ Critical Methodologies, 11*, 129–138.

Matsuda, M. (1993). *Words that wound: Critical race theory, assaultive speech, and the First Amendment.* Boulder, CO: Westview Press.

Muñoz, J. E. (2006). Stages: Queers, punks, and the utopian performance. In D. S. Madison & J. Hamera (Eds.), *The SAGE handbook of performance studies* (pp. 9–20). London: Sage.

Pathak, A. (2010). Opening my voice, claiming my space: Theorizing the possibilities of postcolonial approaches to autoethnography. *Journal of Research Practice, 6*(1), Art. M10.

Pollock, D. (1998). A response to Dwight Conquergood's essay: 'Beyond the Text: Towards a Performative Cultural Politics.' In S. J. Dailey (Ed.), *The Future of performance studies: Visions and revisions* (pp. 37–46). Washington, DC: National Communication Association.

Pollock, D. (2006). Memory, remembering, and histories of change: A performance praxis. In S. Madison & J. Hamera (Eds.), *The SAGE handbook of performance studies* (pp. 87–105). London: Sage.

Schechner, R. (1998). What is performance studies anyway? In P. Phelan & J. Lane (Eds.), *The ends of performance* (pp. 357–362). New York: New York University Press.

Shoemaker, D. (1998). Speaking unspeakables: There's no place like home. From *The Politics of Feminist Performance as Autoethnography: Blurring Genres*. Unpublished Master's Thesis, University of Texas at Austin.

Shoemaker, D. (2011). Mamafesto! (Why superheroes wear capes). *Text and Performance Quarterly, 31*, 190–202.

Spry, T. (2006). A "performative-I" copresence: Embodying the ethnographic turn in performance and the performative turn in ethnography. *Text and Performance Quarterly, 26*, 339–346.

Warren, J. T. (2006). Introduction: Performance ethnography: A TQP symposium. *Text and Performance Quarterly, 26*, 317–319.

Chapter 27

Teaching Autoethnography and Autoethnographic Pedagogy

Bryant Keith Alexander

In response to what I have called elsewhere "a two-voiced assignment" that requires students to have an intimate engagement with scholarly texts through an embodied, experiential, and expressive mode (Alexander, 2002), a young light skinned African American woman offered a brief autoethnographic performance about her brother who died from AIDS entitled " A Daughter/Sister Speaks." The performance, a partial elucidation of David Román's (1998) "Pomo Afro Homos' *Fierce Love*: Intervening in the Cultural Politics of Race, Sexuality and AIDS"— was not just about her, her brother, or the essay, but also the caldron of culture and community in which identity politics of race and sexuality simmer, stew, and cook (and sometimes burn). Danielle walked into a space cleared of chairs in a black box style performance-media space. She self describes her entrance as *"Daughter walks in angry at her mother, carrying a yellow flower in her hand."*

Daughter Speaks.

Ugh, I hate my mother. Ever since my father left she has been so over-protective. Like I was five minutes late for curfew. Five minutes. If my brother Darius were here he would have covered for me. One minute after ten I could always count on Darius to be waiting there with the back door open. He always covered for me and I loved that about him.

You know what else I loved about Darius? It was his beautiful, smooth chocolate skin. I used to sit in the tub for hours trying to scrub off my freckles just so my skin

Handbook of Autoethnography, edited by Stacy Holman Jones, Tony E. Adams, and Carolyn Ellis, 538–556. © 2013 Left Coast Press, Inc. All rights reserved.

would be like Darius's. It never worked. Oh, and you know what else I loved about Darius was that he was so good at football. Everybody said that he could have made it in the league but Darius didn't want to play professional football. Darius was so smart. I loved how wherever we went somewhere, he would always carry a book with him. Reading about something I couldn't pronounce. And you want to know what else I loved about Darius? He could sing. And I don't mean Chris Brown or Trey Songz. I mean the boy could sing like Tevon Campbell. Whenever I was having a bad day, Darius knew exactly how to cheer me up. He would give me pieces of candy or sing a song to me, or even draw. Darius could draw so well. I loved how Darius drew. He even drew this tattoo (looks down at arm remembering a picture that Darius drew for her).

We had a lot of good times together or at least I thought we did. But now he left me here all alone to deal with "her."

You know what I hated about Darius? I hated that he was gay. Mama said that daddy wouldn't have left us if Darius wasn't gay. She said something about it was too hard to deal with having his only son gay. And Preacher Thompson said that Darius was testing God's mercy by being gay. Oh, and my teacher, Mrs. Bert, said that Darius wouldn't have caught that awful disease that killed him if he wasn't gay. And he would still be here with me.

[At this point the flower is drawn to attention as she looks at it and speaks. On each of the following lines she pulls a petal from the flower, and they fall and pool at her feet.]

You know what I love about flowers? [pluck] *I love their petals.* [pluck] *It's almost like God crafted each petal to represent the different personalities of this one flower.* [pluck] *Without all the petals, the flower wouldn't be as beautiful.* [pluck] *Darius was like a flower.* [pluck] *He was my flower.* [pluck leaving only one petal and stamen of the flower]

You know what I hated about Darius's funeral? It was that everyone was focusing on this one thing about Darius, this one petal. They weren't even talking about every thing that made him—him. It's sad to think that the world won't be able to celebrate the true beauty of "my flower."

○

Danielle's performance elucidates many aspects of the Román (1998) chapter in a manner that reanimates the performative intent of the theatre troupe, Pomo Afro Homos. Her performance speaks to the relational dynamics of a singular experience in the cultural contexts of a Black family, church, and school linked to the particularity of Black gay identities and HIV/AIDS—issues of a complicated and *fierce love* that is sometimes nurturing but can also be deadly. She engages autoethnographic performance as a *corroboration*, *collaboration*, and *cooperation* with the informing text, her own experience, and my impetus as a Black gay male professor to include this text in the course—in ways that are personal, professional, and political. Her work gives further *voice, visibility,* and *viability* to the issue of HIV/AIDS in the Black community, but it does something more than simply reiterate her comprehension of the Román chapter. The immediacy and actuality of Danielle's performance forced the class *to feel* the issues.

Through her autoethnographic performance her classmates were able to palpably *feel the real*; this is key because at times students (these particular students, mostly minority and first-generation college students at a predominately Hispanic-serving campus) seem to distrust scholarly texts that do not speak to the immediacy of their experiences. The assignment forces them to filter lived experience through scholarly texts (and back) as a form of rehydration, like trying to move a prune back to a plum; knowing how they exist in their own existential space but how they are informed by the other. These students attempt to use their own sensed and critical reflection on experience as the hydrating liquid of both embodied and scholarly knowing. In this sense, "as a method, and not just an object of investigation, performance can generate knowledge about the subject matter animating the performance," of the essay sure, but maybe more importantly, of personal experience (Gingrich-Philbrook, 2005, p. 303).

Not fully knowing what would emerge from these performances, on this day I was prepared to perform my short autoperformance, "Standing at the Crossroads" (Alexander, 1999b)—a text which depicts my experience of losing a brother to AIDS and a text I have performed for other classes. But Danielle' s performance did the work of the moment as the learning outcomes of a planned instructional engagement were made manifest. In collaboration, I merely shared aspects of my parallel experience with the particular concern that sometimes in the Black community there is a perceived preference to assuming that the Black man who contracts HIV/AIDS is an intravenous user or contracted the disease through oral sex with an infected female (or blood transfusion as a stretch)—anything but through unprotected same-sex sexual activity, which would mar an already socially constructed perception of an exclusively heteronormative Black phallus. I gave students directions to the published version of my story, and not as act of "merely" sharing. This is a moment of outing the personal as a component of an autoethnographic pedagogy; a pedagogy of not just teaching autoethnography but a means through which teachers share intimate aspects of lived experience with critical intention; breaking the fourth wall of an assumed objectified teacher/ student engagement, furthering an argument that teachers always and already teach through the personal (Karamcheti, 1995). It was also a way for me to further queer the classroom and autoethnography (Adams & Holman Jones, 2008).

o

The title of this chapter signals the reciprocating relationship of both teaching autoethnography and engaging an autoethnographic pedagogy as embodied practice. Teaching and the attending notion of pedagogy are informing concerns of interconnected processes. In *Teaching Against the Grain: Texts for a Pedagogy of Possibility* (1992) Roger Simon articulates the notion of pedagogy as *a practical synthesis of the question,* "What should be taught and why? With considerations as to how that teaching should take place" (pp. 55–57). Applied to *teaching autoethnography and autoethnographic pedagogy*—such a definitional approach could imply engaging a dynamic and reciprocal process of both searching for knowledge and gaining knowledge *from an acquired position or location of lived and cultural experience.* Such a position could be located and positioned in what Cheryl Johnson (1995) refers to as the "triangle or trinity of race, gender, and pedagogy" in which the particularlity of selves and lived experiences are explored in the context of culture—with intention of both learning and teaching (p. 130).

Teaching autoethnography and autoethnographic pedagogy foregrounds that a critical explication of human experience often results in building theories and theorems of knowing that are always cross-applied in everyday living and can serve as evidence of academic knowing through the body. Such an approach leads to the development of a sophisticated vocabulary of terms and terminologies that give voice to experience as a means of realizing, personalizing, foregrounding, and sharing histories and happenings that matter in assisting us—teachers and students—in seeing ourselves in relation to the politics of culture and scholarship with the ability to use our shared experiences through performance as templates of sociality and tools of critique. Danielle's performance evidences a sophisticated simplicity of applying and building theories of race and gender bias. She engages a critical reflexivity to locate personal experience in a particular cultural context of knowing, and she "turn[s] the internally somatic into the externally semantic" in a complicated confluence of mourning and memorializing her brother (Spry, 2011a, p. 47).

This chapter will outline a philosophy of autoethnographic pedagogy, offer further considerations of autoethnography as methodological tool, and offer future directions/challenges/concerns for exploration in teaching autoethnography and engaging an autoethnographic pedagogy.

Developing a Philosophy of Teaching Autoethnography/Autoethnographic Pedagogy

The notion of a "teaching autoethnography and autoethnographic pedagogy" establishes an integrative relationship between why one uses or engages autoethnography in the classroom as assignment and critical methodology for student-learning and what might undergird commitments embedded in such a teaching philosophy. What follows could serve as a beginning list of contributing commitments in building a philosophy of teaching autoethnography or autoethnographic pedagogy.

An Autoethnographic Pedagogy Acknowledges the Importance of Critical Performative (Communicative) Pedagogy.

Critical performative pedagogy promotes an active embodiment of doing as a key component of a pedagogical practice used towards libratory ends. Specifically such practices are geared to having students (and participants) perform the possibilities of progressive cultural politics by exploring counternarratives to the master narratives of everyday and educational life (Bamberg & Andrews, 2004; Giroux, Lankshear, McLaren, & Peters, 1996), engaging students in active rehearsals of social justice (Adams, Blumenfeld, Castañeda, Hackman, Peters, & Zúñiga, 2000; Lea & Sims, 2008; Massey, 2012; O'Donnell, Pruyn, & Chavez, 2004), and promoting a dialogical performance. "The aim of dialogical performance," which becomes *sine qua non* for any approach to critical performative pedagogy, "is to bring self and other together so that they can question, debate, and challenge one another" on both the local and global level (Conquergood, 1985, p. 9). Hence the fact that autoethnography is centered within the critical articulation of lived experience as a pedagogical engagement means there must be a deep philosophical commitment to encouraging students to explore how their experiences, in a wide range of social encounters and political happenings, matter. It is a teaching philosophy that is grounded in students bringing their lived experiences into the classroom and having those experiences bear upon and infuse the critical content and processes of education.

Grounded in a performance-based methodology, the practical and theoretical construct of *critical performative pedagogy* is used in diverse yet interlocking ways. For example, performance studies scholar Elyse Pineau (1998, 2002) uses the term "critical performance pedagogy" to reference a body-centered experiential method of teaching that foregrounds the active-body-knowing. Her conceptualization of critical performance pedagogy, heavily supported with precepts from critical pedagogy, "acknowledge[s] that inequities in power and privilege have a physical impact on our bodies and consequently must be struggled against bodily, through physical action and activism" (2002, p. 53). Her performative methodology engages the body as a primary site of meaning making, of ideological struggle, and of performative resistance. Hence, bodies are put "into action in the classroom" as a means of exercising and engaging a liberatory practice that extends beyond the borders of the classroom into everyday citizenship (2002, p. 53). Autoethnography becomes the particular methodological engagement of articulating bodily experience and knowledge.

Pineau's approach is what cultural studies scholar Lawrence Grossberg (1996) might refer to as *the act of doing*. In particular, critical performative pedagogy (in this case in/as autoethnography) in the classroom is used to illuminate and embody social politics "intervening into contexts and power...in order to enable people to act more strategically in ways that may change their context for the better" (p. 143). In this way, critical performative pedagogy (autoethnography) is a rehearsal process for actualizing possibilities outside the classroom (Boal,

1979). Communication and sociology scholar Norman Denzin (2003) approaches *critical performance pedagogy* as a cluster of performative and emancipatory strategies. It includes Pineau's construction but extends further into a "civic, publicly responsible autoethnography that addresses the central issues of self, race, gender, society, and democracy" (p. 225). The expanse of his survey includes performance ethnography, autoethnography, performative cultural studies, reflexive critical ethnography, critical race theory, and the broader sociological and ethnographic imagination, all of which are undergirded in his expansion of Freirean (1974, 2002) politics, pedagogies, and possibilities of hope.

These methods and autoethnography in/as critical performative/performance pedagogy are all empowered with the ability to open up spaces of pain to critical reflection on self and society. Hence, they exist in that tensive space of being radical and risky—radical in the sense that they strip away notions of a given human condition, and risky in that our sense of comfort in knowing the world is laid bare and vulnerable. Such critical engagements of performance in/as pedagogy give way to the possibility of knowing the world differently. They open a possibility of hope encouraged by social responsibility, political activism, and engaged participation in a moral science of humanistic discourse. This cluster of performative strategies that Denzin refers to as *critical performance pedagogy* (echoing others) is all centered in the active body doing, the active mind knowing, and an activated civic responsibility that collectivizes and promotes democracy and human rights (Alexander, 2010; Warren, 2011).

Denzin's construction signals Henry Giroux's (2001) search for a project and the utopian politics of hope when he discusses "strategies of understanding, engagement, and transformation that address the most demanding social problems of our time. Such projects are utopian" (p. 7). Denzin refers to the utopian as indicating an ideal state of human social relations but also uses utopian to indicate a particular and practical strategy of gaining insight into cultural selves and others in order to (re)build community. In this utopian sense, Spry (2011b) writes:

> Performative autoethnography views the personal as inherently political, focuses on bodies-in-context as a co-performative agent in interpreting knowledge, and holds aesthetic craft of research as an ethical imperative or representation....[For me] it has been about dropping down out of the personal and individual to find painful and comforting connection with others in sociocultural contexts of loss and hope. (p. 498)

And in this sense, I also offer the words of John T. Warren (2011), writing on social justice and critical/performative/communicative pedagogy as a

> desire to research, to get it right, to name the practices that promote effective learning that is centered in critical, embodied, and liberatory theory and politics to the effect that desire and loss (and the intermingling of them) have on the teacher body [and the student body] who lives and feels outside of the classroom. (p. 32)

An Autoethnographic Pedagogy Acknowledges the Political Importance of a Border Pedagogy

Teaching autoethnography provides the opportunity for students to critically articulate conflicting cultural experiences, especially in the between spaces of culture, schooling, and the places that they call home. In *Postmodern Education: Politics, Culture, and Social Criticism*, Stanley Aronowitz and Henry Giroux (1991) discuss the construct of *border pedagogy*.

> Border pedagogy offers the opportunity for students to engage the multiple references that constitute different cultural codes, experiences, and languages. This means educating students to read these codes critically, to learn the limits of such codes, including the ones they use to construct their own narratives and histories. (pp. 118–119)

It is a logic that promotes students to bleed the borders of the classroom with lived experience. In more specific terms, Aronowitz and Giroux write that border pedagogy helps students to understand that "one's class, race, gender, or ethnicity may influence, but does not irrevocably predetermine, how one takes up a particular ideology, reads a particular text, or responds to particular forms of oppression" (p. 121). Hence, there is the potential of seeing the links that bind humanity and not the borders of difference that we presume divide us. Border pedagogy asks teachers to engage students in the places and ideological spaces of their own experiences as they try to make sense of culture and curriculum—while practicing a voice long subdued and silenced in the classroom. Such a performance-based critical method demands a new level of engagement that crosses borders between the knowing and the known (Giroux & Shannon, 1997).

In these ways, autoethnographic engagement can move education and teaching toward a pedagogy that strategizes purposeful learning with an awareness of the social, cultural, and political contexts in which learning and living take place. Autoethnography as a particular pedagogical strategy can then move even further to encompass a *critical pedagogy* by revealing, interrogating, and challenging normalizing social and cultural forms and opening spaces for additional voices in a meaningful human discourse. Such an act would always be moving toward becoming a *revolutionary pedagogy* that helps to enact the possibilities of social transformation by bleeding the borders of subjectivity and opening spaces of care (McLaren, 1999).

An Autoethnographic Pedagogy Acknowledges the Importance of Public Pedagogy

In both Pineau's (2002) and Denzin's (2003) approaches to critical performative pedagogy, there is a hope that the embodied, reflective, and reflexive process of performative pedagogy becomes what Giroux (2001) constructs as *a public pedagogy*, a process in which the efforts and effects of such critical processes are not limited to the sterilizing confines of the classroom or traditional educational discourse (e.g., textbooks, scholarly research, standardized curriculum), but are presented to and enacted in the public sphere in ways that work to transform social life. Giroux writes,

> Defined through its performative functions, public pedagogy is marked by its attentiveness to the interconnections and struggles that take place over knowledge, language, spatial relations, and history. Public pedagogy represents a moral and political practice rather than merely a technical procedure. (p. 12)

Through the performed engagement of a cultural dialogue, autoethnography (as linked with performance ethnography) becomes a public pedagogy with several characteristics: It is designed to make public the often privatized, if not secularized, experiences of others. It is designed to begin the painstaking process of deconstructing notions of difference that often regulate the equal distribution of humanistic concern. It makes present and visible the lived experiences of self and others—giving students, performers, and audiences access to knowledge that one hopes will open spaces of possibility.

An Autoethnographic Pedagogy Acknowledges the Importance of "A Performance of Possibilities"

D. Soyini Madison's (1998) construction of *the performance of possibilities* offers both validity and direction for performance ethnography in general, giving gravity to the particular practice of autoethnography. The *performance of possibilities* as applied to autoethnography invokes an investment in politics of "self, other, and self as the Other," always negotiating the tensions and tensiveness between *cynics and zealots*. The *performance of possibilities* as applied to autoethnography takes the stand that the articulation of lived experience matters because it does something in the world by illuminating personal experience and activating social consciousness. The *performance of possibilities* as applied to autoethnography moves away from prediction and control toward understanding and social criticism as both process and product. The *performance of possibilities* as applied to autoethnography does not accept being heard and included as its endpoint but only as a starting point to present and represent self and other as products and producers of meaning, symbols, and history in their fullest sensory and social dimensions. Therefore, the *performance of possibilities* as applied to autoethnography is a performance of voice wedded to experience, of critical thinking wedded to the emotionality of remembrance, and of the power of invoking presence that *moves away from facts (pure and simple) and toward meaning (ambiguous and complicated)*.

In its fullness, Madison's (1998) construction of possibilities might also resonate with José Esteban Muñoz's (2006) delineation between possibility and potential. Muñoz writes: "Possibilities exist, or more nearly, they exist within a logical real.... Potentialities have a temporality that is not in the present but, more nearly, in the horizon, which we can understand as futurity" (p. 11). Madison's possibilities make salient Muñoz's potentialities, which I believe directs an essential value in autoethnographic work, in that the critical reflection and articulation of lived experience offers potential emancipatory ends to both performers and others.

Methodological Considerations in Teaching Autoethnography

In this section I offer a brief sketch of one approach to teaching autoethnography used for both undergraduate and graduate classes in performance studies with courses, in my experience, that were often cross listed between a Department of Communication Studies and a Department of Theatre Arts and Dance that places the rhetorical/epistemic importance and the aesthetic crafting of performance in dialogue (Gingrich-Philbrook, 2005). I offer a brief and partial application to Danielle's performance for the reader to understand the nuanced stages of how this methodology might manifest into such performances.

1. First I ask students to recall a kernel moment, a narrative fragment, *lexias* of a happening, an incident, or occurrence that left a palpable impulse in you; an experience *that changed your life*, a *transformative moment* (Spry, 2011a, p. 122); an "epiphany" that had a significant impact (Alexander, 2009; Bochner & Ellis, 1992; Couser, 1997; Denzin, 1989; Ellis, Adams, & Bochner, 2011) that you seek to theorize, to make sense of in a broader socio-cultural-political context. In the case of Danielle's performance, which I showcase in the beginning of this chapter, her kernel moment might have been, "the family and community response to my brother Darius's death from HIV/AIDS."

2. After identifying the kernel moment and outlining the details of the happening, I encourage working through the logics in telling of the experience. How is the story specific and *contingent* upon particular variables and the actuality of the happening? How might you relay the facts of the story but also occasion the story as an analogy to offer the reader or listener multiple points of entry into the story, to see the experience from differing perspectives? In Danielle's performance, she uses the flower and its petals as an analogy of the multiple qualities of her brother's beauty and character.

3. I ask: Who or what is the socio-cultural-political context for this kernel moment? To whom and what is the story being told in relation to (e.g., family, religion, government, particular cultural practices and expectations, cultural politics of race, gender, sexuality, and so forth)? What are the assumed logics, expectations, power systems, norms, values, and beliefs within these locations? In Danielle's performance it becomes clear that she is speaking in relation to family, church, and school while making a larger argument about the social construction of gay identity.

4. I ask students to then begin to build a story about the kernel moment by establishing context through critical self-reflection.

   - The dramatistic questions of when, where, why, how, what—are good guides in developing the specificity of both the past and present.

   - What are the details of the happening that are key (for the audience) to understand the social, cultural, and political milieu/context of the happening?

   - What are the power structures at play in these moments (e.g., time, place, relationships between players)? What is your relation/ship to/in those structures?

   - What is your location, positionality in the story, to the story, to the happening? What is your sense of empowerment or entrapment, agency of oppression in this situation/context?

   - Who are the players in the story, in the happening? What was your orientation to them and how did they impact the nature of the experience? What are the connections between the persons *at/in* play with socio-cultural-politics that you have defined?

   - How do you intend to represent or characterize these particular others in the story? What is your ethical responsibility and commitment to representing these others relative to critical remembrance of how they existed and the impact of the happening (Conquergood, 1985)?

In Danielle's performance she outlines and fleshes out the factual and emotional components of her experience by listing and detailing things that she loved and hated about Darius; strong emotional binaries. While the performance is a celebration of her brother, she also uses the binary of love and hate to reflexively engage her orientation to her brother being gay, an orientation that she also evidences as culturally constructed. She lists the many qualities of what she loved about her brother, and how she also hated him because he was gay. She provides the evidence and origins of that hate: her mother's suggestion that her father left because his only son was gay, her preacher's suggestion that her brother being gay "tested God's mercy," and her teacher's equation that Gay = HIV/AIDS. Each of her articulations offers evidence and reasoning towards a particular raced and cultural orientation towards HIV/AIDS that she becomes complicit in yet resists; in particular she resists reducing her brother to the particularity of his gendered identity and the disease that took his life. The story that she tells is not just the charting of a narrative plot but also the crafted sharing of experience that draws the audience into a critical emotional field of knowing and experiencing. The petals on the floor at the end of the performance serve as symbolic residue of a broader cultural experience, as is the abject body of her brother in the performance that is presented as eulogy, elegy, and effigy in the performance—actions and accomplishments that were directly signaled from her initiating kernel moment, "the family and community response to my brother Darius's death from HIV/AIDS."

5. I ask students to establish the argument of the story, not as a form of persuasion but as structure of intent:

    • The descriptive details of the story from the preceding steps can begin to serve as the evidence.

    • The rationale of sense making as you tie the variables together in the story can serve as the reasoning.

    • The conclusion is the logical intention of telling the story, which may only fully emerge as the process unfolds.

Danielle's performance speaks to and argues against the reductive construction of her brother's identity relative to him being gay, and having contracted HIV/AIDS.

6. In the process I ask students to invoke emotionality, contingency, and activism. How are you positioned within these factors? What is your emotional response to the original happening and how do you imagine or intend an audience to respond? Could your intention be a less exclusively empathic connection with the experience; a refashioning of the self in the other, and maybe a display of your own critical sense-making that produces an analytically rich and accessible text that reflects their personal change and found knowledge through the process, as an offering to an interested audience for purposes of potential change (Holman Jones, 2005, p. 764)? Is there a charge or further invitation to the audience in this performance?

Danielle's performance reveals how aspects of her own emotional response to the loss of her brother were contingent not only upon the social and cultural context of family and religion to his gay identity, but also upon how she resisted the limitations of her brother's character. In part, her closing line is both private regret as well as a public critique.

7. I ask students to explore the residual effects of the experience. How do you negotiate the "snaking temporality," the shift in time between when the experience occurred and the time of the current telling; "between tellers and audiences," between the person you were and the person you are approaching in the assignment (Gingrich-Philbrook, 2005, p. 305)?

Danielle's performance works with and through time. The performance is clearly *reflective*, as she recalls a past happening. The performance is *reflexive* as she critically makes sense of a happening and her own self-implication in that happening. The performance is also *refractive*, as she bends time between the there and then, and the here and now—to shift the directionality of effect and meaning of the happening. In the process she is both a character inside the story being told, as well as a critical observer outside of the story offering insight and interpretation. Hence, Danielle's performance also responds to these questions:

8. I ask students: How can you draw upon memory to inform the current moment in a reflexive mode that provides you both connection and critical distance to share experience without being consumed in the moment of reliving or replicating experience, but instead uses that sensed knowing to provide the audience with access to an experience worth sharing? What do you come to know differently through critical reflection on the particular experience?

   Separate from the recounting of actual events in the process of critical reflection, are there any unforeseen elements (truths/realities/experiences) you wish to recall? Maybe the story you discovered, or the memory that you recovered is not the one you seek to tell, but a story that now demands telling. What other emergent possibilities of telling the story circulated around the same kernel moment? In other words, are there other versions of this story to be told?

9. Where and how is your body in this critical remembrance, and in the critical retelling of experience? How was your body situated and read in the happening (e.g., gender, race, skin color, body type, ableness)? Did the reading or situatedness of your body play a unilateral or bilateral role in the happening? In other words, the body as *unilateral* references the one-sided physical postures of being, and the body as *bilateral* represents the duality of the body as a site of critical sense making.

In the case of Danielle's performance we see a performance of melancholy in face and body posture as well as the body in a critical mode of response, as she engages the flower as trope of her brother and a problematic cultural practice of assessment.

10. I then ask students to tie together these elements into a meaningful whole in a voice or mode that is uniquely theirs (e.g., narrative, poetry, song, choreographic movement)—recognizing that any good story has a beginning, middle, and end; a crafted argument that is revealed in both intent and form, hence the unification of the two must be "read/understood" by your audience.

Danielle's performance engaged a complex simplicity; a short and well-crafted narrative staged in a bare space. The starkness of the moment directed the audience to focus on the interstates of her negotiating the happening the evidence that she provides and her reasoning and her conclusions, which were private and public as well as singular and plural as a directed cultural critique.

11. Up to this point the considerations listed in this assignment have mostly been about conceptualizing, structuring, and writing the autoethnographic narrative. Once these questions have been addressed and the narrative has been written, how are you (the student) planning on performing the autoethnographic narrative: How is the performance staged?

   • In 9, I offered the possibilities of narrative, poetry, song, choreographic movement. These are all possibilities noting that each aesthetic mode is possible, with the necessity of a verbalized story interspliced in or within choreographic movement.

- How does the student establish the mood and mode of the story through embodiment? Is the performance engaged primarily standing or sitting with a dependence on the oral presentation? Is the performance staged in metaphorical movement or action? Is the performance situated in a created place and space?

- What is the body doing in the performance? In addition to the use of provocative and evocative language—what do you want your audience to see during the performance?

Within this assignment I often establish "a kernel story circle" (a group of three to five students) in the class where students share their initial kernel story (or stories) and students within the group can ask questions. The nature of the questions gives each student cues to the types of information—factual content, details or examples that their classmates might be interested in knowing—relative only to the kernel story, and may help the student decide which kernel story will become the foundation for addressing the assignment. The teller of the kernel story is not required to answer the questions—only listen and take the questions into consideration as he or she engages the process of writing.

Future Directions/Challenges/Explorations

My concern within this chapter has been to outline the pedagogical trajectories of "teaching autoethnography and autoethnographic pedagogy." A particular challenge in teaching autoethnography (for me) has been the relational nature of the "I" as that is posited in relation to culture; noting that autoethnography is both singular (auto) and plural (the cultural community or communities to which it speaks) and the sense that in writing autoethnography one "cannot stand alone" (Holman Jones, 2005, p. 763); but also that the "I" in autoethnography is never singular—relative to time, place, and the politics of telling. This becomes the epistemological stickiness that begins to separate or make apparent (for me) a shift from personal narrative and autobiography—one's own life story—to placing autoethnography in a broader cultural, historical, and political context. I find that the emerging discussion of the *performative "I"* and deepening discussions on reflexivity in *auto/ethnography* (Berry & Clair, 2011) to be clear developments in discussing the plural nature of the "I" found in autoethnography. In practical terms, the performative linked with performativity references the emergence of meanings and identities relative to time, place, and action that is always dialogic as a sociocultural dynamic of meaning making and assumptions of the real that are consistently regenerated in/through performance.

In her essay, "The Labor of Reflexivity," D. Soyini Madison (2011) writes that "the ethnographer not only contemplates his or her actions and meanings in the field (reflective) but also she or he turns inward to contemplate *how* she or he is contemplating actions and meaning" (p. 129). Applied to autoethnography, reflexivity is key to assisting students in seeing and knowing themselves in relation to culture and community; it is key to helping students to recognize their moral and ethical accountabilities and the origins of their logics. So, while teaching autoethnography and engaging an autoethnographic pedagogy, I remind students that *they are not telling stories about what other people did to them. They are telling on themselves in the context of culture,* as I believe that when I share stories of my own experiences—I am not a folklore hero but someone complicit in the politics of social and cultural happenings. In such case, discussing the co-presencing in/of the *performative-I* Tami Spry (2006, 2011a) writes: "Performative autoethnography is a critically reflective narrative representing the researcher's personal and political intersections/engagements/negotiations with others in culture/history/society" (2011a, pp. 53–54).

For me, this co-presencing in/of the "I" creates a challenge for students to begin thinking about issues of accountability and representation of particular others within the context of their autoethnographies in ways in which they also become mindful of the complicity of culture that has shaped their sensibilities. It also makes students mindful of how and to what they may be performing resistance to at any given time. In addition to the framing questions of the assignment previously outlined, in an accompanying analysis paper I further ask them: What role did you play in the happening that you are narrating? What function does the telling of this experience accomplish? What do you come to know about yourself differently after engaging this project and telling your story in public?

But here I also want to invoke Dustin Goltz's (2011) approach to "frustrating the 'I'" that he both laments and celebrates in the challenges of telling a coherent and consistent narrative of experience. A "frustrating I," for me, is about positionality, the political location of the teller and the told that might question the reliability of the story in its multiple iterations and the impetus to tell in shifting contexts. This becomes particularly telling within the context of the classroom when the telling of stirring personal narratives might create tension between what might be actual happenings and the requirements of an assignment that might bolster the necessity for students to tell better stories.

In "frustrating the I" in performing autoethnography, students come to know that there are multiple versions of a story. The challenge is that the "I" is never singular but embodies multiple selves competing for the authority to interpret a story for their own benefit. So as Goltz (2011) writes,

> Still the issue cannot be to speak or not to speak, who can or who should speak (or who needs to just sit quietly and listen) but a continual dialogue and interrogation of *how* we speak, *for whom* we speak, *to whom* who speak, and, always, who is *not* speaking. (p. 403)

In addition to the complexity of negotiating the "I" in autoethnography, I believe that these are the challenges and hopes of teaching autoethnography and autoethnographic pedagogy:

- *Creating a space and opportunity* in which students and others can practice their voices, knowing that they can and should tell their stories—to explore the deep recesses of their experience that "mean to provoke, to raise questions, and implicate" others, always engaging in a critical reflexivity that recognizes their own fallibilities and accountabilities (Hughes & Román, cited in Holman Jones, 2005, p. 784).

- *Encouraging critical stories of experience* that provide students and others with the opportunity to explore self in relation to culture; culture as a dynamic constellation that is hybrid and inbred; culture as practices, surroundings and the politics of their own being and becoming.

- *Asking students how their engagements can be radical acts* of both giving *testimony and witnessing* that place them at the scene of the crime and the precipice of social change; a location that "might act as a doorway, an instrument of encounter, a place of public and private negotiations" (Salverson, cited in Holman Jones, 2005, p. 784). Hence, *asking students how their stories can serve as narrative poetics and performative interventions* (Madison, 2008).

- *Teaching students and others how they can "recognize the power of the in-between"*—capitalizing on the interaction of the critical processes of self-knowing and the critical pleasures of aesthetics (Holman Jones, 2005, p. 784; Spry, 2011a).

- *Recognizing how teaching autoethnography can provide critical opportunities and safe spaces* for such explorations with liberatory goals. One of the challenges of doing autoethnography is the vulnerability of exposure, of students not only opening themselves to critique the self but to expose themselves to critique.

So What Are the Evaluative Criteria of Autoethnography?

I have laid out a series of variables that inform teaching autoethnography and autoethnographic pedagogy, variables that are always grounded in compassion and care. It is a pedagogy that seeks to validate meaningful effort without evaluating articulated experience. It is pedagogy that embraces risk and validates the fallibility of human vulnerability—not simply to tell a story but to *be* the story being told. An autoethnographic pedagogy is fundamentally grounded in a teacher's ability to not only clearly outline expectations but to also embody these commitments in the fullness of pedagogical engagement. I want to challenge you by saying that *teaching autoethnography is most effective when*:

- Autobiographic/autoethnographic engagement is not relegated to an isolated assignment such as "a" performance of autoethnography assignment, but is integrated throughout a pedagogical context that always invites students to critically reflect on lived experience and then filter that knowing as a means of testing theory and applying theory to make sense of personal experience.

- There is a commitment to a critical exploration of culture and positionality that is integrated throughout a pedagogical context (e.g., classroom, community-based activism, human services, therapeutic contexts) or even across the curriculum as a primary methodology (Pineau, 1994, 1998).

- A teacher or instructional guide engages autoethnography as a method of modeling and engendering trust through a reciprocal process of sharing autoethnographic work/processes, marking the fact that pedagogy is always and already personal and political; such engagements of autoethnographic teaching as embodied pedagogy expose the infrastructure of teaching intent and the positionality of the teacher in those processes (Fassett & Warren, 2010).

- The varying modes of using autoethnography as methodology (e.g., mode of research/inquiry, mode of re/presentation, mode of critique and resistance, mode of activism) are integrated and not isolated from the intentionalities of each.

- Teaching embraces "the epistemological connection between creativity, critique, and civic engagement [as] mutually replenishing, and pedagogically powerful" (Conquergood, 2004, pp. 319–320).

- Autoethnography is taught as an *engaged performative pedagogy* that consistently interrogates the metaphor of teaching as performance (Pineau, 1994); a form of teaching as an *engaged performance*—bodies as participating agents of change in community (Cohen-Cruz, 2010); a form of teaching that uses performance as a critical engagement in both teaching and responding to student performances in class; as an active doing (Alexander, 1999a).

I believe that these are only some of the directions/challenges/explorations of a methodology that does *give a lot of permission* but also demands a lot of accountability, for a lot is at stake, ranging from the vulnerability of experience and exposure to the potential of personal and political transformation. The possibilities are worth the risk.

Conclusion

I am taken back to my class and to the struggled engagements of my students to enter scholarly texts and the spaces of opening that performance provides them to explore, embody, and empathically connect with through their own storying of experience which often matches the intellectual rigor of the scholarly texts with which they initially grapple. I always asked the class to do a "reading" of the performance—a reading of what they experienced through the performer's crafted abstract of the informing text, and through their own initial reading of the full essay/chapter. After experiencing performance their voices are alive with energy and they begin to *talk a talk* that is seasoned and informed with rearticulated eyes that help them to see the informing text anew—performance becomes a critical analytic of seeing. The students pause and re-collate acts/actions in performance with a triggered understanding of a quote or argument in the text that was made bare in performance. They often speak of what the articulated story does differently for them than the essay—yet how it, meaning the performance, speaks in a seamless dialogue in language that is also theoretical and academic.

I am taken back to Danielle's performance of "A Daughter/Sister Speaks" and the ease with which she glided on the stage and shared her story and how we were captivated by the crafted telling of experience. At the end of her performance, she retreated in the direction of her initial arrival; the floor surrounding the area of her performative stance was encircled with yellow petals from the flower, remnants of a performance, symbolic remnants of life laid bare.

The themes outlined in this chapter pivoted between conditions and motivations of autoethnographic labor, knowings from acquired positions (academic or autoethnographic), speculations on method/methodology, motivating and undergirding philosophies of doing and knowing—all become most salient in the classroom, in the audiencing of autoethnography, a performance of possibility striving for the potential of the horizon.

References

Adams, M., Blumenfeld, W. J., Castañeda, R., Hackman, H. W., Peters, M. L., & Zúñiga, X. (2000). *Readings for diversity and social justice: An anthology on racism, antisemitism, sexism, heterosexism, ableism, and classism.* New York: Routledge.

Adams, T. E., & Holman Jones, S. (2008). Autoethnography is queer. In N. K. Denzin, Y. S. Lincoln, & L. T. Smith (Eds.). *Handbook of critical and indigenous methodologies* (pp. 391–405). Thousand Oaks, CA: Sage.

Alexander, B. K. (1999a). Moving toward a critical poetic response. *Theatre Topics, 9,* 107–125.

Alexander, B. K. (1999b). Standing at the crossroads. *Callaloo: A Journal of African American and African Arts and Letters, 22,* 343–345.

Alexander, B. K. (2002). Intimate engagement: Student performances as scholarly endeavor. *Theatre Topics, 12,* 85–98.

Alexander, B. K. (2009). Autoethnography: Exploring modalities and subjectivities that shape social relations. In J. Paul, J. Kleinhammer-Tramill, & K. Fowler (Eds.), *Qualitative research methods in special education* (pp. 277–334). Denver: Love.

Alexander, B. K. (2010). Critical/performative/pedagogy: Performing possibility as a rehearsal for social justice. In D. Fassett & J. T. Warren (Eds.), *Handbook of communication and instruction* (pp. 315–340). Thousand Oaks, CA: Sage.

Aronowitz, S., & Giroux. H. (1991). *Postmodern education: Politics, culture & social criticism.* Minneapolis: University of Minnesota Press.

Bamberg, M., & Andrews, M. (2004). *Considering counter-narratives: Narrating, resisting, making sense.* Philadelphia: John Benjamin.

Berry, K., & Clair, R. (2011). Special Issue: The call of ethnographic reflexivity: Narrating the self's presence in ethnography. *Cultural Studies ↔ Critical Methodologies, 11,* 95–209.

Boal, A. (1979). *Theatre of the oppressed.* New York: Urizen Books. (Original work published 1885.)

Bochner, A. P., & Ellis, C. (1992). Personal narrative as a social approach to interpersonal communication. *Communication Theory, 2,* 165–172.

Cohen-Cruz, J. (2010). *Engaging performance: Theatre as call and response.* New York: Routledge.

Conquergood, D. (1985). Performing as moral act: Ethical dimensions of the ethnography of performance. *Literature in Performance, 5,* 1–13.

Conquergood, D. (2004). Performance studies: Interventions and radical research. In H. Bial (Ed.), *The Performance studies reader* (pp. 311–322). New York: Routledge.

Couser, G. T. (1997). *Recovering bodies: Illness, disability, and life writing.* Madison: University of Wisconsin Press.

Denzin, N.K. (1989). *Interpretive biography.* Newbury Park, CA: Sage.

Denzin, N.K. (2003). *Performance ethnography: Critical pedagogy and the politics of culture.* Thousand Oaks, CA: Sage.

Ellis, C., Adams, T. E., & Bochner, A. P. (2011). Autoethnography: An overview. *Forum: Qualitative Social Research, 12*(1).

Fassett, D. L. & Warren, J. T. (2010). *The SAGE handbook of communication and instruction.* Thousand Oaks, CA: Sage.

Freire, P. (1974). *Education for critical consciousness* (M. B. Ramos, Trans.). New York: Continuum.

Freire, P. (2002). *Pedagogy of the oppressed* (M. B. Ramos, Trans.). New York: Continuum.

Gingrich-Philbrook, C. (2005). Autoethnography's family values: Easy access to compulsory experiences. *Text and Performance Quarterly, 25,* 297–314.

Giroux, H. A. (2001). Cultural studies as performative politics. *Cultural Studies ↔ Critical Methodologies, 1,* 5–23.

Giroux, H. A., Lankshear, C., McLaren, P., & Peters, M. (1996). *Counternarratives: Cultural studies and critical pedagogies in postmodern spaces.* New York: Routledge.

Giroux, H. A., & Shannon, P. (1997). *Education and cultural studies: Toward a performative practice.* London: Routledge.

Goltz, D. B. (2011). Frustrating the "I": Critical dialogic reflexivity with personal voice. *Text and Performance Quarterly, 31,* 386–405.

Grossberg, L. (1996). Toward a genealogy of the state of cultural studies. In C. Nelson & D. Parameshwar (Eds.), *Disciplinary and dissent in cultural studies* (pp. 97–107). New York: Routledge.

Holman Jones, S., (2005). Autoethnography: Making the personal political. In N. K. Denzin & Y. S. Lincoln (Eds.), *Handbook of qualitative research* (pp. 763–791). Thousand Oaks, CA: Sage.

Holman Jones, S., & Adams, T. E. (2010). Autoethnography is a queer method. In K. Browne & C. J. Nash (Eds.), *Queer methods and methodologies: Intersecting queer theories and social science research* (pp. 195–214) Surrey, UK: Ashgate.

Hughes, H., & Román, D. (1998). O solo homo: An introductory conversation. In H. Hughes & D. Román (Eds.), *O solo homo: The new queer performance* (pp. 1–15). New York: Grove Press.

Johnson, C. (1995). Disinfecting dialogue. In J. Gallop (Ed.), *Pedagogy: The question of impersonation* (pp. 129–137). Bloomington: Indiana University Press.

Karamcheti, I. (1995). Caliban in the classroom. In J. Gallop (Ed.), *Pedagogy: The question of impersonation* (pp. 123–146). Bloomington: Indiana University Press.

Lea, V., & Sims, E. J. (2008). *Undoing whiteness in the classroom: Critical educultural teaching approaches for social justice activism.* New York: Peter Lang.

Madison, D. S. (1998). Performance, personal narratives, and the politics of possibility. In S. J. Dailey (Ed.), *The future of performance studies: Visions and revisions* (pp. 276–286). Annandale, VA: National Communication Association.

Madison, D. S. (2008). Narrative, poetics and performative intervention. In N. K. Denzin, Y. S. Lincoln, & L. T. Smith (Eds.), *Handbook of critical and indigenous methodologies* (pp. 391–405). Thousand Oaks, CA: Sage.

Madison, D. S. (2011). The labor of reflexivity. *Cultural Studies ↔ Critical Methodologies, 11,* 129–138.

Massey, G. M. (2012). *Ways of social change: Making sense of modern times.* Thousand Oaks, CA: Sage.

McLaren, P. (1999). *Che Guevara, Paulo Freire, and the pedagogy of revolution.* Lanham, MD: Rowman & Littlefield.

Muñoz, J. E. (2006). Stages, queers, punks, and the utopian performative. In D. S. Madison & J. Hamera (Eds.), *The SAGE handbook of performance studies* (pp. 9–20). Thousand Oaks, CA: Sage.

O'Donnell, J., Pruyn, M., & Chavez, C. R. (2004). *Social justice in these times.* Greenwich, CT: Information Age.

Pineau, E. L. (1994). Teaching is performance: Reconfiguring a problematic metaphor. *American Educational Research Journal, 31,* 3–25.

Pineau, E. L. (1998). Performance studies across the curriculum: Problems, possibilities, and projections. In S. J. Dailey (Ed.), *The future of performance studies: Visions and revisions* (pp. 128–135). Annandale, VA: National Communication Association.

Pineau, E. L. (2002). Critical performance pedagogy: Fleshing out the politics of liberatory education. In N. Stucky & C. Wimmer (Eds.), *Teaching performance studies* (pp. 41–54). Carbondale: Southern Illinois Press.

Román, D. (1998). *Acts of intervention: Performance, gay culture, and AIDS.* Bloomington: Indiana University Press.

Salverson, J. (2001). Change on whose terms? Testimony and an erotics of inquiry. *Theater, 31,* 119–125.

Simon, R. I. (1992). *Teaching against the grain: Texts for a pedagogy of possibility.* New York: Bergin & Garvey.

Spry, T. (2006). A "performative-I" copresence: Embodying the ethnographic turn in performance and the performative turn in ethnography. *Text and Performance Quarterly, 26,* 339–346.

Spry, T. (2011a). *Body, paper, stage: Writing and performing autoethnography.* Walnut Creek, CA: Left Coast Press, Inc.

Spry, T. (2011b). Performative autoethnography: Critical embodiments and possibilities. In N. K. Denzin & Y. S. Lincoln (Eds.), *The SAGE handbook of qualitative research* (4th ed., pp. 497–511). Thousand Oaks, CA: Sage.

Warren, J. T. (2011). Social justice and critical/performative/communicative pedagogy: A storied account of research, teaching, love, identity, desire, and loss. *International Review of Qualitative Research, 4*(1), 21–34.

Chapter 28

Autoethnography as a Praxis of Social Justice
Three Ontological Contexts

Satoshi Toyosaki and
Sandra L. Pensoneau-Conway

My Mother's Critique of and Hope for Higher Education

My mother and I talk quite a lot on the phone. She is in Japan, and I am here in the United States. In 1993, she had to become a mother of an international student. She had to learn alphabets and their correct arrangements in order to mail letters to her son. She is a junior high school graduate. Her father did not allow her to go to high school. As a girl, he thought she needed to learn how to knit and tailor clothes instead of tailor alphabets (Toyosaki, 2007). Nowadays, she listens to and watches international news, worrying about and wishing for my wellbeing in the United States. When a tornado hits near where I live, she calls to make sure I am OK. Many times, *she* informs *me* about what is going on in the world—perished young lives of soldiers in various conflicts, natural disasters and their recovery efforts (or lack thereof), deaths of innocent children, and so on.

One day she says to me, "It is quite strange, you know. Humans are supposed to be getting smarter and smarter. Look at how education has become available. And many more people go to colleges and universities. But I don't think people are getting smarter." She tells this to her son, who has earned the highest degree in his field and now teaches and researches in and about higher education. I think to myself: "What is she really trying to say?" Probing questions emerge in my mind. "Am I not getting smarter? Am I not teaching my students to become smarter?" But I do not ask her these questions, nervous about her answers. Also,

Handbook of Autoethnography, edited by Stacy Holman Jones, Tony E. Adams, and Carolyn Ellis, 557–575. © 2013 Left Coast Press, Inc. All rights reserved.

coming from a high-context culture, my mother and I do not ask a lot of questions. Ending my silent probing, she continues, "Look at what humans do to each other in the world. We can go to the moon, but we cannot even understand each other." She pauses. I remain silent, unsure of how to respond, feeling my identity as an academic under attack in this conversation. Her pause continues. Then she quietly murmurs, "This is kind of sad, isn't it?"

Shortly after, over lunch, a colleague relates a telling fact about human beings that he heard on the radio: In the past century, more humans have lost their lives at the hands of other humans than in the previous centuries combined. At the lunch table, I do not challenge him; I think that this fact could be true as the painful images of the Holocaust and WWII flicker through my mind. My mother may be right; we humans may not be getting better at understanding each other even though formal education has become more accessible.

My mother's untrained (academically speaking) critique of higher education is sharp precisely because she uses her motherly love as the criterion for evaluating education. While implicit, she was speaking about neoliberal education (Giroux, 2003; Saunders, 2010) where practical and professional skills are privileged while the education of human love and caring are often hindered. Even in qualitative inquiry, we tend to privilege the head, leaving our body and emotions behind (Ellis & Bochner, 2006). Slowly but surely, I come to understand her educational critique as a call for me, as an academic in higher education, to teach my students and myself to become "smarter," to self-reflexively examine what we do *to* each other, and to care about each other like a mother cares about her son.

My mother asks us to "look at what we do to each other." The evidence is right there in front of us, everywhere, everyday. In our histories, in the statistics (wars, crimes, hate crimes, suicides, abuses, and so forth), in the bruises on our bodies and hearts we feel the call to better educate ourselves. We need to work collectively to become smarter for each other. My mother's critique is harsh but telling.

We live in a world we need to change. We need a way to understand ourselves critically and carefully, for us, for others, and for all of us together. We need critical scholarship that "make[s] a difference in the world and, where necessary, [changes] people" (Ellis & Bochner, 2006, p. 439). Warren (2010) says,

> Critical scholarship needs more than sharp critique in order for it to be useful. Combined with the sharp critical eye, one needs mechanisms of interruption; places where we can begin to make that critique matter in ways that provide hope and possibility.

We see autoethnography as the critical scholarship that does the labor of sharp critique, interruption, and hope—labor that helps us become smarter for us, for others and for all of us together. I believe my mother will see such scholarship and pedagogy—the doing of autoethnography—as education that helps us better understand each other. In other words, we see "doing" of autoethnography as the praxis of social justice.

World-making and having faith in humanity are critical ingredients of doing autoethnography. What if global leaders in the world were autoethnographers? What if educators were trained to engage their students autoethnographically in classrooms? What if oppressors and the oppressed dialogued through their autoethnographies? We get excited about the idea that autoethnography becomes our way of life, an ethical code of being *in* the world, being *with* others, and being there *for* others. In other words, we get excited about the idea of autoethnography as social justice. We wonder how different the world would be, how differently we would move through such a world, if autoethnography were a way of being in the world. This chapter engages a move toward our everyday performance of autoethnographic social justice. We believe that understanding autoethnography as social justice—or, put another way, as a response to social *in*justice—is a move towards actualizing the imaginative function of the questions. In many ways, this begins with the (simple) act of recognition, or what Fraser (1996) terms a "justice of recognition." Here, efforts are directed towards acknowledgment and validation of the other as a person, as a human being deserving of the basic necessities of living. Fraser identifies the goal of recognition as "a difference-friendly world, where assimilation to majority or dominant cultural norms is no longer the price of equal respect" (p. 3). We frame our chapter in this fashion in order to explore how autoethnography might function as an articulation of the justice of recognition.

With this in mind, we ask readers to move with us as we situate the ontological and praxiological[1] commitments of autoethnography. Doing so sets up ways we might privilege autoethnography not merely as a way to know, but also as a way to critically act in the world (praxiology), and a way to understand the processual construction of the self (ontology). A praxiological and ontological approach allows us to demonstrate our understanding of autoethnography as the praxis—as a theoretically informed practice—of social justice within three different micro and macro ontological contexts: an intersubjective context, a relational context, and a community context. Our undergirding perception of autoethnography is that it is a way to orient ourselves towards the world as both an enactment of social justice and a response to social injustice.

Autoethnographic Ontology and Praxiology

When we think of autoethnography as a research methodology, we might risk understanding it solely in epistemological terms—in terms that mark autoethnography as a way of knowing. Scholars (see Anderson, 2006; Ellis, 2004) promote discussion in the epistemological frame, perhaps prompted by our trained "academic" conventions. Moreover, autoethnographers, us included, explain well the axiological, or value-based, commitments of doing autoethnography (see Ellis, 2004; Ellis & Bochner, 2006). In this chapter, we hope to extend gifts of "doing" autoethnography beyond the epistemological and axiological frames. Kiesinger (2002), Lockford (2002), and Toyosaki (2012) argue that autoethnography is/

does more than function as a way of knowing. Our "doing" of autoethnography helps us, autoethnographers, come to know (epistemology), evaluate (axiology), become (ontology), and do (praxiology) our selfhood—our sense of being—in the world; our foci in this chapter are ontology and praxiology—becoming and doing. We focus on autoethnography's constitutive nature; that is, selfhood is constituted—examined, revised, and renewed—and becomes connected with others through the doing of autoethnography (Bochner & Ellis, 1995; Ellis, Kiesinger, & Tillmann-Healy, 1997; Toyosaki, Pensoneau-Conway, Wendt, & Leathers, 2009).

This move to the constitutive nature of autoethnography is key in thinking of autoethnography as the praxis of social justice. At first, the idea of the self as fundamental to social justice may seem contradictory. However, while social justice may be fundamentally *social*, our argument for autoethnography as the praxis of social justice entails an examination of the self who engages in social justice/responds to social injustice. Gandhi's oft-referenced adage, "Be the change you wish to see in the world," is not simply cliché. In order to demonstrate this argument, we theoretically merge autoethnography and a praxis of social justice.

o

I am fortunate to sit on the board of a local group for LGBT youth and their friends who are allies. When I completed the form to be on the board, I had to respond to the question of why I desired such a position. I offered:

> In working to understand my own shifting sexual identity over the years, and in my work with education and youth, I find that there can never be too many people to tell young people that they are loved, that they are respected, and that they are valuable. This is particularly true for those who experience shame and bullying as a result of their (perceived or avowed) sexual identity, or even those who may not be sure of their sexual identity. Being on the board will allow me to better equip myself to continue as an advocate for *all* youth—as we know that when we are able to accept the continuum of sexual identities and experiences we are opening up space for all youth to have positive, affirmative identity formation and relationships. As a not-so-young person anymore, my interaction with the youth (even if indirectly as a board member) will help me to understand the struggles and triumphs that youths of today face.
>
> Finally, as a mother of a two-year-old, I have to admit that I am being a bit selfish. I want her to grow up in an environment that respects and learns from difference, rather than claiming that we're all alike or even outrightly shaming others. Joining the board is a way to practice what I preach.

Admittedly, I fight the feeling of contradiction I know I create for myself in the context of this group, especially among the other board members, many (if not all) of whom identify as sexual minorities. I know I am free to take advantage of the many unearned privileges I receive as a result of my legally recognized relationship with my partner. The ring on my finger, the jointly filed tax return, and the various examined and unexamined ways we move through the world all attest to how I may not belong in this meeting. Tonight, the conversation at our meeting turns to the new film, *Bully* (Lowen, 2011), which came to our small town for a limited run. I did not—would not—see the film. I do not need to be convinced that bullying happens, that it is an epidemic in the United States, that it manifests in visible and invisible ways, and that it is horrendous. Though I don't know I could identify any experience I've had as an experience in bullying (either as doing or receiving), I cannot help but wonder how I may have been a bully. I cannot help but wonder what sort of bullying my daughter may engage in or experience. I cannot imagine feeling anything other than helplessness, pity, and anger, and I am in a social position to avoid those feelings. I do not need to be convinced. But as the group around me begins to express their identification with the film, I feel something more than contradiction; I feel a great sense of inadequacy.

What does it mean for me to not see the film? What does it mean for me to sit here, amongst people who *lived* the film, and in that living, experience the film in ways certainly different than my (non-)experience of it? This inadequate contradiction feels at once responsive and selfish; I desired to and now sit on the board because it is one way I can respond to social injustice, yet I purposefully chose not to see a film that surely (I assume) has great relevance for everyone around me, likely including the youth whose lives I am hoping to positively influence. How might I use this moment of inadequate contradiction to transform my own learning and socially response-able processes? How might I make productive use of my listening in on this conversation about *Bully*?

○

In approaching social (in)justice, we underscore the minute-ness of our performative moments of making and remaking social injustice in our micro-social everyday contexts. Each of these ephemeral moments of identity production is particular (Warren, 2008) and political (Holman Jones, 2005) and the very roadblocks which make possible social injustice. Here comes a shift in our thinking: Maybe seeking social justice is not only about seeking social justice, but about critiquing and interrupting the minute moments of social injustice that permeate our everyday identity performances, and hoping for a better tomorrow with others in our lives. Warren (2011) writes, "For me, social justice is about seeing the world in all its loss and imagining ways of healing" (p. 30). While productively ambiguous, social justice derives from our human—cognitive, affective, and behavioral—capacity to heal from social injustice, be that as victims, doers, spectators, and accomplices of social injustice. This healing process is always intersubjective, always rhizomatic by virtue of its intersubjectivity—a condition from which our sense of self arises. Therefore, efforts towards "a work of justice" are not for the benefit of one person only. Further, seemingly individual acts of justice can converge in an effort to effect social change. The work we do is meant for the *collective* greater good (a collective of which I may be a part). Social justice must necessarily be enacted in the spirit of *with* (not *for*) others. And so while I may have consciously chosen to NOT see the film *Bully* (an act of social injustice as identified through self-reflexion), my conscious choice to ally myself with this LGBT youth organization may be a more meaningful response to social injustice (even my own act of social injustice), done *with* others, rather than occupying a singular seat in a darkened movie theatre. Perhaps my listening-in on the *Bully* conversation at the board meeting is what I, a straight-identified member of a heteronormative society, need to do in order to understand my place in a bully culture. In the micro-level space of recognition of heterosexual privilege, the ways this recognition informs my interactions with others who narrate bullying (and even who narrate social injustice of varying kinds) is an example of the social/relational/macro consequences of social justice work.

We understand autoethnography to originate in a micro-social context. That is, the very nature of the project begins from individual experience (micro), though that experience is situated in a larger, macro-social context. When we do autoethnography, we aim to engage micro-level experience (my experience) as it is intersubjectively embodied within a macro-social context. In other words, *social justice* isn't simply about speaking before congress, or starting a charitable organization, or protesting on the streets, though those all could potentially be social justice work. It is also about asking how the performance of listening can be a response to social injustice, and therefore, a move toward social justice. How might our autoethnographies, as projects that engage a tripartite relationship of writer-reader-text, function as micro-moments of social justice that move out-ward into macro-contexts? Each of our autoethnographies serves as a thread of the micro-social labor against social injustice, a thread that weaves together with others to actualize social change. They are our collaborative emplotments—the active, conscious, narrative placing of the self as a temporal being within the narrative present—of our selves in micro-contexts working towards our goal of social justice. Autoethnography serves as a critical mechanism for working with micro-social acts and sites of social injustice and towards productively ambiguous social justice in the spirit of *with* others. In exploring the relationship between the micro and macro as they intersect with autoethnography and social justice, we discuss three ontological contexts of doing autoethnography: becoming (the self), relating (with relational others), and making community (together), all of which collaboratively promote autoethnography as a praxis of social justice.

Doing Autoethnography as a Praxis of Social Justice

For us, doing autoethnography is a life of self-emplotment. Autoethnographers engage the possible rather than settling in the actual. We do not simply accept the present as it is; rather, we continuously and critically gesture towards how the present might be differently understood in its temporality, in its coming from the past, and in its look toward the future. Autoethnography is the very labor that textures our (inter)subjective selves, the relationships in which we engage, and the communities of which we become a part through autoethnographic storytelling. In this section, we trace critical connections between self-emplotment and social justice in the contexts of intersubjectivity, relationships, and community.

Becoming: Autoethnographic (Inter)subjectivity

One day, my partner says, "You say that a lot these days. I don't like it when you say that." I have been saying, "It is what it is," quite often these days. We confide in each other, try to listen well to each other, seek and give advice to each other, and grow with each other. We are socially minded individuals, always conscious (at least trying to be) of racism, sexism, oppression, and social injustice; this social consciousness is one of many reasons for our initial attraction to each other. I am struggling with ubiquitous social oppressions, some voluntary and others imposed. The world around me is swirling, and I accept the majority of these oppressions just to survive and keep going.

⚬

A small boy, maybe five or six years old, whom I have never met before, walks toward me. I tune into him with an inviting smile. With an innocent smile, he asks, "Do you speak English? Do you speak Spanish?" In moments like this, I say, "It is what it is."

⚬

My friend and I are playing tennis without shirts on because it is an extremely hot day in small-town southern Illinois. Two boys, maybe ten and six years old, pass by on their bikes. The older boy screams out, "Put your shirt on, faggot." In moments like this, I say, "It is what it is."

⚬

A student drops my course after learning my—the teacher's— "abnormal" (non US-American sounding) last name. In moments like this, I say, "It is what it is."

⚬

I have to pass my students' suspicious examination on the first of day of every semester: Can he speak understandable English? I have to pass an examination at the end of semester as the student evaluation asks if I "spoke understandably" in this intercultural communication course, a course that purports to value diversifying our beings through multiple modes of communication and understanding. In these moments, I say, "It is what it is."

⚬

A journal reviewer criticizes my English for not sounding "natural" (Toyosaki, 2011). I do not have the ability to speak and write in natural English, as I was born and raised in Japan speaking Japanese. I really don't know what "natural" English actually means, as English has a tremendous variety in regional and international use. Whose English is natural and normal? And what do we "do" to make and maintain that English as dominant and unquestionable? Also I don't experience and code my life in "normal" English. Indeed, I experience myself in this world and code those lived experiences in choppy, *un*natural English. I feel oppressed in this moment of linguistic critique; yet, I have to learn the (perceived and somewhat mysterious) linguistic oppressors' language to make sure my lived experiences are legible to them. The voices in "natural" English are broken voices to me because I am not a natural English speaker. In these moments, I say, "It is what it is."

○

Furthermore, I have to bite my critical and sympathetic tongue while I inflict the same pain I experience in this linguistic politics on my non-native English speaking international graduate students who are about to enter the publication world of our academy. While I don't know a remedy for these linguistic politics, I feel we need a more collaborative way to deploy our English languages—plural—to create a more diverse academic discourse where our cross-cultural understanding is conceptualized as a matter of caring, love, and collaboration. In my office, my non-English native international students confide their frustration. I say, "We have to keep trying. Who said change is easy?" In this moment, I feel that the saying "It is what it is" is not enough.

○

I tell myself, over and over, "It is what it is." My repetitive reminder helps me to keep going on with and surviving in my life. I have come to use "It is what it is" like a period that punctuates my thoughts. In the moment of this utterance, I feel hopeless and defeated. In the moment of this utterance, I lose—or forfeit— my social agency. Within every moment of this utterance—the liminal present between the past and future—my personhood stands "in peril" (Schrag, 1997, p. 37), hopelessly.

What does it mean for me to experience myself and consciously perform my selfhood in the liminal present? How do I perform personhood in the present, critically examining how the "it" becomes it and carefully entertaining my own (inter)subjectivity for the hoped-for future—not the better future *for* me but a hoped-for future *with* others? Autoethnographers cannot afford to say "It is what it is." We live with the critical and careful fantasy of "what it can be and how" as our doing of autoethnography is a praxis of social theories and justice. As a project that works toward actualizing possibility, autoethnography locates itself at the critical juncture of naming social injustice and engaging acts of social justice. Autoethnography as a research methodology provides cultural and social justice workers both a platform and the critical instruments to interrogate the political, historical, social, and cultural injustice within their lived experiences. Autoethnography further infuses the act of writing with hope for embodied and personally implicated understandings between writer and reader.

The present self is a temporal condition, always coming from the past and moving toward the future (Schrag, 1997). In this temporal movement of self-construction, the present forms a pivotal point. In doing autoethnography, we engage in this implicated present—a present that implies both the past and the future—in order to interrogate our own identity performance-in-production and its reproductive social mechanisms of injustice. We must engage in the present, a simultaneous absence of the "already" and the "not yet" (Schrag, 1986, p. 146), and this living present is the opportunity for our identity interrogation, interruption, and change. It is the opportunity to move from "It is what it is" to "What can it be and how?"—the opportunity for social justice, the opportunity for a response to social injustice.

Further, we cannot comprehend our identity without accounting for how identity is enmeshed in a context, and more specifically, in the context of embodied social relationships. These relationships provide the epistemological and ontological foundations for coming to know the self and the other (Pensoneau-Conway, 2012). "'I' am never just 'I,' but I am 'I' because I am in a relationship with 'you,' creating 'we.' Likewise, 'we' are never just 'we,' because we are situated in a larger social... context" (Pensoneau-Conway, 2012, p. 35). We are intersubjective beings.

Also, it is essential to consider that the self is never a private entity. "Intersubjectivity does not derive from subjectivity, but the other way around" (Giddens, 1991, p. 51). Our being is both social (in relationship with others) and fluid (capable of changing at any moment), and always already intersubjective. However, this anti-autonomous self should not "downplay the significance of its capacity to act, to inaugurate real changes in the world" (Dauenhauer, 2002, p. 155). Thus, autoethnographers are already social authors. They rely on the convention of the intersubjective, social practice of narrativity in creating their understandings of their lived experiences. Moreover, narrativity invites readers into stories with hope that readers can connect (both the story and the autoethnographer) in a highly personal, self-reflexive, and critical way. Autoethnographers are producers, critics, and evaluators of social theories. Doing autoethnography is inherently and always already a labor of social theories; therefore, autoethnographers as intersubjective, social, and dialogical selves possess potential in rendering a critical impetus to promote social justice.

Carol Rambo's (2005; Rambo Ronai, 1995) work accentuates the intersubjective self. Her development of the layered account embodies the messiness of intersubjective identity interrogation. In a layered account, the author takes readers on a non-linear journey with and in the fragmented self of the author, moving the reader through the temporal condition of the living present. Rambo provides an account of a partial, incomplete—layered—sense of self, and underscores the self as an amalgamation of experiences and relationships, each informing the "self" in a unique way. Each of the layers never fully constitutes the self because the self is not defined by any given layer; at the same time, each layer inevitably leaves its impression upon the self (Rambo, 2005). In the fissures where identity finds itself incomplete, the layered account welcomes readers to "fill in the spaces and construct an interpretation of the writer's narrative. The readers reconstruct the subject, thus projecting more of themselves into it, and taking more away from it" (Rambo Ronai, 1995, p. 396), rendering both author and reader intersubjective beings, social authors, and social actors.

Layers of voice reflect layers of self and experience. Even the very act of writing produces an "ad-hoc self" (Rambo Ronai, 1995, p. 399) that establishes a mechanism for social criticism, drawing upon seemingly isolated experiences in order to critique unjust systems. In an example of what we identify as autoethnographic scholarship in the service of social justice, Rambo speaks the unspeakable. She articulates experiences that largely go unnarrated, untold, and in effect, are left un-mattered. Her detailed and graphic sketches of the sexual abuse she suffered at the hands of her father (Rambo Ronai, 1995), along with the abuse enabled by her mentally retarded mother (Rambo Ronai, 1996) and inattentive and emotionally absent grandmother (Rambo, 2005), leave little to the imagination. Subjects such as these are often reduced to a series of statistics, directives for leaving abusive situations, censored accounts stripped of emotional impact and evocative truth, advertisements for recovery procedures. And yet, Rambo complicates each of these taboo topics, adopting a multi-perspectival position. Her writing interrupts everyday moments of injustice. Her work challenges others to take up and respond to moments of social injustice. Just as the moments of the injustice add up, so, too, do the responses. Rambo's interruption may not interrupt the moments of her past, but through the interaction of the reader with Rambo's texts, Rambo's interruption is potentially taken up by others. Rambo creates space, and this space of recognition functions as a resource often denied to marginalized populations. Rambo employs an autoethnographic layered account to boldly carve out space in which to claim the experiential, unfinished, intersubjective self in the context of social injustice, effectively validating the humanity of those who live with such injustice.

Relating: Autoethnographic Relationships

We take several graduate seminars together in our doctoral program at Southern Illinois University Carbondale—rhetorical theory, ethnography, education and culture, autoethnography, and so on. We sit next to each other as close friends do. Our friendship has been formative to our personhoods, our lives, and our worldviews.

Ron Pelias's autoethnography class changes our friendship and how we understand our international/cultural relationship. We (Toyosaki & Pensoneau, 2005) join those who value autoethnography's capacity to carefully examine personal and cultural issues through relational and dialogic investigation. Bochner and Ellis (1995) and Ellis and Bochner (1992) study their abortion experience through their dialogic autoethnography. Ellis, Kiesinger, and Tillmann-Healy (1997) demonstrate how dialogic, collaborative, and relational autoethnography can help researchers produce a careful study of eating disorders, including the social and cultural issues that surround them.

In these projects and others, the autoethnographers recognize a self constituted in relationship with others and dialogue as an interrogative method to explore the intersubjective nature of our self-constructions. Autoethnographic partners collaboratively investigate their shared experiences, self-reflexively examine their individual perspectives, treat each other's experiences and interpretations as resources for further understanding the issue at hand, and finally, understand their active role in strengthening their relationships.

These relationship-based autoethnographies embody a "dialogic encounter" (Schrag, 1986, p. 125) in which relational partners transform from "I and you" into "we." Dialogical participants exchange perspectives and responses in an ongoing and simultaneous way. "Your response," continues Schrag (1986), "is one of incorporating what I have said, by either acceptance, rejection, or modification. Then I respond by incorporating your response into my initial claims" (p. 125). Intentionality underscores this dialogic encounter, as "the 'I' and the 'you' [are] seen as coemergent" in the "fabric of intersubjectivity" (p. 125). The curiosity that undergirds such an intersubjective, dialogic, narrative encounter evokes in the relational partners a desire to know one another, to recognize one another in a way that respects difference as an ontological and epistemological necessity (Pensoneau-Conway, 2012). This stands akin to Fraser's (1996) "difference-friendly world" through the justice of recognition (p. 3).

We (Toyosaki & Pensoneau, 2005) employ co-constructed narrative in investigating one intercultural, interpersonal conflict between us. We also (Toyosaki & Pensoneau, 2005) study how two people of different nationalities work toward constructing our friendship in such a way that it transcends those national borders and cultural differences (such as communication styles, whiteness, race, and so on). We further challenge our taken-for-granted privileges (linguistic, cultural, geographic, and political). Our friendship is complex; Satoshi was born and raised in Japan, exhibits Japanese cultural characteristics, speaks English as his second language, and is male. (Japan is a highly masculine-oriented culture.) Sandy was born and raised in the United States, exhibits "US American" characteristics, speaks English as her native language, and is female. We both live in the United States and develop/maintain our friendship in English. Our friendship is imbued with and implicated by the global politics of language, whiteness, gender, and geographic privilege.

In this project, we narratively study one conflict we experience (Toyosaki & Pensoneau, 2005). In moments of conflict, it is difficult to "recognize" where the other is coming from. We are often inclined to use our own cultural logic to judge each other, resulting in a "What's wrong with her/him?" posture. In this moment, we fail to recognize each other. We enter a conflict as two I's, as isolated subjects, monologically rationalizing our own culture as a dogmatic hermeneutic system and failing to acknowledge and validate our relationship partner's presence.

The participants in relational autoethnography have a responsibility to each other—a responsibility to be response-able and response-willing, an obligation to recognize the other as a *partner* in dialogue. Relational, autoethnographic encounters encompass an ongoing invitation for each partner to make legible the other's lived experience of and through the relationship. Thus, "central to consciousness is not only being authored by Other, but additionally, authoring Other. Consciousness can thus be viewed as a mutual process of authoring, an ongoing dynamic of joint action" (Baxter & Akkoor, 2008, p. 27). Relational autoethnography helps researchers achieve the justice of recognition within a mutual and dialogical authoring of each other. Further, it funds the construction of a relational consciousness. Social justice crystallizes our recognition of each other's presence in the communicative space of intersubjectivity. Thus, social injustice is a problem "we"—a collective of intersubjective selves—have and for which we all are response-able and response-willing to each other in resolving.

○

I read Sophie Tamas's *Life after Leaving: The Remains of Spousal Abuse* (2011), having assigned it as a text in my autoethnography course. She and her co-participants negotiate the articulation of their experiences of various forms of abuse. A poetic orchestra fills the pages of her text, with an aria here claiming the title of *survivor*, a coda there searching for repetition of experience to find community and commonality. A Picardian third pushes for resolution, a solution, an acceptable ending that fits the social narrative of trauma-victim-who-overcomes.

But the verse that resonates with me is the critique of the recovery paradigm and the valorization of therapy. Tamas (2011) takes to task the discourse of recovery and medicalization of experience placed upon those who live through and with trauma. Her co-participants find that they have to re-narrate their abusive experience to social workers, to family and friends, to their children's teachers, to their employers. They are oftentimes told that owning the experiences, and making sense of them, contributes to their recovery. Time spent in therapy purports to inform transcendence, the experience of moving through and beyond. But, as Tamas so beautifully and poignantly calls attention to, making-sense-of is all too often, really, an exercise in explaining away. Making-sense-of indicates that there is sense to be made. But there is no sense to be made of certain phenomena, including abuse. We should not make sense of some things. Sometimes, there is no sense to be made, in the sense that we cannot, and should not, explain away. It is okay to not re-cover these experiences, to not cover them up in the veil of sense-making.

My heart is heavy after I read this critique. My heart is heavy when I re-member, when I put back into my body, the times I told loved ones that they needed help, that making sense was in the best interests of our family, that sense could be made of abuse, of neglect, of trauma. My heart is heavy when I re-member the ways I moved through the world placing the responsibility for sense making on the recipients of abuse, neglect, and trauma. Tamas's critique of the recovery paradigm calls me to live my life differently as a relational other. Where I previously argued that making sense is not only for the good of the person, but also of the person's family and friends, I now try to understand the potential negative implications of making sense in the first place. My mode of being a relational other has shifted from a compellation to help and to fix, to a patient availability where I begin with an open heart and attentive ear.

o

Relational autoethnography, as we have described it here, is a way to respond to social injustice through narrative. It is a way to respecify our relationships as relational others. It is a way to dialogically identify, critique, and change unjust social structures, both metaphorically—as in the sense of how we may understand relational others differently, and thus, change our own performances of self in those relationships—and literally—as in the form of co-authored autoethnographies; for example, narrative co-construction. This sort of relational orientation to autoethnography, and a relational consequence of autoethnography, is at the heart of a justice of recognition in the context of a relationship.

Bochner and Ellis (1995) explain their narrative co-construction process and its methodological merits, which prove instrumental in undertaking social justice in the context of an autoethnographic relationship. Narrative co-construction rests upon two fundamental assumptions about relationships. First, "relationships between people are jointly authored, incomplete, and historically situated" (p. 204), leaving relationships inherently unfinished and fluid. Second, the authors hold that the very act of co-construction becomes a part of the relationship and is not simply *about* the relationship. Partners in a relationship are intersubjectively constructed as partners of each other, actively "participat[ing] in each other's existence" (p. 204).

Through narrative co-construction, relational partners directly face their differences in narrating the relationship. They come to affirm and accept each other's whole being, becoming more whole for themselves and one another. This method teaches autoethnographers the importance of being fully present for each other. By virtue of its relationship-centeredness (not just self- or other-centeredness), this way of being in relationships with others is a foundation of social justice: to be fully present for others and to become more fully human with each other. This is the embodiment of a justice of recognition. This is a relational foundation—a concrete communicative and relational praxis—that helps us challenge and interrupt social injustice.

Gathering: Autoethnographic Community

The community context of autoethnographic social justice projects draws upon Frey, Pearce, Pollock, Artz, and Murphy's (1996) and Novak's (2000) inclusion of the ever-important "with" in their description of social justice. Social justice cannot be by some*one for* someone else. Social justice is a collective effort of a group of individuals working with/in the framework of social critique and social change. This community of others may take the form of a collage of mundane interruptions of everyday social injustice. Ontologically speaking, autoethnography substantiates a life lived in community, where stories are the stuff of the relationships we form—those fleeting relationships in moments of the everyday, and those ongoing relationships with "close, meaningful others" (Adams, 2011, p. 132). Indeed, Schrag (1997) contends that the self constituted in communicative praxis is simultaneously "called into being within a community" (p. 77). Ellis (2009) champions "good" autoethnography for the ways it "works toward a communitas, where we might speak together of our experiences, find commonality of spirit, companionship in our sorrow, balm for our wounds, and solace in reaching out to those in need as well" (pp. 229–230). As a project in affect, analysis, and change, community formed through autoethnography is built upon the web of stories Frey et al. (1996) hold as crucial to social justice. "People's ethical and political judgments are contingent on the webs of the embodied narratives of individuals and communities" (p. 111). To claim an orientation toward social justice, and yet ignore the story/ies of the communities of which we are a part and with which we struggle, would constitute an injustice in itself.

Autoethnography, in its various forms and contexts, is more than a written account of an experience, as evidenced throughout this Handbook. Autoethnography moves, acts, and labors in how writers and readers live the stories written and read. Denzin (2003) holds that texts, contexts, and cultural practices (performances) are indubitably connected (p. 196), and the sense made, however partial, of that tripartite connection happens in the act of reading and relating (Richardson & St. Pierre, 2005, p. 960). Our autoethnographies, then, are unquestionably community-based performance texts—active, living texts—with the potential to incite change through the very performances of our writing, others' reading, and the ensuing dialogues.

Frank (2005) identifies the interconnectedness of stories in creating a community of experience. This does not necessarily mean that a singular story is literally authored by a community of people (though this certainly is a possibility), but that a singular story has the potential to resonate with an infinite number of people in an infinite number of ways, creating a web of stories. For example, when I read

Bochner's (2002), Kiesinger's (2002), and Pelias's (2002) works, I cannot *not* think of my own relationship with my father. While the nature of my familial issues is dramatically different from theirs, I leave their pieces wanting to envision an autoethnographic engagement in my relationship with my father. These pieces, not explicitly but surely, encourage me that I can do this as well and that "It is what it is" is no longer an option. My autoethnographic interactions with my father (Toyosaki, 2012) render minute "differences" in our father-son relationship. While he does not have any knowledge about what autoethnography is and does, something about our relationship has been shifting as a result of my work on my identity as my father's son. In this way, the autoethnographic spirit that Bochner (2002), Kiesinger (2002), and Pelias (2002) pour into their writing travels through my autoethnographic work and my doing of "my father's son" differently.

The partiality of each story creates space for connections with other stories. Stories, storytellers, and story audiences draw upon one another in understanding both the self and the other. Thus, one story does not begin where a previous one ended; to speak of a story's beginning and ending preserves a false sense of completion (Toyosaki, 2007). Rather, stories hinge upon one another, find life in the relationship amongst themselves in what Frank (2005) calls "*perpetual generation*" (p. 967). The analysis of stories "can never claim any last word about what a story means or represents" (p. 967); perpetual generation allows us to respond to one another in a loving, hopeful, community-making mode that exclaims, "I see you. You matter." Perpetual generation engages a social justice of recognition.

Engaging the Possible

We find in autoethnography fertile ground for social justice projects largely because autoethnography assumes a stance of incompleteness of the self, of the other, and of the relationship, thus allowing for intersubjectivity. In the moment of autoethnographic intersubjectivity, persons find themselves as incomplete social actors, always in temporal process, always being made and re-made within relationships, always capable of responding to social injustice. In the moment of relational autoethnography, relational partners grapple with difference, including difference that may manifest in unjust ways. In the moment of autoethnographic community, narratives travel in rhizomatic fashion to bring to light issues of social justice. Autoethnography happens with an attitude of perpetual possibility, and what is social justice if not a collective journey to actualize the possible rather than accept the actual as finished?

It is in the move towards actualizing hoped-for possibilities, towards world-making, towards social criticism, where autoethnography finds it thrust. McKerrow (1993) argues that the goal of a social critic is not to produce master narratives that intend to fix social problems and social conditions. Instead, he argues that the goal of a social critic is to "pull together those fragments whose intersection in real lives has meaning for social actors" (p. 62). This meaning provides the potential to embody those social conditions in new ways. A text of social criticism, then, "functions to enable historicized subjects to alter the conditions of their lived experience" (p. 62). The presence of the possible, of how things could be different and what that difference might be, is what moves social criticism. Autoethnography writes experience in such a way as to make difference present, rather than attempting to make difference disappear. That is, autoethnography works as "a method of inquiry" (Richardson & St. Pierre, 2005) and an ontological and praxiological positioning wherein the processes of writing and living are perpetual processes of possibility, ongoing glimpses into life lived differently, continuous encounters with how social conditions may be otherwise, interruptions of everyday injustices (see Bochner, 2002). Autoethnographers author narratives of experiences as remembered, and in the authoring, write experiences anew in dialogue with others (as reader, as co-author, as co-participant in the experience, as co-constructors in humanity), as an experience of possibility.

Here autoethnographic community emerges when we pledge our personhood—mind, body, and emotion—to and truly live in our endless pulling together (McKerrow, 1993) of the autoethnographic pieces produced and consumed in the world we work to change. Each autoethnographer—indeed, each autoethnography—is incomplete, intersubjective, and relational. Autoethnographies require our continuous pulling together into a discursive stream that textures our lives and communities as we work to effect social change. This community-making is an intense labor of us autoethnographers and, we argue, is praxiological evidence of social justice-oriented communities. We believe that this autoethnographic community—both the concept and the praxis—creates a different world.

Experiences of oppression—both as oppressor and as oppressed, separated only by an oftentimes blurry (at best) thin line—can draw people together in a hopeful, loving relationship with one another as incomplete beings who long for possibility actualized, who yearn for change taking shape, who work—and it is *work*—towards transformation and identification with one another and with the not-yet. An enterprise that aims to change the world certainly does so with a hopeful spirit. And one does not need to look far to see that autoethnographers invest in the capacity for transformation (interruption, transgression, disruption, movement) through autoethnographic narrative (Adams & Holman Jones, 2008; Denzin, 2003; Ellis, 2009; Holman Jones, 2005)—one story, one person, one self/other at a time. One does not set out to create change without being hopeful of actualizing that change; autoethnography makes us smarter.

Critical Reminders before We Depart

Frey et al. (1996) remind us that scholars working within the realm of social justice have no blueprint to follow, no set of criteria to meet, no absolute *telos* by which to measure whether or not they have reached social justice, engaged in research approaching social justice, or created just change. Nor, the authors caution, should they. However, we are heartened by their directive that in order for our work to matter, we need to develop a "sensibility" for social justice (p. 110). The idea of a sensibility is precisely what we argue for here through situating autoethnography as an orientation towards social justice. More than a method—which, by the very term, implies a process in a procedural sense—we hope readers will understand that the autoethnographic life necessitates a sensibility for social justice in the moments of the self, the relationship, and the community.

We challenge scholars of social justice, researchers of social injustice and social inequality, and activists for social change to fully embrace autoethnography for its ontological and praxiological—hence, transformative—potential. We implore scholars, researchers, and activists to fully and whole-heart-edly embrace love and hope as guiding principles as we encounter sites of autoethnographic intersubjectivitiy, relationship, and community. We see autoethnography as a concrete communicative and intersubjective praxis (Schrag, 1986) of social justice, and applaud its capacity to draw upon, engage, and preserve the ontological space of the *with* that situates it in the service of social justice.

Note

1. Throughout this essay, we will expand upon the term *praxiology* and its various forms. In short, the term involves the nature of doing. For us, the suffix *–ology* situates the term within the discourse of epistemology, ontology, and axiology. While it is also sometimes spelled "praxeology," we argue that using the lesser-used "praxIology" visually emphasizes the root *praxis* while retaining its relationship to the other "ologies."

References

Adams, T. E. (2011). *Narrating the closet: An autoethnography of same-sex attraction*. Walnut Creek, CA: Left Coast Press, Inc.

Adams, T. E., & Holman Jones, S. (2008). Autoethnography is queer. In N. K. Denzin, Y. S. Lincoln, & L. T. Smith (Eds.), *Handbook of critical and indigenous methodologies* (pp. 373–390). Thousand Oaks, CA: Sage.

Anderson, L. (2006). Analytic autoethnography. *Journal of Contemporary Ethnography, 35*, 373–395.

Baxter, L. A., & Akkoor, C. (2008). Aesthetic love and romantic love in close relationships. In K. G. Roberts & R. C. Arnett (Eds.), *Communication ethics: Between cosmopolitanism and provinciality* (pp. 23–46). New York: Peter Lang.

Bochner, A. P. (2002). Perspectives on inquiry III: The moral of stories. In M. L. Knapp & J. A. Daly (Eds.), *Handbook of interpersonal communication* (3rd ed., pp. 73–101). Thousand Oaks, CA: Sage.

Bochner, A. P., & Ellis, C. (1995). Telling and living: Narrative co-construction and the practices of interpersonal relationships. In W. Leeds-Hurwitz (Ed.), *Social approaches to communication* (pp. 201–213). New York: The Guilford Press.

Dauenhauer, B. P. (2002). Schrag and the self. In B. Beck Matušik & W. L. McBride (Eds.), *Calvin O. Schrag and the task of philosophy after postmodernity* (pp. 152–164). Evanston, IL: Northwestern University Press.

Denzin, N. K. (2003). The call to performance. *Symbolic Interaction, 26*, 87–207.

Ellis, C. (2004). *The ethnographic I: A methodological novel about autoethnography*. Walnut Creek, CA: AltaMira Press.

Ellis, C. (2009). *Revision: Autoethnographic reflections on life and work.* Walnut Creek, CA: Left Coast Press, Inc.

Ellis, C., & Bochner, A. P. (1992). Telling and performing personal stories: The constraints of choice in abortion. In C. Ellis & M. Flaherty (Eds.), *Investigating subjectivity: Research on lived experience* (pp. 79–101). Newbury Park, CA: Sage.

Ellis, C., & Bochner, A. P. (2006). Analyzing analytic autoethnography: An autopsy. *Journal of Contemporary Ethnography, 35,* 429–449.

Ellis, C., Kiesinger, E., & Tillmann-Healy, L. M. (1997). Interactive interviewing: Talking about emotional experience. In R. Hertz (Ed.), *Reflexivity and voice* (pp. 119–149). Thousand Oaks, CA: Sage.

Frank, A. W. (2005). What is dialogical research, and why should we do it? *Qualitative Health Research, 15,* 964–974.

Fraser, N. (1996, April 30–May 2). *Social justice in the age of identity politics: Redistribution, recognition, and participation.* [Lecture]. The Tanner lectures on human values (pp. 1–68). Standford, CT: Stanford University.

Frey, L. R., Pearce, W. B., Pollock, M. A., Artz, L., & Murphy, B. A. O. (1996). Looking for justice in all the wrong places: On a communication approach to social justice. *Communication Studies, 47,* 110–127.

Giddens, A. (1991). *Modernity and self-identity: Self and society in the late modern age.* Stanford, CT: Stanford University Press.

Giroux, H. A. (2003). Utopian thinking under the sign of neoliberalism: Towards a critical pedagogy of education hope. *Democracy & Nature, 9,* 91–105.

Holman Jones, S. (2005). Autoethnography: Making the personal political. In N. K. Denzin & Y. S. Lincoln (Eds.), *The SAGE handbook of qualitative research* (3rd ed., pp. 763–792). Thousand Oaks, CA: Sage.

Kiesinger, C. E. (2002). My father's shoes: The therapeutic value of narrative reframing. In A. P. Bochner & C. Ellis (Eds.), *Ethnographically speaking: Autoethnography, literature, and aesthetics* (pp. 95–114). Walnut Creek, CA: AltaMira Press.

Lockford, L. (2002). Breaking habits and cultivating home. In A. P. Bochner & C. Ellis (Eds.), *Ethnographically speaking: Autoethnography, literature, and aesthetics* (pp. 76–86). Walnut Creek, CA: AltaMira Press.

Lowen, C. (Producer), & Hirsch, L. (Director). (2011). *Bully* [Motion picture]. United States: The Weinstein Company.

McKerrow, R. E. (1993). Critical rhetoric and the possibility of subject. In I. Angus & L. Langsdorf (Eds.), *The critical turn: Rhetoric & philosophy in postmodern discourse* (pp. 51–67). Carbondale: Southern Illinois University Press.

Novak, M. (2000). Defining social justice. *First Things, 108,* 11–13. Retrieved from www.calculemus.org/lect/FilozGosp04-05/novak.html

Pelias, R. (2002). For father and son: An ethnodrama with no catharsis. In A. P. Bochner & C. Ellis (Eds.), *Ethnographically speaking: Autoethnography, literature, and aesthetics* (pp. 35–43). Walnut Creek, CA: AltaMira Press.

Pensoneau-Conway, S. L. (2012). Understanding identity through dialogue: Paulo Freire and intercultural communication pedagogy. In N. Bardhan & M. P. Orbe (Eds.), *Identity research in intercultural communication* (pp. 33–50). Lanham, MD: Lexington.

Rambo, C. (2005). Impressions of Grandmother: An autoethnographic portrait. *Journal of Contemporary Ethnography, 34,* 560–585.

Rambo Ronai, C. (1995). Multiple reflections of child sex abuse: An argument for a layered account. *Journal of Contemporary Ethnography, 23,* 395–426.

Rambo Ronai, C. (1996). My mother is mentally retarded. In C. Ellis & A. P. Bochner (Eds.), *Composing ethnography: Alternative forms of qualitative writing* (pp. 109–131). Walnut Creek, CA: Sage.

Richardson, L., & St. Pierre, E. (2005). Writing: A method of inquiry. In N. K. Denzin & Y. S. Lincoln (Eds.), *The SAGE handbook of qualitative research* (3rd ed., pp. 959–978). Thousand Oaks, CA: Sage.

Saunders, D. B. (2010). Neoliberal ideology and public higher education in the United States. *Journal for Critical Education Policy Studies, 8*, 41–77.

Schrag, C. O. (1986). *Communicative praxis and the space of subjectivity.* West Lafayette, IN: Purdue University Press.

Schrag, C. O. (1997). *The self after postmodernity.* New Haven, CT: Yale University Press.

Tamas, S. (2011). *Life after leaving: On the remains of spousal abuse.* Walnut Creek, CA: Left Coast Press, Inc.

Toyosaki, S. (2007). Communication sensei's storytelling: Projecting identity into critical pedagogy. *Cultural Studies ↔ Critical Methodologies, 7*, 48–/3.

Toyosaki, S. (2011). Critical complete-member ethnography: Theorizing the dialectics of consensus and conflict in intracultural communication. *Journal of International and Intercultural Communication, 4*, 62–80.

Toyosaki, S. (2012). Praxis-oriented autoethnography: Performing critical selfhood. In N. Bardhan & M. P. Orbe (Eds.), *Identity research in intercultural communication* (pp. 239–251). Lanham, MD: Lexington.

Toyosaki, S., & Pensoneau, S. L. (2005). YAEZAKURA—Interpersonal culture analysis. *International Journal of Communication, 15*, 51–88.

Toyosaki, S., Pensoneau-Conway, S. L., Wendt, N. A., & Leathers, K. (2009). Community autoethnography: Compiling the personal and resituating whiteness. *Cultural Studies ↔ Critical Methodologies, 9*, 56–83.

Warren, J. T. (2008). Performing difference: Repetition in context. *Journal of International and Intercultural Communication, 1*, 290–308.

Warren, J. T. (2010, April). *Performative pedagogy as a pedagogy of interruption: Difference and hope.* Paper presented at the annual meeting of the Central States Communication Association, Cincinnati, Ohio.

Warren, J. T. (2011). Social justice and critical/performative communicative pedagogy: A storied account of research, teaching, love, identity, desire, and loss. *International Review of Qualitative Research, 4*, 21–33.

Chapter 29

Personal/Political Interventions via Autoethnography

Dualisms, Knowledge, Power, and Performativity in Research Relations

Keyan G. Tomaselli, Lauren Dyll-Myklebust, and Sjoerd van Grootheest

Keyan discovered autoethnography by accident. Stuck in the middle of the Kalahari Desert with a group of students due to engine failure, he started writing about the experience as it unfolded. Ten days later, having fished for spare parts and tires over hundreds of kilometers and fixed the vehicle, they proceeded to their research site, still a day's drive in deep sand. His diary later formed the basis for an article. When the article was submitted to *Cultural Studies ↔ Critical Methodologies,* the editor, Norman Denzin, responded that he could "smell the dust" (see Tomaselli, 2001). Not previously aware of autoethnography, Keyan then introduced the method to his students and colleagues.

The twenty-year Kalahari project has involved successive cohorts of students and their supervisors, numbering over 200. These researchers elaborated the method into something of a hindsight explanation of what we had been doing. Autoethnography is not just about "us," but is used as a way of reducing the distance between our hosts/subjects/informants/research partners[1] and our research teams. We are wearing two kinds of subjectivities here. The first concerns our own identities in relation to Others, and we draw on reflexivity to guide our research positions and ensuing narrative. The second is that we write about autoethnography in the third person in order to offer an analytical voice on autoethnography as political/personal interventions, thus mapping its concerns, themes, and practices.

Handbook of Autoethnography, edited by Stacy Holman Jones, Tony E. Adams, and Carolyn Ellis, 576–594. © 2013 Left Coast Press, Inc. All rights reserved.

Autoethnography and (WE)IRDNESS: Us, Them, and We

Lauren and Keyan, both South Africans, have been grappling with issues of subjectivity, identity, and methodology in both research and teaching within a Eurocentric, Cartesian-based institution. In approaching the contradictions resulting from the very heterogeneous composition of our student and research teams—which are simultaneously multiracial, multilinguistic, multireligious, multiethnic, multigendered and multidisciplinary—we realize that the usual research conventions that analytically separate Subject and Object could not be assumed. Making sense of these multiple, shifting, and different identities in doing research is difficult when one is constantly negotiating positivist responses from often bewildered academic peers. Conversely, where our peers dismiss autoethnography, our research partners revel in writing and research relationships with which they can identify, in which they can "see themselves," and in which they can trust (see Bregin & Kruiper, 2004; *SUBtext*, 2011[2]). Autoethnography for us thus applies to the relationship, as well as the negotiations as part of this relationship, between observers and observed.

Observing ourselves observing others observing us led us to an article on weirdness. Researchers largely inhabit Western, Educated, Industrialized, Rich, and Democratic (WEIRD) societies (Henrich, Heine, & Norenzayan, 2010). These societies assume that they are the "normal" minority that secures the majority of the world's academic attention and which generates most of its research—mostly about itself. We three authors are products of a WEIRD world. We learned WEIRD ways as students, and for a long time we accepted WEIRDNESS and its associated positivism as normal.

Our experiences all over Africa, however, called WEIRDNESS and positivism into doubt. Stuck in the Kalahari was Keyan's "eureka" moment. Doing cultural studies in non-WEIRD Africa required liminality, and a "reverse cultural studies"[3] (Tomaselli, 2001, 2005) was born. We accepted that in Africa nothing is as it seems, that White, Western, Cartesian assumptions rarely prevail, and that some academic practices require methods that integrate Subject and Object.

Autoethnography in the kind of contexts in which 96 percent of the non-Western world lives, loves and dies needs to be recognized in studies published in the North-West (Europe, North America). Those of us who live in largely non-WEIRD societies straddle worlds that often make little sense to WEIRDs (except as tourists and the Northern academic). We are the Other for our European colleagues. Why do they want to know about "us" we wonder? Hosting Sjoerd, a visual anthropology graduate from The Netherlands, offered the opportunity for a European to study an African sub-culture (Durban fishermen), and to learn how he identified himself with regard to both his object of study and his research partners.

Analysis is conducted via relationships. We thus problematize our researcher position while critically engaging homogenizing Eurocentric theory. We also resist attempts to place ourselves at the center of our analysis. The fishermen case study is written in the first person by Sjoerd as it stems from his master's research where he theorized this data from his research sites. However, the other examples are written in the collective "we" as they are team-based projects within the wider Rethinking Indigeneity project.[4]

No matter who one is, what one does, or where one lives, researcher and lived relations are always about negotiating insider-outsider dichotomies. We will examine how we as researchers negotiate these dichotomies—how We are inter-pellated[5]/positioned by Them. Researchers tend to affect asymmetrical observer-observed power relations by concealing the contradictions and imponderables they encounter in the field itself. Autoethnographic approaches highlight these contradictions, mobilize through them, and then explain them. Autoethnography excavates researchers' hidden transcripts[6] (Scott, 1990) concealed by the positivist conventions of objectivity and statistical data analysis. Later in this chapter we explain how and why autoethnography is a useful method as an interrogation of the research process and the relationships (both personal and political) involved. We approach this in terms of both our subjectivist (first person) and analytical (third person) practice. In other words, we are negotiating both discourses simultaneously—the auto and the impersonal.

Autoethnography allows us to meet the challenge of including our research partners as "experts" in the research process (see *SUBtext,* 2011). The typical division between Us (researcher or research partner depending on from whose perspective one is looking) and Them (researcher or research partner depending on from whose perspective one is looking) is blurred in some of our projects conducted with the ≠Khomani Bushmen[7] in the Northern Cape of South Africa. For example, at the Biesje Poort rock art site ≠Khomani crafters were employed as the indigenous "experts" by the multicultural and multidisciplinary team.[8] Their role was to provide local knowledge and stories that they perceived as linked to the rock art images and material culture found at the site. Whether these stories were scientifically validated or historically correct was not important. Rather, what was important is that our team shared their knowledge (whether past or contemporary) with each other.

Autoethnography enables what Nhamo Mhiripiri experienced as the Us-as-Them identity (in a singular sense the me-as-Other identity). He felt excluded from the research group during an encounter at OstriSan[9] due to his subjectivity as a tall (twice as tall as many ≠Khomani), Shona-speaking Zimbabwean male. Nhamo made use of both the autoethnographic, as well as 'silent authorship' voice. He remembers that fellow researchers Vanessa Dodd and Nelia Oets met with the ≠Khomani 'informally' on the first day they visited OstriSan, and reported that the interactions between themselves and the ≠Khomani had been pleasant and friendly (see Oets, 2003, pp. 48–49). The following day the mood was icy and constrained (Mhiripiri, 2009); "The ≠Khomani women seemed uncomfortable in their traditional outfits, bare breasted, by presence of the *African man* in our group; they crouched over, covering themselves with their crossed arms. The easy interaction of the day before was gone and there was a definite distance between 'us' and 'them'" (Oets, 2003, p. 49, emphasis ours). Mhiripiri (2009) concluded:

> I was *the African man* of that day. There was also another man from my research group, Keyan Tomaselli, *a white (South) African man*. Nelia and Vanessa are white too; *white African women*. Danie Jacobs, who acted as our guide during the encounter with the Bushmen, was yet another *white Afrikan/er man*... Perhaps the observation by Nelia Oets is correct that I, a black African man, was the unlikely "tourist" in our motley group of the day, and induced discomfort by my presence especially that I could not speak the ≠Khomani self-performers' languages. (pp. 150–151)

While his gaze may have been estranging for the ≠Khomani, Nhamo himself also felt alienated from the ≠Khomani (and those members of the research group who were South African, or could speak the language). The encounter illustrates how, in the field, researchers become the Them to our research partners. Autoethnography allows Us to explore our simultaneous inclusion and exclusion from the field and our research partners' lives.

Autoethnography and its affiliation with personal/political interventions both for researchers and the researched, or in the relationship between these two groups, could offer a research practice that can assist in breaking away from endistancing or colonizing applications and consequences.

"The Personal is Political"

Carol Hanisch's (1970) phrase, "the personal is political,"[10] highlights an often neglected conjuncture. Our examples include: 1) a small group of subsistence fishermen, third generation South Africans of Indian extraction living in Durban, South Africa's third largest city; and 2) a slightly larger group of "inconvenient indigenous" (Saugestad, 2001) ≠Khomani Bushmen. Both groups feel (and are) marginalized by structures over which they have little or no control. Personal problems become political problems and then researchers' problems, also. For example, the withdrawal of fishing rights (personal) is sourced to the Durban City manager, leading the fishermen to engage in a (political) struggle (see Bond, 2012). For the ≠Khomani working as cultural performers at a remote desert tourist lodge, not being invited to a meeting (personal) is viewed as a social and political affront. This sense of exclusion affirms their suspicion that even in the twenty-first century they are not perceived as modern citizens. As we will come to see and discuss, the expectation is often that the researchers can fix this exclusion.

Historically, both of these groups have been victims of apartheid's systematic oppression. Their (personal and political) exclusion is still felt today. The fishermen were, several months prior to the 2010 FIFA World Cup, removed from

Durban's beach piers as they were accused of despoiling these public facilities. Whether autoethnography can assist both researcher and researched in making sense of this exclusion and obstruction depends on whether subject communities acquiesce to researchers working in their communities or whether they deploy strategies to resist research and researchers. The ≠Khomani, in particular, resent "research for research's sake," which they see as egotistical careerism on the part of opportunistic academics, journalists, and TV producers who are accused of getting rich by "stealing" their (indigenous) knowledge, their time, and their stories. Nhamo shares his understanding of how this resistance plays out in the field: "We do not always know when we are being duped or sent on a wild goose chase.... Some of the stories we are told are to extract sympathy cash from us, money which is often not well-spent" (Mhiripiri, 2009, p. 71).

Taking steps to ensure the conditions for well-intentioned research is one benefit of autoethnography (see Tomaselli, McLennan-Dodd, & Shepperson, 2005). Through getting to know us via our regular return visits, our reports back on our research, and employment of some community members as co-researchers, our partner communities identify with us as empathetic individuals, rather than as representatives of remote organizations. Nhamo reflects on this too:

> Notwithstanding my moments of soul-searching, I was consoled that the people often disclosed that they respected the CCMS team because we "respected people and the Bushmen in turn respected us" (Kruiper, V. & Kruiper, B. personal communication, April 2002). We do not just take from the community, but in our humble ways we contribute to the community through sending back photographs, completed dissertations and publications that used our research communities as subjects. (Mhiripiri, 2009, p. 91).

These are the *reasons* we use an autoethnographic approach, but then *how* do we *use* autoethnography?

Autoethnography in Application

Autoethnographic writing reveals multiple layers of consciousness, connecting the personal to the cultural (Ellis & Bochner, 2000). Exposing a "vulnerable self" is considered an indulgence on the researcher's part whose unempirical dwelling on his/her own subjectivity/emotions/ignorance/self-doubt/exclusion is conventionally considered unscientific. Positivism, in its "rigorous application" of "instruments" to "generate" objective "data" by "eliminating bias" and arriving at "dispassionate" findings has its obvious uses. However, interpretive research also "applies" its own "rigorous epistemological procedures" in its *performativity, multivocality, reflexivity* and *constructedness* whereby "researcher position can be used productively as *tensional* starting points of thinking about the human encounter" (Mboti, 2012, p. 56). Next we will define these procedures and illustrate how employing them adds to the autoethnographic nature of our research.

Performativity

Performance ethnography and performative writing show emotion and existing conditions witnessed in the field by writing in the ongoing dialogue between Self, his or her research partners, and the world (see Holman Jones, 2005, p. 767). Our Centre uses research to dramatize the issues and existing conditions that policy-makers maintain they do not know about (for example, issues of exclusion by a marginalized community, as will be illustrated with the World Cup example). In this way interpretation, in the critical cultural and action research[11] that we employ, becomes performative[12] (Mboti, 2012).

The challenge of performativity is to "create texts that unfold in the inter-subjective space of individual and community and that embrace tactics for both knowing and showing" (Holman Jones, 2005, p. 767; Jackson, 1998; Kemp, 1998). "Voices of the Kalahari" (Lange, 2003[13]/2007) meets this challenge. It is an ethnographic encounter mediated via a bilingual (English and Afrikaans[14]) and multiperspectival mystery play with characters named: Confused, Youth, Authority, and People. The identities stand for the multiple personalities of each of the researchers as each tried to make sense of the liminal.

Multivocality

Our understanding of multivocality, or diversity of voice and perception, is illustrated by Sonja Laden and Nate Kohn (2003):

> Each of the researchers...write[s] reflexively about a single event, which gives us multiple perspectives on one encounter with San communities....Each researcher sees the events somewhat differently, each reads individual Bushmen in highly individual and contradictory ways giving us a nuanced picture of people and place...[as] a testament to the complexity of the human condition [and] the vagaries of interpretation. (p. 1)

This multivocality extends to include the multiple voices of our research partners. This inclusive approach creates a multidimensional image of the field (see Lange, 2007, 2011; Lange, Kruiper, & Tomaselli, 2007; Morris, 2007), and what we seek to study reflects not only the place and its people but also the procession of viewers, recorders, and researchers in these partner's communities and the impact they may have.[15]

Multivocality also extends to our commitment to conducting and producing research that is empowering and transformational for our subjects and that has use-value for them. For example, Lauren's PhD thesis (Dyll-Myklebust, 2012) developed an action research model for public-private-community partner-ships (PPCPs) in community-owned and privately-operated lodge tourism. The use-value here is the provision of a schematic that aids dialogue and decision making that acknowledges the role and voices of all partners.

Focusing on the power relations in !Xaus Lodge[16] operations between the conservation authority, operator, lodge management, community owners, hospitality staff, and cultural studio crafters was vital in developing a PPCP model that considered all stakeholders. The model sets out the importance of dialogic communication and cultural relativity in development projects. It suggests that possible differences in a stakeholder's history, epistemology and ontology should be considered if a project is to negotiate the demands of both commercial viability and the symbolic and spiritual needs of the community partners. The research thus adopted the autoethnographic commitment to *multivocality*. Engaging with, listening to, and documenting the stories, expectations, and skills of different members of the stakeholder groups valorized the *multivocality* of the assumptions and preconceptions they brought to the development project. These assumptions and preconceptions were analyzed within participatory communication theories (Cornwall, 2008; Kincaid & Figueroa, 2009; Quarry & Ramirez, 2009), as well as "lessons learned" from tourism-as-development literature (Ashley, Goodwin, & Roe, 2001a, 2000b; Ashley & Haysom, 2006; Rogerson & Visser, 2004). These were configured into the model that suggests best practices within a multi-stakeholder lodge development project. In this way, our research lives up to the call for a more open-minded form for exploring "multiple ways of seeing and making sense of the world" (Kincheloe & Steinberg, 2008, p. 150; see also Finlay, 2009). The research embraces "autoethnography as a radical democratic politics—a politics committed to creating space for dialogue and debate that instigates and shapes social change" (Holman Jones, 2005, p. 763; Reinelt, 1998) and is conscious of what research needs to say and do on broader social and political levels that lead to social action.

Reflexivity

Reflexivity occurs when researchers "systematically and rigorously reveal their methodology and themselves as the instrument of data generation" (Ruby, 1980, p. 153). Our application of autoethnography offers a strategy that assists us in understanding how we work with research participants. We (researchers) are also positioned by our research partners. Thus, in some ways we adopt and adapt to the subaltern's political, social, and personal agendas (see Dyll, 2007; Mhiripiri, 2009; Tomaselli, Dyll, & Francis 2008). Both groups thus have the potential for agency in the encounter in which power dynamics are constantly shifting and being re-negotiated through dialogue about methods and interpretation.

The re-negotiation occurs in the questioning of *objectivity* that seeks to eliminate the researcher from the researcher-researched relation. What is safeguarded in objectivity is the Self/researcher's vulnerability, thus maintaining not only his/her traditional authority, but also his/her "right" to know others while he/she is effectively insulated from being known (Mboti, 2012). *Reflexivity* offers a step towards fracturing this insulation and the researcher's institutional authority. In working with communities Other to their Self, researchers "have an ethical, political, aesthetic and scientific obligation to be reflexive and self-critical" (Ruby, 1977, p. 3; see also Berry, this volume). Being reflexive does not simply require one to be self-conscious but to know what parts of oneself to reveal to the reader as the *producer*, to help the reader understand the process that was used in constructing the end *product* (Fabian, 1971; Ruby, 1977). As we come to see in the following examples, reflexivity thus aids us in illuminating the *constructedness of representation*.

Constructedness

We make a commitment to highlighting the *constructedness* of research as it is empirically experienced, not just read or written in some kind of endistancing text. Our approach identifies the researcher and how he/she deals with the central fact of critical mediation and interpretation (Mboti, 2012, p. 63).

Autoethnographers negotiate power relations by engaging, recording, and reflecting on them. Autoethnography thus assists us in examining via self-reflexivity the *dynamic lived contexts* encountered in the field.

Autoethnography's humanistic and experiential approach allows researchers to ponder and "write in" the nature of the encounter and the research process, thus illustrating how a research outcome is always *constructed*—made, negotiated, and renegotiated by both researchers and researched who are involved in the *process*. Our subjects' experiences are not drowned out by our own or by theory. They specifically ask us to relay their grievances to authorities who they claim ignore them, to have their stories entered into the official record. For example, when a Botswanan, who has adopted a "Bushman" identity, was asked if he would allow us to video him, he replied:

> I want to do it because we Bushmen are a people....There are people who don't know what a Bushman is, or what sort of nation a Bushman is. It would be better if they had such pictures. And I who am a Bushmen, can show these pictures to people and then tell them and then I must also point out the pictures to them, myself also, yes, because I'm a Bushman. (G. Orileng, personal communication, June 1999)

Gadi considers video about the Bushmen, with him as one of their spokespersons, to be a means through which Bushmen can voice their concerns about land rights and social resources, so that these concerns may in some way become part of the official record (see Tomaselli, Dyll, & Francis, 2008). Autoethnography thus allows partners to recognize themselves within the academic text and to understand the uses to which this text can be put (in the service of their interests).

Evidence of the mundane (everydayness) strengthens research discourse through situating the act of research as fully cultural, reflexive, contextual, active, process-based, personal, political, wholly uncertain, and thoroughly *lived*. Methodology and theory are thus at the service of life and not the other way round (Mboti, 2012, p. 59). Lived texts such as the fishermen's protests are empirically verifiable.

Thus far we have defined and briefly demonstrated the four "epistemological procedures" that, for us, illustrate autoethnography: *performativity, multivocality, reflexivity* and *constructedness*. The following case study on the FIFAWorld Cup and a poem written by a graduate student on her research encounter will further illustrate these autoethnographic points and procedures in practice.

Making Sense of Exclusion in the FIFA World Cup 2010 Context

In 2004, South Africa was elected to host the FIFA World Cup 2010. Extensive preparations preceded the event, including the renovation of three beachfront piers. On completion, the general public was allowed back onto the piers, but the fishermen who had historically fished on these facilities were now prevented from doing so. From early 2010, I (Sjoerd) heard rumors that the fishermen were preparing to utilize the World Cup to contest their fishing ban from the piers. As the general attitude towards the World Cup was mostly celebratory, I was struck by the intensity and frequency of public actions of discontented groups in South Africa at large (see Bond, 2010). That the workings of democracy can be located in the public sphere (Fraser, 1997) made this study particularly relevant as it would enable me to elaborate on the structures of power in the workings of representation in modern democracies. I made contact with the protesting fishermen when stories on their plight gained momentum in the press well in advance of the World Cup.

The fishermen inhabited a variety of class positions, racial identities, and religious affiliations and offered contesting explanations for their categorical exclusion. They cited unfair treatment by the state (particularly during the World Cup), stigmatizing tendencies in the media, and class-based division between themselves and surfers who are typically middle class and were not excluded. Bob, an unemployed subsistence fisherman, acknowledged the surfers' right to use the same space, and described the situation in terms of differentiation and discrimination:

> Now, regarding the fishing, 90% of the fishermen are Indian. So, if you look at it now, based on the facts that we are paying a license every year to fish on the pier, we pay for bait license for pumping bait, fishing license, the pier now is closed for us, but it is open for the surfers. That is blatant discrimination against us, whereas they do it for fun, we do it for a living. (van Grootheest, 2011a, p. 69)

The process of gaining access to these fishermen is illustrative of how I became tied up with the political activities and interests of a subject community. The gatekeepers among the fishermen regularly invited me to public gatherings or meetings with journalists and/or public officials. The first meeting was called to discuss newly installed light poles on the beachfront piers and the resulting ecological light pollution. I was introduced to a municipal official as "Stewart" (a name that would more or less stick throughout the research period). I became a political actor and source of power for the fisher leadership, as my being "from

University" arguably added legitimacy to their struggle. In addition to writing the thesis, I produced a documentary entitled *The Bay of Plenty* (van Grootheest, 2011b). My presence in this context was perceived as beneficial to the community and informed my analysis of their understanding that a documentary representing their side of the story was crucial in effectively negotiating their exclusion.[17] The way in which the fishermen positioned me as (leading to) a potential source of power by providing access to means and channels of communication in the academic domain facilitated rapid access to them. Public action was their job, not mine. I wanted to explore *how* the fishermen perceived the enclosure of this public space from which they had historically fished, how they organized, and in some instances failed to organize, to resist their exclusion.

In musing about how I was positioned by the fishermen, I was required to reflexively problematize my own subjectivity, position, and relationships with and within this community by exposing my research methods and how I responded to circumstances in the field. Reflexivity exposes method (Ruby, 1977), which was written into my thesis and demonstrated in sections of the video where fishermen directly addressed me, which demystified the conventional "invisible" filmmaker. Was I a fly-on-the-wall, or, interpellated through the camera, was I the "fly-in-the-soup" (Crawford, 1992, p. 79)? Where did my loyalties lie? How did the fishermen view me? These were the questions of which I was mindful, but which I never fully resolved. The question, then, is how to reflexively problematize this frothy researcher position where I often found myself pulled between being a propagandist for the fishermen on the one hand and engaging in conventional academic inquiry on the other.

When filming *The Bay of Plenty* (van Grootheest, 2011b) the camera was largely welcomed as the fishermen saw the *use-value* of my research and the legitimation brought to their struggle. The camera signified the importance of their participation in public processes of representation. My identity as a researcher and cameraman became a further (re)source of power in that the fishermen were increasingly able to take control over their representation. While I videoed, the fishermen continuously directed the camera and thus in a way also *constructed* my analysis. In one instance, Aman, a recreational fisherman, is seen outside the Human Rights offices in central Durban holding two different newspaper articles featuring the same photograph of the Bay of Plenty pier. He discusses the media's misrepresentation of the fishermen's adherence to the fishing ban, angry that a dated photo is used in a current newspaper article as "proof" that fishermen were still fishing. He believed that my documentation of this was essential in "setting the story straight" and addresses the camera:

> Stewart, I need you to take the photo of this...both pictures, alright? See, it's the same picture, the old picture has been used. Why are they using an old picture? They are lying. They are misleading the public. They are using an old picture when the fishing was permitted. (van Grootheest, 2011b)

Rather than an additional method to "access the data," the documentary triggered a process that created knowledge of a different order (see Jenssen & Crawford, 2009), one based on *performativity*. In highlighting how the personal is political, Holman Jones (2005) urges us to ask ourselves, "How well does the work create a plausible and visceral lifeworld and charged emotional atmosphere as an incitement to act within and outside the context of the work?" (p. 773). The documentary is *performative* in that it captures and *shows* the fishermen's personal narratives recorded in their homes, on the piers, and during protests, depicting their struggle. The *performativity* of these personal narratives can be considered a personal/political intervention in that identity and experience are symbiotic of performed story and the social relations in which they are embedded. Personal narrative performance is especially crucial to those communities excluded from the privileges of dominant culture, and who are without voice in the political sense (Langellier, 1999, p. 129).

Explaining the differences between the two different research outputs—the written thesis and the documentary—must therefore rest to some extent on the nature of visual anthropology. In conventional science, the researcher is (presumably) objective, separated from that which he or she is studying and writing, a fly-on-the-wall so to speak. In contrast, my drawing on visual anthropology strategies, which ideally respect the intrinsic experience of research partners, locates me/the videographer within the web of relations being studied, as a fly-in-the soup.

Autoethnography is about fishing for relations, juggling and connecting explanations, before they get processed, systematized, and sanitized in the factory that is called the academy. Who is determining whom? Being referred to as "Stewart, who is here to help us," I soon came to recognize the political nature of my presence. The documentary is my version of the fishermen's version of the story. The *performativity* of my work, then, lies in the creation of *The Bay of Plenty*—a documentary created in the inter-subjective space between myself and the fishermen with the objective to show the fishermen's lifeworlds to audiences in order to resist the stigmatized images circulated in the media and to protect their access to the piers.

Performativity is also useful in facilitating a more personal form of autoethnography. The poem below was created by a South African female Zulu student in her exploration of the researcher-researched relationship, deriving from an encounter in the Kalahari Desert.

A Poem to Negotiate Researcher-Researched Relations

I am a young woman caught in a rhythm of a world I know nothing about.
A world I'm told is the root of my existence. A world with many eyes
and many questions carved on the ground.
A world I'm coerced to accept as my own, as who I am, coerced by the history
and the many eyes who marvel at this world, at this identity I am told is mine.

I am a woman torn by the inequities of the past
Enraged!
Confused!
By the expectations, by the pressures that care not to ask about my own
thoughts but instead gaze at my world in amusement and daze before
disappearing into their own worlds,
capturing these perceptions in fancy history books
silencing the real struggles of my world, locking me in,
holding me prisoner.
I am a young Bush woman, a descendant of the #Khomani
I have many faces, a skin colour with many layers
And speak many tongues except my own.

I do not fit into any box, these people, my people
each have travelled many paths, arrived at destinations far different
from those of their forefathers. But still they hang on. I hang on...
to a thread that continues to dangle, far from its root.
Yet still the writings in the sand continue to call **Them** *and* **Me** *by name.*

Wandile Sibisi wrote this poem after meeting a ≠Khomani woman, Vinkie, during her first research trip in 2010. This poem was just one step in Wandile's attempt to construct a framework for making sense of the encounter. The process involved multiple steps: 1) experiencing the *encounter*; 2) writing the *poem* in reflecting on the encounter; 3) conducting a follow-up *interview* with Vinkie; 4) *performing* the poem at a research seminar in Durban; and 5) writing her research project in which she reflexively analyzed the nature of the encounter within the framework of visual anthropology (Sibisi, 2010).[18]

To make the personal political we should draw on the lessons that the turn toward personal narrative and performance has taught us—writing our stories as they are constructed in and through the stories of others (Holman Jones, 2005). The encounter was an informal first interaction in the desert, unplanned and unexpected. The poem was a creative outcome of this encounter. Does Wandile's poem constitute a story that is constructed in and through the story of another by writing from the assumed perspective of Vinkie as the Other? Writing performatively was a strategy used by Wandile to *think through* the connections she felt with Vinkie as well as the life and expectations of an-Other person. In so doing she learned something about herself (her assumptions, prejudices, hopes) and how she understood the research encounter.

Conducting the interview in order to gain further insight into Vinkie and her life and then analyzing the interview (as well as the poem) were important steps to revealing the poem's constructedness. It allowed her to "test" the assumptions she initially brought with her to the encounter. Wandile reveals:

I assumed a position of dominance and power, as I recreated Vinkie and her identity as a Bushman, a woman, and her dreams and ambitions. For instance I immediately assumed that by having a coloured[19] identity, Vinkie would be confused about who she is only to discover during an interview...that she was quite content with who and what she is, identifying herself without any hesitation only as a Bushman. (Sibisi, 2010, p. 19)

Wandile's poem is therefore a contested space where its creation and performance included a flurry of assumptions, imagination, and an awareness of the socio-cultural and political context in which both she and Vinkie were situated. At first, Vinkie seemed impossible to understand based on how different her desert life appeared to be. But in using performative autoethnography Wandile, the educated urban sophisticate, discovered that there were more similarities than differences between them. Her poem thus attests to the idea that "performativity is inseparable from politics, autobiographical performance, personal narrative, and performative auto/ethnography enmesh the personal within the political and the political within the personal in ways that can, do, and must matter" (Homan Jones, 2005, p. 774).

Wandile "reflected on [her] world" (Freire, 1970/1990, p. 52) and on her cultural identity as a young modern Zulu woman engaged in the difficult juggling act of "staying true" to her tradition, which often feels foreign to her, while being a modern and sophisticated urban woman. However, she felt that because she, like Vinkie, is from an indigenous South African community, they shared a connection. In writing about this connection Wandile reflected on herself within broader South African social relations: "From what position am I able to make sense of my experience in the Kalahari? What is my own identity? As I write I find I cannot escape these questions. I must confront them, despite the fact that I'm not sure of the answers or simply afraid to confront them" (Sibisi, 2010, p. 22).

Performativity helps to explain Wandile's encounter where she uncovered personal aspects of Vinkie and herself.

Vinkie is a member of the "inconvenient indigenous" (Saugestad, 2001) ≠Khomani group. The Bushmen are viewed by some governments as "inconvenient" as they insist on their First People's status, and thus demand special recognition over other population groups. Where the ≠Khomani can claim United Nations declarations as legitimation of their struggles, the fishermen have no such global leverage. Both groups, however, can be considered "inconvenient" interlopers, the fishermen with regards to the city council and the ≠Khomani with regard to national government.

Both the ≠Khomani and the fishermen are involved in a rebellion against what they see as an over-determining structure that suppresses the human(istic) element in society (inhibiting and disempowering them). Both communities work willingly with us due to the self-reflexive, participatory, and autoethnographic methods we have evolved in consultation with them (for examples, see Bregin &

Kruiper, 2004; *SUBtext,* 2011; Tomaselli, 2007). In fact, as discussed earlier, the ≠Khomani at times *subvert* formal research due to the perceived lack of immediate benefit for them. Researchers are often pejoratively othered by their subjects, simply seen as a source for material gain by subjects to whom to sell their stories (Tomaselli, 2003). The Durban fishermen, in contrast, saw tactical opportunity in working with Sjoerd. Researchers are associated by the marginalized with the WEIRD, people who can be helpful but also dominating. We conclude with some observations on this relationship.

Conclusion: (Auto)ethnographic Flukes

In addressing the issue of anthropologists from the "North" working in the "South," Andrew Causey (2012, p. 147) observes that European and American-based anthropology traditions of the global North entail an often premature mapping and articulation of research agendas and methodologies. Thoughtful analysis of events occurring at the edges of carefully planned ethnographic work can transform not only the research itself, but also the individual and the character of our written presentations.

This is exactly what we have been doing. Like us, (Causey, 2012) concludes that "the work of an ethnographer is rarely so structured and controlled as the final published experiences might imply" (p. 127). Autoethnography allows us to embrace the "potentials of chance" (Causey, 2012, p. 127), to follow the side-roads that lead away from formally intended research. Many of our colleagues, students, parents, and administrators remain uneasy with this approach. They want certainty, predictability and clarity (see Sabloff, 2010; Woolf, 1997). In many ways, clarity is a way of *being* rather than of finding, cataloguing, and indexing; for us, clarity is found in the live interrogation of the identities of *both* researchers and researched, and of being courageous enough to handle the outcomes. It is in this nexus that reflexive research and autoethnography find their relevance, as is illustrated in this chapter.

Our organizing themes in this chapter were *performativity, multivocality, reflexivity* and *constructedness.* What we want to stress in terms of our own practice is the *relationship* between Self and Other, researchers and researched, observer and observed, indeed, the entire nature of the encounter, and more specifically within personal/political interventions that these procedures are made possible and materialize possibilities. *Performativity* enables the shifting back and forth between Self and Other to examine what comes out in the wash (as in Wandile's poem). *Multivocality* requires connection to an object/subject of study (what can be verified, author-subject centered). *Reflexivity* requires explicit description of method, not just its application as a hidden *transcript.* At the end of the day autoethnography, like any genre, is *constructed.* The difference is that this form is explicitly self-aware and far more flexible in addressing the portents of increasingly heterogeneous societies.

Notes

1. While there are many terms that the academy uses to refer to people visited and researched, we refer to them primarily as "research partners" as this implies an active role in the research process as opposed to the terms "research subject" or "research informant."

2. Available at: ccms.ukzn.ac.za/images/Subtext/subtext%.202011.pdf. These are examples of where our research partners have written about their own experiences, as well as about the research that they take part in.

3. This form of cultural studies goes beyond deconstruction and towards connecting with the material and ontological (nature of being) conditions on the ground. It inverts the power relations of the (typically) more powerful Self over the Other by understanding and 'writing in' the Other's perspective and demonstrating that they have agency in explaining their development concerns, needs, and solutions. In this way reverse cultural studies "offers an autoethnographic framework in which verification is made possible, in which prior research is acknowledged and respected (and engaged), and in which triangulation (via the reporting of different researchers on the same observations/encounters) is encouraged" (Tomaselli, Dyll, & Francis, 2008, p. 356).

4. The Rethinking Indigeneity project originated in collaboration with the University of Leeds, Centre for Postcolonial Studies (see Nicholls, 2009), and extended from Tomaselli's previous projects that have been ongoing since 1995. This project offers analyses on: cultural/heritage tourism; the politics of representation; tourist/host and researcher/researched relations; as well as development communication. Its objective is to debunk the assumption that indigeneity entails marginalized communities reverting to a 'traditional' self-representation or lifestyles in 'resistance' to influences of the globalized world. Research is therefore set within a participatory framework whereby participant community members can discursively engage and negotiate the perceptions, expectations, and, at times myths, that the media, researchers, lodge operators, and tourists may impose (see Dyll-Myklebust, 2011).

5. Interpellation is the process whereby individuals recognize themselves as subjects through ideology, thus illustrating how subjects can be complicit in their own domination (Althusser, 1971).

6. Scott (1990) focuses on the way that subaltern people resist domination and that their everyday resistance demonstrates that they have not consented to dominance. "Transcripts" stands in for the encoding, reading, and interpreting of the discourse of political struggle and the dilemmas of making and writing history from below, particularly in extreme forms of subordination. Domination dramatizes itself with what Scott calls a "public transcript"—the open performance of power and a deliberate display of its signs (Greenhouse, 2005). The "hidden transcript" is the other side of that power—instances of critique of traditional power by social observers, "rebels," and the subaltern. Typically located "backstage," a hidden transcript is difficult to locate and read, at least until it has been consolidated as a coherent symbolic statement among a unified group of people (Scott, 1990, p. 135).

7. The term "Bushman" first came into use in the Cape area in the 1600s by early Dutch settlers, where "Bojesman/Bossiesman" signified "outlaw." "San" is generally traced to the Khoi word "Sonqua," signifying "original people" or "foragers" (Barnard, 1992), although both Gordon (1992) and Barnard (1992) make a case for its derogatory sense of "bandit" or "rascal." Barnard (1992) further explains that "although 'San' is gaining wide acceptance among non-specialists, several ethnographers who formerly used it have now reverted to 'Bushman'" (p. 7). The primary reason that we use the term Bushman, however, is that our research partners refer to themselves as "Bushmen," thereby subverting those who seek to re-name them without consultation.

8. The team included a co-ordinator and representative of an arts for peace non-profit organization, ARROWSA; landscape architects from the Universities of Cape Town and Pretoria to facilitate cultural mapping; and an archaeological team from the McGregor Museum.

9. A cultural tourism venture in the North West Province that employed ≠Khomani as performers.

10. "Political" here refers to the broad sense of the word as pertaining to power relationships, not the narrow sense of electoral politics.

11. Action research "is a participatory, democratic process that enables practical knowing in the pursuit of worthwhile human purpose. It brings together action and reflection, theory and practice,

in participation with others, in the pursuit of practical solutions to issues of pressing concern to people, and more generally the flourishing of individual persons and their communities (Reason & Bradbury, 2001, p. 1).

12. Performativity refers to how, "through our writing and our talk, we enact the worlds we study. They instruct our readers about this world and how we see it" (Denzin, 2006, p. 422). In objection to positivism's focus on the verifiability of statements, Austin (1962) introduced "the performative" as a new utterance category that has no truth value as it does not describe the world, but rather acts upon it. "While the words of a performative do in some sense 'fit' the world, conforming to the conventions that govern their success, they also constitute it, so that by their very utterance the world is also made to fit the words" (Hall, 2000, p. 185). Gender, for example, is performative in that it constitutes "the identity it is purported to be. In this sense, gender is always a doing, though not a doing by a subject who might be said to pre-exist the deed" (Butler, 1990, p. 25). "There is no prediscursive identity, as even our understanding of biological sex is discursively produced" (Hall, 2000, p. 186). In the same vein autoethnographers are called to examine how researched and researchers alike manipulate the regulatory framework or ideologies with which they enter the encounter.

13. This paper was originally published in the *Current Writing* (2003) theme edition, and was later included in Tomaselli (2007).

14. The *lingua franca* of the areas where we meet out Bushman research partners.

15. For more information on the value of *multivocality* in research read about our project at the Biesje Poort rock art site where the research team is multicultural (≠Khomani crafters, Afrikaans academics, English academics, Xhosa museum employees) and multi-disciplinary (archeology, landscape architecture, cultural studies) (see *SUBtext*, Autumn 2011).

16. See www.xauslodge.co.za.

17. The same occurred with my co-supervisor (Tomaselli) who had to subvert municipal regulations, by-laws, and bureaucracy in ensuring due access to public spaces for the camera that I used to document my interactions. Some events relating to the World Cup were off-limits to protestors and the cameras they brought in, as permits were required for beach locations. This situation thus implicated my supervisor also in "wrong doing," a factor whose likely consequences needed to be assessed in broader institutional terms. (Cameras were fair game under apartheid, and Tomaselli spent much of his time in the 1970s and '80s attempting to secure return from the Security Police of cameras belonging to him and his students.)

18. Student research is incorporated into our publications with acknowledgement and in terms of the participatory practices of the Rethinking Indigeneity project. While Wandile is not a co-author of this particular chapter, her and other students' work provides experiential snippets that enable our collective methodological discussions. The poem is part of an unpublished essay which is indicative of an encounter; she has given permission for us to mobilize it as an example on autoethnography.

19. The term *colored* refers to an ethnic group who have a diverse heritage, including lineage from the sub-Sahara, although not enough to be considered black under apartheid (or post-apartheid) categories. Although the term emerged in early colonial history as a racial classification, it evolved into a specific cultural and linguistic identity largely dominant in the Western Cape province (Crawhall, 2001). The ≠Khomani resent the "colored" classification imposed on them by the previous apartheid state, and indeed the new post-apartheid one.

References

Althusser, L. (1971). Ideology and the ideological state apparatuses. In L. Althusser (Ed.), *Lenin and philosophy and other essays*. London, New Left Books.

Ashley, C., Goodwin, H., & Roe, D. (2001a). *Pro-poor tourism strategies: Making tourism working for the poor*. London: Overseas Development Institute.

Ashley, C., Goodwin, H., & Roe, D. (2001b). *Pro-poor Tourism Strategies: Expanding opportunities for the poor*. London: Overseas Development Institute.

Ashley, C., & Haysom, G. (2006). From philanthropy to a different way of doing business: Strategies and challenges in integrating pro-poor approaches into tourism business, *Development Southern Africa, 23,* 265–280.

Austin, J. L. (1962). *How to do things with words.* Cambridge, MA: Harvard University Press.

Barnard, A. (1992). *Hunters and herders of Southern Africa: Comparative ethnography of the Khoisan Peoples.* Cambridge, UK: Cambridge University Press.

Bregin, E., & Kruiper, B. (2004). *Kalahari rainsong.* KwaZulu-Nata, South Africa: University of KwaZulu-Natal Press.

Bond, P. (2010). South Africa's Bubble Meets Boiling Urban Social Protest, *Sociologias.* Available at sociologias-com.blogspot.com/2010/07/south-africas-bubble-meetsboiling.html

Bond, P. (2012, January 3). Durban hopes for a better future. *The Mercury, 7.*

Butler, J. (1990). *Gender trouble: Feminism and the subversion of identity.* New York: Routledge.

Causey, A. (2012). Critical side-roads: exploring ethnographic flukes, *Critical Arts, 26,* 147–149.

Cornwall, A. (2008) Unpacking 'Participation': Models, meanings and practices. *Community Development Journal, 43*(3), 269–283.

Crawford, P. I. (1992). Film as discourse: The invention of anthropological realities. In P. I. Crawford & D. Turton (Eds.), *Film as ethnography* (pp. 66–82). Manchester, UK: Manchester University Press.

Crawhall, N. (2001). *Written in the sand. Auditing and managing cultural resources with displaced Indigenous Peoples.* Cape Town, South Africa: SASI/UNESCO.

Denzin, N. K. (2006). Analytic autoethnography or déjà vu all over again? *Journal of Contemporary Ethnography, 35*(4), 419–428.

Denzin, N. K., & Lincoln, Y. S. (2008). Preface. In N. K. Denzin, Y. S. Lincoln, & L. T. Smith (Eds.), *Handbook of critical and indigenous methodologies* (pp. ix–xv). London: Sage.

Dyll, L. (2007). In the sun with Silikat. In K. G. Tomaselli (Ed.), *Writing in the san/d: Autoethnography among indigenous Southern Africans* (pp. 117–130). New York: AltaMira Press.

Dyll, L. (2009). Community development strategies in the Kalahari—an expression of moderniza-tion's monologue? In P. Hottola (Ed.), *Tourism strategies and local responses in Southern Africa* (pp. 41–60). Wallingford, UK: CAB International.

Dyll-Myklebust, L. (2011). Blurring the lines at Biesje Poort Heritage Site: Mapping the future of rethinking indigeneity research. In *SUBtext.* The Centre for Communication, Media and Society. Available at: ccms.ukzn.ac.za/images/Subtext/subtext%.202011.pdf

Dyll-Myklebust, L. (2012). *"Lodge-ical" thinking and development communication: !Xaus Lodge as a public-private-community partnership in tourism.* Unpublished PhD thesis. The Centre for Communication, Media and Society. University of KwaZulu-Natal, Durban, South Africa.

Ellis, C., & Bochner, A. P. (2000). Autoethnography, personal narrative, reflexivity. In N. K. Denzin & Y. S. Lincoln (Eds.), *Handbook of qualitative research* (2nd ed., pp. 733–768). Thousand Oaks, CA: Sage.

Fabian, J. (1971). Language, history and anthropology. *Philosophy of Social Sciences, 1,* 19–47.

Finlay, K. (2009). The un/changing face of the ≠Khomani: Representation through promotional media. *Visual Anthropology, 22,* 334–361.

Fraser, N. (1997) *Justice interruptus: Critical reflections on the postsocialist condition.* London: Routledge.

Freire, P. (1970/1990). *Pedagogy of the oppressed.* London: Penguin Books.

Gordon, R. J. (1992). *The Bushman myth: The making of the Namibian underclass.* Boulder, CO: Westview Press.

Greenhouse, C. J. (2005). Hegemony and hidden transcripts: The discursive arts of neoliberal legit-imation. *American Anthropologist, 107*(3), 356–368.

Hall, K. (2000). Performativity. *Journal of Linguistic Anthropology, 9* (1–2), 184–187.

Hanisch, C. (1970). The personal is political. In S. Firestone & A. Koedt (Eds.), *Notes from the second year: Women's liberation* (pp. 152–157). New York: New York Radical Feminists.

Henrich, J., Heine, S. J., & Norenzayan, A. (2010). The weirdest people in the world? *Behavioral and Brain Sciences, 33,* 61–135.

Holman Jones, S. (2005). Autoethnography: Making the personal political. In N. K. Denzin & Y. S. Lincoln (Eds.), *Handbook of qualitative research* (pp. 763–791). Thousand Oaks, CA: Sage.

Jackson, S. (1998) White noises: On performing white, on writing performance. *Drama Review, 42,* 49–65.

Jenssen, T., & Crawford, P. I. (Eds.). (2009). *Behind the eye: Reflexive methods in culture studies, ethnographic film, and visual media.* Højbjerg, Denmark: Intervention Press.

Kemp, A. D. (1998). This black body in question. In P. Phelan & J. Lane (Eds.), *The ends of performance* (pp. 116–129). New York: New York University Press.

Kincaid, D. L., & Figueroa, M. E. (2009). Communication for participatory development: Dialogue, action, and change. In L. R. Frey & K. N. Cissna (Eds.), *Handbook of applied communication research* (pp. 506–531). London: Routledge.

Kincheloe, J. L., & Steinberg, S. R. (2008). Indigenous knowledges in education: Complexities, dangers, and profound benefits. In N. K. Denzin, Y. S. Lincoln, & L. T. Smith (Eds.), *Handbook of critical and indigenous methodologies* (pp. 135–156). London: Sage.

Laden, S., & Kohn, N. (2003). Introduction. Part 1: Representing representation. *Current Writing: Text and Reception in Southern Africa, 15* (Special issue), 1–7.

Lange, M. (2007). Voices from the Kalahari: Methodology and the absurd. In K. G. Tomaselli (Ed.), *Writing in the san/d: Autoethnography among Indigenous Southern Africans* (pp. 73–86). New York: AltaMira Press.

Lange, M. (2011). *Water stories and rock engravings: Eiland women at the Kalahari Edge.* Amsterdam, Netherlands: SAVUSA.

Lange, M., Kruiper, B., & Tomaselli, C. (2007). Meeting points: Symbiotic spaces. In K. G. Tomaselli (Ed.), *Writing in the san/d: Autoethnography among Indigenous Southern Africans* (pp. 87–104). New York: AltaMira Press.

Langellier, K. (1999). Personal narrative, performance, performativity: Two or three things I know for sure. *Text and Performance Quarterly, 19,* 125–144.

Mboti, N. (2012). Research, method and position: What are we doing? In K. G. Tomaselli (Ed.), *Cultural tourism and identity: Rethinking indigeneity* (pp. 53–70). Amsterdam, Netherlands: Brill Academic.

Melkote, S. R., & Steeves, H. L. (2001). *Communication for development in the Third World: Theory and practice for empowerment* (2nd ed.). London: Sage.

Mhiripiri, N. (2009). *The Tourist viewer, the Bushmen and the Zulu: Imaging and (re)invention of identities through contemporary visual cultural productions.* PhD Thesis. The Centre for Communication, Media and Society, University of KwaZulu-Natal, Durban, South Africa.

Morris, D. (2007). Snake and veil: On the rock-engravings of Driekopseiland, Northern Cape, South Africa. In G. Blundell, C. Chippindale, & B. Smith (Eds.), *Seeing & knowing: Understanding rock art with or without ethnography* (pp. 37–54). Johannesburg, South Africa: Wits University Press.

Nicholls, B. (2009). Indigeneity, visuality and postcolonial theory: The case of the San. In G. N. Devy, G. V. Davis, & K. K. Chakravarty (Eds.), *Indigeneity: Culture and representation* (pp. 203–212). New Delhi: Orient Black Swan.

Oets, N. (2003). From myth to reality to somewhere in between. *Current writing: Text and reception in Southern Africa, 15,* 43–56.

Quarry, W., & Ramirez, R. (2009). *Communication for another development: Listening before telling.* London: Zed Books.

Reason, P. & Bradbury, H. (2001). *Handbook of action research: Participatory inquiry and practice.* London: Sage.

Reinelt, J. (1998). Notes for a radical democratic theatre: Productive crisis and the challenge of indeterminacy. In J. Colleran & J. S. Spencer (Eds.), *Staging resistance: Essays on political theater* (pp. 283–300). Ann Arbor: University of Michigan Press.

Richardson, L., Adams S. T., & Pierre, E. (2005). Writing: A method of inquiry. In N. K. Denzin & Y. S. Lincoln (Eds.), *Handbook of qualitative research* (pp. 959–978). Thousand Oaks, CA: Sage.

Rogerson, C. M., & Visser, G. (2004). Tourism and development in post-apartheid South Africa: A ten year review. In M. Rogerson & G. Visser (Eds.), *Tourism and development issues in contemporary South Africa* (pp. 2–25). Pretoria, South Africa: Africa Institute of South Africa.

Ruby, J. (1977). The image mirrored: Reflexivity and the documentary film, *Journal of University Film Association, 29,* 3–18.

Ruby, J. (1980). Exposing yourself: Reflexivity, anthropology and film, *Semiotica, 30*(1/2), 153–179.

Ruby, J. (2000). *Picturing culture: Explorations of film and anthropology.* Chicago: University of Chicago Press.

Saugestad, S. (2001). *The inconvenient indigenous: Remote area development in Botswana: Donor assistance and the first people of the Kalahari.* Uppsala, Sweden: Nordic Africa Institute.

Sabloff, J. A. (2010). Where have you gone, Margaret Mead? Anthropology and public intellectuals. *American Anthropologist, 113,* 408–416.

Scott, J. C. (1990). *Domination and the arts of resistance: Hidden transcripts.* New Haven, CT; London: Yale University Press.

Sibisi, W. (2010). "I am Bushman": A close encounter with "the Other." Honours Research Project. The Centre for Communication, Media and Society, University of KwaZulu-Natal, Durban, South Africa.

SUBtext. (2011). *SUBText* research editorial, Autumn issue. South Africa: The Centre for Communication, Media and Society, The University of KwaZulu-Natal. Available at ccms.ukzn.ac.za/images/Subtext/subtext%20autumn%202011.pdf

Tomaselli, K. G. (2001). Blue is hot, red is cold: Doing reverse cultural studies in Africa. *Cultural Studies ↔ Critical Methodologies, 3,* 283–318.

Tomaselli, K. G. (2003). Stories to tell, stories to sell: Resisting textualisation. *Cultural Studies, 17,* 856–875.

Tomaselli, K. G. (2005). *Where global contradictions are sharpest: Research stories from the Kalahari.,* Amsterdam, Netherlands: Rozenberg.

Tomaselli, K. G. (Ed.). (2007). *Writing in the san/d: Autoethnography among Indigenous Southern Africans.* Walnut Creek, CA: AltaMira Press.

Tomaselli, K. G. (2011). Stepping stones into the future, *SUBtext, 15.* Available at: ccms.ukzn.ac.za/images/Subtext/subtext%.202011.pdf

Tomaselli, K. G. (forthcoming). A personal journey into different kinds of writing. *Visual Anthropology.*

Tomaselli K. G., Dyll, L., & Francis, M. (2008). "Self" and "Other": Auto–reflexive and indigenous ethnography. In N. K. Denzin, Y. S. Lincoln, & Y. T. Smith (Eds.), *Handbook of critical and indigenous methodologies* (pp. 347–372). London: Sage.

Tomaselli, K. G, McLennan-Dodd, V., & Shepperson, V. (2005). Research to do, results to sell: Enabling subjects and researchers. *Society in Transition, 36,* 24–37.

Van Grootheest, S. (2011a). *Resistance and representation: The organization of protest by subsistence and recreational fishermen during the FIFA World Cup 2010.* M.A. thesis. The Centre for Communication, Media and Society. University of KwaZulu-Natal, Durban, South Africa.

Van Grootheest, S. (2011b). *The bay of plenty.* South Africa: The Centre for Communication Media and Society, University of KwaZulu-Natal. 52 mins.

Woolf, S. H. (1997). Preserving scientific debate and patient choice, *Journal of the American Medical Association, 278,* 2105–2108.

Chapter 30

Musings on Postcolonial Autoethnography

Telling the Tale of/through My Life

Archana Pathak

Introduction

Writing autoethnography is not an easy task. To examine oneself and one's life in a way that fosters thoughtful, engaged, genuine, and rigorous critique requires immense time, introspection, honesty, and courage. And given the scientific imperialism (Pathak, 2008) of the academy, it also requires, at the very least, a disruption of the intellectual training that most of us have received.

For these two reasons, I engage in autoethnography through a postcolonialist frame. Postcolonial methods allow the autoethnographer to analyze herself as both the subject of study and as a product of larger social, political, and cultural systems. At the same time, postcolonial methods presume and expect that the scholar will critique the very system of knowledge production that drives our academic enterprise. Thus, postcolonial autoethnography has the capacity to achieve two intertwined goals: the creation of a scholarship that serves to reveal and disrupt dominant structures of oppression and the recognition that the process of knowledge production itself must also continuously be scrutinized to assure that the scholarship does not reproduce the very systems it is working to dismantle (Pathak, 2008).

In an attempt to meet the goals of revealing and disrupting structures of oppression while recognizing the process of knowledge production, this essay explores the ways in which one can engage in postcolonial autoethnography through a postcolonial autoethnographic text. Despite the pressing mandate of

Handbook of Autoethnography, edited by Stacy Holman Jones, Tony E. Adams, and Carolyn Ellis, 595–608. © 2013 Left Coast Press, Inc. All rights reserved.

scientific imperialism to be objective, distant, and squarely in the middle of the statistical norm, I find myself drawn relentlessly to the margins, singing a harmony that is off from the rest of the voices around me about the unique ways my experiences reveal and reflect a larger world. This voice is discordant in that it does not blend into the mainstream academic chorus. Though when it is sounded as a unique voice, I finally begin to hear its beauty and the ways it reflects a larger world. This essay articulates the potential possibilities in singing a postcolonial autoethnography.

One important success of autoethnography is the way it has worked to decenter the chorus of variable analytics as the primary/most accurate form of knowledge production. Autoethnography centers knowledge in narratives of self, allowing for the ways individual stories serve as platforms for greater social critique (Bochner, 2001; Bochner & Ellis, 2002; Ellis, 2004; González, 2000). While positioning narrative as a form of knowledge works to disrupt the scientific imperialism endemic in the social sciences, it also continues to reinforce the false binary of knowledge as either intellectual *or* embodied.

This false binary of intellect/embodiment upholds a colonialist paradigm in which "native" knowledge is seen as "lore" embodied (Grosz, 1993, p. 187). Embodied "knowledge is relegated to the realm of the exotic, fantastic world of the indigenous and their myths. And, implicit in that derailment is the reinforcement of western, white, male intellectual knowledge as scientific, universal, and true" (Pathak, 2010, p. 4).

Thus, "'lore' in some ways reinforces its position vis-à-vis western knowledge" (Pathak, 2010, p. 4). The question here, however, is not whether such native knowledge has value. Indeed, Edward Said (1978) argues that celebrating diversity is in actuality a tool of empire. The question becomes one of measuring the validity and reliability of lore and embodied knowledge. To "know is to fully engage an experience with one's mind, body, and heart" (Pathak, 2010, p. 4). Knowledge is a more multi-dimensional realm than what we are taught to accept. Acknowledging this allows us to consider how it is possible for a person to have both intellectual and experiential knowledge (Alexander & Mohanty, 1997; Mohanty, 1987; Stone-Mediatore, 2000).

Employing a Postcolonial Frame in Autoethnography

To examine the ways that postcolonial autoethnography might address these questions about the value and legitimacy of experiential knowledge, we must first understand "postcolonial" and I must locate myself within that discourse. And, we need to explore the ways in which postcoloniality intersects/informs both autoethnography and South Asian communities.

Postcolonial is a term that has taken on quite a well-regarded stance in the academy. Indeed, it is centrally positioned in most critical cultural studies movements. And at the same time, the question of the "post-colonial" has also come under serious scrutiny (Dirlik, 1994; McClintock, 1992; Shohat, 1992). These critiques warrant attention. Specifically, Ella Shohat (1992) and others critique the ways in which postcolonial studies have taken on a tone of acceptability in the academy because of the ways they have served to homogenize the colonial question and present the ahistorical, universalizing, and depoliticizing implications of colonial experiences.

While Shohat (1992) has several valid points, I nevertheless elect to identify myself and my writings as postcolonial, specifically because of what she identifies as the "in-between framework of the post-colonial" (p. 107). This "in-betweenness" allows me to explore the ways in which positionality shifts and changes through geopolitical contexts. As a South Asian academic with a family history firmly rooted in the Indian Independence movement, my experiences are best articulated as postcolonial. For me the term illuminates the realities of the end of "traditional" colonialism in India and the problematic complexities of India's subsequent and ongoing nationalist movement; postcolonialism points to the ways in which the movement through colonialism and neocolonialism is overdetermined through contemporary migration experiences. As a diasporic Indian who continues to benefit from class and caste privilege, I cannot claim shared spaces of neocolonialism with those for whom colonialism continues to manifest in particular ways. Nor can I articulate a sense of imperialism as India as yet is not positioned against U.S. geopolitics in ways similar to nations such as Egypt.[1] *And, at the same time,* through the language of the postcolonial, I can articulate the amorphous, ambiguous in-betweenness of being a brown person, an immigrant, an NRI (non-resident Indian) and a naturalized U.S. citizen who is neither of her homeland nor well situated in the U.S. race matrix. Ruth Frankenberg and Lata Mani (1993) articulate this idea by explaining that the postcolonial does not operate on its own but is, in effect, "a construct internally differentiated by its intersections with other unfolding relations" (p. 294). Peter Hulme (1995) continues by positing:

> If "post–colonial" is a useful word, then it refers to a *process* of disengagement from the whole colonial syndrome which takes many forms and is probably inescapable for all those whose worlds have been marked by that set of phenomena: 'post–colonial' is (or should be) a descriptive not an evaluative term....[It is not] some kind of badge of merit. (p. 122)

Thus, it is possible that postcolonial is not a study of colonialist histories, nor is it merely a response to colonialist study. Indeed, I attempt to re-engage the subversive moves of the postcolonial by articulating it as a process, manifestation, and engagement of the ways those of us who come from former colonial worlds are continuously pushed up against each other through and because of our colonial histories (regardless of the vast differences between those histories), the ways in which colonialism has been, continues to be, and is a pervasive presence in a "postcolonial" world and as a way of employing the language of the academy in rebellious ways that disrupt the academy's comfort. Indeed, my choice to use the term serves to ease the liberal academy into reading my work with a sense of righteousness without my signaling that it is this very positionality I will ultimately critique. Raka Shome and Radha Hegde (2002) address this very question in their caution that telling the story of colonialism is *not* postcolonial scholarship. For scholarship to serve the postcolonial paradigm, it must engage the colonialist *question*:

> Its commitment and its critical goals, first and foremost, are interventionist and highly political. In its best work, it theorizes not just colonial conditions but why those conditions are what they are, and how they can be undone and redone (although more work is needed on this latter aspect). This is important to keep in mind for it emphasizes that not every study of colonialism would necessarily qualify as a post-colonial study. Merely describing or chronicling the facts of colonialism, without taking an emancipatory political stance, and without offering interventionist theoretical perspectives through which to examine the violent actions and erasures of colonialism, does not make a study post-colonial in its critical impulse. (Shome & Hegde, 2002, p. 250)

Post-colonial autoethnography allows me to engage both *the* story and *its* story. Specifically, in extending Maria Cristina González's (2003) four ethics for post-colonial ethnography to autoethnography I posit a methodology that "a scholar of color can utilize to disrupt the false binaries that drive her away from the work that impassions her while holding true to the mandates of 'rigor' that pervade the academy and its evaluative bodies" (Pathak, 2010, p. 7).

The Four Ethics

González (2003) explains that it is not easy to write from a post-colonialist positionality. Given our training, we often inadvertently reproduce the colonialist voice. González explains:

> Colonialism, as I have framed it, along with religious-political imperialism, results in a form of silencing in scholarly writing. This silencing is insidious in that along with the obvious explicit censorship of texts and writings, it helps create the illusion of a free exchange of ideas. (p. 80)

This silencing is clearly seen in the ways that academic journals call for scholarship on diversity and at the same time utilize arbitrary standards of "reliability" or "validity" to discount (and not publish) such scholarship based on the premise that it does not engage in reliable or valid "method." Postcoloniality provides a space that not only invites exchange of ideas, but also allows one to name the ontology, axiology, and methodology that shape one's voice (see Conquergood, 1985, 1991; Shome, 1996).

As González (2003), explains, the postcolonialist scholar articulates ideas that both explain and disrupt the very nature of colonialism:

A post-colonial ethnography, therefore, is not merely an act of defiance, but one of great courage, in that unlike pre-colonial awareness, there is now a sense of coexisting within social systems that may or may not still be fully or partially in the creative grasp of the colonial fist. (p. 81)

González (2003) offers four ethics for postcolonial ethnography that serve the ethnographer in her endeavors to disrupt colonialist systems: accountability, context, truthfulness, and community. Accountability calls for the scholar to explicitly articulate how she came to know the story she is telling. Context calls for the naming of the social, political, economic, and cultural forces that shape the story being told. Truthfulness demands that the scholar push herself to tell even the invisible parts of the story—those that might go unnoticed, unrecognized. Finally, community calls to the very people whose stories are being told; it reminds the scholar that the story and her work are not separate from those whom they are about. These four ethics are inextricably intertwined and create a synergy through which one engages in postcolonial autoethnography. Central to each of these ethics is the process of the autoethnographer navigating the delicate, fragile dance between self/group, researcher/researched. These ethics account for the ways in which the scholar must continuously, reflexively test her writings and ideas to assure that the colonist voice is not being reproduced and simultaneously layer that reflexivity into the larger story. It is imperative, then, to examine these ethics specifically in the ways they are interconnected as we explore how to engage them in autoethnography through an autoethnographic tale.

Musings on a Postcolonial Life

If I am to honestly write about what it means to be a child of the Indian diaspora, I must first own who I am. I am a 1.5er. You know her—that child who was born somewhere else, but raised in the United States. But I'm surely not an FOB[2]—my English has a distinct valley girl intonation, and most Indians who meet me are perplexed by my presence. They can't figure out how I am actually Indian. I can't even rightfully be called an ABCD[3] since I wasn't born in the United States. And I own that this is my story of my memories about others who may or may not remember, interpret, or acknowledge these stories in any way similar to mine.

When we talk about the Indian diaspora, it's often articulated as an all-encompassing hug that incorporates all Indians. But it doesn't. I'm a particular breed. I have to acknowledge that I am an immigrant who comes from an established bourgeois family. We had/have class, caste, educational, and economic status, which is important to know because Indianness then ultimately gets defined as a space that reifies a Hindu, Brahmin, white collar terminally educated community. It reveals a liberal elite of India who had the wherewithal to migrate to America. Of course the Indian diaspora in the United States is much more diverse than that, especially now. However, those who came in the post–1965 migration wave overwhelmingly tended to be upper caste and upper class and held terminal degrees.

These immigrants struggled, worked two and three jobs to make ends meet, found ways to celebrate their culture even though there was no community to speak of, and modified their cooking to mimic the well-loved meals of their homeland. They came from a land of the poor with only seven dollars in their pockets and the blessings of their elders to sustain them.[4] But these struggles led to a life of success. And this success was both part and parcel of their hard work and all that they brought with them—their status, their education, their class standing, their names. Indian-Americans became the epitome of the American Dream. It's a great story. And it's a true story.

But underneath is another story—one that we rarely articulate. These post-1965 immigrants came from families of wealth and status. They came with, right before, or right after siblings and others from their towns, villages, and caste. They found each other in America and supported each other in getting settled. They were allowed to keep their names and some if not all of their education. And even if their formal education went unaccounted and unaccredited, its effects aided them in maneuvering middle-class America. The "model minorities" were the perfect foil against which to judge and condemn already established communities of color in the United States (Bhatt, 2003).

These immigrant families came together in living rooms across the United States to celebrate their culture through music, dance, food, and celebration. They shared a common language, common histories, and common careers. This allowed for a community to quickly come into being and to be sustained through gatherings, shared narratives, and common experiences. The small living room gatherings grew into social organizations, community organizations, political organizations, and the symbol of Indian-America. Such an amalgam of identities then became the marker of Indianness. For me and for many who were a part of the post–1965 migration wave, "Indian" becomes synonymous with Hindu, traditional joint family (made up of three, even four patrilineal generations living together, working together, existing together), North Indian, heterosexual, middle/upper middle class identity. And the unspoken part? We were (are) a community far removed from the African–American and Latino communities already in the United States; becoming American meant continuing to distance ourselves from these communities of color (Bhatt, 2003).

My understanding of what it meant to be Indian wasn't simply a manifestation of a selective nostalgia on the part of my parents. It was, instead, a postcolonial sensibility that ultimately led to the immigrant generation (my parents' generation) embracing a "model minority" politic through which they conflate conservative U.S. political values with Indian family values, tie their bourgeois sensibilities to the solidly conservative U.S. white middle class, and attempt to achieve social acceptance through producing a class of children who embody the "best" of both the Indian and American worlds.

Is it any wonder, then, that I couldn't figure out who the hell I was as a child? I looked in the mirror and saw someone who looked nothing like the white, middle-class children in her suburban Illinois elementary school. Nothing in the world around me was like the India I had left behind. Indeed, everything that made me feel safe and connected to that far-away land—my language, the smells, my clothes, my way of moving, everything—was mocked. And all of the sudden, the sensations I associated with India—the smell of mustard seeds popping in hot oil, the lilting cadence of Gujarati, the soft brush of a sari as my mother walked by me—went from being warm hugs that comforted me to being rigid walls that closed me in and separated me from the outside world while policing me to assure I was a "good Indian girl."

The Indian immigrant community was so caught up in proving their worth to the American West, holding onto a culture that was so incredibly far away geographically and in time (Pathak, 2008) and securing success for their children (read, culturally "authentic" and successful by normative U.S. standards of success), that they ultimately recreated the very Victorian/colonial Indianness they had worked so hard to expel from their motherland. Being Indian meant showing ourselves and everyone else that we were successful, reliable, and culturally unobtrusive while simultaneously offering up our culture as an exotic artifact for the consumption of American whites. The message was loud and clear: "See! You were right to let us in. We will act well, bolster your economy, and keep our cultural selves private unless you ask for a show." And in doing so, India's magnificent complexity, multiplicity, diversity, conundrums were erased. Just like that.

All of this serves as background for my story as a scholar. From childhood until well into my graduate career, I didn't know I wanted to be a scholar, nor did I think I really had the capacity to do so. Honestly, I didn't even know what a scholar was.

As a child, I wasn't a good student. I was easily distracted, I didn't really like math, and I cared more about watching people and becoming friends than studying, listening to the teacher, or doing my work. This was a serious cultural crisis for my family. I carried my family's reputation on my shoulders. My success meant that everything they had given up to come to America was ultimately worth it. And any lack of success meant that I had personally failed, that I had acted inappropriately. I do not know if my parents believed that I was completely at fault (or at fault at all), but their responses to my failures definitely implicated me. In India, school meant studying. Children go to school to be trained in terms of their intellect and academic discipline. The idea that children go to school to learn how to play just didn't compute to my parents.

My parents sent me to my new school in Illinois in the best of Indian fashion: my long plaits well oiled and neatly braided, in my best dress with matching socks, my Indian food lunch deftly packed in my lunchbox and my school supplies comfortably tucked into my school bag. I came home to recriminations: How did my dress get so dirty? Why were my socks not pulled up? Where was the ribbon that held my plait? How had I dared to rip pages out of my school book?

The situation only got worse when my parents were called in to see the principal, Dr. Honel. I hadn't been doing well. The other children laughed at me, refused to play with me, and I wasn't performing well in the mandatory socialization that is central to U.S. kindergarten pedagogy. I now realize that Dr. Honel was a smart, thoughtful administrator who understood that this new family in his school needed cultural adaptation training; but then, his calling my parents in to see him was the first in a lifetime of acts I would commit that embarrassed and dishonored my parents (at least in the moment).

I've never found out what exactly happened at that meeting between my parents and Principal Honel. But I do remember what changed in my life. I no longer wore dresses to school. I no longer got in trouble for tearing out pages from my school workbook. And I started seeing the school psychologist. I can't remember her name; it started with a C. I saw her until I left the school in the fifth grade. My inability to fit in was designated a psychological problem. The school psychologist was the first of many authority figures in my life who would define my way of being as abnormal, unhealthy, and inept. My mother also began monitoring my baths every morning after that meeting. My parents told me that my classmates had complained that I smelled, and my parents were appalled, thinking that I hadn't been bathing properly. I now realize that the offensive smell my classmates complained about was my hair oil, something that my parents didn't even consider, given the natural, enjoyable presence of that smell in our day-to-day lives.

It's important to note that my parents did not say I failed, per se. But I believed I failed. And I believed that *they* believed I failed. Of course, I knew that my success was the family's success and that succeeding was the least I could do given all that my parents had given up and continued to give up for me. But I also can look back now and see how these moments were incredibly difficult for my parents as they attempted to learn how to move in a world completely foreign to them without even an iota of the support they had had back home in India. And that difficulty was compounded by the fact that in their worlds, they had always moved with success and achievement. Failure was, quite literally, a foreign concept.

My parents represented the elite of Indian society. Materially, this meant that they had class status, caste status, and educational status; that they lived in urban spaces and that they were multilingual/English speaking. In coming to the United States, they not only traveled many geographic miles, they also traveled many social miles. I can see how their confusion, frustration, and hurt were the threads that pulled me toward a lifetime of trying to understand the structures of privilege, disprivilege, and oppression. They are such amazing people, and they work so very hard. Why couldn't the people around us see that? Why did my mother have to keep taking the test to become a dentist? Why didn't my father practice medicine in America? Why did they seem to beg people to accept them? My actions may have embarrassed them, but their actions also embarrassed me. As a five-year-old, I didn't have the language; my adult self can give words to the feelings coursing through me—I wanted my parents to yell "FUCK YOU!"

to those who attacked them, mocked them, denied them, dismissed them, and ignored them, instead of trying to fit in and be enough.

But try to fit in they did. And they did so because they couldn't understand how it was possible that they didn't fit in. In their minds, hearts, and souls, they belonged. They were of privilege. They could not fathom being disprivileged, not in any truly embodied sense (Hill Collins, 2008). Even as members of the Independence movement in India, their community saw their status as that of privilege and the British as usurpers. The move to end colonialism wasn't aimed at earning privileged status in their society; it was a move to reclaim the privilege that was rightfully theirs. Indeed, that is also the very reason that many upper-caste, Hindu Indians were ultimately opposed to Gandhi's idea of a casteless, secular India. Gandhi not only wanted to rid India of its external colonizers, he also wanted to rid India of its colonial read/interpretation of its religious and cultural history (Gandhi, 1993). Gandhi posited that the ideas of caste as practiced in contemporary India were a result of colonial interpretations of ancient Hindu texts. That in actuality, the ways of caste were not hierarchical. Gandhi also posited that democracy had to be secular; no one religion could serve as the premise of the government. These two ideas dislocated upper caste and upper class Hindus in ways that they had not experienced. Even in India's colonial epochs (Moghul, Arayan, British) upper caste Hindus had been afforded a certain degree of status. Indeed, this very status allowed colonial forces to stay intact as these upper caste, upper class Indians were often used to manage and control the masses. It is no surprise, then, that Indian immigrants to the United States, such as my parents, attempted to utilize the age old techniques to find a way to survive in a foreign world. And, it is no surprise that as a diasporic Indian who saw herself as a part of the U.S. race matrix, I wanted my parents to claim their place as members of a community of color in the United States.

This story is only a small part of a much larger story, but it illuminates particular ways in which the four ethics can be articulated in autoethnographic writing.

Accountability

González (2003) writes, "The ethic of accountability addresses both the story being told and the way that the ethnographer came to know that story" (p. 83). This means that if I want to tell my story, I must be accountable to the multiple stories that position me as an immigrant. There is *the* story and *its* story, and there may be other stories beyond these stories. For me, these threads emerge at times as a double helix—two strands intertwined and independent—stories told within and through each other. This emerges in my story as I weave together the stories of the post–1965 Indian immigrant with my own familial history. And at other times, these two stories stand as twin trees, each full in and of itself, but together presenting a synergy of interconnectedness. In sharing my stories about coming to America and the ways my family found their place in this new world, I simultaneously tell the story of the how and why the voices of people of color must be incorporated into academic discourses to allow for the multiple realities of those who do not represent the hegemonic norms of our society. I do this through stories about my own desire and need to seek an explanation for my experiences, a way to locate my experiences as meaningful in that they are shared by others.

Context

The ethic of context "mandates that the storyteller name the systems that shape, constrict, disrupt, inform both the story and the storyteller" (González, 2003, p. 84) in autoethnography. This particular ethic foregrounds a postcolonialist frame. The telling of the experiences through a critical frame of establishing context also serves to hold me accountable to a tale that is both about my experience and about the process of telling tales.

Attending to context, the autoethnographer works to resist an insular narcissism that narrows the story to merely herself, her experiences, and her thoughts. It reminds the autoethnographer that her story is important precisely because it is a story about how her story lives in the larger world (e.g., Bochner & Ellis, 2002; Chang, 2008; Visweswaran, 1994). This is most evident as I position the tale of the post–1965 Indian immigrant up against the backdrop of the U.S. race matrix and ongoing U.S. imperialism. These contexts shape my story in particular ways and also allow for others to see how such political, social, economic, and other structures may also shape their experiences. This is, in many ways, a primary tenent inherent to postcolonial practice: engaging in scholarship/theory for the conscious political purpose of radical change. Providing the context allows for me to explicitly name and critique the very systems that attempt to name and critique me.

Truthfulness

The third ethic of truthfulness exemplifies a sort of radical openness that allows for the telling of a reality that is often rendered invisible to those who benefit from the colonialist frame (Mohanty, 2003). Radical openness is most evident in the ways that presenting postcolonial autoethnography calls for a brave telling of what it means to be colonized and how one navigates the echoes of that history in her life. This ethic requires the autoethnographer to not rest comfortably in her version of the story. Radical openness pushes me to think about how the moments that were so salient for me may or may not have held any meaning for others in the story. And, in examining the possibility that some points in my story are mere reflections of my own narcissism, I am pushed to continually contextualize each moment to solidify its value in the tale.

This is not to say each moment of my story (anyone's story) isn't important. But the process of postcolonial autoethnography demands that we continue to move through our stories so that we can present them as tools for radical change.

Such movement necessitates that I must always consider how my story can serve a larger purpose and the ways in which it might do so. For me, particularly, this larger purpose includes writing into the void of silence that scientific imperialism (Pathak, 2008) creates by privileging aggregate data as the most valuable data. In telling my tale I engage in an act of rebellion against a system that says my story does not hold any particular value. At the same time, I present a story that illuminates the ways in which colonialism continues to echo through the lives of postcolonial peoples. In my tale, this is best seen through the ways I bank on the exotic value of my story while utilizing that exoticness to reveal the deeply colonialist paradigm that "allows" me to tell the story. This is further seen in the ways that I strive to articulate the distinct particularities of my own colonial and postcolonial history. My story cannot be used to tell the story of a Latina, a West Asian/Arab/Middle Easterner, or a South American woman. Though there are hopefully commonalities echoed in our stories. Thus, I must push myself to honestly articulate the contextualized realities of my particular colonial history while also recognizing that the specificities of my story may not be a part of the larger postcolonial tale.

Community

And finally, "the ethic of community implies that once we step forward with an ethnographic tale, we can no longer feign separation from those with whom we have shared the story" (González, 2003, p. 85). This ethic demands that one's story cannot be told alone. For the autoethnographer, it demands that the story be told not only of a person who is an example of the world, but of a person who exists within a larger world—someone who is part and parcel of a larger story (hooks, 1994; Visweswaran, 1994). I tell my story not only because I want/need my story to be told (indeed, it often actually causes me much embarrassment and is quite painful to commit to paper) but because it reveals components of the lived experiences of concepts that are often only discussed in the abstract: racism, sexism, patriarchy, and eurocentrism. My story is but one example of the ways in which racism, sexism, eurocentrism, and patriarchy are operationalized in our day-to-day lives. My story shows moments where I am defined through my race, where I am discriminated against as a woman, where I am encouraged to work at being more white, where being a woman positions me as less than.

These ethics offer autoethnography a postcolonial frame through which it can locate itself as a rigorous methodology in the social sciences. Through these four ethics we see the potential of developing autoethnographies that serve to both illuminate a story and present the larger story in a context that is often unrecognized and/or silenced.

Conclusion

Postcolonialism, while contested, holds a critical, necessary place in the academy and serves as an ideal frame through which to move our academic endeavors into a space of activism and radical change. For this reason, I find the potentialities of intertwining the post–colonial critique with autoethnography particularly appealing. I'm glad that I've always struggled with my story. Not because I don't deserve to have my story told, but because the struggle pushed me to find ways to engage beyond the traditions I was taught. My academic training was firmly entrenched in logical positivist social science, inviting me to speak to my "diversity" but only legitimating the scholarship that reproduced the normative, aggregate data of variable analytics.

Despite not finding any space for my voice in my traditional training, I am glad I was trained in a variety of intellectual traditions. This training allowed me to understand the depth of the colonialist enterprise in the academy and develop ways in which to actively, rigorously transcend it.

Autoethnographers must continue to write so that there is a growing body of literature that provides examples of rigorous scholarship and offers legitimate methodological articulations of the value of autoethnography. This writing serves as a foundation for future scholarship in which we disrupt the colonial mindset that method exists a priori, without a need to articulate its roots, its assumptions, and its origins (Feyerabend, 1993).

Finally, postcolonial autoethnography opens the door for more rigorous, critical positivistic scholarship. It is not the goal of postcolonial scholarship to get rid of positivistic scholarship; only to allow it to hold its space so that other methods may hold their spaces, allowing for a rich, diverse, complex matrix of scholarship. In doing so, we then push all methodologies to be utilized to their greatest value, in the best and most applicable ways, to ends that serve a greater good. By doing so, we uphold the postcolonial enterprise of engaging in research for radical change.

Acknowledgments

The author would like to thank Stacy Holman Jones, Tony Adams, and the anonymous reviewers whose insightful comments served to strengthen this essay.

Notes

1. This is not to say that there is no neocolonialism or imperialism in terms of India. I am responding specifically to the critiques Shohat (2008) presents in her article regarding the vast differences between colonial histories and contemporary imperialist relations between the United States and various postcolonial nations.
2. FOB: "Fresh off the boat" refers to Indians who are newly arrived immigrants and/or those immigrants who have been in the United States for much shorter periods of time.

3. ABCD: "American born confused desi" refers to Indian-Americans who were born in the United States and seemingly lack cultural identity. The term *desi* is a Hindi word meaning "of the homeland." This term is particularly used for those who are read as lacking "cultural authenticity and connection." The terms FOB and ABCD are used in conjunction with each other.

4. India's currency was not worth much up against the dollar, and the United States would only let immigrants bring in a small amount of money when entering the country, so the immigrants did not have much financially when they arrived. Despite that, because they were of wealth and status in India, they carried with them the "invisible weightless knapsack" of class privilege, which would ultimately help them navigate the United States (McIntosh, 1995, p. 130).

References

Alexander, M. J., & Mohanty, C. T. (1997). *Feminist genealogies, colonial legacies, democratic futures.* New York: Routledge.

Bhatt, A. J. (2003). Model minority as a colonial system: Asian Indians in the United States. In E. Kramer (Ed.), *The emerging monoculture: Assimilation and the "model minority"* (pp. 203–220). Westport, CT: Praeger/Greenwood.

Bochner, A. P. (2001). Narrative's virtues. *Qualitative Inquiry, 7*, 131–157.

Bochner, A. P., & Ellis, C. (Eds.). (2002). *Ethnographically speaking: Autoethnography, literature and aesthetics.* New York: AltaMira Press.

Chang, H. (2008). *Autoethnography as method.* Walnut Creek, CA: Left Coast Press, Inc.

Conquergood, D. (1985). Performing as a moral act: Ethical dimensions of the ethnography of performance. *Literature in Performance, 5*, 1–13.

Conquergood, D. (1991). Rethinking ethnography: Towards a critical cultural politics. *Communication Monographs, 58*, 179–194.

Dirlik, A. (1994). The postcolonial aura: Third world criticism in the age of global capitalism. *Critical Inquiry, 20*, 328–356.

Ellis, C. (2004). *The ethnographic I: A methodological novel about autoethnography.* New York: AltaMira Press.

Feyerabend, P. (1993). *Against method* (3rd ed.). New York: Verso.

Frankenberg, R., & Mani, L. (1993). Crosscurrents, crosstalk: Race, 'postcoloniality' and the politics of location. *Cultural Studies, 7*, 292–310.

Gandhi, M. K. (1993) *Gandhi: An autobiography: The story of my experiments with truth.* Boston: Beacon Press.

González, M. C. (2000). The four seasons of ethnography: A creation-centered ontology for ethnography. *International Journal of Intercultural Relations, 24*, 623–650.

González, M. C. (2003). An ethics for postcolonial ethnography. In R. P. Clair (Ed.), *Expressions of ethnography* (pp. 77–86). Albany, NY: State University of New York Press.

Grosz, E. (1993). Bodies and knowledge: Feminism and the crisis of reason. In L. Alcoff & E. Potter (Eds.), *Feminist epistemologies* (pp. 187–216). New York: Routledge.

Hill Collins, P. (2008). *Black feminist thought: Knowledge, consciousness and the politics of empowerment.* New York: Routledge.

hooks, b. (1994). *Teaching to transgress: Education as the practice of freedom.* New York: Routledge.

Hulme, P. (1995). Including America. *ARIEL, 26*, 117–123.

McClintock, A. (1992). Third world and post-colonial issues. *Social Text, 31/32*, 84–98.

Mohanty, C. T. (1987). Feminist encounters: Locating the politics of experience. *Copyright, 1*, 30–44.

Mohanty, C. T. (2003). *Feminisms without borders: Decolonizing theory, practicing solidarity.* Raleigh, NC: Duke University Press.

Pathak, A. A. (2010). Opening my voice, claiming my space: Theorizing the possibilities of postcolonial approaches to autoethnography. *Journal of Research Practice, 6*(1), Article M10. Retrieved May 1, 2012, from jrp.icaap.org/index.php/jrp/article/view/231/191

Pathak, A. (2008). Being Indian in the U.S.: Exploring the hyphen as an ethnographic frame. In L. A. Flores, B. J. Allen, & M. P. Orbe (Eds.), *Intercultural communication in a transnational world* (pp. 175–196). Washington, DC: National Communication Association.

Pathak Bhatt, A. (2008). The Sita syndrome: Examining the communicative aspects of domestic violence from a South Asian perspective. *Journal of International Women's Studies, 9*(3), 155–173. Retrieved August 24, 2010, from www.bridgew.edu/soas/jiws/May08/Sita.pdf

Said, E. W. (1978). *Orientalism.* New York: Vintage.

Shohat, E. (1992). Notes on the 'post-colonial.' *Social Text, 31/32,* 99–114.

Shome, R. (1996). Postcolonial interventions in the rhetorical canon: An "other" view. *Communication Theory, 6,* 40–59.

Shome, R., & Hegde, R. S. (2002). Postcolonial approaches to communication: Charting the terrain, engaging the intersections. *Communication Theory, 12,* 249–270.

Stone-Mediatore, S. (2000). Chandra Mohanty and the revaluing of "experience." In U. Narayan & S. Harding (Eds.), *Decentering the center: Philosophy for a multicultural, postcolonialist, and feminist world* (pp. 110–127). Indianapolis: Indiana University Press.

Visweswaran, K. (1994). *Fictions of feminist ethnography.* Minneapolis: University of Minnesota Press.

Chapter 31

Evaluating (Evaluations of) Autoethnography

Craig Gingrich-Philbrook

Attracted by the movement, Traf, my 6-year old Rat Terrier, stands on her back feet and gently paws my arm. She wants kisses; I oblige. I rarely refuse, no matter what I'm doing. It's my nod to the importance of living in the present. (Ellis, 2000, p. 273)

1.

The world doesn't make very much sense to me, right now, but that doesn't surprise me. I recognize this crisis as what William Beardslee (1990) described as a conflict between orienting and disorienting stories. When I found his essay articulating this difference, having just begun presenting queer performances of my personal narratives, I felt like I had located the confirmation I had searched for in a world in which I often had to run from the imminent explosion of a house full of lies. Briefly put, orienting stories tell us things like: our success depends upon our effort, everyone in the United States has equal opportunity, corporate research and development create a better tomorrow, our families will always love and protect us, and education trains people to question consensual reality. Just for instance; the world moves via the coordination of millions of other orienting stories, also. I'd wager some of them popped into your mind, too, as you read this.

Disorienting stories, by contrast, narrate those occasions when the orienting stories fail to predict—and sometimes actively mask—our actual experience in the world: the roadblocks to success encountered by even the most industrious

Handbook of Autoethnography, edited by Stacy Holman Jones, Tony E. Adams, and Carolyn Ellis, 609–626. © 2013 Left Coast Press, Inc. All rights reserved.

among us; the discrimination and inequalities many of us face, to varying degrees, at work, at school, seeking medical care, and so forth; the profit-driven destruction of our planet and extinction of species, fueled by industrial advancement; the intimate violence, abuse, and rejection many experience from family members, often including banishment from home because the person(s) they love is/are the "wrong" race, class, sex, nationality, religion, and so forth; and the closure of knowledge in the name of censorious political and epistemic orthodoxies way too certain about who we are, what we should value in one another, and which kinds of knowledge should "count."

After coming this far in this Handbook, I think most readers can recognize that autoethnography has a stake in the disorienting story and its critical potential, even if we find it more useful to say that any given story will have both orienting and disorienting aspects. Hard work does matter, even if it cannot guarantee success; without valuing equality, we have no reason to work toward it; science gave us antibiotics that save lives, even as they prompt the development of resistant strains of illness-bearing organisms; some members of our families, often the youngest and most vulnerable, sometimes take up our cause or protect us from others; and committed educators will always fight back against corporatization and unbelievably bizarre efforts to ban critical thinking, such as that occurring in the state of Texas as I write this (Haley, 2012). Beardslee himself acknowledges the need to resist thinking of orienting/disorienting as a binary absolute, an either/or.

Autoethnography works this territory, this space between the orienting and disorienting story. When I say at the beginning of this essay that the world doesn't make much sense to me right now, I say that as someone with a personal history and academic history that refuse to remain separated, a refusal many autoethnographers identify with. As I have worked on this chapter, I have struggled in the midst of a very particular contest between orienting and disorienting stories about the role of the personal in academic settings, the censorious impulses that sometimes punish the resistant personal voice, and the politics of disciplinary responses to difficult situations. Villanova University, a Catholic institution, recently disinvited my friend Tim Miller, a queer performance artist, after asking him to give a workshop that would help students tell their own life stories about identity and critical moments in power relations (Miller, 2012; Rose, 2012). Despite what one might think, if one naturalized the incompatibility of Catholicism and the avowal of an out, queer identity, Villanova's initial invitation made a great deal of sense; it complemented the orienting story of the university's Mission Statement. Speaking in a collective voice, that story says, among other things,

> [We concern] ourselves with developing and nurturing the whole person, allowing students, faculty and staff to grow intellectually, emotionally, spiritually, culturally, socially and physically in an environment that supports individual differences and insists that mutual love and respect should animate every aspect of university life. (Mission Statement)

Villanova's president withdrew Tim's invitation after an email campaign conducted by a right-wing group, The Cardinal Newman Society (a society named after the same person as the Newman Centers at many universities, but not associated with them). The group told a misleading story about Tim, saying that he had done things he hadn't done, characterizing his work in sensationalizing ways, and describing ACT UP—a protest group to which he belongs and that works on behalf of people with HIV/AIDS and promotes awareness and preventative education—as "anti-Catholic."

To be sure, ACT UP has taken issue with the church's resistance to *anyone* providing accurate information about AIDS prevention and access to condoms, most notably in the notorious "Stop the Church" action at St. Patrick's cathedral in New York. But, despite the Newman Society's claims to the contrary, Tim did not take part in that demonstration; he was thousands of miles away, in California. ACT UP *has never* protested against Catholicism in its own right, never advocated laws against Catholics, never rallied people to oppose the marriage of Catholics, never sought the legal right for GLBTQ people not to hire Catholics, never lobbied for the legal right of gender-variant children to bully Catholic children, and so on, as some—by no means all—Catholic organizations have in what I would describe as only the most recent political turns in their centuries-old war against GLBTQ people and their freedom of expression (Gingrich-Philbrook, 2012). To characterize ACT UP as simply "anti-Catholic" misleads readers and incites violence; it defames an organization that works to protect an excruciatingly vulnerable population from prejudices that continue to fuel the HIV-AIDS epidemic, stigmatizing those who contract it and who hope merely to live.

In the press release announcing the cancellation, the president of the university echoed many of the Newman Society's false characterizations of Tim and his work. Disorientingly, then, the president's actions did not demonstrate much support for individual difference, failing to "insist" that the Newman Society and Villanova treat Tim with the "mutual love and respect" Villanova's mission statement claims "should animate every aspect of university life." I guess that "every aspect" really just means "some aspects."

I spent a lot of time looking blankly out of windows over these last months, thinking about that exclusionary "some." I saw a fox once, loping in a wide circle around the brush pile in the back, searching for something or running from something. Who can say? I guess he or she was a quicksilver bright side to all that staring, and for that I am grateful.

Life is funny. Well, strange, anyway; by coincidence, I sat on the planning committee for a conference on the "ethics and economies of performance" that Villanova planned to host a few months after this incident. Sometimes one disorienting story overlaps with another, just to remind us to notice our interdependence and the systemic nature of power relations. The conference meant to gather members of the National Communication Association's Performance Studies Division, a group of people very interested in stories and in making sure everybody gets to tell them. It felt excruciatingly hypocritical for me to go. I told the hardworking primary host I didn't think I could attend, felt I should withdraw from the planning committee, and had prepared a statement—prepared a story, in other words—for the division's email list explaining why. She asked me to wait before sending it and said her department chair would like to speak to me; she arranged a phone call between us for later that evening.

When the phone rang, I had some hope, but after the first few minutes of pleasantries, I felt the chair had begun lecturing me about how complicated the situation was. I don't disagree with that assessment, only that it justified inaction. He didn't let me speak much, or I didn't feel able to; I want to own my share of my silence. I spent a lot of time listening in the near dark to arguments about the timing of efforts for justice that I have heard a thousand times. I sat by my aquarium, the only light in the room, watching the little tetras move in and out of the clump of java moss that takes up a corner of the tank, searching for something or running from something. In the end, after attempting to justify the necessity of the president's actions with the fact that he was really a good person and probably didn't mean what he said, probably was just following orders, the chair asked me what felt like an insincere question, at least under the circumstances: "Craig, how do we help people deal with their homophobia?" All I could answer was, "Well, usually what we do is invite people to come to campus and tell stories drawn from their life, which is precisely what the president has prevented." Like Tami Spry (2011), I believe that "It is in the *coperformativity of meaning with others* that I find myself as a performative autoethnographic researcher, in the constant negotiation of representation in always emergent, contingent, and power-laden contexts" (p. 39). When we exclude the bodies of others from on-campus proximity with students, even those others whose views we find unruly, we deny everyone involved the opportunity to experience this "coperformativity of meaning with others." By contrast, written and performed autoethnography has the power to *actually* insist on mutual respect in embodied and textual encounters between ourselves and those "others" our cultures and beliefs have alienated and misrecognized.

We hung up as cordially as we could, and I sat there a minute, catching my breath before switching off the light in the tank and heading to bed with my partner, Jonny, who also cares deeply about Tim, and performance, and stories, and treating people with love and respect. We withdrew from the conference, waited for a promised statement from the department defending Tim or the mechanism for addressing the issue open and honestly to appear in the conference schedule on its website. Several months later, these things had still not appeared, and our names remained on the program, so we took to the division's email list, finally telling the story we had previously withheld in good faith. We explained why we weren't attending, and we asked others to consider staying away as well. We told that story more forcefully than many liked, less forcefully than some felt necessary. Other people also stayed away, sharing our sense that going would allow an institution that had behaved badly to use our participation as an alibi, as proof that it really was interested in mutual love and respect for all, rather than for just some.

But other people felt that, however badly Villanova had treated Tim, the larger story of the discipline's need to meet and discuss its future trumped the irony that the university's departure from its mission seemed based on the unethical desire to avoid the economic consequences of alienating wealthy donors. Unlike Jonny and me, they felt that the very real needs of our discipline outweighed the potential value of creating a nationally visible counter-story about the purpose of performance in an educational setting and the necessity to resist the chilling effects of organizations like the Newman Society. Those chilling effects. though, are excruciatingly real; the society's own president, Patrick J. Reilly, recently boasted in *The New York Times* that many Catholic universities, hoping to avoid controversy, now secretly seek his approval for guest speakers before inviting them (Goodstein, 2012). In other words, Catholic universities outsource co-curricular decisions, seeking ideological approval for the stories they bring to campus. Censorship, after all, performs the harshest evaluation of a life story. It says, "we would prefer it if you did not exist to tell your story, so we will create the artificial appearance that you have vanished."

I can't tell you how many times I sat staring at the screen or the tablet and just had to look away from the drafts of this essay during this time. When this kind of thing happens, I make room for my cat to jump up on my lap. When he arrived yowling at the front door years ago, I named him O.W., after my grandfather, himself named after the Wright Brothers: Orville-Wilbur. My grandfather and my grandmother, Margaret, took me in after I ran away from the house of lies at home before it blew apart. As a kitten, O.W. liked to steal his namesake's shaving brush from my bureau and carry it around the house. I have never known what to make of that synchronicity. Now, twelve years later, an old gentleman with a chin as white as my grandfather's, he senses something about my struggle to write; stands on my lap, front paws on my chest; and presses his forehead into mine in contemplative consolation.

I try to stay in the present, but some days I felt so disoriented about the future of autoethnographic essays and performances and how they get evaluated that I didn't know how to proceed. Often in these last few months, writing seemed futile. What orienting story could I tell about evaluation, when it so often provides the occasions for disorienting experiences? I want to say that even holding a notebook hurt on those days—that the wiring in my finger tips, lit up with the rest of my nervous system by everything going on and bruised by all the typing of petitions, position statements, and email, couldn't even bear the texture of *paper*. But, of course, that isn't literally true, even though saying it helps communicate the extremity of what I felt, bodily, in such a world as this. My discipline, devoted to telling disorienting stories and breaking the canon of literature open to welcome excluded voices, forgave (or appeared to forgive) an institution's unconscionable treatment of someone who fought all the way to the Supreme Court for the right to speak one's truth to power in autobiographical performance.

Great.

But people who went to the conference, many of whom I love—genuinely, deeply, materially—tell another story about what their participation did and did not mean. And here's the thing: I have to honor that. The conflict between our stories doesn't make any of them disappear, doesn't make any of them less important to understand. If you laid them side by side and tried to evaluate which of our stories about this whole affair mattered most, at least to you, you might choose different ones depending upon whether your evaluative criteria privileged the sources used, the poetic language, their political investment, their commitment to witnessing, which account really offered the biggest bigger picture, and so on. Using those same criteria, many people you love—genuinely, deeply, materially in your own way—might well come to conclusions different than yours. Each of us involved in this controversy could write an autoethnography about these events; many of us will. They won't match. They won't move in a linear way toward a single, collective truth. We'll write about what the situation revealed to us as we experienced it unfolding in our awareness. I think it's useful, too, to flip the order of that sentence to more poetically and unexpectedly capture the autoethnographic impulse to have agency in the present by articulating the context of the past: each of us could write an autoethnography about what *we revealed* to these events. Each of us felt the struggle cue different histories, memories, needs, and contingencies. We lived through, and continue to feel, the ways the events challenged our sense of ourselves and what we think performance, storytelling, and autoethnographic reflection accomplish in both university life and wider, public cultures that sometimes underestimate and/or actively demean the value of another's experience.

I want to say, "And that divergence of stories is good."

I believe it is good, I really do.

But I can't say it doesn't trouble me. I can only surrender the belief that I am entitled to live an untroubled life if others do not share that entitlement. Autoethnography helps me fashion this surrender, and that may be my most useful evaluation of it.

2.

We tell stories, but we also hear them, and some of the ones we hear describe the impact of the ones we've written on how people evaluate others. Someone told me once that an essay I wrote, "Autoethnography's Family Values: Easy Access to Compulsory Experiences," was placed, repeatedly and anonymously by one or more people, in an autoethnographer's departmental mailbox as a kind of punitive, bullying harassment. I experienced the piece as "for" rather than "against" autoethnography, and I still do. I wanted to offer an aesthetic challenge rather than a condemnation, teasing out the creative double bind between the impulse to create knowledge and the impulse to create art. A double bind isn't a binary so much as an acknowledgment of the necessity to mix and mingle "equally valued and equally insufficient messages" (Peterson & Langellier, 1982, p. 243) in a world that does not guarantee that one's ultimate result will win the approval of those in charge. Still, people used the essay to bully and condemn, and their "targets" have received it in that spirit. I can understand that. Really. So much so that the story of that mailbox violence threw me off writing for a while. I did it still, a little; but my heart wasn't in it like before. See, I've gotten stuff in my mailbox with that kind of mean intention before. Someone signed me up to receive newsletters and funding appeals from a staunchly homophobic Catholic organization. I'd get little crucifixes wrapped up like promotional Easter Seals address labels in requests for donations to "help stop the sodomites from ruining America." My mailbox became another house of lies that could explode any day, sending shrapnel into my psyche. I learned to approach it slowly, cautiously. All of this happened at about the same time that the essay came out and found its way, over and over again, into the mailbox of another human being.

The story I was told, whether true or false, requires me to acknowledge that evaluations of autoethnography, including my own, capture the efforts of real people and deploy them in arguments advancing the evaluator's own paradigm, psyche, and professional identity-work. For that matter, so do evaluations of those evaluations; I can't say that I've always recognized the essay I thought I wrote in the way people have evaluated it, either. We should expect this, to some degree, but I appreciate the reminder that evaluations (and evaluations of evaluations) of autoethnographies work in a shared world, not at an Archimedean remove from what they evaluate, even if they don't always share its worldview.

I want to take the time to theorize this "shared world" by thinking about Jacques Lacan's frequent observation that "There's no such thing as a metalanguage" (e.g., 1975/1998, p. 118). Doing so will help me describe evaluation as a communicative materiality, an important step in making our performance of that materiality ethical and efficacious, that is, to make it useful for people in a fair way. Now, I know, in our shared world, that sometimes people read "Lacan" and tune out. I get that; sometimes people use his work in very cerebral ways that can feel disconnected from the physical emergencies of lived experience. And I certainly don't agree with everything he says, nor everything psychoanalysis maintains; but neither his specific body of work nor psychoanalytic literature in general agrees internally, so we're even. I don't particularly endorse the opposition of language and the body, the cerebral and the experiential, either (Gingrich-Philbrook, 2001). I'm not alone in this. Stacy Holman Jones and Tony E. Adams (2010) also argue that,

When we say, "No theory, no politics, just stories," we forget the differentiating, strange-making impulse of critical inquiry and scholarship. Instead of stories *or* theory, emotionalism *or* explanation, seeking *or* representation, aesthetics *or* knowledge, we need a language that unsettles the ordinary while spinning a good story. We need the shifting, refiguring, and excessive talk of *maybe,* about what *matters,* that says something *queer.* (p. 137)

My *experience* with reading *theory,* Lacan in particular, helps me explain why I resist that opposition so much. Lacan has held my attention since I read this sentence one afternoon in grad school: "The unconscious is the sum of the effects of speech on a subject, at the level at which the subject constitutes himself [or herself] out of the effects of the signifier" (1973/1978, p. 126). I lay down on the floor in the living room, hands over my face, and wept. I didn't care about the stinky old rug. I just bawled. I stayed on the floor for what seemed like hours, thinking, watching the light change in the room as twilight fell, and then the dark. Tears have a reasonably contested place in autoethnography and its evaluation, including my own evaluations. In "Family Values," I described autoethnography's sometimes extreme emotion as "emotional kitsch," likening some of it to "the big eyes on those sad little cats in dime store paintings" (p. 307).

I can be such an ass sometimes.

To be sure, there's something very privileged about being in grad school and having the kind of time to read and lie down for a good cry. And no, the tears we shed don't prove much, in themselves; I want that to be what I meant with that remark about the cats, and in the context of the essay it's a little more subtle than I'm portraying it here. When we write and evaluate autoethnographies, though, I think we forget that sometimes, not always, an episode like this signals a gestalt— an "aha" experience something like a cross between a light bulb popping on over one's head and being hit in the face with a water balloon: everything feels suddenly somehow different; we see an enormous pattern. Like looking at the Grand Canyon, we face the sublime and struggle to keep up with a new, unforeseen experience-of-understanding-experience that we may struggle for weeks, years, a lifetime to fully communicate to ourselves, let alone another person. The gestalt is the news, not the tears; however real they are, it's what they reveal that's worth marking as a writer and really looking for, as a reader, between the lines of a piece.

Lacan's observation about the unconscious and language acknowledged, like no one and nothing before it did for me, that everything I had heard and read was in me somewhere. Every homophobic slur and secret profession of love; every lullaby my mother sang and every news story about how an animal species whose name I had learned on a flash card faced extinction. The death of Harvey Milk; Harvey, who said, "You've gotta give 'em hope." My mother's strange stories about what God had told her about my birth, about how I would rise up and fight the Anti-Christ. My grandmother telling me that my father had died. Walt Whitman *and* Jerry Falwell; Joan Didion, Emily Dickinson, Jorie Graham, Virginia Woolf, *and* Anita Bryant. In a wet flash, I understood my odd combination of shyness and love of public speaking. I understood them as the material consequences of both feeling unwelcome in the day-to-day world as a queer kid with a love of language, and also enjoying the, as it turns out, somewhat conditional love of coaches and advisors who helped me learn to say things on platforms and stages, even if those things weren't always what they wanted to hear. In other words, I understood why I still felt hurt by words, still sensed in physical violence against me and others the words our bashers had heard about the disposability of queers. I think that's why I took the Villanova president's remarks about Tim so seriously, why they registered so deeply: I understood that their readers absorbed those words into the unconscious part of themselves that might perpetrate future violence and allow them to feel justified. I also can't let this paragraph end without noting how White the sources of my unconscious were at the time, how exclusionary my education was, how I've tried to rectify that in ways that will always feel belated.

So, yeah, my sense of Lacan is an embodied, material experience. That's why, in the midst of the email list discussion of the Villanova conference, I had his formula for fantasy, $\$ \diamond a$, tattooed on my left forearm, why I made it a part of my body (see "Lacanian Formula" if you're curious about what it means). While not every autoethnographer would put it this way, I feel drawn to the method because I feel stronger in the company of people offering a reflexive, albeit never exhaustive, account of the making and unmaking of their psyches in the course of material events; people navigating how others encourage them to understand themselves resisting the less useful understandings by writing back against the grain of the taken for granted; people reaching out in coalition to help others do so, too.

So when I read "There's no such thing as a metalanguage," I feel Lacan knock—no, *help*—theory off its pedestal into the world it incorrigibly shares *with* experience because it *is* experience. When we theorize autoethnography and try to create models for its evaluation, we have an experience of trying to think carefully about something that matters. Autoethnography may feel different from the experiences we *apply* it to, but our practice of it remains a human practice, just like getting a tattoo, adopting a child, taking a boat-trip, or losing a partner. It feels meta when we write about it, but it isn't, at least not in my reading of Lacan's perspective.

Further, we theorize in a shared world where we dispute *how* a given something matters, doing so in a language that can never achieve the collective understanding it craves. "To say that there is no such thing as a metalanguage is to say that the task of constructing such a universal discourse could never be completed" (Cutrofello, 2002, p. 142). Lacan's sentence fascinates me because it sounds as if it were speaking an observation from outside. It's pretty sure of itself, after all, with that "There's no such thing..." But if I take it seriously, from its own standpoint on the impossibility of getting outside of language existentially, experientially, I hear Lacan taking a situated stand, making a strong evaluation of our closure within language. He's willing to express his conviction without guarantee.

What we think of as evaluation, then, never stands above autoethnography. Instead, it always occurs alongside, on the same plane and in the same world as the autoethnographic work under consideration, whether it contests or reaches out to that work in coalition. Sometimes, perhaps even most times, it does a little of each in some ratio or synergy that different people experience as tipping more one way than the other. In more conversational terms, an evaluation always tells—whatever else we might say about it—"just another personal story."

I don't mean to minimize personal stories with that word "just." Why would I do that? I just told you a bunch of stories. Instead, I want to equalize autoethnography and its evaluation, ontologically and epistemically. Let me start by asking, "How does evaluation convince us otherwise? How do we come to believe that, merely by virtue of its being 'an evaluation,' it has an epistemic advantage over what it evaluates?" One way to answer this question involves thinking about time. As turns in larger cultural conversations about knowledge, the university, and strategies for inquiry, evaluations seem, by virtue of coming after autoethnographies, to possess the benefit of history and reflection. But the fact that an evaluation focuses on a given autoethnography does not guarantee that it stands in any epistemologically privileged temporal relation to it. Often, as many of us can attest, the evaluation can feel as if a pre-programmed machine had written it, merely reinforcing, through repetition, the always-already historically prior orienting values the autoethnographer hoped to respond to, critique, and disorient in the first place.

We can also answer this question by thinking about how a *person* becomes an *evaluator*. An evaluation seems to have an advantage because it comes from someone the orienting story of the academy has delegated/assigned a judgmental authority, asking that person to identify with that authority and to enact its sometimes arbitrary, although very consequential, prerogatives, enhancing or degrading a real living person's life chances (Goffman, 1963). A person in this role can simply say the insurgent, disorienting story has failed to make its case, like every other resistant story before it. It's kind of like how only the person temporarily fulfilling the role of "it" can tag someone in a game of tag. We agree to there being an "it" when we play the game. Certainly, we expect a person in this role to offer some good reasons for a claim that an autoethnography has failed, but if we feel the story told in the piece offends us, undermines our privilege, or threatens our love of the orienting story it contests, we may be too quick to accept any reason, rather than hold out for good reasons, to reject it. Any evaluation of autoethnography, then, is simply another story from a highly situated, privileged, empowered subject about something *he or she* experienced. To evaluate autoethnography in a genuinely useful way, you have to open yourself to being changed by it, to heeding its call to surrender your entitlement.

Now, at one level, this is terribly obvious, even as it is horrifically paradoxical. If I argued that the promise and logic of autoethnography demand an end to evaluation as we know it, I'd run into some trouble. Up close, let's think about this argument from the position of someone reading this Handbook for a course. Budding autoethnographers may very well want the reassurance of a checklist outlining things a good autoethnography does, the qualities it possesses, because that might help them decide when they have finished a piece they're working on. Wouldn't it be great to have a kind of cross between an existential oven-timer and a drag-queen fairy godmother to look over our shoulder at the screen and say, "Bing! You're done, Honey; this shit is *baked*; anyone tells you different, I will come over and stomp their ass"?

But such a checklist makes so much more sense as something developed over time and experience, something that changes and grows, adapts to different writers, writing different projects, for different purposes, at different times. Because we don't have an existential-oven-timer-drag-queen-fairy-godmother, we can confuse a checklist for a metalanguage, something universally endorsed. Too quickly, we can convert it into a magic contract for power relations with professors making and grading an autoethnography assignment, editors and their editorial reviewers making publication assessments, disciplinary committees making award judgments, colleagues writing tenure and promotion letters, and/or the administrators deliberating about what those letters and the publication record do or do not prove about a faculty member's likely future contributions to the goals their university has outlined in its mission statement—goals that, as we have seen, some (not all) administrators reinterpret or simply ignore when framing counterintuitive, prejudicial decisions about who gets to stay in the Big Brother House and who gets sent home.

Power relations appeal to our desire for such a contract, a desire to know what the rules are in order to avoid the punishment breaking them brings, a desire cultivated by decades of schooling. This desire confuses fairness in the face of difference with standardization and uniform procedures of anonymity and multiple points of evaluation. Anonymity, the orienting story tells us, encourages objectivity and the suspension of the reviewer's individual interests. But anonymity may just as easily shield interest and bias from accountability. Anonymity can sponsor the bomb in our mailbox, in other words; anonymity is sociality's off-hours, when anyone can slip us something lethal without many witnesses, the few who do exist themselves being sworn to secrecy. The anonymity of evaluations also helps them appear to come from a higher order of thinking; unsigned, they can appear to come as if from nature, as unassailable as a rock in the yard.

Evaluations also appear to have priority another way; they often come in a pack. The call for multiple points of anonymous evaluation, *in a way reminiscent of a quintessential logic of quantitative research,* wants to solve for outliers and their bias, eccentrically positive or negative assessments. In essence, someone, an editor or anyone with a vote who looks at a tenure file, "averages" assessments to see which responses dominate the results, as if we could more rationally trust the more popular response and central (that is, centric, rather than eccentric) tendencies in a set of evaluations. I don't mean that this is always "bad"; I just want to look at it plainly and examine its assumptions. Sometimes, often perhaps, someone looking at a tenure file or a set of article reviews has the good sense to throw out the review that needs to be thrown out, or to look past a crowd of dismissive reviews that offer few good reasons to see the lone positive review teasing out the real contributions of a piece or body of work that may seem unfamiliar to most readers.

But the fact that the process works sometimes doesn't mean that this preference for centrism shouldn't give those of us resisting the orienting story's common sense, in order to reveal the disorienting story's subjugated knowledge, some legitimate pause. Once we enter the territory of standing evaluative criteria for multiple anonymous evaluators to use, we may already have forfeited much of autoethnography's potential. Patricia Clough (2000) points to that forfeiture as a danger of what I would describe as accepting an orienting story about autoethnography:

> Of course, setting such criteria may only conventionalize experimental writing or make more apparent the ways in which experimental writing has already become conventional. It may become increasingly difficult to think that what has been called experimental ethnographic writing still is experimental. And so, the bad news is that in normalizing experimental writing, what may be forgotten is that experimental ethnography was once thought to be "bad" writing, improper sociology and inappropriate for publication in recognized sociological journals. (p. 278)

In other words, if some of the autoethnographies from the past were good even when they were viewed as bad, might some of the ones that are viewed as bad even now really be good?

However many evaluators consider the conventional/orienting value of an essay or body of work, then, whether the traditional three or one hundred, all may miss its improper/disorienting value to other readers. Consider some of those "other" readers whom the standing procedures don't require us to consult and who have never seen the checklist—publics and constituencies often given lip-service in the university mission statements that nominally guide tenure and promotion decisions. For example, it's hard to know how many of our disciplinary colleagues assign our essay; what the essay meant to how many students who read it, how many of them used it in their own writing, let alone if it made even one of them lie down and cry and figure something out. It's hard to know how many of those colleagues and students shared our essay with a friend, especially one outside the academy. We don't know who performed our essay on the public speaking/forensics competition circuit, or how their audiences felt about it. We don't know who talked with whom about our essay over coffee or a beer; after or before making love; with a parent or family member in an explanation or defense of their disciplinary choice that allows them to stay in a given major rather than face parental disapproval, and so on. I'm just scratching the surface here.

Instead, most evaluating practices measure the popularity of the piece in excruciatingly narrow ways that imagine every scholar knows every essay of every other scholar and makes an informed decision about what to cite or ignore. Given the explosion of outlets for scholarship that has attended the rise of a publish-or-perish mentality, fueled by a proliferation of delivery mechanisms and digitally based alternatives to print, this assumption is simply untenable (see Striphas, 2010). We try to keep up, of course; I'm not licensing tuning the conversation out because there are so many conversants. But still, even in the Fantasyland where we have read everything, *not* citing something we're aware of isn't always a vote against it; the piece may not be right for the nuanced focus we mean to create in our own essay.

In spite of all of this, many people have proposed sets of criteria for evaluating autoethnography. An important collection of these appeared as a special focus in an issue of *Qualitative Inquiry* (see Bochner, 2000; Clough, 2000; Denzin, 2000; Ellis, 2000; Richardson, 2000). Others have also entered the discussion (Faulkner, 2007; Pelias, 2011; Pollock, 1998; Spry, 2011). I honor those attempts to influence evaluation, at least in part because they move hesitantly, almost apologetically, slowly toward offering their version of what autoethnography should do. Pelias (2011) exemplifies the contingency with which these authors often speak:

> I wish to articulate what I like and what I don't without imposing my evaluative stance but acknowledging that I have one that guides my practice as a reviewer, teacher, and writer. I leave open the possibility of other evaluative and more productive schemes. (p. 666)

In a way, these generous attempts both want to and don't want to enhance inter-rater reliability. They ask, "How might we bring all of our judgments into alignment? How might we craft a metalanguage that knows it isn't one, so to speak?" Read them. They elaborate the aesthetics, ethics, and politics of representation in autoethnography in moving ways.

They also take various stands against the checklist, even as they give in and give the gift of sharing their own evaluative topoi, such as asking whether a piece tells a compelling story, shows more than it tells, treats others fairly, reflects on the privilege of the author, holds out hope, and/or changes the fortunes of the disenfranchised. The autoethnographic literature has no shortage of essays that tell the would-be practitioner what to do. We are soaking in advice about what to do before we click "print" that last time or go on stage with our stories. We don't always know what to do when, having done all of those things in craft's orienting story, things go to hell because someone feels otherwise about stories; refuses to see what we have shown; lies about our actions to characterize them as unfair, as victimizing the dominant culture; sees our self-reflexivity as a weakness to exploit or a sign that we won't fight back; has no interest in our hope; and/or prefers the disenfranchised to stay where they are, or to kneel down further, thank you very much.

Still, sometimes soaking in the good stuff isn't so bad.

3.

Tim likes to go float in the ocean at Venice Beach. He floats when he's happy; he floats when he's sad. Sometimes he, his partner Alistair, and their little dog Frida just walk along the shore. A California boy myself, I grew up loving the field of waves, feeling my body rise and fall among them, buoyed on the surface of their mystery. I taste the Pacific when Tim talks or writes about an afternoon soak, or whenever I think about her, really. I should apologize here, to those concerned by my gendering of the ocean this way; I can't hold a conception of the ocean as an "it" in my mind for very long before she becomes female again. I try to think critically about feminizing the Pacific, and yet there she moves, in my mind, full, generative, two-thousand miles west. Maybe I just see the ocean being so exploited and used as a dumping ground for so much of our metaphorical and literal shit that my ecofeminist leanings come rushing to the fore. I feel like we treat the ocean the way my stepfathers treated my mother; sooner or later, it will be difficult to recognize her, impossible to save her, but I hope we will keep trying.

As a kid, I wanted to become an oceanographer, specializing in ichthyological taxonomy. I loved the Latin names of fishes, each a little poem about their color, shape, or habits; or sometimes an homage to their so-called discoverer. I asked a ninth-grade English teacher why she corrected the word "fishes" to "fish" in one of my papers when the titles of my aquarium books always said "fishes." She did some research, sharing her discovery that "fishes" is appropriate when referring to more than one species. If I have twenty tuna, I have fish. If I have twenty tuna and a mackerel, I have fishes. "Fishes" marks a pluralist plural, then, reminding the reader to be alert to differences in the accumulating bodies in the intersecting schools.

With this history, I know full well that, at the very least, if the Pacific is not herself a being, she and the other oceans and seas with which she mingles and exchanges information teem with a variety of creatures. They engage in complicated evolutionary contests and partnerships, predatory and symbiotic and changing slowly over time as their struggles with and for one another converge and divide like the waves above them. I know that the diminishing number of these beings face the grave consequences of our indifference to their peril in a world where media coverage of ocean acidification is forty times less than the airtime devoted to this or that Kardashian and what she has done or said to this or that other Kardashian (Theel, 2012). *Forty times.* All around the world, whole cultures, ways of life, and species disappear, evaporate because we prefer some stories to others and apportion our attention accordingly. We sacrifice some possibilities for others, often, but not always, in the name of our own comfort or numbing distraction.

I know Tim cares about the ocean, and me, and certainly performance and the sharing of life stories; anyone who knows him knows how many people he looks after, checks in with, encourages. I know he knows I care about him, too, and about whether or not he and Alistair are safe in a country that won't allow them to marry, only settle for a civil union that won't protect Alistair from deportation the way marriage does the foreign-born spouses of straight folks. I know that his outspokenness about this—not just on his own behalf, but, and this is crucial, using his experience as a doorway to empathy with others—is, in part, what led to his banishment from Villanova as if we were living in some other century. The existential-oven-timer-drag-queen-fairy-godmother in me wants to shout, "Cue the torch bearers, Shug, because the ages are getting dark, AGAIN!" But I don't like that use of "dark" to signify a lack of intelligence, compassion, or simply wonder. It's racist. I've been trying to get that usage out of my head for twenty-five years. Talk about the sum effect of language upon the unconscious. Instead, I'll just say that the ages are getting mean.

The brutal evaluative politics of how stories come and go often naturalize their exclusions of important stories precisely on the grounds of these stories failing to become popular. Tim's performances aren't popular with very conservative Catholics, so he wasn't allowed to teach young Catholic students how to talk about their own lives, even if his workshop might help them tell the mysterious story of their experiences with faith—the unforeseen moments of answered prayers and comfort found in the grace extended by another person's forgiveness and understanding. Villanova excluded his stories about how to tell stories because the truth of Tim's life and his perspective made some uncomfortable. Many would rather hear about a family of marginal celebrities than how we're killing the ocean Tim floats on, let alone his stories about how the orienting story of heteronomativity damages so many lives. His stories and those ocean stories, stories about our shared stake in one another and the world in which we live, get pushed to the brink of intellectual extinction. This exclusion offers a microcosm for the macrocosm of biological extinction ahead of us on land and beneath the sea if we don't change our ways.

How, then, could these stories have the kind of "impact factor" that universities increasingly demand scholars prove, using the number of times someone has cited their work and the popularity of the journals in which that work appears? How could these stories, excluded from the get-go, demonstrate "persistence," the fact of being cited over a long period of time, when so many feel so licensed to turn away from them *before hearing them*? Autoethnographers recognize that, even if a statistic can't capture the power of the stories they tell, those narratives still accumulate. They form the patterns of interacting waves that constitute our fluid identities; animate our participation in dynamic, sometimes predatory, cultural contests; support our reaching out to create symbiotic coalitions to protect mutual values; and gesture toward the evolution of what we "know" about knowing over the passage of time. When one speaks about identity this way, it helps to remember that "fluid" doesn't mean immaterial or immune to history; and it certainly doesn't mean "gentle," particularly if one considers the rip tides formed when flows come together; the tsunamis generated by deep, sudden shocks and shifts; or the corrosive power of tides eroding a shore over the centuries.

Sometimes, hope has a Darwinian time-scale.

4.

It's the fourth of July, hot and sticky, and I'm trying to make sense of the orienting story of freedom. We're having a heat wave. I don't know whether it's tropical or not, but the temperature's rising; it isn't surprising if you've paid any attention at all to the disorienting story of climate change. I can sense this essay reaching that temporary closure that feels like an end, even though there will always be so much more to say. When I click "save" and go downstairs for a break before the proofreading begins, I have to go outside and change the water in the bucket I put out for the deer and other creatures. I haven't seen the fox again, but I'm hopeful setting out some water might make that more likely. When I see him or her this time, I'll try not to want anything, search for anything, but what the fox is becoming, what I am becoming, looking at the fox. I'll try not to look at the fox in a way that suggests I'm running, retreating in a mania to be elsewhere and distracted from the difficulty. I will try to live in the present. Perhaps, in setting this agenda for myself, I have already botched that project, or perhaps I've just recognized it as a possibility. We'll see how it turns out.

A friend of mine used to say that the only way out was through. I agree, but that isn't an excuse for unkindness or foolishness, my own or anyone else's. It doesn't cancel out this observation to acknowledge that telling the kind from the unkind often requires time, and that what once appeared foolish may later prove itself wise—or vice versa, for that matter. Evaluations (of evaluations) of autoethnographies tell just another story, often a very important story, but a story we should not grant any unearned advantage to speak about the value of someone's work for all of time. All real evaluation is formative; the summative evaluation is an artifact of particular constellations of power and ignorance about our immersion in dominant culture's illusory mastery of time. We'll see how I feel about that strong statement in a couple of years.

In talking about evaluations of autoethnography, it seems reasonable to me to ask evaluators to declare their biases, rather than letting those illusions simmer beneath the surface. I'm not a big fan of anonymous reviewing, for reasons I've explained, so, where possible, part of that disclosure of bias should, from my perspective, include the disclosure of the evaluator's identity so that her or his life-history isn't masked. When considering multiple reviews, administrators and editors should, in my perspective, give the benefit of the doubt to the survival of a story over its extinction or banishment, otherwise we'll end up with Kardashians, rather than turtles, all the way down. If, like Villanova, the university authorizing the evaluation of a body of an autoethnographer's work has a Mission Statement that includes phrases about things like diversity, mutual respect, and a commitment to critical thinking, administrators would do well to protect those values from being merely the orienting talk that masks their disorienting walk. The Mission Statement, rather like The Declaration of Independence, announces an intention, but it guarantees nothing unless we live up to its promise of breadth and protect the unpopular from the brutality or faddish pastimes of the majority.

Any evaluation that proceeds without attending to these principles is hypocritically flawed. I offer this perspective as someone much more comfortable avowing the identity of "autoethnographer" than I once was, knowing my perspective enjoys no entitlement to remain untroubled. Nonetheless, I reserve the right, sharing a world with, standing alongside friends and colleagues with whom I do not always agree, to join them in autoethnography's continuing commitment to trouble the disequilibrium in the distribution of entitlements. One of those entitlements, not the least among them, is the right to tell one's story.

I look forward to yours.

I hope you get to tell them.

Call me if anybody tries to stop you.

Dedication

For Carolyn.

References

Beardslee, W. A. (1990). Stories in the postmodern world: Orienting and disorienting. In D. R. Griffin (Ed.), *Sacred interconnections: Postmodern spirituality, political economy, and art* (pp. 163–175). Albany: State University of New York Press.

Bochner, A. P. (2000). Criteria against ourselves. *Qualitative Inquiry, 6,* 266–272.

Clough, P. T. (2000). Comments on setting criteria for experimental writing. *Qualitative Inquiry, 6,* 278–291.

Cutrofello, A. (2002). The ontological status of Lacan's mathematical paradigms. In S. Barnard & B. Fink (Eds.), *Reading Seminar XX: Lacan's major work on love, knowledge, and feminine sexuality* (pp.141–170). Albany: State University of New York Press.

Denzin, N. K. (2000). Aesthetics and the practices of qualitative inquiry. *Qualitative Inquiry, 6,* 256–265.

Ellis, C. (2000). Creating criteria: An ethnographic short story. *Qualitative Inquiry, 6,* 273–277.

Faulkner, S. L. (2007). Concern with craft: Using *Ars Poetica* as criteria for reading research poetry. *Qualitative Inquiry, 13,* 218–234.

Gingrich-Philbrook, C. (2001). Bite your tongue: Four songs of body and language. In L. C. Miller & R. J. Pelias (Eds.), *The green window: Proceedings of the Giant City Conference on Performative Writing* (pp. 1–7). Carbondale: Southern Illinois University.

Gingrich-Philbrook, C. (2012). ACT UP as a structure of feeling. *Quarterly Journal of Speech, 98,* 81–88.

Goffman, E. (1963). *Stigma: Notes on the management of spoiled identity.* New York: Prentice-Hall.

Goodstein, L. (2012, May 16). New fight on a speaker at a Catholic university. *The New York Times.* Retrieved from www.nytimes.com/2012/05/17/us/new-fight-on-a-speaker-at-a-catholic-university.html

Haley, G. (2012, June 27). Texas Republican Party seeks ban on critical thinking, other stuff. *Austinist*. Retrieved from austinist.com/2012/06/27/texas_republican_party_seeks_ban_on.php

Holman Jones, S., & Adams, T. E. (2010). Autoethnography and queer theory: Making possibilities. In N. K. Denzin & M. D. Giardina (Eds.), *Qualitative inquiry and human rights* (pp. 136–157). Walnut Creek, CA: Left Coast Press, Inc.

Lacan, J. (1978). *The four fundamental concepts of psycho-analysis*. (A. Sheridan, Trans.). New York: W. W. Norton. (Original work published 1973.)

Lacan, J. (1998). *The seminar of Jacques Lacan, book XX: On feminine sexuality, the limits of love and knowledge 1972–1973*. (J. Miller, Ed.; B. Fink, Trans.) New York: W. W. Norton. (Original work published 1975.)

"Lacanian Formula for Fantasy, The." The Boundary Language Project. Pennsylvania State University. Retrieved from art3idea.psu.edu/locus/fantasy_formula.pdf

Miller, T. (2012). The V effect. *Liminialities, 8*(2). Retrieved from liminalities.net/8-2/veffect.html

"Mission Statement." Office of the President. Villanova University. Retrieved from www1.villanova.edu/villanova/president/about_university/mission.html

Pelias, R. J. (2011). Writing into position: Strategies for composition and evaluation. In N. K. Denzin & Y. S. Lincoln (Eds.), *The SAGE handbook of qualitative research* (pp. 659–668). Thousand Oaks, CA: Sage.

Peterson, E., & Langellier, K. (1982). Creative double bind in oral interpretation. *The Western Journal of Speech Communication, 46*, 242–252.

Pollock, D. (1998). Performing writing. In P. Phelan (Ed.), *The ends of performance* (pp. 73–103). New York: New York University Press.

Richardson, L. (2000). Evaluating ethnography. *Qualitative Inquiry, 6*, 253–255.

Rose, H. (2012). Breathing, again. *Liminialities, 8*(2). Retrieved from liminalities.net/8-2/breathing.html

Spry, T. (2011). *Body, paper, stage: Writing and performing autoethnography*. Walnut Creek, CA: Left Coast Press, Inc.

Striphas, T. (2010) Acknowledged goods: Cultural studies and the politics of academic journal publishing. *Communication and Critical/Cultural Studies, 7*, 3–25.

Theel, S. (2012, June 27). "STUDY: Kardashians get 40 times more news coverage than ocean acidification. Media Matters for America. Retrieved from mediamatters.org/blog/2012/06/27/study-kardashians-get-40-times-more-news-covera/186703

Chapter 32

Twitch

A Performance of Chronic Liminality

Carol Rambo

I keep rewriting the opening. There is no opening because there is no closure. There is only falling through.

○

It is the spring of 1999; I have been in therapy for about a month. I am an incest survivor with a physically and sexually abusive father and a mentally disabled mother. I have done research and written on both topics (Rambo Ronai, 1995, 1997). One of my papers won an award. The other one got me featured on the cover of a magazine, written up in other major media outlets, and even got me a spot on CBS News's *Public Eye on America* with Bryant Gumbel. I am an "expert." Even though I just got tenure, I don't seem to be doing well. I have developed some embarrassing obsessions and compulsions, and I think about suicide often. I have decided to see a therapist in case my issues have to do with the incest (which I have never gotten treatment for; I never needed to). I expect that the psychological perspective will give me some tools to help me reframe my experience. As a qualitative sociologist, I have an "insider understanding" about what therapy is going to be like. A therapist is someone who will help me sort through my stories of self, weeding out the ones from the past that don't work so that I can internalize better stories that work for the present day. The therapist has given me a lot of books to read, and I am going through them rapidly. I am quite thrilled; I am doing well at this—A plus. Not that they give out grades or anything. If I just

Handbook of Autoethnography, edited by Stacy Holman Jones, Tony E. Adams, and Carolyn Ellis, 627–638. © 2013 Left Coast Press, Inc. All rights reserved.

read enough and really understand it, I know I can beat this thing. I'm really glad I came to see the therapist. Once I get through therapy (I know I'll get through it quickly), I'll be an even better writer than I was before. I just know it.

○

I am on a beautiful sailboat coming in from a spectacular day. The water is clear and blue green. The sensation of gliding, the breeze, the sunny cloudless sky, everything is beyond perfect. I am thoroughly happy; saturated with happiness. I haven't felt an inner peace this solid, ever. Everything is going to be all right.

As the boat comes in to dock, I ready myself to exit. Before I can put my foot on the dock, I fall backwards hard.

"I am so damn clumsy, I have spoiled everything," I think to myself.

Flailing, I crash through the bottom of the boat. As I sink backwards into the silent depths, for a split second I still see everything as beautiful. Then I panic at the falling debris and breathe water into my lungs. As I thrash about, above me, the remnants of the hole I fell through are rapidly dispersing, lost in the chaos of the boat splintering apart and sinking. I turn to swim towards the dock, but it, too, is splintering apart. I am drowning, lost in chaos, with the destroyed boat descending rapidly upon me and no idea which way to swim. I'm not going to make it. In a fit of stark terror, I wake up from this dream. I am never the same again. I am destroyed.

○

Knowing is the problem.

○

From 2008 to 2011, I was the editor-in-chief for the journal *Symbolic Interaction*. During that time, many authors submitted autoethnographic manuscripts for consideration. More than once, I had to write letters that contained something like the following:

Dear Autoethnographer,

I am inviting you to revise and resubmit. Your manuscript has an "under baked" quality to it. Sometimes this happens because a draft was handed in too early and the writing needs more work. At other times an author has not had adequate time to process the events in question. As a result, the author's voice becomes muddled, and his or her perspective lacks insight.

○

I let you know, for the sake of impression management, that I was recently an editor of an academic journal. I cloak myself in its legitimacy and whatever legitimacy that you, the reader, attribute to the academy itself. I am a tenured associate professor at a state university. I have so-called "quirks" I am going to write about that may not seem to match my professional identity. While I look over what

I have written and realize I am still dealing with shame, I strongly suspect my experience is more common than most would suppose. Exploring the nature of my experience gives me an insight into the inner workings of the social world that I might not have otherwise cultivated. But I am getting ahead of myself…

○

I am unsure I have the right to write about this topic. I may be writing about it too early, much like the authors I advised to revise and resubmit. Carolyn Ellis (1995) in her autoethnographic work about her husband's death kept a journal and collected other documents while the experience was going on. Only later, after his death and after she had some distance on the experience, did she attempt to sift through her notes and documents and write her book. One could argue that my lack of clarity about what is going on means that I do not, yet, have a workable, livable resolution to write about. So why write about this? I cannot even label it.

There are some experiences that take a long time to resolve, or they never resolve at all. That is the nature of them—they are chronically liminal. On the face of it, no story or situation is ever permanently resolved; the story can always be rewritten later, even when we think we have resolution (Ellis, 2009). Furthermore, others can rewrite them after our death. My perceived lack of resolution opens up a void that leaves me struggling to fill a narrative gap in my personal story line. A successful narrative would create boundaries and a definition of the situation. Definitions, in turn, provide useful formulas and recipes out of which to construct lines of action (Blumer, 1969). Right now, I still struggle with how to think and act towards what has been going on, even though I have been aware of it for well over ten years.

If I am mindful, if I am reflexive about the process of writing these experiences, I believe it is possible to give voice and representation to something that is in the active process of being "worked on." I have decided it is okay that I do not know what is "really" going on and that I may never know. I have decided it is okay for the reader to think I am lying or making it up (I have wondered if I am, too, why shouldn't he or she?). I have also decided that autoethnography and a layered account format is an excellent platform from which to explore the nature of Twitch and the experience of living with chronic liminality or "not knowing."

○

I kind of don't want to tell you about her—kind of. I wonder if writing about her is a form of prostituting her and I am pimping her out for your consumption, for a publication. I wonder how she feels about me writing this about her. I could ask her, but it is not that easy. Then there is the stigma; you will think differently of me after you read this. There are also questions I will not be able to answer. Is it multiple personality disorder (MPD), which has been reclassified as dissociative identity disorder (DID)? Is it an abreaction that has not worked its way through my body, a body memory that is kind of stuck? Is it Posttraumatic Stress Disorder (PTSD) with dissociative features? I am not sure. All of these have been suggested to me by therapists, including the idea that it is a dissociated personality fragment rather than a fully developed, separate personality. This is the neighborhood of concepts I am in if I wish to define what the topic of this chapter will be. But this chapter is also a short performance (Denzin, 2003; Pelias, 1999; Spry, 2011) of chronic liminality as I struggle with the psychoanalytic narrative and my own story line.

As I live from day to day, Twitch is compartmentalized away from me, not a problem—much. I decided to name her, to give her agency. But her name also reflects what she does. Every now and again she surfaces and I am afraid of what she will do. She has not been *too* weird, not gone *too far* over the line, nor has she ever put me into a social situation I could not handle. I used to hear a small childlike voice in my mind, several times a day, sometimes several times an hour, saying, "I want to die." I think that was her, back then, before I had any of the conceptual tools on board to attempt to frame the experience.

That was before I went into therapy to deal with the impact of being raised by my father, who was a sex offender (Rambo Ronai, 1995), and my mentally disabled mother (Rambo Ronai, 1997). My father has a long record of offending against children. My mother was tested by mental health care professionals and determined to have an I.Q. somewhere near 75. I am oddly fortunate that this documentation exists. Survivors of childhood trauma do not always have this kind of external validation for their memories.

Most of the time, I hardly know Twitch is here.

○

She curls through me, both inside and out. If I released totally into her, I might well be in a fetal position right now. A small sensation occurs first in my right shoulder (almost always the right shoulder), though sometimes it will show up as either of my hands flopping about. "It" is here; "she" is here. Then my right shoulder violently shrugs upwards towards my ear, involuntarily, a coiled, winding energy that has been sprung. When I release into it, the curling takes over, winding its way through more and more of my body.

I stop typing to feel for a moment. Both shoulders come up to my ears and both hands cross in front of my face. My head turtles into my chest. The coiling feels tighter and tighter, as if drawing me into myself. I cannot go with it for too long because it gets so tight I am physically uncomfortable and headed for pain. I consciously give myself permission to stop, and I do. I shake my head and arms and rotate my shoulders to get the feeling of the coiled energy out of my body. It is only then that "I" feel like I have control again.

I write, trying to be, and trying to describe. I kind of can't, I sort of can. The more I write like this, typing reflexively regarding my experience, the more she goes away. But she is here. She is a like a cat—if I am still, she might come out. I am not always sure I want her. She probably knows this.

○

I reread what I wrote above and my right shoulder twitches and my arms flail about wildly. If I reread it more, it happens more violently. I call this (as does the psychology literature) being "triggered." Twitch can be triggered by many things: the cold, a story of childhood sexual abuse, a story about a child being beaten, hearing someone describe her experience of something like Twitch, or thinking about Twitch for a while. Sometimes when I am deeply relaxed, she arises from seemingly nowhere. She does not typically use words to talk, yet I am sure she understands words just fine. I am not "understanding it" for her. She reacts energetically (through my body) to things she does not agree with (or things she does). In order to understand I must slow down, become quiet, and ask her (me?) why she reacted that way. The killer is, I usually agree with her in the final analysis. And yet I resist her.

I must emphasize my experience of this. I am not doing this; "it" is. The experience is of an "other." Not big drastic other. Not "movie of the week, I'm taking over the show" other. But other. To my horror, she has been triggered during class lectures. In one situation no one noticed. In the other, students wrote off what my body did as an extreme reaction to something one of them had said (and technically it was) and laughed. Twitch is not trying to destroy me.

Elements of Twitch were starting to show up before I went in for therapy. I was acting so oddly I could not fool myself that I was "okay" any more. Later, she showed up more overtly when I started therapy. For this reason I have often wondered if somehow, either by accident or on purpose, my therapist helped me to co-construct her into existence. There is a large literature on false memories, theoretically implanted by therapists (Loftus, 2003), so why not a "false entity?" I did not take this literature lightly; it could be that I had read so much that I had made this whole thing up and was somehow enacting a script, subconsciously. I hinted to a trusted friend about my experiences, and she suggested that it did not matter if it was real or not. That was also what my therapist said when I challenged him regarding it. "Just go with it," they both said. I took away from these interactions that the process of getting to a better place, whatever it took, was what was important. So I tried to relax and not worry...

○

It happens over and over again; in my therapist's office, at home in bed, or on the living room floor. I am choking, my throat shut, my shoulders pinned to the ground, this is happening "to" me. If I clamp down on all of it, I can stop it and come out of it, usually.

My therapist urges me to relax and not fight it. I shake my head then breathe in deeply and lie back down. I extend my arms out to my sides, palms up, and straighten my legs and let them drop open as I settle back on to the floor. It seizes me again, rolling me to the left, twisting to the right, tossing, turning, struggling, even as my shoulders stay pinned.

I pull out of it and start to weep, "What the fuck is this? What is wrong with me?" I question my therapist incessantly to see if he has ever had anyone in his office who acts like me. He reassures me he has.

He comments, "When things happen before there are words for them, sometimes the body remembers it where the mind does not. This is the body's way of telling the story."

"Why don't I know that people do this? Why isn't this commonly understood about how people are? Do you understand how freaky this is?" I ask.

He knowingly nods yes.

○

I cannot write about this without my throat closing up on me. I thought I had processed this, but it is still here. The punch line is simple, or so I thought. My father would straddle me, pinning my shoulders to the ground with his knees (I can clearly remember this; it was one of the regular ways he controlled me). He would tell my mother to go away or he would hurt her, too. At other times he did this when she was not there. He would choke me. I know that! Why isn't this over with? Why does my throat do this as I write? The idea is that once you figure it out, once you have the narrative, or the insight, you should be able to move on. Why can't I move on? Why does my body still do this to me?

○

Once you "know," the idea is that the reaction should be extinguished and the PTSD should become resolved. According to Joseph (2011, pp. 60–61):

> In a sense, extinction is like rewiring the connections in the brain. The reason that some people continue to suffer from posttraumatic stress is that they do not get this extinction experience. They understandably prefer to avoid reminders of their trauma—but what they miss out on is the experience of learning that these reminders no longer represent danger.

If I frame my experience as a reaction to my trauma history, then I am avoiding processing the trauma in such a manner that I can experience a successful "extinction" reaction. I believe I know what happened. Or even what probably happened. So why am I like this?

○

I have been told by a psychologist that the part of the self that is typically disowned and the hardest to get in touch with is the one that was helpless, the one that took the abuse. This part splits off (there are a number of ways it is described in the literature) because the child cannot contain the experience and exist in day-to-day life at the same time. It is physically overwhelming—too much stimulation for a child to process at the neurobiological level. What may be even more overwhelming for a child is living with the awareness that her parent, the one she is dependent on, may kill her. If that is the case then she has to live with the knowledge that she is alone in the world.

○

"A part splits off," Jeezus! Sounds like a bunch of shit to me—bull fucking shit.

○

Please do not think I do not see my aggression for what it is, a way to armor against and distance myself from what is going on. At the same time, it sounds like psychobabble—a part split off—give me a Goddamn break. I remember so much, so clearly. I was there. Don't tell me otherwise.

As I write, reread, and think about the events, it seems likely that my father could have forced oral sex on me. He sometimes coerced my mother into it, and he and my mother tricked me into it. This I remember.

○

We live in an abandoned house with no power or running water, on a Pennsylvania mountain in Amish country. There are two dumpsites near, one almost immediately outside the house, and one a little further from the house in the woods. The place is literally a dump.

It is likely that I am three or four years old. My father has me on the mattress, between his legs, masturbating him. The atmosphere has a veneer of "playfulness." My father and mother often gallivant through the house naked, laughing, only to collapse into a heap and have sex later. Sometimes I would just go on playing, while at others I would quietly go elsewhere, sensing that they could drag me into it. When I was included, sometimes it seemed loving enough that I participated willingly. At other times I didn't want to do what he wanted. This was one of those flashpoints at which I could get beaten; I had to be very careful. This particular time I am uneasy and suspicious. I don't want to do this, but I don't want to make him angry.

They instruct me regarding how to handle my father's penis. I don't want to handle it at all, but stroking it did not seem to be a big deal. Then my father says, "Put it in your mouth."

I say, "I don't want to."

He says in a tone that even I know is artificial, "It's fun." The tension is high, as if there is a rattlesnake in the room, but no one will speak of the snake for fear it will strike.

He continues the fake Mr. Rogers's happy voice as he says to my mother, "Tell her how she can do it, Suzy."

Perhaps nervous, perhaps oblivious, my mother laughs and says, "There's two ways you can do it. You can lick it like an ice-cream cone."

"Show her," he says, interrupting her. She makes a gesture with her hands and mouth, as if she is licking the sides of an ice-cream cone.

"Or you can suck it like a lollypop," she says, gesturing as if she were putting a whole lollypop into her mouth.

"Which would you like to do?" my father asks.

I do not want to do any of it, but I must be strategic. I decide that pretending it is an ice-cream cone is a much better idea because I know what comes out of the tip of that thing, and it ain't ice cream. Putting my mouth around his penis, like a lollypop, is just plain foolish; a good way to choke, and even more nasty than just licking it.

o

These are the facts as I remember them. I know he would chase me through the house, beat me, and/or have other kinds of sexual relations with me. I know this. I have these odd things my body does without my volition powering it. I have this swelling thing that happens in my throat. Why am I unable to accept that he probably forced me to perform oral sex on him? Nothing else explains this as well. That is the narrative many in the psychological community would expect to be the correct one.

I do not accept it because I cannot remember it. I refuse to claim that something happened when I cannot remember it. There are so many horrible things I have finally remembered clearly, why wouldn't I remember this?

o

I do not want this to be happening. I do want the insights that Twitch offers. I wish I could get around this process. There is usually a tremendous amount of affect with this experience. Put more simply, I cry hard for a long time.

When I am inside "it," depending on the events, I may choke or gasp, or struggle, or cry out. I have had the back of my head, neck, and shoulders jammed into the floor while the rest of my body was arched up off the ground, and my feet were scooting me backwards. Anything can go. At times it is difficult to stay with it and not hurt myself or my therapist. Later, when I cry, I feel how desperately alone and helpless I was in the situation. Inside remembering and crying, I feel it once again (or something similar, how can I know if the experience replicates what it was "really like"?).

I am an adult now. I am safe. My father is dead, but even if he were alive, he could not do those things to me anymore. Inside the safety, I can handle deep introspection and recall; it is no longer as threatening as when the abuse was originally occurring. All that is left are the feelings. When I allow the remembering and the crying, a piece of myself comes back to me and I am more than I was as a result. The world feels fresh and alive. Sounds, sights, and sensations have a crisp sharpness, intensity, and clarity; more so than in my day-to-day life. Present in the here and now, I have compassion for the kid I was (I was so little with no one to help me and no idea that I needed to or could ask for help). While I often think I am "fucked up," I have made choices that were the best ones I could make given the understandings and survival strategies I had cultivated living with that particular family. I did the best I could with what I had. With this comes a deep compassion that gets generalized to everyone. Like me, they, too, are doing the best they can with what they have. So many of us are screwed up disasters inside because we are not given safety and the space to process trauma and heal from it. These truths are both sad and beautiful.

○

Some experiences never come to a happy story-closing resolution—they are chronically liminal. The lack of a specific definition of the situation feels problematic; constantly open to question and speculation. Yet life goes on whether we have a satisfying story about what is happening that we can live with, or not. Many situations are chronically liminal. A partial list includes trying to identify the unknown source of a chronic pain or chronic illness, not knowing who your parents were, not knowing what happened to a child you regret placing for adoption, or not knowing if a lost loved one is dead or alive such as in the case of war, kidnapping, or natural disaster. In all of these situations there is the perception that a real answer can be known and the ability to know is blocked somehow. Perhaps the real problem is the concept of truth; the "real" source of the pain or illness may not be treatable by modern medicine, the "real" parents, child, or loved one may be dead, but there is no record of it. One can search or wonder all one's life when, in reality, nothing can be found, there is no explanation or label, the situation just is.

Furthermore, in a deeper sense—sociologically, psychologically, and linguistically—we are all doomed on any quest for the truth. Shopping for labels—DID, PTSD, body memories, abreactions, splinters, fragments—these are all sensitizing concepts, not "real" in any obdurate way. They are useful ideas to help sort and categorize experiences. The "tell" regarding how this works resides in the fact that the American Psychiatric Association keeps revising their Diagnostic and Statistical Manual of Mental Disorders (DSM) every few years based on the utility of the concepts for both clients and practitioners. Changing words and psychological paradigms evolve as they both "capture" and fail to capture lived experience in a Foucaultian sense.

Foucault's (2003) work emphasized the idea that knowledge was an expression of the power of society itself. With the medical "gaze" come medical words and frames that embody and animate individual subjectivity. By looking to "experts" for "the truth" about what is happening to me, it is as if I am seeking to sacrifice my freedom, my sovereignty, for the sake of the safety of a "definition." I want to be captured by the experts and have my experience ranked, spatialized, taxonomized, and tamed into submission. I keep trying to violently "pin it down" so to speak. But this will not happen.

As I spend time spinning my wheels, looking through the DSM IV and combing the internet and research papers for clues about what is happening to me, none of the descriptions I read match my experience precisely, anyway. People with DID are passive and have a lot of memory gaps and time they cannot account for. I do not fit that. The idea that I am having body memories or abreactions is not so farfetched, except, honest to God, Twitch is something I can dialogue with (or more to the point she/it dialogues with me). So if I take this search for a label to its conclusion, I am left wondering, "Am I the only one?" or "Am I somehow making this up?" Two therapists have said no. So there is no closure even there, only the validation that something is "up."

So am I just stuck? Am I writing this article too early? Will the story of my situation always be in a perpetual state of "revise and resubmit?" Or has the psychological community left me out of their categorization schemes? Do they need to "revise and resubmit?" Foucault might tell me to enjoy the openness, the freedom, the fact that I don't know, and the fact that the situation is in play. In other words, I should not worry about it. But it is not that easy.

Another difficulty I have working with this aspect of myself is the culture I find myself located in. I am afraid of the stigma. According to Goffman (1963) a person with stigma "is thus reduced in our minds from a whole and usual person to a tainted, discounted one....It constitutes a special discrepancy between virtual and actual social identity" (p. 3). I have the ability to write this with some safety because of my position in the academy—I am tenured. But at the same time there is a disjuncture between what I present to the world and what I have chosen to keep to myself all these years. I am afraid of the consequences of what others might think. This is part of my motivation for writing this; I should not be afraid. Being afraid keeps us quiet. Keeping quiet keeps this out of the mainstream discourse. Everyone should know that these kinds of things happen—many of the psychologists and psychiatrists do. By writing about Twitch, I hope to help bring the experience out of the ghettoization of analysts' offices and the marginalizing discourse of psychoanalysis and into the normalizing light of day.

Body memories, abreactions, and DID are considered by the psychological community to be normal reactions to trauma, yet they are pathologized. According to the literature (see David Baldwin's Trauma Information Pages for an exhaustive collection of articles on trauma and its effects [www.trauma-pages.com]) these are some of the ways that the body deals with the overwhelming stimulation that accompanies a traumatic event. The body records the trauma experience, but the mind does not have the time or ability to process it all at once. In a life or death situation, the mind must concentrate on staying alive. The experience is still recorded, but not processed. Later, when the crisis has passed, the mind and body attempt to process the trauma. When the mind will not let it happen, the body persists in trying to process it anyway. PTSD, which can include invasive flashbacks, abreactions, and more, results when the attempts to process the trauma are blocked

(Gradus, 2007). Alcoholism and drug abuse are methods of self-medicating away the discomforts that arise from this struggle.

These normal responses to trauma are problematic; they interfere with the smooth functioning of social interaction. It is more efficient in a modern production and consumption driven society to pull the individuals in question out of the society and put them into "therapy," "treatment," or even hospitalize them. This specialization and marginalization not only sequesters the individual from the group, it also sequesters the knowledge from the group. Other cultures, usually ones considered to be "primitive," that move at a slower pace (such as Shamanistic cultures), make room for these experiences. The knowledge about the effects of trauma is part of the participants' everyday understandings. Trauma survivors are embraced as they participate together in specific rites and rituals that bring the community together for the sake of healing an individual in distress. There is no stigma, no need to hide. There is acceptance.

My so-called "quirks" are not so quirky. Childhood trauma is quite common (for statistics see the website for the National Child Traumatic Stress Network). Trauma touches most of our lives at one time or another. PTSD is also common, and with soldiers returning to their homes from wars all over the globe, its incidence promises to become even more prevalent (Gradus, 2007). I do not pretend that I can generalize my experience to all trauma survivors. I am willing to speculate that many people have aspects of themselves, like Twitch, that are disowned. They surface in these people's daily lives as extreme aversive reactions or more subtle unconscious biases. They are little bits and pieces of unprocessed trauma, impacting people's consciousness and their lives. Sex and violence in movies, drugs, alcohol, video games, sports, television, and most other forms of consumption that I can think of are artifacts of a culture built up around anesthetizing the pains, small and large, of unprocessed stress and trauma.

Near the opening of this chapter, when discussing chronic liminality, I stated, "A successful narrative would create boundaries and a definition of the situation." Maybe the search for the story is "the problem" at times. Maybe there is too much closure already, where I "think" I know but I do not. Maybe success, for now, is leaving my story open and not creating boundaries.

References

Blumer, H. (1969). *Symbolic interactionism: Perspective and method*. Berkeley: University of California Press.

Denzin, N. K. (2003). *Performance ethnography: Critical pedagogy and the politics of culture*. Thousand Oaks, CA: Sage.

Ellis, C. (1995). *Final negotiations: A story of love, loss, and chronic illness*. Philadelphia: Temple University Press.

Ellis, C. (2009). *Revision: Autoethnographic reflections on life and work*. Walnut Creek, CA: Left Coast Press, Inc.

Foucault, M. (2003). *The birth of the clinic.* London: Routledge

Goffman, E. (1963). *Stigma: Notes on the management of spoiled identity.* London: Penguin.

Gradus, J. (2007). Epidemiology of PTSD. *United States Department of Veteran's Affairs.* Retrieved December 28, 2011, from www.ptsd.va.gov/professional/pages/epidemiological-facts-ptsd.asp

Joseph, S. (2011). *What doesn't kill us: The new psychology of posttraumatic growth.* New York: Basic Books.

Loftus, E. (2003). Make believe memories. *American Psychologist, 58,* 867–73.

Pelias, R. J. (1999). *Writing performance: Poeticizing the researcher's body.* Carbondale: Southern Illinois University Press.

Rambo Ronai, C. (1995). Multiple reflections of childhood sexual abuse. *Journal of Contemporary Ethnography, 23,* 395–426.

Rambo Ronai, C. (1997). On loving and hating my mentally retarded mother. *Mental Retardation, 35,* 417–432.

Spry, T. (2011). *Body, paper, stage: Writing and performing autoethnography.* Walnut Creek, CA: Left Coast Press, Inc.

Chapter 33

A Glossary of Haunting

Eve Tuck and C. Ree

Act so that there is no use in a centre. A wide action is not a width. A preparation is given to the ones preparing. They do not eat who mention silver and sweet. There was an occupation. A whole centre and a border make hanging a way of dressing. This which is not why there is a voice is the remains of an offering. There was no rental.

Gertrude Stein, Rooms, Tender Buttons, *1914 (2007), p. 39*

The derealization of the 'Other" means that it is neither alive nor dead, but interminably spectral.

Judith Butler, Precarious Life, *2006, p. 33*

Ghosts are never innocent: the unhallowed dead of the modern project drag in the pathos of their loss and the violence of the force that made them, their sheets and chains.

Avery Gordon, Ghostly Matters, *1997, p. 22*

Handbook of Autoethnography, edited by Stacy Holman Jones, Tony E. Adams, and Carolyn Ellis, 639–658. © 2013 Left Coast Press, Inc. All rights reserved.

A

Alphabet of terms

This is a glossary written by two women, both theorists and artists, in the first person singular. A glossary ordinarily comes after a text, to define and specify terms, to ensure legibility. Glossaries can help readers to pause and make sense of something cramped and tightly worded; readers move from the main text to the back, and forth again. In this case, the glossary appears without its host—perhaps because it has gone missing, or it has been buried alive, or because it is still being written. Maybe I ate it. It has an appendix, a remnant, which is its own form of haunting, its own lingering. This glossary is about justice, but in a sense that is rarely referenced. It is about righting (and sometimes wronging) wrongs; about hauntings, mercy, monsters, generational debt, horror films, and what they might mean for understanding settler colonialism, ceremony, revenge, and decolonization. In the entries of this glossary I will tell the story of my thinking on haunting. Yet this glossary is a fractal; it includes *the particular and the general*, violating the terms of settler colonial knowledge which require the separation of the particular from the general, the hosted from the host, personal from the public, the foot(note) from the head(line), the place from the larger narrative of nation, the people from specific places. This glossary is a story, not an exhaustive encyclopedia (which is itself a container), and this story includes my own works of theory and art as well notations on film and fiction. It is a story that seethes in its subtlety—the mile markers flash-faded instantly from exposure. Pay close attention, and then move very far away. I am only saying this once.

Am I telling you a story?

In telling you all of this in this way, I am resigning myself and you to the idea that parts of my telling are confounding. I care about you understanding, but I care more about concealing parts of myself from you. I don't trust you very much. You are not always aware of how you can be dangerous to me, and this makes me dangerous to you. I am using my arm to determine the length of the gaze.

At the same time that I tell, I wonder about the different endings, the unfurled characters, the lies that didn't make it to the page, the anti-heroes who do not get the shine of my attention. Each of the entries in this glossary is a part of the telling. Together, they are the tarot—turn this one first, and one divination; turn another first, and another divination. Yes, I am telling you a story, but you may be reading another one.

American horror, as depicted in film

This is what I can't help but notice. Mainstream narrative films in the United States, especially in horror, are preoccupied with the hero, who is perfectly innocent, but who is assaulted by monstering or haunting just the same. Part of the horror of US horror films is the presumed injustice that a monster or ghost would tamper with the life of a decent person. We, the audience, are meant to feel outrage in the face of haunting, we are beckoned to root for the innocent hero, who could be us, because haunting is undeserved, even random. The hero spends the length of the film righting wrongs, slaying the monster, burying the undead, performing the missing rite, all as a way of containment. This story arc has the same seduction as math, a solution to the problem set of injustice. The crux of the hero's problem often lies in performing that mathematics. Chainsaw the phantom + understand the phantom = a return to the calm of our good present day…Until the next breach, which triggers the next round of problem solving.

Select recent Japanese horror films disrupt the logic of righting past injustice or reconciliation, instead invoking a strategy more akin to wronging, or revenge. In *Dark Water*, Hideo Nakata's popular 2002 Japanese horror film (discussed in more detail in this glossary under entry **D, Dark Water**), an unsubdued and vengeful ghost haunts tenants in a leaking apartment building—in particular a newly single mother and her daughter, whose relationship the ghost covets and resents. At the end of the film, to spare her own daughter, the mother accepts the inevitability of the haunting and assumes the role of the ghost's mother; her daughter, in turn, suffers the same maternal abandonment that triggered the first ghost's horrific fury; rather than a heroic slaying, there is an anti-heroic relinquishing. Rather than resolution, deferment.

Similarly, in *Ringu* (Nakata, 1998) and its American remake *The Ring* (Verbinski, 2002), the main character, again a mother, attempts and fails to put a ghost spirit to rest. In the films, a mother and son watch a viral video of disturbing imagery which contains another sort of contagion: A vengeful ghost of a murdered girl turns the act of seeing her trauma into a violent curse, and anyone who views it dies horrifically a week later. As part of the main character's desperate search to save her son, she uncovers the story of the girl's psychic powers and the murder by her fearful father, finds her body in a well and properly buries it; however, the ghost is unappeased by ceremonial closure and continues to kill. The mother discovers the only way the ghost will spare someone is to copy the tape and make sure yet another person sees it, all of which the mother frantically prepares to do at film's end.[1] Until every person has witnessed the tape, the curse continues. At work is a logic of personal rescue through social contamination, a twisted outcome. Rather than spectral containment, spectral dissemination.

The difference between notions of justice popularized in US horror films and notions of justice in these examples of horror films from Japan is that in the former, the hauntings are positioned as undeserved, and the innocent hero must destroy the monster to put the world in balance again (though predictably, several of the hero's companions who are women or people of color will likely be sacrificed along the way). In the latter, because the depth of injustice that begat the monster or ghost is acknowledged, the hero does not think herself to be innocent, or try to achieve reconciliation or healing, only mercy, often in the form of passing on the debt.

American anxieties, settler colonial horrors

Colonization is as horrific as humanity gets: genocide, desecration, poxed-blankets, rape, humiliation. Settler colonialism, then, because it is a structure and not just the nefarious way nations are born (Wolfe, 1999), is an ongoing horror made invisible by its persistence—the snake in the flooded basement. Settler colonial relations are comprised by a triad, including a) the Indigenous inhabitant, present only because of her erasure; b) the chattel slave, whose body is property and murderable; and c) the inventive settler, whose memory becomes history, and whose ideology becomes reason. Settler colonialism is the management of those who have been made killable, once and future ghosts—those that had been destroyed, but also those that are generated in every generation. "In the United States, the Indian is the original enemy combatant who cannot be grieved" (Byrd, 2011, p. xviii). Settler horror, then, comes about as part of this management, of the anxiety, the looming but never arriving guilt, the impossibility of forgiveness, the inescapability of retribution.

Haunting, by contrast, is the relentless remembering and reminding that will not be appeased by settler society's assurances of innocence and reconciliation. Haunting is both acute and general; individuals are haunted, but so are societies. The United States is permanently haunted by the slavery, genocide, and violence entwined in its first, present and future days. Haunting doesn't hope to change people's perceptions, nor does it hope for reconciliation. Haunting lies precisely in its refusal to stop. Alien (to settlers) and generative for (ghosts), this refusal to stop is its own form of resolving. For ghosts, the haunting is the resolving, it is not what needs to be resolved.

Haunting aims to wrong the wrongs, a confrontation that settler horror hopes to evade. Avery Gordon (1997) observes,

> Haunting is a constituent element of modern social life. It is neither premodern superstition nor individual psychosis; it is a generalizable social phenomenon of great import. To study social life one must confront the ghostly aspects of it. This confrontation requires (or produces) a fundamental change in the way we know and make knowledge, in our mode of production. (p. 7)

Social life, settler colonialism, and haunting are inextricably bound; each ensures there are always more ghosts to return.

B

Beloved

As a young child, Beloved was killed by a mother determined to free her from slavery. Now grown, she returns to haunt the broken bits of her family, first as an angry house spirit, then later as a stranded young woman, whom they take in, drawn by a strange attraction to her. Furious, plaintive, consuming, wheedling, childlike, clever, Beloved's haunting is no ordinary rattling. Hers is a familial possession, a cleaving of her hungry violent soul to theirs. As Beloved's insatiability grows, her mother wastes away to feed the lost child she finally recognizes with gifts, food and attention. Beloved seduces her stepfather who can no longer stop his nightmares of slavery from crashing into his waking thoughts. They are avoided by the rest of town who know about the monstrous mother and her ghost child. As Toni Morrison's (1987) novel layers fragments of voices, memories, and dreams, the violent past and the haunted present seep into the narrative until it is slavery itself in its multiplying psychic forms that haunts the family and readers, the horror and haunting of today. Beloved is not a ghost appeased by remembering, nor a ghost to erase. In the end, a now pregnant Beloved disappears amidst the confusion of a visit from a group of concerned women and her mother's flashback of a slave owner's return. Morrison ends her story with a note on circulation and silence: "This is not a story to pass on" (1987, pp. 274–275).

But why haunting?

Haunting is the cost of subjugation. It is the price paid for violence, for genocide. Horror films in the United States have done viewers a disservice in teaching them that heroes are innocent, and that the ghouls are the trespassers. In the context of the settler colonial nation-state, the settler hero has inherited the debts of his forefathers. This is difficult, even annoying to those who just wish to go about their day. Radio ads and quips from public speakers reveal the resentment some settlers hold for tribal communities that assert claims to land and tribal sovereignty. This resentment seems to say, "Aren't you dead already? Didn't you die out long ago? You can't really be an Indian because all of the Indians are dead. Hell, I'm probably more Indian than you are." Sherman Alexie (1996) warns, "In the Great American Indian novel, when it is finally written, all of the white people will be Indians and all of the Indians will be ghosts" (p. 95).

Erasure and defacement concoct ghosts; I don't want to haunt you, but I will.

C

Composite narrator/Combined-I

I chose to write in the first person singular to double-fold my wisdom and mask my vulnerabilities. I use the bothness of my voice to misdirect those who intend to study or surveil me. My voice is thus (and always was anyway) idiosyncratic, striated, on the brink. When I write to you, it is sometimes to you, the other woman, and other times it is to you, my reader. I am a becoming-specter, haunting and haunted, a future-ghost, a cyclops, a stain.

Cyclops

She is the monster blinded by the heroic sea explorer Odysseus who eyes the Cyclopes' island and sheep for himself. In Homer's telling, the Cyclopes are a race of gigantic one-eyed cave dwellers, man-eating, barbaric, and easily fooled. Odysseus bamboozles the Cyclops, robs her sheep, maroons her in blindness, betrays her with language ("Nob'dy has destroyed me!"), and becomes celebrated for centuries for his conquests. One the classic monster, the other the epic hero, names easily twisted into cannibal and provider, native witch and colonizer, pre-modern and modern, unsettler and settler.

In my telling, the Cyclops's story is a revenge story. She is the anti-hero, anti-host. She wants to be left alone. Her enormous eye sees through deceptive Odysseus who feigns codes of hospitality to receive the sheep as gifts. She will keep her land and sheep out of reach, a thing of myth. She does things that are monstrous to violate the colonizer and to wage vengeance for future ghosts, none of which is legible to Homer. Invaders want to be hosted; she will imprison them in her cave. Hungry Odysseus dreams of stealing her beloved sheep; she will devour his beloved men with wine. But…

Let me tell you the end of this story again, from my mouth. While Odysseus is happily restored at home and publicly celebrated, the Cyclops's story continues. She walks the vastness of his kingdom, slowly becoming a ghost. Her emptied socket becomes a mask. Her revenge feeds her, making her opaque, anti-gravity, a black hole. Odysseus is blind to her, no longer able to see the Cyclops as when he coveted her land and food. She hides in plain sight and crafts her haunting. She will orphan Odysseus as she has been orphaned, but not of family, land or body. She will strand Odysseus in constant unease, bereft of his cherished and clever reason. His house will leak. The walls will sag. He will dream of sheep. He and everyone around him will forget his name; he will become an unremarkable shadow of Nob'dy, the clever alibi and source of his fame.

Revenge requires symmetry with the crime. To the (purported) (would-be) hero, revenge is monstrous, heard but not seen, insatiable, blind with desire, the Cyclops robbed of her eye. To the self-designated hero, revenge hails a specter of something best forgotten, a ghost from a criminal past.

To the monster, revenge is oxygen.

D

Dark Water, v.5

I made *Dark Water*, a series of art installations, in response to Hideo Nakata's popular 2002 Japanese horror film of the same title, in which a persistent ceiling leak in a new apartment is not only a yellow stain on the fantasy of a fresh start for a single mother and child; the leak's increasing seepage and its migration toward the mother's bed threaten to reveal an unfathomable and supernatural horror

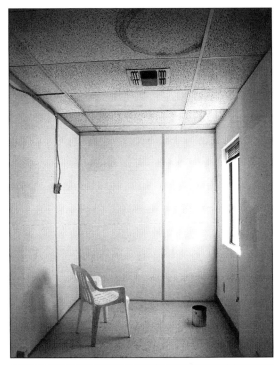

Figure 33.1
Dark Water, v.2, 2009—
school trailer, water, bucket.
Photo by author C. Ree.

Figure 33.2
Dark Water, v.5, 2010—
suspended ceiling, water,
buckets. An installation piece
that remade a portion of the
gallery's suspended ceiling.
Over the course of two weeks,
fifteen gallons of water slowly
leaked through the ceiling
fragment into buckets below.
The show culminated with the
ceiling's collapse.
Photo by author C. Ree.

residing directly above. Nakata's simple device of the leak expresses the horror of walls transgressed, physical structures made permeable and violated of their visual promise of protective boundaries. *The roof over our heads* suddenly becomes the very source of a profound anxiety.

The inception of the leak in *Dark Water* (the film) is the return of a furious ghost accidentally drowned while left unattended by a working mother. The child-ghost's possessive rage first presents as a leak and crescendos in a tidal wave of water emanating from the walls, ceilings, elevators, and plumbing, a deluge representing the ghost's uncontainable weeping rage. The entire building gushes through its pores with the ghost's inexorable will to subvert the main character's mother-daughter bond. At the same time, worldly conditions have already initiated a different sort of encroachment on the relationship between mother and daughter—a job with long hours at odds with school pickup times, school leaders who criticize her daughter's behavior as a symptom of living with a single working mother, and a hostile divorce in progress with custody over the daughter as the central dispute.

In the culmination of the film, as a means of saving her child, the main character resigns herself to joining rather than vanquishing the ghost. Abandoning her daughter and her former life, she enters a quasi-spectral alternate realm to become the lost mother the ghost has craved all along, thereby bartering a sort of truce. Mothering the ghost becomes a way to live with ghosts.

Nakata recasts social dysfunction and common anxieties as symptomatic of everyday ruins. His film suggests no resolution to these hauntings but rather coexistence, deferral, and even an embrace of this anxiety. Nakata's horror connects everyday dysfunction, historical violence, the paranormal and the futility of conquering the dead.

My art installation (*v.2, 2009*) in response to *Dark Water* began as a carefully placed drip from my studio ceiling, at the time located in a trailer (the sort used in overcrowded public schools) on a university campus. The moment water seeped through the ceiling, the leak marked the school site as an everyday space of possible horror and dysfunction. Constructed yet also really seeping water, the leak caused visitors to question whether the space was an artwork or a living, breathing problem. It was this disturbance of certainty into openings for horror and anxiety that became the heart of the *Dark Water* works.

Since then, the seed idea of the *Dark Water* installation has been mutating into different pieces that activate misrecognition, ruin, and the fantastic—works which inflect our surroundings with the horror and irrational of the everyday, which glance sideways at specters and the sociological traumas that they haunt. In *Dark Water v.5 (2010)*, I installed a floating ceiling beneath the gallery ceiling and dripped fifteen gallons of water slowly over the course of two weeks; eventually the water-logged floating ceiling collapsed into a monumental heap. As in the first installation, visitors alternately walked unawares below, or with alarm at the "water problem," or in confusion as to what and how the thin filament of ceiling could leak.

The experience of misrecognition by those who saw the installations is important to me. I want to confront them with the presence of a site that is simultaneously a ruin and a remake, is haunted and haunting, is horrific and very plain, that foregrounds the Now of dripping and the slow stuttering time of grasping at comprehension as buckets fill with water, a place "we do not yet or no longer understand" (Abbas, 2010). I want you to sense the unrecognizable as you might experience seepage, to see the coordinates of the familiar change from underneath and overhead, to trouble the real into a space that momentarily houses ghosts and into a time and place that is unexplainably urgent.

Decolonization

As much as the discourse of decolonization has been embraced by the social sciences over the last decade, the decolonial project rarely gets beyond the conceptual or metaphorical level. I want to slip a note into some people's pockets, "Decolonization is not metaphor," because at some point, we're going to have to talk about returning stolen land. My guess is that people are going to be really reluctant to give up that ghost. Fanon (1963) told us that decolonizing the mind is the first step, not the only step. Decolonization necessarily involves an interruption of the settler colonial nation-state, and of settler relations to land. Decolonization must mean attending to ghosts, and arresting widespread denial of the violence done to them. Decolonization is a recognition that a "ghost is alive, so to speak. We are in relation to it and it has designs on us such that we must reckon with it graciously, attempting to offer it a hospitable memory *out of a concern for justice*" (Gordon, 1997, p. 64, emphasis original).

Decolonization is a (dearly) departure from social justice. Honestly, I just sometimes have trouble getting past that phrasing, "social justice." Listing terrors is not a form of social justice, as if outing (a) provides relief for a presumed victim or (b) repairs a wholeness or (c) ushers in an improved social awareness that leads to (a) and (b). That is not what I am doing here, saying it all so that things will get better. Social justice is a term that gets thrown around like some destination, a resolution, a fixing. "No justice, no peace," and all of that. But justice and peace don't exactly cohabitate. The promise of social justice sometimes rings false, smells consumptive, like another manifest destiny. Like you can get there, but only if you climb over me.

Desire

Damage narratives are the only stories that get told about me, unless I'm the one that's telling them. People have made their careers on telling stories of damage about me, about communities like mine. Damage is the only way that monsters and future ghosts are conjured.

I am invited to speak, but only when I speak my pain (hooks, 1990). Instead, I speak of desire. Desire is a refusal to trade in damage; desire is an antidote, a medicine to damage narratives. Desire, however, is not just living in the looking glass; it isn't a trip to opposite world. Desire is not a light switch, not a nescient turn to focus on the positive. It is a recognition of suffering, the costs of settler colonialism and capitalism, and how we still thrive in the face of loss anyway;

the parts of us that won't be destroyed. When I write or speak about desire, I am trying to get out from underneath the ways that my communities and I are always depicted. I insist on telling stories of desire, of complexity, of variegation, of promising myself one thing at night, and doing another in the morning. Desire is what we know about ourselves, and damage is what is attributed to us by those who wish to contain us. Desire is complex and complicated. It is constantly reformulating, and does so by extinguishing itself, breaking apart, reconfiguring, recasting. Desire licks its own fingers, bites its own nails, swallows its own fist. Desire makes itself its own ghost, creates itself from its own remnants. Desire, in its making and remaking, bounds into the past as it stretches into the future. It is productive, it makes itself, and in making itself, it makes reality.

E

Equinox, by Joy Harjo, an excerpt[2]

> *I must keep from breaking into the story by force*
> *for if I do I will find myself with a war club in my hand*
> *and the smoke of grief staggering toward the sun,*
> *your nation dead beside you.[3]*

F

Future ghost

I am a future ghost. I am getting ready for my haunting.

M

Making-killable

I recently had a wonderful visit with Donna Haraway who suggested I consider the process of making-killable (as well as interspecies ethnography) when it comes to my Cyclops and her cave of sheep. Haraway and others describe making-killable as a way of making sub-human, of transforming beings into masses that can be produced and destroyed, another form of empire's mass production. Making-killable turns people and animals into always already objects ready for violence, genocide, and slavery.

Mercy

Mercy is a temporary pause in haunting, requiring a giver and a receiver. The house goes quiet again, but only for a time. Mercy is a gift only ghosts can grant the living, and a gift ghosts cannot be forced, extorted, seduced, or tricked into giving. Even then, the fantasy of relief is deciduous. The gift is an illusion of relief and closure. Haunting can be deferred, delayed, and disseminated, but with some crimes of humanity—the violence of colonization—there is no putting to rest. Decolonization is not an exorcism of ghosts, nor is it charity, parity, balance, or forgiveness. Mercy is not freeing the settler from his crimes, nor is it therapy for the ghosts. Mercy is the power to give (and take). Mercy is a tactic.[4] Mercy is ongoing, temporary, and in constant need of regeneration. Social justice may want to put things to rest, may believe in the repair in reparations, may consider itself an architect or a destination, may believe in utopic building materials which are bound to leak, may even believe in peace. Mercy is not any of that. Mercy is just a reprieve; mercy does not resolve or absolve. Mercy is a sort of power granted over another. Mercy can be merciless.

Monsters

People who deny the persistence of settler colonialism are like the heroes in American horror films, astonished that the monster would have trouble with them. Denial is a key component of the plotlines, the evil might get you if you look too deeply at the horror. You can only look between fingers on a hand that covers your eyes.

The promise of heroic resolution is a false assurance. Revenge films provide another more useful storyline for addressing the following questions: What is a monster? (A monster is one who has been wronged and seeks justice.) Why do monsters interrupt? (Monsters interrupt when the injustice is nearly forgotten. Monsters show up when they are denied; yet there is no understanding the monster.) How does one get rid of a monster? (There is no permanent vanquishing of a monster; monsters can only be deferred, disseminated; the door to their threshold can only be shut on them for so long.)

~~Mother~~

~~Somewhere between monsters and mutual implication.~~

Mutual implication

Mutual implication, or *nos-otras*, is a way of describing how the colonized and the colonizer "'leak' into each other's lives" (Torre & Ayala, 2009, p. 390, citing Anzaldúa, 1987) after centuries of settlement. Mutual implication is evidenced by *leaking*.

Agent O [prelude]

I am Agent O and she is mine. I made her in order to theorize a different sort of justice—one that dismantles, one that ruins—in the flesh. In this ongoing art and performance work, Agent O is embodied and makes appearances in mundane places, aiming to unsettle them. I made her, but she is already outside of me.

I created Agent O to be both law and transgression (Morrison, 1993), to dig with her fingernails to unearth the relationship of psychic-paranormal knowledge to state-official knowledge. Though her body takes different forms, Agent O is an elderly psychic woman produced through exposure to Agent Orange as a child in Vietnam, and now passes time as a corner psychic advising on simpler affairs. Agent O is a symbol of the constitutive nature of wartime, peacetime, state control, and apocalypse in everyday life.

Agent O is part monster, part residue of war, part paranormal figure outside of law, part opaque agent within the western project. She destroys ceilings, appears in bathhouses, and wears a face visor. A psychic once told me "You may win the lottery one day. But you will only win $2 to buy another ticket." She was probably Agent O. (See Appendix O on the haunting of the form O.)

Agent O [melisma]

As soon as a ceiling goes up, I want it to stop being what it is, to become something out of reach. A teacher once told me, "We owe it to ourselves to make our own medium." After seeing a recent piece, which moved from ceiling installation, to a non-public performance, to its destructive aftermath, to video and photographs, he remarked that my medium might actually be refusal.

So far there have been seven ceiling pieces. Each has included a moment of collapsing. Agent O is often the agent of this collapse—sometimes as saboteur, sometimes as enabler. She has destroyed a room-size ceiling in the middle of the night; she has released a water-logged ceiling to the ground during gallery hours. The why of her agency is always unclear. I only know she is motivated. I have never shown her to the public; or rather, the public never knows she is there as part of the ceiling piece. She seems to muddy the clarity—so I let the ceiling work seem clear. *Isn't this work about architecture, capitalism, and/or social dysfunction?* But I like that she was there, her whiff of strange agency left behind in a room of critique. Except for now (in this telling of this story), she is a secret.

P

Psychic

A psychic told me, "You're a good girl. A lot of people love you. But you don't care."

R

Rattlesnakes saving as ceremony

In Silko's (2010) memoir, *The Turquoise Ledge*, readers are confronted with Silko's preoccupation with rattlesnakes. Her stories of encounters with rattlesnakes are relentlessly accounted in the book, and at the podium. In many tales, she risks

Figure 33.3
Agent O
and the
dropped
ceiling.
*Photo by
author C.
Ree.*

her own safety and comfort in order to rescue a rattlesnake, or even welcome a rattlesnake to make a home near or in her home. At the 92nd Street Y, she told us that her obsession with saving rattlesnakes derived from seeing her father kill a rattlesnake when she was a girl. As her reader (her corner psychic), it seems to me that she exposes herself to danger, to the possibility of the poison, as a fulfillment of a generational debt that originated in her father's killing of the snake, and her witnessing of it. Her attendance to rattlesnakes snared by wire fences, caught in modernity, her wrists bared to the venom; all her penance, her ceremony to recognize the snakes that haunt her.

Red

In Anne Carson's *Autobiography of Red,*[5] "Geryon is a monster everything about him was red" (1999, p. 37). Geryon[6] is a young boy who is red, who is winged. At the age of five, he begins writing his autobiography, recorded in a fluorescent covered notebook. In it, Geryon observes that Herakles, his lover, his enemy, will kill him one day, and get his cattle, and kill his little red dog. In a parent-teacher conference, Geryon's teacher wonders if Geryon's stories will ever feature a happy ending. Geryon goes to his desk and with a pencil writes a happy ending: "All over the world, beautiful red breezes went on blowing hand in hand" (p. 38).

Revenge [recapitulation]

Unruly, full of desire, unsettling, around the edges of haunting whispers revenge. The rage of the dead, a broken promise, a violent ruin, the seeds of haunting, an engine for curses. It can and cannot be tolerated. Not like justice. Everyone nods their head to justice. Who can disagree with justice? Revenge on the other hand... Revenge is necessarily unspeakable to justice. We have better ways to deal with revenge now. But revenge and justice overlap, feed and deplete the other. In heroic films, justice and revenge slip and slide, exchanging names. Revenge goes drag as justice, or justice reveals its heat from revenge—the renegade civilian, the passionate lawyer, the rogue cop, the violated mother with shotgun on her hip. In ghostly horror films like *The Shining* (Kubrick, 1980) and *Poltergeist* (Hooper, 1982), the site of spectral terror, the terrible place, is often a cemetery buried underneath a contemporary mansion; the injustice is literally in the foundation and produces a haunting based on revenge (Clover, 1992, p. 30). The outlines of wrong and right, usually so Hollywood clear, shift out of focus the crime of history, the crime of fact (building over the dead) and instead assert the larger crime of desire that spills outside norms (vengeance). Justice and revenge—both invoke and refuse the other. Revenge is one head of the many-headed creature of justice.

Resolution

Last winter, when I was pregnant but hadn't told anyone yet, I went to an event featuring Maxine Hong Kingston, Leslie Marmon Silko, and Toni Morrison, at the 92nd Street Y.

Kingston's work (1989) is meaningful to me because my mother tugged my ears to return from bad dreams, too. Kingston's work (2004) is meaningful to me because our family home burned in the same fire, too. Morrison opened the night by talking about the friendship shared by the three of them. Silko and Kingston read from their recent memoirs, which were both in many ways about making wrong right again. Kingston stood on a box to read at the podium. Silko's hair kept falling on her pages. Speaking of their long friendship, Kingston said that Silko taught her that ceremony is the only resolution.

Ruin

These ceilings haunt my work. The ceilings I'm thinking about—the ones with acoustic tiles that slowly brown with leaky stain marks—always everywhere but in their own nowhere space. School buildings, grocery stores, office spaces, police stations, libraries, converted basements, temples, sometimes galleries and high-end boutiques. I never see them, but rather, I sense them. I can walk into a space and know without looking if the ceiling, *that ceiling*, is there. Designed to look like a reassuring solid plane, they are in fact an aluminum grid filled with lightweight tiles, suspended by wires here and there. Nothing holds the tiles in place but gravity and the grid. Their cheap, disposable, modular, flexible design was a breakthrough and ensured their spread throughout buildings today, and in many ways, their invisibility. "The building and rebuilding suggest that space is almost like a kind of very expensive magnetic tape which can be erased and reused....What is erased are cultural memories; what is rebuilt are more profitable buildings" (Abbas, 1994, p. 452). The tiles' swappable nature is also touted as a low-cost strategy for hiding leaks. Simply replace evidence of water damage with a new clean tile.

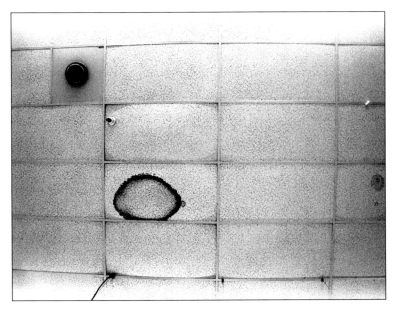

Figure 33.4 Albertsons, 2009, photograph, 4" × 6". Part of a photographic series on evidence of ceiling leaks in public spaces such as schools, department stores, and corporations. If you are reading this in an office building, look up, you may see your own leak stain. This particular leak was in the frozen food section of a popular grocery chain in Southern California. *Photo by author C. Ree.*

Yet, every time I glance overhead, a brown rusty stain looks back, unattended to and forgotten, hinting at leaks which threaten to press through in the next rain. "The ruins look back" (Caws, 1997, p. 303). I hear the downpour and wonder if I will see clear water seeping through from overhead. *Maybe next to the brown circle from the last leak. Will I see the water or feel it first? Which bucket will I throw underneath? Maybe the leak got fixed. Maybe it got fixed, but the fixing won't hold.* This anxiety about leaks is what I dwell on—their source, our inability to keep up with them, the rot they produce, the dysfunction of our ceilings, how they unsettle our sense of space—as well as how unnoticed they can go, how water stains dot most of our institutions. I think of Hurricane Katrina and horror movies, toxic schools, and suburban decay. The leak to me is a sort of sign, the ghost's *memento mori*, that we are always in a process of ruin, a state of ruining. Our ruins are not crumbled Roman columns, or ivy covered abandoned lots. Our ruins lie within the quick turnover of buildings, disappearing landmarks, and disposable homes, layered upon each other and over again.

And in the tradition of the symbolism of horror, the ruin always points to the scene of ghost-producing violence. The ruin is not only the physical imprint of the supernatural onto architecture, but also the possessed or deluded people wandering amidst the ruin who fail to see its ruinous aspect. The idealistic homeowners who move into the haunted home; the humans who do not recognize the living dead until it is too late. In these layered always-ruining places, our ghosts haunt, and we are blind to it. They are ghosts birthed from empire's original violence, the ghosts hidden inside law's creation myth (Benjamin, 1986 p. 287), and the new ghosts on the way as our ruins refresh and mutate. They are specters that collapse time, rendering empire's foundational past impossible to erase from the national present. They are a source of persistent unease. This is what suspended ceilings try to hide but only uncover.

S

Suspended, ceilings

Ceilings which leak. Ceilings which stare back. Ceilings which crash down.

W

Wrongs, righting the
Wrongs, writing the
Wrongs, wronging the

This is the last entry for now, only a temporary stay. More entries wait to be written, and not always patiently. Over our lifetimes, you and I have been told in many different ways that we should try to right wrongs, and certainly never wrong wrongs. Revenge is wronging wrongs, a form of double-wronging. You, like me, have been guided/good-girled away from considering revenge as a strategy of justice. To even consider revenge might be deemed dangerous, mercenary, terrorizing. At the same time, righting wrongs is so rare. Justice is so fleeting. And there are crimes that are too wrong to right. Avery Gordon (1997) writes that our task is to "look for lessons about haunting when there are thousands of ghosts; when entire societies become haunted by terrible deeds that are systematically occurring and are simultaneously denied by every public organ of governance and communication" (p. 64).

Wronging wrongs, so reviled in a waking life, seems to be the work of nightmares and hauntings and all the stuff that comes after opportunities to right wrongs and write wrongs have been exhausted. Unreadable and irrational, wronging wrongs is the work of now and future ghosts and monsters, the supply of which is ever-growing. You'll have to find someone to pull on your ears to bring you out of the nightmares, to call you home and help you remember who you are, and to hope that the ghosts will be willing to let you go [*see also,* **Mercy**].

Notes

1. In the Verbinski version, the curse is passed by videotape to strangers.
2. "Equinox," from *How We Became Human: New and Selected Poems: 1975-2001* by Joy Harjo. Copyright © 2002 by Joy Harjo. Used by permission of W. W. Norton & Company, Inc.
3. These same words you passed to me when my father died, because someone sent them to you when your father died. I sent them to you then, too. These words, another dissemination of loss, and that lingering disappointment.
4. In *Secret Sunshine,* a Korean film, (yet another) mother decides to forgive her son's murderer but becomes furious to learn he's found God and forgiven her first. This fury exposes how mercy granting is used to wield power, how one can covet the power to be merciful and feel betrayed when subjected to it.
5. Written in verse, Anne Carson's (1999) work is (or performs) as much about autobiography and language as mythic monsters. To me, her myth feels slippery and true. "I will never know how you see red and you will never know how I see it. / But this separation of consciousness / is recognized only after a failure of communication" (p. 105). Her monster Geryon is stuck in his red monstrosity, obsessed with his own famously bad ending from Greek legend. He self-chronicles, alternating between a notebook and photos, depicting a life desiring his mythic enemy Herakles. Carson's telling, which includes translations, word puzzles, and fragments, advises of both a life's irreducibility to language, and language's power to perform a life, that words can have many folds and be duplicitous, that I am free to rename and unname, that there may be a way to self-write which will not haunt me forever, that stories and their various attachments while they are being put together should also feel like they are on the verge of unraveling, that desire even wrong-desire, is a part of it.
6. In Greek myth, Geryon is the fearsome many-headed monster with a two-headed dog, both slayed by Heracles for his cattle during his Tenth Ordeal.

References

Abbas, A. (1994) Building on disappearance. *Public Culture, 6,* 441–459.

Abbas, A. (2010, January). *Space, cinema, architecture.* Lecture presented at University of California at Irvine, Irvine, California.

Alexie, S. (1996). *The summer of black widows.* Brooklyn, NY: Hanging Loose Press.

Benjamin, W. (1986). Critique of violence. In P. Demetz (Ed.), *Reflections* (pp. 277–300). New York: Harcourt Brace.

Butler, J. (2006). *Precarious life: The powers of mourning and violence.* London: Verso.

Byrd. J. (2011). *The transit of empire: Indigenous critiques of colonialism.* Minneapolis: University of Minnesota Press.

Carson, A. (1999). *Autobiography of red.* New York: Vintage Books.

Caws, M. A. (1997). *The surrealist look: An erotics of encounter.* Cambridge, MA: MIT Press.

Clover, C. J. (1992). *Men, women and chain saws: Gender in the modern horror film.* Princeton, NJ: Princeton University Press.

Fanon, F. (1963). *The wretched of the earth.* New York: Grove Press.

Gordon, A. (1997). *Ghostly matters: Haunting and the sociological imagination.* Minneapolis: University of Minnesota Press.

Harjo, J. (2008). Equinox. *On winding through the milky way.* [CD]. Sante Fe, NM: Fast Horse Recordings.

hooks, b. (1990). Marginality as a site of resistance. In R. Ferguson, M. Gever, T. T. Minh-ha, & C. West (Eds.), *Out there: Marginalization and contemporary cultures* (pp. 241–243). Cambridge, MA: MIT Press.

Hooper, T. (Director), Spielberg, S. (Writer), & Grais, M. (Writer). (1982). *Poltergeist* [Motion picture]. United States: Metro-Goldwyn-Mayer.

Kingston, M. H. (1989). *Woman warrior: Memoirs of a girlhood among ghosts*. New York: Vintage Press.

Kingston, M. H. (2004). *The fifth book of peace*. New York: Vintage Press.

Kubrick, S. (Director, Writer), King, S. (Novelist), & Harlan, J. (Executive Producer). (1980). *The shining* [Motion picture]. United States: Time Warner Company.

Morrison, T. (1987). *Beloved: A novel*. New York: Knopf.

Morrison, T. (1993). Nobel Lecture, December 7, 1993. In S. Allén (Ed.), *Nobel lectures literature 1991–1995* (pp. 47–56). Singapore: World Scientific.

Nakata, H. (Director), Hara, M. (Executive Producer), Takahashi, H. (Writer), & Suzuki, K. (Novelist). (1998). *Ringu* [Motion picture]. Japan: Omega Project.

Nakata, H. (Director), Ichise, T. (Producer), Suzuki, K. (Novelist), Nakamura, Y. (Writer), & Suzuki, H. (Writer). (2002). *Dark water* [Motion picture]. Japan: ADV Films.

Silko, L. M. (2010). *The turquoise ledge*. New York: Viking.

Stein, G. (2007 [1914]). *Tender buttons*. Sioux Falls, SD: Nu Vision, LLC.

Torre, M. E., & Ayala, J. (2009). Envisioning participatory action research entremundos. *Feminism and Psychology, 19*, 387–393.

Verbinski, G. (Director), Kruger, E. (Writer), & Suzuki, K. (Novelist). (2002). *The Ring* [Motion picture]. United States: Dreamworks.

Wolfe, P. (1999). *Settler colonialism and the transformation of anthropology: The politics and poetics of an ethnographic event*. New York: Cassell.

Appendix O (on the Haunting of the Form O)

The Haunting of the Form O

To continue our way backward, sideways and in between, we begin with our letter of the day, "O," rather unchanged from the Latin O, itself from Greek o *omicron*, in turn from the Phoenician *ayin*, likely derived from the Arabic ع *'Ayn*, which all hail from the Egyptian *ir*, a sound whose hieroglyph was ◁▻. In ancient Egyptian, this glyph was not simply passive sight, but also meant to do, to make or one who enacts. Vision was realizing. In the Eye of Horus or *Wedjat*, the eye was both goddess and a mathematics. The oldest known fractional system, the *wedjat's* different broken parts were also glyphs representing $1/2 + 1/4 + 1/8 + 1/16 + 1/32 + 1/64$, parts which equaled one when reassembled into an intact eye.

In Greek, *omicron*, "little o" or "o-micron," was a letter but also a number, 70. Likewise, *Omega*, big O or "o-mega," began as a doubled omicron (and eventually became, Ω, or ω). Omega took its shape from the mouth forming the long 'oh' sound, and was also a letter and a number equal to 800. It also came to signify finality or the end because of its terminal position in the Greek alphabet. With omega and omicron, the O and the o, the eye and the mouth began to share a shape.

Any consideration of O must also consider the void and the circle. The study of the circle drove the development of geometry, calculus, astrology, astronomy, and at multiple points in time, the circle and mathematics itself were considered divine pursuits, knowledge so sacred and powerful that its secrets were guarded by math initiates and priests on pain of death.

Whereas these sciences considered the circle as perfection, a path or a volume, the concept of zero played funnier games. In fact, zero's (0) very number status confounded the Greeks

"How can nothing be something?" Yet zero's null point forms the base for counting in positive or negative directions, the ironic ground for the figure of numbers themselves. Although zero may have wandered from India, to China to Islamic countries and eventually to Greece, its etymological and representational root is Arabic, both as a small circle o, and described by the word صفر *ṣifr*. Here zero's social potential manifested itself more ingeniously. *Sifr* meant empty, void, devoid, as well as the numerical concept of zero. However, as Arab mathematics spread globally, *ṣifr* alluded to secret knowledge, a code, encryption. In language, computing, math, *cipher* is empty and full, a way to transform in order to conceal, a void masking a presence.

As a side note, another parallel and earlier development of zero started with the Olmecs, a pre-Mayan civilization accredited with first using zero in their Long Count Calendar in 32 BCE. Similar to the Arabic use of zero as a decimal ordering system, and different from Roman zero as simply another place on a string of numbers, Olmec zero made possible a veritable matrix, a computing system. With the Olmecs, zero was also fundamentally temporal, simultaneously marking the beginning of a cycle of time, and its end.[1] Interestingly, whereas all other numbers in the Olmec counting system were represented by some combination of a dot (•) or a horizontal line (-), the zero was neither point or line or any abstraction at all. Rather peculiarly, zero was depicted as a round shell 🐚, hardness shaped by an emptiness within.

Letters that are numbers, mouths that are eyes, voids that hide - the O and the cipher have strange communion with the Korean character ㅇ, also born as a drawing of a mouth, an outline of the throat. When found at the beginning of a character, ㅇ is silent, a null consonant. Placed at the end it commands a -ng, a sound more like a fist in the throat.

The Korean spoken language is one of only a few which is believed to be a "language isolate," likely born without a shared genealogy to any other language. This status,

---

[1] The Long Count Calendar has been made recently famous by misinterpretations of an apocalypse scheduled for December 2012. In fact, according to many scholars, this is not the end of all things, but a resetting of the Long Count to year zero to mark the beginning of another age, in which the world will be recreated through war or conflict.

conferred after intense study, moves a language from "unclassifiable" to that of linguistic orphan or hermetically generated (or dropped down by alien spaceships). If the source of spoken Korean defies history, then written Korean was born without one. In 1443, King Sejong mandated the creation of a simple writing system for the nation. The resulting system, *hangul,* and the 24 geometric letters of its alphabet were developed as a system for the future. King Sejong gifted this language to a country largely illiterate from the impossibility of learning the labyrinthine pictograms of Chinese, itself a mark of Korea's colonial past and a living barrier between the elite and the peasants. *Hangul* could be learned in hours, corresponded to the actual sounds of spoken Korean, and once released, was initially taken up mostly by women and the poor. Each letter was designed to be a map for the speaker's mouth - with one look, a person would know how to shape the lips, place the tongue, tighten the throat and deliver the sound. Eye, mouth, breath. Vision as action. Whereas Egyptian hieroglyphs haunt letter O so many epochs later, Sejong's alphabet was conceived as modern technology, born fresh and unmarked with the same logic as computer code – to be modular, robust, flexible and intuitive. With *hangul,* Sejong completed the Korean language's strange linguistic sovereignty - Korean language as isolate, language as science fiction, language as orphan.

O and the eye – connected from the beginning. The shadow of the eye, even in letters shaped like mouths. O that means something and nothing, a phantom vision no one sees. And all this bring us to *Outis* (**ΟΥΤΙΣ**). Odysseus' veil and alibi, the name assumed to trick Cyclops, a name translated as "Nobody," *Outis* could not have begun with a more perfect letter.

Oracle, somewhere in the Matrix, baking cookies in an apartment project, delivering riddles for a savior, waiting for him to get it. She the cynical but secretly hopeful sister of

Onibaba, masked samurai-chopping hag, converts the weapons of her murdered victims into cash for the barest of life in the wake of war's awful hangover. Destroyer of war's logic, deliverer of warriors to the round hungry pit. Onibaba, whose wooden mask horrifically cleaves to her face so she, in the end, can only see and be seen through a monstrous screen.

Obaltan (Stray Bullet) – Korea's most famous film, the wandering lost after the Korean war, haunted by old Hollywood films and the nowhere of liberation. A note on Obaltan - it is considered the best Korean film of all time. But

before what it is now, in its first life, it was banished by the post-war government. In the little window before it was destroyed, it had been sent to the SF International Film Festival in 1963. When Korean cinema became something folks wanted to excavate and archive, people searched high and low and found this one last copy hidden away, subtitled in English for festival viewing. This one copy is the source for the thousands of DVD copies now available. As a result, however, the subtitles have become a permanent tattoo on Obaltan, impossible to remove, present in every screening, marking its resurrection and second life. The subtitles are always striking - their odd font, their odd translation, their odd history. Like a bug in the soup.

Orestes, meaning 'mountain,' held up for killing his mother at the behest of Apollo - either to avenge his war hero father Agamemnon like a good son or to remove Clytemnestra's matriarchy forever like a good man. Afterward goes irrevocably mad.

And finally,
Some say translation is always a kind of betrayal, an excess of meaning which haunts the impossibility of equivalence, an Egyptian eye of action hidden in the Greek O of the mouth. If translation is not only the movement of meaning from one language into another, but also movement between forms, *orphan,* our last word for the day, is both the figure of translation and its transgression. *Orphan*'s marooned quality, the figure of the fatherless child comes from its Proto Indo European root **orbh-* or being stranded, bereft. However, **orbh-* and its derivate forms in Greek also meant to change allegiance, to move into a class unconnected to others, to lose free status. This translation from biological to legal father, from free to slave, from stranded to bonded, sees a further development in modern European words for work or labor, such as German *Arbeit* "slave, or work." In Slavic languages where leading vowel and consonants were reversed over time, *orbh* became modern day Russian *rabota* "work." In fact, in 1921 science fiction writer Karen Čapek used the Czech word *robota* ("drudgery," "slave") when creating his vision of autonomous labor machines – *robots.* In the finale of his play *R.U.R. (Rossum's Universal Robots),* the laboring robots, unhappy with their servitude, overthrow and destroy the human race. Capek's robots, the strange great great grandchildren of *orphan,* move from slave to sovereign, and enact translation's ultimate betrayal. From family through law to science fiction: orphan, slave, robot, overthrown finally and strangely free again.

Chapter 34

An Autoethnography of What Happens

Kathleen Stewart

Autoethnography can be a way of doing something different with theory and its relation to experience. The prospect is unsettling for some, a relief for others. The promise or threat of writing theory through the device of a self elicits a visceral split reaction. In part, the difference in reactions is an effect of how comfortable a person is, for whatever reason, with the compositions of worlds made obvious in writing. Where one person might be transported into a resonance with compositions of her or his own: "Ah, you are *that* person, I know what you're doing"— another might be negatively startled, and perhaps even disappointed, to see the world presented starkly as a composition of elements thrown together into something with texture, density, and force. The fullness of compositionality might seem to present an alter explanation for how things are the way they are without laying out just what this might mean (what it might do) in the scheme of how we think and feel about things. Compositionality itself is strange—a stranger. It might be expected in reading fiction or watching television, but that's one thing. Not the kind of thing you expect in a talk or an article. On the extreme end of the negative startle response, people can feel vertigo, nausea, an almost traumatic fight and flight response. In my experience, this last, extreme response is usually experienced by men and is fairly common for whatever reason. It is certainly not that a gross and essential category, men, is without imagination or experience, and yet there may be something gendered happening.

Handbook of Autoethnography, edited by Stacy Holman Jones, Tony E. Adams, and Carolyn Ellis, 659–668. © 2013 Left Coast Press, Inc. All rights reserved.

Reactions, like the compositions that set them in flight, are assembled with speed. They are thrown together, really, and out of a grab bag of disparate elements. Whatever form a particular reaction takes, some kind of reaction is part of the process of autoethnography. You write from a place in which the world is reacting to something; it's animated, incited, thrown together into something; you react to this thrown together world; the audience, drawn into this circuit of reaction, also reacts—to that world, to your thrown together response. The question of composing worlds is a question, then, of how forces of all kinds take form and how forms take on a charge and enter circuits of reaction.

One thing that can happen in these circuits of reaction is an almost nostalgic search for what seems to be slipping away or transmogrifying into something harsh and loud. Things seem to be becoming too much of themselves or fading away altogether. Wishes flood in for a naturalized scaffolding of thought. There may be a search for stable matter and for a concept pure and simple that explains it or speaks of it to others in a calm and quiet zone of conversation about the things of the world. This reaction to loss and excess can do many things. It can turn the stomach. It can set off a flight of thought. Or it can call forth the revival of "the critical" in its basest form—the search for stains and scars. Once lines of fault-finding are set in motion, terms like the reflexive, the anecdotal, or the performative are hurled as weapons against imagined states of mind—navel-gazing, narcissism, a will to dominate others through the force of words. Against an unfamiliar spark, a defense can flower into its own compositional excesses. The room then throws itself together into a melodrama in which specters lurk; sins against intellectual right-thinking and bodily comfort have to be blanched or tempered. A utopic public sphere of academic exchange gathers its ghostly self to propose a restraint on writing itself. Now it seems that there are dangers in writing going too far, being too intense, setting off on its own tracks, digressing, embodying, pulling the wool over otherwise sharp eyes. Suddenly, writing is a dictator, an assault.

I am not exaggerating (that is, letting writing run away with me). I have seen this dynamic leap into form for decades. A friend once said academics like writing that tells them 95 percent of what they already know and 5 percent of something new. So when the noise of composition becomes audible, the room gets moody. Against the kind of theory and knowledge that takes place in writing, real scholarship appears, in retrospect, as something solid. In the circuit of reaction, writing is always being reinscribed as something that is and should be epiphenomenal—a means of expressing what has already been garnered by real research. Thought that emerges in forms of writing is an unrecognizable object; its corralling scores over and conserves a limited repertoire of theory-making: the politics and poetics of suspicion, the obvious knowledges of critical thinking, a grab bag of mantras—everything is socially constructed, everything is discursive, everything is about power, everything is cultural. We're back on solid ground. We love the concept of grounding.

But if the effort is not just to ground theory/writing in a punishingly flattened real world but to actually pull it into alignment with phenomena, autoethnography can be a form of writing that works, or at least does *some* work. Detouring into descriptive eddies, it might slow the naturalized relationship between subject, concept, and world (Latour, 2007). It might note the incommensurateness of the elements throwing themselves together. It might become attuned to the throwing together itself. It might become a hinge onto the commonplace labors of becoming sentient to whatever is happening. It might skid over the surface of something that feels like something, or pause on one strand of a phenomenon as it moves together with other strands or falls out of sync, becoming an anomaly or a problem. It might describe something's qualities, trajectories, and duration or try to follow how things accrue or how they lose steam. In short, it can be a way to hone in on the singularities in which things actually take place. It's also risky, and of course it can fail miserably.

Autoethnography, in other words, is one way of reimagining the subject-object in scenes of the composition of some kind of world, whether that world is a lived identity, a prismatic structure of feeling or thought, a historical present, or the force of potentiality animating something. The objects of autoethnography are tellingly diffuse yet precise—a tone of voice, a form of labor, a sleepless night, unsignified intensities. An attachment circulates across bodies of all kinds—human bodies, bodies of thought, plant and animal bodies, bodies of pain and pleasure—assemblages of histories and politics, forms of caring and abuse solidified into models.

Autoethnography is one route into a broader-ranging, more supple exploration of what happens to people, how force hits bodies, how sensibilities circulate and become, perhaps delicately or ephemerally, collective. It describes the qualities of connection and impact in recognizable situations. It composes a world perturbed by the singularities of events in ways that can be generative.

Here, as an exemplar, I write of a death and the way that death disturbs but also activates the self-world relation. Autoethnography here is an endurance, a shift in attunement, a painful, scraping, scoring over of unbearable shifts in the self-world relation. It is a bell ringing, a reduction (a cooking down) to painful truths, a shared zone of impossibility.

When a Life Ends...

When a life ends it's as if it bursts, leaving wet weights all over the landscape. The living live in a state of dispersal.

What happened to her toothbrush?

Where are the little pearl earrings she wore through the long duration of a decade of life in the process of losing itself one quality at a time?

The line between self and other, subject and object, person and event, is smeared, rubbed out like a child's crayon experiment. The distinctions between things are flooded by the unspeakable dullness of sheer loss. The body surges sluggishly. It tries, half-heartedly, to push itself up to the high flood plain where the detritus of loss dirties the bereft landscape. This used to be a world. You used to be in it. Now things are in slow motion.

Knowledge is a breathless, drowned forensics.

The question of what happened circles recursively around the lifeless body.

The living are in a heavy float, without so much as a detail to get stuck on or a melodrama to snap things into a narrative arc.

Words are a wallpaper, a muffling.

The eyes listlessly track moving objects.

Your body tries to dwell in the scene of the last time you touched her. She was blind, paralyzed, deaf. Her fingers would walk down her starving body to find your hand. You would just sit, hold the hand until it became restless again. You would bring your lips to her forehead. Then what happened? The aides said she died in her sleep, her hands folded over her chest. You are grateful for this miraculous scene of peace but you can't quite fathom it, knowing, as you do, how all the nights before this final night went. Not well, in short. She agonized over her dead, once drunken and violent, father's apparitions in the room, the sense of stain left like a residue once the surge of living had failed her, leaving her alone with no way now to talk, no way to get home, no way to see the hill outside the window or the faces leaning in from time to time, no way to care for and no way to receive the care now only occasionally drifting by at a distance—the mini deeds that now only gesture at soothing and suturing while the blanketing unworlding empties the weight of the world into a crushing blankness.

They say there are stages of grief. It starts with phone calls in the middle of the night, which you don't get because you only have cell phones now and you turn the ringers off to sleep, for meetings; yours is almost always off because you forget to turn it back on. You are hostile to the phone, though you love it, too. It is unreliable, though always with you. You expect so much of it, try to control its every move, and somehow, as a result of all this, you always receive news long after the fact. Your mother's phone was hard wired to the wall in her kitchen for over fifty years. You had to answer that phone; you had to make rules for its social use; "I'm sorry, we're having dinner. Can she call you back?" Now, and for the longest time, you have not been able to take that phone number off your cell phone—917-688-5444—because you want it to still be in existence in some form.

Now it's 5:47 AM and you are alone with your cell phone in the dark. You see the calls—more than one. Your brother, your sister again and again at 2 AM and 2:20 and 2:45. Then they stopped. There's a voice message. You make calls; you cry; you walk around saturated with alarm and under the watery weight. You can't bear to make travel arrangements or to do anything else that takes patience or needs decisions. You make a stupid decision to cremate, like that was obvious. You don't realize that means there won't be a body to see, kiss.

Realizations are bodily and, as a class, sickening and unbearable and after the fact.

Obviously you can't think things through. But that's not because you're on pause; it's because thoughts pass through you like bullets through flesh. It's all patching things up all the way down.

You start with the obituary, the eulogy. You think, well, you'll write. But writing, it turns out, is not catharsis or distance, but a stain. That stain. A theft. A sinking. Everyone is scrambling at the tipping point where the weight of death's unbearable impact is already slipping away, leaving in its place the blank stare of the nothing. Fault is hardening up on the fault line. The siblings are vying desperately for the place at the dead center of her. There's been an unforgivable omission in the obituary. Now you're in the church in the middle of the eulogy having included the stolen words of everyone you can think of—the sisters, every one of the grandchildren, the children, there's mention of the friends, and your aunts' hawk eyes are trained on your family body—look at Katie's arms! She's got the Stewart fatty tumors! You're trapped in a bruising theatre, already mouthing the words that are earning you your final report card from the family.

Eulogy for Mama

It's time to say goodbye… This one loved potatoes, ripe summer tomatoes and corn, winter squash, the smell of green onions, a cold beer before supper, her town, her neighborhood, her house, a cup of tea with a little bit of milk, the blues and purples of a winter sky, to take a walk, to sit and talk, windows open to let in the air.

She would pull her feet up on the stool in front of her, ready to hear what a visitor had to say for herself. She had the gift of gab. She took an impersonal pleasure in people and what comes out of their mouths. She could size you up in a glance, cut you to the quick with a killer phrase.

Claire went first into the world, and first out of it. People watched her, gravitated to her, followed her around, waddled behind her like ducks into whatever new territory she opened. She had her projects, encounters, labors. Always. The poor kids she taught, the poverty everywhere, the dark side always felt yet put in its place to make room for the work of composition, the children she raised, the antique furniture she salvaged from Vermont barns when the dairy business collapsed and then painstakingly refinished in the driveway year after year. She became the life-long loyal steward of these tables and chairs. She made lamps and lampshades that filled her house, her children's houses, and her friend's houses. She doodled beautiful drawings of bombshell women while she talked on the phone. She painted scenes on boxes and plaques. She deposited her whole paycheck into a college fund for thirty years. She savored the weight of the world "like a tender shred of chicken close to the bone" (Longsong, 2009, p. 31).

As a child, she had the Shirley Temple curls and the spring in her step. People passing on the street would do a double take, just to make sure she wasn't somebody. The men at the market would lift her onto the counter to dance The Good Ship Lollipop dance. She learned to drive at ten; by the time she was fourteen, she was driving all her little sisters and cousins all over town in her father's pick-up truck. As an adult, people basked in her presence. When she bought a camp in New Hampshire, others started looking at property there, too. She grew miraculous geraniums and a jade plant so big and healthy people said it must be five hundred years old. Those plants flourished through the freezing winters and a month at a time without water, clinging to their windows with southern exposure.

People always said there was something about her. She could listen. She could hold on. She could write a world out of a collection of characters spinning through landscapes, atmospheres, a look in the eye, the fate of the body. She would do anything if she was in it with others.

Her oldest grandson, Justin, remembered a crazy spontaneous trip to Barre, Vermont, one cold winter day towards the end.

An adventure to go rediscover a place we both knew for different reasons. She shared stories of a different time when her kids were kids, then teenagers. Stories that made me laugh. Sad stories of friends lost. Adventures when she was young, when Grandpa was young. Early love, and later on love. Stories that explained the path that led us to this crazy day trip to Vermont when she was already so sick and frail. We visited stone carving sheds, shared lunch, and then drove home late through a major blizzard, somehow knowing we would be safe no matter what happened. That day I knew how much she so truly loved her world. She always taught me that this world was a tough place. But she wanted so much to stay in it with us.

After

I sleep hard. I am awakened by bad dreams every few minutes. But then, as if drugged, I have fallen asleep again and have had another dream. My mouth is dry as sand. I get up to pee again, then fall back into the bed like an animal. I snap my stiff neck back into alignment with a quick, careless gesture like a neck headache is nothing, and a neck is nothing, maybe it will just snap off and that will be the end of this. It's like everything is just a gesture now. And now and I'm back down. In the excursions from bed to bath I see myself as really old, grotesque. I shuffle my feet. Then I remember, oh, but they're paralyzed, I can't actually walk at all. I am my mother's body. I am living without distinctions. I am exhausted but laboring still, an empty, gesturing laboring, looking for what needs to be done now even though I do not care.

The Near Past in Long Durée

There were a dozen years of episodes, realizations, adjustments—a frantic, moving labor dragging denial in its wake. A gearing up to respond, become agentive, that never quite found its groove. We would find ourselves taking stock of one new situation after another thinking "Oh! This is as bad as it gets." Then the prism of suffering and terror would shift into something unimaginably worse. We would learn again what to do with our bodies. We would dream up labors that might help in some way or maybe just distract us for a minute from the hardest labor of just sitting with a misery that wailed in a dark, bereft world. Even then things had started to become merely gestural. We were tainted by this incapacity, this unwillingness, this half-motion, that slowly became clear as the last accounting of what we would be able do for our mother. Not enough. We were witnesses to a shredding in which we were complicit.

My notes to the nurses and social workers and administrators at the time are insanely long and detailed lists of conditions and episodes aimed at getting something done that would make things better. Getting her back into the nursing home or out of it or on morphine or off of it or under a regime of care or out from under it. There were always moments when a choice seemed simple and like a real choice, but then came the inevitable smudging. We thought about her physical security and isolation (she can't stay alone in the apartment; she keeps falling), but in so many ways the nursing home made everything worse; her frailty bloomed into devastating disability. We thought the morphine would take her out of her misery, but it just took from her the last shred of energy to stay connected to a world. Eventually the lists failed me. We were unmoored together in a sheer seriality—this happened and then that. Moments of mooring now stood in sharp relief to the ordinary endurance of the unbearable. Occasionally, a visit from an old friend would pull her up into a world of other people's problems, the possibility of modes of attention, her role as the good listener others rotated around. For a long time there were brief escapes out into the spring air to be near the flowers I would try to describe, to sit under a fall tree together, she in an unwieldy padded wheelchair that reclined, moving, with great effort on my part, great fear on her part, over the uneven sidewalk and through doorways. Agency became, for all of us, the sheer labor of staying sentient to something.

Now the only labor left is the compulsion to give the wet weights a skin. A gesture of loyalty to love and horror. I am in a state of attunement, on alert. The ordinary itself piles up around me as the detritus of now disloyal projects and casual investments that hold no interest. The very existence of these things is amazing to me, but only passively. I cannot muster any energy to throw in their direction. People are looking into my eyes for sympathy, a little weepy, and I'm thinking "Oh, I know, but it's so much worse than you think." I'm snapping back and forth between big pause, deer-in-the-headlights sympathy for all the watery eyes around me and speed processing. Just snapping. In time, all this will turn to unblinking rage. And then the rage will turn into something flat but harsh and rickety. From here, the wisdom of age comes into focus as a sobering up. I recognize it as the hard-won, violent, and strange outcome of giving up a long struggle with increasingly unbearable weights. Its sad slackening, shot through with weirdness and surprise, is a way of living through things, but certainly not unsullied.

When the Ordinary Sidles Up Again
(It's All Gestures All the Way Down)

So when the ordinary finally sidles up again, it's flattened but jumpy. I try to find ways to describe what happened. The way practices and routines became hollow, gestural, and how much these gestures mattered as such. I remember a day when my mother was still living in her house. My sister and I walked with her to the library to find an audio book. She couldn't make it on her own anymore. She ran into a friend, and the two old ladies sat on a bench outside in the park for two hours while the sun went down. That was joy. Victory. When she moved to assisted living, I put her artwork and photographs up on the walls and installed what lamps would fit. I hoped for a restoration and she proclaimed it so, but it wasn't. When I cooked in her apartment, it brought her to the relief—her life made good—even though she knew the half-effort in the poorly stocked kitchen was just a sad gesture. My efforts (and others') jump-started her own gestural economy of learning the ropes, keeping going in some very small way—one foot in front of the other.

Over time, undoable projects crystallized, lending a sharp, cruel texture to the living through of what counted as life. Living on was a sheer will to live weighted with now vague potential (but still something). There were fictions, luminosities; loud and heavy narratives with punch lines and tips for living right. These formed an erratic rhythm whose obvious construction both released and annoyed residents. The tiny white Christmas lights on the bushes by the front door and the garlands strung around the balustrade of the grand staircase in the lobby added beauty under the guise of a seasonal atmosphere. There are beautiful art prints on the walls. On one long hallway they are all in blue. There were fires in the fireplaces. The alarms were being pulled in residents' apartments every night. Ambulances quietly came and went, unremarked. It took some digging, some enduring attention, to discover even the deaths. But the end was an infrastructural undercurrent like the buzzing of the dimmed hall lights through the night. There was always the kissing, the compliments and jokes repeated close to the deafening ears—You look beautiful! What a hat! Are you taking a trip? Are you going to a party?

A guy named Mike came every other month or so. His booming voice led the residents in song at Tuesday afternoon tea with hand-painted flowered teapots and cups. Sometimes he brought an animal show and told loud, strong jokes and stories. He had a red Brazil bird that was never going to grow up. That bird was a devil. He would close himself in the kitchen cabinet and tear the labels off the cans and shred them. He ate by dipping his whole body in a gooey nectar, licking it off his wings, and then shaking like a dog. So you had to have a plexiglass cage. You had to clean it every day. Imagine! Self-help information was reassuring even when it wasn't practical or relevant anymore. There were little puzzles to be solved if you could muster the energy to recognize them. There were things you could do and objects to wonder about, take pleasure in (the birds are beautiful), or judge—"Oh! I don't like mice." One of Mike's keeps escaping the ball it's housed in as it rolls across the floor.

Conclusion

Philip Lopate (1997), a master of the personal essay, writes often about the writing of an author, a self, a life "exposed on the stage of the world" (p. 50). Such writing might include the minutia of the everyday life of an historical present, or the ramblings of a consciousness obsessed with gender, drugs, death, or a self-serving narrative of a life. A broad range of forms of writing have the capacity to pull a subject onto the stage of a world, to world the subject, to subject a world. The compositional complicity of subject-world is, for me, the first question of autoethnography. It is a way of calling up the textures and densities of worlds of all kinds formed out of this and that—identities, situations, scenes, sensory conditions, bodies, meanings, weights, rhythms, absence. A way of sidling up to the interesting or unbearable atmospheres and events of those worlds. A hinge onto a moment of some world's legibility. Can it tell us anything about the way things circulate and get animated? What kinds of attachments does this relation make possible or foreclose? How does it emerge in particular, and what remains? What would it mean to think of it as an always emergent phenomenon—one in the process of forming up or throwing up forms? Can it be a form of exposure? Of what?

Autoethnography is motivated, strategic, and prolific in our historical present. Here, I have tried to suggest that it can be a way to forge a linkage between self and world, the abstract and concrete, the massive and minute, the fuzzy or smudged yet precise. It is a composing that attunes to forces coming into form.

I wonder, with Joan Didion, then, what it means to find a perfect detail. One that is, perhaps, one of the countless materialities, jumps, and strands of thought that constitute links between self and world.

The cracked crab that I recall having for lunch the day my father came home from Detroit in 1945 must certainly be embroidery, worked into the day's pattern to lend verisimilitude; I was ten years old and would not now remember the cracked crab. The day's events did not turn on cracked crab. And yet it is precisely that fictitious crab that makes me see the afternoon all over again. (Didion, 2006, p. 103)

In autoethnography, it may sometimes be possible for a detail to remain a detail. It does not have to become the symbol of a meaning. It hinges not onto a logic per se but more fundamentally onto the tactile compositions of the living out of things. This is theory's labor, pulling into proximity to the ordinary work of becoming sentient to a world's bodies, rhythms, ways of being in noise and light and space (Nancy, 1997). Depending absolutely on its angle of approach and the way it catches light, writing becomes an energetics of what happens and a carapace of spent and living forms.

References

Didion, J. (2006). *We tell ourselves stories in order to live: Collected nonfiction.* New York: Alfred A. Knopf.

Latour B. (2007). *Reassembling the social.* Oxford: Oxford University Press.

Longsong, L. (2009). *Imagine a door.* Cincinnati, Turning Point Press.

Lopate, P. (1997). *The art of the personal essay.* New York: Anchor Press.

Nancy, J-L. (1997). *The sense of the world.* Minneapolis: University of Minnesota Press.

Conclusion

Storying Our Future

Tony Adams, Stacy Holman Jones,
and Carolyn Ellis

Where Stories Take Us

It's no wonder that, after coming to autoethnography, authors feel an immediate connection, a desire to read and write and share personal stories in their research. It's no wonder that scholars say, again and again, autoethnography is *the* method, *the* practice, *the* way of life for them. Neurological science teaches that stories offer us an experience that is, as far as the brain is concerned, parallel to encountering a person or an event in life (Murphy Paul, 2012). Stories also offer us something more, something remarkable: the ability to enter and engage deeply in another's experiences, thoughts, and feelings, and in turn create a map of our futures—a theory of mind and relation—that brings us into each other's beliefs, desires, and intentions without obscuring what makes us different from or holds us apart from others (Murphy Paul, 2012).

And so, stories invite us not to *describe* the world as it is, but instead to *move* and *live into* the world with others to try to shape a future together. Living the autoethnographic life allows us to story a future marked by compassion, by solidarity and communion, by change and justice, and by hope. We'd like to conclude this wonderful collection of essays about and examples of autoethnography by mapping where our individual and collective stories might take us.

Handbook of Autoethnography, edited by Stacy Holman Jones, Tony E. Adams, and Carolyn Ellis, 669–677. © 2013 Left Coast Press, Inc. All rights reserved.

Stacy

Autoethnography has offered me a way of writing, experiencing, and understanding a number of moments, turns, and absences in my life: the power of story in my life as a scholar; the resonance and dissonance among women's stories of power and stories of resistance; story as a performance that tells my relationship with my adopted child into being; telling, too, the story of coming into a new, queer identity; and turning to story as a way to offer a memorial to those I have loved. Always, writing autoethnography has been a way for me to find out, to know and to tell, to come out and to say no to other ways of life, and to honor and grieve relationships—those chosen and those lost.

Recently, autoethnography has offered me a way to write into the future—to story the life and relationships I would like to know and have into being. For me, writing is a space for engaging in *communion* with self in relation to others. Writing autoethnography with others—with Tony and Carolyn, with the authors of this Handbook, with colleagues, with students, with family—is a practice of deeply relating in body and heart and word. Writing autoethnography with those in my life and work—most notably my child, now eleven years old—is a practice of introspection and connection that asks me to consider the relational ethics of research and invites us to embrace language and story as a means for connecting on a new and exciting level. These, though, are my words about the power of story in our connection. Here are the words we—my child and I—write together: *Stories make you curious. They tell you about yourself and other people, they help you figure things out, and they show you how to live life.* This curiosity—this asking and searching and finding out—are where story takes us as we tell our future together.

Tony

I have many hopes, desires, and expectations for my future autoethnographic work.

I hope to continue to disrupt harmful social silences and dissatisfying relational experiences. For instance, I grow weary of worrying about disclosing my same-sex attraction to others and tired of having my sexuality and the relationship I have with my (male) partner relegated to the periphery of social interaction. In my future autoethnographic work, I hope to describe and offer strategies for eliminating these silences and for changing these experiences.

I also want to make my work as honest and hopeful as possible, telling as much as I can remember in ethically responsible ways. While I will sometimes describe the happy and joyful moments in my life, I will prioritize the painful and problematic experiences that I feel are in need of dire change.

I will acknowledge and interrogate the ethics of researching others, particularly how others will be probed and prodded, what questions will be asked, and how their information will be used. While I do not believe that autoethnography is the only way to do research, I appreciate the heightened attention that many autoethnographers devote to the nuances, ethics, and possible ethical violations of research practice.

I will continue to learn about the craft of writing with the hope of making my autoethnographic work more accessible and engaging. While I do not expect my articles to be read by millions or even tens of thousands of people, I do expect my work to be more readable, humane, and engaging than more traditional, impersonal, and emotionally sterile research reports.

I hope to use autoethnography to improve the significant relationships in my life and use the writings in this Handbook to propel me into new ways of being. I want to be impacted by others' stories and I want my stories to have an impact on others. Such reciprocity will continue to enhance the theorizing of relationships as well as provide us all with better "equipment for living" (Burke, 1974)—better stories to use when making sense of difficult, complicated, and uncertain everyday affairs (Bochner, 2001; Coles, 1989).

Carolyn

Sometimes now the past looms larger than the future. When I imagine the past, it is filled with experience and autoethnographic stories that interpret, reinterpret, and revision that experience. For more than two dozen years, autoethnography has been my companion, comforting me in my disappointments and losses and reminding me to celebrate achievements and attachments. I am thankful for the moments, hours, days, and years I have spent reflecting and writing autoethnographically to understand the colorful and varied life I have lived and to figure out how to live as fully and meaningfully as I can. In these ways, autoethnography has made my life and work more rewarding.

For me, autoethnography always has been a relational practice. To do autoethnography well means that I examine my experiences in the context of emerging and ever-changing relationships and enter the world of others as much as I try to understand the self. I locate myself through their eyes and hearts, consider their alternative points of view and interpretations, and try to feel their plights as fully as I can. In these ways, autoethnography has contributed to making my relational life deeper and more satisfying.

Writing with Stacy and Tony—and alongside the authors in this Handbook— paves the way into the future, and I find myself as excited about autoethnography now as I was when it first began. I'm also engaged by the research I've been doing for the last few years, which involves taking the autoethnographic perspective into collaborative research with non-academics. In this research, relational autoethnography provides a way to contribute directly to the lives of others, especially those who feel unwarranted pain and anguish. I feel called now to be a secondary witness for Holocaust survivors, to assist in their telling and meaning making, to listen intimately and respond from my heart to stories that are too terrifying and painful to remember in isolation. My work now and for the future focuses on collaborative stories that will be read, remembered, and retold by future generations hoping to stem the possibility of such tragedies as the Holocaust happening again.

Through the kind of ethical, collaborative witnessing suggested by Stacy, Tony, and me, as well as others in this volume, autoethnography contributes to social justice, social and political change.

○

As our individual narratives suggest, in story, we can be lovingly, critically, contingently, and reflectively present to and for each other. In story, we are called not only to give an account of ourselves, but also to be accountable to one another. In story, we can write ourselves into a more promising, more equitable future. Storying our connections as autoethnography, as Butler (2005) writes, "does not have as its goal the establishment of a definitive narrative but constitutes a linguistic and social occasion for self-transformation" (p. 130). Answering to and engaging with others, telling our stories, and giving an account of ourselves and being accountable to each other is—time and again—a chance "to be moved, to be prompted to act" (p. 136).

Contributions of this Handbook

As evidenced by this Handbook, we have great hope for autoethnography as a way of working and living. And we're not alone. More and more journals and publishers accept autoethnographic work, and more and more academic programs are producing, or helping create, autoethnographic projects. There have been numerous conferences devoted significantly and exclusively to the method, including the International Congress of Qualitative Inquiry, the emerging Ethnographic Friendships Conference, and the Doing Autoethnography graduate student conference. There are ongoing efforts to create the *Journal of Autoethnography*, an interdisciplinary publication solely devoted to theorizing and applications of the method. These efforts, in conjunction with the rich history of autoethnographic theory, instructional guides, and exemplary texts, provide a stage for the contributions this Handbook makes to the work of those just coming to autoethnography as well as to those living the autoethnographic life.

To begin, we believe this Handbook contributes to long-standing efforts to legitimate autoethnography as a method, approach, and way of looking at and living in the world. Throughout, contributors show how and why autoethnography matters, not with the intent to seek "daddy's approval" from arbiters of traditional social scientific standards and philosophies (Gingrich-Philbrook, 2005), but instead to illustrate the purposes, practices, and possibilities of autoethnographic research. We also hope the Handbook will encourage others to do the work that they find meaningful and important, as well as illustrate what autoethnographic texts can contribute to research and to the living of life. Further, we hope that personal experience will continue to inform research practice, not because personal experience is better or more truthful or more generalizable, but rather because it can humanize research and make research more relevant, accessible, and meaningful to others.

We also believe the Handbook models a variety of ways to do and conceive of autoethnography. While we do not advocate for any definite, prescriptive criteria for doing autoethnography, we do believe that the personal and theoretical essays about autoethnography included in the Handbook show what the method and approach are as well as what autoethnographic projects can and should do. This Handbook includes a range of discussions and justifications for autoethnography, as well as many exemplars that illustrate how autoethnography might look. These should not be used as definitive typologies, but instead as maps of the key discussions in autoethnographic inquiry and representation. Further, while there are criteria used to evaluate autoethnographic texts (see Bochner, 2000; Clough, 2000; Denzin, 2000; Ellis, 2000; Pelias, 2011; Pollock, 1998; Richardson, 2000, 2009; Spry, 2011), these criteria are more focused on strengthening the power and accessibility of the text; rarely are the criteria used to determine right or wrong, as life is much more complicated than such a binary construct.

Further, many essays in this Handbook illustrate the feminist, queer, indigenous and dialogic sensibilities of autoethnographic practice. Autoethnography is feminist with its focus on lived, personal experience, its appreciation of difference and intersectionality, and its valuing of rationality, emotionality, and multiple ways of knowing; queer in its attempts to fill necessary gaps in social and academic discourse, disrupt harmful assumptions of normalcy, foreground identity politics, and take an activist-oriented, critical sensibility to understanding experience; indigenous in the multiple ways it focuses on the ethics of representing others, its valuing of multiple ways of knowing and representing information—of not just using prose, but also poetry, art, and music; and dialogic in the method's call for collaboration as well as in its emphasis on finding ways to give back to others.

Given such sensibilities, we hold autoethnography to be one of the most ethical methods of and approaches to research, especially because it recognizes and tries to accommodate procedural, situational, and relational ethics (Ellis, 2007). We acknowledge and follow the procedural guidelines laid out by institutional review boards, yet understand that is only the beginning of doing ethical research. Thus, we concentrate in our projects on maintaining relationships of trust and respect. We try to be aware of those moments and situations that call into question how we are going about our research and how we are honoring and taking care of those others (and ourselves) who are part of—or affected by—the work we do. As an ethical research practice, autoethnography humanizes research processes and products and works to be more inclusive of how life is lived and how experience is storied.

The contributions of the Handbook authors and the expansion of autoethnography in numerous disciplines and in multiple publication venues point to the idea that more and more scholars and artists are coming to autoethnography with passion and energy, rather than with reluctance or fear about the career and personal implications of engaging in personally meaningful research. These events also point to the promise of autoethnography to imagine communal lives lived differently, fully, and justly. The acceptance, development, and hope of autoethnographers allow us to consider autoethnography a "what if" practice—a method for imagining, living into, and sharing our collective future. As we move into this future, we must be cognizant of the needs and limitations of autoethnography, including the approaches and examples presented in this Handbook. We offer these needs and limitations as a challenge to both current and future autoethnographers.

Needs and Limitations of this Handbook

While we have tried to capture portraits of autoethnographic life from scholars around the globe and from a variety of disciplines, there are some notable gaps. First, with the exception of a few chapters (e.g., Bartleet; Metta; Mingé; Tuck & Ree), this is a text-heavy collection. Writing continues to be the primary way of knowing in many areas of the academy, but we need to find ways to emphasize and appreciate non-text-dominant ways of knowing and representing research. We also need to nurture platforms for sharing non-text-based autoethnographic work, such as online journals, including *Liminalities, Forum: Qualitative Social Research,* and the "Alternative Scholarship" section of *Women and Language*, all of which can accommodate images, sounds, film and other interactive formats, And we would applaud seeing autoethnography work—text-based or arts-based—in popular venues such as StoryCorps recordings, the *It Gets Better Project*, or on *This American Life.*

In addition to expanding the media, formats, and venues for presenting autoethnographic work, we need to bridge the gap between approaches to conducting and presenting autoethnographic research, addressing the perceived cleavage among analytic and social scientific approaches and experimental and performative works. As the essays in this collection suggest, differences in our training, research commitments, and approaches to both writing and ethics guide and govern the written products of our work (see Allen-Collinson; Boylorn; Chang; Colyar; Denzin; Gingrich-Philbrook; Hernandez & Ngunjiri; Mingé; Tamas; Tullis). However, we must not let differences in training, commitments, and approaches limit and restrict the unifying potential of our work. Rather than proclaiming allegiance to one approach over the other, autoethnography can benefit from the strategic and integrative use of all manners of research approaches in producing work that engages and matters to audiences. We look forward to the day when analytic and arts-based autoethnographers work, write, create, and perform in collaboration.

Last, while this Handbook represents the interdisciplinary reach of autoethnography in numerous contexts, we take seriously the challenge issued by several authors: Western people, experiences, values, and desires are not and should not be the sole interest or province of qualitative research, including autoethnography

(Basu & Dutta; Crawley & Husakouskaya; Pathak; Tomaselli, Dyll-Myklebust, & van Grootheest; Tuck & Ree). To that end, we encourage non-Western writers and scholars working in non-Western contexts to consider how autoethnography might be used in telling other and different stories, as well as how the practice of autoethnography can be shaped and refined through the insights of non-Western storytellers.

There are surely other limitations to be found in this Handbook and other needs to address within and among the community of autoethnographers. Taken together, the needs and limitations we have identified here help direct us into the next era of autoethnographic research, and we welcome a new generation of autoethnographers.

Future Directions in Autoethnography

There are several new directions for future autoethnographic researchers and the next generation of autoethnographers to consider and pursue. One such direction is to engage in autoethnography as a process of collaboration—with other scholars as others as well as with the persons we love, work with, and study. Many of the authors in this collection (Anderson & Glass-Coffin; Crawley & Husakouskaya; Douglas & Carless; Dutta & Basu; Hernandez & Ngunjiri; Tomaselli, Dyll-Myklebust, & van Grootheest; Toyosaki & Pensoneau-Conway; Tuck & Ree; Wyatt & Gale) offer models for doing collaborative work (see also Ellis & Rawicki, in press a, b; Chang, Ngjuri, & Hernandez, 2012). Consider how we can embrace and expand the idea of collaboration among scholars by developing interdisciplinary projects and by seeking research and writing collaborations with the non-scholar collaborators in our work and our lives.

As we move into the future we must continue to develop ways of ethically engaging research and storymaking; we must not separate the experiences we are writing (or dancing, or singing, or painting) from the goals of the work, the judgments we might make of a story's impact or success, or the persons we become as storytellers (see Alexander; Berry; Chawla; Gannon; Richardson; Giorgio; Pelias; Poulos; Rambo; Shoemaker; Stewart). As autoethnographers, we must recognize that we are not removed or separate from the other human beings who populate our tales. Instead we must remain connected and committed to a position of autoethnographic engagement and humility inside and outside the story; as Craig Gingrich-Philbrook says in his essay, "Autoethnography may feel different from the experiences we *apply* it to, but our practice of it remains a human practice."

And finally, we urge autoethnographers to turn their attention to experiences of exclusion, degradation, and injustice, and in so doing, create work that not only makes the case for change but also embodies the change it calls into being. Several essays included in this Handbook (e.g., Dutta & Basu; Gingrich-Philbrook; Tillmann) enact the change they seek to make in the world in their stories, their orientation to writing, and the responsibilities of authorship. Further, these authors call on readers to fulfill their responsibilities to engage and to "write to right" (Bolen, 2012). For example, Tillmann urges allies and readers to "uphold each person's basic human rights—the right to safe, nutritious food; to clean air and water; to secure housing; to meaningful work; to health care; to be free from discrimination and violence; and to loving relationships."

To Tillmann's list we would add that the *right to story* is among each person's basic human rights. And so we issue the following call to action to all autoethnographers.

A Call to Action

While the journey of this Handbook is nearly complete, the autoethnographic exploration of selves, cultures, and worlds is just beginning. As you make your way into that world, we ask that you:

- Continue to further establish autoethnography as a rich and viable method for social research by teaching, talking about, and writing autoethnography.

- Continue to support others doing autoethnographic work by reading their research and including it on course syllabi and reading lists.

- Seek funding sources that support qualitative, artistic, and narrative-based research and apply for support for your autoethnographic research projects.

- Recognize and carefully consider critiques of the method (Atkinson, 1997; Atkinson & Delmont, 2010; Buzard, 2003; Coffey, 1999; Delamont, 2009; Tolich, 2010). Find ways to address these critiques, or put the critiques aside when they come from those who would never believe in autoethnography and for whom a "good" autoethnography would most likely never exist.

- Turn your attention toward the harm being done to us and to others and use autoethnographic research to tell and right stories of injustice.

- Write stories of compassion, of solidarity and communion, of change and justice, and of hope. These stories—your stories—are the future of autoethnography.

○

In closing, we hope that autoethnography continues to be more than a research method. We believe that autoethnography provides us with a way of telling the story of our future together. And we are confident that autoethnography will continue to be a way for us to live and to write life honestly, complexly, and passionately.

References

Atkinson, P. (1997). Narrative turn or blind alley? *Qualitative Health Research, 7,* 325–344.

Atkinson, P., & Delamont, S. (2010). Can the silenced speak? A dialogue for two unvoiced actors. *International Review of Qualitative Research, 3,* 11–17.

Bochner, A. P. (2000). Criteria against ourselves. *Qualitative Inquiry, 6,* 266–272.

Bochner, A. P. (2001). Narrative's virtues. *Qualitative Inquiry, 7,* 131–157.

Bolen, D. M. (2012). *Toward an applied communication relational inqueery: Autoethnography, co-constructed narrative, and relational futures.* Unpublished doctoral dissertation, Wayne State University, Detroit, Michigan.

Burke, K. (1974). *The philosophy of literary form: Studies in symbolic action* (3rd ed.). Berkeley: University of California Press.

Butler, J. (2005). *Giving an account of oneself.* New York: Fordham Press.

Buzard, J. (2003). On auto-ethnographic authority. *The Yale Journal of Criticism, 16,* 61–91.

Chang, H., Ngunjiri, F. W., & Hernandez, K-A. C. (2012). *Collaborative autoethnography.* Walnut Creek, CA: Left Coast Press, Inc.

Clough, P. T. (2000). Comments on setting criteria for experimental writing. *Qualitative Inquiry, 6,* 278–291.

Coffey, A. (1999). *The ethnographic self: Fieldwork and the representation of identity.* London: Sage.

Coles, R. (1989). *The call of stories.* Boston: Houghton Mifflin.

Delamont, S. (2009). The only honest thing: Autoethnography, reflexivity and small crises in fieldwork. *Ethnography and Education, 4,* 51–63.

Denzin, N. K. (2000). Aesthetics and the practices of qualitative inquiry. *Qualitative Inquiry, 6,* 256–265.

Ellis, C. (2000). Creating criteria: An ethnographic short story. *Qualitative Inquiry, 6,* 273–277.

Ellis, C. (2007). Telling secrets, revealing lives: Relational ethics in research with intimate others. *Qualitative Inquiry, 13,* 3–29.

Ellis, C, & Rawicki, J. (in press a). Collaborative witnessing of survival during the Holocaust: An exemplar of relational autoethnography. *Qualitative Inquiry.*

Ellis, C., & Rawicki, J. (in press b). Collaborative witnessing in conversations with Holocaust survivors. In S. High & H. Greenspan (Eds.), *Beyond trauma and testimony.* Vancouver: University of British Columbia Press.

Gingrich-Philbrook, C. (2005). Autoethnography's family values: Easy access to compulsory experiences. *Text and Performance Quarterly, 25,* 297–314.

Murphy Paul, A. (2012, March 17). Your brain on fiction. *The New York Times.* Retrieved from www.nytimes.com/2012/03/18/opinion/sunday/the-neuroscience-of-your-brain-on-fiction.html?pagewanted=all

Pelias, R. J. (2011). Writing into position: Strategies for composition and evaluation. In N. K. Denzin & Y. S. Lincoln (Eds.), *The SAGE handbook of qualitative research* (pp. 659–668). Thousand Oaks, CA: Sage.

Pollock, D. (1998). Performative writing. In P. Phelan & J. Lane (Eds.), *The ends of performance* (pp. 73–103). New York: New York University Press.

Richardson, L. (2000). Evaluating ethnography. *Qualitative Inquiry, 6,* 253–255.

Richardson, L. (2009). Tales from the crypt. *International Review of Qualitative Research, 2,* 345–350.

Spry, T. (2011). *Body, paper, stage: Writing and performing autoethnography.* Walnut Creek, CA: Left Coast Press, Inc.

Tolich, M. (2010). A critique of current practice: Ten foundational guidelines for autoethnographers. *Qualitative Health Research, 20,* 1599–1610.

Index

About the Authors

Tony E. Adams is Associate Professor in the Department of Communication, Media and Theatre at Northeastern Illinois University. He attended private Catholic school from age four until eighteen, worked as a bartender at Yellowstone National Park and a teller supervisor at a bank, and has been a vegetarian since 1998. Currently, he studies and teaches about interpersonal and family communication, qualitative research, communication theory, and sex, gender, and sexuality; he has published more than thirty articles, book chapters, and reviews in these areas. His book, *Narrating the Closet: An Autoethnography of Same Sex Desire* (2011), received the 2012 National Communication Association Ethnography Division Best Book Award and the 2012 Organization for the Study of Communication, Language, and Gender Outstanding Book Award. He is in the process of authoring another book about autoethnography with Stacy and Carolyn.

Bryant Keith Alexander serves as Dean of the College of Communication and Fine Arts at Loyola Marymount University, where he is also a Professor in the Department of Communication Studies. His interdisciplinary scholarship contributes to the fields of communication studies, cultural studies, gender and queer studies, African American Studies, race and sexuality studies, as well as performance and pedagogical studies. He is coeditor with Gary Anderson and Bernado Gallegos of *Theories in Education: Power, Pedagogy, and the Politics of Identity*. His book *Performing Black Masculinity: Race, Culture, and Queer Identity* won the 2007 Best Book Award from the National Communication Association's Ethnography Division. His scholarship appears in a wide range of journals and books, and in a series of juried, state-of-the art handbooks, including the *Handbook of Critical and Indigenous Methodologies*; the *Handbook of Performance Studies*; the *Handbook of Qualitative Research* (3rd edition); the *Blackwell Handbook of Critical Intercultural Communication*; and the *Handbook of Communication and Instruction*. He has published chapters in collections including: *Men and Masculinities: Critical Concepts in Sociology*; *Opening Acts: Performance in/as Communication and Cultural Criticism*; *Black Queer Studies: A Critical Anthology*; *Queer Theory and Communication: From Disciplining Queers to Queering the Discipline(s)*; *From Bourgeois to Boojie: Black Middle-Class Performances*; and *The Black Professoriate: Negotiating a Habitable Space*, and is included in the *Beacon Best 2000: Best Writing of Men and Women of All Colors*. His work in auto/ethnography includes "Rhetorics of Loss and Living: Adding New Panels to the AIDS Quilt as an Act of Eulogy" in the book *Remembering the AIDS Quilt* and a series of essays in collaboration with Claudio

Moreira and Hari Stephen Kumar, the first of which is titled "Resisting (Resistance) Stories: A Tri-Autoethnographic Exploration of Father Narratives Across Shades of Difference," published in *Qualitative Inquiry*. His next book project is the forthcoming *The Performative Sustainability of Race*, which will appear in Peter Lang's "Black Studies and Critical Thinking" book series.

Jacqueline Allen-Collison is Reader in the Sociology of Sport at the School of Sport & Exercise Science, University of London, where she has the (arduous) role of Director of Studies for the degree in Sport & Social Sciences. She has specialized in qualitative methodologies since her early doctoral days and is particularly interested in autoethnography—and now—autophenomenography. Her current research interests cohere around sociological and feminist phenomenological analyses of the body, including gendered and sporting bodies; symbolic interactionist approaches to identity, "identity work," and disrupted identities; and lived experiences of intimate partner abuse and violence. She has published in a wide range of international journals in both mainstream sociology and sports sociology and serves on various editorial boards, including the Editorial Associate Board of *Sociology* (the journal of the British Sociological Association) and the Editorial Board of *Sociological Research Online*. For her, one of the great delights of "teaching" (if that is the correct term!) autoethnography and autophenomenography is seeing—and feeling—the huge impact it can have on students' and researchers' lived experience.

Leon Anderson is a Professor of Sociology and Head of the Department of Sociology, Social Work, and Anthropology at Utah State University. He is the co-author, with David A. Snow, of *Down on Their Luck: A Study of Homeless Street People* and with John Lofland, David Snow, and Lyn Lofland, the fourth edition of *Analyzing Social Settings*. Prior to pursuing a career in sociology and higher education, he worked a variety of jobs in the Northwest, including forest fire fighting in Oregon, crab cannery work in Dutch Harbor, Alaska; and grave digging in Montana. In the early 1980s he worked as a youth counselor in Anchorage and wrote feature stories for the *Anchorage Daily News*. In 1983 he entered graduate school at the University of Texas, where he pursued qualitative research under the mentorship of David Snow. From 1988 until 2011, he taught at Ohio University in Athens, Ohio. He began to seriously pursue autoethnographic research and writing in the early 2000s as he sought to reinforce what he felt were the often unacknowledged connections between traditional Chicago School ethnography and contemporary autoethnographic writing. He is currently working on a sociology of deviance textbook and an ethnography of sport skydiving, while trying to balance life as a scholar, department head, outdoor enthusiast, and grandfather. He can be reached for comment at leon.anderson@usu.edu.

Brydie-Leigh Bartleet is a Senior Lecturer at the Queensland Conservatorium Griffith University, Australia. She was Research Fellow on the Australia Research Council funded project *Sound Links* (2007–2008), one of Australia's largest studies into community music. Her current research projects include an Australia Research Council funded project *Captive Audiences* (2012–2013), which explores performing arts rehabilitation programs in prisons, and an Australian Government Office for Learning and Teaching funded project, *Enhancing Indigenous Content in Performing Arts Curricula Through Service Learning with Indigenous Communities* (2011–2013). She serves on a range of international and national boards, including the International Society for Music Education's *Community Music Activities Commission*, the Music Council of Australia, and the editorial board for the *International Journal of Community Music*, and she has served the Musicological Society of Australia for a number of years in various national and state positions. She has over eighty publications on topics that explore the contemporary realities of music making, such as community music, women's music, cross-cultural music projects, conducting practice and pedagogy, and music autoethnography. She has published her work in a number of high profile international journals, including the *International Journal of Music Education, British Journal of Music Education, Journal of Contemporary Ethnography, College Music Symposium*, and the *International Journal of Community Music*, and has presented at a number of international and national conferences and symposia. She has also co-edited three books on music-related topics—*Music Autoethnographies: Making Autoethnography Sing/Making Music Personal*; *Musical Islands: Exploring Connections between Music, Place and Research*; and *Navigating Music and Sound Education*, as well as a special issue of the *International Journal of Community Music* on music in the Asia Pacific region. As a community music facilitator she has conducted bands, orchestras, choirs, and jazz ensembles from Australia, Thailand, Singapore, and Taiwan, and has also worked as a sessional lecturer at the University of Queensland and as a multi-instrumental teacher in schools in Brisbane and Bangkok.

Ambar Basu is an Assistant Professor in the Department of Communication at the University of South Florida. His research focuses on health communication, culture, the environment, and marginalization. Specifically, his research positions culture and health communication within the transformational politics of broader theoretical and methodological frameworks such as postcolonial and subaltern studies and critical ethnography. He was awarded the Janice Hocker Rushing Early Career Research Award for 2011 by the Southern States Communication Association. He has published in journals including *Communication Monographs, Human Communication Research, Health Communication, Qualitative Health Research*, and in books such as *Learning Race and Ethnicity: Youth and Digital Media* and the *Routledge Handbook of Health Communication*.

Keith Berry is an Associate Professor in the Department of Communication at the University of South Florida and recently served as Chair of the National Communication Association's Ethnography Division. His work draws together phenomenology and diverse (auto)ethnographic methods to examine communication, culture and identity, particularly the constitution of subjectivity across diverse relational and cultural scenes. He has published in journals such as

Cultural Studies ↔ Critical Methodologies, Qualitative Inquiry, International Journal of Qualitative Methods, and *Liminalities: A Journal of Performance Studies,* and in books such as *Identity Research and Communication: Intercultural Reflections and Future Directions.*

Arthur P. Bochner took the narrative turn in the 1980s and has never looked back. As fate would have it, a chance encounter with one Carolyn Ellis in 1990 inspired a partnership in love and work that inspired two jointly edited volumes and numerous chapters, stories, and essays aimed at opening a space of inquiry into what it can mean to know one is alive, to care about what one can do to make life better, and to pay greater attention to the difficulties, hardships, and injustices that permeate the human condition. "I am honored to have earned the highest rank of Distinguished University Professor at the University of South Florida and to have been selected as an NCA (National Communication Association) Distinguished Scholar. I have been blessed to live a life of learning and teaching. The son of working class parents, I am grateful for the opportunities I was given by them and by mentors and colleagues to live productively through the golden age of university education. My autoethnography of my life in school, *Coming to Narrative: Method and Meaning in a University Life,* will be published in 2013 by Left Coast Press, Inc. My 'other life' includes a passion for raising and caring for peonies and dahlias, and for my canine pals, Buddha and Zen, who remind me to live in the moment with joy and appreciation for life's many gifts and pleasures."

Robin M. Boylorn is Assistant Professor of Interpersonal and Intercultural Communication in the Department of Communication Studies at the University of Alabama. Her research focuses on issues of diversity and social identity, and the intersections of race, class, and gender/sex. Her work, utilizing her personal lived experience(s) and creative and performative writing, offers social and cultural critiques of representations of black women. Her publications include articles in *Cultural Studies ↔ Critical Methodologies, Qualitative Inquiry, International Journal of Qualitative Methods,* and *Critical Studies in Media Communication.* Her first book, *Sweetwater: Black Women and Narratives of Resilience,* was published by Peter Lang in 2013.

David Carless is a Reader in Narrative Psychology in the Research Institute for Sport, Physical Activity and Leisure at Leeds Metropolitan University, UK. In his interdisciplinary research—which draws on psychology, sociology, and performing arts—he uses storied forms of communication to understand and represent human experience. Through a variety of narrative, performative and arts-based methods, this work explores the ways identity and mental health are developed, threatened, or recovered in physical activity and sport related contexts. His work has been published in two-dozen different international journals, and he is co-author with Kitrina Douglas of *Sport and Physical Activity for Mental Health* (2010).

Heewon Chang is Professor of Organizational Leadership and Multicultural Education at Eastern University in Pennsylvania. She was born to education, is married to education, and breathes education. Her educational journey began in South Korea, where she was born to two professors of education. Since she started first grade, she has been in school over four decades, either learning or teaching. After completing a bachelor's degree in education at Yonsei University in South Korea, she came to the University of Oregon to pursue an MA and PhD in educational anthropology under the tutelage of Harry Wolcott. During graduate school, she found a soul mate. Perhaps it is not surprising that her soul mate, born to two math educators in Germany, turned out to be a math professor. She breathes education daily, whether she works with her PhD students or teenagers in her church, and lives her belief that all can be educated and good and equal education for all can improve an entire society.

She joined Eastern University in 1994 as a member of the faculty in the MEd in multicultural education and currently holds a joint faculty appointment in the PhD in Organizational Leadership as well. Since she joined Eastern University, she has founded two online journals. Currently she serves as Editor-in-Chief of the *International Journal of Multicultural Education,* an open-access peer-review scholarly e-journal. She has authored or edited four books, including *Adolescent Life and Ethos: An Ethnography of a US High School* (1992), *Autoethnography as Method* (2008), *Spirituality in Higher Education: Autoethnographies* (co-edited with Drick Boyd, 2011), and *Collaborative Autoethnography* (co-authored with Faith Ngunjiri and Kathy-Ann Hernandez, 2012). Her research agenda includes qualitative research methods, including autoethnography, leadership mentoring, educational equity and justice, multicultural education, and anthropology of education.

Devika Chawla is Associate Professor in the School of Communication Studies, Ohio University. Her scholarly research focuses on communicative, performative, and narrative approaches to family identity in the South Asian Indian context. Her areas of intellectual interest include postcolonial and transnational studies, performance, ethnography, interpretive research, and memoir. Her essays have been published in numerous communication and interdisciplinary periodicals and a number of edited volumes. She is the author of two books: *Intercultural Communication: An Ecological Approach* (with Amardo Rodriguez, 2010) and *Liminal Traces: Storying Performing, and Embodying Postcoloniality* (2011). She is currently at work on a monograph about narratives of home, travel, and identity in cross-generational oral histories of refugees in India's Partition.

She lives in the rolling hills of Athens County in Appalachian Ohio. She walks daily.

Julia E. Colyar is an Assistant Professor in the Department of Educational Leadership & Policy at the University at Buffalo, where she teaches courses in student affairs administration and higher education. She previously worked as an academic advisor for undergraduate students and has taught undergraduate courses in composition and literature. Her research focuses on access and transitions to college for low-income, underrepresented students; in particular, she is interested in the ways student identities are shaped by college environments. In 2009, she co-edited a book with William G. Tierney called *Urban High School Students and the Challenge of Access.* Recently, she has written about the constructions of "remedial" and "elite," two labels increasingly applied in higher education, but not always in productive ways. She also thinks and writes about qualitative research and narrative methods. Her writing can be found in *Qualitative Inquiry, Educational Researcher,* and *Theory into Practice.* She completed a master's degree in English Literature at the University of Toronto, and a PhD in Higher Education at the University of Southern California.

Sara L. Crawley is Associate Professor of Sociology at the University of South Florida, and also regularly teaches in the Department of Women's and Gender Studies. Trained in both qualitative sociology and women's studies, she focuses on the interdisciplinary space compelled by feminist and queer theories, especially on topics of the body and bodily experience, and regularly employs autoethnography as method. Her book *Gendering Bodies* (coauthored with Lara J. Foley and Constance L. Shehan) adds interpretive sociology to gender and sexualities theories to explain how gender gets written on and produced by bodies in interaction. Having published autoethnographic work in *Feminism and Psychology, Feminist Teacher, Journal of Lesbian Studies, Journal of Contemporary Ethnography,* and *Cultural Studies ↔ Critical Methodologies,* she recently was invited to hold workshops on feminist theory, queer theory, and interpretive methods in Ukraine for scholars from post-Soviet countries; some of her works have recently been translated into Russian.

Norman K. Denzin is Distinguished Professor of Communications, College of Communications Scholar, and Research Professor of Communications, Sociology, and Humanities at the University of Illinois, Urbana-Champaign. He is the author or editor of more than two dozen books, including *Custer On Canvas; The Qualitative Manifesto; Qualitative Inquiry Under Fire; Searching for Yellowstone; Reading Race; Interpretive Ethnography; The Cinematic Society; The Voyeur's Gaze*; and *The Alcoholic Self.* He is past editor of *The Sociological Quarterly,* co-editor (with Yvonna S. Lincoln) of four editions of the *Handbook of Qualitative Research,* co-editor (with Michael D. Giardina) of five plenary volumes from the annual Congress of Qualitative Inquiry, co-editor (with Lincoln) of the methods journal *Qualitative Inquiry,* founding editor of *Cultural Studies ↔ Critical Methodologies* and *International Review of Qualitative Research,* and editor of three book series.

Kitrina Douglas's background is eclectic, revealing a meandering history in professional sport, journalism, commentary work for the BBC and Eurposport, alongside a desire to understand and make sense of life (her own and others'). As an independent researcher she has carried out research for a variety of agencies, including the Department of Heath, NHS Trusts, UK sport, the Addiction Recovery Agency, and the Women's Sport and Fitness Foundation. The research she has been involved with reflects her interests in physical activity and mental health, reflexivity, narrative inquiry, and creative performative methodologies. She has a Visiting Fellowship in the Centre for Exercise Nutrition and Health Sciences, School for Policy Studies, University of Bristol, where she earned her PhD.

Mohan J. Dutta is Professor and Head of the Department of Communication and New Media at the National University of Singapore and the Founding Director of the Center for Culture-Centered Approach to Research and Evaluation (CARE). He holds an adjunct appointment with the Brian Lamb School of Communication and with the Center on Poverty and Health Inequities (COPHI) at Purdue University. His research specialties are grassroots activism for social change, culture-centered approaches to global public relations, Marxist theories of social change, new media and social change, and postcolonial and subaltern studies approaches to communication. He is the winner of the PRIDE award for the best published article in public relations in 2005, and he was recognized as a University Faculty Scholar by Purdue University for his scholarly excellence. He has published over 150 journal articles and book chapters and is an author or editor of six scholarly books.

Lauren Dyll-Myklebust is Lecturer and Graduate Supervisor at The Centre for Communication, Media and Society at the University of KwaZulu-Natal in South Africa. She lectures graduate modules in development and public health communication (with an emphasis on social and behavioral change). She is a key contributor to the Kalahari research project entitled *Rethinking Indigeneity,* within which both her MA and PhD are based. Her research interests and publication topics include: development communication, cultural tourism with particular emphasis on issues of identity as well as stakeholder relationships, critical indigenous qualitative research including autoethnography, and mediagraphy as methodology.

Carolyn Ellis is first and foremost an autoethnographer who lives and loves the autoethnographic life. She is honored to have received the 2012 Lifetime Achievement Award in Qualitative Inquiry from The International Center for Qualitative Inquiry. She knows she is fortunate to have one of the best jobs in the world as Distinguished University Professor in the Department of Communication at the University of South Florida. Her most recent books include *The Ethnographic I: A Methodological Novel about Autoethnography*; *Revision: Autoethnographic Reflections on Life and Work;* and *Music Autoethnographies: Making Autoethnography Sing/Making Music Personal.* She has thoroughly enjoyed working on this Handbook with Stacy and Tony and is now excited to begin writing another autoethnography book with them, which will be published by Oxford University Press. She has published numerous articles, chapters, and personal stories situated in emotions and interpretive representations of qualitative research, particularly autoethnography. Her current research focuses on listening to Holocaust testimonies, and sharing authority in a collaborative research process with first- and second-generation survivors. Soon to be chair of her department, she hopes to keep her optimistic spirit and continue to write. Most definitely she will need many long mountain walks with her partner Art and their dog companions, Buddha and Zen.

Ken Gale works as a Lecturer in Education in the School of Education at Plymouth University. His main teaching and research interests can broadly be contextualized within the philosophy of education. More specifically, he is interested in the spaces of inquiry that open up when the work of post structural theorists—in particular Deleuze and Guattari, but also Foucault, Derrida, Butler, Irigaray and others—is used in relation to and in conjunction with creative approaches to the performance of the self and others. His collaborative and performative teaching and research practices connect with narrative and autoethnographic forms of inquiry, and he works to apply these to theory/practice or conceptual/contextual relations as a means of exploring and inquiring into a number of areas of interest, including subjectivity, friendship, gender, teaching and learning, and professional identity and practice style.

He has published widely and presented at a number of international conferences in all the above fields. He was part of a funded project to develop online resources on collaborative writing for early career researchers and faculty: www.writeinquiry. org. With Bronwyn Davies, Susanne Gannon, and Jonathan Wyatt he recently co-authored the book, *Deleuze and Collaborative Writing: An Immanent Plane of Composition* (Peter Lang, 2011), and more recently, with friends and colleagues Jonathan Wyatt, Tami Spry, Ron Pelias and Larry Russell, he has co-authored the book *How Writing Touches: An Intimate Scholarly Collaboration* (Cambridge Scholars). He is an associate member of the Higher Education Academy, a member of the International Association of Qualitative Inquiry and the Narrative Inquiry Centre at the University of Bristol, where he is also a Visiting Fellow.

He has three children, Katy, Reuben and Phoebe; has recently become a grandfather to Rohan James; and lives and nurtures, and sustains his soul in Cornwall in the UK.

Susanne Gannon is an Associate Professor in the School of Education and Centre for Educational Research at the University of Western Sydney (UWS), Australia. With other members of the Centre she is interested in how issues of equity, globalization, and place contribute to sustainability in the broadest sense. She was a secondary English teacher and curriculum adviser in various locations in Australia before returning to university for higher degree research. She began working with Bronwyn Davies in her Masters (with honors) and PhD, and this continued for some years within a highly productive but now defunct research group, Narrative, Discourse and Pedagogy, at UWS. Her expertise in teaching includes a diverse array of qualitative research methodologies and English education, particularly pedagogies of writing. Although she would rather write literary texts than academic ones, her output in the former remains slim and in the latter prolific. Nevertheless, she tries to bring a literary sensibility and attention to the aesthetics, ethics, and affective potentialities of texts to everything she writes.

Her publications include several co-edited and co-authored books: *Deleuze and Collaborative Writing: An Immanent Plane of Composition* (with Wyatt, Gale, and Davies, 2011); *Place Pedagogy Change* (with Somerville, Davies, Power, and Carteret, 2011); *Pedagogical Encounters* (with Davies and others, 2009); and *Doing Collective Biography* (with Davies and others, 2006). She is currently working on a book on collective biographies of girlhood with Marnina Gonick of Mount Saint Vincent University, Nova Scotia, Canada. She has also published numerous book chapters and journal articles. Although she critiques the intensification of academic labor in the performative university, she simultaneously incorporates its practices into her everyday life, demonstrating the paradoxical relationship of submission and mastery that Judith Butler writes about and the disciplinary technologies that Michel Foucault writes about. In much of this work she finds poststructural theory helpful to think through taken for granted normative discourses, and she hopes to find "lines of flight," to borrow from Gilles Deleuze, that might help her cope with the territorializing practices of contemporary academic life. For example, she chooses to live with parrots and possums in the beautiful Blue Mountains west of Sydney, tries sporadically to grow vegetables, and likes to sing in a community choir on Tuesday nights.

Craig Gingrich-Philbrook is an Associate Professor of Performance Studies in the Speech Communication Department at Southern Illinois University, Carbondale (SIUC). His work has appeared in such journals as *Text and Performance Quarterly, Communication Theory, The Quarterly Journal of Speech, The Journal of Homosexuality, Cultural Studies*, and *Liminalities: An Online Journal of Performance Studies*. At SIUC he teaches courses in performance studies, queer theory, and creative collaboration, and holds the William and Galia Minor Professorship in Creative Communication. He has presented his autobiographical performance work at universities around the country and at performance art venues, including Dixon Place and SUSHI. In 2008, he received the National Communication Association's Irene Coger Award for Outstanding Performance.

Grace A. Giorgio directs the writing programs for the Department of Communication at the University of Illinois. Her research, writing, and teaching examine communication practices in interpersonal and public domains, with the intention of bridging the personal and the political. She studies the experimental use of qualitative research methods to investigate the intersection of self, culture, and the public sphere. Her research interests include using writing as a method of inquiry to creatively and critically explore the cultural expectations and tensions in interpersonal and family communication contexts. She is particularly interested in the healing powers of writing in all of its creative and experimental formations. Her autoethnographies explore these subjects through the short story format and include "The Wedding Dress" (2008), "Gigi's Tipis" (2010), "The Hermit and the Old Goat" (2010), and "In His Own Time" (forthcoming). Living in rural Illinois has brought her to also study questions of sustainability in public policy discourse. Her work also explores what James Howard Kunstler (2005) calls the Long Emergency, a time of contraction in resources and capital and of climate change. Her writings and public policy course attend to how we will manage these exigencies and the demands they place upon our culture; she hopes her work will help us imagine and manifest a more sustainable way of life. She also teaches gender communication courses and has published critical essays and *Contesting the Utopia: Power and Resistance in Lesbian Relationships* (2010).

Bonnie Glass-Coffin is Professor of Anthropology at Utah State University. She came to autoethnography as a preferred method for sharing her research with readers because of her early work with female shamans (called *curanderas*) in Northern Peru. While she was conducting dissertation research, her informants insisted that it is only through the lens of personal awakening and through validating everyday life "experience" as sacred that healing occurs. They challenged her to write of her own experiences in the field and her own transformations as she discussed their work and their lives. Her first book, *The Gift of Life: Female Spirituality and Healing in Northern Peru* (1998), intentionally wove her personal story of healing together with a more academic treatment of gender and shamanism to honor what she learned from these women. Since then, she has written herself into many of her scholarly articles, even as she has expanded her interests to explore more generally the roles played by personal experience and transformation in ethnographic writing, as a model for learning in university classrooms, and as a mandate for ethical interaction with the multiple worlds in which we live. She has published her work in English and in Spanish in book chapters and journals such as *Ethnohistory*, the *Journal of Ritual Studies, Zygon, Anthropology and Humanism*, and *Anthropology* of *Consciousness*. She can be reached for comment at bonnie.glasscoffin@usu.edu.

H. L. (Bud) Goodall, Jr. (September 8, 1952–August 24, 2012) was a Professor in the Hugh Downs School of Human Communication at Arizona State University. A pioneer in the field of narrative ethnography, he wrote many books about culture, including *Casing a Promised Land* (1989), *Living in the Rock n Roll Mystery* (1991), and *Writing the New Ethnography* (2000). His memoir, *A Need to Know: The Clandestine History of a CIA Family* (2006), won the Best Book of 2007 Award from the Ethnography Division of the National Communication Association. He also applied theories of communication and narrative to counter ideological support for terrorism, resulting in the edited volume, *Weapons of Mass Persuasion: Strategic Communication and the War of Ideas* (with Corman and Trethewey, 2008). His recent work consisted of an autoethnographic blog called *The Daily Narrative*, where he invited readers to accompany him on his fifteen-month journey with pancreatic cancer, in what he called Cancerland. There he demonstrated with emotional honesty, generosity, and utmost tenderness the absolute best that autoethnography can be as he explored and provided insights about the meaning of life, loving, and living well, and dying a good death. His words touched us deeply, including those of us who had never met him, and he brought us all together into a community who cared about him and each other. Many of his colleagues and students contributed to *Celebrating Bud: A Festschrift in Honor of the Life & Work of H.L. "Bud" Goodall, Jr.* (edited by Sarah Amira de la Garza, Robert Krizek, and Nick Trujillo, 2012). Bud's friends and colleagues are deeply saddened by the loss of this inspiring narrative ethnographer and autoethnographer who touched so many lives so profoundly.

Kathy-Ann Hernandez is passionate about books and well-crafted stories! Growing up in the twin island Republic of Trinidad and Tobago, she was an avid reader. Her father and grandmother nurtured this love. Her dad filled their house with books.

Her grandmother's house did not have many books as she did not need them. At night, her grandmother entertained them with fanciful folktales as they sat on long wooden benches on the moonlit verandah. She knew that she wanted to tell stories and see them printed in books. She wanted her stories to captivate others the way her grandmother's tales would charm listeners and elicit the response: "Tell us another one, Ma… Please!!"

In the process of making a career, somehow this early passion got slightly derailed. She did end up in the academy—certainly a place where books abound. However, something did not feel quite right. Her field of study, educational psychology, is steeped in the positivistic paradigm and elevates objectivity as the sine qua non of rigorous research. In elementary school, her teachers often complemented her writing abilities, but in graduate school, one of her first papers, which she wrote with meticulous care, came back with lots of red marks. Several words were circled, and her professor had written the terse comment: "Avoid literary terms." She did not need to be told twice; she learned quickly to silence her lyrical voice. In 2008 she was introduced to autoethnography by her colleague, Heewon Chang. Here was an approach to research that was antithetical to everything she had been taught in graduate school. Was this legitimate research? She was not sure, but she was intrigued. At the core, she still values research that challenges her to address the nomothetic function of science. However, she has a visceral connection to a line of inquiry that allows her to tell the untold side of her research agenda. This approach celebrates the ideas, feelings, and perceptions of researchers who are themselves critical to the research process, yet often find their own voice silenced in their scholarship. Finally, the chance to speak in her own voice!

At Eastern University, she teaches courses in research methods and is the Director of Research for the Loeb School of Education. Her research targets the Black diaspora and issues affecting disengagement and underachievement of students, experiences of women of color in the academy, and spiritual affiliation and constructions of Black masculinity. She has written a number of book chapters and articles in line with her research interests. She was also a co-editor for a special issue of the *Journal of Research Practice* on autoethnography (2010), and is a co-author of *Collaborative Autoethnography* (with Heewon Chang and Faith Ngunjiri, 2012). Together with her husband, she owns and manages a consulting practice in Philadelphia. Through autoethnography, she is learning how to unite her scholarship with her early passions—to tell stories that elicit the welcome request: "Tell us another one… Please!"

Stacy Holman Jones is Professor, Graduate Coordinator, and Co-Director of the Performance Ensemble at California State University, Northridge (CSUN). Prior to joining the faculty at CSUN, she was Associate Professor and Graduate Director at the University of South Florida. She received a BA in Distributed from Iowa State University, her MA in Communication Studies from California State University, Sacramento, and her PhD in Performance Studies from the University of Texas at Austin. Her research focuses broadly on how performance constitutes socially, culturally, and politically resistive and transformative activity; how gender and desirous and desirous identities are created, made known, and negotiated; and how the work of feminism gets done in and though interpretive methods, especially cultural critique, critical autoethnography, and performative writing. She is the author of *Kaleidoscope Notes: Writing Women's Music and Organizational Culture* (1998) and *Torch Singing: Performing Resistance and Desire from Edith Piaf to Billie Holiday* (2007). She is co-editor, with Tony Adams and Carolyn Ellis, of this Handbook and *Autoethnography*, part of Oxford University Press's Understanding Qualitative Research Series (forthcoming, 2014). She has published essays in *Text and Performance Quarterly, Qualitative Inquiry, Cultural Studies ↔ Critical Methodologies,* and the *Journal of Contemporary Ethnography.* She is the recipient of several research and teaching/mentoring awards, including the Janice Hocker Rushing Early Career Research Award and the Organization for the Study of Communication, Language, and Gender's Feminist Teacher/Mentor Award. She teaches graduate courses in performance, feminist studies, and qualitative methods, including performing ethnography and autoethnography. She loves working with Carolyn and Tony and hopes to get to do so for a long time to come. After years of listening to torch singers, she still enjoys a sad song. She is an avid and aspiring writer, reader, home cook, and foodie, though her most cherished avocations are being a mom and partner.

Nadzeya Husakouskaya (Nadya Gusakovskaya/Надежда Гусаковская/ Надзея Гусакоская) is a lecturer at European Humanity University (EHU), Belarusian university in exile in Vilnius, Lithuania. She is also an Associated Researcher and Board Member of the Centre for Gender Studies at EHU. After closure of the University in Minsk, Belarus, in 2004, She followed the re-established institution to Lithuania, where over the course of the past six years, she has been teaching gender-related courses, including *Foundations of Gender Theory, Theory and Practice of Feminism, Gender and Capitalism,* the first such courses offered for Belarusians. Her academic interests include gender and queer theory, focusing on the body and sexuality, feminist methodology, critical pedagogy, and, recently, migration. She has been published in Russian in collective volumes such as *Belarusian Format: Invisible Reality* (2008), *Relevant Problems of Social and Human Science* (2007), *Gender and Transgression in Visual Art* (2007), *Variation on Gender* (2004). After migrating to Lithuania in 2006 she kept working with gender issues, targeting Belarusian NGOs. From 2008 till 2011 she collaborated with the International Organization for Migration to conduct a series of gender training sessions. In 2011 she headed a one-year project hosted by Belarusian Human Rights House in Vilnius and aimed to form and foster a new group of opinionated women activists dealing with the ideas of gender sensitivity and gender equality in Belarus.

Although her professional focus has largely been on theory, the many activities that enrich her life and work have taken place largely outside of the classroom. In 2006 she worked as Student Affaires Office Manager at EHU, facilitating the transition and adaptation of Belarusian students to Lithuania. For four years starting in 2007, she led a large social and educational project—*LitPro*—launched at EHU and supported by the Ministry of Foreign Affaires of the Republic of Lithuania and aimed at developing an intercultural dialogue between Belarus and Lithuania. While in Lithuania, she initiated and managed a varied set of social and cultural events focusing in particular on gender, representation, visibility and migration issues, including a theatrical project, *In-Between,* *K.V. Shorts Festival,* focusing on inconvenient issues and a social project, *FotoLab.Exclusion,* dealing with anti-discrimination issues.

She has always been fascinated by writing practices—writing diaries since age nineteen. She was one of the winners of the Belarusian National Competition of Young Writers in 2000. She co-founded and worked as editor and author of the e-zine *Takaya* launched by the Center for Gender Studies at EHU in Minsk in 2003. Currently pursuing her life experience and academic interests in gender and migration, she entered the Erasmus Mundus MA program on Migration and Intercultural Relations. In 2012 she joined the African Centre for Migration and Society at the University of the Witwatersrand in Johannesburg, South Africa, as a visiting researcher studying migration and sexuality in urban space.

Marilyn Metta is a feminist academic in the School of Social Sciences and Asian Languages at Curtin University in Perth, Western Australia. She has an interdisciplinary background and has taught across a wide range of disciplines, including women's studies, social sciences, gender studies, social work, cultural studies and counseling. She is a practicing psychotherapist at the West Leederville Counselling Centre in Perth. Her counseling work with individuals, families, and children has been important in informing her research and teaching work and vice versa. Her research interests are in lifewriting, feminist and gender studies, domestic violence, ethnic/migrant identities, Asian Australian studies, and psychotherapy. She has researched extensively in the areas of family and domestic violence and feminist lifewriting. Her upcoming research is an ethnographic study of the Burmese Chin women refugees living in Malaysia.

She is the author of *Writing Against, Alongside and Beyond Memory. Lifewriting as Reflexive, Poststructuralist Feminist Research Practice* (2010), which won the International Congress of Qualitative Inquiry 2011 Qualitative Book Award. The book explores how memory, embedded in our scripts of the past, inscribed in our bodies, and reflected in the collective memory of every family, group, and community, occupies one of the most controversial and contested sites over what constitutes legitimate knowledge-making. Using a reflexive feminist research methodology, the book engages in memory-work in creating three life narratives written in different narrative styles: her mother and father's biographies and her autobiography/autoethnography. By exploring the intersections of race, gender, ethnicity, and culture in the social and cultural constructions of identities in the lifewriting, this book maps the underlying politics of storytelling and storymaking, and investigates the political, social, pedagogical, and therapeutic implications of writing personal life narratives for feminist scholarship, research, and practice.

She is a Malaysian-born Chinese Australian, has two children, and lives in Perth, Western Australia.

Jeanine Marie Mingé's areas of interest include performance studies, feminist theory, queer theory, community art, and arts-based inquiry. All of her work is dedicated to cultivating social justice. She is equally enthralled by and creates the communicative presence of visual imagery, poetry, installation art, narrative, and performance. Her book, co-authored with Amber Lynn Zimmerman and part of Routledge's "Innovative Ethnographies" series, is entitled *Concrete and Dust: Mapping the Sexual Terrains of Los Angeles* (2013). This book is an arts-based autoethnography of place and sexualities in Los Angeles. She is developing a solo performance based on the manuscript and will be touring this work nationally. In April 2011, she was invited to give the Keynote Address on this work at James Madison University's 33rd Annual Communication Studies Conference. A recently published article in *Text and Performance Quarterly* entitled "Not Exactly the Same Parenting Story: Or, How Do We Live in the Academy" was an invited review of a performance by scholar/artist Deanna Shoemaker. She has also published work in *Qualitative Inquiry* and *Studies in Symbolic Interactionism*.

Faith Wambura Ngunjiri received a bachelor's degree in education in Language and Literature and a master's degree in Missions Studies, both from universities in her native Kenya. In 2003, she came to the United States to undertake further studies, and earned a Masters of Organization Development and an EdD in Leadership Studies, both from Bowling Green State University. This diverse educational experience has produced varied interests, mostly focused on leadership: women and leadership; women and religious leadership; spiritual leadership; servant leadership; and culturally responsive research approaches. Autoethnography has proved to be a valuable research approach to studying these subjects.

Since mid-2008, she has been teaching leadership studies and research design courses to graduate students at Eastern University, a Christian college located in the lush suburbs west of Philadelphia. She loves the part of her job that involves teaching, guiding dissertation research, serving on the Institutional Review Board, and working with mostly warm, friendly, and supportive colleagues. Then there's the part of the job she hates—the soul-killing, ego-driven, micro-aggressive behaviors that leave an African immigrant woman professor feeling unwelcome in the environment. But, that's not a line for the bio… it's a line in an autoethnography on experiences of minority women of color in academia.

Along with her responsibilities of teaching, service, and research (in that order), she is also the inaugural Director of Research at the graduate college. Her responsibility involves cajoling an unwilling administration to provide more resources for faculty research and encouraging frustrated and overworked faculty to engage in scholarly publishing. She has published articles in the *Journal of Research Practice*, the *International and Intercultural Communication Annual*, the *Journal of Business Communication*, the *Journal of Pan African Studies*, and the *Journal of Educational Administration*, among others. She has also published book chapters, one solo authored book, *Women's Spiritual Leadership in Africa* (2010), and one co-authored book, *Collaborative Autoethnography* (with Heewon Chang and Kathy-Ann Hernandez, 2012).

Archana A. Pathak is Assistant Professor of Gender, Sexuality & Women's Studies at Virginia Commonwealth University. She is also President of the Board of The Conciliation Project, a social justice theater organization. She identifies as a post-colonialist feminist scholar who examines issues of race, class, gender, sexuality, nationality, and scientific imperialism from a social justice perspective.

Ronald J. Pelias teaches performance studies in the Department of Speech Communication at Southern Illinois University, Carbondale. He works on the stage primarily as a director and on the page as a writer committed to non-traditional forms of representation. His most recent books exploring qualitative methods are *Leaning: A Poetics of Personal Relations* (2011) and *How Writing Touches: An Intimate Scholarly Collaboration* (2012) with Ken Gale, Larry Russell, Tami Spry, and Jonathan Wyatt.

Sandra L. Pensoneau-Conway is Assistant Professor of Speech Communication at Southern Illinois University Carbondale. She holds a BS (cum laude) in Speech Communication from Southern Illinois University Edwardsville (1999), an MS in Speech Communication from Southern Illinois University Carbondale (2001), and a PhD in Speech Communication from Southern Illinois University Carbondale (2006). After teaching for over six years at Wayne State University in Detroit, Michigan, she returned to Carbondale. Her teaching and research interests include critical communication pedagogy, communication and identity, and automethods. She is also the Director of the SPCM 101 Introductory Communication course. She is currently working on several projects, including a qualitative study that explores Freire's conceptualization of semi-intransitive, naïve transitive, and critical transitive consciousness as it relates to understanding privilege among first-year college students.

She has been nominated for and/or received numerous awards for teaching and research. Most recently, she was nominated for the Outstanding Faculty Award in Speech Communication. Prior to that, she was awarded the Harriet Dowdell Bantz, Sandra Petronio, & Charles R. Bantz Faculty Research Award, the Commitment to Excellence in Graduate Education Award, and the Graduate College Teaching Award (all at Wayne State University). She was also nominated for the President's Award for Excellence in Teaching at Wayne State University. She has presented research at local, regional, national, and international conferences. Her recent publications appear in the *International Journal of Qualitative Methods*, along with essays in the edited books *Communication Centers and Oral Communication Programs in Higher Education: Advantages, Challenged, and New Directions* (2012) and *Identity and Communication Research: Intercultural Reflections and Future Directions* (2012).

Christopher N. Poulos is Associate Professor and Chair of Communication Studies at the University of North Carolina at Greensboro. An ethnographer and philosopher of communication, he teaches courses in relational and family communication, ethnography, dialogue, and film studies. His book is *Accidental Ethnography: An Inquiry into Family Secrecy* (2009). And his work has appeared in *Qualitative Inquiry, Communication Theory, Southern Communication Journal,* and in several edited books.

Carol Rambo is Associate Professor of Sociology at The University of Memphis, and a former editor of *Symbolic Interaction*. Carol has published in journals such as *Deviant Behavior, Mental Retardation, Qualitative Inquiry,* and *Journal of Aging Studies*. Her research interests include the intersection of trauma, narrative, the economy, and the environment.

C. Ree has practiced in the arts for the past seventeen years as artist, programmer, curator, and teacher. Her past projects include a focus on non-normative art spaces, including audio sessions with transnational psychic women, haggling at the counter with corporations, street racer organizing, art centers with disabilities, and youth-driven art practices inside schools. Her *Dark Water* series on the monstrous and fantastic has exhibited in galleries in Los Angeles, San Francisco, and Orange County. She is currently curating short films for the San Diego Asian Film Festival and collaborating with UCLA on sensory data technologies, youth participation, and the LA State Historical Park. She resides in California.

Laurel Richardson is Professor of Sociology at The Ohio State University and an internationally renowned qualitative researcher with specialties in arts-based research, writing-issues, gender, and contemporary theory. She has modeled alternative representation of research through writing by publishing her work as essay, poetry, ethnodrama, and autoethnography. Her innovative work has brought her to Denmark, Italy, Canada, Finland, France, Iceland, and Australia, and she has been honored with awards for her writing, mentoring, teaching, and community outreach. She is engaged now with a series of two interlaced ethnographic essays: "Seven Minutes from Home" and *Kissing in the Dark—A Nonfiction Novel*. On good days, she writes, walks her Papillion dogs, and writes some more.

Deanna Shoemaker is Associate Professor of Communication and Performance Studies at Monmouth University, where she serves as the faculty advisor for COMMWORKS: Students Committed to Performance. She received her PhD in Performance Studies from The University of Texas at Austin in 2004. She is also a performer and theatre director who has worked in Chicago and in Austin, Texas, as a member of Salvage Vanguard Theatre. As a scholar/artist, her research interests include feminist/activist performance practices; adaptations of contemporary literature; performance auto/ethnography; cultural and aesthetic representations of gender, race/ethnicity, sexuality, and class; and activist and performance pedagogies. Her work has been published in *Text and Performance Quarterly, Liminalities,* and *Cultural Studies ↔ Critical Methodologies*. Her most recent original performances include "Mamafesto" (solo) and "Hauntings: Marking Flesh, Time, Memory" (co-written and performed with Tessa Carr).

Andrew C. Sparkes is Professor of Sport, Physical Activity and Leisure in the Research Institute for Sport, Physical Activity and Leisure, Carnegie Faculty, at Leeds Metropolitan Universityin England. His research interests revolve around the ways that people experience different forms of embodiment over time in a variety of contexts. Recent work has focused on performing bodies and identity formation; interrupted body projects (e.g., spinal cord injury) and the narrative reconstruction of self; aging bodies and physical culture; and sporting auto/biographies as narrative maps of being. These interests are framed by a desire to develop interpretative forms of understanding via the use of life history, ethnography, and narrative approaches.

Kathleen Stewart is Professor and Chair of Anthropology at the University of Texas, Austin. Her first book, *A Space on the Side of the Road: Cultural Poetics in an 'Other' America* (Princeton University Press, 1996) was based on two years of ethnographic fieldwork in the fragments of coal-mining camps in southern West Virginia. An experiment in evoking the density and texture of cultural poesis in the camps and an effort to pull theory into alignment with it, *A Space on the Side of the Road* won the Chicago Folklore Prize and was also recognized by the Victor Turner Award for Best Ethnography. *Ordinary Affects* (Duke University Press, 2007) approaches ordinary intensities as a plane of expressivity that is more than representational. It provokes attention to the forces of all kinds that give everyday life the quality of a continual motion of relations, scenes, contingencies, and emergences. Her current book project, *Worldings*, is an effort to approach an ethnographic present in the United States in which little worlds of all kinds are proliferating. Ranging from the tiny and temporary to the earth-shatteringly complete, the prolific generativity of such worlds says something about the way that people are now living through their presents by tweaking on forms—the possibility of forms, the loss of forms, the sense of potential and threat in the very phenomenon of forms emergence in refrains and rhythms that score over the social-cultural-political-theological-entertainment terrain like tracks to follow. The widespread phenomenon of worlding opens the question of a post-humanist phenomenology in which difference and singularity matter all the way down but only because things stick, flatten, grow dense in the rote, the ordinary, and even the determinate and generic. Agency, perception, context, and the subject exist in situ—not just situated but compositionally immanent to rhythms and moods, atmospheres and energetics. As an experiment in writing, this book is written as a prismatic fan of aspects of worlding, or angles, including atmospheres, forms of attachment and attunement, materialities and their registers, precarities, refrains, regionalities, the color red, life itself, animacy, and mood.

She has done ethnographic work in Appalachia, Las Vegas, New England, California, and Austin, where she lives with her husband and two children and all their animals (three cats, a dog, snails, a lot of fish in tanks, hundreds of stuffed animals). She writes early in the morning, before the day. Work is good but there's too much of it. They travel a lot. And there are plenty of bad things that happen. She is of a small town in Massachusetts, a big family. She has been the recipient of fellowships from the National Endowment for the Humanities, the School of American Research, the Institute for the Humanities at the University of California, Irvine, the Rockefeller Foundation, and the Center for Cultural Studies at the University of California, Santa Cruz.

Sophie Tamas is a Postdoctoral Fellow in Emotional Geography at Queen's University (Kingston, Canada) and an Instructor in the School of Canadian Studies at Carleton University (Ottawa, Canada). Her first book, *Life after Leaving: The Remains of Spousal Abuse* (2011) was published by Left Coast Press, Inc.

Barbara Tedlock is currently Research Associate at the Museum of International Folk Art in Santa Fe, New Mexico, and Distinguished Professor of Anthropology at the State University of New York at Buffalo, where she has served as Chair of Anthropology and Associate Dean of the College of Arts & Science. Her honors include appointments to the National Humanities Faculty; a Senior Fellowship at the Center for the Study of World Religions at Harvard University; a Fellowship from the American Philosophical Society; a Grant-in-aid from the Wenner-Gren Foundation; a Weatherhead Resident Fellowship at the School of American Research; the Charles Borden, Geoffrey Bushnell, and Juan Comas Prize for the best paper in linguistics at the International Congress of Americanists; two NEH fellowships; an American Council of Learned Societies (ACLS) Senior Fellowship; and a visiting appointment at the Institute for Advanced Study in Princeton. She has published more than one hundred articles, essays, and reviews based on her extensive field research among the Zuni of New Mexico; the Maya of Guatemala, Mexico, and Belize; and her own people the Ojibwe of Saskatchewan. Her books are *Time and the Highland Maya* (recently reissued in a revised and expanded edition and translated into Spanish); *Teachings from the American Earth: Indian Religion and Philosophy* (translated into German and reissued in English); *Dreaming: Anthropological and Psychological Interpretations; The Beautiful and the Dangerous: Dialogues with the Zuni Indians* (translated into French and reissued in English); and *The Woman in the Shaman's Body: Reclaiming the Feminine in Religion and Medicine* (translated so far into German, Danish, Spanish, Italian, Portuguese, and Turkish).

Lisa M. Tillmann is Professor of Critical Media and Cultural Studies at Rollins College. Her published work, much of it centered on LGBT identities, relationships, and civil rights and on women's relationships to their bodies and to food, explores intersections between politics and lived, embodied experience.

Keyan G. Tomaselli is Senior Professor in, and Director of, The Centre for Communication, Media and Society, University of KwaZulu-Natal, Durban, South Africa. He is a Fellow of the University and of the International Communicology Institute. He edits *Critical Arts: South-North Cultural and Media Studies* and is founder and co-editor of *Journal of African Cinema*. The books he has written and or edited in which he has developed his autoethnographic approach include: *Cultural Tourism, Methods and Identity: Rethinking Indigeneity* (2012); *Writing in the San/d:*

Autoethnography amongst Indigenous Southern Africans (2007*); Encountering Modernity: 20th Century South African Cinemas* (2006); *Where Global Contradictions are Sharpest: Research Stories from the Kalahari* (2005); and *Appropriating Images: The Semiotics of Visual Representation* (1999). His other books include *The Cinema of Apartheid* (1988), and the co-edited *Political Economy of Media Transformation in South Africa* (2011), *Cultural Icons* (2009), and *African Cultural Studies and Difference* (2011).

He has been a Fulbright Scholar and Visiting Professor at Michigan State University, has contributed to media studies programs in Kenya, Ethiopia, Malawi, and other African countries, is a regular contributor to the Bayreuth International Graduate Programme in African Studies, and has consulted for UNESCO and other agencies.

Satoshi Toyosaki was born and raised in Japan. He came to the United States in 1993 when he was twenty years old with a goal of learning English. Later in his undergraduate program, he became interested in international and intercultural communication, and subsequently pursued his degrees in communication studies. He holds a BA in Speech Communication from Eastern Illinois University, an MA in Communication Studies from the University of Central Missouri, and a PhD in Speech Communication from Southern Illinois University. In his doctoral program, he specialized in international and intercultural communication, critical and qualitative research methodologies, and critical pedagogy. He received the Thomas J. Pace Award for Outstanding Graduate Teaching in 2004 and the Excellence in Graduate Student Research/Creative Activity Award in 2005. After completing his doctoral degree, he taught at the University of Wisconsin-La Crosse for three years. He is currently an Assistant Professor in the Department of Speech Communication at Southern Illinois University, Carbondale, where he researches and teaches international and intercultural communication from interpretive and critical perspectives. Among others, he teaches seminars in critical and interpretive methods, ethnography, self in communication, and communication, love, and social justice. He employs various ethnographic methods, particularly autoethnography, in his research. He has presented numerous papers at regional, national, and intercultural conferences in communication and education. In 2012, he received the Top Paper Award from the Intercultural Communication Interest Group of the Central States Communication Association. Recently, he has been focusing his scholarship on critical selfhood performance in intercultural contexts and hopes to develop an automethodological and praxiological approach to intercultural communication. His essays appear in publications such as *Identity and Communication Research: Intercultural Reflections and Future Directions*, the *International Journal of Qualitative Methods*, the *Journal of International and Intercultural Communication*, *Cultural Studies ↔ Critical Methodologies*, the *International and Intercultural Communication Annual*, and the *International Journal of Qualitative Studies in Education*.

Eve Tuck is Assistant Professor of Educational Foundations at the State University of New York at New Paltz. Her recent work is concerned with settler colonialism, Native feminist theories, the politics and ethics of research, youth resistance to educational injustices, land education, and refusals of settler colonial research. She is the author of "Suspending Damage: A letter to Communities" in *Harvard Educational Review,* "Breaking up with Deleuze: Desire and Valuing the Irreconcilable" in the *Journal of Qualitative Studies in Education*, and *Urban Youth and School Pushout: Gateways, Get-aways, and the GED* (Routledge, 2012). She is an enrolled member of the Tribal Government of St. Paul Island, Alaska, and she resides in New York.

Jillian A. Tullis is Assistant Professor of Communication Studies at the University of North Carolina at Charlotte. Her research focuses on communication about serious illness, dying, and death. She studies communication at the end of life in health care settings such as cancer centers and hospices. In the classroom, she teaches about health communication, spirituality, culture, and communication theory. Her professional career started at a Burger King in Sacramento, California, when she was fifteen. While her work ethic was honed making Whoppers, she's convinced there is no better job in the world than being a college professor, except for maybe the job of being her loyal pit bull mix, Amber.

Sjoerd van Grootheest graduated at the University of Amsterdam with a BA degree in Cultural Anthropology. He then graduated with a full research MA from The Centre for Communication, Media and Society at the University of KwaZulu-Natal in South Africa. His MA study encapsulates his research interests and methodologies which include: subaltern representation, social movement organization, and visual methods, particularly ethnographic and documentary filmmaking. He has produced two documentaries, *The Bay of Plenty* and *Vasile Nedea,* which were both screened at international film festivals. He is currently active as a director for a video production company in the Netherlands.

Mary E. Weems is a poet, playwright, imagination-intellect theorist and social foundations scholar working in interpretive methods. She was the Poet Laureate of Cleveland Heights from 2007 to 2009. She is the author and/or co-editor of several books, including her educational text *Public Education and the Imagination-Intellect: I Speak from the Wound in My Mouth*; *Working Hard for the Money: America's Working Poor in Stories, Poems, and Photos*; and a book of poems titled *An Unmistakable Shade of Red and the Obama Chronicles*. Her book of poems, *For(e)closure*, a finalist in the 2011 Main Street Rag Poetry contest, is in press. She has been widely published in journals, including *Qualitative Inquiry, The African American Review,* and *xcp: Cultural Poetics*. Her work has also appeared in numerous anthologies, most recently, *Go, Tell Michelle: African American Women Write to the New First Lady*. She has had numerous articles, performance texts, and book chapters published in the field of education, including: "The E in Poetry Stands for Empathy" in *Poetic Inquiry: Vibrant Voices in the Social Sciences*, "Sadie Stories" in the *International Journal of Qualitative Studies in Education,* and "Constructions of Childhood: Globalized Homelessness and Poverty, and Race is 'not' an Additive," part of a special issue of *Cultural Studies ↔ Critical Methodologies*. She won the Wick

Chapbook Award for her collection *white,* has been nominated for a Pushcart Prize, and her play *Another Way to Dance* won the Chilcote award for The Most Innovative Play by an Ohio Playwright. She is currently an Assistant Professor in the Department of Education and Allied Studies at John Carroll University. She also works as a language-artist-scholar through her business *Bringing Words to Life.* Programming includes "The Sankofa Project, Don't Be Afraid to F.L.Y. (Find Love in Yourself)." Her new multi-authored book, *Writings of Healing and Resistance: Empathy and the Imagination-Intellectis,* is forthcoming. Weems also designs and facilitates professional development workshops.

Jonathan Wyatt is Head of Professional Development and a Research Fellow at the University of Oxford, based respectively at the Oxford Learning Institute and the Department of Education. He worked a day a week as a counselor within the National Health Service for ten years until 2011 and now has a small private practice.

His research interests focus, firstly, on academic writing (collaborative writing, writing as inquiry, performative writing, autoethnography and collective biography) and, secondly, on the experience of loss. In both these areas he draws primarily from poststructural theory, particularly Gilles Deleuze. He is involved in a number of research collaborations: with Ken Gale (University of Plymouth) in a continuation of their work on Deleuzian collaborative inquiry, including a co-edited special issue of the journal, *International Review of Qualitative Research*; with Ken Gale, Larry Russell, Ronald Pelias and Tami Spry on collaborative performative writing, which has spawned three journal articles and a recent book *(How Writing Touches: An Intimate Scholarly Collaboration,* Cambridge Scholars, 2012); with Tony Adams co-editing a recent special issue of *Qualitative Inquiry* on the theme of sons and fathers; and with Sophie Tamas co-editing a special issue, again of *Qualitative Inquiry,* looking at the intersections between research and therapy. With Jane Speedy, Nell Bridges and Ken Gale, he was part of funded project to develop online resources on collaborative writing for early career researchers and faculty: ww.writeinquiry.org. And with Bronwyn Davies, Susanne Gannon and Ken Gale he co-authored another recent book, *Deleuze and Collaborative Writing: An Immanent Plane of Composition* (Peter Lang, 2011).

He continues to work on experiences and understandings of loss, using autoethnography, writing as inquiry, and other embodied practices. He is collaborating with Beatrice Allegranti on a practice-based interdisciplinary research project, Moving Voices, which explores loss and the boundaries between the art form, therapy and performance. He is an accredited member of the British Association for Counselling and Psychotherapy, and a member of the International Association of Qualitative Inquiry, the Narrative Inquiry Centre at the University of Bristol, where he is a Visiting Fellow, and the Centre for Arts Therapies Research, University of Roehampton, where he is a Visiting Lecturer. He lives in Abingdon, near Oxford, with his partner Tessa; their two adult children (Joe and Holly) are out in the world somewhere, making their way. Life's priorities feature coffee and football.